Johan van der Walt
The Horizontal Effect Revolution and the Question of Sovereignty

Johan van der Walt

The Horizontal Effect Revolution and the Question of Sovereignty

DE GRUYTER

LDD *Johan van der Walt*, Professor of Philosophy of Law, University of Luxembourg.

ISBN 978-3-11-024802-9
e-ISBN 978-3-11-024803-6

Library of Congress Cataloging-in-Publication Data
A CIP catalog record for this book has been applied for at the Library of Congress.

Bibliographic Information published by the Deutsche Nationalbibliothek
The Deutsche Nationalbibliothek lists this publication in the Deutsche Nationalbibliografie; detailed bibliographic data are available in the Internet at http://dnb.dnb.de.

Printing and binding: CPI books GmbH, Leck
♾ Printed on acid-free paper
Printed in Germany

www.degruyter.com

For Frank Michelman, Joe Singer and André van der Walt

It is habitually assumed, from a contemporary perspective, that the concept of statehood as territorial sovereignty was first devised to consolidate the form of the state against external forces. It is, therefore, widely argued that the early idea of territorial sovereignty coincided with the intensification of an exclusionary/international dimension in politics: that is, that states claimed sovereignty to defend and assert themselves against other states. In fact, however, the converse is the case. The territorialisation of political power was, in the first instance, a process in which power was linked (or projected itself as being linked) to one place and to one geographically-localised group of institutional actors in order to reduce the privatistic transaction of political power within a particular society, which typified the political dimensions of feudalism: that is, to prevent the alienation of lands, cross-boundary ownership of land, indiscriminate fusion of private and public resources, and the private seigneurial disposition over political goods. In this respect, the principle of statehood as territorial sovereignty was inextricably bound to the articulation of power as a resource that was detached from private or particular status or control, that was abstractly constructed as applicable to an entire society, and that effectively included society and all its members in relatively uniform fashion. The consistent fusion of territory and statehood, in other words, was an expression of a formatively underlying process of *political inclusion* ... In this process, power broke through the super-imposed private/public forms of later feudalism, and it identified *territory* as the primary unit of socio-political inclusion."

Chris Thornhill "The Future of the State" 358.

Preface

The American state action doctrine and the German and European concept of the horizontal effect of fundamental rights would appear to be *opposing* principles. The state action doctrine basically negates the horizontal effect of fundamental rights and the principle of the horizontal effect of fundamental rights basically dispenses with the requirement that some specific instance of state action be identified for fundamental rights to have effect in the relations between private persons. However, there is a significant body of German scholarly and judicial opinion that also understands horizontal effect as ultimately a reflection of either the *factual reality* of some or other state involvement in the relations between private citizens, or the *normative principle* that such state involvement should be assumed whenever claims to fundamental rights violations are at stake. German scholars and judges refer in this regard to the constitutional duty of the state to protect the fundamental rights of its citizens and residents. American scholars on the other side of the Atlantic who are critical of the use of the state action doctrine as a procedural device with recourse to which state involvement in and responsibility for in some or other alleged fundamental rights violation can be denied so as to deny the violation of the rights as such, basically do so on the same grounds on which German scholars base the principle of horizontal effect. These critical American scholars also believe fundamental rights violations in relations between private individuals turn on either the empirical recognition of real state involvement in the violation, or the normative recognition that the state should be considered involved in that violation. On a number of rare occasions, American judicial opinion, even if only by implication, also reflected this view.

All the arguments in this book pivot on an unequivocal endorsement of this critical American and standard German understanding of the state action and horizontal effect doctrines, hence the connection between horizontal effect and state sovereignty that it posits as its fundamental point of departure. This is the first key structural point that will be stressed in this regard: Horizontal effect of fundamental rights is indeed *an effect* of state sovereignty and state sovereignty is likewise *an effect* of the horizontal effect of fundamental rights between the citizens and/or residents of a state. The latter part of this statement suggests intentionally that states cannot truly call themselves "sovereign" when their judiciaries do not recognise the horizontal effect of fundamental rights. A properly sovereign state, this book argues, unflinchingly owns up to its factual or normatively assumed involvement in all fundamental rights violations that come to pass within its territorial boundaries. The historical genesis of this principle is masterfully captured by Chris Thornhill in the epigraph to this book: historically, the internal sovereignty of states *that resulted from* the inclusionary protection of the fundamental rights of all citizens and residents present *within* the territorial boundaries of the state, precedes their sovereignty vis-à-vis other states. This is the first leg on which this book stands.

The second leg stands as a response to the question regarding the kind of sovereignty modern or postmodern states can claim when they move to comply with their sovereign constitutional duty to protect the fundamental rights of their citizens. States who move to protect the kind of rights that are generally contemplated when the concept of fundamental rights is at issue, should want to call themselves liberal democratic states. And liberal democratic states, argues the second half of this book, cannot embody monolithic or monistic conceptions of sovereignty. Liberal democratic states only remain *liberal* democratic states for as long as their sovereignty remains a register of the social divisions and cultural pluralisms that characterise modern societies. The sovereignty of liberal democratic states must thus always consist in the sustenance of constitutionally sound relations between democratic majorities and minorities. The one thing that the sovereign sustenance of democratic majority-minority relations demands from liberal democratic states, is to *generally* avoid expansive invocations of objective value orders that demand endorsement from all citizens and residents. Modern societies would not have been socially and culturally as deeply divided as they are, if they could be said to generally endorse the same set of values that for reasons of this general endorsement constitute an objective value order. And this, unfortunately, is exactly where the German horizontal effect jurisprudence articulated in the famous *Lüth* decision of the GFCC went astray and also led many other jurisdictions of the world astray.

With its invocation of an objective constitutional value order that radiates through all spheres of law, the court in *Lüth* engaged in a kind of judicial review that American legal theorists call substantive due process review. American judges have in theory but not always in practice become consciously wary of substantive due process judicial review ever since the notorious decision of the United States Supreme Court (hereafter USSC) in *Lochner v New York* in 1905. Horizontal effect jurisprudence can and should learn from this wariness. There are always exceptional cases in which the judicial assertion of certain minimum substantive constitutional protections is unavoidable and indeed required if the principle of sovereignty is to remain meaningful. One crucial part of the endeavour of this book is to explain why and when this is sometimes necessary, but another equally crucial part of this endeavour is to explain why and when this kind of judicial review must be avoided if a judiciary means to remain the judiciary of a liberal democratic state that respects the deep social, cultural and political differences that prevail between its citizens and/or residents.

The substantive due process horizontal effect judicial review articulated in *Lüth* is today ironically threatening the very future of *Lüth* in Germany, because of the way the European Court of Justice (hereafter ECJ) has basically taken on a horizontal effect jurisprudence of the kind articulated in *Lüth* to assert a de facto sovereignty in Europe that is arguably not quite contemplated de jure by the European Union Treaties. This has come to pass in four judgments that are generally known now as the *Laval* quartet, the *Laval* and *Viking* judgments of 2007 and the *Rüffert* and *Luxembourg* judgments of 2008. What these judgments announced unequivocally, as especially the *Rüffert* judgment makes clear, is the relegation of *Lüth* to secondary of marginal significance in Germany. The sovereignty that *Lüth* used to effect de jure and de facto in Germany, has now been assumed de facto by a different court, notwithstanding the de jure insistence of the German constitutional judiciary that the sovereign protection of German fundamental rights in Germany is still its untouched prerogative.

Problematic in this development is not the de facto assumption of sovereignty by the ECJ in the *Laval* quartet as such. Transfers of sovereignty are always de facto transfers before they eventually become de jure transfers. We learn this from both Schmitt and Kelsen. Transfers of sovereignty are usually first precipitated by factual and historical revolutionary progressions, the process of which is generally completed with the eventual sedimentation of de jure sovereignty. In this regard, one can talk about a veritable horizontal effect revolution in the jurisprudence of the ECJ. At issue in this revolution is not just the culmination of the jurisprudential revolution that expanded the effect of fundamental rights from state-subject to subject-subject relations in the course of the twentieth century (the semantic revolution that is firstly contemplated by the title of this book), but also a veritable judicial-political revolution that effectively transfers sovereignty from the Member States to the Union. Perhaps this is just the way the eventual federalisation of Europe has to proceed if it is to proceed at all.

Bothersome, however, is the kind of sovereignty that might ensue from this development, for it is doubtful at this stage whether the kind of sovereignty that is asserted in the jurisprudence of the ECJ aims to comply with the liberal democratic demand regarding the respect for social, cultural and political divisions. Not all revolutions are progressive revolutions, as the conservative revolutionary movement in the time of Weimar Germany showed clearly. For the moment, the jurisprudence of the ECJ would seem to espouse a substantive due process conception of judicial review that is, both in form and substance, conspicuously similar to the Herbert Spencer substantive due process articulated by the USSC in *Lochner v New York* in 1905. There would seem to be a clear connecting line running from *Lochner* to *Lüth* to *Laval.* And as far as continental European history is concerned, this substantive due process judicial review of the ECJ – assuming for now that it is informed by ordo-liberal principles, as many observers believe it is – would also seem not to be that unrelated to the conservative revolutionary movement of Weimar.

The aim of this book is firstly to articulate a coherent understanding of the relation between horizontal effect jurisprudence and sovereignty that might contribute to an advancement of legal theory that could be globally useful and interesting. But its second aim is to also invite careful thought and circumspection regarding the substantive due process conception of horizontal effect that ultimately links *Lüth* and *Laval* to *Lochner.* And in doing so, it also hopes to point out a different direction – *another heading* – that especially Europe and Europeans might want to consider *today* as far as the future of their sovereignty is concerned.

The first step towards a regard for this other heading would consist in a horizontal effect jurisprudence that rehabilitates for horizontal effect cases the classical three-step proportionality test that generally applies in the judicial review of legislation. The evaluative judicial balancing processes that became the hallmark of horizontal effect ever since *Lüth* is an aberration of this classical proportionality test and the root of the substantive due process problems to which it gives rise. This step may well appear to represent a simple plea for a return to orthodoxy in judicial review procedures. In some respects it surely is that. But appearances may well also be deceptive in this case. For the arguments that will be forwarded in this regard are the outcome of jurisprudential moves that many orthodox constitutional scholars would consider unorthodox.

These moves, moreover, rely heavily on dissenting judicial opinions that have never become "good law" anywhere. And if one adds to this that these dissenting opinions come from cases that no orthodox constitutional scholar would consider as horizontal effect cases – namely the dissenting opinion of Justices Rupp-v. Brünneck and Simon in the *Erste Abtreibung* case that the GFCC decided in 1975 and the dissenting opinion of Justice Grimm in the *Reiten im Walde* case that the same court decided in 1989 – it should become clear that this book is in many respects an experiment. It takes liberties with hegemonic legal doctrine that a constitutional lawyer would be less inclined to take. The aim of doing so is to offer a different perspective on the meaning and significance of contemporary constitutional review that may help it deal better with the deep social, cultural and political divisions that inform constitutional conflicts today. Liberal constitutional theory all too often still conceives of constitutionalism as essentially a safeguard against the abuse of political power and the concomitant abuse of state machinery. It has not yet come round to appreciate the state as an essential safeguard for constitutionalism. This is what liberal constitutional theory can learn from the questions with which the horizontal effect of fundamental rights confronts it. And what it can learn in this regard is crucial for an age in which constitutional jurisdictions are marked by deep social, cultural and political differences.

This book evidently pays homage to liberal democracy and the liberal democratic state. Its hope is to make a contribution to a consistent theory of liberal democratic constitutional review. Having worked on it from 2009, I finally finished this book (assuming just for the moment that a book like this can ever be "finished") with intensive work between September 2013 and January 2014. These were months during which the Edward Snowden revelations confronted many of us who believed that we lived in exemplary liberal democracies with the sobering if not disheartening reality that this is far from true. We live in a time during which arcane reasons of state again seem to draw the limits of liberty in no uncertain terms. A book that extolls the liberal democratic state under these circumstances – especially one that understands liberal democratic states as states in which popular democracy has divested the state of all separate reasons of state that are not reducible to reasons of citizens – exposes itself to accusations of serious naivety. Assuming that *critical inquiry* is a defining element of significant social, political and legal science, it would appear more apposite right now to concentrate one's efforts on studies that engage more realistically with the dark reality of the "deep state." There is much merit in this observation.

And yet, it is not with naivety that the pages of this book hold on for life to the ideal of liberal democracy. Liberal democracy may well be little more than an ideal. It may well have little purchase in hard reality. It nevertheless remains an ideal of which modern *legal* theory cannot afford to let go without forfeiting one of its defining conditions. Theories of law that would dismiss the constitutional ideals of the Enlightenment – individual liberty, equality, inviolable dignity of the person – as myths, would turn legal studies into historical reflections on contingent power relations. Such reflections may well be worthy and interesting undertakings in their own right. But they would no longer constitute theories of *law* if we understand under "law" the modern endeavour to arrange and organise societies on the basis of Enlightenment ideals of moral autonomy, liberty and equality. The idea that contemporary legal theory can again come to seriously conceive of personal power relations as "law" in the way pre-modern (feudal) legal theory could still do with some plausibility, is unthinkable, notwithstanding disconcerting flirtations with such conceptions of law evident in current conceptions of private governance and societal constitutionalism. There is a point where legal theory must take leave of some of its claims to social science for the sake of remaining theory of law.

Seen from this perspective, evidence of deep states or the deep state (perhaps there is only one) with which the Snowden revelations confront legal theory so starkly is only relevant to the way we think about law to the extent that this evidence threatens and undermines the courage to hang on to the concept of law. It cannot affect the concept of law as such. It can only undermine the courage, hope and trust required to presuppose its validity, in the way Kelsen instructed us to do. Evidence of the deep state that ultimately operates below or above or beside the law surely makes it difficult to believe in the concept of law in the way this book evidently still does. Perhaps one should concede that this book can right now be little more than a reminder of the promise contained in the modern concept of law and an expression of hope that it will become easier to believe in this concept again than it is at the moment. But if legal theorists were to lose faith completely in the promise of law or at least the promise of the concept of law, they would evidently have to give up the business of legal theory and turn to theology (or redeeming literature) for the sake of sustaining what faith might still be sustainable in the idea that the heavens, at least, still regard all mortals as equal and free. It is remarkable that the concept of liberal democratic law – so modest and non-utopian in its aspirations, so fatally compromising with regard to demands of substantive justice – has attained an almost utopian quality at the beginning of the twenty first century.

Contents

Acknowledgements and Disclaimers — XIX

Introduction — 1

I The Horizontality Revolution — **1**
II Two Histories, Four Questions, Twelve Cases, Two Scholarly Debates — **6**
III Liberal Democratic Constitutionalism — **13**
IV Liberal Democratic Sovereignty — **19**
V Liberal Democratic Historicity — **21**
VI Liberal Democratic Constitutional Review — **25**
VII Outline of Arguments and Chapters — **31**

Part One: Horizontal Effect

Chapter One: Erased Baselines and Inversed Coordinates: 19th Century Backgrounds of the Horizontality Question — 37

I Introduction — **37**
II The Privatisation of Constitutional Rights in America — **41**
III The Nineteenth Century Transformation of Private Law Rights in America — **48**
IV The Privatisation of Constitutional Rights in Germany — **59**
V The Nineteenth Century Transformation of Private Law Rights in Germany and its Impact on Early Twentieth Century German Public Law — **66**
VI The Baseline of Erased Baselines — **74**
VII Inversed Coordinates — **78**

Chapter Two: Twelve Pivotal Cases — 85

I Introduction — **85**
II *The Civil Rights Cases* (and their Unlikely South African Echoes) — **86**
III *Shelley v Kraemer* — **92**
IV *Labour v Swing* and *New York Times v Sullivan* — **98**
V *RWDSU v Dolphin Delivery Ltd* — **102**
VI *Lüth* — **107**

VII *Du Plessis v De Klerk* — **114**
VIII *Flagg Brothers, Inc. v Brooks* — **120**
IX *DeShaney v Winnebago County Department of Social Services* — **124**
X The Duty to Protect: *Roe v Wade* and *Erste Abtreibung* — **130**
XI *Reiten im Walde* — **151**
XII Summary Reflections — **155**
1 Vicissitudes of the State Action Doctrine — **155**
2 The Contradictory Legacies that Informed *Du Plessis* — **156**
3 The Dismantling of *Swing*, *Shelley* and *Sullivan* in *Flagg Brothers* and *DeShaney* — **157**
4 Shifting Horizontal Effect Jurisprudence from Private to Legislative Relations — **157**
5 Substantive and Procedural Due Process and the Question of Sovereignty — **158**
6 Constitutional Histories of Peoples — **163**

Chapter Three: State Action — 166
I Introduction — **166**
II Michelman's "Hohfeldian Point" — **168**
III Wechsler and Tribe: Two Readings of *Shelley* — **172**
IV Seidman's Reading of *DeShaney* — **181**
V One Way out of the American Conceptual Impasse — **190**

Chapter Four: Drittwirkung — 201
I Introduction — **201**
II Nipperdey's Position — **203**
III Dürig's Position — **207**
IV Leisner's Position — **212**
V Schwabe's Position — **222**
VI Canaris' Response — **227**
VII Schutzpflicht and/or Drittwirkung? — **230**

Part Two:
Sovereignty

Chapter Five: Uninterrupted Sovereignty — 235
I Introduction — **235**
II Divided Sovereignty — **241**

III Between Deism and Deontology – Europe and Ordo-Liberalism — 246
IV Dispersed Sovereignty – Government and Governance — 252
V Dispensed Sovereignty – The Davidsonian Road to Luhmann — 260
VI Uninterrupted Sovereignty – A "Luhmannian" Return to Hegel — 275

Chapter Six: Différantial Sovereignty — 293
I Introduction — 293
II Coercive Enlightenment Ideals — 296
III Carl Schmitt's Unitary Substantive Due Process and Indirect Horizontal Effect Jurisprudence — 300
IV Hans Kelsen and the Open Duality of the Constitutional Democratic Whole — 315
V Leisner's "Kelsenian" Horizontal Effect Jurisprudence — 323
VI Différantial Sovereignty — 327

Chapter Seven: Sovereignty and the Dual Destiny of *Lüth* in Europe — 334
I Introduction — 334
II The Rise of European Union Sovereignty — 338
III The Demise of German Sovereignty and the Marginalisation of *Lüth* in Germany — 348
IV European Union Sovereignty – Vertical and Monistic or Horizontal and Différantial? — 352

Chapter Eight: Liberal Democratic Constitutional Review — 361
I Introduction — 361
II The Recognition of Sovereignty — 366
III Liberal Democratic Sovereignty — 368
IV Substantive and Procedural Due Process Constitutional Review — 369
V The Proceduralisation of Minimum Substance and the First Proportionality Question — 374
VI The Second Proportionality Question: Rationality and Effectiveness — 379
VII The Third Proportionality Question: Minimal Intrusion — 381
VIII The Difference between Ordinary and Constitutional Law — 386
IX Social Liberal Democracy? — 390

Bibliography — 401

Abbreviations — 419

Index of Persons — 420

Subject Index — 423

Acknowledgements and Disclaimers

The appreciation for Hegel's political philosophy – which articulates the *raison d'être* of the modern state in terms of institutional subordination of all pursuits of self-interest in civil society to the Kantian demands of moral autonomy – that is evident throughout this book was kindled many years ago by Marinus Schoeman, a philosophy lecturer during my undergraduate years who later also supervised my Masters dissertation on the philosophy of Kant and Hegel and since then has become a dear friend. I wish to thank him again here for the instruction and inspiration during those formative years.

I started working on the question of the horizontal effect of fundamental rights just after the judgment of the South African Constitutional Court in the case of *Du Plessis v De Klerk* in 1996. Between then and 2008 I published a number of articles on horizontal effect in South African law journals. Apart from copying a couple of quotes from them and rethinking some of the thoughts contained in them, I have not relied on the texts of those articles in this book and the position on horizontal effect that I am taking in this book also differs in many respects from the position that I developed in those articles. But I learned much from the work I did in those years and would like to thank the editors of those journals, especially the *South African Journal on Human Rights* and the *Journal for South African Law* for the opportunity they gave me to publish my earlier thoughts on this subject.

I would also like to thank all the South African colleagues with whom I had frequent exchanges of thoughts in those times. They were many and any attempt to thank them individually would only end up with a very long list that would still be too short. So I will refrain from doing so. However, there is one South African whom I would like to thank expressly here. I was fortunate to have occasional contact with Justice Johann Kriegler in the course of many years. I do not know whether he ever got to know about the rather sharp critique of his "dissenting" opinion in *Du Plessis v De Klerk* that I articulated in several journal articles. If he did he never let on that he did. Some elements of that critique have again found their way into this book, but they have now, I think and hope, attained a different character. I think the engagement with the puzzling passages from Justice Kriegler's opinion in *Du Plessis v De Klerk* now, at long last, reflects the fact that they have in many respects remained unfading sparks that have kept on inspiring me to return to the question of horizontal effect. If those passages got some signals crossed, as they may well have done, they surely constituted the most productive judicial "mistakes" that any legal theorist can hope for. For those "mistakes" have in many respects kept my thinking busy for close to twenty years now. I adorn the word "mistake" with scarecrows here because I do not think or no longer think of those puzzling passages as mistakes in the common sense of the word. At issue in them, I have come to realise over the years, are much rather instances of those rare original thoughts that leave the register of correct- and incorrectness so as to allow one to confront the deeper puzzles of our existence, in this case, the deeper puzzles of the threshold of the law by which we live. Only a shallow soul would think of these thoughts as mistakes. I do not think I understood this well when I started writing about them almost twenty years ago and I hope and trust Justice Kriegler would pardon me for that. I hope the re-engagement with those puzzling parts of his opinion in *Du Plessis* in this book does now, after all these years, begin to reflect some of the depths that they allow one to explore.

I studied German *Drittwirkung* case law and the German academic debate on *Drittwirkung* from February 1999 to January 2000 as a Humboldt scholar in Cologne. Klaus Stern was a generous host during that year and also guided my reading of the German literature on horizontal effect patiently during that time. I wish to thank him again for that.

I started writing this book in 2009 while still working at the University of Glasgow. I left Glasgow in 2011, but in the relatively short time from 2007 when I arrived till 2011, I had instructive scholarly exchanges with many colleagues in especially Glasgow and Edinburgh but also from elsewhere in the United Kingdom. I again learned much from many people during this time and a list of names would here again be much too long and much too short. However, I do wish to single out two colleagues from these Glasgow years whose work and thought have influenced the writing of this book very specifically, namely Emilios Christodoulidis and Chris Thornhill. I would like to thank both of them, not only for the countless exhilarating academic exchanges in the course of which many of the thoughts articulated in this book took form, but also for the inspiring friendship that resulted from these exchanges.

I started working at the University of Luxembourg in September 2011 and thus came to know the remarkable bunch of fine scholars who make up the Research Unit for Law at this institution. I wish to express my appreciation to all of them for contributing to a vibrant, pleasant and friendly working environment. I wish to thank my three European law colleagues, Eleftheria Neframi, Jörg Gerkrath and Herwig Hoffmann in particular for much needed advice and guidance with regard to some developments in European law that I discuss in Chapter Seven.

In the course of 2012 and 2013 the Research Unit in Law of the University of Luxembourg hosted three workshops on constitutional developments in Europe in which a number of Europe's finest constitutional, legal and social theorists participated. Among them were Monica Claes, Emilios Christodoulidis, Michelle Everson, Dieter Grimm, Christian Joerges, Hans Lindahl, Ulrich Preuss, Fritz Scharpf, Bert van Roermund, Scott Veitch and Neil Walker. On one occasion, two fine legal theorists from South Africa, Danie Brand and Karin van Marle, were also among our guests. I wish to thank all these scholars (and again also colleagues from Luxembourg who participated) for their contributions to the discussions we had, many of which had a direct bearing on the thoughts articulated in this book. Of these scholars I wish to thank Dieter Grimm, Christian Joerges and Eleftheria Neframi in particular for kindly reading and advising me on some or other chapter or some pages from earlier drafts of the manuscript that eventually became this book.

I wish to express another word of thanks to Ulrich Preuss for generously hosting me at the Hertie School of Governance for three months in 2010 during which I studied works of Carl Schmitt and Hans Kelsen. The insights regarding these authors that he shared with me during this time were invaluable and inspired many of the thoughts about Schmitt and Kelsen articulated in especially Chapter Six.

I dedicate this book to Frank Michelman, Joe Singer and André van der Walt. The three of them have been the most generous of mentors and friends for many years. Their influence on the way I think about law is simply immense and this book surely reflects that. I also thank them for reading and commenting on parts of an earlier draft of the manuscript.

Michelman's writings have over many years made key contributions to both the questions that I bring together in the two parts of this book, the question of state action and horizontal effect, on the one hand, and the question of liberal constitutionalism as a response to political difference and conflict, on the other. In this respect I would like to think of this book as particularly a tribute to what I have learned from him.

The thoughts articulated in this book were nevertheless developed independently (assuming one can still say something like this after Foucault). Responsibility for any shortcoming or failures of understanding reflected in them cannot be attributed to any of the colleagues or friends acknowledged above. Those who kindly read parts of the text only read parts and not the rest. And whether the final draft printed here responds adequately to their many recommendations and critical questions is something they could not check in the end.

I thank my friend Etienne van Zyl for reading early parts of the text and sifting out many of those clumsy sentences that always hide themselves so well only to become glaringly conspicuous in print. Those that still slipped through I of course take for my account.

I wish to thank Jeff Ellsworth, Richard Mailey, Brian Nail and Mikel Trako for their assistance during the final stages of polishing and finishing footnotes, checking the bibliography, proofreading and indexing. A special word of thanks is due to Brian Nail for taking the lead in this and for spending many hours working closely with me during the last days to tie up last loose ends.

More gratitude than I can ever express is due to my wife Sibylle who had to live with this project for more than four years and for graciously allowing me to use every spare minute between September 2013 and January 2014 to bring it to completion.

Johan van der Walt, Luxembourg, January 2014

Introduction

I The Horizontality Revolution

The Dutch constitutional theorist Luc Verhey refers to "a silent revolution" that has been taking place in the jurisprudence of the European Court of Human Rights (hereafter ECHR) in Strasbourg over the years. *Een stille Straatburgse revolutie*, Verhey calls it.[1] At issue, for Verhey, is the extensive reading of human rights by the ECHR in a number of decisions that identified a range of *positive duties* on states party to the Convention to protect the Convention rights of their citizens, on the one hand, and effectively created a *general personality right* on the basis of Article 8 of the Convention, on the other.[2] The revolutionary element in this development, contends Verhey, consists in the way the identification of these positive duties and general personality right widens the traditional vertical state-citizen relations embodied in human rights so as to include a significant range of horizontal citizen-citizen relations among them. The quietness of this revolution pertains to the deliberate tendency of the Strasbourg Court not to address the question of the horizontal application of the Convention rights expressly.[3] This deliberate skirting of the horizontal application question is, according to Verhey, strikingly evident in the Court's observation in *Vgt Verein gegen Tierfabrieken* that it is neither desirable nor necessary "to elaborate a general theory concerning the extent to which the Convention guarantees should be extended to relations between private individuals *inter se*."[4]

1 "Horizontale Werking van Grondrechten: de Stille Straatsburgse Revolutie," in *Geschakeld Recht: Verdere Studies over Europese Grondrechten ter Gelegenheid van de 70ste Verjaardag van Prof. mr. E.A. Alkema*, ed. Tom Barkhuysen, M.L. van Emmerik, and J.P. Loof (Alphen aan den Rijn: Kluwer, 2009), 534.

2 The key cases to which Verhey refers are the following: *Costello-Roberts v. The United Kingdom* (1995) 19 E.H.R.R. 112; *Marckx v. Belgium* (1997) 24 E.H.R.R. 143; *VgT Verein gegen Tierfabriken v. Switzerland* (2002) 34 E.H.R.R. 4; *Hatton and Others v. the United Kingdom* (2002) 34 E.H.R.R. 1; *Von Hannover v. Germany* (2005) 40 E.H.R.R. 1; *Appleby and Others v. the United Kingdom* (2003) 37 E.H.R.R. 38; *Gustafsson v. Sweden* (1996) 22 E.H.R.R. 409.

3 Verhey, "Horizontale Werking van Grondrechten: de Stille Straatsburgse Revolutie," 534.

4 *VgT Verein gegen Tierfabriken v. Switzerland* (2002) 34 E.H.R.R. 4. For an instructive attempt to systematise the judicial practice of the Strasbourg Court despite its express refusal to articulate a general theory (malgré le refus de la Cour de Strasbourg "d'élaborer une théorie générale des obligations positives), cf. Frédéric Sudre, "Les 'obligations positives' dans la jurisprudence européenne des droits de l'homme," in *Protection des Droits de l'Homme: la Perspective Européenne : Mélanges à la Mémoire de Rolv Ryssdal*, ed. Paul Mahoney (Köln: Carl Heymanns, 2000), 1359–1376. For other insightful discussions of the Strasbourg jurisprudence regarding

This statement of the ECHR, as phrased here in *Vgt Verein*, is partially understandable. A general theory concerning the *extent* that fundamental rights such as the Convention guarantees might affect individuals is of course not possible or desirable, for this extent will vary from case to case. Sometimes fundamental rights will affect horizontal relations incisively and even dramatically. Sometimes their effect on horizontal relations will be negligible. A general rule or principle cannot absolve a court from the very real decision-making and solution-finding that are required in this regard and will at best obscure and at worst undermine this work. But a general theory regarding the general principles and concepts on the basis of which this real decision-making and solution finding work must commence can facilitate and enhance the decision-making work required here. This is especially so, as we shall presently see, because a general theory regarding the application of fundamental rights in the private sphere has in fact emerged in case law and scholarship in many countries of the world, one which does more harm than good and therefore requires fundamental revision.

That the Strasbourg "revolution" – just one instance of the *horizontality revolution* that is at issue in this book – has reverberated strongly through European countries party to the Human Rights Convention is common course now. And many European countries have been experiencing similar reverberations independently of the Human Rights Convention under the auspices of their national constitutions, as we shall presently see. Similar tremors have made themselves felt elsewhere in the world. A particularly interesting narrative of horizontal application has been unfolding in South Africa in recent years. And in the background of all these histories, still looms the old man among them, the American state action doctrine that sprung its source in 1883 (surely neither horizontal nor revolutionary at the time) and cascaded into white waters in the 1940s (to become truly revolutionary and truly horizontal, if only for a short while). The hor-

positive duties, cf. also Dean Spielmann, "Obligations Positives et Effet Horizontal des Dispositions de La Convention," in *L'Interprétation de La Convention Européenne des Droits de l'Homme*, ed. Frédéric Sudre (Brussels: Nemesis/Bruylant, 1998), 133–174 and Achim Seifert, "L'effet Horizontal des Droits Fondamentaux : Quelques Réflexions de Droit Européen et de Droit Comparé," *Revue Trimestrielle de Droit Européen* 48 (2012): 801–826. The first important element of the Strasbourg jurisprudence that both Sudre and Spielmann emphasise concerns the effectiveness of the Convention rights (l'effectivité du droit) and the role the state plays in guaranteeing this effectiveness. This point plays a crucial role in the "Hegelian" arguments that will ultimately be forwarded in this book. At issue in this regard is a conceptual shift away from the identification of the state as the principal threat to fundamental rights towards an identification of the state as the principal guarantor of fundamental rights. See in this regard especially Chapter Five.

izontality revolution, or its absence, has clearly become a crucial and wide-ranging concern of contemporary legal systems.

The horizontality revolution has not always been silent though. Unlike the ECHR, many jurisdictions of the world have been grappling and still grapple expressly and vociferously with their horizontality revolutions. They regard the horizontal application of fundamental rights as a problematic, complicated and basically anomalous legal phenomenon that must be explained and best be explained away at that. For this purpose, their judiciaries and scholars have mostly converged approvingly around the notion of *indirect horizontal effect.* According to these scholars and judiciaries, indirect horizontal effect establishes a sound middle way. It avoids the extremes of the direct invocation of constitutional rights in private disputes, on the one hand, and the complete denial of the normative relevance of constitutional rights to private legal disputes, on the other. The notion of indirect horizontal effect has established a pervasive grip on contemporary legal consciousness. It has indeed become one of the defining characteristics of orthodox legal consciousness today and has therefore turned into a fundamental jurisprudential or legal theoretical concern. It is no longer a merely doctrinal concern. It concerns the way mainstream jurists think about law today.

As the vast literature on the subject has surely explained well enough by now, indirect horizontal effect basically turns on the idea that constitutional rights and principles relevant to disputes between private citizens should never be invoked *directly* in the pleading and judicial resolution of these disputes. They should only be invoked *indirectly.* Pleadings may assert that existing private law is irreconcilable with constitutional principles and accordingly demand from judges an application of private law that accords with and promotes all relevant constitutional law that affects it. As a significant current articulation of the idea puts it, *judiciaries must develop private law so as to give effect to and promote constitutional values in private disputes.*[5]

This principle of indirect horizontal application is usually supplemented by or employed in combination with a second principle that has become another pervasive feature of contemporary judicial reasoning and scholarly inquiry, namely, the idea of *positive duties on states to protect the constitutional rights*

5 Art 8(3) of the South African Constitution of 1996. This is also the central idea developed in the *Lüth* case in Germany, in the *Dolphin Delivery* case in Canada and the *Du Plessis* case in South Africa. Cf. *Lüth* BVerfGE, 7 198 (1958), hereafter cited as *Lüth*; *RWDSU v. Dolphin Delivery,* 573 2 (S.C.R. 1986), hereafter cited as *Dolphin Delivery*; *Du Plessis v De Klerk,* 1996 (5) BCLR 658 (CC), hereafter cited as *Du Plessis.* Cf. Chapter Two for detailed discussions of and full references to these cases.

of their citizens. As we saw above, Verhey highlights this idea or principle as one of the pillars of the ECHR jurisprudence. Some scholarly doubt has been raised regarding the question whether these two ideas actually belong together.[6] This book does not go so far as to suggest the two notions have nothing to do with one another, but it endorses the *positive duty* approach as by far the better approach and questions key aspects of the indirect horizontality approach incisively. Suffice it nevertheless simply to observe, for now, that the *indirect horizontal effect approach*, either alone, or supplemented by the *positive duty approach*, has established itself as a dominant characteristic of judicial reasoning in many countries of the world. Alongside the jurisprudence of the ECHR, European states party to the Human Rights Convention predominantly follow this approach or combination of approaches, in their national jurisdictions. This is surely true for German case law, the key decision of which will receive extensive attention in this book,[7] but also for the majority of European jurisdictions.[8]

---

6 Cf. the discussion of *Drittwirkung*, Chapter Four.

7 Spielmann suggests that the German distinction between direct and indirect horizontal application (unmittelbare/mittelbare Drittwirkung) influenced the Strasbourg Court's jurisprudence significantly as is evident from Strasbourg's parallel distinction between the direct applicability of the Convention rights to private persons, on the one hand, and the positive duty on states to guarantee these rights, on the other. Cf. Spielmann, "Obligations Positives et Effet Horizontal des Dispositions de La Convention," 154.

8 Several panaromic comparative studies of horizontal effect in Europe and elsewhere are available that convey this message clearly. Andrew Clapham, *Human Rights Obligations of Non-State Actors* (Oxford: Oxford University Press, 2006); Clapham, *Human Rights in the Private Sphere* (Oxford: Clarendon Press, 1993); Daniel Friedmann and Daphne Barak-Erez, eds., *Human Rights in Private Law* (Oxford: Hart Publishing, 2001); Jörg Fedtke and Dawn Oliver, eds., *Human Rights and the Private Sphere: A Comparative Study* (Abingdon: Routledge-Cavendish, 2007); Jörg Neuner, ed., *Grundrechte und Privatrecht aus rechtsvergleichender Sicht* (Tübingen: Mohr Siebeck, 2007); Gert Brüggemeier, Aurelia Ciacchi, and Giovanni Comandé, eds., *Fundamental Rights and Private Law in the European Union – Vol. I: A Comparative Overview* (Cambridge: Cambridge University Press, 2010). Spain seems to be an exceptional case. Article 9(1) of the Spanish Constitution determines that "citizens and public authorities are subject to the Constitution and to the rest of the legal system." Article 9(1) would therefore seem to constitute a direct horizontal effect regime in Spain, very similar to the one effected by article 8(2) of the South African Constitution of 1996. Andrea Rodriquez Liboreiro surprisingly does not take article 9(1) as a self-evident textual basis for direct horizontal effect and she also indicates significant disagreement between Spanish theorists in this regard. Cf. Liboreiro, "Spain – A Jurisdiction Recognising the Direct Horizontal Application of Human Rights," in *Human Rights and the Private Sphere: A Comparative Study*, ed. Jörg Fedtke and Dawn Oliver (Abingdon: Routledge-Cavendish, 2007), 389. Juan María Bilbao Ubillos, "Die Einwirkung der Grundrechte auf das spanische Privatrecht," in *Grundrechte und Privatrecht aus rechtsvergleichender Sicht*, ed. Jörg Neuner (Tübingen: Mohr Siebeck, 2007), 119–158 makes a similar assessment of the situation in

This book articulates a comprehensive and incisive critique of this pervasive indirect horizontal effect approach and of the vague jurisprudence that accompanies it. The main argument on which the critique pivots is this: The indirect horizontal application doctrine effects an obfuscation of the key questions that the effect of constitutional rights in the private sphere raises for the theory and practice of constitutional review, on the one hand, and for an incisive understanding of liberal democratic constitutionalism in our time, on the other. The argument will proceed by highlighting four of these key questions that emerge from a narrative of twelve key horizontal application cases that have been decided by constitutional judiciaries in the United States, Canada, Germany and South Africa. The significance of these questions, however, only becomes apparent when one takes into consideration the nineteenth century backgrounds from which the horizontality revolution sprung. Chapter One therefore first takes a close look at the main features of the nineteenth century jurisprudential backgrounds from which the horizontality revolution took leave in the course of the 20th century. The jurisprudential histories that are selected for this purpose are those of the United States and Germany. These two histories also inform the two scholarly debates about horizontal effect, the German and the American, with reference to which the main theses of this book are articulated.

Spain. In its decision in *Engel v Engel* of 17 January 1985, Luxembourg's Cour Supérieure de Justice (Cour de Cassation) followed the positive duty approach that the European Court of Human Rights articulated in its *Marckx* decision. Cf. Spielmann, *L'effet potentiel de la Convention européenne des droits de l'homme entre personnes privées*, 53; Patrick Kinsch, "Dean Spielmann, *L'Effet Potential de la Convention Européenne des Droits de l'Hommage entre Personnes Privées,*" *Annales du Droit Luxembougeoise*, (1995): 493–496, (Review of Dean Spielmann *L'Effet Potential de la Convention Européenne des Droits de l'Hommage entre Personnes Privées*), Annales du Droit Luxembourgeoise, 1995, 494. An implicit recognition of horizontal effect is also evident in the decision of the Cour de Cassation of 10 July 1992. Cf. Spielmann, "Obligations Positives et Effet Horizontal des Dispositions de la Convention," 166–167. Cf. the Bibliography at the back of this book for further references to literature on horizontal effect in Europe, and especially to the many contributions to the debate in the United Kingdom. The approach to horizontal effect in the UK turns on the question whether the alleged abridgment of one of the rights entrenched in the Human Rights Act of 1998 can be attributed to a public authority in terms of Section 6(1) of the act. Cf. *Aston Cantlow Parochial Church Council v Wallbank* [2003] UKHL 37. However, since Section 6(3) also identifies a court or tribunal as a public authority, applications and interpretations of the common law by UK courts must remain consistent with the rights entrenched in the Act, hence also the remarkable judicial development of the common law remedies for breach of confidence into a veritable right to privacy in *Douglas v Hello* [2005] EWCA Civ 595.

II Two Histories, Four Questions, Twelve Cases, Two Scholarly Debates

The picture of nineteenth century jurisprudence that emerges from the development of nineteenth century law in America and Germany traced in Chapter One testifies to the two major distinctions and divisions that came to structure jurisprudence towards the end of the nineteenth and beginning of the twentieth century, namely, the distinction and division between private and public law, on the one hand, and the distinction and division between law and socio-economic history, on the other. The former division resulted from the revolutionary and democratic expulsion of social hierarchies from public relations. The latter division, concludes Chapter One, led to a remarkable inversion of the coordinates on which the former division turned. The expulsion of social hierarchies from public relations – the final consolidations of which were the removal of all class and gender restrictions on voting rights and the termination of significant hereditary rule – should have impressed upon political and legal theory and legal systematics the conception that public relations are horizontal. This was not to be. The separation of law from socio-economic history on which late 19th century jurisprudence came to insist programmatically – when jurisprudence came to ignore socio-economic baseline questions dogmatically, as Chapter One puts it – made it plausible to look upon public law relations as vertical power relations (between superiors and inferiors) and upon private law relations as horizontal relations (between equals). It is only when early twentieth century jurisprudence again began to take cognisance of the historical realities reflected in socio-economic baseline questions that the inverse reality of public and private law relations became apparent. Proper cognisance in *realist* and *sociological* approaches to law and jurisprudence of the socio-economic realities that informed late nineteenth and early twentieth century law began to reveal the extent to which private law relations were becoming increasingly vertical and hierarchical. And it was only against this background that jurisprudence could again begin to look towards public law and public relations as the real locus and promise of horizontal relations.

Nineteenth century liberal democratic societies insisted increasingly that any tolerance of hierarchies in public life must be subjected to express and conscious justification. On the other hand, they also insisted that private hierarchies must generally be tolerated as natural outcomes of virtuous diligence and natural talent. These two broad normative attitudes became increasingly difficult to reconcile with one another when private hierarchies evidently became oppressive enough to render the democratic insistence on the absence of public hierarchies increasingly shallow and meaningless. It is to this socio-historical reality that the horizontality revolution in twentieth century constitutional jurisprudence responded by insisting on adequate subordination of the former to the latter, that is, adequate subordination of vertical private law relations to the horizontality of public law relations. Seen from this perspective, the horizontality revolution in constitutional review must be understood as a move towards the horizontalisation or re-horizontalisation of private law relationships, and not as a move towards applying constitutional demands *to* horizontal relations. To the extent that it has *horizontalising effect*, the horizontality revolution in constitutional review concerns a horizontalisation of private relations, and not an interference with relations that are already horizontal.

Whether the horizontal effect revolution in constitutional review has significant *horizontalising* effect remains doubtful. It has largely remained a conceptual or jurisprudential revolution. In other words, it has at best been a conceptual revolution of sorts. It has not brought about a social revolution with real horizontalising historical significance. The horizontal effect jurisprudence of the European Court of Human Rights in Strasbourg may well be one of the socially more progressive examples of horizontal effect jurisprudence. However, it is exactly with regard to the jurisprudence of this court that Sudre observes with dismay the failure to ensure socio-economic rights in Europe.[9] Sudre cites and comments upon the observation of Justice Thór Vilhjálmmsson in his dissenting opinion in the *Airey* decision in this regard:

> "One can hardly win the war against poverty by interpreting the European Convention of Human Rights." However, it would nevertheless appear preferable not to add to this economic and social exclusion also a juridical exclusion."[10]

As if Strasbourg's failure to promote a robust egalitarian horizontal effect jurisprudence required insult upon injury, the ECJ has, exactly by means of horizontal effect of the fundamental liberties guaranteed by the European Union Treaties, come to articulate what many academic observers perceive to be an anti-egalitarian and anti-social jurisprudence in a series of judgments (*Laval*, *Viking*, *Rüffert*, *Luxembourg*) to which we return in Chapter Seven. This jurisprudence of the ECJ would indeed seem to be undermining levels of social security and

---

9 Cf. Sudre, "Obligations positives," 1366: "Il n'est guère supportable que le droit européen des droits de l'homme ne puisse intégrer, au titre des droits garantis, le droit de vivre dans des conditions conformes à la dignité de la personne humaine."

10 Cf. Sudre, "Obligations positives," 1366: "'On ne peut pas gagner la guerre contre la pauvreté en interprétant largement la Convention européenne des droits de l'homme.' Il paraît, néanmoins, souhaitable de ne pas ajouter l'exclusion juridique à l'exclusion économique et sociale."

equality guaranteed by the national constitutions of some European Union Member States.[11] The quiet horizontal effect revolution that Verhey invokes has therefore by no means convincingly brought about anything close to a social revolution. The horizontalising potential of horizontal effect is not yet on the horizon of European horizontal effect jurisprudence or any other horizontal effect jurisprudence. We return to this distressing reality in Chapter Eight. It is important to note already here, however, that the social consequences of the ECJ's jurisprudence in the *Laval*-series of cases are not conclusively clear. There are some who argue forcefully that the freedom of movement that the findings in these cases promote at the expense of social security measures and structures in some host states, may actually serve the goal of (invisible hand) social redistribution in Europe.

This argument will not convince those who believe that the destruction of minimum social security guarantees that were achieved after decades (or longer) of painstaking political processes, will only spread vulnerability with no real gain in general social security. Chapter Seven returns to this deep difference of

11 As mentioned we return to these cases in Chapter Seven. We shall also see then that the GFCC has remarkably not observed any serious discrepancy between German constitutional jurisprudence and the jurisprudence of the ECJ in these cases in its *Lisbon* judgment. But it is exactly with reference to a similar observation in its *Maastricht* judgment of 1986 that a former judge of the GFCC recently pointed out the potential for increasing tensions in this regard. Cf. Dieter Grimm, "Prinzipien statt Pragmatismus" *Frankfurter Allgemeine Zeitung*, 6 February 2013: "Fehlt es dem Gericht jedoch an Gelegenheiten, seine grundsätzlichen Positionen in konkrete Entscheidungen umzusetzen, könnte es dazu kommen, dass sich das "noch hinnehmbar" perpetuiert. Was ihm unter diesen Umständen bliebe, wären die kleineren Korrekturen im Bereich der Anwendung der Verträge, also das Halt bei eindeutigen Kompetenzverletzungen oder gravierenden Grundrechtsdivergenzen. Das erste würde eine Revision der Mangold-Entscheidung voraussetzen, wonach selbst in eindeutigen Fällen von fehlender EU-Kompetenz ein europäischer Rechtsakt nur dann unanwendbar sein soll, wenn er zu einer Gewichtsverschiebung im Machtgefüge von EU und Mitgliedstaaten führt. Die zweite würde eine Aktivierung der Solange-Rechtsprechung verlangen, derzufolge das Bundesverfassungsgericht europäische Rechtsakte am Maßstab der nationalen Grundrechte messen darf, wenn die EU es an einem adäquaten Grundrechtsschutz fehlen lässt. Gegenwärtig ruht diese Kompetenz, weil das Bundesverfassungsgericht 1986 erklärt hat, dass der europäische Grundrechtsschutz dem deutschen im Wesentlichen entspricht. Mit fortschreitender Integration treten aber vermehrt Divergenzen zutage. Tendenziell prüft der EuGH nationales Recht streng, europäisches dagegen grosszügig. Tendenziell wiegen in seiner Rechtsprechung die wirtschaftlichen Freiheiten stärker als die personalen und kommunikativen. In der Rechtsprechung des Bundesverfassungsgerichts ist es umgekehrt. Ob sich daran durch die nunmehr in Kraft befindliche Grundrechte-Charta der EU und den bevorstehenden Beitritt zur Europäischen Menschenrechtskonvention etwas ändert, muss sich zeigen. Vorerst bleibt es ein Feld, auf dem das Bundesverfassungsgericht noch eine Wächterrolle zu spielen hat."

opinion, but not to take part in it or resolve it. In the final analysis, the social consequences of the ECJ's horizontal effect jurisprudence may well be unfathomable. Chapter Seven returns to these conflicting perceptions to make a different point: Whatever the social consequences of the ECJ's *Laval* jurisprudence, this jurisprudence as such has dramatic consequences for the locus of sovereignty in the European Union, for the *Laval* jurisprudence effected a decisive shift in Europe as far as political sovereignty is concerned. In this regard, the horizontality revolution evident in the ECJ's *Laval* jurisprudence is quietly bringing about a significant political revolution. Verhey may well want to refer one day to the *stille Luxemburgse revolutie* – the quiet political revolution – that came to a head in Luxembourg in December 2007 with the *Laval* and *Viking* decisions of the ECJ, as Joseph Weiler has in fact done long before these cases.[12]

The arguments in this book ultimately accept or concede that the horizontal effect revolution in constitutional jurisprudence will probably never effect progressive social revolutions or reforms. If progressive social revolutions or reforms still stand any real chances in this world, they stand them with progressive social movements and electoral politics, not with judicial review. However, it is for the sake of indeed giving such progressive politics a better chance (or at least an equal chance) that this book resists the kind of horizontal effect review that the ECJ conducted in the *Laval* and *Viking* cases. It consequently aims to articulate an understanding of horizontal effect review that *generally* defers to legislative outcomes when confronted with questions of substantive social justice, something that the ECJ surely did not do in *Laval*, *Viking* or *Rüffert*.

However, the arguments in favour of general deference to legislative outcomes that will be forwarded in this book do accept and underline the possibility of exceptional cases in which deference to legislation is not the appropriate judicial response. The decision of the USSC in *DeShaney v Winnebago County Social Services Department* will be the prime example in this book of how things can go seriously wrong in this respect. The conception of horizontal effect review articulated in this book firstly resists the aberrational judicial deference of the kind displayed in *DeShaney*. But it also resists the aberrational judicial activism that the ECJ exemplified in the *Laval*-series of cases. In other words, the conception of horizontal effect review that will be offered in this book aims to promote an understanding of constitutional review that will resist abdications of sovereignty, on the one hand, and juristocratic usurpations of sovereignty, on the other.

---

12 Cf. Joseph Weiler "A Quiet Revolution. The European Court of Justice and its Interlocutors," *Comparative Political Studies*, 26 (1994) 510–534.

Let us return now to the conceptual or semantic revolution at stake when one invokes "the horizontal effect revolution" in the context of constitutional review. Chapter One traces this conceptual revolution to the French Revolution, that is, to the new way in which the revolutionary generation came to think about law at the end of the eighteenth century. If the conceptual revolution at stake in the notion of the "horizontal effect revolution" is ultimately to become a coherent reflection of its political revolutionary origins, it will need to effect a historically significant *substantive political* horizontalisation of private relations and a subordination of all private relations to *fundamentally public* norms and concerns. This is what the French Revolution was all about, at least conceptually. The horizontal effect revolution in twentieth century constitutional review has thus far shied away from this potential political historical significance by allowing itself a fundamental equivocation that leaves it more or less meaningless. It has settled on a self-understanding that pivots on vague and ambiguous notions of a private sphere that remains untouched by or shielded from constitutional norms, on the one hand (hence the pervasive rejection of direct horizontal effect of constitutional norms), but nevertheless influenced by constitutional norms (hence the pervasive endorsement of indirect horizontal effect), on the other. Seen from this perspective, the horizontal effect revolution has not even lived up to the conceptual revolution that it promised or promises, let alone the social or political revolution that one may have wanted to expect from it. It is in response to this conceptually vague, ambiguous and ultimately self-negating jurisprudence that this book seeks to develop a sounder understanding of horizontal effect. And it commences to do so by posing four key questions that emerge from the equivocation that goes by the name of indirect horizontal effect:

1) Why has horizontal application at all been identified as a separate and new development in constitutional review, considering the fact that constitutional review is always performed by a court of law and therefore always involves a branch of government and organ of state that is subject to ordinary constitutional review? One can call this the *Shelley* conundrum, given its dramatic exemplification in the United States Supreme Court decision in *Shelley v Kraemer.* [13]
2) Why has horizontal application at all been identified as a separate and new development in constitutional review if all law is subject to constitutional review and private law or common law is surely part and parcel of law?

13 334 U.S. 1 (1948), hereafter cited as *Shelley.*

One can call this the *Swing* and *Sullivan* conundrum, given its curious manifestation in the cases of *Labour v Swing*[14] and *New York Times v Sullivan.*[15]

3) It is trite that laws that proscribe crimes such as murder, rape, assault and theft are as applicable in the most private of private spheres (private homes and private bedrooms – here too one is not allowed to murder, rape, assault or steal) as they are outside these private spheres. Why is there nevertheless such a strong perception afoot in horizontal application jurisprudence that there are pockets of sheer privacy that lie beyond the reach of the law and therefore beyond the application of constitutional rights? We shall call this the Kriegler conundrum because of the particularly striking way the former South African constitutional judge Johann Kriegler articulated the argument. However, an engagement with case law and scholarly literature in the United States and Germany will show that this perception is not just a South African curiosity.
4) How can one distinguish clearly between private law disputes and constitutional law disputes in order to avoid turning constitutional courts into final courts of appeal in all private law matters? (One can call this the "extra appeal court" conundrum.)

This book traces the ways in which these questions have emerged from twelve key state action or horizontal effect cases decided by constitutional judiciaries in the course of the twentieth century. The cases – seven from the United States, one from Canada, three from Germany and one from South Africa – were not selected because they are more significant than all other high profile horizontal effect cases decided in the world in the course of the previous century. They were selected solely for reasons of the sufficient significance and exemplarity that one can draw from them. They are exemplary instances of the horizontal effect jurisprudence of the twentieth century on the basis of which one can construct the dominant narrative of horizontal effect jurisprudence that unfolded in the course of this century. This exemplarity, however, surely does not eradicate the significant margin of arbitrariness that also played a part in their selection for this narrative. They could easily have been replaced by many other cases, but all possible selections would have ended up being arbitrary in some way or another.

What, however, is at stake in the exemplarity invoked here? Exemplarity is after all itself a notion that is always informed by various degrees of choice and decision. It is never a simple reflection of the way "things are." The choice and

14 312 U.S. 321 (1941), hereafter cited as *Swing.*
15 376 U.S. 254 (1963), hereafter cited as *Sullivan.*

decision that informed the perception of exemplarity in the cases selected for discussion in this book concerns the way these cases exemplify the problematic relation between private liberty and state sovereignty that still bothers jurisprudence and legal theory, now well more than three and even four centuries after the first modern articulations of this relation in the thought of political philosophers such as Jean Bodin (1530 – 1596), Thomas Hobbes (1588 – 1679) and John Locke (1632 – 1704). The question whether politically significant liberty is a natural given that limits sovereign authority (natural liberty as conceived by Locke) or a product of sovereign authority (civil liberty as conceived by Hobbes and arguably also by Bodin) is one that would continue to inform and define modern constitutional thought and the institutional practice of constitutional review. And after having been stabilised somewhat in the field of classical vertical constitutional review that governs the relations between states and citizens, the question would again raise its head in rather unruly fashion with the doctrines of state action and horizontal effect or *Drittwirkung* that the USSC and the GFCC would precipitate with their respective judgments in *The Civil Rights Cases* in 1883 and *Lüth* in 1957. In terms of dominant or formative developments in legal theory, these two cases and their consequences can plausibly be argued to have turned the twentieth century into the century of state action and horizontal effect constitutional review.

The ten other cases discussed in Chapter Two have been selected for the way they allow one to trace or construct the destiny of the *The Civil Rights Cases* and *Lüth* and certain key moments in the history of horizontal effect jurisprudence in the course of the twentieth century. Chapter Seven later adds three more cases to the discussion – the *Laval*, *Viking* and *Rüffert* cases decided by the ECJ in 2007 and 2008. These cases allow one not only to trace the twentieth century development of horizontal effect into the twenty first century, but also to illuminate the way it would contribute to the significant transfer of sovereignty that would result from the process of European integration.

The two theoretical or scholarly debates about state action or horizontal effect that are discussed in Chapters Three and Four have also not been selected because they are more important than similar debates elsewhere in the world. As already pointed out above, a significant horizontal effect debate has also unfolded in recent years in South Africa in response to the challenge to think through the transformation demands stipulated by the South African Constitutions of 1993 and 1996. Similar socially and politically pertinent horizontal effect debates can surely also be found in other countries of the world. The American and German debates were nevertheless selected for discussion because these debates did coin a number of key concepts that would also come to dominate debates elsewhere in the world. And the American and German debates also developed these concepts in ways that allow one to link them to the broader legal and political theoretical questions regarding the relation between sovereignty and liberty mentioned above.

None or very few (I am not aware of one) of the many panoramic discussions of horizontal effect that are available today have made the crucial move to discuss this problematic in the broader context of the deeper political and legal theoretical concerns that lurk in the question of horizontal effect.[16] This is what this book seeks to do now by linking the question of horizontal effect expressly to a broader theoretical concern with the structuring concepts of liberal democratic constitutionalism, foremost among them being the concept of liberal democratic sovereignty.

III Liberal Democratic Constitutionalism

In other words, the aim of this book is to explain the deep conceptual problems that keep on plaguing the question of the horizontal effect of fundamental rights in terms of the deeper tensions that emanate from the *apparently* contradictory or paradoxical aspirations of liberal constitutional democracy. These "contradictory" or "paradoxical" concerns of liberal constitutional democracy are usually articulated in terms of the tensions between *constitutionalism*, on the one hand, and *democracy*, on the other, or, between the *sovereignty of the constitution* and *popular sovereignty*.[17] This book offers a decidedly different view. It believes the real tensions at issue here are between *liberal* constitutionalism and *democratic* constitutionalism. The ideas of liberalism and constitutionalism can easily be squared or reconciled with one another, as liberal political and legal theorists maintain convincingly. There is nothing contentious about this claim. Contentious would only be the more expansive claim that constitutionalism can be reconciled and squared with *nothing but* liberalism. This claim would, in fact, not only be contentious. It would be wrong. Popular sovereignty and constitutionalism can be squared as well, as is evident from the sufficiently coherent and plausible framework of anti-liberal jurisprudence that Carl Schmitt developed in his constitutional theory. A people's constitution can be the embodiment of its exis-

16 There are many publications available that provide admirable and reliable encyclopaedic and introductory overviews of this field of law. Cf. again footnote 8.

17 Martin Loughlin and Neil Walker, eds., *The Paradox of Constitutionalism: Constituent Power and Constitutional Form* (Oxford: Oxford University Press, 2008).

tential endorsement of popular sovereignty, argued Schmitt, without falling foul of basic demands of logic and coherence.[18]

What appears to defy reconciliation and synthesis, however, are the evidently insurmountable tensions and differences between *liberal* constitutionalism, on the one hand, and the *popular-sovereign* or *democratic* constitutionalism of the kind that the likes of Schmitt articulate and promote, on the other. In other words, it is the apparently irresolvable nature of the tensions and differences between two completely different and distinct concepts of constitutionalism, namely, the concept of democratic constitutionalism and the concept of liberal constitutionalism, that has come to plague legal and political theory with the erroneous idea of the irresolvable paradoxes or contradictions of a third and again entirely different and distinct concept of constitutionalism, namely *liberal democracy* or *liberal democratic constitutionalism.*

The first of the concepts of constitutionalism invoked here, *democratic* constitutionalism, can of course also be understood and described as *constitutional sovereignty*, that is, in terms of the sovereignty of a people that is defined, articulated and embodied in its constitution. Considering the twist Schmitt has given to these terms, one can also describe the constitutionality at issue in *constitutional sovereignty* as the concrete *existential embodiment* or concrete *bodily existence* of sovereignty. Chapter Six pays more attention to Schmitt's conception of constitutional embodiment or embodied constitutionalism and contrasts this conception with Kelsen's *disembodied* concept of constitutionalism. Most of the key arguments forwarded towards the end of this book are based squarely on the latter. Suffice it nevertheless to state for now that *constitutional sovereignty* or the *sovereignty of the constitution* should not be applied exclusively to either popular-democratic or liberal constitutionalism. It applies to both. It applies to both the embodied Schmittian and disembodied Kelsenian conceptions of constitutional sovereignty that will be distinguished and contrasted in this book. And it also applies to the third conception of constitutional sovereignty that this book ultimately develops on the basis of Kelsen's disembodied concept of constitutionalism, namely, the conception of *liberal democratic constitutionalism* or *liberal constitutional democracy.*

However, liberal democratic constitutionalism should not be misunderstood as a simple compound of liberal constitutionalism, on the one hand, and democratic constitutionalism, on the other. It is a completely different concept that must be understood on its own terms. And it is on the basis of this completely different concept of liberal democratic constitutionalism that this book will ad-

---

18 Carl Schmitt, *Verfassungslehre* (Berlin: Duncker & Humblot, 2003).

dress the problems that plague the theoretical conceptualisation of the horizontal effect of constitutional principles. It is only and exactly from the background of the first two concepts of constitutionalism, the two monolithic conceptions of constitutionalism in terms of either liberal constitutionalism or popular sovereignty, that the third, the concept of liberal democratic sovereignty, appears unworkable. It is only from the perspective of simplistic conceptions of liberal constitutionalism, on the one hand, and simplistic conceptions of popular-sovereign constitutionalism, on the other, that the more complex (and conceptually exponentially more refined) idea of *liberal democracy* or *liberal democratic constitutional sovereignty* appears incoherent, paradoxical, contradictory, etc. And it is from this unfortunate vantage point that contemporary constitutional review jurisprudence has run into the conceptual trouble in which it finds itself today. Simplistic and unrefined understandings of *liberal constitutional democracy* or *liberal constitutional democratic sovereignty* as a brittle compound of two monolithic substances (liberal constitutionalism, on the one hand, and democratic constitutionalism, on the other) that chemically resist cohesion have caused the conceptual havoc evident in contemporary horizontal effect judicial review.

It is not important whether this unfortunate background conception of liberal democratic constitutionalism as an unstable compound of two mutually resistant substances has been or is entertained expressly or just implicitly in horizontal effect jurisprudence. It usually amounts to little more than a silent background conception that informs horizontal effect discourses vaguely. It is nevertheless important to grasp that this unfortunate background conception has led consciously or sub-consciously to the hegemony of the well-meaning but ultimately insidious notion of the *indirect horizontal effect of constitutional rights*. This is the key contention with which this book commences:

The notion of indirect horizontal effect is the result of a discourse through which judiciaries, ill informed by notions of irresolvable tensions between liberal and democratic sovereignty, obfuscate the way horizontal effect adjudication apparently confronts them with either a liberty deficit or a sovereignty deficit.

This key contention can be articulated in more or less the same way with regard to the state action doctrine:

The varying vicissitudes of state action doctrine adjudication (which have led some observers to view it as a conceptual disaster area) are likewise a function of judicial and scholarly failure to come to terms with the apparently incircumventible choices between sovereignty deficits and liberty deficits that arise whenever the question of the private violation of constitutional rights raises its head.

It is important to take a closer look at each of the two deficits that are at issue here by relating them to the four key horizontal effect questions pointed out above. The first three questions result from jurisprudential endeavours to avoid liberty deficits. The fourth question results from the jurisprudential regard for the unjustifiable sovereignty deficits that will result from any attempt to limit the effect of constitutional law to public spheres.

The liberty deficit

The first two of the four key questions pointed out above, respectively tagged as the *Shelley v Kraemer* and *Swing and Sullivan* conundrums, confront judiciaries with the elementary reality that unitary systems of statehood and unitary systems of law must surely be governed through and through by the fundamental normative concepts on which these unitary systems of statehood and law turn. These fundamental normative concepts are usually articulated in state constitutions. No branch of government and no branch of law can be exempted from the general normative framework that state constitutions impose on unitary systems of statehood. The judiciary is surely such a branch of government that is part and parcel of a system of unitary statehood. Judiciaries can thus also not be exempted from the normative constitutional frameworks that inform systems of statehood. Private law is surely a branch of law that is part and parcel of unitary statehood. Private law can thus also not be exempted from the normative constitutional frameworks that inform systems of statehood. Some judiciaries nevertheless experience grave difficulty when they are required to face up to these elementary facts of statehood, and the contortions of state action or horizontal effect jurisprudence are the direct results of this difficulty. Judiciaries experience this difficulty because they are haunted by the idea that due recognition of these elementary principles and facts of statehood must culminate in negations and destructions of essential elements of personal liberty that liberal democracies must safeguard and respect. According to these judiciaries, these essential elements of personal liberty therefore require that the recognition of the unitary normativity of unitary systems of state be ignored or suspended when the effect of constitutional norms on private relations and private legal relations is at stake. Some kind of special exception must be made for private spheres and private law if the liberty promised by liberal democracy is to be safeguarded, for private individuals will somehow no longer be able to consider themselves free if they are subject to the constitutional norms that underpin the unitary system of statehood.

However, to remain coherent, this judicial exemption of private individuals from constitutional norms for the sake of safeguarding spheres of private liberty obviously also has to ignore the reality reflected in the third key question pointed out above, the question tagged as the *Kriegler conundrum*. The criminal codes and criminal laws of liberal democracies very obviously impose fundamental and demanding normative demands on the most private of private spheres. No defence to a criminal charge can stand on an argument that the crime at issue was committed in the private sphere and may thus not be prosecuted. Why should this defence then somehow become viable when a violation of a constitutional norm is at stake? Should there be any good reason for the viability of this defence against charges of constitutional violations, that reason cannot turn on the blank or blanket notion that liberal democracies should not impose normative demands of statehood on private spheres, for they regularly do so in the case of criminal law. It will have to turn on some other reason and it is one of the key aims of this book to determine whether and how such an other reason can be articulated coherently.

The sovereignty deficit

There are nevertheless some judges and judiciaries that conspicuously endorse, without much ado at that, the insight that private spheres are as subject to the effects of constitutional law as they are to the effects of criminal law. They see no reason why private spheres should be exempted from any of these effects. According to them, such exemption would make as much nonsense of the idea of constitutional law as the general exemption of private spheres from criminal law would make sheer nonsense of the idea of criminal law and ultimately of the idea of law as such. For these judges, such exemptions would amount to fundamental denials of sovereign statehood, fundamental denials of the fundamental concept of the complete territorial rule of the sovereign's law or the complete territorial rule of sovereign law. According to these judges, any attempt to exempt private spheres from the demands of constitutional law must result in sovereignty deficits that undermine basic principles of statehood and the rule of law.

We shall see in Chapter Two that the judges who presided in *Shelley v Kraemer, Labour v Swing* and *New York Times v Sullivan* and the judiciary that presided in *Lüth* were not bothered by the liberty deficits that clearly haunted the judges in *RWDSU v Dolphin Delivery Ltd* and *Du Plessis v De Klerk*. Why were they not bothered by the liberty deficits that so haunted the judges in *Dolphin* and *Du Plessis?* They were not bothered thus, because, we shall argue, according to them, the concept of sovereignty in terms of complete territorial rule does not threaten liberty. To the contrary, it safeguards it. They obviously subscribed to the Hobbesian understanding of sovereignty as the source of civil liberty, not its termination or antithesis. That is why they were more concerned with sovereignity deficits than they were with liberty deficits.

The endorsement of a coherent concept of statehood and of sovereignty as complete territorial rule nevertheless raises a question that the judges in

Swing, *Shelley*, *Sullivan* and *Carmichele* and the judiciary in *Lüth* have not faced properly and incisively, even though *Lüth* raised the question expressly. The question at issue is the fourth of the key questions pointed out above: How can one distinguish clearly between private law disputes and constitutional law disputes if all private relations and all private law relations are, in accordance with the principle of the sovereign rule of law, in principle subject to constitutional review? How can one avoid turning constitutional courts into final courts of appeal in all private law matters when one endorses the complete territorial rule of sovereign law? This question can be answered satisfactorily, however, when one maintains a consistent regard for the relations between sovereignty and liberty within liberal democracies. In the same way that liberal democratic sovereigns would allow for wide spectra of conduct that are not burdened by criminal sanctions, it would also allow for wide spectra of conduct that are not burdened by constitutional sanctions. The rejection of the notion of any a-priori or natural spheres of private conduct that are in principle exempted from constitutional law that a coherent concept of statehood and sovereignty requires, does not amount to the idea that all private conduct is constitutionally relevant. A liberal democratic sovereign would as little "constitutionalise" vast spectra of private conduct as it would criminalise vast spectra of private conduct. The liberal democratic sovereign, John Rawls teaches us well, is, neither in its criminal law nor in its constitutional law, in the business of enforcing comprehensive worldviews that subject every aspect of life to questions of right and wrong. The liberal democratic sovereign is only in the business of maintaining and enforcing a number of essential principles, principles of public reason Rawls calls them, without which liberal democracies cannot function properly.[19]

The horizontal effect of constitutional rights does accordingly not concern the blanket question whether constitutional norms apply to private relations. It concerns the more specific question whether they apply to the specific private conduct at stake. At issue under horizontal effect is thus not the general question "whether" but the specific questions "when and when not." Only once the "when and when not" question can be approached on sound foundations will it become clear that the recognition of the complete and uninterrupted rule of the sovereign's law need not turn all private disputes into constitutional disputes and need not turn constitutional courts into highest courts of appeal in all pri-

19 John Rawls, *Political Liberalism* (New York: Columbia University Press, 1996). It is noteworthy that Hobbes already recognized that a wise sovereign governs no more than is absolutely necessary to govern. "Unnecessary laws are not good laws," he observed. Cf. Hobbes *Leviathan* in William Molesworth (ed) *The English works of Thomas Hobbes of Malmesbury*, Vol. III (London: John Bohn, 1839), 239–40.

vate disputes. Properly considered as a specific "when and when not" instead of a general "whether" question, horizontal effect becomes a question of *the historical case* and the *definitive historicity* of liberal democracy. We will take a closer look at this definitive liberal democratic historicity below. But we first need to take a closer look at the liberal democratic sovereignty that underpins this definitive historicity.

IV Liberal Democratic Sovereignty

A picture should already be emerging now as to how the arguments in this book endeavour to resolve the conceptual problems of horizontal effect by resituating them properly in a context of liberal democracy. As already indicated above, the whole endeavour seeks to steer clear of current views regarding the paradoxes or contradictions of liberal democracy. It does so by taking the concept of liberal democracy out of the fatal or paralysing crossfire between monolithic conceptions of liberal constitutionalism, on the one hand, and democratic constitutionalism, on the other. It articulates, instead, a concept of liberal democratic constitutionalism that presents it as an independent third concept of constitutionalism. In other words, it presents liberal democratic constitutionalism in its own terms, and not in terms that are parasitic upon monolithic conceptions of either liberal or democratic constitutionalism. And it is from the vantage point of this independent concept of liberal democracy that the arguments in this book seek to remedy the liberty and sovereignty deficits of current conceptions of the horizontal application of fundamental rights. It will not be so bold as to claim that these deficits can be erased entirely. But it will claim that their scope can be narrowed significantly and satisfactorily.

The claim that liberal democracy can and should be contemplated independently of simplistic conceptions of liberalism, on the one hand, and democracy, on the other is surely not new. Jürgen Habermas, to name just one prominent example, has put forward an extensive argument regarding the co-origination of rights and democracy that echoes this claim in many respects.[20] The present argument will, however, not take recourse to Habermas' endeavours in this regard. It is content to regard itself, at least in some respects, as a fellow traveller as far as Habermas is concerned. It nevertheless takes its main inspiration and instruction from a very simple but remarkably effective argument that

20 Jürgen Habermas, *Faktizität und Geltung – Beiträge zur Diskurstheorie des Rechts und des demokratischen Rechtsstaats* (Frankfurt am Main: Suhrkamp, 1992), 112–135; 167–187.

Hans Kelsen developed in *Vom Wesen und Wert der Demokratie.*[21] Kelsen's argument receives full attention in Chapter Six. Suffice it to announce here the rudimentary elements of the moves Kelsen makes in this regard.

A simple conceptual analysis leads Kelsen to contend that the concept of a democratic majority presupposes the co-existence of a democratic minority, and vice versa. The constitutional principle of minority protection therefore comprises, in the same breath, the constitutional sustenance of democratic majorities. Without the constitutional protection of minorities, democratic majorities lose their *majority* status. They may of course still enjoy the physical capacity or sheer avaricious power to present and assert themselves as superior social forces and accordingly impose themselves on weaker social forces. They will, however, no longer be able to rely on the linguistic concept of "majority rule" when they do. And they will accordingly no longer enjoy the *constitutional freedom* to call themselves *majorities.* Or, to put the matter more precisely, they will no longer have the *liberal democratic constitutional freedom* to do so. They will not be liberal democratic majorities.

Liberal democracy, contends Kelsen, consists in the maintenance of majority-minority relationships. This concept of liberal democracy clearly does not at any moment in time, not even as a matter of abstract principle, contemplate the monolithic protection of natural or a-priori liberty against democratic majorities. It endorses the principle of democratic majority rule in no uncertain terms. But it surely also dismisses the monolithic franchising of popular sovereignty at the expense of minorities and minority rights. Kelsen's concept of liberal democracy is not in any way parasitic upon either monolithic liberalism or monolithic popular-sovereignty. Liberal democracy, conceived in Kelsenian terms, is therefore not an unstable compound of two elements that resist proper integration. Separated from one another, neither of the two elements of "liberty" and "democracy" invoked here ever contribute anything meaningful to the completely different and exponentially more textured fabric called *liberal democracy.*

The textured concept of liberal democracy that comes to the fore in Kelsen's work also allows for a textured conception of liberal democratic sovereignty. This conception of liberal democratic sovereignty provides liberal democratic constitutional theory with an understanding of the relationship between sovereignty and liberty that steers clear of both the sovereignty deficits and the liberty deficits that emerge from current judicial and scholarly conceptions of the horizontal effect of fundamental rights. From Kelsen's conception of constitutionalism in terms of the maintenance of minority-majority relations emerges an understand-

---

21 Hans Kelsen, *Vom Wesen und Wert der Demokratie* (Aalen: Scientia Verlag, 1981), 53, 57–58.

ing of sovereignty that premises the legitimate political power of majorities on the liberty of minorities, and vice versa. What emerges from this conception is, in fact, an understanding of sovereignty as fundamentally differentiated or fundamentally informed by a differentiation intrinsic to itself. But this intrinsically differentiated sovereignty need not translates into sovereignty deficits. It simply requires the recognition of *different* and *differing* manifestations of sovereignty in the overall texture of liberal democratic sovereignty. It is helpful to introduce here the concept of a *différant* or *différantial* liberal democracy in terms of which the political *differing* that takes places between majorities and minorities also *defers* the respective identities of both majorities and minorities.[22] The political differences between minorities and majorities do thus not result from preexisting majority and minority identities. Political majorities and minorities receive their respective identities from the way they differ. Their identities always come later. They are constantly postponed or deferred by the differences that call them into existence.

Sovereignty thus defined by the way it sustains fundamental rights and liberties and powers of both minorities and majorities, allows one to understand these fundamental rights and liberties themselves as crucial expressions of sovereignty. The provision that liberal democratic constitutional review must make for these minority rights and liberties need not and must thus not translate into sovereignty deficits. And it likewise needs to recognise that the legitimate sovereignty that becomes manifest in the political power of liberal democratic majorities no longer translates into liberty deficits. It is important to take a closer look now at the concept of liberal democratic liberty that is at issue here. It goes by the name of *historicity.* At issue is the concept of *liberal democratic historicity.*

V Liberal Democratic Historicity

The context of liberal democracy with reference to which this book seeks to resolve the conceptual problems that attach to the question of horizontal effect should be clear now. The task of resolving the questions that attach to horizontal effect should therefore also be clearer now. At issue is the endeavour to resituate the horizontal effect question in the majority-minority relations that define liberal democratic constitutionalism. It seeks to resituate the problematic of horizontal effect in the differing and deferring texture (or texturing) of liberal democracy. And the crucial insight to which this relocation of the horizontal effect

22 Jacques Derrida, *Marges de La Philosophie* (Paris: Les Éditions de Minuit, 1972), 1–29.

question leads, is this: *Not all questions of private law and not all private law disputes can be situated in the context of majority-minority relations.* Private law most often only addresses relations and disputes between individuals, the social-political pertinence of which does not extend beyond the relationships between the individuals directly involved. The personal may sometimes be political, as a contemporary political slogan with sound aspirations contends (and with which the horizontality revolution in constitutional review has much in common). But the personal is not always political.

Disputes between individuals do sometimes have social-political significance that extends beyond the relations of those directly involved. They do so when they relate to some or other significant social minority-majority dispute such as the disputes regarding gay marriage that have come to the fore so dramatically in several liberal democracies in recent years. When they do raise such majority-minority tensions, they evidently raise constitutional questions. They then self-evidently also raise questions regarding the constitutionality of any private law rule or principle that may apply under the circumstances at issue. When they do not raise constitutional issues, when the disputes at issue evidently have no broader political dimension, they can at most raise questions regarding the correct application of private law that have no business in a constitutional court and no business with constitutional jurisprudence.

The need to maintain a clear regard for the difference between cases in which disputes between individuals have broader social political significance and cases in which they do not is one of the key insights that this book aims to contribute to horizontal application jurisprudence. This insight stresses a crucial difference between constitutional law and private law, as we saw above, but does not take anything away from the fact that private law is always subject to the normative demands of the constitution. As such it provides a crucial answer to the fourth key question listed above. It explains why some private disputes do not and should not enjoy the attention of constitutional judiciaries. They concern truly private disputes about private law rights and private law liberties, and concern nothing but these private disputes, because they do not concern and do not raise political questions. All private law is surely systematically subject to the norms of the constitution and potentially subject to constitutional review, but not all private law disputes are interesting or relevant as far as these constitutional norms are concerned.

The distinction between constitutionally relevant and constitutionally irrelevant private disputes expounded here also goes a long way towards explaining why liberal democratic constitutional review need not be as vulnerable to accusations of juristocratic usurpations of sovereignty to which horizontal effect review understandably exposes it. Accusations of juristocratic usurpations of sovereignty are understandable as a result of the highly problematic notion of indirect horizontal effect that has established itself in the discourse of constitutional review. The concept of indirect horizontal effect indeed affords judges vague powers of review that render the whole enterprise of constitutional review highly questionable. It is therefore one of the main aims of this book to dismantle this notion of indirect horizontal effect. We return to this point shortly. Suffice it for now, however, to stress the following: The restriction of constitutional review to questions that obviously relate to social minority-majority tensions not only protects judiciaries against accusations of undue interference with private spheres. It also provides them with much clearer and therefore far less contentious criteria for the decisions that are demanded from them when liberal democratic constitutional review is really at stake.

There is a spectrum of human conduct that is often described in terms of natural or private liberty. At issue is a sphere of purely domestic affairs and relations that have no significance outside this domestic sphere. "Domestic" should not be confused here with the family home. It includes the family home, but it also includes, for instance, domestic arrangements in a corporate office block. Here too one finds arrangements regarding the placing and operation of coffee machines, or arrangements regarding the number of weeks within which an insurance claim must be submitted, etcetera. At issue here is the sum total of private conduct that is simply uninteresting to the constitution, a range of conduct that can perhaps be described in terms of the maxim *de minibus non curat lex constitutionis*. At issue is the range of private liberty that the constitution considers trivial for reasons of being void of any fundamental constitutional question, however high the private and even private law stakes of such conduct may be. One can imagine terrible kitchen quarrels about the placement or misplacement of carving knives. They could even end up in a divorce court. Similar kitchen quarrels can break out in commercial relations. One could have a serious quarrel about the late registration of an insurance claim,[23] or about who may and who may not take photographs at the wedding of celebrities.[24] Quarrels such as these could end up in court and could easily run through the whole assortment of private law appeal courts available and still remain unresolved. The fact that they have run through the whole assortment of private appeal courts available does not thereby turn them into constitutional questions. They remain irreducibly irrelevant as far as constitutional values are concerned. Private liberty is a term

---

23 Cf. *Barkhuizen v Napier* 2007 (5) SA 323 (CC).
24 *Douglas v Hello* [2005] EWCA Civ 595.

that describes areas of constitutional irrelevance. *De minibus non curat lex constitutionis.*[25]

The constitution wakes up from its well-deserved slumber (it needs its rest, it has to last for ages), however, when a private dispute raises questions of social historical significance. And the question of horizontal effect concerns this social historical awakening. The notion of liberty attains a new meaning in this context. It becomes political liberty. It then concerns the liberty to raise matters of fundamental social historical interest. This liberty is rare, or at least rare when compared to the everyday phenomenon of domestic or private liberty. The moments of political liberty concern the disclosure of significant histories. They concern, one might say, the liberty of history to reveal itself differently, the liberty of history to bring to the fore new questions of social existence that galvanise citizens into new democratic minorities and majorities. One can surely refer to these moments as constitutional moments.[26] At issue in these moments is the fundamental *historicity* of liberal democracy, the *defining historicity* of liberal democracy.

The jurisprudence of the state action doctrine and of horizontal effect, we shall see in especially Chapters Three and Four, has run into paralysing conceptual problems because of the way it has been confusing historical liberty with private or natural liberty and historicity with an a-historical domesticity. An in-

---

25 *Barkhuizen v Napier* would seem to be a clear case of *de minibus non curat lex constitutionis. Douglas v Hello* is somewhat more complex but also leans sharply in the direction of *de minibus non curat lex constitutionis.* One can go quickly to the essential issue at stake here. Had Hello published photos that the Douglasses wanted no-one to publish for reasons of unwanted disclosures of their personal or intimate lives, a fundamental right to privacy may well have been at stake. To the extent that the dispute only concerned the unauthorised publication of photographs that another magazine such as OK had the rights and consent to publish, the dispute could at best have been a private law dispute and indeed one between OK and Hello. The problem is that Hello published photographs without consent that were, as far as we know, not significantly more "intrusive" or "disclosing" than the photographs that OK published with consent. And the question is whether this lack of consent alone really raises a constitutional question that can be distinguished from a mere private law question. This does not mean, however, that a constitutional norm, supposing for the moment that article 8 of the Human Rights Act constitutes a constitutional norm, cannot also be used as a private law norm or to develop a private law norm where it is necessary and convenient to do so. That it can be used thus is argued well by Walter Leisner, as will be shown in Chapter Four. Whether *Douglas v Hello* and *Barkhuizen v Napier* raised *constitutional* issues is a question to which we return in Chapter Two. And the background to this question will be a concern with the trivialisation of constitutional issues that threatens to take place when all private disputes come to be regarded as constitutional disputes.

26 Cf. Bruce A. Ackerman, *We the People: Foundations* (Cambridge: Harvard University Press, 2000).

cisive regard for the fundamental historicity of liberal democracy, we shall now see, can help us recover a coherent understanding of liberal democratic constitutional review.

VI Liberal Democratic Constitutional Review

It should have become clear from the conceptual steps taken above that the concept of liberal democracy as a way out of the present conundrums of horizontal effect jurisprudence turns on two fundamental constitutive qualities or moments. It turns, on the one hand, on a conception of sovereignty that is intrinsically differentiated. And it turns, on the other hand, on a conception of historical liberty or liberal historicity. In terms of this conception of liberal historicity, liberty is no longer understood in terms of a natural sphere of private liberties, the parameters, scope and meaning of which are more or less self-evident. It is understood, instead, in terms of the infinitely open scope of possible histories that can come to inform liberal democracy.[27]

The disclosures of the new histories that may come to inform liberal democracy are never self-evident. Their evidence requires critical hermeneutic intervention to become "self-evident." There is, in other words, a fundamental hermeneutic or ontological circle at work in the relation between the liberal democratic historicity and liberal democratic sovereignty that is at issue here. Liberal democratic historicity is a function of liberal democratic sovereignty and vice versa. Liberal democracy pivots on this circularity. And the circle or circularity at issue here turns on acts of interpretation; hence, ultimately, the hermeneutic dynamic or dynamism of this circle. The critical interpretive or hermeneutic question that liberal democracy constantly faces is basically always a variation of this one: Should the historical offing of new minority-majority relations be suppressed or sustained? For instance, should abortions that are not medically indicated be criminalised or decriminalised, notwithstanding the fact that a democratic majority has already decided the matter in one way or another? Only once an interpretation has been forged and a decision has been made does a history become or fail to become evident.

Abortion is indeed the question that this book takes as its key example of the liberal democratic constitutional review with reference to which horizontal effect

27 At issue here is a concept of liberty akin to that which Jean-Luc Nancy articulates, that is, the liberty of existence to reveal itself freely (Jean-Luc Nancy, *L'expérience de la liberté* (Paris: Galilée, 1988).

should be understood. That is why it includes two cases in its discussion of horizontal effect that are rarely properly considered in horizontal effect jurisprudence, namely the decision of the USSC in *Roe v Wade* and the decision of the GFCC in *Erste Abtreibung*. The significance of these cases consists in the way they show up the fundamental deficiency of one of the world's most typical and most exemplary horizontal effect judgements, namely the judgement of the GFCC in the case of *Lüth*. *Lüth* surely plays a pivotal role in the narrative of twelve horizontal effect cases that will be developed in Chapter Two. It is portrayed there as a superior instance of horizontal effect jurisprudence because of the way it stresses the uninterrupted reach of liberal democratic sovereignty. The jurisprudence in *Lüth* surely does not entertain or tolerate sovereignty deficits. But *Lüth* raises another problem, one that is disastrous for the concept of liberal democratic constitutional review that this book offers as an alternative to current conceptions of horizontal effect jurisprudence. The concept of a single objective value order that *radiates* through all aspects and strata of law – surely one of the key notions in *Lüth* – is largely (not completely, we shall soon see) irreconcilable with the intrinsically differentiated sovereignty on which liberal democracy turns.

The notion of a single objective value order is incompatible with the Kelsenian concept of minority-majority relations introduced above. The latter obviously suggests the co-existence of multiple "objective" value orders, at least two of which have engaged in significant conflict by the time constitutional review enters the scene. *Lüth* confronts the significant and deep social divisions that characterise contemporary liberal democracies with a monolithic form of substantive due process review that should be dismissed as seriously out-dated. The substantive due process approach to horizontal effect review in *Lüth* should be replaced with a procedural due process approach to horizontal effect. The analysis of *Roe v Wade* and *Erste Abtreibung* towards the end of Chapter Two aims to put horizontal effect jurisprudence on this new track. It does so, by identifying the horizontal effect or *Drittwirkung* relation in abortion cases, not in terms of the relation between a pregnant woman and an unborn child, but between majority and minority legislative positions regarding the question whether the rights of a child or a human person should at all be considered as relevant as far as the constitutionality of abortion is concerned. It follows, in other words, the minority opinion in *Erste Abtreibung*.

It is nevertheless true that no liberal democracy, however socially divided it may be, can claim to be completely devoid of a number of essential substantive legal norms that govern every stratum of social existence. The definition of common crimes in criminal codes would not have been possible had this not been the case. The normative relativism and pluralism of contemporary liberal democracies usually come to a halt when questions of common murder, theft, assault, etcetera, come into play. Something like an objective value order does exist or is at least assumed or presupposed to exist in liberal democracies when the definition and identification of common crime is at stake. There is, in other words, an "illiberal" moment in liberal democracy. Without this "illiberal" assumption of substantive normative convictions regarding common criminality, liberal democracy's claim to sovereignty would simply evaporate. And this "illiberal" assumption of an undivided sovereignty for the sake of sustaining the minimal substantive order without which sovereignty simply evaporates is, moreover, not restricted to questions of criminal law. It also concerns fundamental questions of constitutional law. In fact, the close proximity between criminal law and constitutional law comes to the fore in this regard, because questions of criminalisation are quintessentially also questions of constitutional law. Nothing may be criminalised in liberal democracies unless their constitutions demand such criminalisation. Private law is very different in this regard. As we saw above, there are many questions that private law can settle in ways that do not interest the constitution. But some coercive areas of private law, the law of torts or civil delict for instance, are also tied up with substantive normative values that even liberal democratic constitutions impose "illiberally" on everyone.

How should a consistent theory and practice of liberal democratic constitutional review deal with this complex mixture of multiple normative orders, on the one hand, and the single normative order that informs or is presupposed to inform criminal law and at least some areas of coercive private law, on the other? The answer that will be offered to this question is this one: Liberal democratic constitutional review should always proceed with the presumption of prevalent majority-minority relations. It should therefore proceed by first inquiring whether the dispute under scrutiny is informed by the prevalence of significant social minorities. When the outcome of this inquiry turns out to be negative, the assumption of a single substantive normative order becomes legitimate. Having drawn this maxim from the reading of *Roe v Wade* and *Erste Abtreibung*, Chapter Two eventually returns to test it on *DeShaney v Winnebago County Social Services*. The remarkable upshot of this test is that one can plausibly construe Justice Rehnquist's opinion in *DeShaney* as based on an assumption of a rather bizarre minority-majority configuration in the United States regarding 14th Amendment protection in the case of a state's negligent failure to prevent serious bodily harm. Justice Rehnquist's opinion in *DeShaney* suggests that one of the following three possibilities may have prevailed in Wisconsin at the time *DeShaney* was decided:

1) A fully unanimous conviction that a state's negligent failure to prevent serious bodily harm should not be burdened by tort liability;
2) A constitutionally legitimate democratic majority conviction that a state's negligent failure to prevent serious bodily harm should not be burdened by tort liability.
3) A constitutionally protected minority conviction that a state's negligent failure to prevent serious bodily harm should not be burdened by tort liability.

This construal of *DeShaney* is not capricious. It is firmly anchored, we shall see in Chapter Two, in Justice Rehnquist's assertion that "[t]he people of Wisconsin ... should not have [a system of State liability for failure to act in situations such as the present one] thrust upon them by this Court's expansion of the Due Process Clause of the Fourteenth Amendment."[28] This statement only makes sense in conjunction with an assumption that there may possibly be a constitutionally significant endorsement of state immunity to tort liability in Wisconsin that the people should be free to articulate for themselves if they have not done so yet. What Justice Rehnquist is honouring with the assertion at issue here, is the possibility that a people may want to deny their own sovereignty, for that is surely what a blanket endorsement of state immunity to tort liability amounts to in the final analysis. The blanket endorsement of state immunity to tort liability amounts to a negation of the very rationale of civil sovereignty as conceived by Hobbes and the whole political tradition that he founded with this conception.

When a judiciary prefers to interpret a state's failure to provide adequate protection of fundamental rights not as a failure that must be rectified, but as an expression of that state's deliberate and constitutionally legitimate will not to provide such adequate protection, that judiciary no longer engages with the sovereign task of assessing the state of majority-minority relations with reference to which popular sovereignty must be defined. It thus does not serve but disserves popular sovereignty. It basically declares, on behalf of the state, a legitimate unwillingness to exercise one of the essential functions of state sovereignty. This is indeed how Chapter Two and the rest of this book read Justice Rehnquist's legacy as far as the state action doctrine is concerned. Together with his opinion in *Flagg Brothers, Inc. v Brooks*,[29] Justice Rehnquist's jurisprudence in *DeShaney* constitutes an abdication of sovereignty on behalf of the people of Wisconsin as well as the people of the United States. And the distinction be-

---

28 489 U.S. 189 (1989), 202–203, *hereafter cited as DeShaney.*
29 436 U.S. 149 (1978), hereafter cited as *Flagg Brothers.*

tween abdications of sovereignty, on the one hand, and the constitutional protection of minorities or the honouring of majorities, on the other, is surely one of the most pressing questions with which this book engages.

Be that as it may, it should already be clear from the above that the recasting of horizontal effect review in terms of a due consideration of majority-minority relations allows one to avoid the vague substantive due process review that the *Lüth* decision has bequeathed to the world under the label of indirect horizontal effect. It allows one to avoid the nebulous assumption of a single set of substantive values that radiates through the legal system as a whole. It allows one to cast even the minimum levels of substantive due process that condition criminal and tort liability in terms of the relatively simple assessment whether there is a morally and rationally sane minority that would and could seriously and legitimately oppose the constitutionality of a number of essential criminal and tort law sanctions without which no civil state can exist. One would think that the tort liability considered in *DeShaney* belongs to this category of essential tort law sanctions that no sane minority or majority can be imagined to doubt. Again, this would appear, bizarrely, not to be the case in the United States, as Chapter Two will show. Suffice it nevertheless to observe here that the Kelsenian conception of liberal democratic constitutionalism allows one to turn even inevitable substantive due process considerations in liberal democracies into procedural due process considerations. The assumption of minimal substantive norms that all citizens share and which accordingly warrant the constitutional subordination of all law to these minimal substantive norms can be translated into procedural inquiries. They can be turned into realistic and reasoned acts of judicial imagination, duly informed by the opposing arguments of counsel, that are ultimately required to do one thing only, namely to confirm the simple and factual absence of any morally and rationally sane majority or minority that rejects the existence of these norms. Once such inexistence has been confirmed, the norm that survives this judicial procedure can be enforced as if it were a substantive norm that everyone endorses. The question at stake here is a relatively simple and highly empirical one and does not allow for wide margins of judicial fluffing.

However, the question at stake here is of course not always so simple. History does sometimes confront one with extreme times and situations. One knows that there have been times – dark times Hannah Arendt calls them – during which not only some minorities, but also "majorities" (the word becomes questionable here when one follows Kelsen consistently) have evidently come to entertain substantive normative convictions that one would want to consider as insane, deranged and irreconcilable with the ideals of civil statehood. A certain substantive due process judicial review, either during the reign of such deranged "majorities" (if there are courageous judiciaries around who can still face up to this task) or after such reign has finally come to an end (in the form of war crime tribunals, etc.) then appears to be inevitable.

Chapter Eight engages with this apparent inevitability of a minimum of substantive due process without which liberal democracies cannot be contemplated. It ultimately proposes an understanding of this inevitable minimum of substantive due process review in constitutional review procedures in terms of which this "minimum substance" can be seen to meet the requirements of an "adequate proceduralisation." With the resulting presentation of constitutional review as fundamentally a practice of procedural due process, the minimal substantive remainders of which can at least be proceduralised adequately for purposes of avoiding most of the trouble one associates with substantive due process review procedures, this book surely responds in some respects to some of the forceful *democratic* critiques of judicial review that have been forwarded in recent years. Notable in this regard are the critiques articulated in the work of Mark Tushnet, Jeremy Waldron and Ran Hirschl.[30]

The critique of the "vague" notion of "indirect horizontal effect" that has come to dominate much of horizontal effect jurisprudence is central to the arguments forwarded in this book. And this critique surely resonates to some extent with the arguments of especially Waldron and Hirschl. The critique of "indirect horizontal effect" articulated in this book surely cautions against "juristocratic" impositions of substantive constitutional values on walks of life that do no call for them. Elements of this call for caution should also be evident in an endorsement of André van der Walt's articulation of a subsidiary relation between legislation and judicial review that I have articulated elsewhere.[31]

30 Cf. Jeremy Waldron, *Law and Disagreement* (Oxford: Oxford University Press, 1999); Waldron, *The Dignity of Legislation* (Cambridge: Cambridge University Press, 1999); Ran Hirschl, *Towards Juristocracy: The Origins and Consequences of the New Constitutionalism* (Cambridge: Harvard University Press, 2004); Mark Tushnet, *Taking the Constitution Away from the Courts* (Princeton: Princenton University Press, 1999).

31 Cf. Johan van der Walt, "Constitution-Making as a Learning Process: Andrew Arato's Model of Post-Sovereign Constitution-Making," *South African Journal on Human Rights*, 26 (2010): 1–18 at 13 fn. 21. I engaged here with a debate between André van der Walt and Karl Klare that is of much significance for democratic critiques of constitutional review. Cf. André van der Walt, "Normative Pluralism and Anarchy: Reflections on the 2007 Term," *Constitutional Review*, 1 (2008): 77–128 and Karl Klare, "Legal Subsidiarity & Constitutional Rights: A Reply to AJ van der Walt," *Constitutional Review*, 1 (2008): 129–154. For a more systematic and comprehensive articulation of the subsidiarity thesis, cf. also André van der Walt, *Property and Constitution* (Pretoria: Pretoria University Law Press, 2012) 35–112.

VII Outline of Arguments and Chapters

The arguments and themes introduced above will be elaborated in the course of two parts and seven chapters that make up the body of this book. Part One concentrates on horizontal effect and state action jurisprudence in the United States and Germany. Part Two concentrates on the question of sovereignty in liberal democracies.

Part One, titled *Horizontal Effect*, comprises four chapters. Chapter One articulates the historical background that informs the horizontal effect and state action jurisprudence in Germany and the United States with reference to the conceptions of private and public law that informed nineteenth century legal consciousness. Chapter Two turns to state action and horizontal effect case law, mostly in the United States and Germany, but it adds to the selection of American and German cases one Canadian and three South African cases on which the German and American cases discussed had a significant influence. As already observed above, the selection of cases discussed in Chapter Two reflects a degree of arbitrariness. And the inclusion of the Canadian and South African cases in the selection of cases discussed in Chapter Two would seem to add an additional element of arbitrariness to this list. The American and German cases were nevertheless chosen, we said, because of the way they coined key terminology and developed it in a way that allows one to relate them to the broader theoretical issues that this book seeks to address. And the Canadian and South African cases were added to the list because they contribute significantly to a clear understanding of the main questions and issues that would emerge from the German and American case law. Chapters Three and Four turn to scholarly discussions of state action and horizontal effect in the United States and Germany. What ultimately emerges from the four chapters in Part One is a clear recognition of the need to reflect more incisively on the relation between horizontal effect review and state sovereignty, and this is what Part Two then sets out to do.

Part Two, titled *Sovereignty*, comprises another four chapters. Chapter Five develops the concept of *uninterrupted sovereignty* further with reference to a recent contribution to the horizontal effect debate by Ralph Christensen and Andreas Fischer-Lescano. Christensen and Fischer-Lescano's outstanding book *Das Ganze des Rechts* takes the *Drittwirkung* debate into a new direction and warrants the considerable attention that Chapter Five pays to it. It nevertheless also prompts a somewhat different understanding of some of the key authors that they discuss, especially of Hegel and Luhmann. Chapter Five relies heavily on exactly Hegel and Luhmann in order to develop a concept of uninterrupted coercive sovereignty. This concept of uninterrupted coercive sovereignty allows and indeed requires taking leave of the conception of horizontal effect that Christensen and Fischer-Lescano propose. Horizontal effect review, claims Chapter Five, cannot be conceptualised consistently without invoking both the uninterrupted reign and general coerciveness of sovereignty, both of which are basically rejected by Christensen and Fischer-Lescano.

The concept of total or uninterrupted coercive sovereignty that Chapter Five espouses does nevertheless not at all imply an endorsement of authoritarian conceptions of sovereignty. The elaboration of the concept of différantial sovereignty in Chapter Six aims to make this clear. Chapter Six elaborates the concept of différantial sovereignty with reference to key elements of the constitutional theories of Carl Schmitt and Hans Kelsen. It takes a close look at the relation between the concept of unitary sovereignty that Carl Schmitt develops in his *Verfassungslehre* and the concept of adjudication that he developed in his 1933 essay *Volk, Bewegung, Staat*. It is especially from this concept of adjudication that Schmitt articulated in 1933 that this book extracts an alert against the substantive due process *Ausstrahlungs* or radiation jurisprudence that the GFCC developed in *Lüth*.

Chapter Six articulates a sharp recognition of the need for an understanding of uninterrupted sovereignty that differs fundamentally from the concept of sovereignty that Schmitt articulates. The uninterrupted sovereignty that sovereign states must assert in order to give effect to the fundamental aims and functions of territorial sovereignty should be conceived in terms of a deeply differentiated sovereignty, not the monolithic and unitary sovereignty that Schmitt contemplates. And it is for purposes of articulating a concept of uninterrupted but deeply differentiated sovereignty that Chapter Six then turns to take a close look at the relation between Hans Kelsen's understanding of liberal democratic constitutionalism and his *Stufenbau* understanding of adjudication. What one learns from Kelsen on both counts, argues Chapter Six finally, is embodied in a striking way in both the fundamental conception and method of horizontal effect adjudication that Walter Leisner developed in his early contribution to the *Drittwirkung* debate in Germany. Leisner's contribution to the debate clearly pivots on a double rejection of the jurisprudence in *Lüth*. It turns on a rejection of the notion of an objective value order, and a rejection of the notion of the radiation effect or *Ausstrahlungseffekt* of this objective value order. Leisner's rejection of an objective value order goes hand in hand with another of his key insights, namely, his acute regard for the fact that constitutional review is always a matter of horizontal constitutional review. Leisner ultimately erases the distinction between horizontal and vertical effect in a remarkable way that echoes Kelsen's concept of majority-minority relations in fundamental respects. And this erasure, contends Chapter Six, is crucial for the consistent procedural due process concept of constitutional review that this book proposes for a future constitutional review. The move from a substantive to a consistently procedural due process conception of constitutional review implies and requires a fundamental dismantling of the very notion of the vertical effect of fundamental rights. There is an irreducible link between substantive due process and vertical effect.

Chapter Seven returns to a discussion of case law. It analyses the judgments of the ECJ in the *Laval* and *Viking* cases of 2007 and the *Rüffert* case of 2008 and identifies these cases as a significant moment in the transfer of sovereignty from the European Union Member States to the European Union. The de facto European Union sovereignty that is emerging from this transfer of sovereignty from the Member States to the Union, argues Chapter Seven, is by far not yet the kind of horizontal sovereignty that Chapter Six described as différantial sovereignty. The sovereignty that seems to be emerging in the case law of the ECJ, argues Chapter Seven, is the product of a substantive due process horizontal effect jurisprudence that pays insufficient attention to the normative and political differences with which sovereignty in Europe will need to engage.

Chapter Eight takes stock of the concepts and insights developed in the preceding chapters of this book. It concludes the book with an articulation of a coherent concept of liberal democratic sovereignty, on the one hand, and liberal democratic constitutional review, on the other. It emphasises again the need to rid constitutional review as far as conceivably possible, from the substantive due process review developed in *Lüth.* It proposes, in other words, a concept of horizontal effect and liberal democratic constitutional review that turns squarely on a consistent conception of procedural due process review and it elaborates this concept in terms of a consistent judicial application of a simple proportionality test in all cases of constitutional review. In the vast majority of these cases the proportionality test will turn on empirical considerations that judges will hardly be able to fluff. Only in exceptional cases will the procedural proportionality test at issue in constitutional review turn abstract and Kantian (that is, only rarely will they come to turn on conceptions of universal validity that cannot be proved empirically). But the moral and rational sanity of those who would, under the exceptional circumstances at issue in these cases, find this Kantian morality questionable, would surely itself be questionable enough to merit the response of a coercive and sovereign dismissal. Also in consistently *liberal* liberal democracies are there, regrettably for liberal democrats, dark times during which an abstract Kantian morality simply decides the exceptional case.

Part One: **Horizontal Effect**

Chapter One: Erased Baselines and Inversed Coordinates: 19th Century Backgrounds of the Horizontality Question

I Introduction

The political imagination of America and Europe was captured by an unprecedented spirit of radical change and revolution towards the end of the eighteenth century. Hannah Arendt argues that the two revolutionary sprits were fundamentally different. Whereas the French Revolution was fuelled by a moral concern with equality and compassion with the poor, the American Revolution was fuelled by the ideal of political freedom. The ideal of political freedom, she contends, was not only concerned with *liberation from* the British Crown. It was also and fundamentally informed by the ideal of public freedom, the *freedom to* partake in political action. "Positive freedom" Isaiah Berlin would come to call the concern at issue here, contrasting it clearly with negative freedom, *freedom from* external constraints.[1] The latter freedom, freedom from any kind of external interference with one's life, is the essence of private liberty. Seen from this perspective, the American revolutionaries, or at least some of them, had much more than private liberty in mind when they rebelled against the Crown. According to Arendt's somewhat romantic vision, they were and wanted to be men of action who took charge of their own affairs not just for the sake of their own affairs but for the sake of taking charge.[2]

Not all of the American revolutionaries were so public minded though. There was ambivalence in the revolutionary spirit that also accommodated a strand of thinking that was indeed intent only upon establishing stable forms of government under the auspices of which private liberty could flourish. Simplifying matters somewhat, one can distinguish in this regard between the Adamsonian and Madisonian lines of thinking. The former stressed the ideal of public freedom;

---

1 Isaiah Berlin, *Four Essays on Liberty* (London: Oxford University Press, 1969). Berlin of course already published his essay on positive and negative liberty in 1958, in other words, five years before Arendt first published *On Revolution* in 1963. The roots of the distinction can be traced to earlier sources, among them Kant. For an overview, cf. Ian Carter, "Positive and Negative Liberty," in *The Stanford Encyclopedia of Philosophy*, ed. Edward N. Zalta, 2012, http://plato.-stanford.edu/archives/spr2012/entries/liberty-positive-negative/.

2 Hannah Arendt, *On Revolution* (New York: Penguin Books, 1963).

the latter stressed the ideal of stable government that would foster private liberty. Nineteenth century American legal history tells the story of how the latter gradually gained the upper hand over the former. The state action doctrine, coined in 1883 in the *Civil Rights Cases*, was not just about the relation between federal and state governments, as Justice Bradley suggested in the majority opinion of the court. And it was not just about racism, as Charles Black would later suggest.[3] It was surely also very much, perhaps more than anything else, about entrenching the Madisonian vision of minimal politics and maximum private autonomy in American law. In fact, the racist elements of the state action doctrine, which surely existed, became possible because of the way they dovetailed with the Madisonian ideal of private liberty.

Sections II and III of this chapter relate two narratives that tell the tale of the historical victory of the Madisonian over the Adamsonian conception of freedom in striking fashion. The first narrative concerns the transformation of the institution of property in American law from a minimal concern with a basic condition for political participation to a maximal concern with private autonomy. Section II relates this narrative with reference to the work of Jennifer Nedelsky[4] and Elizabeth Mensch.[5] The second narrative concerns the transformation of American law that took place in the development that Duncan Kennedy calls "the rise of Classical Legal Consciousness."[6] This transformation is also related in Morton Horwitz's account of the transformation of American law between 1780 and 1860.[7] Paul Atiyah's account of the "rise of freedom of contract" is the classical statement of a parallel development in English contract law.[8] Section III brings to the fore key aspects of the historical development related in the work of Kennedy, Horwitz and Atiyah regarding the "rise of classical legal consciousness" and "freedom of contract."

Sections IV and V then turn to two accounts of 19th century German law that echo the American narratives of Nedelsky, Mensch, Kennedy, Horwitz and Atiyah in significant respects. Section IV highlights key points of Walter Leisner's ac-

---

3 Cf. Charles Black, "The Supreme Court, 1966 Term – Foreword: State Action, Equal Protection, and California's Proposition 14," *Harvard Law Review* 81 (1967): 69–109.

4 Jennifer Nedelsky, *Private Property and the Limits of American Constitutionalism: The Madisonian Framework and Its Legacy* (University of Chicago Press, 1990).

5 Elizabeth Mensch, "The History of Mainstream Legal Thought," in *The Politics of Law: A Progressive Critique*, ed. David Kairys (New York: Pantheon Books, 1998), 23–53; "The Colonial Origins of Liberal Property Rights," *Buffalo Law Review* 31 (1982): 635–736.

6 Duncan Kennedy, *The Rise & Fall of Classical Legal Thought* (Cambridge: AFAR, 1998).

7 Morton J. Horwitz, *The Transformation of American Law, 1780–1860* (Cambridge: Harvard University Press, 1977).

8 Paul Atiyah, *The Rise and Fall of Freedom of Contract* (Oxford: Clarendon Press, 1979).

count of the historical development of German constitutionalism during the 19th century. Leisner's account of the history of German constitutionalism portrays a privatisation of constitutional rights in 19th century Germany that echoes the privatisation of constitutional rights in 19th century America in significant respects. Leisner's narrative of the reduction of the broad concern with political liberty prevalent at the time of the French Revolution to the narrow conception of economic liberty that ultimately prevailed in the *Paulskirche* constitution of 1848 surely echoes the American narrative that Nedelsky and Mensch relate. Section V turns to the rise of conceptualist jurisprudence or *Begriffsjurisprudenz* in 19th century German private law theory in the work of the German Pandectists. This development reflects the German counterpart of the "rise of classical legal consciousness" and "freedom of contract" that Section III related with reference to Kennedy, Horwitz and Atiyah.

The aim of all the historical narratives in this chapter is threefold. The first concern is, as already stated, to show how a broad concept of political liberty made way for an economical concept of liberty in the course of the 19th century in both America and Germany. The second is to show that this reduction of political to economic liberty created an abstract concept of legal subjectivity that deliberately ignored all elements of historical and social context in legal relationships. This abstract legal subjectivity surely reflected the liberation of the legal subject from the historically entrenched hierarchies of feudal Europe and feudal law. The emancipatory potential and quality of this abstract legal subjectivity can therefore not be denied. However, once removed from the shackles of historical feudal hierarchies, this abstract legal subjectivity would become the source of new social stratifications and new social hierarchies that could henceforth claim to be exempted categorically from all historical and contextual social scrutiny, given that abstraction from context and history had become an emancipatory virtue with self-evident legitimacy. Thus could classical legal consciousness maintain the "legitimate" reduction of law to the facilitation of abstract will-formation that deliberately ignored baseline political and historical conditions and considerations.

A regard for this depoliticising and de-historicising process of conceptual abstraction brings into sight the third and main concern of this chapter. Under cover of the normative abstraction performed by legal conceptualism, formalism or *Begriffsjurisprudenz*, new social hierarchies could develop and entrench themselves "surreptitiously," at least as far as legal theory and doctrine was concerned. These social hierarchies, however, did not manage to entrench themselves "surreptitiously" outside circles of scientific legal theory. Rising social discontent in the course of the 19th century attested to tangible oppression and patent deprivations of liberty that surely rendered this entrenchment of new hierarchies conspicuous enough. But they, these hierarchies, enjoyed the advantage of a conceptually acute but empirically blind Iustitia under cover of which "innocent" or "neutral" business could carry on as if it had no bearing on the social and political questions of the time. The question whether Iustitia's symbolic blindness, her impartiality, was in fact only possible and credible by virtue of acute percipience of social historical conditions, was a question that legal theory and doctrine would only begin to ask in the twentieth century.

This then was the 19th century framework of private law that eventually came to precipitate the horizontality revolution in twentieth century constitutional review and constitutional theory. It was a framework that promoted the development of unprecedented social hierarchies and social inequality under cover of legal doctrine and jurisprudence that adhered strictly and exclusively to conceptualist or abstract conceptions of social equality. In terms of this framework, private law relationships were held to be *horizontal*. Unlike the *vertical* relationship between citizens and state or citizens and public authorities, private law relationships were considered relationships among equals. This dogma not only turned on the programmatic erasure of baseline questions from the attention of legal doctrine, it also turned on an inversion of the core coordinates of law that informed the Enlightenment imagination and symbolism of the revolutionary generation towards the end of the 18th and beginning of the 19th century. This revolutionary imagination considered *political* relations to be fundamentally equal. Political relationships, held the revolutionary credo, tolerate no natural or metaphysical hierarchy or authority that command unquestioned respect. As such they also demand that private inequality play no role in political authority. In fact, they ideally demand that private inequality play no significant role in any social relationship. As we shall soon see towards the end of this chapter, the revolutionary generation designated *to the state* the political responsibility to destroy the social inequalities that previously passed under claims to royal and feudal privileges. By the end of the 19th century however, social elites could again rely on law to preclude public scrutiny of private inequality and, moreover, could rely on law to focus on public authority as the only real threat to liberty and social equality.

Public relations thus again became "vertical" towards the end of the 19th century, as if the great democratisations of early modernity had never happened. And thus could private relations plausibly come to present themselves as horizontal. The nineteenth century framework of law that informed the horizontality revolution in the twentieth century thus pivoted on two fulcrums: *Erased baselines and inversed coordinates*. This historical background requires careful reflection on the terminology that has come to be associated with the application of constitutional rights in the sphere of private law. When one refers to the application of constitutional rights to private relations as the *horizontal effect of constitutional rights*, one surely cannot claim to denote the application of constitutional rights to horizontal relations. One can at best claim to denote the application of *horizontalising* norms to vertical relationships.

Constitutional rights are the last vestiges of the great discourse of horizontality and horizontalisation that the epochal revolutions of modernity bequeathed to modern societies. If these rights were to apply meaningfully to anything, they would logically have to apply to something that is at odds with or in tension with the horizontality that they embody. They would apply to some instance of social verticality, that is, to some manifestation of social hierarchy, irrespective of whether the manifestation of hierarchy at issue marches under the banner of public authority or entrenched private wealth. And their *application* would logically imply *horizontalisation*. Constitutional theory and language would gain miles of consistency if this simple principle would become and remain clear: The *horizontal effect* of constitutional rights concerns the *horizontalising* application of constitutional rights. This is the core contention that this chapter seeks to elaborate.

II The Privatisation of Constitutional Rights in America

James Tully argued in 1980 that Locke's political philosophy was, unlike the voluntarist philosophy of Hobbes, fundamentally inspired by the Thomist notion of the *suum*. The third pillar in the triad of life, liberty and estate that constituted the core of Locke's political theory, contended Tully, was not an expression of property in the modern sense of the word. It was an expression of the *suum*, the essential means to which every individual was entitled for purposes of sustaining life and limb.[9] Richard Tuck forwarded a similar interpretation of Locke in 1979.[10] It is doubtful, however, whether Tully and Tuck's interpretations of Locke conclusively trump C.B. Macpherson's 1962 contention that Locke's political theory was as much an expression of possessive individualism as that of Hobbes.[11] It is more likely the case that Locke's understanding of property was

9 James Tully, *A Discourse on Property: John Locke and His Adversaries* (Cambridge: Cambridge University Press, 1980).

10 Richard Tuck, *Natural Rights Theories: Their Origin and Development* (Cambridge: Cambridge University Press, 1979).

11 Crawford B. Macpherson, *The Political Theory of Possessive Individualism: Hobbes to Locke* (Oxford: Oxford University Press, 2010).

deeply ambiguous and that Tuck, Tully and Macpherson simply teased out two different strands in Locke's thinking that were deeply at odds with one another.

Seeing the matter in this way would offer us a clue as to why the American revolutionary imagination allowed both the Adamsonian and Madisonian fractions to compete for the soul of the American nation. The concept of property that Locke bequeathed to the American Revolution was simply ambiguous enough to allow for both these lines of constitutional thinking. And this ambiguous Lockean legacy would also explain why the *common law* concept of property was capable of the transformation or mutation that it went through in the course of the nineteenth century without being left behind like an empty shell or breaking apart completely. The common law concept of property all along sustained a semantic ambiguity that would allow it to serve quite different social ideals in different times. We turn to the nineteenth century transformation of American common law in the next section. Let us first take a closer look at the transformation of the constitutional concept of property rights in the course of the nineteenth century.

In terms of both their feudal background and the background of the political revolution in seventeenth century England, proprietary rights in England were inseparable from the question of the legitimate powers of government and of participation in government. In Germany, argued Joachim Rittstieg in 1976, more or less along the same lines that Walter Leisner already argued in 1960, liberty was a function of property, a state of affairs which rendered both liberty and property private matters. In England, by contrast, property was a function of liberty, a state of affairs which made both property and liberty political issues. It is against this background that Locke's position regarding the duty of the state to safeguard and respect life, liberty and property must be understood, argued Rittstieg. When Locke speaks of property in the context of liberty, Rittstieg wrote, it is not private property (*privates Eigentum*) that is at issue. At issue for Locke is thus not a legal relation between private legal subjects, but the boundary of legitimate royal action that individuals had the liberty to co-determine.[12] Ritt-

---

12 The feudal concept of freehold still informed the understanding of property in seventeenth century England, however much this land was already transferable by means of sale. The unity of dominium and imperium in feudal land relations, if not indeed still largely applicable at the time, was something of the immediate past from which freehold acquired through market transactions had just emerged. This unity of imperium and dominium was appropriated by big land owners represented in parliament by even bigger landowners. Rittstieg explains that the new relation between the king and freehold landowners after 1688 did not simply consist in the curtailment of the king's sovereignty in the sense that he henceforth had to respect a set of conclusively defined proprietary rights but otherwise left him free to do as he pleased with

stieg's contentions in this regard clearly tap into the line in Locke's thinking that, respectively three and four years later, Tuck and Tulley would trace back to the Thomist influences in Locke's thought. All three of them, Tuck, Tulley and Rittstieg, may well be offering us a too narrow or too one sided understanding of Locke, but the line of Locke's thinking that they prioritise in the process does explain an essential element of both the English and American revolutionary imaginations. Locke's association of property with liberty clearly reflected the Whig political philosophy that triumphed in the Glorious Revolution and led to the entrenchment of property alongside liberty as a constitutional principle in England.[13] This Whig sensibility, however, was not something that would remain confined to England. It was pervasive among the colonists who settled in America. "Americans did not have to be told that liberty and property were inseparable," observes John Reid. They commonly assumed this inseparability. There may well have been "no eighteenth-century educated American who did not associate defense of liberty with defense of property." "What have in the twentieth century become separated may have been so united in the eighteenth century that one could not be conceived of existing independently of the other."[14]

In fact, as was the case in the Glorious Revolution, the defence of property against the Crown's right to claim taxes from the colonists again became a central issue in the American Revolution and Declaration of Independence. And being so intimately linked to the birth of the American people as a nation, it

---

regard to matters which did not involve the proprietary rights of his subjects as they were defined at that stage. The new situation after 1688 was rather that of two sovereign spheres existing alongside one another. The proper boundaries between these two spheres had to be determined anew by parliament with every new issue that would arise between them. The dominium of the holders of freehold land can therefore clearly be seen to have included a political sovereignty or imperium. "Property" in this context was clearly not just a matter of defining private legal relations. It was something concomitant with the liberty of political decision-making. Relevant in this regard is also the fact that both active and passive voting rights were at this time still determined with reference to minimal requirements of income and land ownership. Cf. Helmut Rittstieg, *Eigentum als Verfassungsproblem: zu Geschichte und Gegenwart des bürgerlichen Verfassungsstaates* (Darmstadt: Wissenschaftliche Buchgesellschaft, 1975), 33–36, 41.

13 Cf. John Phillip Reid, *Constitutional History of the American Revolution: The Authority to Legislate* (Madison: Univ of Wisconsin Press, 1986), 28. However, Locke's conception of these rights as natural rights and not as historical rights indicates that his theoretical position also differed in important respects from the typical Whig stance. Cf. also the discussion of Locke's relation to the Whig tradition and Burke's relation to Locke in Frederick A. Dreyer, *Burke's Politics: A Study in Whig Orthodoxy* (Waterloo: Wilfrid Laurier Univ. Press, 1979), 68–84.

14 Reid, *Constitutional History of the American Revolution*, 33.

is not surprising that liberty and property would become fundamental principles in the American constitution. The fifth as well as the fourteenth amendment reiterate Locke's triad of "life, liberty and property" to the letter. A similar expression would again be employed, only a few years after the drafting of the Fifth Amendment, in article 2 of the *Déclaration des droits d'homme et du citoyen* of 1789. The irony of this development should not be missed. In awe of the realization of political liberty in America, the French revolutionaries, in their own effort to break with their feudal past, took over the association of liberty and property that derived from the Whig reliance upon ancient feudal rights in the English revolution.

However, it is important also to note that the articulation of property as a *droit inviolable et sacre* in article 17 of the *Déclaration* did not as such constitute a private law institution and was therefore also not yet conceived as a vehicle for private liberty. The entrenchment of property as an inviolable and sacred right in the *Déclaration* was, at the time, yet another restatement of a "Lockean" principle of political freedom. The *Déclaration* was solely concerned with political liberty and equality. It is only towards the second half of the nineteenth century that economic liberalism became a prominent social principle in Europe and it is only then that the importance of property as a private law institution became significant. And the property clause in the *Déclaration* could also not yet be understood as a private law institution.[15] For a post-revolutionary definition of property as a private law institution in France, one has to look to the *Code Civil* and not to the *Déclaration*. And it is only to be expected that the definition of property in Article 544 of the Code Civil, articulated in 1804, only fifteen years after the declaration, would also not yet evince the "purely private" or purely "self-interested" character that would later be associated with property as a private law institution. It was virtually a restatement of Bartolus of Saxoferrato's 14th century definition of dominium and as such expressed a different understanding of property that was arguably much less concerned with purely private concerns and much more concerned with the demarcation of feudal powers.[16] As will become clear in Sections IV and V below, the "purely private law" conception of property

15 G. C. J. J. van den Bergh, *Eigendom: Grepen uit de Geschiedenis van een Omstreden Begrip* (Deventer: Kluwer, 1988), 52.

16 "La propriété est le droit de jouir et disposer des choses de la manière la plus absolue, pourvu qu'on n'en fasse pas un usage prohibé par le lois ou par les règlements." Quoted from Alfons Bürge, *Das französische Privatrecht im 19. Jahrhundert: zwischen Tradition und Pandektenwissenschaft, Liberalismus und Etatismus* (Frankfurt a.M: Vittorio Klostermann, 1991), 3.

would only enter French private law with the influence of German Pandectism in the second half of the nineteenth century.[17]

The political understanding of property that informed the revolutionary discourses towards the end of the 18th century nevertheless mutated into the private law conception of property in the course of the 19th century. Soon after the revolution, argues Elizabeth Mensch, the Whig association of liberty with property underwent a fundamental transformation. Initially, the colonists' revolutionary rejection (in the name of liberty) of the king's dominium over their land went hand in hand with the establishment of local communal structures and institutions. As Mensch puts it, "[the colonists] found themselves saying 'Damn the king' as they set up their own local courts, designed to protect the freedom of their labour on their land."[18] The marked feature of property rights that were claimed in this development was their social character. They were much rather an expression or function of communal life and interaction than a reflection of private entitlements. Property arrangements in the Long Island towns in the state of New York were exemplary in this regard. Land was distributed in these towns in more or less equal sizes or on the basis of the size of the settling families. And although the settlers preferred to own and work these lots for themselves against payment of substantial mortgages rather than lease the land at a cheaper rate, the degree of individualism evinced by this "private ownership" was subject to pervasive restrictions and responsibilities regarding communal requirements and needs. Land was not to be held solely for the purpose of speculative profit. Absenteeism led to forfeiture and contracts to sell unimproved land could be voided. Land in these towns could further only be held as property on condition that the owners participated in community projects such as the maintenance of common pastures, road building and grain mills. Settlers could even be asked to give back a portion of their land for the purpose of accommodating new settlers. An incident that came to pass in the village of Middleburgh underlined the non-private character of land use evident in these arrangements. One of the inhabitants of the village was imprisoned for refusing to give up a portion of his land to accommodate new settlers. The magistrates nevertheless convinced him in the process that the land was "granted to the village in common" and he later confessed to having been disobedient as a result of an "ungovernable passion

17 Cf. Bergh, *Eigendom*, 52. as well as the reference to Bürge in note 16 above. The association of the property clause in the Declaration with the property clause in the Code Civil in J.H. Lokin and W.J. Zwalve, *Hoofdstukken uit de Europese Codificatie-Geschiedenis* (Groningen: Tjeenk Willink, 1992), 173, must therefore be approached with some caution. One must recognise both the significant difference and evident proximity between them.

18 Mensch, "The Colonial Origins of Liberal Property Rights," 733.

roused by [the] belief that the land belonged to him absolutely, by virtue of patent and conveyance..."[19]

This communal understanding of land use that was pervasive before the revolution did not prevail after the revolution. Instead of an embodiment of political liberty and communal responsibility, the erstwhile Whig association of political liberty with property turned into a barrier against participatory politics and executive interference after the Revolution. It is instructive to quote Mensch extensively on this point:

> "In the years after the Revolution, one can see the emergence of the elements from which [the liberal conception of private, individualized rights in stark confrontation with a potentially oppressive sovereign power and the Gothic elegance of classical legalism in which it culminated] was later fashioned. First, the 'sovereignty of the people' was lifted out of the local, concrete community that was central to the authentic republican vision. The will of the people became only an abstract idea, embodied in a written constitution, the interpretation of which was divorced from the direct will of the people who ostensibly created it – and from the will of any concrete people at any particular time. In effect, 'the people' became that vaguely mystical body which stepped onto the political stage only once, distributed its sovereignty within the spheres delineated by the constitution, and was never seen again.
>
> Similarly, the notion of property was lifted out of the community of voluntary labor and active participation from which it had once derived its meaning. Rather than an expression of popular will, property as an abstract constitutional right was conceptually insulated from the will of the people standing as a right in opposition to participation. Moreover, after the Revolution the link between property and liberty was asserted, ironically, not on behalf of republican communitarianism, but most often on behalf of hierarchical power relations – yet without hierarchy's traditional ethical claims."[20]

The argument that the constitutional right to property deformed American politics and turned the concern with property into a pursuit of private concerns is also central to Jennifer Nedelsky's account of the 19th century constitutional developments in America. Nedelsky relates the tension between the safeguarding of economic hierarchy and democratic political participation to the political arguments and stances of the participants at the 1787 Constitutional Convention, especially those of John Madison, Governor Morris and James Wilson. Both Madison and Morris argued for a constitution the fundamental purpose of which would be the protection of the property rights of the wealthy few against the democratic will of the propertyless masses.[21] Wilson, on the other hand, al-

19 Ibid, 648.

20 Ibid, 734.

21 Cf. Nedelsky, *Private Property and the Limits of American Constitutionalism*, 16–95.

though not completely averse to the protection of property as a fundamental right, stressed democratic political participation of the people in government as the fundamental purpose of the constitution to be drafted.[22] The Madisonian stance won the day. The American Constitution, argues Nedelsky, is essentially a Madisonian legacy. According to her, the Madisonian concern with the protection of property rights which shaped the Constitution of 1787 led to the neglect of two crucial political issues: "the means of fostering popular participation in government and the relationship between economic and political power."[23]

The combined result of these two neglected issues, argues Nedelsky, was the constitutional insulation of social inequality from democratic transformation and a common conception that redistribution was irreconcilable with the constitutional principle of limited government.[24] The bottom line of Nedelsky's argument is that this constitutional model no longer makes sense in the paradigm of the welfare state that succeeded the era of liberal capitalism. Government interference in what was formerly regarded as the private sphere has become the order of the day. Private property therefore no longer provides "the conceptual boundary to the legitimate scope of government." The result of the demise of property as a conceptual criterion for the limits of legitimate government is, in other words, that we no longer have a proper conceptual basis for constitutional government:

> "In many crucial respects, we have accepted the New Deal but rejected its conceptual underpinnings. As a country, we routinely engage in redistribution to ameliorate social ills, but we have not simply accepted property as a mere social construct to be redefined or redistributed without constraint. The status of property as boundary lingers despite its disintegration as a constitutional concept. We countenance redistribution as a means, but we have no consensus on a vision of the state that clearly defines redistribution as a legitimate goal. And we tacitly rely upon, but have no clear means of justifying, this distinction between means and goal. In short, because the original structure of constitutionalism rested on an effort to prevent democratic control of property, our post-New Deal state requires a rethinking not just of the meaning of property, but also of the scope and purpose of the state. As such, it requires new foundations for constitutionalism."[25]

Louis Seidman, we shall see in Chapter Three, makes a very similar claim in the context of the American state action doctrine. Americans, he argues, have not yet come to terms with the implications of the New Deal for the private/public dis-

22 Cf. Ibid, 96–140.
23 Ibid, 2.
24 Ibid.
25 Ibid, 3.

tinction; hence the continuing shambles of the state action doctrine.[26] The discussion of the state action doctrine in Chapter Three will return to these claims. For now, let us take a closer look at the concept of private law rights that prevailed towards the end of the nineteenth century, the concept of private law rights, in other words, that constituted the private law background when the American Supreme Court articulated the state action doctrine in 1883.

III The Nineteenth Century Transformation of Private Law Rights in America

In 1975 and 1977 Duncan Kennedy and Morton Horwitz respectively articulated two deeply resonating and highly influential narrative accounts of the history of 19th century American private law. A number of key developments can be distilled from these narratives. Most of them are also clearly traceable in Paul Atiyah's 1979 account of the rise and fall of freedom of contract in English law. I shall rely on all three of these narratives in this section for purposes of an elementary and concise description of the framework of private law and private law thinking that was current when the state action doctrine was articulated in 1883, but Kennedy's narrative will do most of the work in the outline articulated below.

The first key development that can be distilled from Kennedy's, Horwitz's and Atiyah's narratives concerns the general shift from property to contract as the central organising principle in the system or framework of private law. The second development concerns the "purification" of contract law by expelling from proper contract law all elements of non-consensual coercion such as "implicit contracts," quasi-contracts and torts. The sifting out of all these non-consensual elements that were still evident in earlier frameworks of contract law allowed for the apotheosis of a voluntarist or will-based understanding of private law in terms of which all or almost all instances of "coercion" in private law could be pushed to the margins. A third key development was the rise of a legal formalism and conceptualism that quite evidently began to undermine the consensual voluntarism on which the whole framework of contract-based private law claimed to turn. As Atiyah points out well, there was something deeply paradoxical if not downright contradictory to the insistence of late nineteenth century judiciaries that the true consensus between contracting parties had to be determined strictly with reference to the express terms of the contract

26 Cf. the extensive discussion of Seidman's views in Chapter Three.

and not at all with reference to any evidence to the effect that the express terms did in fact not express such consensus.[27]

The apotheosis and hypostasis of contractual voluntarism towards the end of the 19th century also reflected another deep transformation of law and legal thought in the course of the nineteenth century. The institution of property law that organised 18th century private common law was largely based on principles of natural reason and reasonableness. The property law based systems of 18th century American private law was in this respect closely related to the tradition of natural law and the insistence of this tradition on the intrinsic reasonableness of proper social and legal relationships. The consensual voluntarism that would become dominant in the course of the nineteenth century would replace this natural law principle of intrinsic reasonableness with the reasonableness of autonomous rational choice: It was "reasonable" to expect that adult legal subjects with regular legal capacity would generally promote their own interests in ways that are best for them. Should they occasionally fail to do so, they would learn from their failures and do better the next time.[28] This shift in focus from the intrinsic reasonableness with which all legal relationships had to comply to the principle of rational choice as the guiding criterion for valid and enforceable legal relationships, explains Horwitz, expressed the interests of the entrepreneurial and mercantile ethics of the 19th century that replaced the static agrarian culture of the 18th century.[29]

The overarching shift from the relatively static conception of property concomitant to 18th century agrarian land usage to the dynamic industrial and entrepreneurial use of property in the 19th century already goes a long way towards explaining the replacement of property by contract as the central organising principle in private law. It is nevertheless instructive to take note of the technical developments in legal thought that facilitated this process. Kennedy's narrative of 19th century American law is organised around different configurations of binary oppositions that informed different phases of American law. He would become famous inside and infamous outside the Critical Legal Studies movement for his analysis of modern legal consciousness in terms of a rule-standard oppo-

---

27 Cf. Atiyah, *The Rise and Fall of Freedom of Contract*, 459 "[W]hy should the courts have wished to couple a bargain theory of contracts with this hard objectivism. At the very same time that the Courts were insisting that contracts should be construed so as to give effect to the intention of the parties, they were also adopting rules which often precluded a search for any real intent."

28 Ibid, 437.

29 Horwitz, *The Transformation of American Law, 1780–1860*. This is the story of the whole book, but cf. the succinct statement at 211.

sition that respectively conveyed self-interest and altruism as the two driving concerns of the law.[30] Eighteenth century legal consciousness or pre-classical legal consciousness, as Kennedy calls it, worked with a significantly different set of binary oppositions and different ways of resolving the tensions between them. One of these binary oppositions was that between *technicality* and *liberality*.

The tension between *technicality* and *liberality* played a major organising role in the specific period of pre-classical legal thought during which property was the over-arching organising concept. *Liberality* was employed to bypass and override the maze of *technical* feudal restrictions on the alienation of property in order to promote the free alienation of property. Feudal restrictions on alienation were still vigorously upheld by a social ethics informed by the interests of proud and distinguished families intent on keeping property in the family and not having it squandered by descendants. *Liberality*, informed by the interests of the developing market economy in the free and simple exchange of property, bypassed the technical feudal restrictions on alienation and thus paved the way for the major shift from pre-classical to classical legal consciousness.[31] *Liberality* would ultimately destroy the pre-classical assumption of pre-existing and timeless social relations, reflected especially in old trans-generational property relations, by ushering in the subjective freedom of individual owners to alienate and appropriate property at will as the central organising force in property relations. In other words, *liberality* paved the way for the centrality of *will-based legal relations* in classical legal thought. It paved the way for the ascendance of contract as the central organising principle in 19th century private law. The elimination of restraints on alienation and the liberation of the subjective will of owners to appropriate, use and alienate their property as they deemed fit led to contract eventually displacing and eventually replacing property as the core organisational principle in legal relationships. Neither Blackstone nor Kent considered contract or torts as separate fields of law and provided no separate headings for them in their classificatory schemes. Contract was subsumed and dealt with under the ways in which *personal* property could be alienated. Torts were similarly dealt with in terms of remedies for private wrongs, central to which were remedies for infringements of property rights.[32] As Kennedy puts it:

---

30 Cf. especially Duncan Kennedy, "Form and Substance in Private Law Adjudication," *Harvard Law Review* 89, no. 8 (June 1, 1976): 1685–1778.

31 Kennedy, *The Rise & Fall of Classical Legal Thought*, 144–150.

32 Ibid, 125–127.

> "Tort and contract, as we see them, were perceived embedded in the elaborated social contexts of status and land holding. Because they were relatively unimportant *concepts*, they could simply be tacked onto the larger structure of the *Commentaries*."[33]

It was understandable that the elimination of constraints on alienation and the concomitant rise of a free property market would change things and bring contract into the centre of legal doctrine's organising scheme. Tort, we shall see soon, would have its day only much later. Important to note now is the fact that contract already began to gradually displace property in the pre-classical mind-set. Initial signs of this shift were already evident in Blackstone's distinction between implied and express contracts and in the judicial opinion of Lord Mansfield in *Moses v Macpherlan*.[34] "What Mansfield did," argues Kennedy, "was to suggest not a new cause of action for restitution, but a new general theory of the basis of contractual liability." "Mansfield's approach ... was the basis of the emergence of contract in place of property as the main organising concept of mid-nineteenth century law."[35] The approach was resisted by traditional common lawyers for another 70 years, but it came into its own with Parsons' treatise *On Contract*. Parsons phrased the matter as follows:

> "The Law of Contracts, in its widest extent, may be regarded as including nearly all the law which regulates the relations of human life. Indeed, it may be looked upon as the basis of human society. All social life presumes it, and rests upon it; for out of contracts, express or implied, declared or understood, grow all rights, all duties, all obligations, and all law. Almost the whole procedure of human life implies, or, rather, is, the continual fulfilment of contracts..."[36]

At the time that Parsons wrote this passage, however, the understanding of every aspect of life in terms of an array of contracts was plausible only by virtue of a set of fictions that portrayed a myriad of non-contractual and non-consensual legal relationships as implicitly contractual. The notion of *implied contracts* came to explain the force of legal relationships that were patently non-contractual and automatically attached to the simple state of things and status of people. Thus, for instance, did the intrinsic natural reasonableness that 18th century law attached to the duties of support and maintenance that fathers owed to children and husbands to wives change into a matter of implicit consensus. And so

---

33 Ibid, 127.

34 Ibid, 165.; Horwitz, *The Transformation of American Law, 1780–1860*, 170.; Atiyah, *The Rise and Fall of Freedom of Contract*, 482.

35 Kennedy, *The Rise & Fall of Classical Legal Thought*, 165.

36 Ibid, 165–166.

did the vicarious liability for employees who worked under the control of their employers come to rest on implied contractual relationships dictated by natural reason.[37] Even tort liability was considered to be the implication of an overarching social contract. Parsons relied on Blackstone to make this point:

> "'Implied contracts,' says Blackstone (Vol ii, p 443), 'are such as reason and justice dictate, and which, therefore, the law presumes that every man undertakes to perform.'"[38]

Parsons' concept of contract was clearly not yet that of Classical legal thought. Contract was not yet for him exclusively a matter of the pure expression of a subjective will, as the Classics would come to see it. It was evidently too mixed up with notions of involuntary bonds that could not be altered by the subjective will of the individual. For this to happen, the involuntary bonds had to be sifted out from the purely voluntary domain of contract. "The Classics created ... by subtraction," writes Kennedy to characterise the apotheosis of the will theory of contract that would take place between 1867 and 1880.[39] In contrast to Parsons' imperialistic claim that every social relation turned on a contract, either express or implied, classical legal theorists such as Leake, Langdell, Pollock, Holmes, Markby and Holland purged all involuntary legal relations implied and imposed by law from the subject of contract in the course of the 1870s. This was the culmination of a development that commenced, after an early anticipation in the 1856 case of *Herzog v Herzog*, with the publication of the second edition of Austin's *Jurisprudence* in 1860 and Maine's *Ancient Law* in 1861. The essence of the development consisted in weeding from the concept of contract all notions of implied contracts so as to eventually construct a wholly separate category of "quasi-contracts" that included all legal relations that formerly were subsumed under implied contracts. In the *Herzog* case the court already distinguished contracts that, according to it, embodied the intention of the parties, but did not do so properly. In such cases the intention of the parties had to be inferred from the factual evidence available. At issue were contracts that were *implied in fact*. These contracts, argued the court in *Herzog*, had to be distinguished from contracts that were *implied by law*. The latter contracts were "merely constructive contracts, while the former [were] truly implied ones."[40]

This first break in American case law with Parsons' inclusive or overarching understanding of contract entered American legal theory in Holmes' first *Amer-*

37 Ibid, 166–175.
38 Ibid, 166.
39 Ibid, 213.
40 Ibid, 179.

ican Law Review article in 1871 and his publication of the 12th edition of Kent's commentaries in 1872. In the latter Holmes added a footnote to Kent's initial definition of contract in which he referred to the *Herzog* case and affirmed the distinction between contracts implied in fact and contracts implied by law. The latter were mere legal fictions that were no longer needed after the abolition of the forms of action, argued Holmes.[41] However, the main impetus for this shift came from the publication of the second edition of Austin's *Jurisprudence* in 1860 and Maine's *Ancient Law* in 1861. Both these works engaged with Roman law, but unlike earlier engagements with Roman law, they focused not on the mass of ancient and medieval Roman law rules, but on the theory behind these rules. According to Austin and Maine, Roman legal theory distinguished clearly between legal relationships determined by the will of the parties and legal relationships determined by the will of the state. The latter relationships were grouped under the categories of quasi-contract and delict or tort.[42] This led to the importation of the concept of quasi-contract into subsequent American legal thinking. The most important treatises on contract after Parsons' and before that of Williston's were those of Bishop and Page. Both Bishop and Page devoted much attention to the distinction between quasi-contract and contracts proper. Keener completed the development with his *Treatise on the Law of Quasi-Contracts*. Keener portrayed the notion of quasi-contracts as unscientific and theoretically wrong. He listed under these quasi-contracts many items that Parsons still included under his inclusive conception of contract such as the obligations of common carriers and innkeepers; obligations of incapacitated persons to pay for benefits; obligations of parents to children and of husbands to wives; liability for benefits received under voided express contracts and liability for money paid by mistake. The subtraction of all these obligations from the proper domain of contract took place under the general principle of unjust enrichment.[43]

The emergence of torts as a separate field of private law marks a decisive phase in the development of classical legal consciousness.[44] In Parsons' framework, tort was simply an important part of every aspect of contract and especially of implied contracts. It concerned the proper standards of behaviour that the law imposed on contractual parties. This treatment of torts obfuscated the distinction between duties that were properly contractual and duties that were imposed on parties by the sovereign.[45] The Classical reaction to this obfuscation of

41 Ibid, 180.
42 Ibid, 179; cf. also Atiyah, *The Rise and Fall of Freedom of Contract*, 481–482.
43 Kennedy, *The Rise & Fall of Classical Legal Thought*, 180.
44 Ibid, 181–190; Atiyah, *The Rise and Fall of Freedom of Contract*, 501–505.
45 Kennedy, *The Rise & Fall of Classical Legal Thought*, 182.

sovereign and private wills was to define a separate field of torts. The first ever separate treatise on Torts remarkably only appeared in 1859 with the publication of Francis Hilliard's *The Law of Remedies for Torts*. Hilliard's innovation consisted in taking torts out of their connection with specific remedies and forms of action and by developing a general concept of tort on the basis of interconnected principles. Thus did the first ever general theory of tort emerge from America. The first English treatise on tort, Charles Greenstreet Addison's *Wrongs and Their Remedies, A Treatise on the Law of Torts*, would follow in 1860. Both treatises commenced with a broad Roman law distinction between obligations *ex contractu* and obligations *ex delictu* but neither managed to construct a consistent theory of delict or tort as distinct from contract.

Holmes 1873 article "Theory of Torts" was the first to delink tort effectively from contract. Holmes argued that torts arose from a number of specific non-contractual relations between parties. Melville Bigelow took Holmes' theory further. He articulated a tripartite categorisation of torts in 1875 by distinguishing between torts that arise from contractual relations between parties, torts that arise from relations incidental to contractual relations that need not be dealt with as contracts, and most importantly, torts that merely arose from the fact that a wrong was committed by someone who was a member of the state. The invocation of state membership as a source of obligation prepared the way for Wigmore to define the whole of private law in terms of a collection of recusable and irrecusable obligations. Both recusable and irrecusable obligations concerned "relations between members of the community regarded as being ultimately enforceable by the political power," but the latter also originated from the will of the political power whereas the former originated only from the will of the individuals involved in the relation. The former included "Contract (in the narrow sense) and the latter "Torts (so called)" and "Enrichment (a part of Quasi contracts as now treated."[46]

The last important development that consolidated classical legal consciousness and classical freedom of contract consisted in the purging of all considerations of personal status from the main body of *pure contract* law.[47] Roman law was organised around family relations and the status of the paterfamilias, on the one hand, and the lack of this status of other family and household members, on the other. This status or lack of status of the paterfamilias still played a

46 Ibid, 185–186.

47 Ibid, 191–212; Atiyah, *The Rise and Fall of Freedom of Contract*, 259. This was the process that Henry Maine famously called "from status to contract." Cf. Maine, *Ancient Law. Its Connection with the early History of Society and its Relation to Modern Ideas* (London: John Hopkins, 1920) 336–7.

definitional or "operative" role in the whole spectrum of legal relations as conceived by Blackstone and Kent, but also in the contractualist versions of preclassical legal thought as articulated by Parsons, Metcalf and W.W. Story. Combined with or grasped as part and parcel of a spectrum of implied contracts, the status of specific persons such as husbands and fathers, on the one hand, and wives, children, servants and other persons who lacked the status of the father and husband, on the other, played a central role in the understanding of all legal relationships. Private law as conceived from Blackstone to Parsons paid no or at best indirect attention to private law rules in the abstract. Up to Parsons, private law rules would always be understood as closely connected to the status of the parties involved.[48] This framework changed fundamentally in the wake of Austin's and Maine's treatment of the Roman law conceptualisations of status.

Austin referred in this regard to the "exploded definition" of status, "formerly current with modern civilians," in terms of a quality that conferred different rights on different kinds of individuals (status est qualitas, cujus ratione homines diverso jure utuntur). In contrast to this "formerly current" definition, Austin offered a new definition in terms of which status was nothing more than the quality inherent in a person that had no intrinsic but at most a consequential impact on the rights, duties, capacities or incapacities of the person.

> "But, according to the definition which I am now considering, the rights or duties, capacities or incapacities, are not themselves the status: but the status is a quality that lies or inheres in the given person, and of which the rights or duties, capacities or incapacities, are merely products or consequences."[49]

This move made it possible for Austin to bring to the fore "the existence, at the core of the legal order" of a general body of private law pertaining to persons "with no peculiarities of status."[50] In Austin's own words, this allowed for the advantage of brevity and clarity:

> "[T]he general rules and principles with which the Law of Things is properly or directly concerned, are preserved detached and abstracted from everything peculiarly relating to particular classes or persons; they are, therefore, presented more clearly than if they were interspersed with that more special matter. Each rule or principle is apprehended more easily and distinctly than if the modifications which it receives from that more special matter, were appended or annexed to it. Being brought together more closely, their mutual relation

48 Kennedy, *The Rise & Fall of Classical Legal Thought*, 191–193.
49 Ibid, 194.
50 Ibid, 195.

> and dependency is more easily perceived. The brevity, therefore, which this division of the corpus juris produces, tends also to its clearness."[51]

Kennedy distils from this statement of Austin's the emergence of the classical legal structuration of the fundamental contradictions of law in terms of core and peripheral aspects of law. The Classical scheme, however, was not yet complete in Austin's writings. The notion of status itself had to be rid of symbolic meanings and reduced to nothing more than "variations in capacity." This second move was accomplished by Holland in 1880. The last nuance that Kennedy adds to this development concerns the way Maine's progressivist concern with the elimination of the despotic paternal powers in legal relations translated into an individualist laissez-faire vision of the law. At the time the Classical theorists pushed paternal powers along with status to the margins of the law, these powers no longer embodied the arbitrary despotic will of the paterfamilias, but principles of "communal solidarity," namely parental and spousal obligations of support and vicarious liability of masters for the torts of servants.[52] In other words, the purging of the last remnants of status from contract law paved the way for the laissez-faire conception of freedom of contract that came into its own in the second half of the nineteenth century. As Kennedy puts it:

> "Thus wrenched from its content, Maine's law of progress became a slogan of laissez-faire. The important thing was not the opposition of the law of persons to abstract contract law, but that of legal relations whose terms the parties controlled to legal relations the state treated in a regulatory, paternalist, communal and informal manner. Once the situation was described and understood in these terms, it followed as a matter of course, unless one was a socialist, that the category of pure contract, ruled by ideals of facilitation, self-determination, autonomy and formality, was the norm, and the end of the historical development."[53]

Classical legal consciousness thus ultimately came to arrange the two fundamentally contradictory concerns of law – individualist self-interest (and its concomitant set of values, facilitation, self-determination, autonomy and formality) and communal altruism (and its concomitant set of values regulation, paternalism, community and informality) respectively – in terms of the pure contractual core of the law and the peripheral rests of sovereign interventions into this core domain. The sovereign interventions into the domain of pure contract served only to curb the anti-social excesses to which pure contractual law might give

51 Ibid, 195–196.
52 Ibid, 195–199.
53 Ibid, 199–200.

rise. In other words, categories of private law such as torts or delict, quasi-contracts and the law of persons figured like units of public law within private law. They expressed the will of the sovereign to keep private law and individual legal relations compatible with communal concerns and values. The relegation of communal concerns and values to the margins of law in order to reserve the centre of private law for the contractual clash of wills would soon move the sovereign to intervene more actively and centrally in private law. This return of the will of the sovereign to leave its mark on private law would find expression in expanding social welfare and consumer protection legislation that would come to mark the end of the 19th and the beginning of the 20th century. This development marked the turn of the century in all the industrialised countries of the world. In America it finally led to Roosevelt's New Deal.

There is one development within the common law, however, that constituted a remarkable return of the sovereign's concern with communal values *within* private law, namely, the renewed prominence the law of tort or delict would attain with the decision of the House of Lords in *Donoghue v Stevenson*.[54] Atiyah points out

> "how the absence of a separate category of general tortious liability combined with the principle of privity of contract deprived many victims of their claims for negligent damages towards the end of the 19th and beginning of the 20th centuries. In the absence of a general principle of tortious liability, persons not party to a contract could have no claims for damages in terms of contract, and had no general cause of action beyond the terms of contract. This situation would only come to an end in 1932 with the watershed case of *Donoghue v Stevenson*. Lord Atkin's decision in *Donoghue* would suddenly cast the net of non-contractual liability for damages much wider than classical laissez-faire conceptions of law would tolerate."[55]

Horwitz's, Atiyah's and especially Kennedy's narrative of the development of nineteenth century law show clearly how this development compounded the shift from the Whig concern with legal rights as embodiments of political liberty, still common among the American settlers in the period leading to the American Revolution, to a concern with rights as embodiments of private liberty in the course of the nineteenth century. All legal rights, common law rights included, could in a certain sense be seen as constitutional or political rights (constitutive of political liberty and sovereignty) up to and around the time of the revolution. These rights, however, slowly but surely transformed into purely private law rights in the course of the nineteenth century. And this process of de-politicisa-

---

54 [1932] A.C. 562.
55 Atiyah, *The Rise and Fall of Freedom of Contract*, 502–504.

tion that gave rise to the purely private law conception of rights went further. Not only did legal rights lose their political and constitutional nature in the course of the nineteenth century so as to become private law rights concerned only with the enforcement of private legal relationships. The nineteenth century development of private law also saw to it that the private law rights that displaced the political and constitutional conception of rights were thoroughly rid of all other elements of law that reflected the coercive imposition of a communal sovereign will on the liberty of private individuals to contract with one another without external constraints.

In other words, a double de-politicisation is evident in the rise of classical legal consciousness. It consisted firstly in the gradual removal of political elements *from* rights and secondly in the gradual removal of communal political interference *with* rights. The first removal was effected by the shift from a property based understanding of private law (pivoting predominantly on early common law constraints on free alienation of property) to a contract based concept of private law (pivoting on freedom of contract and thus on the free alienation of property). However, the concept of freedom of contract that emerged from this first removal was still heavily constrained by a considerable array of non-contractual concerns with status or non-contractual conditions of legal capacity and other quasi-contractual or implied-contractual relations such as tort liability. The first removal thus demanded a second. It demanded the removal of all objective constraints on the capacity to contract. This second removal was effected, firstly, by the reduction of the concept of legal capacity to a set of minimum constraints dictated by minimal requirements of legal capacity, and secondly, by the categorical subjection of the concerns of tort law to the concerns of the law of contract. The marginal role that tort liability came to play during the heyday of freedom of contract (torts were little more than remedies for breach of contract) completed the picture of the sovereign's withdrawal from the substance of private law and private legal relations. The marginal role of tort liability toward the end of the nineteenth century thus also completed the narrative of the erasure of concerns with political liberty from the concerns of law.

The eventual return of communal sovereignty and political liberty as an essential concern of law would ultimately take place in four ways. It would begin with the extensive legislative constraints on freedom of contract (consumer laws, labour laws, social security laws). It would also come to the fore in a heightened concern with standards of good faith in contract law. It would be extended by the rise in prominence and significance of tort law within common law (*Donoghue v Stevenson* would become the famous beacon). And it would be consolidated with the explosion of the state action doctrine in the years that followed the New Deal. Chapters Two and Three will tell the story of this explosion of the state action doctrine in the Supreme Court decisions of *Swing v Labour*, *Shelley v Kramer* and *New York Times v Sullivan*. The explosion of the state action doctrine and the unlimited expansion of the horizontal effect of constitutional rights that these cases brought about, we shall see then, effected nothing less than the uninterrupted return of the will of the sovereign to all private legal relationships. Suffice it to grasp for now that this development in twentieth century United States constitutional law consolidated the return of communal sovereignty and political liberty as fundamental concerns of law after the eclipse of these concerns in the course of the nineteenth century. Let us now take a look at a similar eclipse and eventual return of communal sovereignty and political liberty in nineteenth and twentieth century German law.

IV The Privatisation of Constitutional Rights in Germany

Walter Leisner points out that the *Déclaration des Droits de l'Homme et du Citoyen* was not aimed against the state but against private legal subjects whose actions could not be reconciled with the principles of reason embodied in the *Déclaration*.[56] Far from a protection against the state, it was a call upon the state to fulfil its task of subjecting all private concerns to the demands of reason. The state was not suspected of unreasonable action at the time of the revolution, even when it acted forcefully and harshly. It was relied upon as a transformative vehicle of reason that would eradicate all unreasonable exercises of private power. Included under these exercises would especially be all hereditary privileges that were irreconcilable with the basic equality of all individuals.[57] "Abusive police action may also have come into the sight of revolutionary action, but it was mostly against the estates and the patrimonial state that the revolution acted." "Against landlords even more than against the princes" did the revolution object. What they pursued was in the first place the fundamental liberty of equal access to land, to the natural benefits of their environment and to commerce, all of which landlords claimed for their exclusive use on the basis of ancient and intransparent private law entitlements. In the first phase of the Revolution, this reaction against private powers overshadowed whatever resistance against public power may also have been evident at the time.[58]

---

56 Walter Leisner, *Grundrechte und Privatrecht* (München: Beck, 1960), 22.
57 Ibid, 23.
58 Ibid.

The principles of reason and basic equality that informed the *Déclaration* derived from natural law. These principles, Julius Ofner would emphasise in 1911, "only turned against nobility and church, *not against the state.*" "It recognised the state as an organised community and provided it with new scientific support."[59] Ofner's observation regarding natural law principles as the scientific basis of the organisation of the state goes to the heart of Leisner's thesis regarding the origin of natural law principles. These principles, he argued, derived from the reasonable self-organisation of pre- or early-modern communities on the basis of which they endeavoured to establish the highest levels of personal freedom that circumstances would allow. They derived from the organic or organisational order of communal life itself.[60]

We need not establish the precise extent to which this evidently Gierkean beginning of Leisner's narrative is accurate. It is surely accurate enough as a general observation regarding the general inclination of all communities to organise themselves as rationally and as fairly as unobserved or unreflected cultural and ideological constraints would allow. However, one should surely not overestimate the freedom-promoting thrust of pre-modern European communities and communal life. It is doubtful whether the self-organisational dynamics of pre-revolutionary European communities were quite as conducive to personal liberty as Leisner suggests. Be it as it may, it is important to bear this beginning of Leisner's narrative in mind to come to grips with his thesis regarding the fundamental semantic change (*Bedeutungswandel*) that befell the concept of natural rights in the 19th century. His argument is, namely, that the self-organisational social role that natural law principles played in pre- and early-modern times transformed into negative rights against the state in the 19th century. With this claim Leisner seeks to refute Jellinek's assertion regarding the essential state-orientation (*Staatsrichtung*) or vertical effect of fundamental rights.[61] According to Leisner, this state-orientation of fundamental rights only materialised in the 19th century and lasted only until the catastrophic demise of constitutionalism in the first half of the 20th century rendered these constitutional rights obsolete. When constitutionalism re-emerged in Germany after World War II, the exclusively state-oriented or vertical application of fundamental rights would no longer characterise the German constitutional framework. The GFCC would take leave of this framework in no uncertain terms in 1957.

---

59 Ibid, 23–24.
60 Ibid, 5–10.
61 Ibid, 3–4.

To the extent that the *Déclaration* addressed the state, continues Leisner's argument, it called upon it to enact civil law legislation on the basis of which one could also employ private law to dismantle the ancient privileges and intransparent titles that dominated feudal legal relationships.[62] Here then, does one find the origins of the idea of the state's duty to protect and promote the fundamental rights of individuals, also against possible abridgment by other individuals. This idea, we shall soon see, would become the core of German constitutional and *Drittwirkung* jurisprudence in the second half of the twentieth century.

The French revolutionaries also considered the principles of natural law as the basis of all law and therefore the unifying force in the legal system. They were absolute principles that stood above all positive law.[63] But the idea that laws enacted by the state – conceived as self-evidently the vehicle of liberty and reason – could be at odds with the basic rights articulated in the *Déclaration* was almost inconceivable at the time; hence the failure of all the attempts at the time to introduce any form of constitutional review of legislation. Legislation was simply assumed to give expression to the will of the people, as Carré de Malberg explained in his classical engagement with this issue.[64] This assumed harmony between state conduct and fundamental rights may have been a fiction or a figment of the revolutionary imagination of the time, but it sustained the idea that the fundamental unity of private and public law was rooted in the fundamental unity of liberty itself, and this unity rendered the horizontal effect of public law principles or fundamental rights self-evident. This self-evidence, however, did not survive Napoleon's seizure of power. The unity of the law thereafter no longer inhered in the unity of freedom, but in the unity of the imperial will. The revolutionary ideals were still evident in the substance of the Napoleonic Civil Code, but the Civil Code could no longer claim to be directly rooted in the principles of political freedom. This was the first crack in the unity of the law, argues Leisner. It was the first step towards the increasing insulation of private law from public law principles and the first step towards an increasingly technical understanding of the problems of private law.

The first comprehensive expression of this post-revolutionary separation of private law from public law would nevertheless not yet surface in the Napoleonic Code itself. It would come to the fore in the *Allgemeines Bürgerliches Gesetzbuch* of Austria of 1811. The Austrian Code precipitated a development that would culminate in the formalist conceptions of private law of the German Pandectists in

62 Ibid, 24.

63 Ibid.

64 Raymond Carré de Malberg, *La Loi Expression de la Volonté Générale* (Paris: Economica, 1931), 16–19.

the second half of the nineteenth century. And only then would the end product be exported to France again, and subsequently also to the rest of Europe and the United States. It is worthwhile to trace this development briefly from the first codification of the law in Prussia, via the Austrian Code, to the later civil codifications in Europe.

The natural law idea of the unity of the law that is rooted in the unity of freedom was still clearly evident in the first Prussian Codification of the law, the *Preussisches Allgemeines Landrecht* of 1794, commissioned by the enlightened King of Prussia, Frederick II. The *Allgemeines Landrecht* contained criminal, family, public and administrative law, but was mainly conceived as a civil code. However, Carl Gottlieb Svarez, who along with Ernst Ferdinand Klein authored the codification, was as clearly guided by a natural law philosophy of the state as he was by technical-empirical conceptions of private law. His conceptions were clearly informed by the fundamental rights articulated in the first human rights declarations and the political explosion in France also led to the entrenchment of these ideas in the final editorial stages of the project.[65]

The reign of Frederick II (he died in 1786) surely was enlightened for the times and the reign of his successor, Frederick William II, may have been, if not quite enlightened (in the Enlightenment sense of the word – he was a Rosicrucian), at least benevolent. Prussia, however, was still an absolutist monarchy at the time. The natural law ideas of personal liberty that guided Svarez's codification of the law could therefore not yet find expression in the public law sections of the code. Svarez thus resorted to the civil code to embody his conceptions of natural liberty in the codification. At this stage then, quite in contrast to the notion of the radiation effect of fundamental rights in private law (*Ausstrahlungswirkung der Grundrechte im Privatrecht*) that would come to mark German constitutional jurisprudence in the twentieth century, the fundamental principles of natural liberty radiated from within private law into other fields of law. Private law therefore provided the unitary natural law spirit of the law in the *Allgemeines Landrecht* and did so in a way that led to a widely lamented "despotism of fairness" at the time.[66]

The situation changed significantly with the codification of Austrian law in the *Allgemeine Bürgerliche Gesetzbuch* of 1811. The drafting of the Austrian codification went through two distinct stages that were respectively marked by the leading figures Karl Anton Freiherr von Martini, on the one hand, and Franz von Zeiller and Joseph von Sonnenfels, on the other. Martini produced a first

65 Leisner, *Grundrechte und Privatrecht*, 16.
66 Ibid, 17.

draft of the codification that was saturated by the natural law ideas of the Prussian *Allgemeines Landrecht* and the principle of the unity of the law – the unity of public and private law – that stemmed from these ideas. However, Martini's natural law ideas were systematically removed from the draft by a first revision commission. The commission simply stripped the first eight paragraphs that contained the principles of natural law from the draft. Sonnenfels also offered an early draft as alternative to Martini's first concept. Informed as it was by the conviction that private law had its origin in public law, it also contained ten introductory natural law paragraphs that were to apply to both public and private law. These paragraphs also fell under the axe of the revision commission. When Zeiller took over the leading role from Martini in 1797 he expressly pursued a rigorous and systematic division between public and private law in terms of which he restricted public law to the relation of the individual to the whole state (*das Verhältnis des einzelnen zum Ganzen*). He advocated an "essential difference" between political and civil legislative spheres (*Wesensverschiedenheit des politischen vom bürgerlichen Gesetzgebungsbereich*).[67] This division between public and private law signalled the first defeat of general natural law principles as far as the European civil codifications were concerned and precipitated the technical isolation of private law from public and constitutional law in subsequent legal developments.[68]

At the time that Zeiller was effecting this first significant division between private and public law in the history of European law, the technical isolation of private law was not yet inspired predominantly by the idea of an essential technical difference between private and public law. This idea only became dominant later when the scientific theories of private law began to advance it increasingly. At the time of the Austrian codification, the separation between public and private law, and the isolation of private law from the general principles of natural law, were driven by an anti-revolutionary phobia that came from the side of public law and the Court of the King.[69] However, the Historical School, the precursor of the Pandectist approach to legal science, already took the first legal theoretical step towards a closed system of private law rights and concepts. In doing so, it entrenched the separation of private law from natural law.

The Historical School did not expressly reject or deny the natural law ideas of liberty, but simply began to ignore them. By focusing exclusively on the sphere of private law, it effectively rendered the natural law ideas obsolete, spending no

67 Ibid, 20.
68 Ibid.
69 Ibid, 21.

time on expanding the individual autonomy warranted by private law principles into the public sphere.[70] The method of the Historical School consisted in rationalising the mass of private law materials inherited from the past with reference to core concepts and principles derived from Roman law.[71] The substantive content of natural law principles that was already embodied in these legal materials survived the rationalisations of the Historical School, but did so in significantly reduced forms. The fundamental and unitary freedom of the person emphasised by natural law would henceforth only find expression in concepts of property (*Eigentum*), freedom of contract (*Vertragsfreiheit*) and freedom of testation (*Testierfreiheit*). Isolated from its natural law origins, the general idea of freedom started suffocating under the constraints of these concepts. At first, only one significant mode of expression remained open for the revolutionary concern with freedom, namely, the defence of negative liberties against the state. However, the rise of the social movements of the nineteenth century must also be understood against the background of this suffocation of freedom in the private sphere and in private law. As Leisner sums up this development:

> "This was the tragic mistake of the 19th century; failure to recognise an enduring dynamic of freedom in private law, neglecting to distil a holistic foundation of the legal order from the spirit of liberty that was defended so courageously against the state."[72]

Thus came into existence the conservative liberal legal order that would later largely welcome the restoration movements in the second half of the 19th century. Another nail in the 19th century coffin of natural law principles of freedom, contends Leisner, was the Hegelian political philosophy of the time that stressed the sovereignty of the state vis-à-vis its subjects. This assessment of Hegel turns on a contentious interpretation of his political philosophy to which Chapter Five will pay further attention. Suffice it to state for now that Hegel's philosophy remained much closer to the ideals of the French Revolution than Leisner appears to appreciate. Be it as it may, as Leisner sees the matter, the 1848 Revolution and the Frankfurt Constitution also fell far short of the revolutionary ideals of 1789. The 1848 Revolution and Frankfurt Constitution, he avers, were more informed by the drive towards German unity than it was by the natural law ideals of the French

---

70 Ibid, 31.

71 Cf. note 101 below.

72 Leisner, *Grundrechte und Privatrecht*, 31: "Dies war der tragische Irrtum des 19. Jahrhunderts: die Verkennung einer andauernden Freiheitsdynamik im Privatrecht, die Vernachlässigung der *Gesamtgrundlegung* der Rechtsordnung aus dem Geist der Freiheit, die man gegen den Staat so tapfer verteidigte."

Revolution. To the extent that fundamental rights were embodied and emphasised in the 1848 Constitution, they were exclusively aimed against the state. They had no role to play in the private sphere and left this proto-liberal society to its own private law devices.

This then is how the fundamental semantic transformation (*Bedeutungswandel*) of fundamental rights in 19th century Germany (and Austria) came to pass. Commencing as principles of natural law that informed the self-organisation of society, they became conceptual and normative building blocks for the German Federation (*Deutscher Bund*) and, eventually, the German empire. The impact of the Frankfurt Constitution on private law was negligible. Abolition of hunting privileges, free sub-divisibility of property and the cancellation of fideicommissionary guarantees (the constraints on alienation that the previous section also highlighted with reference to Kennedy's narrative of 19th century American law) were achieved after intense battles in the plenum of the *Paulskirche*. But when it came to pushing through some fundamental social rights against the state, as the French revolutionaries did in 1848, the liberal conservative majority began to fear for the freedom of economic competition which they deemed non-negotiable, notwithstanding the fact that social rights against the state could at most impact only indirectly on this freedom of competition. Thus did a very conservative liberalism emerge as the real and enduring winner of the *Paulskirche* debates.[73] The Restoration would eventually undo whatever progressive public law principles came out of Frankfurt in 1848, but it would not touch the private liberties that had come to establish themselves in the meantime. For these liberties posed no threat to the return of monarchical and imperial rule. To the contrary, it offered the imperial government and its imperialist designs a very lucrative source of income.[74]

---

73 Ibid, 36–37.

74 Leisner does not touch on this point, but Locke and Kant already recognised the link between the wealth produced by a free market economy and imperial military potential. Cf. John Locke, "Two Treatises of Government," in *The Works of John Locke*, vol. 5 (Aalen: Scientia Verlag, 1963), sec. 42; Immanuel Kant, "Mutmasslicher Anfang der Menschengeschichte," in *Werke in 10 Bänden*, ed. Wilhelm Weischedel, vol. 9 (Darmstadt: Wissenschaftliche Buchgesellschaft, 1983), 98. Arendt makes the point regarding capitalist and imperialist expansionism very clear. Cf. Hannah Arendt, *The Origins of Totalitarianism: Imperialism* (New York: Harcourt Brace Jovanovich, 1968), 126, 135: "Imperialism was born when the ruling class in capitalist production came up against national limitations to its economic expansion. The bourgeoisie turned to politics out of economic necessity; for it did not want to give up the capitalist system whose inherent law is constant economic growth, it had to impose this law upon its home governments and to proclaim expansion to be an ultimate political goal of foreign policy." "What imperialists actually wanted was expansion of political power without the foundation of a body politic.

V The Nineteenth Century Transformation of Private Law Rights in Germany and its Impact on Early Twentieth Century German Public Law

Between 1840 and 1849 Savigny presented his monumental eight volume study and systematisation of inherited Roman legal materials under the title *System des heutigen römischen Rechts*. The fulcrum on which the Pandectists' work turned was the concept of "subjective rights." Savigny's own conception of subjective rights can be extracted from two key paragraphs in the *System*. The first paragraph defines the concept of a legal relation. The second describes the essential feature of individual power embodied in this relation. Savigny phrased the paragraphs as follows:

> "The essence of the legal relationship was determined as a sphere of independent reign of the individual will."[75]

> "We call this power the right of a person, which also means 'capacity.' Many call it a 'right in the subjective sense of the word.'"[76]

This conception of subjective rights became the core organising principle in the work of other Pandectists such as Von Jhering, Puchta and Windscheid. Windscheid ultimately defined subjective rights as follows:

> "A right is the power or supremacy of the will as warranted by the law."[77]

Imperialist expansion had been touched off by a curious kind of economic crisis, the overproduction of capital and the emergence of 'superfluous' money, the result of oversaving, which could no longer find productive investment within the national borders." Cf. in this regard also Carol Rose, "The Ancient Constitution vs. the Federalist Empire: Antifederalism from the Attack on 'Monarchism' to Modern Localism," *Faculty Scholarship Series* no. Paper 1823 (January 1, 1989): 80, http://digitalcommons.law.yale.edu/fss_papers/1823. I borrowed this footnote from Johan Van der Walt, *Law and Sacrifice: Towards a Post-Apartheid Theory of Law* (London: Birbeck Law Press, 2005), 187, fn. 112.

75 F.C. von Savigny, *System des heutigen Römischen Rechts*, Vol I (Berlin: Deit und Comp, 1840), par 53 (334): "Das Wesen des Rechtsverhältnisses wurde bestimmt als ein Gebiet unabhängiger Herrschaft des individuellen Willens."

76 Von Savigny, *System des heutigen Römischen Rechts*, Vol I, par 4 (7): "Diese Macht nennen wir ein Recht dieser Person, gleichbedeutend mit Befugnis. Manche nennen es das Recht in subjectiven Sinn."

77 B. Windscheid, *Lehrbuch des Pandektenrechts* (Aalen: Scientia Verlag, 1963), vol I par 37 (156): "Recht ist eine von der Rechtsordnung verliehene Willensmacht oder Willensherrschaft." Consider also G.F. Puchta, *Vorlesungen über das heutige römische Recht* (Leipzig: Verlag von Bernhard Tauchnitz, 1862), Vol I, par 22 (56): "Subjecte von Rechtsverhältnissen sind die Menschen als rechtlich freie. Die rechtliche Freiheit aber ist die, welche dem Menschen als reinen

That the Pandectists did not consider this power of the will warranted by law to be constrained by any moral considerations external to the legal system of positive legal rights was abundantly clear. Savigny stressed that the law was concerned only with the "external world" and "the sphere of external co-existence" ("... *weil das Recht, seinem Wesen nach, dem Gebiet des ausseren Zusammenlebens angehort*") and thus only concerned with the "external liberty" (*ausseren Freyheit*) of the individual.[78] He therefore distinguished emphatically between law and morality. The task of the law was not to prescribe moral principles, only to ensure that everyone remained free to decide moral issues for himself.[79]

This positivist separation between law and morality has its origin in Kant's distinction between law (*Legalität*) and morality (*Moralität*). Kant defined the law as "the sum total of conditions under which the arbitrary exercise of one's will could be reconciled with the arbitrary exercise of the will of others under a general law of liberty."[80] This conception of law played a very specific role in his practical philosophy. The law had to ensure the existence of the external or objective conditions that would enable every individual in society to act outwardly according to the demands of the categorical imperative. The categorical imperative was the moral command that everyone should listen to the voice of his own conscience and thus remain his own lawgiver. The law, Kant argued, had nothing to do with any moral decisions made in this autonomous fashion. The law was in no way concerned with the enforcement of morality.[81] It simply had to establish and maintain the external relations between individuals in society in a manner that would ensure the inner moral autonomy prescribed by the categorical imperative for each and everyone. In other words, the law had to ensure that everyone's outward behaviour remained consistent with the moral

---

Willenssubject zukommt, sie ist die reine Macht (Wille in der Potenz), die Moglichkeit, einen Gegenstand auf sich zu beziehen, sich zu unterwerfen." Cf. also Rudolf Von Jhering, *Geist des römischen Rechts auf den verschiedenen Stufen seiner Entwicklung* (Leipzig, Breitkopf und Härtel, 1894), vol 2 par 31, 140 "Der Inhalt eines jeden Rechtsverhältnisses, wenn man dasselbe des Beiwertes entkleidet und auf seinen juristischen Kern zurückführt, ist Willensmacht, Herrschaft, die Unterschiede der Rechtsverhältnisse sind Unterschiede der Herrschaft."

78 Cf. Von Savigny, *System des heutigen Römischen Rechts*, vol I par 59 (410); vol I par 8 (18).

79 Cf. Von Savigny, *Vermischte Schriften* (Aalen: Scientia Verlag, 1968), vol 5, 285: "Sittlichkeit zu erzwingen, ja selbst Unsittlichkeit zu verhindern, liegt ausser der Macht des Gesetzgebers, und er ist dafür nicht verantwortlich."

80 Immanuel Kant, *Metaphysik der Sitten*, in *Werke in 10 Bänden*, ed. Wilhelm Weischedel, vol. VII (Darmstadt: Wissenschaftliche Buchgesellschaft, 1983), 21.

81 Cf. Ibid, 35: "Also ist das allgemeine Rechtsgesetz: Handle äusserlich so, dass der freie Gebrauch deiner Willkur mit der Freiheit von jedermann nach einem allgemeinen Gesetze zusammen bestehen könne..."

principle of self-legislation and therefore with the right of everyone to the arbitrary exercise of his or her will.

The influence of Kant on the Pandectists is well documented in legal historical and theoretical scholarship.[82] Suffice it to note here only Leisner's observation regarding Kant's influence – "*antinaturrechtlich gewerteten Kantschen Erkenntnissen (etwa Trennung von Recht und Moral)*" – in Zeiller's and Sonnenfels' erasure of Martini's natural law principles in the first draft of the Austrian *Allgemeines Bürgerliches Gesetzbuch.*[83] Many questions abound here. The first surely concerns Kant's optimism that a formal system of legal rules would enduringly suffice to safeguard the freedom of everyone to heed the demands of morality. Habermas has noted in this regard that Kant was in this respect clearly informed by the optimistic *laissez-faire* economic theories of his time.[84] He therefore did not and perhaps could not foresee the extent to which severe economic disequilibrium might come to deprive masses of people of the external liberty to make the decisions required to give expression to their internal liberty or moral autonomy.[85] Kant was, however, also not naive in this regard. He acknowledged that his definition of the law in terms of the general system of rules that would reconcile the external liberty of individuals turned on an ideal or idealistic construction of law.[86] As was the case later with Hegel, Kant's definition of law turned on an *idea* of law, not the historical reality of law.

---

82 Julius Binder already asserted in 1907 that Savigny's system was undoubtedly constructed on the fundamental principles of Kantian philosophy. For this reference to Binder and a further discussion of the relationship between Kant and the Pandectists, cf. Hans Kiefner, "Der Einfluss Kants auf die Theorie und Praxis des Zivilrechts im 19. Jahrhundert," in *Philosophie und Rechtswissenschaft: Zum Problem Ihrer Beziehung Im 19. Jahrhundert* (Frankfurt a.M: Jahrhundert, Vittorio Klostermann, 1969), 5. Cf. also Franz Wieacker, *Privatrechtsgeschichte der Neuzeit: unter besonderer Berücksichtigung der deutschen Entwicklung* (Göttingen: Vandenhoeck & Ruprecht GmbH KG, 1967), 352.

83 Leisner, *Grundrechte und Privatrecht*, 21.

84 Jürgen Habermas, *Strukturwandel der Öffentlichkeit* (Frankfurt a.M: Suhrkamp, 1990), 188–189.

85 Kant had already published his practical philosophy when the poor appeared on the scene, to borrow somewhat from Arendt (cf. *On Revolution*, 48: "[T]he multitude, *appearing for the first time in broad daylight*..."). He was seventy years old when the revolution broke out and died in 1804. We cannot impute too much knowledge of modern poverty to him. But he was surely not unfamiliar with poverty, and we must assume that he was in typical bourgeois fashion just not deeply bothered by the relation between physical poverty and the ability to make moral decisions.

86 Kant, *Metaphysik der Sitten*, 336: "Was Rechtens sei (quid sit iuris), d.i. was die Gesetze an einem gewissen Ort und zu einer gewissen Zeit sagen oder gesagt haben, kann er noch wohl angeben; aber, ob das, was sie wollten, auch recht sei, und das allgemeine Kriterium, woran man

The stage of history nevertheless changed dramatically soon after Kant died. Hegel, notwithstanding his grand attempt at constructing a system of law that was no less idealistic than Kant's, could no longer ignore the dark shadows that began to haunt legal systems that were strictly or predominantly based on individual autonomy. He was acutely aware of the destitute masses – the *Lumpenproletariat* – for whom the idea of individual autonomy had become meaningless. Hegel studied the political economists incisively and understood well that the pursuit of self-interest and the fulfilment of needs in civil society would eventually subject every aspect of life to the logic of merciless competition, thus dooming those who could no longer compete to abject squalor.[87] When Savigny expounded his understanding of modern Roman law between 1840 and 1848, he surely was in a position to take notice of the serious side effects of formal systems of law that left individuals to their own devices. He opted not to do so. Against the background that he was writing, his legal theoretical voice surely resonated well with the conservative liberalism that triumphed in the *Paulskirche* in 1948 and resisted the introduction of social rights into the Frankfurt Constitution. This is surely even more decidedly the case for the later Pandectists who wrote their treatises on Roman law in a time when the critical mass of social discontent was sufficient to precipitate the rise of broadly significant social and socialist movements. As Wieacker observed, the Pandectists took no notice of either Hegel or the social questions of their time.[88]

The Pandectist systems of private law were the dominant force in German legal doctrine during the second half of the 19th century and the main source of the thinking that went into the codification of German private law in the *Bürgerliches Gesetzbuch* of 1896 (BGB). The private law contained in the BGB would therefore quite understandably come to evince all the significant traits of a liberalism that was much less concerned with democratic freedom than it was with economic freedom. Principles of communal solidarity that would ensure and sustain a broad base of individual autonomy were largely absent from it. It thus became a vehicle for the conservative liberalism that triumphed in the

---

überhaupt Recht sowohl als Unrecht (iustum et iniustum) erkennen könne, bleibt ihm wohl verborgen, wenn er nicht eine Zeitlang jene empirischen Prinzipien verlässt, die Quellen jener Urteile in der bloßen Vernunft sucht...um zu einer möglichen positiven Gesetzgebung die Grundlage zu errichten. Eine bloß empirische Rechtslehre ist ... ein Kopf, der schön sein mag, nur schade ! daß er kein Gehirn hat." The distinction between empirical or positive law and the idea of law runs like a golden thread through Kant's theory of law.

87 Joachim Ritter, "Hegel und die französische Revolution," in *Metaphysik und Politik* (Frankfurt a.M: Suhrkamp, 2003), 183–255.

88 Franz Wieacker, *Privatrechtsgeschichte der Neuzeit: unter besonderer Berücksichtigung der deutschen Entwicklung*, 415. I return to this reference in Chapter Five where it is quoted fully.

Frankfurt constitutional debates and it did little to temper the all-consuming dynamics of civil society that Hegel saw so well.[89]

The Pandectists presented their work to the world as modern systematisations of Roman law. A deep irony attaches to their work in this regard. For the understanding of private law rights in terms of a systematised set of abstract rights unrelated to context was not present at all in Roman law. The legal theorist and historian who articulated this fundamental difference between Roman and modern law most consistently in the twentieth century is undoubtedly Michel Villey. We need not go into the details of Villey's thesis regarding the origins of the subjective conception of rights in modern law. His central contention relates to clear evidence that the word "*ius*" with reference to which the Pandectists linked their theories of subjective rights to Roman law, did not at all pertain to the capacity or powers of individuals, but to "*rei,*" that is, to things. The word "*ius*" pertained to things or constellations of things to which the law attached sufficient significance to award entitlements and remedies. These awards and entitlements were embedded in a holistic cosmology that informed all of social life as well as the natural environment. Roman law had no or little regard for the notion of an individual wilfulness that exceeded its cosmological and socio-cosmological embeddedness. For that, Roman law was much too deeply rooted in the Aristotelian and Stoic thinking of its time.[90] And this is exactly what can no longer be said of modern and especially nineteenth century subjective rights. These rights were abstracted from all contextual specificities. This abstraction was the very aim of the Pandectist method. Already early in the second half of the nineteenth century did Rudolph von Jhering refer to this logical formalisation and abstraction of the law as the specific task (unsere Aufgabe) of his generation of private law theorists (scientists).[91] In the process they created generic systems

---

89 Cf. further the discussion of Hegel's assessment of the relation between state and civil society in Chapter Five.

90 Michel Villey, *La Formation de la Pensée Juridique Moderne* (Paris: Quadridge/PUF, 2009), 420.

91 Von Jhering articulated this task in his essay "*Unsere Aufgabe.*" The essay was the first contribution to the first issue of the *Jahrbücher für die Dogmatik des heutigen römischen und deutschen Privatrechts* that appeared in 1857. I refer here to the reprint of the essay in Von Jhering *Gesammelte Aufsätze aus den Jahrbüchern für die Dogmatik des heutigen römischen und deutschen Privatrechts Bnd I* (Jena: Gustaf Fischer, 1881). Von Jhering's description of the new scientific method distinguished between lower and higher jurisprudence. Lower jurisprudence concerned the collection and study of a mass of relevant legal rules and materials. Higher jurisprudence concerned the abstraction of the spirit of these rules through the construction of general legal concepts. Cf. *Gesammelte Aufsätze* 8: "Der Gegensatz der höheren zur niederen Jurisprudenz bestimmt sich durch den Gegensatz des Rechtsbegriffes zu der Rechtsregel, und

of abstract rights that became ideal vehicles for historically dis-embedded capitalist economies, to use Carl Polanyi's terminology.[92] It is important to note another irony in this regard. At the very time that legislators and public authorities in Europe and America began to appreciate the need to subject capitalist economies to historical considerations that transcended the abstract and a-historical logic of free-market principles, public law theory began to imitate the formalism of the Pandectists. At the very time that at least some private law theorists – notably among them Von Jhering[93] – began to discern the emaciation of individual liberty that the formal concepts of law wreaked, public lawyers started using this scientific approach of nineteenth century private law theorists to re-articulate the field of public law. Georg Jellinek, the theorist who according to Leisner can be singled out as principally responsible for limiting the application of constitutional rights to conduct of the state, was an exponent of this movement, but the pioneering figures were Paul Laband (in Germany) and Vittorio Emanuele Orlando (in Italy).[94] Laband articulated the task of public law as follows:

---

den Uebergang des Rechts aus dem niedern in den höhern Aggregatzustand vermittelt die juristische Konstruction, indem sie den gegebenen Rohstoff zu Begriffen erhebt."

92 Karl Polanyi, *The Great Transformation: The Political and Economic Origins of Our Time* (Boston, MA: Beacon Press, 2001), 60, 74, 227, 279.

93 Cf. Von Jhering *Im Begriffshimmel der Jurisprudenz* in *Scherz und Ernst in der Jurisprudenz: eine Weihnachtsgabe für das juristische Publikum* (Leipzig: Breitkopf und Härtel, 1909), 259: "Bedeutung der [juristischen] Probleme für das Leben? Gibt es hier denn ein Leben? Hier herrscht nur die reine Wissenschaft, die Rechtslogik, und die Bedingung ihrer Herrschaft und all der Herrlichkeit, die sie aus sich entlässt, besteht gerade darin, dass sie mit dem Leben nicht das mindeste zu schaffen hat." That the young Von Ihering already discerned how removed this jurisprudence was from reality is clear from his excessive response to this issue in "*Unsere Aufgabe.*" Cf. *Gesammelte Aufsätze* 15: "Auch darin trifft der Vergleich mit der Naturwissenschaft zu, dass es nicht ein unmittelbar praktischer Zweck war, oder dass wenigstens nicht ausschliesschlich dieser es war, welcher die Untersuchung veranlasste und leitete, sondern dass es zugleich ein rein wissenschaftliches Interesse galt, bei dem schon die Lust und Freude an Entdeckungen den Forscher weiter trieb. Aber wie die Entdeckungen der Naturwissenschaft, so kommen auch hier die Entdeckungen der Jurisprudenz dem Leben zu gute. Nicht gerade sofort, nicht gerade in dieser Form. Vielleicht liegt mancher von den gefundenen Rechtssätzen ein Jahrhundert lang unbenutzt, bevor sich der erste Fall ereignet, auf den er angewandt werden kann, vielleicht kann er nie auf eine solche unmittelbare praktische Verwerthung hoffen, aber er leistet seinen Dienst, indem er die Brücke zu anderen wirbt, oder indem er sie trägt, stützt, ergänzt. Und wäre auch gar kein Nutzen abzugeben, so ist er eben da seiner selbstwegen, er existirt, weil er nicht nicht-existiren kann, und weil die Jurisprudenz nicht Jurisprudenz sein und ihren praktischen Beruf nicht erfüllen könnte, wenn sie nur das unmittelbar Praktische suchen wollte."

94 Cf. Massimo La Torre, "'Rechtsstaat' and Legal Science. The Rise and Fall of the Concept of Subjective Right," *Archiv für Rechts- und Sozialphilosophie* (1990): 50–68.

> "The scientific task of the doctrinal study of a specific area of positive law consists in the construction of legal institutions, in tracing back specific legal rules to general principles and inferring from these principles general implications. This is, apart from the initial research that identifies the applicable legal rules (that is, the acquisition of complete knowledge and mastery of the subject matter), a purely logical activity of the mind. For the fulfilment of this task there is no other means available than logic. I cannot accept any other purpose for legal doctrine (*Dogmatik*) apart from the conscientious and complete identification of positive legal material and the logical mastery of this material through concepts." [95]

The system of public law rights that Jellinek would articulate in the spirit of the systems of private law rights articulated by the Pandectists was part and parcel of this move to re-articulate public law scientifically. Public law science would ultimately go much further than private law science. The definition of a right as a "sphere of subjective power" that was current among the Pandectists apparently still had too much sovereign blood in its veins for a system of public law that aimed to subject public legal subjects (public authorities) to the strictly logical and normative legitimacy of the state. The system of public law rights developed by Jellinek and others consequently had to make way for a system of logically coherent legal norms. Hans Kelsen's theory of public law and general theory of law is usually regarded as the high water mark of this development.[96] That Kelsen's normative positivism can be interpreted markedly differently – that his legal constructivism is in fact much more historical and sociological than is generally understood, even more political than the legal theory of his antagonist, the legendary champion of *political* legal theory, Carl Schmitt – will become clear from Chapter Six. Suffice it nevertheless to observe for now that early twentieth century constitutional theory in Germany became marked by a deep split between radical "historicist" and strictly conceptual or normative approaches to

95 Laband, *Das Staatsrechts des Deutschen Reiches Vol 1* (Tübingen: J.C.B. Mohr (Paul Siebeck), 1911) ix: "Die wissenschaftliche Aufgabe der Dogmatik eines bestimmten positiven Rechts liegt aber in der Konstruktion der Rechtsinstitute, in der Zurückführung der einzelnen Rechtssätze auf allgemeinere Begriffe und anderseits in der Herleitung der aus diesen Begriffen sich ergebenden Folgerungen. Dies ist, abgesehen von der Erforschung der geltenden positiven Rechtssätze, d. h. der vollständigen Kenntnis und Beherrschung des zu bearbeitenden Stoffes, eine rein logische Denktätigkeit. Zur Lösung dieser Aufgabe gibt es kein anderes Mittel als die Logik.... [I]ch kann es nicht als richtig anerkennen, wenn jemand der Dogmatik andere Aufgaben stellt als die gewissenhafte und vollständige Feststellung des positiven Rechtsstoffes und die logische Beherrschung desselben durch Begriffe." Also quoted by La Torre "*Rechtsstaat*" and Legal Science," 61.

96 Hans Kelsen, *Reine Rechtslehre* (Aalen: Scientia Verlag, 1994).

constitutional law. A Hegelian synthesis between concept and history did not appear possible in German legal theory at the time.

A neo-Hegelian wave of constitutional thinking eventually emerged during the Weimar period. One of the key figures in this return to Hegel in legal theory during Weimar was Rudolf Smend. It would become the merit of Smend to launch a mode of constitutional thinking that is both rigorously conceptual and sufficiently historical. And it is this neo-Hegelian historical conceptualism that ultimately came to inform the horizontal effect jurisprudence that the GFCC would develop in *Lüth*.[97] The theory of horizontal effect that will be articulated towards the end of this book will avoid certain aspects of the Schmendian neo-Hegelianism that informed the *Lüth* jurisprudence. It will become clear in Chapter Two that there are many problematic elements in the jurisprudence that the GFCC launched with *Lüth*. But it will also become clear in the last section of this chapter that *Lüth* took an important step away from the a-historical formalism that 19th century legal science bequeathed to 20th century constitutional theory. *Lüth* can be understood as the opening call for a historical or historicist re-contextualisation of private and public law, a re-contextualisation of both private and public law through constitutional review.

It is not surprising that a certain Hegelianism or neo-Hegelianism would become a key ingredient of the call for the re-contextualisation of law articulated in *Lüth*. Hegel was acutely aware that an idealistic system of law based on the Kantian ideal of individual moral autonomy would not necessarily guarantee such moral autonomy in actual legal relationships. His acute engagement with political economy made him realise that actual legal relationships were more likely to destroy moral autonomy than safeguard it. For Hegel, empirical reality no longer sustained the idea that a legal system that turned on a strict separation of legality (Legalität) and morality (Moralität) would somehow continue to safeguard the conditions for morality, as it may still have done for Kant. In response to this empirical foundering of Kantian morality he took his "grey-in-grey" recourse to the state, or at least the *idea* of the state, as the ultimate resort for whatever Kantian moral autonomy might be sustained in this world.[98] Chapter Five will return to and endorse this Hegelian recourse to the state as the last vestige and guarantor of Kantian morality. Chapter Five and the rest of this book can and will surely be read as a neo-Hegelian conception of constitutional review. If it is true that *Lüth* represents a Smendian neo-Hegelianism, this book surely

97 Ralph Christensen and Andreas Fischer-Lescano, *Das Ganze des Rechts – Vom hierarchischen zum reflexiven Verständnis deutscher und europäischer Grundrechte* (Berlin: Duncker & Humbolt, 2007), 37–47, 59–66.
98 Ritter, "Hegel und die französische Revolution," 183–255.

does not shy away from this neo-Hegelianism. To the extent that it does take leave of *Lüth* in the end, it does not take leave of the neo-Hegelian *statism* reflected in *Lüth*.

We have reached the end of the two 19th century narratives, American and German, that this chapter set out to trace. The rest of this chapter will highlight the essential outcomes of these narratives in two further sections. Section VI will firstly reflect on the baseline of erased baselines that emerged from 19th century legal science. Section VII will secondly look at the inversed coordinates of this legal science.

VI The Baseline of Erased Baselines

Two observations regarding the American state action doctrine cast the horizontal effect question in a nutshell. The first is Cass Sunstein's observation that the state action doctrine (the refusal to acknowledge the horizontal effect of the Federal Constitution) turned on the assumption of a fundamental "status quo neutrality," that is, the assumption of existing economic distributions as "natural" and therefore not subject to political questioning or reflection.[99] The second is Charles Black's reference to the state action doctrine as "one of the last unexpunged clauses of America's gentleman's agreement on racism."[100] It is important to grasp the intrinsic connection between Sunstein's and Black's observations. The insistence embodied in the state action doctrine that the common law be taken as the starting point or baseline for all private law questions is exactly what renders the status quo neutral and natural. The common law does not speak to race or any other social status. As we saw above, the 19th century development of American private common law pivoted on the purification of all baseline questions of personal status from the concerns of law. Nineteenth century legal science distilled from the trappings of erstwhile status concerns an abstract legal subject, a legal subject exclusively characterised by a politically and socially de-contextualised will or agency that engaged in neutral economic competition with other such abstract legal subjects. If the state action doctrine pivots

99 Cass R. Sunstein, *The Partial Constitution* (Cambridge, Mass.: Harvard University Press, 1993) 74–75, 159–161; Cf. Stephen Gardbaum, "The 'Horizontal Effect' of Constitutional Rights," *Michigan Law Review* 102, no. 3 (December 1, 2003): 415.

100 Black, "The Supreme Court, 1966 Term – Foreword: State Action, Equal Protection, and California's Proposition 14," 97. Cf. also the discussion of Black's views in this regard in Chapter Three.

on the baseline of the common law, as Sunstein claims, it in fact pivots on the erasure of baseline questions.

The culmination of 19th century legal science and 19th century law in the mind-set that Kennedy calls "classical legal consciousness" created a veritable matrix under the sway of which all particular personal embodiments that involved some or other social specification played no role. As long as this matrix could be maintained, there would be no chance of race, class, gender or socio-economic concerns re-entering the common law; hence the attempt in 1883 to reintroduce questions of race into private law through the 14th Amendment. The fact that this attempt failed, the fact that baseline questions were by design of the state action doctrine prevented from re-entering the law underlines three important issues. It firstly shows how and the extent to which the common law insistence on abstract legal will and abstract legal subjectivity, as the threshold condition for all significant legal questions, triumphed over any understanding of the equal protection concerns of the Federal Constitution that might reintroduce questions of status or race or gender into private law reasoning. It thus also shows how the state action doctrine entrenched the matrix created by classical legal consciousness. And it shows further, on a more specific level, how questions of private racism were written out of the law. Private racism was prevented from becoming a constitutional question by the state action doctrine *and* disqualified from becoming a common law question by the common law insistence on abstract legal subjectivity and abstract will as threshold conditions or significant legal questions. Under these conditions, one surely did not need substantive common law rules such as "Blacks cannot buy property" that would give the game away and expose itself all too evidently and flagrantly to the 14th Amendment. The principle of abstract legal agency, abstract legal subjectivity and abstract contractual will-formation kept the substantive baselines effectively and efficiently out of sight for business to proceed as usual. Thus did private racism become a non-legal matter, a gentleman's agreement that could not be exposed to legal scrutiny.

German Pandectism likewise culminated in the doctrinal construction of an abstract legal subjectivity that was no less disembodied than its American counterpart, namely, the abstract contractual will that classical American legal consciousness distilled from the trappings of status and implied reason that still informed 18th century law and legal thought. As we saw above, the major Pandectists defined subjective or private law rights as nothing but the abstract will power that is granted by general law. The private law system that civil law theorists and judiciaries built on the glassy framework of four private law rights retained nothing of the contextuality or embeddedness that attached to the institutions of Roman law from which these rights were derived. The Pandectists presented their private law systems as modern Roman law, but these presentations surreptitiously performed an expulsion of essential features of Roman law in the same way that Austin and Maine used Roman law distinctions (contractus, quasi contractus, delictum) to create a system of law that could hardly be further removed from the rich contextual rationality of Roman law. Maine was aware of this. He knew that there was a huge difference between the modern conception of rights as subjective powers and the Roman conception of rights as a particular kind of relationship.[101]

With its *Lüth* decision of 1957 the GFCC moved exactly in the opposite direction that the USSC did in 1883 when it coined the state action doctrine in the *Civil Rights Cases*. The USSC actively and deliberately de-contextualised the law with the state action doctrine articulated in the *Civil Rights Cases*. The GFCC actively and deliberately re-contextualised the law with the *Drittwirkung* doctrine articulated in *Lüth*. The *Lüth* decision effectively decided in favour of re-opening the baseline questions that come into play before some or other specific rule of law presents itself in the circumscribed spotlights of strict neutrality and general application. The reasoning employed in *Lüth* may have been questionable in many respects, as we shall see in Chapters Two and Six. But the *Lüth* judgement made a clear decision in favour of contextualising the abstract conception of wrongful competition in the BGB (that rendered the boycotting of Veit Harlan's film wrongful or *sittenwidrig* as the trial court found) so as to take into account the historical circumstances of post-war Germany.[102] It considered the embeddedness of the legal dispute in painful and shameful circumstances; it considered the various ways the subjectivity of the disputing parties could not be severed from these circumstances; it considered all the concerns that prevented the parties from claiming abstract existence in a context-free zone of economic competition. On this count alone *Lüth* brought about the jurisprudential revolution that allowed the return of historical and political baseline questions to the judicial resolution of conflicts that are, in fact, not abstract and not devoid of political and historical considerations. Conflict, and legal conflict is no exception in this regard, often constitutes the essential concretisation of the political and the historical.

---

101 H.S. Maine, *Ancient Law: Its Connection with the Early History of Society and Its Relation to Modern Ideas* (London: John Murray, 1920), 336–337; H.S. Maine, *Dissertations on Early Law and Custom* (London: John Murray, 1891), 365.

102 Cf. Thomas Henne and Arne Riedlinger, eds., *Das Lüth-Urteil aus (rechts-)historischer Sicht: die Konflikte um Veit Harlan und die Grundrechtsjudikatur des Bundesverfassungsgerichts* (Berlin: Berliner Wissenschafts-Verlag, 2005).

The concretisation of the political and the historical consists, in fact, always in fracturing the glassy surfaces that society obtains from legal abstraction. It consists in the eruption of the murky depths that the slick surfaces of legal abstraction obscure. The task of the law consists in this abstraction and, ultimately, in this obscuration.

The law is always abstract. It is the essence of the law to perform abstraction and to present conflicts in the light or clarity of abstraction. In this respect Marx's assessment of law as a system of abstract analogy that ignores particular differences is of course as correct as an assessment of water as wet.[103] And one may prefer, as Marx did, to get out of the water, but there is nothing one can do about water's wetness while one is in it.[104] The essential abstraction that defines all law was also significantly true for the categories of Roman law. No system of law can entertain the absolute specificity of context and biography and remain law. It would turn misguidedly into another enterprise should it seek to do so. It would turn into the enterprise of literature and the literary exploration of the deep secret of all instances of individual life and every individual thing that, on the other extreme end of the spectrum, also explode context and the very concept of context for the sake of absolute individualised justice.[105] The law cannot and should not attempt to do this. The question of context and contextualisation that the horizontality revolution returned to jurisprudence must therefore be understood in terms of the exigency of selecting adequate levels of abstraction and adequate levels of contextualisation in the resolution of conflicts. The horizontal effect of fundamental rights can thus be argued to turn on the maintenance and regulation of the tension between concept and context. It turns on the mainte-

---

103 Karl Marx, "Critique of the Gotha Programme," in *Karl Marx Friedrich Engels: Collected Works Vol. 24* (London: Lawrence & Wishari, 1989), 75–99. The original German text reads: "Das Recht kann seiner Natur nach nur in Anwendung von gleichem Maasstab [sic] bestehn; aber die ungleichen Individuen (und sie wären nicht verschiedne Individuen, wenn sie nicht Ungleiche wären) sind nur an gleichem Massstab messbar, so weit man sie unter einen gleichen Gesichtspunkt bringt, sie nur von einer *bestimmter* Seite fasst, z. B. im gegebnen Fall sie *nur als Arbeiter* betrachtet, und weiter nichts in ihnen sieht, von allem andern absieht." Cf. Karl Marx, "Kritik des Gothaer Programms," in *Karl Marx und Friedrich Engels: Werke-Artikel Entwürfe*, by Friedrich Engels (Berlin: Dietz Verlag, 1985), 14.

104 For those who believe living with law is an incircumventible condition of humanity, Marxism can *at best* be a literary affair. For further reflection on this thought, cf. Jean-Luc Nancy, *La Communauté désoeuvrée* (Paris: Christian Bourgois, 1999), 175–198.

105 Cf. Johan van der Walt, "Law, Utopia, Event," in *Law and the Utopian Imagination*, ed. Austin Sarat (Stanford: Stanford University Press, 2014); Johan van der Walt, "Law and the Space of Appearance in Arendt's Thought," in *Hannah Arendt and the Law*, ed. Marco Goldoni and Christopher McCorkindale (Oxford: Hart Publishing, 2012).

nance and regulation of the tension between the erasure and reconstruction of historical and political baseline questions in legal reasoning.

VII Inversed Coordinates

There is a prominent view among legal theorists that private law is really just a sub-division of public law. Georg Jellinek articulated this view as follows:

> "All private law is only possible on the basis of the recognition of the personality of the individual, or more strictly speaking, through recognition of specific aspects of the individual, with recourse to which he is able to mobilise the authority of the state. All private law rights are connected to a public law claim to recognition and protection."[106]

According to this definition, all private law rights, horizontal as they may appear, ultimately depend on the vertical relation between the state and the individual. A number of legal theoretical observations are nevertheless required to attain to an understanding of the vertical/horizontality relation or the relation between state and civil society that is at issue here. These observations will make clear that the private/public law distinction is much more complex than Jellinek's view would suggest. Jellinek himself makes it clear that the relation between private and public law is extremely complex and that it is often quite difficult to point out this distinction in a-priori fashion when one deals with concrete cases. He points out in this regard that the state itself often stands in a private law or private economic relation to its "subjects" or citizens. The state often enters into contracts with private individuals and often incurs tort or delictual liability to pay compensation for damage to private individuals and thus becomes involved in two of the core legal relations that constitute the field or system of private law. In these cases, the state must be seen to act as a private legal subject.[107]

However, the complexity of the relation between private and public law that comes to the fore when more general legal theoretical principles are considered concerns another issue. It concerns the question whether the relation between

106 Georg Jellinek, *Allgemeine Staatslehre* (Berlin: Julius Springer, 1922), 385: "Alles Privatrecht ist nur möglich auf Grund der Anerkennung der individuellen Persönlichkeit, näher gefasst durch Anerkennung bestimmter Qualitäten des einzelnen, vermöge deren er in den Stand gesetzt ist, in seinem Interesse die Staatsgewalt in Bewegung zu setzen. Alle Privatrechte sind mit einem öffentlich-rechtlichen Anspruch auf Anerkennung und Schutz verbunden."
107 Ibid.

state and citizen should not, at a more fundamental level of reflection, rather be regarded as a *private law* relationship, notwithstanding the accuracy of Jellinek's view that no private law and no private legal capacity are possible without state recognition and support. Put more simply: The automatic assumption that law pertaining to the state is public law can and must be questioned in the first place. Private law may well be part and parcel of the law pertaining to the state and the legal capacities of the state, as Jellinek asserts, but there is no self-evident reason why the law pertaining to the state should be regarded as public law in the first place. Broader legal theoretical and legal historical considerations provide one with good reasons to think that the law pertaining to the state could in many respects be regarded as part and parcel of "private law," as the long history of feudal legal relations would suggest. These theoretical and historical considerations become evident when one scrutinises public and private legal relationships from the perspective of their alleged verticality and horizontality.

Standard or mainstream legal theory regularly assumes private law relations between private law subjects as horizontal relations whereas public law relations are taken to be vertical in view of the subordinate position of the citizen or subject to the state and public authorities. This view regarding the horizontal character or horizontality of private legal relations and the vertical character or verticality of public legal relations is a standard feature of public law textbooks, but let us again turn to Jellinek for a typical articulation:

> "The opposition between private and public law can be traced to the fundamental idea that private law regulates the relations between individuals who face one another horizontally (*Nebengeordnete*), while public law regulates the organisation and function of public authorities, the relation between these authorities themselves, as well as the relations between these authorities and their subjects (*Unterworfene*)."[108]

The key words in Jellinek's passage that imply the horizontality of private relations between citizens and the verticality of public relations between citizens and public authorities are *Nebengeordnete* and *Unterworfene*. This view regarding the horizontality of private and the verticality of public law relations is well established and entrenched in standard legal systematics, doctrine and history.

108 Ibid, 384: "Der Gegensatz von Privat- und öffentlichem Recht kann auf den Grundgedanken zurückgeführt werden, daß im Privatrecht die einzelnen als grundsätzlich Nebengeordenete einander gegenüberstehen, es daher die Beziehungen der einzelnen als solcher ordnet, während das öffentliche Recht Verhältnisse zwischen verschiedenen Herrschaftssubjekten oder die Organisation und Funktion der Herrschaftssubjekte und deren Beziehungen zu den Herrschaft Unterworfenen regelt."

The view that public law relations are vertical relations has its historical origins in the very symbolism of law and politics of the pre-modern age that fell into disarray with the rise of the nominalist and Newtonian self-understanding of the modern age. Within the framework of pre-modern symbolism, political rulers such as kings, princes and other nobles enjoyed an elevated status in the complete cosmological scheme of heaven and earth. As representatives of God on earth, the king enjoyed a position at the very top of the great *chain of being*.[109] The relation between the king and his subjects was therefore self-evidently of a vertical nature. Similarly vertical were the relations between the rest of the privileged nobility (who took their seats just below the king in the big scheme of things[110]) and the lower orders of pre-modern European societies.

Now, the historical legacy of the great political revolutions of the modern age (especially the American and French revolutions) consisted precisely in their concerted attempts to dismantle the vertical or hierarchical constructions of pre-modern Europe so as to establish a truly horizontal communal order in terms of which no one would stand in a vertical relation to any one else and everyone would be truly *equal* before the law. The function of early modern constitutionalism was to contribute to and promote this fundamental horizontalisation of social relations. The horizontal effect of constitutional principles on private law, which contemporary jurisprudence has come to regard as a secondary if not anomalous manifestation of constitutional review, can thus plausibly be argued to constitute the original and primary form of constitutional review.[111] As Walter Leisner articulated the point strikingly in the German horizontal effect de-

---

109 For insightful descriptions of this symbolism, cf. James Daly, "Cosmic Harmony and Political Thinking in Early Stuart England," *Transactions of the American Philosophical Society* 69, no. 7 (1979): 1–41; Walter Ullman, *The Individual and Society in the Middle Ages* (London: Methuen and Company, 1967); Walter Ullmann, *Medieval Political Thought* (Baltimore: Penguin, 1975); George Duby, *The Three Orders: Feudal Society Imagined* (Chicago: University of Chicago Press, 1982).

110 Often in equal power relations – first instances of rule of law like *magna charta* were about horizontal agreements between the king and nobility that the king also had to honour. In these earlier times the pope was the only real sovereign with ultimate authority over all earthly rulers. The position of the king as absolute sovereign and therefore as completely at the top of the hierarchy only materialised towards the end of the middle ages and especially during the reformation with the maturation of the idea of the divine right of kings. This idea was a result of the king eventually winning the long battle between state and church for ultimate authority on earth. For the classic discussion of this development cf. John Neville Figgis, *The Divine Right of Kings* (London: Cambridge University Press, 1934), 17–65.

111 I use constitutional review in a loose sense here. Strictly speaking it is the legacy of the jurisprudence that developed in the wake of the decision of the United States Supreme Court in *Marbury v Madison* 1 Cranch 5 US 137 (1803).

bate, it was hardly conceivable to direct constitutional review against the state at the time of the French Revolution. The state was perceived as the revolutionary agent that would progressively destroy the unconstitutional remains of the inequalities that pertained to Europe's old status based societies:

> "The French Revolution was not primarily a reaction against the state: It was directed against abuses of the royal executive, not against the state itself, as the increase of state power at the time of the revolution shows. The point of departure was therefore less the questioning of state power as such, but much rather the reaction against the exercise of power over people in a private law-like, arbitrary fashion of which the outgoing monarchy made itself guilty, often relying on police methods. Also the reaction against the state was juridically speaking only a private law struggle against the state as a third party... Equality was so much on the foreground that it was constantly recognised with amazement that although state intervention became much sharper as time passed, it was tolerated in the knowledge that state power was exercised here in a stately way."[112]

It is of course true that the old symbolism or political theology of the pre-modern age would re-emerge very soon in post-revolutionary Europe. Especially Michelet would, by articulating a revolutionary or post-revolutionary mysticism, soon again view the secular state as an earthly God or the representative of God on earth[113] and it surely did not take long for hereditary rule to return to France and Europe. But the idea of horizontal constitutionalism would survive all the nineteenth century waves of restoration and would continue to inform the concept of constitutionalism that survived the cataclysmic eclipses of constitutionalism in the first half of the twentieth century. However, concomitant to the re-

---

112 Leisner, *Grundrechte und Privatrecht*, 22: "Die französische Déclaration war nicht primär eine Reaktion gegen 'den Staat': sie richtete sich gegen gewisse Übergriffe der königlichen Exekutive, nicht gegen den Staat an sich, wie die gleichzeitige Verstärkung der staatsgesetzlichen Allmacht beweist. Ausgangspunkt war deshalb weniger die Infragestellung eines staatlichen Machtsanspruchs als solchen, sondern vielmehr die Reaktion gegen die Ausübung der Gewalt über Menschen in einer privatrechtsähnlichen, willkürlichen Weise...dessen sich das niedergehende Königtum mit manchen Polizeimethoden schuldigmachte. Auch die antistaatliche Reaktion war rechtlich nur ein 'drittgerichteter,' privatrechtlicher' Kampf....Die 'Gleichheit' stand so sehr im Vordergrund, dass immer wieder mit Verwunderung festgestellt worden ist, dass die Eingriffe staatlicherseits später oft weit schärfer waren, aber ertragen wurden in der Erkenntnis, dass hier Staatsgewalt in staatswürdiger Weise ausgeübt wurde." This point has been made by numerous scholars. For more references, cf. Klaus Stern, *Das Staatsrecht der Bundesrepublik Deutschland*, vol. Band III/1 (München: C.H. Beck, 1988), 1515–1516.

113 Cf. especially the classic essay of Claude Lefort, "Permanence du Théologico-politique?," in *Essais sur le Politique XIXe-XXe siécles* (Paris: Seuil, 1986), 275–329; Claude Lefort, "The Permanence of the Theologico-Political?," in *Democracy and Political Theory* (Minneapolis: University of Minnesota Press, 1988), 213–255.

turn of monarchy and imperial rule in nineteenth century Europe emerged the idea of politically neutral civil societies and free markets. Increasingly unconstrained by politics or the theological symbolism of pre-modernity, and much rather bolstered by a new social symbolism of thrift and deserved entrepreneurial success,[114] this new world would give rise to the most hierarchical or vertically ordered "private spheres" imaginable.

The systems of private law that emerged towards the end of the 19th century pivoted, as we saw above, on abstract legal subjectivity or abstract will-formation. Abstract will-formation could nevertheless not found its own forcefulness and power. It could not explain the capacity of legal subjects to sustain themselves in a competitive environment, let alone procure ascendancy in this environment. Contractual will-formation surely turns on some degree of personal power play and psychological arm wrestling, but the real force that constitutes the capacity to conclude contracts as a vehicle of contractual freedom derives from backgrounds of wealth and financial power. It is these backgrounds that ultimately underpin contractual freedom, not the personal ability to sign one's name unflinchingly. Only the impecunious deal with the impecunious. If the hierarchies of medieval power were symbolised by the towering spires of Gothic cathedrals, castles and palaces, they surely find their match in the spiralling heights of latter day corporate architecture. And these heights surely constitute the hermetic altitudinal boundaries between boardroom and park bench deals. True, had he lived today, Anatole France may well have observed that the boardroom deal can also be concluded on a park bench. But the reverse is surely not true. The world of private law, exemplified as it is today by corporate culture, is not a horizontal world. And if some law is to ensure that some park benches remain available for park bench dealers, if some law is to ensure that at least some parks remain unincorporated into corporate office parks, that law will not be private law.[115] Private law creates, sustains and increases hierarchies. This is its proper and legitimate aim. It cannot be expected to do what it is not meant and designed to do. It cannot be expected to keep its hierarchical contours in check, let alone reduce them. Those who wish to resist the hierarchical world of private law can of course also do so legitimately. But they cannot expect pri-

---

114 As Max Weber observed with reference to the connection between protestantism and capitalism. Cf. Max Weber, "Die protestantische Ethik und der Geist des Kapitalismus," in *Gesamtausgabe*, ed. Horst Baier, Wolfgang J. Mommsen, and Rita Aldenhoff, vol. 18 (Tübingen: Mohr Siebeck, 1993).

115 Cf. Johan van der Walt, "Johannesburg: A Tale of Two Cases," in *Law and the City*, ed. Andreas Philippopoulos-Mihalopoulos (Routledge-Cavendish, 2007), 221–236.

vate law and private lawyers to do that for them. Again, one may want to get out of the water, but one cannot complain about its wetness.

An unfortunate implication of the indirect approach to horizontal effect of constitutional rights, we shall see in Chapters Two and Four, is indeed the expectation it imposes on private law to do what it is not designed to do. Indirect horizontal effect seeks to impress upon private law judges, lawyers and theorists the responsibility to apply private law against the grain of its own logic, to counter-act its own hierarchical tendencies. If something is designed to subject the towering heights of private law hierarchies to the requirements of minimal levels of horizontality and equality, constitutional rights are. This is what the horizontal effect of constitutional rights is all about. It concerns the restriction and even the undoing of private hierarchies. It concerns the constitutionally required levelling and horizontalisation of these hierarchies.

In a paradoxical way, the horizontal effect of constitutional rights may even come to serve what may once have been the truth of the will theory of private law. It may come to see to it that the free will of individuals and not just established wealth determines the relationship between them. "The classics created by subtraction," writes Kennedy. Horizontal effect might demand one day, with Roberto Unger, the one crucial subtraction that might make the will theory of private law attain to the element of truth that may well inhere in it, but has largely remained hidden up to now. It may one day come to demand the subtraction of inheritance law from the domain of private law.[116] The arbitrary inheritance of significant wealth sustains private hierarchies and frustrates the free will formation of new generations. And it does so beyond the lifespan of anything that can still be called the *living will* of a testator. Mortal will formation cannot survive itself. The suggestion that it can is an anti-social fiction.

Modern law relies on nasciturus fictions to afford unborn life equal access to legal protection. The nasciturus fiction affords it whatever equality of life chances remains possible after birth. As such, the nasciturus fiction enhances the ideal of horizontal legal relationships. This is not true in the case of fictions that do the opposite. Fictions that impute posthumous wills to the dead, wills, moreover, that sustain excessively unequal life chances, are democratically deeply questionable. The horizontalising application of constitutional rights may well one day come to subtract inheritance law from the domain of private law and turn inheritance into a matter of communal, public or political deliber-

---

116 Cf. Roberto Unger's resistance, in the name of democracy, to property claims beyond death as embodied in the law of succession. Cf. Roberto Mangabeira Unger, *Democracy Realized: The Progressive Alternative* (New York: Verso, 1998), 144; Roberto Mangabeira Unger, *What Should Legal Analysis Become?* (New York: Verso, 1996), 14.

ation. As things stand, however, the world of free competition that private law sustains is much like a chess tournament in which the players have to start new games without the pieces they have lost in previous games, and even without the pieces their mothers and fathers lost in games long forgotten. Is it any wonder then that some players end up entering the fray without a single pawn to field? Is it any wonder that some players never even enter the fray, never come to take part in the game? Those who conceive the world of private law in terms of horizontal legal relationships are deeply deluded.

Chapter Two: Twelve Pivotal Cases

I Introduction

The question of the horizontal effect of constitutional rights is broadly speaking the question whether the violation of a constitutional right of one private individual by another private individual is actionable in law. The question has its positive legal origins in the state action doctrine developed by the United States Supreme Court in the wake of its decision in the *The Civil Rights Cases.*[1] This chapter will study the legacy of the *The Civil Rights Cases* by taking a close look at this historical judgment as well as at eleven other cases, six of which are also United States Supreme Court decisions. The journey starts with *The Civil Rights Cases*, then moves on to the next three United States cases, namely *Shelley v Kraemer*,[2] *Labour v Swing*[3] and *New York Times v Sullivan.*[4] It then plots a course through Canada, Germany and South Africa with *RWDSU v Dolphin Delivery Ltd*,[5] *Lüth*[6] and *Du Plessis v De Klerk.*[7] After *Du Plessis* the focus returns to the United States for a close look at *Flagg Brothers, Inc. v Brooks*[8] and *DeShaney v County Department of Social Services*,[9] and then moves off-shore again to take up a mid-Atlantic position between the United States and Germany with a comparison of *Roe v Wade*[10] and the *Erste Abtreibung* (*First Abortion*) decision of the GFCC.[11] The chapter ends with a discussion of the GFCC's decision in the *Reiten im Walde* case.[12] *Roe*, *Erste Abtreibung* and *Reiten im Walde* are not generally regarded as state action or horizontal effect cases. The engagement with them in this chapter will nevertheless show that they can and should be read as horizontal effect cases.

---

1 109 U.S. 3 (1883), hereafter cited as *The Civil Rights Cases.*
2 334 U.S. 1 (1948), hereafter cited as *Shelley.*
3 312 U.S. 321 (1941), hereafter cited as *Swing.*
4 376 U.S. 254 (1963), hereafter cited as *Sullivan.*
5 [1986] 2 S.C.R 573, hereafter cited as *Dolphin Delivery.*
6 7 BVerfG 198, hereafter cited as *Lüth.*
7 1996 (5) BCLR 658 (CC), hereafter cited as *Du Plessis.*
8 436 U.S. 149 (1978), hereafter cited as *Flagg Brothers.*
9 489 U.S. 189 (1989), hereafter cited as *DeShaney.*
10 410 U.S. 113 (1973), hereafter cited as *Roe.*
11 1 BVerfG 39 (1975), hereafter cited as *Erste Abtreibung.*
12 80 BVerfG 137 (1989), hereafter cited as *Reiten im Walde.*

II *The Civil Rights Cases* (and their Unlikely South African Echoes)

The American state action doctrine concerns a deep resistance against the notion that private individuals can violate the constitutional rights of other private individuals. This deep resistance characterises a broad juridical frame of mind in the United States. Many judges, lawyers and scholars have resisted this frame of mind over the years and it has come under considerable pressure at times, especially around the middle of the twentieth century, that is, in the New Deal and post-New Deal years. But it has never been conclusively or even significantly dislodged from the American juridical imagination. It can still be said to reflect a dominant if not the predominant frame of mind among American jurists, as is clear from the as yet seemingly unassailable legacy that Justice Rehnquist would bequeath to the people of the United States in cases like *Flagg Brothers, Inc. v Brooks* and *DeShaney v County Department of Social Services*. The essence of this juridical frame of mind is already evident in fully-fledged form in the key dictum of Justice Bradley in the majority opinion of the court in the *Civil Rights Cases*. This dictum can for all relevant purposes be singled out as the historical source of the state action doctrine. This is how Justice Bradley phrased it:

> "In this connection it is proper to state that civil rights, such as are guarantied by the Constitution against State aggression, cannot be impaired by the wrongful acts of individuals, unsupported by State authority in the shape of laws, customs, or judicial or executive proceedings. The wrongful act of an individual, unsupported by any such authority, is simply a private wrong, or a crime of that individual; an invasion of the rights of the injured party, it is true, whether they affect his person, his property, or his reputation; but if not sanctioned in some way by the State, or not done under State authority, his rights remain in full force, and may presumably be vindicated by resort to the laws of the State for redress. An individual cannot deprive a man of his right to vote, to hold property, to buy and to sell, to sue in the courts, or to be a witness or a juror; he may, by force or fraud, interfere with the enjoyment of the right in a particular case; he may commit an assault against the person, or commit murder, or use ruffian violence at the polls, or slander the good name of a fellow-citizen; but unless protected in these wrongful acts by some shield of State law or State authority, he cannot destroy or injure the right; he will only render himself amenable to satisfaction or punishment; and amenable therefor to the laws of the State where the wrongful acts are committed. Hence, in all those cases where the Constitution seeks to protect the rights of the citizen against discriminative and unjust laws of the State by prohibiting such laws, it is not individual offenses, but abrogation and denial of rights, which it denounces, and for which it clothes the Congress with power to provide a remedy. This abrogation and denial of rights, for which the States alone were or could be responsible, was the great seminal and fundamental wrong which was intended to be remedied. And the remedy to be provided must necessarily be predicated upon that wrong. It must assume that in the

> cases provided for, the evil or wrong actually committed rests upon some State law or State authority for its excuse and perpetration."[13]

Several convictions or concerns informed this insistence that civil rights can only be violated by states and not by the private wrongs or crimes of individuals. The matter turned firstly on a close and literal reading of the 14th Amendment of the United States Constitution that states:

> "*No State* shall make or enforce any law which shall abridge the privileges or immunities of citizens of the United States; nor shall any *State* deprive any person of life, liberty, or property without the due process of law; nor deny to any person within its jurisdiction the equal protection of the laws."[14]

The issue in the Civil *Rights Cases* was nevertheless not yet, as it would become later, simply whether the 14th Amendment applied directly to individuals who infringe the civil rights of other individuals. At issue was the constitutionality of Sections 1 and 2 of the Civil Rights Act of 1875. The constitutionality of these sections fell subject to scrutiny as a result of having been invoked as causes of action by five claimants who alleged that their civil rights had been violated by a number of other individuals.[15] Section 1 of the Act sought to give proper effect to the 14th Amendment by stipulating that "all persons within the jurisdiction of the United States shall be entitled to the full and equal enjoyment" of all public accommodations.[16] Section 2 provided further that any person found guilty of

---

13 *The Civil Rights Cases*, 17.

14 Emphases added.

15 In one case the plaintiff, Robinson, had brought an action against the defendant on the grounds that the defendant, Memphis and Charleston RR, had refused to allow his wife into the ladies' car because she was of African descent. In two other cases the complaints concerned the refusal of the defendants, Stanley and Nichols, to grant persons of colour the accommodation in and privileges of an inn or hotel. And in the last two cases the complaints concerned the refusal of the defendants, Ryan and Singleton, to grant persons of colour the privileges and accommodations of a theatre. The review of these cases by the Federal Supreme Court all turned on the question of the constitutionality of Sections 1 and 2 of the Civil Rights Act. The cases of Stanley, Nichols, Ryan and Singleton came up for review because of certificates of division of opinion in the trial courts regarding the constitutionality of Sections 1 and 2. Robinson's case was reviewed in response to a writ of error filed by Robinson.

16 The full text of Section 1 reads as follows: "That all persons within the jurisdiction of the United States shall be entitled to the full and equal enjoyment of the accommodations, advantages, facilities, and privileges of inns, public conveyances on land or water, theatres, and other places of public amusement; subject only to the conditions and limitations established by

a violation of Section 1 would have to pay compensation of five hundred dollars to the aggrieved person and would be punishable by a fine or a term of imprisonment.[17]

According to Justice Bradley and the majority of the court, the constitutionality of these sections turned on the question whether the 14th Amendment empowered Congress to enact primary legislation that applied directly to citizens of the United States. In other words, the majority of the court turned the matter into a question regarding the proper relation between the sovereignty of the federal government of the United States and the subsidiary sovereignty held by the member states with which the federal government could not interfere. And their answer was that the 14th Amendment did not warrant the primary legislation evident in these sections of the Civil Rights Act. The ill that the 14th Amendment sought to remedy, the majority argued, was *state action* that abridged the privileges or immunities of citizens of the United States. The 14th Amendment thus empowered Congress to enact legislation that remedied any state action that abridged the privileges and immunities of citizens. But it did not empower Congress to remedy such abridgment by and among citizens themselves.[18] Hence

---

law, and applicable alike to citizens of every race and color, regardless of any previous condition of servitude."

17 The full text of Section 2 read as follows: "That any person who shall violate the foregoing section by denying to any citizen, except for reasons by law applicable to citizens of every race and color, and regardless of any previous condition of servitude, the full enjoyment of any of the accommodations, advantages, facilities, or privileges in said section enumerated, or by aiding or inciting such denial, shall, for every such offense, forfeit and pay the sum of $500 to the person aggrieved thereby, to be recovered in an action of debt, with full costs; and shall, also, for every such offense, be deemed guilty of a misdemeanor, and upon conviction thereof shall be fined not less than $500 nor more than $1,000, or shall be imprisoned not less than 30 days nor more than one year: Provided, that all persons may elect to sue for the penalty aforesaid, or to proceed under their rights at common law and by state statutes; and having so elected to proceed in the one mode or the other, their right to proceed in the other jurisdiction shall be barred. But this provision shall not apply to criminal proceedings, either under this act or the criminal law of any state: And provided, further, that a judgment for the penalty in favor of the party aggrieved, or a judgment upon an indictment, shall be a bar to either prosecution respectively."

18 It is worthwhile taking a good look at the crucial dicta of Justice Bradley in this regard. Cf. *The Civil Rights Cases*, 11–12 and 13: "Positive rights and privileges are undoubtedly secured by the fourteenth amendment; but they are secured by way of prohibition against state laws and state proceedings affecting those rights and privileges, and by power given to congress to legislate for the purpose of carrying such prohibition into effect; and such legislation must necessarily be predicated upon such supposed state laws or state proceedings, and be directed to the correction of their operation and effect ... Of course, legislation may and should be provided in advance to meet the exigency when it arises, but it should be adapted to the mischief and wrong which the amendment was intended to provide against; and that is, state

the court's conclusion that, apart from actual acts of enslavement,[19] a private wrong or crime committed by one citizen could not violate the civil rights of another citizen.

Was it just rigorously conceptual and technically exact legal reasoning that led the court to this conclusion, or was there more to this decision than just technical correctness? According to Justice Harlan's dissenting opinion the exacting conceptual jurisprudence of the technical legalism of the majority opinion very conspicuously circumvented the obvious aim of the 14th Amendment to guarantee to every citizen of the United States, regardless of colour or class, the equal protection of the law. And when the aim or end is as clear as the 14th Amendment made it, the means follow as a matter of course. The aim of the 14th Amendment clearly empowered Congress to take whatever measures it deemed necessary to secure to all the equal protection of the laws, as long as these measures were not prohibited. As Justice Harlan put it:

> Congress is not restricted to legislation for the execution of its powers expressly granted; but, for the protection of rights guarantied by the Constitution, it may employ, through legislation, such means, not prohibited, as are necessary and proper, or such as are appropriate, to attain the ends proposed." [20]

Against the background of this common sense avoidance of technical legalism to give effect to the self-evident aim of the 14th Amendment, the "rigorous" reading of this same Amendment as a restrictive stipulation that limits the legislative

---

laws or state action of some kind adverse to the rights of the citizen secured by the amendment. Such legislation cannot properly cover the whole domain of rights appertaining to life, liberty, and property, defining them and providing for their vindication. That would be to establish a code of municipal law regulative of all private rights between man and man in society. It would be to make congress take the place of the state legislatures and to supersede them."

19 Consider the other part of the majority opinion that the 13th Amendment of the Constitution did authorise Congress to enact primary legislation to ensure that no citizen engaged in acts of slavery, given the absolute proscription of slavery contained in it. But the court held that the abridgment of civil rights in this case had nothing to do with slavery. Cf. *The Civil Rights Cases*, 20–25. Akhil Amar would argue more than a century later that many state action problems could be circumvented by recasting them into Thirteenth Amendment concerns. Cf. "Remember the Thirteenth," *Constitutional Commentary* 10 (1993): 403. We live in different times from those in which Justice Bradley's strong rejection of this argument, but it is doubtful whether it stands a much better chance today.

20 *The Civil Rights Cases*, 28–29. Cf. also Justice Harlan's insistence that this is the broad and liberal construction of the Constitution that the Supreme Court has always endorsed (*The Civil Rights Cases*, 52). Cf. also his reliance on Chief Justice Marshall's statements to this effect in *McCulloch v Maryland*, 17 U.S. 316 (1819).

powers of Congress to remedy only *state* abridgments of civil rights begins to appear more artful than rigorous. And one need not search long for plausible reasons for this artfulness. The robust racialist and segregationist spirit of the time had already been articulated clearly in *Dred Scott v Sandford*[21] twenty-five years earlier (1856) and would continue to assert itself conspicuously thirteen years after *The Civil Rights Cases* in *Plessy v Ferguson*[22] (1896). Against this background, Justice Bradley's reasoning can hardly confound anyone. Truly confounding, however, would be the resurfacing of his reasoning more than a hundred years later in South Africa against a completely different socio-political background. In 1995 the South African constitutional judge Johann Kriegler would articulate the following observation in his dissenting opinion in the case of *Du Plessis v De Klerk:*

> "The [Bill of Rights] has nothing to do with the ordinary relationships between private persons or associations. What it does govern, however, is all law, including that applicable to private relationships. Unless and until there is a resort to law, private individuals are at liberty to conduct their private affairs exactly as they please as far as the fundamental rights and freedoms are concerned. As far as the [Bill of Rights] is concerned a landlord is free to refuse to let a flat to someone because of race, gender or whatever; a white bigot may refuse to sell property to a person of colour; a social club may black-ball Jews, Catholics or Afrikaners if it so wishes. An employer is at liberty to discriminate on racial grounds in the engagement of staff; a hotelier may refuse to let a room to a homosexual; a church may close its doors to mourners of a particular colour or class. But none of them can invoke the law to enforce or protect their bigotry. One cannot claim rescission of a contract or specific performance thereof if such claim, albeit well-founded at common law, infringes a Chapter 3 right. One cannot raise a defence to a claim in law if such defence is in conflict with a protected right or freedom. The whole gamut of private relationships is left undisturbed."[23]

What could possibly explain the reasons for this resurfacing of Justice Bradley's reasoning more than a hundred years later in an opinion of a South African constitutional judge who surely would not have been elected to the South African Constitutional Court in 1994 had there been any hint of racialist or segregationist sentiments in his personal or judicial character? To stagger the irony further: What reason could plausibly exist for the resurfacing of this reasoning in a judicial opinion that was expressly aimed at giving effect to the core aspiration of the South African Constitution of 1993 to break with South Africa's history of racial oppression? In Justice Kriegler's own words:

---

21 60 U.S. 393 (1956).
22 163 U.S. 537 (1896).
23 *Du Plessis*, 720 D–G.

> "Our past is not merely one of repressive use of state power. It is one of persistent, institutionalized subjugation and exploitation of a voiceless and largely defenceless majority by a determined and privileged minority. The 'untold suffering and injustice' of which the Postscript speaks does not refer only to the previous forty years, nor only to Bantu education, group areas, security and the similar legislative tools used by the previous government. The Postscript mentions 'a divided society characterised by strife [and] conflict.' That is not a reference to governmental action only, or even primarily. The 'reconciliation and reconstruction' mentioned in the last paragraph relate not so much, if at all, to the oppressed and the oppressive government, but to reconciliation of whites and blacks, to reconstruction of a skewed society. Likewise, when the Preamble speaks of 'citizenship in a sovereign democratic constitutional state' the emphasis immediately falls on racial equality."[24]

When one compares this statement with the opinions voiced in *The Civil Rights Cases* one would think it is the spirit of Justice Harlan speaking now and no longer that of Justice Bradley. Justice Kriegler would in fact also echo Justice Harlan's no-nonsense faithfulness to the clear aim of the constitutional protection at issue:

> "I find it unnecessary to engage in a debate with my colleagues on the merits or demerits of the approaches adopted by the courts in the United States, Canada or Germany. That pleases me, for I have enough difficulty with our Constitution not to want to become embroiled in the intricacies of the state action doctrine, Drittwirkung and the like... Our Constitution aims at establishing freedom and equality in a grossly disparate society. And I am grateful to the drafters of our Constitution for having spared us the jurisprudential gymnastics forced on some courts abroad. They were good enough to say what they mean."[25]

Whether he wanted to or not, Justice Kriegler surely became "embroiled in the intricacies of the state action doctrine" in the course of his opinion. His reading of the South African Constitution of 1993 echoes Justice Bradley's 1883 insistence that the 14th Amendment only authorised Congress to counter state action or state law that abridged constitutional protection in all significant respects. Why would this formidable task-minded liberal spirit stand, on the one hand, for everything Justice Harlan stood for in *The Civil Rights Cases*, only to get hung up, on the other, on a jurisprudence that is effectively that of Justice Bradley's? This is a key question that demands incisive scrutiny. It is a question that comes up again and again whenever liberal and progressive judges who are fully committed to the constitutional values that they serve prefer to do so by means of "indirect horizontal" rather than "direct horizontal" application of these constitutional values. Indeed, it is a core contention of this book that all judges who

24 *Du Plessis*, 717 A–E.
25 *Du Plessis*, 724G–725B.

opt for the indirect approach to horizontal effect are surreptitious ventriloquists of Justice Bradley's jurisprudence, however much they would want to distance themselves from his politics. There are indeed many liberal or progressive Harlans around marching in the Bradley uniform. Why is this so? This is one of the key questions that this book seeks to address and it begins to do so, in the rest of this chapter, by looking closely at a number of key cases in the century of horizontal effect case law that links *Du Plessis* to *The Civil Rights Cases*. And it begins now with the case that the judgment in *Du Plessis* would vociferously dismiss as irrelevant for South African horizontal effect jurisprudence.

III *Shelley v Kraemer*

Scholarly analysis has distilled four basic strands of state action from a wide range of Supreme Court judgments that constitute its state action case law.[26] The first strand concerns the "public function" cases. At issue in these cases is the question whether a private company or corporation has taken over a public or governmental function from the state.[27] The second strand concerns the "sig-

26 The instructive schematisation that follows here is taken from Gardbaum, "The 'Horizontal Effect' of Constitutional Rights."

27 In 1946 and 1968, in its decisions in *Marsh v Alabama* 326 U.S. 501 (1946) and *Amalgamated Food Employees Union Local 590 v Logan Valley Plaza* 391 U.S. 308 (1968) the United States Supreme Court decided that private ownership and control of a whole shopping centre and a whole city actually replaces the political control of public authorities. Such ownership and control must therefore be taken to be subject to constitutional criteria. *Marsh* and *Logan* were the first of a series of Supreme Court decisions that would later become known as the "public function cases." *Marsh* was nevertheless not strictly speaking a public function case. It was decided on the rule that the fundamental rights of the public enjoy precedence over the rights of ownership to the extent that owners make their property available for public use. Four years after the *Logan* decision, the Supreme Court narrowed down the potential application of the public function rule followed in *Logan* considerably by refusing to apply the *Logan* rule in the case of *Lloyd Corp. v Tanner* 407 US 551 (1972). The court distinguished the facts in *Lloyd* on the basis of a rule already stipulated in *Logan*. According to this rule, fundamental rights would only qualify for protection on private property if those rights bear relation to the particular use to which the property is put. Freedom of speech had to prevail in *Logan*, argued the court, because the use of free speech at issue actually concerned one of the businesses in the mall. The free speech claim concerned the picketing against the employment of a strictly non-union staff by Weiss Markets, a company that did business in the mall. This was not the case in *Lloyd*. At issue in *Lloyd* was general political protest against the Vietnam War that bore no specific relation to any of the businesses in the mall. Another four years later, the Supreme Court held in *Hudgens v NLRB* 424 U.S. 507 (1976) that *Lloyd* had actually overruled *Logan*. After *Hudgens*, *Marsh* was the only progressive public function case still left standing in the jurisprudence of the United States

nificant entanglement" cases. The question in these cases is whether some state action such as the provision of some or other public service is inextricably linked to private conduct that abridges a fundamental right.[28] At issue under the third strand are the "significant encouragement" cases. Here the review question is whether the state "provided such significant encouragement, either overt or covert, that the choice must in law be deemed to be that of the state."[29] The fourth strand concerns those cases in which none of the above forms of state action nor any other significant state action can be linked to private conduct that abridges fundamental rights, apart from a court order that finally comes round to honour and enforce some or other curtailment of fundamental rights by a private person. The 1948 case of *Shelley v Kraemer* is the *locus classicus* of this fourth kind of state action in American jurisprudence. And as we shall see below, *Shelley* has also left an indelible mark on horizontal effect jurisprudence elsewhere in the world.[30]

The disputes in *Shelley* turned on the question whether the court enforcement of two restrictive covenants entered into by private individuals constituted state action that was subject to review in terms of the 14th Amendment of the United States Constitution. At issue were the appeals of two black families against the findings of the Supreme Courts of Missouri and Michigan. The Missouri and Michigan courts had been called upon to scrutinise whether restrictive covenants between private property owners in the cities of St. Louis and Detroit were reconcilable with the 14th Amendment. The covenants were designed to prevent those who were party to them from allowing black families to occupy any of the properties subject to the covenants. The Missouri and Michigan courts had scrutinised the covenants and had found them to be consistent with the 14th Amendment.[31] In the appeals against these findings to the Federal Supreme

---

Supreme Court. (The Supreme Courts of New Jersey and California still follow the stance taken by the Federal Supreme Court in *Logan*.) However, the reasoning of the Federal Supreme Court in *Marsh* has in subsequent decisions effectively been limited to apply only in cases of company towns that impose limits on the enjoyment of rights embodied in the Federal Constitution.

28 Cf. *Burton v Wilmington Parking Authority* 365 U.S. 715 (1961); *Moose Lodge No. 107 v Irvis* 407 U.S. 163 (1972); *Blum v Yaretsky* 457 U.S. 991 (1982); *Rendell-Baker v Kohn* 457 U.S. 830 (1982).

29 Cf. *Blum v Yaretsky* 457 U.S. 991 (1982); *Reitman v Mulkey* 387 U.S. 369 (1967).

30 It may be necessary to add a fifth strand of state action to the four that Gardbaum highlights, namely, a range of at least two decisions that took common law rules as embodiments of state action. Cf. the discussion of *Labour v Swing* and *New York Times v Sullivan* below.

31 The first case concerned the enforcement of a restrictive covenant between owners of property on a section of Labadie Avenue in the city of St. Louis that they will not allow their property to be occupied by people of the "Negro or Mongolian Race" [sic] for a period of 50 years. Pursuant to a contract of sale of one of the properties subject to the restrictive covenant,

Court, the respondents in both cases argued that there was no state action involved in the covenants and that the mere enforcement of the covenants by a court of law does not constitute state action for purposes of the 14th Amendment.

The Federal Supreme Court dismissed this argument. A number of key passages from Chief Justice Vinson's articulation of the court's opinion bring the core of the reasoning to the fore on the basis of which the court found that the appellants' 14th Amendment rights had indeed been breached. The remarkable feature of this reasoning is the meticulous way in which it remained faithful to Justice Bradley's opinion for the majority of the court in *The Civil Rights Cases*, but nevertheless effectively rendered this opinion obsolete in startling fashion. Having considered two earlier cases in which it had struck down city ordinances that denied occupancy of property on the basis of race as irreconcilable with the 14th Amendment,[32] the court observed the following problem as far as the current disputes were concerned:

> "But the present cases, unlike those just discussed, do not involve action by state legislature or city councils. Here the particular patterns of discrimination and the areas in which the restrictions are to operate, are determined, in the first instance, by the terms of agreement among private individuals. Participation of the State consists in the enforcement of the restrictions so defined. The crucial issue with which we are here confronted is whether

---

the Shelleys, a "Negro" couple, received the title or deed for the property purchased from the seller in August 1945. In October 1945 other owners of property subject to the covenant sought to obtain an order from the Circuit Court of St. Louis to prevent the Shelleys from occupying the purchased property. The Circuit Court refused to grant the order. The court found that the agreement had never become effective, given the failure of the participants in the covenant to obtain the signatures of all the property owners in the district as the covenant stipulated. The Supreme Court of Missouri overturned the Circuit Court's decision by finding that the covenant had become effective. By the time it did so, however, the Shelleys had already moved into the house they purchased. They now petitioned the Federal Supreme Court to obtain an order that the restrictive covenant violated the 14th Amendment. The second case concerned an essentially similar set of facts regarding property purchased in the city of Detroit. In this case the Circuit Court of Wayne County granted an order that the purchasers, one Ferguson and his wife, must vacate the property within 90 days. They appealed to the Supreme Court of Michigan on the ground that they had been denied the rights protected by the 14th Amendment. The Supreme Court dismissed the appeal on the finding that no 14th Amendment rights had been affected by any of the afore-going events. Cf. also Johan van der Walt, "Abdications of Sovereignty in Horizontal Effect Jurisprudence," in *Boundaries of State, Boundaries of Rights: Human Rights, Private Actors, and Positive Obligations*, by Tsvi Kahana and Anat Scolnicov (Cambridge University Press, Forthcoming).

32 *Buchanan v Warley*, 245 U.S. 60 (1917); *Harmon v Tyler*, 273 U.S. 668 (1927).

> this distinction removes these cases from the operation of the prohibitory provisions of the Fourteenth Amendment."[33]

> "Since the decision of this Court in The Civil Rights Cases the principle has become firmly embedded in our constitutional law that the action inhibited by the first section of the Fourteenth Amendment is only such action as may fairly be said to be that of States. The Amendment erects no shield against merely private conduct, however discriminatory or wrongful."[34]

> "We conclude, therefore that the restrictive agreements standing alone cannot be regarded as a violation of any rights guaranteed to the petitioners by the Fourteenth Amendment. As long as the purposes of those agreements are effectuated by voluntary adherence to their terms, it would appear clear that there has been no action by the State and the provisions of the Amendment have not been violated."[35]

> "But here there was more. These are cases in which the purposes of the agreements were secured only by judicial enforcement by state courts of the restrictive terms of the agreements. The respondents urge that judicial enforcement of private agreements does not amount to state action; or, in any event, the participation of the State is so attenuated in character as not to amount to state action within the meaning of the Fourteenth Amendment."[36]

The court then moved to respond to the respondent's arguments that mere judicial enforcement of a private agreement does not constitute state action for purposes of the Fourteenth Amendment. And in doing so it made the follow finding:

> "That the action of state courts and judicial officers in their official capacities is to be regarded as action of the State within the meaning of the Fourteenth Amendment, is a proposition which has long been established by decisions of this Court. That principle was given expression in the earliest cases involving the construction of the terms of the Fourteenth Amendment."[37]

The earliest cases to which the court was referring here included *Commonwealth of Virginia v Rives*[38] and *Ex Parte Common Wealth of Virginia*,[39] both of which were decided in 1880, as well as *The Civil Rights Cases* of 1883. With regard to the latter, Justice Vinson observed the following:

---

33 *Shelley*, 12–13.
34 *Shelley*, 13.
35 *Shelley*, 13.
36 *Shelley*, 13–14.
37 *Shelley*, 14.
38 100 U.S. 313 (1880).
39 100 U.S. 339 (1880).

> "In the Civil Rights Cases this Court pointed out that the Amendment makes void 'state action of every kind' which is inconsistent with the guarantees therein contained, and extends to manifestations of 'state authority in the shape of laws, customs, or judicial or executive proceedings.' Language to like effect is employed no less than eighteen times during the course of that opinion."[40]

It is important to note that the line of judicial authority for the point that judicial decisions constitute state action for purposes of the Fourteenth Amendment did not end here, but continued to include a long line of Supreme Court decisions between 1881 and 1940.[41] Justice Vinson could of course also have gone back all the way to *Marbury v Madison*[42] to invoke Chief Justice Marshall's emphatic statement that courts are also bound by written constitutions.[43] The conclusion that judicial decisions constitute state action for purposes of the Fourteenth Amendment could therefore hardly have been established more firmly in the jurisprudence of the Supreme Court than it already was. Two more observations are of importance in this regard. Judicial decisions that violated the Fourteenth Amendment were not restricted to cases of procedural unfairness; they often included the mere enforcement of a substantive common law rule by the court.[44] Following these observations, Justice Vinson concluded his scrutiny of the past record of the Supreme Court with these strong words:

> "The short of the matter is that from the time of the adoption of the Fourteenth Amendment until the present, it has been the consistent ruling of this Court that the action of the States to which the Amendment has reference includes action of state courts and state judicial officials... [I]t has never been suggested that state court action is immunized from the operation of those provisions simply because the act is that of the judicial branch of the state government."[45]

In view of the position thus articulated, the Court in *Shelley* found that the decisions of the Supreme Courts of Missouri and Michigan had violated the Four-

---

40 Cf. *Shelley*, 14–15. Cf. also Van der Walt "Abdications of Sovereignty in Horizontal Effect Jurisprudence (forthcoming)."

41 Notably *Twining v New Jersey* 211 U.S. 78 (1908); *Brinkerhoff-Faris Trust & Savings Co. v Hill* 281 U.S. 673 (1930). Justice Vinson cites 13 more cases in footnote 14. Cf. *Shelley*, 15.

42 5 U.S. 137 (1803).

43 Cf. *Marbury v Madison*, 5 U.S. 137 (1803), 180: "[It] confirms and strengthens the principle, supposed to be essential to all written constitutions, that a law repugnant to the constitution is void; and that all *courts*, as well as other departments, are bound by that instrument." Chief Justice Marshall himself added the emphasis.

44 *Shelley*, 17.

45 *Shelley*, 18.

teenth Amendment and ordered them to be reversed. It should be clear from the meticulous scrutiny of the past record of the Federal Supreme Court that the decision in *Shelley* should not have come as a surprise or shock to anyone. But it surely did and the surprise and shock that it would cause in United States constitutional jurisprudence and constitutional jurisprudence elsewhere in the world relates to the way a penny that had been dangling in the air since *The Civil Rights Cases* finally dropped in *Shelley* and dropped in a way that suggested the state action doctrine had all along been much ado about nothing. The penny dangled, dropped, and vanished into what one might call Lebowskian nothingness. In the end there was no ransom money, but neither had there been a kidnapping. If judicial decisions had all along been recognised as state action and if this recognition had informed state action adjudication from its very beginnings in *The Civil Rights Cases,* as Justice Vinson found to be the case in *Shelley,* state action had all along been a veritable non-doctrine. The conditions for its application would have been fulfilled every time a court merely commenced to consider its application in a way that rendered the whole enterprise pointless. A rule that applies without any exception whatsoever is a non-rule, a mirage of a rule, a chimera.[46]

That the sheer nothingness of the long-standing state action doctrine was too much to accept for the Supreme Court's future jurisprudence is clear from the way this jurisprudence commenced to restrict *Shelley's* future application narrowly to the facts in *Shelley.* The rule in *Shelley* is still applicable, but its impact has been curtailed in subsequent case law by means of technical and factual distinctions that not only led to politically regressive results, but also gave rise to a conceptually complicated, convoluted and incoherent jurisprudence. This development of the state action doctrine in the wake of *Shelley* would, moreover, soon also affect or infect horizontal effect jurisprudence elsewhere in the world. Close scrutiny of the three key cases that coined horizontal effect jurisprudence respectively in Canada, Germany and South Africa makes this abundantly clear. Among these three jurisdictions, the German approach to the rule in *Shelley* is the most consistent. As we shall see, the German Constitutional Court turned the rule into a standing formula that eventually came to underpin each and every instance of horizontal effect of the *Grundgesetz.* But we

46 Laurence Tribe presents this as a misconstruction of *Shelley* – one that has in any case been rendered obsolete by the "discriminatory intent" test laid down in *Washington v Davis* 426 U.S. 229 (1976). He also proposes a better understanding of *Shelley* in §16–21 of his book, one that according to him survives the dismantling of *Shelley* in *Washington v Davis.* Cf. Tribe, *American Constitutional Law,* 2nd ed. (New York, N.Y.: Foundation Press, 1988), 1718. Chapter Three will pay more extensive attention to his arguments in this regard.

cannot travel to Germany just yet. We need to stay in the United States for two more cases, then cross its northern frontier into Canada and only then shall we turn to the jurisprudence of the Federal Constitutional Court in Germany.

IV *Labour v Swing* and *New York Times v Sullivan*

Shelley may have been the United States Supreme Court's most spectacular dive into nothingness at the time, but it was not the first conspicuous one. The abyss underneath *Shelley* had already become startlingly visible eight years earlier in *Labour v Swing.* And neither were *Swing* and *Shelley* the last dives into this abyss. Another would follow thirteen years after *Shelley* in the landmark case of *New York Times v Sullivan.*

The judgment of the United States Supreme Court in *Labour v Swing* established the principle that common law constitutes state action. The case concerned an attempt to unionise employees that worked in Swing's beauty parlour. When the attempt failed the union concerned started picketing Swing. Swing applied for an injunction against the picketing in the Circuit Court. The case turned on allegations that the picketing was accompanied by violence and false allegations, but it transpired in the appeal hearing that the case was really about secondary picketing, that is, picketing of a business by members of a union not employed by that business. The Supreme Court of Illinois sustained the finding of the appeal court that the picketing by non-employees was unlawful.[47] The rule against secondary picketing issued from the common law of the state of Illinois and the task of the United States Supreme Court was now to establish whether this common law rule constituted an unconstitutional abridgment of the freedom of expression granted by the Fourteenth Amendment. As Justice Frankfurter put the matter:

> "All that we have before us, then, is an instance of 'peaceful persuasion' disentangled from violence and free from 'picketing en masse or otherwise conducted' so as to occasion 'imminent and aggravated danger.' We are asked to sustain a decree which for purposes of this case asserts as the common law of a state that there can be no 'peaceful picketing or peaceful persuasion' in relation to any dispute between an employer and a trade union unless the employer's own employees are in controversy with him."[48]

47 *Swing*, 324.
48 *Swing*, 325.

Justice Frankfurter overruled the decision of the Supreme Court of Illinois. He found that the common rule against secondary picketing could not be reconciled with the freedom of expression guaranteed by the Fourteenth Amendment:

> "The scope of the Fourteenth Amendment is not confined by the notion of a particular state regarding the wise limits of an injunction in an industrial dispute, whether those limits be defined by statute or by the judicial organ of the state. A state cannot exclude workingmen from peacefully exercising the right of free communication by drawing the circle of economic competition between employers and workers so small as to contain only an employer and those directly employed by him."[49]

Returning for a moment to *Shelley*, it should be clear that *Shelley* could also have been decided on the principle that common law rules constitute state action for purposes of the protection afforded by the Fourteenth Amendment. Henry Friendly suggests it was decided thus,[50] but Frank Michelman contends more convincingly that it was not.[51] Be it as it may, the Supreme Court's judgment in *Swing* suggests that state action had already gone "out of business" seven years before *Shelley*, as Michelman puts the matter with reference to *New York Times v Sullivan*.[52] There had never been any doubt that executive and legislative action constituted state action for purposes of the Fourteenth Amendment by the time *Swing* came to be decided. What *Swing* added was to remove any doubt that may have remained at that stage whether common law constituted state action.

49 *Swing*, 325–326.

50 Cf. Henry J. Friendly, "The Public-Private Penumbra: Fourteen Years Later," *University of Pennsylvania Law Review* 130, no. 6 (June 1, 1982): 1295: "Somehow I cannot escape the conclusion that it was Missouri's maintenance of a rule of common law permitting the enforcement of racially restrictive covenants, not the action of its courts in enforcing the rule, that was the unconstitutional state action in *Shelley*."

51 Cf. Frank Michelman, "The Bill of Rights, the Common Law, and the Freedom-Friendly State," *University of Miami Law Review* 58 (2003): 406: "*Shelley v Kraemer* does not qualify as an instance of the Court's subjecting state common law to Bill of Rights review. It would have, if the Court had addressed itself to the question of the compatibility of Missouri's common-law doctrine of equitable servitude, as applied in *Shelley*, with Fourteenth Amendment norms and concluded, as conceivably it might have, that the state law doctrine as applied there failed an equal-protection test because it gave racial covenants a free pass from certain legal restrictions typically applied to running covenants and servitudes... In fact, however, the Supreme Court's opinion had nothing to say about the compatibility of Missouri's *law* with the Fourteenth Amendment. The Court rather focused on the constitutional permissibility of coercive judicial *enforcement* of a racially discriminatory private arrangement that had been fashioned in the shelter of what might have been – indeed was, for all the opinion had to say about it – a body of utterly race-neutral state contract law doctrine."

52 Ibid, 404.

With common law now also recognised as state action along with legislative and executive action, there was absolutely nothing left that could justify a claim that an abridgement of a right did not constitute state action. State action can thus be considered to have gone out of business truly and officially as early as 1941. And the decision that put it out of business was not a once-off deviation, as *New York Times v Sullivan* would make abundantly clear in 1963.

L. B. Sullivan, then Police Commissioner of the City of Montgomery, brought a civil law libel action against four Alabama clergymen and the New York Times Company on the basis of an advertisement run in the *New York Times* on 29 March 1960.[53] The Circuit Court of the County of Montgomery awarded the plaintiff damages to the amount of $ 500 000 on the basis of the common law of Alabama.[54] The Supreme Court of Alabama upheld the judgment on appeal, but the United States Supreme Court overturned it again and dismissed the claim for damages. Justice Brennan found the Alabama libel law on which the claim turned to fall foul of the First and Fourteenth Amendments.[55] The respondent claimed that his action for damages concerned a civil or private matter on

---

53 The advertisement in the *New York Times* on which the claim was based, did not mention Sullivan by name, but referred to "loads of police armed with shotguns and tear-gas" that ringed off the Alabama State College Campus in order to suppress civil rights protests on the campus. The advertisement also stated, among more allegations, that "the Southern violators have answered Dr. [Martin Luther –] King's peaceful protests with intimidation and violence... have arrested him seven times for 'speeding,' 'loitering' and similar 'offenses,' and 'have [now] charged him with perjury." Sullivan claimed that the article implicated the police, not only in the ringing off of the campus where they were expressly mentioned, but also in all of the latter actions, and by thus implicating the police, also implicated him as commissioner of Montgomery.

54 In the trial court judgment, the judge instructed the jury that the statements in the advertisement were "libelous per se" and "not privileged." In terms of the common law of Alabama, he instructed further, injury is implied by the bare fact of the per se libelous publication. Malice, falsity and general damages are presumed and need not be alleged or proved, and punitive damages may be awarded by the jury if they found that the statements were indeed published maliciously and not just negligently or carelessly. The liability of the defendants therefore ultimately only turned on the questions of whether the jury found the article to have been published by the defendants and whether the statements were made "of and concerning" the plaintiff. The judge rejected the defendants' contention that his rulings abridged the freedoms of speech and of the press guaranteed by the First and Fourteenth Amendments.

55 Justice Brennan's ruling ultimately turned on the finding that common law rules that imposed the burden to prove truth and absence of malice on the defendants in a libel claim cannot be reconciled with the robust freedom of expression granted by the First and Fourteenth Amendments when criticism of public officials and personalities is at stake. The constitutional standard, Justice Brennan decided, requires that the claimant carry the burden of proof of falsity and malice. Cf. *Sullivan*, 297–298.

which the Federal Constitution had no bearing. Justice Brennan responded as follows:

> "We may dispose at the outset of two grounds asserted to insulate the judgment of the Alabama courts from constitutional scrutiny. The first is the proposition relied on by the State Supreme Court–that 'The Fourteenth Amendment is directed against State action and not private action.' That proposition has no application to this case. Although this is a civil lawsuit between private parties, the Alabama courts have applied a state rule of law which petitioners claim to impose invalid restrictions on their constitutional freedoms of speech and press. It matters not that that law has been applied in a civil action and that it is common law only, though supplemented by statute. The test is not the form in which state power has been applied but, whatever the form, whether such power has in fact been exercised."[56]

New York Times v Sullivan put state action "out of business," claims Michelman. If the constitution tolerates neither executive state administration, nor state legislation, nor state common law that falls foul of its guarantees, there is simply no basis left on which a constitutionally unsound contention can enter a court of law and exit that court triumphantly. Yet, anyone who knows something of American law also knows, contends Michelman further, "something persists in [American] jurisprudence that walks and talks like a state action doctrine with teeth."[57] As we saw above, *Sullivan* was in fact already the third declaration of the state action doctrine's bankruptcy. *Swing* and *Shelley* had already put state action out of business twice before. But it kept on trading as if nothing had happened. Chapter Three will return to this after-life of the state action doctrine that in terms of *Swing*, *Shelley* and *Sullivan* should never have had a life to begin with. Suffice it to observe for now that we have set the stage for a border crossing and an encounter with a remarkable border patrol. For just up north from the United States, the Canadian Supreme Court would refuse to grant the contaminating jurisprudence of *Shelley* and *Sullivan* entry into its pristine territories. It would accept that court decisions constitute government action for purposes of Canadian Charter rights protection, but not when the court only acts a neutral arbitrator. It would accept that the common law constitutes government action for purposes of Charter protection, but only when the government is itself involved in common law litigation. The Canadian border patrol marched under the banner of the 1986 case *RWDSU v Dolphin Delivery* and its neat packet of jurisprudential policing would be taken over almost line for line in *Du Plessis v De*

---

56 *Sullivan*, 265. Cf. also Michelman, "The Bill of Rights, the Common Law, and the Freedom-Friendly State," 403 for a similar quotation of this passage.
57 Ibid, 404.

Klerk when the South African Constitutional Court later moved fast to keep *Shelley* also out of South Africa.

V *RWDSU v Dolphin Delivery Ltd*

RWDSU v Dolphin Delivery Ltd turned on the same question that came up in *Swing v Labour.* It turned on the question whether an injunction against secondary picketing (the picketing of any third party not directly involved as an employer in a dispute between employers and employees) obtained under Canadian Common Law constituted an abridgment of the right to freedom of expression guaranteed by Section 2(b) of the Canadian Charter of Rights and Freedoms.[58] Section 1 of the Charter makes provision for reasonable limitations of the Charter rights. Respondent argued that the common law rule constituted such a reasonable limitation of the right to freedom of expression granted by Section 2(b). The appellant argued that the limitation was not reasonable. The Canadian Supreme Court finally dismissed the appeal against the injunction prohibiting secondary picketing granted by the trial court. It nevertheless did so, not only on the ground that the common law rule against secondary picketing constituted a reasonable limitation of right to freedom of expression. It also did so on the ground that the Charter did not apply at all to common law disputes in which the state was not a party.[59]

Justice McIntyre delivered the judgment for the majority of the court. Given the principal lines of argument put to the court by the appellant and respondent,

58 The appellant, a workers union (*Retail, Wholesale and Department Store Union*) acted as bargaining agent for the locked out employees of Purolater, an Ontario-based courier. The respondent made local deliveries for Purolater in its area, at first directly and later through Supercourier, a company connected to Purolater. Appellant had approached the British Columbia Labour Relations Board for a declaration that the Respondent and Supercourier were allies of Purolator. The declaration would have enabled the appellant to lawfully picket the respondent's business premises. The Board declined to hear the application for want of jurisdiction. The lawfulness of the picketing now had to be determined on the basis of the Canadian common law, given the silence of the *Canada Labour Code* on the matter. Under the common law, the matter turned on the rule that secondary picketing (the picketing of any third party not directly involved as an employer in a dispute between employers and employees) was unlawful. The respondent had obtained an injunction *quia timet* on the basis of this rule and the appeal against the granting of the injunction now turned on the claim that the rule constituted an unconstitutional infringement of the right to freedom of expression guaranteed by section 2 (b) of the Charter of Rights and Freedoms.

59 Cf. also my discussion of *Dolphin Delivery* in "Abdications of Sovereignity in Horizontal Effect Jurisprudence," (forthcoming).

Justice McIntyre and his colleagues could easily have let the matter rest on the question of the reasonableness or unreasonableness of the limitation that the common law rule against secondary picketing imposed on a charter right. That they found it necessary to expressly engage with the question whether the Charter applied to common law disputes between private parties reveals their discomfort with a matter that did not really arise in the case as such, but came from elsewhere. It came from down south. Without stating it expressly, Justice McIntyre's opinion made it clear that he was haunted by the spectre of *Shelley*. A brief perusal of the essential steps in his reasoning makes this abundantly clear.

The first step concerned the need to establish whether picketing constituted "expression" for purposes of the right to freedom of expression guaranteed by Section 2(b) of the Charter. The positive response of the court in this regard could not have been firmer:

> "There is, as I have earlier said, always some element of expression in picketing. The union is making a statement to the general public that it is involved in a dispute, that it is seeking to impose its will on the object of the picketing, and that it solicits the assistance of the public in honouring the picket line. Action on the part of the picketers will, of course, always accompany the expression, but not every action on the part of the picketers will be such as to alter the nature of the whole transaction and remove it from *Charter* protection for freedom of expression. That freedom, of course, would not extend to protect threats of violence or acts of violence. It would not protect the destruction of property, or assaults, or other clearly unlawful conduct. We need not, however, be concerned with such matters here because the picketing would have been peaceful. I am therefore of the view that the picketing sought to be restrained would have involved the exercise of the right of freedom of expression."[60]

The second step concerned the question whether the common law ban on secondary picketing constituted a reasonable limitation in terms of Section 1 of the Charter. The court's response could again not be clearer:

> "When the parties do exercise the right to disagree, picketing and other forms of industrial conflict are likely to follow. The social cost is great, man-hours and wages are lost, production and services will be disrupted, and general tensions within the community may be heightened. Such industrial conflict may be tolerated by society but only as an inevitable corollary to the collective bargaining process. It is therefore necessary in the general social interest that picketing be regulated and sometimes limited. It is reasonable to restrain picketing so that the conflict will not escalate beyond the actual parties. While picketing is, no doubt, a legitimate weapon to be employed in a labour dispute by the employees against their employer, it should not be permitted to harm others... It is my opinion then that a lim-

60 *Dolphin Delivery*, par 20.

> itation on secondary picketing against a third party, that is, a non-ally, would be a reasonable limit in the facts of this case. I would therefore conclude that the injunction is "a reasonable limit prescribed by law which can be demonstrably justified in a free and democratic society."[61]

The last dictum quoted here wrapped up the legal question at issue for all practical purposes. According to the case report, neither of the parties raised the question whether the Charter applies at all to common law disputes between private parties. Had the court had any reservations about such application, it could have simply stated such reservations without actually deciding the matter, given that regular judicial practice encourages reticence with regard to deciding matters that are not really raised as a point in contention. But the court wanted to decide this question and it did so by analysing Sections 52(1) and 32 of the Charter. Section 52 expounds the general legal supremacy of the Charter as the supreme law of the land and the principle that no law that is inconsistent with it can have any force or effect.[62] Section 32 expounds and delimits the scope of the Charter's application. It reads as follows:

> This Charter applies
>
> (a) to the Parliament and government of Canada in respect of all matters within the authority of Parliament including all matters relating to the Yukon Territory and Northwest Territories; and
> (b) to the legislature and government of each province in respect of all matters within the authority of the legislature of each province.

Justice McIntyre did not need much time and deliberation to decide that the inconsistency of any law with the Charter at issue in Section 52(1) included any inconsistency of the common law with the charter. He observed:

> "The English text provides that "any law that is inconsistent with the provisions of the Constitution is, to the extent of the inconsistency, of no force or effect." If this language is not broad enough to include the common law, it should be observed as well that the French text adds strong support to this conclusion in its employment of the words "elle rend inoperantes les dispositions incompatibles *de tout autre regle de droit.*" To adopt a construction of s. 52(1) which would exclude from Charter application the whole body of the common law, which in great part governs the rights and obligations of the individuals in society,

---

61 *Dolphin Delivery,* paragraph 30.

62 Section 52(1) reads: "The Constitution of Canada is the supreme law of Canada, and any law that is inconsistent with the provisions of the Constitution is, to the extent of the inconsistency, of no force or effect."

would be wholly unrealistic and contrary to the clear language employed in s. 52(1) of the Act."[63]

However, after having thus established that the *Charter* also applies to the common law, the court immediately retreated from the wide scope of application that this inclusion of the common law signified, by interpreting the provisions of Section 32(a) and 32(b) as restrictive criteria that exempted common law disputes between private persons from the broad application implied by the inclusion of the common law under Section 52(1). It immediately resorted to the notion that only government action could infringe a right granted by the charter. Thus did it import the basic logic of the state action doctrine articulated by the United States Supreme Court in *The Civil Rights Cases:*

"In this way the *Charter* will apply to the common law, whether in public or private litigation. It will apply to the common law, however, only in so far as the common law is the basis of some governmental action which, it is alleged, infringes a guaranteed right or freedom... The element of governmental intervention necessary to make the *Charter* applicable in an otherwise private action is difficult to define. We have concluded that the *Charter* applies to the common law but not between private parties."[64]

One more question haunted the court. What constitutes governmental action or intervention? Does governmental action include a judicial decision that applies and enforces the common law? This was the *Shelley* question to which the court ultimately felt compelled to respond. And it did so with determination to exorcise the spectre of *Shelley*, without raising its name. In the process, however, it also had to take leave of the "troublesome" view of Professor Hogg. Hogg wrote in the second edition of his *Constitutional Law of Canada:*

"The fact that a court order is governmental action means that the Charter will apply to a purely private arrangement, such as a contract or proprietary interest, but only to the extent that the Charter will preclude judicial enforcement of any arrangement in derogation of a guaranteed right. In a sense, the common law authorizes any private action that is not prohibited by a positive rule of law. If the Charter applied to the common law in that attenuated sense, it would apply to all private activity. But it seems more reasonable to say that the common law offends the Charter only when it crystallizes into a rule that can be enforced by the courts. Then, if an enforcement order would infringe a Charter right, the Char-

---

63 *Dolphin Delivery*, paragraph 25, (emphasis added by Justice McIntyre).
64 *Dolphin Delivery*, paragraph 34–34.

> ter will apply to preclude the order, and, by necessary implication, to modify the common law rule."[65]

Justice McIntyre found this view troublesome. As he put it:

> "I find the position thus adopted troublesome and, in my view, it should not be accepted as an approach to this problem. While in political science terms it is probably acceptable to treat the courts as one of the three fundamental branches of Government, that is, legislative, executive, and judicial, I cannot equate for the purposes of *Charter* application the order of a court with an element of governmental action. This is not to say that the courts are not bound by the *Charter.* The courts are, of course, bound by the *Charter* as they are bound by all law. It is their duty to apply the law, but in doing so they act as neutral arbiters, not as contending parties involved in a dispute. To regard a court order as an element of governmental intervention necessary to invoke the *Charter* would, it seems to me, widen the scope of *Charter* application to virtually all private litigation. All cases must end, if carried to completion, with an enforcement order and if the *Charter* precludes the making of the order, where a *Charter* right would be infringed, it would seem that all private litigation would be subject to the *Charter.* In my view, this approach will not provide the answer to the question. A more direct and a more precisely-defined connection between the element of government action and the claim advanced must be present before the *Charter* applies."[66]

As Hogg himself notes clearly in his response to the decision in *Dolphin Delivery,* Justice McIntyre was exorcising the spectre of *Shelley* in this passage.[67] And having exorcised *Shelley's* spectre thus, he moved on to wrap up the whole question regarding the impact of the Charter on private relations as follows:

> "Where such exercise of, or reliance upon, governmental action is present and where one private party invokes or relies upon it to produce an infringement of the *Charter* rights of another, the *Charter* will be applicable. Where, however, private party "A" sues private party "B" relying on the common law and where no act of government is relied upon to support the action, the *Charter* will not apply. I should make it clear, however, that this is a distinct issue from the question whether the judiciary ought to apply and develop the principles of the common law in a manner consistent with the fundamental values enshrined in the Constitution. The answer to this question must be in the affirmative. In this sense, then, the *Charter* is far from irrelevant to private litigants whose disputes fall to be decided at common law. But this is different from the proposition that one private party

65 Peter Hogg, *Constitutional Law of Canada: Vol. II*, 2nd ed. (Ontario: Thomson Carswell, 1985), 678 (as quoted by Justice McIntyre in *Dolphin Delivery*, paragraph 35 – this edition was not accessed here).

66 *Dolphin Delivery*, paragraph 36.

67 Cf. Hogg, *Constitutional Law of Canada: Vol. II*, 5th ed. (Ontario: Thomson Carswell, 2008) 94, footnote 103 where he relates this move directly to the decision in *Shelley.*

owes a constitutional duty to another, which proposition underlies the purported assertion of *Charter* causes of action or *Charter* defences between individuals."[68]

The court found no government action of the kind required to make the *Charter* applicable to the dispute between the parties in casu and dismissed the appeal against the injunction. And in doing so it wrote an important chapter on the historical and global development of horizontal effect that would, as we shall soon see, have a remarkable impact on the application jurisprudence of the South African Constitutional Court way down in the southern hemisphere. But we need to stay in the northern hemisphere a little longer. For the South African Constitutional Court would also rely heavily on the jurisprudence of another northern hemisphere jurisdiction. It relied heavily on the application jurisprudence for which the GFCC would lay the foundations in the *Lüth* case in 1958. It is important to also pick up this northern line before we move south.

VI *Lüth*

The decision of the GFCC in the *Lüth* case concerned the constitutional review of the decisions of the Regional and Appellate Courts of Hamburg. The Hamburg courts had decided that a call by Eric Lüth to boycott the films of the Nazi filmmaker Veit Harlan constituted a civil wrong in terms of both § 823(1) and § 826 of the German Civil Code.[69] Lüth appealed to the GFCC. He claimed that the finding

---

68 *Dolphin Delivery*, paragraph 39.

69 On the 20th September 1958, the constitutional plaintiff, the chairman of the Hamburg Press Club and Senatsdirektor at the time, called upon cinema owners and film distributors to boycott the film *Unsterbliche Geliebte*. The film was produced by Veit Harlan, a German filmmaker well known for his production of National Socialist propaganda films among which the film *Jud Süss* was the most notorious. Domnick-Film-Produktion GmbH and Herzog-Film GmbH, the former as the producer and the latter as the distributor of the film, successfully applied for an interdict in the Hamburg Regional Court (*Landgericht*) that prohibited the defendant from calling film distributors and cinema owners to boycott the film *Unsterbliche Geliebte*. The Regional Court found the boycott to be wrongful (*sittenwidrig*). Harlan's absolution from criminal proceedings against the film *Jud Süsss* and the fact that the post-war denazification directives of the Allied Control Council had subjected him to no restrictions as far as the practice of his profession was concerned, convinced the court that the boycott call was irreconcilable with the democratic legal and moral convictions of the German people (*die demokratische Rechts- und Sittenaufffassung des deutschen Volkes*). According to the court, the wrongfulness of the boycott did not consist in the expression of a denigrating opinion with regard to Harlan, but in the way it tried to move the public to make Harlan's future pursuit of a film-making career impossible. The Appellate Court of Hamburg (*Oberlandesgericht*) subsequently dismissed the appeal against the Regional Court's

of the Hamburg courts violated rights guaranteed by the German *Grundgesetz* (Foundational Law, hereafter cited as the GG). The GFCC upheld the claim. The reasoning that informed its decision turned on six key points:

1) The fundamental rights embodied in the GG are primarily aimed at protecting the individual against abuse from public authorities. They are the defensive rights of the citizen against the state (*Abwehrrechte des Bürgers gegen den Staat*). This is clear, maintained the GFCC, from the spiritual history (*geistesgeschichtliche Entwicklung*) of the idea of fundamental rights in the constitutional development of states in which these rights came to be recognised,[70] and from the fact that the legislator had granted the legal remedies which these rights offered only with regard to actions of public authorities.[71]
2) The GG does not constitute a neutral order, but an objective normative order (*objektive Wertordnung*) that derives its essence from the idea of human dignity and the free development of the person in common social life (*soziale Gemeinschaft*). This objective order underpins all spheres of law. Legislation, state administration and judicial deliberation are therefore subject to its guidelines. This of course also applies to civil law, insisted the GFCC. No civil law principle may contradict it and every civil law principle must be interpreted in the spirit of this objective normative order embodied in the GG.[72]
3) The general clauses of civil law, such as paragraph 826 of the Civil Code (*Bürgerliches Gesetzbuch*), require the assessment of human conduct with reference to considerations such as the good morals of society. These considerations lend themselves especially to the embodiment of constitutional norms in civil law. The assessment of the purport of these general clauses for a particular dispute requires, as a matter of first concern, the consideration of the whole normative order to which a people adheres at a particular point in its spiritual history. The general clauses have therefore correctly been said to be the bridgeheads (*Einbruchstellen*) of the fundamental rights into civil law.[73] The GFCC nevertheless insisted in this regard that the dispute between private individuals remains, procedurally and substantively, a civil law dispute. It requires the interpretation and application of civil law, even

decision and the constitutional plaintiff therefore approached the GFCC (*Bundesverfassungsgericht*) with the claim that the decisions of the trial courts had violated his fundamental right to freedom of speech.

70 *Lüth*, 204–205.

71 *Lüth*, 205.

72 *Lüth*, 205.

73 *Lüth*, 206.

though such interpretation and application must heed constitutional considerations.[74]

4) The influence of constitutional values on civil law is especially at issue when coercive law is concerned. Civil law that governs the relations between individuals without leaving them a choice in the matter clearly constitutes a public order. As such, coercive civil law supplements public law and is therefore closely related to it. Coercive civil law is therefore especially exposed to the influence of the constitution.[75]
5) Trial Court judiciaries must test whether applicable civil law prescripts are affected by the norms embodied in the GG and whether this normative effect requires an amendment of civil law. Any influence that requires such a modification of existing law must be heeded rigorously. That this is so can be gleaned from the fact that Article 1 III of the GG expressly also binds the civil law judiciary to the fundamental rights contained in the Foundational Law. A failure of a judge to heed the influence of constitutional norms on applicable precepts of private law, not only constitutes a transgression of the objective constitutional order, but also constitutes a violation of a fundamental right by a public official. Anyone whose fundamental right is violated in this way may approach the GFCC with a constitutional complaint.[76] Faced with such a constitutional complaint, the Federal Constitutional Court must test whether the reach and effect of the fundamental rights in the sphere of private law has been assessed correctly.
6) The nature of this task to review judicial decisions against which constitutional complaints have been filed also imposes a limit on the GFCC's powers of review in these matters. It is not the task of the constitutional judiciary to test the case against which the complaint is directed for all possible mistakes. Its task is only to assess the radiation effect of the constitution on applicable civil law in order to give proper effect to the constitution in the dispute at issue. In other words, the GFCC is not meant to be an instance of higher review, but it cannot shy away from the duty to scrutinise the constitutionality of a trial court decision.[77]

Having considered the constitutional complaint at issue in view of the six principles outlined above, the GFCC concluded that the decision of the Regional Court could not be reconciled with the values of the GG. It did not reflect a prop-

74 *Lüth*, 205–206.
75 *Lüth*, 206.
76 *Lüth*, 206–207.
77 *Lüth*, 207.

er regard for the fundamental importance of freedom of speech in the German constitutional order. The GFCC accordingly proceeded to pronounce its judgment with a statement that would become nothing less than a standard formula for its later judgments in horizontal effect or *Drittwirkung* cases. A more or less literal translation of this formulaic pronunciation reads as follows:

> "The decision of the Regional Court failed to recognise the significance which the right to freedom of expression enjoys also in those cases where it comes into conflict with private interests. As such it falls short of constitutional criteria and must be deemed to have violated the fundamental right which the plaintiff enjoys in terms of article 5 I."[78]

The first four of the six points highlighted above can be read as confirmation and endorsement of the positions that the United States Supreme Court took in *Labour v Swing* and *New York Times v Sullivan* (*Sullivan* was of course decided six years after *Lüth*). They confirm the principle that all law, common law included, is bound by the rights and norms embodied in the Constitution. Points 5 and 6 confirm the position taken in *Shelley v Kraemer*. They endorse emphatically the finding in *Shelley* that a court decision itself can violate a constitutional right. And if any doubt whatsoever still remains in this regard, the formulaic statement with which the GFCC concluded its judgement surely removes that. As we saw, the court stated expressly that "the decision of the Regional Court ... must be deemed to have violated the fundamental right [of] the plaintiff."

It should also be clear that *Dolphin Delivery* differs from *Lüth* on both counts. The decision in *Dolphin* insisted that common law is only bound to the constitution when the state is party to a common law dispute, not so in the case of disputes between private individuals. And it also rejected expressly the idea that a "merely arbitrating" judiciary is bound by the constitution. There can be no doubt that *Lüth* is much more in line with *Swing*, *Sullivan* and *Shelley* than it is with *Dolphin*. However, *Dolphin* and *Lüth* have one point in common. They both emphasise the point that common law or civil law should be interpreted in a way that renders it reconcilable with the constitution. Constitutional law

---

78 *Lüth*, 230 (emphasis added): "Das Bundesverfassungsgericht ist auf Grund dieser Erwägungen zu der Überzeugung gelangt, daß das Landgericht bei seiner Beurteilung des Verhaltens des Beschwerdeführers die besondere Bedeutung verkannt hat, die dem Grundrecht auf freie Meinungsäußerung auch dort zukommt, wo es mit privaten Interessen anderer in Konflikt tritt. Das Urteil des Landgerichts beruht auf diesem Verfehlen grundrechtlicher Maßstäbe *und verletzt so das Grundrecht des Beschwerdeführers* aus Art 5 Abs 1 Satz 1 GG. The court relied on this wording again and again in subsequent judgments. Cf. 24 BVerfG 278; 25 BVerfG 256; 30 BVerfG 173; 34 BVerfG 35 BVerfG 202; 42 BVerfG 142; 46 BVerfG 325; 54 BVerfG 129; 54 BVerfG 148; 60 BVerfG 234; 61 BVerfG 1; 62 BVerfG 230; 66 BVerfG 116; 73 BVerfG 261.

can and must be allowed to enter civil law through the open principles of the latter so that it can "radiate through" all aspects of civil law. On this last point both decisions evidently took a stance in favour of that which has become known as the *indirect horizontal effect* of constitutional rights.

Lüth is nevertheless more complex than *Dolphin* in this regard. *Lüth's* obvious correspondence and resonance with *Swing*, *Sullivan* and *Shelley* brings it much closer to the *direct horizontal effect* of fundamental rights. To be sure, neither *Lüth*, nor *Swing*, *Sullivan* or *Shelley* suggests private individuals can rely directly on constitutional rights in private litigation. For this they are all too much in line with the angle on state action that *The Civil Rights Cases* bequeathed to United States jurisprudence. But they do suggest that private individuals are *always* bound by the constitution in a way that *Dolphin* does not. This difference is significant, significant enough to suggest a different understanding of the concerns at stake in the distinction between direct and indirect horizontal effect. *Substantively speaking*, all that anyone in favour of *direct* horizontal effect really seeks to achieve is the simple recognition that private individuals are as bound by constitutional rights as states are. Judges and scholars in favour of *direct* horizontal effect object to the idea that individuals are somehow not bound by the constitution when the state is said not to be present in the conflict between them. They want the constitution *to apply*. This is the main thing. How it applies is not unimportant, but it is of secondary importance. And as far as this *substantive* insistence that the constitution applies to all private individuals at all times is concerned, neither *Lüth*, nor *Swing*, *Sullivan* or *Shelley* allows for an exception. If the rules laid down in these cases were to be followed, no private individual would ever again be able to claim that she is not bound by the constitutional rights of others. *Swing* and *Sullivan* and the first four principles in *Lüth* would deprive her of any common law remedy or defence that is at odds with the constitution. And the fifth principle in *Lüth*, as well as the formulaic confirmation of this fifth principle in the articulation of the decision in *Lüth*, would deprive her, just as the rule in *Shelley* does, of any court order that may come to her avail in a way that is at odds with the constitution.

To be sure, the *Lüth* judgment ultimately imparts or seems to impart a mixed message to the discourse of horizontal effect. On the one hand it makes a clear choice in favour of the *indirect approach to horizontal effect* by its insistence that the objective norms embodied in fundamental rights find expression in private law through the medium of directly applicable civil law prescripts (principles 1 to 4 above). On the other hand it clearly also endorses the unexceptional application of constitutional principles to private individuals in the way *Swing*, *Sullivan* and *Shelley* do. The latter endorsement, we saw above, evidently returns to *Lüth* and does so completely unconstrained by the qualifications that the decision in *Dolphin Delivery* would later impose in Canada on cases like *Swing, Sullivan* and *Shelley.* It is this endorsement that turns *Lüth*, at least practically or substantively, into a champion of the direct horizontal effect of constitutional rights. Again, if *Swing*, *Sullivan*, *Shelley* and *Lüth* were to be followed unconditionally, no individual would ever again be able to claim that a constitutional right of another imposes no duty on her, for no common law rule and no court decision at odds with that right would be able to come to her avail.

There is surely more than one way in which one can make sense of these two sides of *Lüth* – its apparent endorsement of both direct and indirect horizontal effect – without just silencing the one side at the cost of the other as has become common practice in the interpretation of *Lüth* as an example of indirect horizontal effect. The most plausible way, however, would be to distinguish between the *form* and *substance* of the *Lüth* decision. A reading of *Lüth* in terms of the form and substance of the jurisprudence that it articulated can be constructed as follows:

i) In *substance*, the norms of the GG apply to every walk of German life, also to conduct and choices of private citizens merely facilitated by civil law. Yes, *Lüth* said "especially" to coercive civil law, and this "especially" is confounding. It is most likely simply meaningless, but irrespective of whatever it might mean, "especially" evidently does not mean "exclusively." Later judgments of the GFCC surely confirmed that facilitative civil law is likewise subject to the demands of the GG.[79]
ii) That the norms of the GG apply thus to every walk of German life, need nevertheless not and must not lead to the replacement of civil law rules and principles by the fundamental rights provisions and discourse embodied in the foundational law. There is a constitutionally prescribed *method* or *form* through which the impact of the foundational law on civil relations must register in law. This method requires the deliberate interpretation of civil law principles, especially the general clauses, in ways that render them *substantially* compatible with the norms of the GG.
iii) Principles 1 to 4 of the *Lüth* decision highlighted above *expressly* reflect and stipulate the *method* and *form* of horizontal effect endorsed in *Lüth:* The impact of the GG on private legal relationships must be channelled through the open principles of private law.
iv) Principles 1 to 4 nevertheless also reflect *implicitly* an important element of the substance of the horizontal effect endorsed in *Lüth*. Principles 1 to 4 clearly suggest that no common law rule is exempt from the impact of hor-

79 For a very significant decision in this regard, cf. 89 BVerfG 214 (the *Bürgschaftsverträge* case).

izontal effect (which implies no private individual will ever have a private law rule to stand on that is inconsistent with the GG). In this regard the decision in *Lüth* echoes the decisions of the USSC in *Swing* and *Sullivan.*

v) Principle 5 and the confirmation of principle 5 by the formula in which the decision is cast expressly reflect another element of the *substance* of the horizontal effect endorsed in *Lüth.* They expressly state that the judiciary is bound by the GG (which implies no private individual will ever have a court decision to stand on that is inconsistent with the GG). In this respect *Lüth* echoes the decision in *Shelley.*

vi) There is *no intrinsic tension* or inconsistency in *Lüth* between the method and form of (indirect) horizontal effect articulated in principles 1 to 4 and the substance of (direct) horizontal effect evident in principle 5 and the formula in which the decision is cast. One can and should thus not discern a tension between the form and substance of the horizontal effect jurisprudence articulated in *Lüth.* The indirect form of horizontal effect stipulated in *Lüth* is nowhere invoked in *Lüth* as a principle that excludes or exempts some private individuals or some private legal relations from the impact of the constitution. Whatever tensions may come to characterise the indirect horizontal effect of constitutional rights in other jurisdictions must therefore derive from the way those jurisdictions impose extrinsic limitations on the indirect horizontal effect of fundamental rights. This is the case, as we saw above, in Canada, because of the way the decision in *Dolphin Delivery* expressly introduced an extrinsic limitation to principles 1 to 4 (the Charter applies to the common law, *but not when the state is not involved in the dispute*) and another extrinsic limitation to principle 5 that also rendered the formula of the decision in *Lüth* unusable (the Charter applies to court decisions, *but not when the court only acts as arbitrator*).

In other words, the *Lüth* decision articulates the demand for a *substantive* correspondence between constitutional law and civil law that respects the *formal* or *methodological* differences between them and vice versa (the form also respects the demanded substance). This understanding of the relationship between private and constitutional law articulated in *Lüth* does not yet constitute a comprehensive or complete assessment of *Lüth.* The analysis offered above has not even begun to engage with the 6th principle extracted from the decision (the insistence that the GFCC should not be considered as a general court of appeal). And it has not yet addressed the highly problematic aspects of the notion that the general principles of private law should be used as bridgeheads for the GG's radiation through private law. We shall return to *Lüth* presently in order to address both these issues. But the analysis pursued above already goes a long way towards a better understanding of *Lüth*. It makes more accurate sense of *Lüth* than standard invocations of *Lüth* as a mere example of indirect horizontal effect have hitherto done.

Had the two different (but complementary) sides of *Lüth* been clearer to the South African Constitutional Court when it proceeded to decide *Du Plessis v De Klerk*, it may have spared itself many interpretive complications and a deep irony. The South African Constitutional Court followed both *Dolphin Delivery* and *Lüth* as if these decisions stood for the same jurisprudence. They did not register that *Dolphin* brought to bear extrinsic considerations on the jurisprudence in *Lüth* that were inconsistent with the intrinsic coherence of this jurisprudence. They endorsed these extrinsic considerations. In the process, they ended up invoking *Dolphin Delivery* against *Shelley* without realising how its reliance on *Lüth* exposed it to a full importation of *Shelley*. Let us now take a close look at how all of this came to pass.

VII *Du Plessis v De Klerk*

Little of *Lüth* ultimately survived in *Du Plessis v De Klerk*. Some loose elements that remind one of *Lüth* could still be seen drifting around like debris in the majority opinion that Acting Justice Kentridge wrote for the court. The one unmistakable piece was the emphasis on the radiation effect – *Ausstrahlungswirkung* of fundamental rights. Some formless and deforming figment of form one might call this loose piece of *Lüth* drifting around in *Du Plessis*. *Ausstrahlungswirkung* channelled through the *Generalklausel* of private law, we saw in the discussion of *Lüth* above, constituted the form in which the Karlsruhe court wanted to cast horizontal effect in Germany. Indirect horizontal effect – *mittelbare Drittwirkung* – was the form or method on which it insisted. But this form or method, we saw above, did not openly undermine the basic substance of *Lüth*, namely, the substantive insistence that no social conduct can claim natural exemption from constitutional scrutiny.

This was not to be the case in South Africa. As a result of the importation of elements of Canadian horizontal effect jurisprudence, elements that could not be reconciled with the jurisprudence in *Lüth*, the SACC ended up proposing a form of horizontal effect jurisprudence in *Du Plessis* that undermines instead of sustains the substantive principle that no social conduct is exempted from constitutional scrutiny. It proposed a form of horizontal effect that undermined and therefore deformed the principle of horizontal effect. And it continued to hang onto this deforming form of horizontal effect after *Du Plessis*, even after the South African sovereign, seeing clearly where things were heading, enacted new constitutional application clauses in 1996 through which it asserted or re-asserted a full territorial constitutional sovereignty from which no one and no sphere of life could claim exemption.

The 1996 Constitution introduced a legal dispensation in South Africa in which the Bill of Rights embodied in Chapter 2, traditionally the cornerstone of public law legal relations, was expressly acknowledged as the cornerstone of all legal relationships in South Africa. Not only did the 1996 Constitution expressly introduce a horizontal effect regime into South African law. As will become clear below, it also introduced a *substantive* horizontal effect regime into South African law that anyone with some understanding of constitutional law would recognise as a *direct* horizontal effect regime. The new application clauses of the 1996 Constitution can convincingly be said to have introduced this *direct* horizontal effect regime clearly, systematically and judiciously. The judicious element of this introduction of direct horizontal effect into South African law was reflected in the way it stipulated clear terms for the resolution of possible conflicts between ordinary and constitutional law, conflicts that it wisely foresaw. And the terms it laid down for the resolution of these potential conflicts between ordinary and constitutional law clearly amounted to the same resolution proposed by the GFCC in *Lüth*. It proposed a *form* of horizontal effect that would rely on the indirect *method* of horizontal effect proposed in *Lüth*, the key concern of which was the development of ordinary law so as to render it compatible with constitutional principles. This indirect method of horizontal effect articulated in *Lüth* also requires critical revision today, as we shall soon see. But this can at least be said of *Lüth:* Its method did not openly or expressly subvert its substance. And such subversion is exactly what came to pass in *Du Plessis*.

Towards the end of 1995, only months before the 1996 Constitution came into force, the SACC judged that the Constitution of 1993, commonly known as the Interim Constitution, applied only *indirectly* to private relations. This was the case of *Du Plessis v De Klerk*. The crucial question at issue in *Du Plessis* was whether a newspaper article that had fallen foul of South African defamation law before the 1993 Constitution came into force could be vindicated by the constitutional right to freedom of expression introduced by Section 15(1) of this Constitution. The court split the question into two separate questions, namely the question whether the 1993 Constitution applied retrospectively to a legal dispute that arose before the enactment of the Constitution and the question whether the Constitution affected private legal disputes at all. The answer to the first question was negative and need not be discussed here. It is *Du Plessis*' complex affirmation of the second question that is scrutinised in what follows.

The decision in *Du Plessis* turned mainly on Section 35(3) of the 1993 Constitution.[80] Section 35(3) stipulated the following:

> In the interpretation of any law and the application and development of the common law and customary law, a court shall have due regard to the spirit, purport and objects of this Chapter [i.e. the Bill of Rights].

Along with this provision, the court bore in mind Sections 7(1), 7(2) and 33(4) of the 1993 Constitution. Section 7(1) made the fundamental rights embodied in Chapter 3 of the 1993 Constitution binding on legislative and executive action. Section 7(2) made the rights in Chapter 3 applicable to all law in force. Section 33(4) stipulated further that Chapter 3 did not preclude measures to prohibit unfair discrimination by bodies and persons not bound by s 7(1). The court inferred the following key implications from these clauses for the question regarding the horizontal effect of the Bill of Rights:

1) Section 33(4) would have made no sense if the Chapter were intended to apply directly to private legal disputes, since such application would have rendered the phrase 'persons and bodies other than those bound in terms of section 7(1)' meaningless.[81]
2) The absence of a reference to the judiciary in s 7(1) was not an oversight. One of its effects is to prevent the importation of the doctrine developed in *Shelley v Kraemer.*[82]
3) Constitutional rights under Chapter 3 may be invoked against an organ of state, but not by one private litigant against another.[83]
4) Private litigants may contend that statutory law or executive acts relied on by the other party are inconsistent with Chapter 3, and therefore invalid.[84]
5) Chapter 3 applies to the common law (only) when government action relies on it.[85] Common-law principles or rules are not to be subjected to constitutional review in private legal disputes, since holdings of unconstitutionality in such cases would leave gaps in the law. Drastic amelioration of the common law is a function of Parliament.[86]
6) Direct horizontal effect would lead to routine referrals of common-law cases to the Constitutional Court. This would militate against the limitation of the

80 *Du Plessis*, paragraph 60.
81 *Du Plessis*, paragraph 46.
82 *Du Plessis*, paragraph 47.
83 *Du Plessis*, paragraph 49(a).
84 *Du Plessis*, paragraph 49(b).
85 *Du Plessis*, paragraph 49(c).
86 *Du Plessis*, paragraph 53.

> jurisdiction of the Constitutional Court to constitutional matters and the preservation of the regular civil jurisdiction of the Appellate Division.[87]

In short, the South African Constitutional Court's judgment in *Du Plessis* committed the court to the position that private disputes could only be taken to court on causes of action or grounds of defence already contained in private law, irrespective of whether these disputes also raised constitutional questions. Once such a private dispute had indeed been taken to court on the basis of some private law cause of action or defence, the parties could expect the courts not to apply such principles or rules in a manner that would be inconsistent with the Constitution. Indeed, they could rely on the court to develop and transform existing law to ensure that it accorded with the principles and values embodied in the Bill of Rights.

Du Plessis evidently endorsed the *indirect horizontal effect* of the Bill of Rights. It is nevertheless important to repeat the caveat already articulated early on in this chapter with reference to Justice Kriegler's "dissenting judgment." The court essentially endorsed the indirect horizontal effect of the Bill of Rights, but it never said so in these terms. The court simply stressed that the constitution only applied vertically to the relation between citizens and the state. Whatever impact the constitution was envisaged to have on private relations was expressed solely in terms of *the radiation effect* of the Constitution through the whole of the legal system, the system of private law included.

Be it as it may, this indirect horizontal or radiation effect approach of the court would continue to condition the court's application jurisprudence well after the 1996 Constitution had changed the application provisions fundamentally. This continuity between the court's pre- and post-1996 application jurisprudence is truly remarkable when one considers the incisive way in which Section 8 of the 1996 Constitution changed the application provisions of the 1993 Constitution.[88] Ironically, however, the SACC's persistence with its *Du Plessis* reasoning after 1996 may well have been more informed by Justice Kriegler's "dissenting opinion" than it was by Justice Kentridge's opinion for the majority.[89]

---

87 *Du Plessis*, paragraph 57.

88 Cf. art 8(2). For a more extensive discussion of this development, cf. Van der Walt, "Progressive Indirect Horizontal Application of the Bill of Rights: Towards a Co-operative Relation between Common-law and Constitutional Jurisprudence," *South African Journal on Human Rights* 17 no 3 (2001): 344–348.

89 The key case that took the *Du Plessis* jurisprudence over for post-1996 horizontal effect cases in South Africa was *Khumalo v Holomisa* 2002 5 SA 401 (CC). *Khumalo* can be argued to have

Justice Kriegler's "dissenting opinion" constituted one of the biggest conundrums of the *Du Plessis* case. As we saw above, Justice Kriegler envisaged a paradoxical horizontal effect jurisprudence that would, on the one hand, heal a society skewed by a racist and segregationist past, and on the other hand, leave much of that skewness intact and "undisturbed" as long as this skewness remains private and does not rely on law in order to prevail. Here are the essential lines of the passage quoted above again:

> "The [Bill of Rights] has nothing to do with the ordinary relationships between private persons or associations. What it does govern, however, is all law, including that applicable to private relationships. Unless and until there is a resort to law, private individuals are at liberty to conduct their private affairs exactly as they please as far as the fundamental rights and freedoms are concerned ... The whole gamut of private relationships is left undisturbed."

Later SACC case law resolved this puzzle by pointing out that procedural law and procedural exceptions against actionability are as much subject to the demands of the Constitution as substantive law is. This happened in the case of *Carmichele v Minister of Safety and Security* when the SACC considered the constitutionality of a procedural exception that a claim for delictual damages does not disclose a cause of action. The defendant in *Carmichele* raised the exception that the claimant had not disclosed the essential elements of the state's legal duty to protect her against the harm (as a result of assault) she had suffered. The SACC considered this exception on further appeal after both the trial court and the Supreme Court of Appeal had sustained it. The SACC found the trial and appeal court hearings wanting for not having considered the reconcilability of the exception with the fundamental rights of the claimant and referred the case back to the trial court for a rehearing that would properly consider the effect of the claimant's fundamental rights on the exception raised by the defendant.

With its decision in the *Carmichele* case, the SACC effectively demolished the notion that a claim for damages (or any other remedy sought) must first cross the frontier of law before constitutional rights can commence to have an effect on the case. The result of the decision is clearly that the question whether the claim has successfully entered the zone of law or not is already subject to the effect of the claimant's constitutional rights. The *Carmichele* saga evidently resolved the Kriegler conundrum. The SACC's decision in *Carmichele* made clear that Justice Kriegler could not have been talking about private fundamental rights violations that

---

turned in significant respects on Justice Kriegler's insistence that the Constitution applied to law and not directly to social conduct.

are *in principle* or *conceptually* unaffected by law (*by law* unaffected by law) when he invoked a "whole gamut of private relations" that the Constitution leaves "undisturbed." He could not have been talking about claims that can *in principle not* be taken to court. He could at best have been talking about violations that *incidentally* have not or will not be brought to a court of law. And if this is indeed what he was talking about, he also could have extended his gory list of "private" constitutional right violations (see again the full passage quoted above) to include the following: A man can have sexual intercourse with his wife without her consent. He can kill her. He can steal his brother's or neighbour's money. He can trash or invade someone's property. He can violently abuse his children. And so forth.

All these things will indeed remain "purely private" matters as long as no one proceeds to subject them to the scrutiny of law. This "whole gamut of private relations" will indeed be left undisturbed by the Bill of Rights as long as no one commences to bring them to book. It is of course a sad fact of life that people sometimes get away with murder. But no one in his right mind would raise this fact as an assurance that the Constitution leaves the "whole gamut of private relations undisturbed." No one in his right mind would invoke simple failures of a state to protect its citizens against criminal and civil harm as an assurance that the Constitution will not interfere with their private lives. We must assume therefore that Justice Kriegler was also not doing this and that he simply got his signals somewhat crossed in *Du Plessis*. But try as one might, one cannot offer this excuse to the justices that signed the majority opinion in *DeShaney v Winnebago County Department of Social Services* to which we turn below. As we will see then, Justice Rehnquist basically said in so many words that a failure of a state to protect its citizens against crime and assault does not warrant an imposition of the 14th Amendment on their private lives. "The people of Wisconsin," he insisted, "should not have [a system of State liability for failure to act in situations such as the present one] thrust upon them by this Court's expansion of the Due Process Clause of the Fourteenth Amendment."[90] The reading of *DeShaney* that is offered below will confirm that this was just another way of saying: Do not be concerned, as long as the state has done nothing to protect you, the 14th Amendment will not interfere with your private lives. The *Carmichele* decision, we saw above, fortunately saved the South African legal community unambiguously from this madness, that is, from this inconceivable refusal of a judge, a state official, to assume the sovereignty entrusted to him and make a

---

90 *DeShaney*, 202–203.

decision that was worthy of this sovereignty.[91] But the disavowal of state sovereignty evident in *DeShaney* could not have come as a surprise to anyone familiar with Justice Rehnquist's jurisprudence. Already eleven years before *DeShaney* did he expressly refuse to acknowledge state sovereignty in a way that surely prepared the way for his judgement in *DeShaney.* This was the case of *Flagg Brothers, Inc. v Brooks.*

VIII *Flagg Brothers, Inc. v Brooks*

Shirley Brooks and her family were evicted from her apartment in Mount Vernon, New York, in June 1973. The City Marshal arranged for the Brooks' furniture and possessions to be stored by Flagg Brothers, Inc. After having been informed of the costs of the removal and storage, Brooks authorised Flagg Brothers to proceed, nevertheless complaining that the price was too high. After further disagreement regarding the amount owed to them, Flagg Brothers informed Brooks that her possessions would be sold if their bill was not paid within 10 days. After

91 By asking the trial court in *Carmichele* to reconsider its finding, the South African Constitutional Court basically instructed the court to return to a principle that the South African judiciary had already recognised and endorsed as a common law principle many years before. The South African Supreme Court of Appeal (it was called the Appellate Division at the time) already recognised and endorsed the principle thirty years before *Carmichele* in the case of *Minister van Polisie v Ewels* (1975 3 SA 590 (A)). With the *Ewels* decision the then Appellate Division rid the South African civil law of delict (tort) of a madness similar to the madness that is written all over *DeShaney.* Before *Ewels*, South African courts also entertained the idea that public legal liability could be avoided as long as no "prior conduct" could be imputed to them. By finally relating the well-established common principle in *Ewels* to the constitutional duties to prevent harm, the *Carmichele* decision can be said to have expanded the doctrine of state action so as to include *state inaction* under *state action. Carmichele* indeed paved the way for a whole series of cases in which the South African common law judiciary began to scrutinise state inaction freshly as possible abridgments of fundamental rights that also demand findings of common law delictual liability. Cf. for instance *Minister of Safety and Security v Van Duivenboden* 2002 6 SA 431 (SCA) and *Van Eden v Minister of Safety and Security* 2003 1 SA 389 (SCA). This veritable expansion of the state action doctrine to also include *state inaction* that fails to protect constitutional rights ultimately undid and made good the rejection of *Shelley* (and *Swing* and *Sullivan*) in *Du Plessis v De Klerk.* Against this background there is absolutely no scope left in South Africa for private conduct that can claim categorical exemption from constitutional scrutiny, for private conduct that violates constitutional rights will always precipitate the question of state inaction, that is, the state's omission or failure to prevent that private conduct. This is what *Carmichele* was all about. This, however, is not the way that state action is understood in the United States, as will become clear from the discussion of *DeShaney* to which we turn now. The American concept of state action does not include state inaction.

further failed negotiations, Brooks filed a class action in the District Court under Section 1983 of Title 42 of the United States Code (42 U.S.C. § 1983) seeking an injunction against the sale of her belongings together with a claim for damages. The action was based on the allegation that the actions of Flagg Brothers violated her 14th Amendment rights. Another evictee, Gloria Jones, whose furniture had also been stored by Flagg Brothers after eviction, joined Brooks in the action. The American Warehousemen's Association and the International Association of Refrigerated Warehouses, Inc., joined Flagg Brothers as defendants.

The District Court dismissed Brooks' action for failure to state a claim for relief under § 1983, given the absence of state action in the dispute between Brooks and Flagg Brothers. The Court of Appeals reversed the order. The District Court had relied on the decision in *Jackson v Metropolitan Edison Co*[92] for its decision, but the majority in the Court of Appeals asserted that the *Jackson* decision in fact suggested that state action can be present in the action of a private party when a function of state sovereignty had been delegated to that party by the state. And it found clear evidence of such a transfer of sovereignty in the case of the actions of Flagg Brothers. It stated:

> "By enacting §7–210 [of the New York Uniform Commercial Code], New York not only delegated to the warehouseman a portion of its sovereign monopoly power over binding conflict resolution citations omitted, but also let him, by selling stored goods, execute a lien and thus perform a function which has traditionally been that of the sheriff."[93]

With this finding, the Court of Appeals clearly avowed the sovereignty of the state of New York. The sovereign can delegate tasks to private parties, argued the Court of Appeals, but it cannot divest itself of that sovereignty in the process. It remains the sovereign and must own up to the consequences of the delegated exercise of its powers. This was not, however, how Justice Rehnquist saw the matter in the USSC hearing of the case. The crux of his opinion is reflected in the following dictum:

> "A warehouseman's proposed sale of goods entrusted to him for storage, as permitted by § 7–210, is not "state action," and since the allegation of the complaint failed to establish that any violation of the respondents' Fourteenth Amendment rights was committed by either the storage company or the State of New York, the District Court properly concluded that no claim for relief was stated by respondents under 42 U.S.C. 1983."[94]

---

92 419 U.S. 345, 95 (1974).
93 Cf. *Flagg Brothers*, 149.
94 *Flagg Brothers*, 155–166.

Justice Rehnquist distinguished the dispute in *Flagg Brothers* from a number of other decisions in which the actions and remedies of creditors had been subjected to procedural remedies.[95] The challenged statute, argued Justice Rehnquist further, did not delegate to the storage company an exclusive prerogative of the sovereign to settle disputes. Other remedies for the settlement of disputes between debtors and creditors are available that are not traditionally regarded as a public function. The dispute in *Flagg Brothers* therefore had to be distinguished from other public function cases where state action could be identified in their conduct.[96] It should be clear from these key points in his judgment that Justice Rehnquist's opinion constitutes a bold rejection of the avowal of state sovereignty by the Court of Appeals. That this is so is not a matter of mere construal. At issue is not just a reading of his opinion. His discussion of the public function cases committed him to make an express statement in this regard:

> "Thus, even if we were inclined to extend the sovereign function doctrine outside its present carefully confined bounds, the field of private commercial transactions would be a particularly inappropriate area into which to expand it. We conclude that our sovereign-function cases do not support a finding of state action here."[97]

Justice Rehnquist wrapped up his argument by covering two more bases. "[M]ere acquiescence in a private action [does not] convert such action into that of the State."[98] And the state law concerned, in this case §7–210 of the New York Uniform Commercial Code, he argued, could not as such constitute state action for purposes of the 14th Amendment.

> "It is quite immaterial that the State has embodied its decision not to act in statutory form. If New York had no commercial statutes at all, its courts would still be faced with the decision whether to prohibit or to permit the sort of sale threatened here the first time an aggrieved bailor came before them for relief. A judicial decision to deny relief would be no less an 'authorization' or 'encouragement' of that sale than the legislature's decision embodied in this statute. It was recognized in the earliest interpretations of the Fourteenth Amendment 'that a State may act through different agencies, either by its legislative, its executive, or its judicial authorities; and the prohibitions of the amendment extend to all action of the State infringing rights protected thereby... If the mere denial of judicial relief is

---

95 *Flagg Brothers*, 157. Cf. *North Georgia Finishing, Inc. v Di-Chem, Inc.* 419 U.S. 601 (1975); *Fuentes v. Shevin* 407 U.S. 67 (1972); *Sniadach v Family Finance Corporation* 395 U.S. 337 (1969).
96 Cf. *Flagg Brothers*, 157–163, which relies expressly on the restriction of *Marsh v Alabama* in *Logan Valley*. Cf. also *Terry v Adams* 345 U.S. 461 (1953); *Smith v Allwright* 321 U.S. 649 (1944); *Nixon v Condon* 286 U.S. 73 (1932). Cf. again fn. 27 above.
97 *Flagg Brothers*, 163.
98 *Flagg Brothers*, 164–166. Cf. *Moose Lodge No. 107 v Irvis* 407 U.S. 163.

> considered sufficient encouragement to make the State responsible for those private acts, all private deprivations of property would be converted into public acts whenever the State, for whatever reason, denies relief sought by the putative property owner."[99]

And one should consider in conjunction with this dismissal of legislative or judicial action that authorises or condones deprivations of property rights performed by private actors another telling articulation of the point in an earlier footnote:

> "It would intolerably broaden ... the notion of state action under the Fourteenth Amendment to hold that the mere existence of a body of property law in a state, whether decisional or statutory, itself amounted to state action ..."[100]

What transpires from the above passages from Justice Rehnquist's opinion in *Flagg Brothers* is a clear acknowledgement that states are obviously involved in legislative, executive or judicial action that fails to grant a remedy against an abridgment of a 14th Amendment right by a private person. However, this acknowledgment is accompanied by explicit assertion that this reality is of no consequence for the private disputes at hand. Justice Rehnquist does not deny the state's involvement in private disputes, but he instructs one "to pretend not to notice it," as Frank Michelman puts it.[101] Against the background of his clear acknowledgment of state involvement in these cases, his instruction that one ignores this involvement amounts to nothing less than a disavowal of the sovereignty avowed by the Court of Appeals. A disavowal of sovereignty that follows directly on the heels of a clear recognition of sovereignty does not constitute a mere negation of sovereignty. It does not amount to a statement that sovereignty has never been at issue here. It is not like saying some territory never formed part of the state. It is much more like saying that the state should stop acting like the sovereign it is when 14th Amendment violations by private persons come into view. The state action doctrine, as articulated by Justice Rehnquist in *Flagg Brothers*, thus constitutes an unequivocal abdication of sovereignty. This abdication would be performed under even more dismaying circumstances in *DeShaney v Winnebago County Department of Social Services*. Justice Rehnquist refused to "expand the sovereign function doctrine" into the "particularly inappropriate area" of "private commercial transactions" in *Flagg Brothers*. In *DeShaney* he would also refuse to expand the sovereign function doctrine

---

99 *Flagg Brothers*, 165.

100 *Flagg Brothers*, 160 note 10. Cf. also Van der Walt, "Abdications of Sovereignty in Horizontal Effect Jurisprudence," (forthcoming).

101 Frank Michelman, "W(h)ither the Constitution?," *Cardozo Law Review* 21 (2000): 1076.

into the area of a state's failure to stop private assault of which it was amply aware. As we shall see now, he also found it "particularly inappropriate" to thrust a public liability tort on the people of Wisconsin.

IX *DeShaney v Winnebago County Department of Social Services*

"The facts of this case are undeniably tragic," states Chief Justice Rehnquist in his opinion for the court in *DeShaney v Winnebago County Department of Social Services.*[102] Joshua DeShaney must have been between two and three years old when the Winnebago County Officials first heard that he might be a victim of violent child abuse in January 1982. Between January 1982 and March 1984 the Department of Social Services (DSS) compiled a considerable record of suspicion that Joshua was being abused violently by his father Randy DeShaney.[103] Chief Justice Rehnquist's summary of the facts of the case records the rest of the story as follows:

> "In March 1984, Randy DeShaney beat 4-year-old Joshua so severely that he fell into a life-threatening coma. Emergency brain surgery revealed a series of haemorrhages caused by traumatic injuries to the head inflicted over a long period of time. Joshua did not die, but he suffered brain damage so severe that he is expected to spend the rest of his life confined to an institution for the profoundly retarded. Randy DeShaney was subsequently tried and convicted of child abuse."[104]

Joshua's mother brought an action on his behalf against the DSS for failing to protect his civil rights as guaranteed by the Fourteenth Amendment. The United States District Court for the Eastern District of Wisconsin entered a summary

102 *DeShaney*, 191.

103 Randy DeShaney's second wife complained to the police, at the time of their divorce, that Randy had previously "hit the boy causing marks and [was] a prime case for child abuse." In January 1983 Joshua was admitted to hospital with multiple bruises and abrasions. The Department of Social Services (DSS) was notified of suspected child abuse and the child was put in temporary custody of the hospital. However, after some investigation the investigating team decided there was not enough evidence of child abuse. They did make some recommendations regarding Joshua's safety with which Randy DeShaney promised to comply voluntarily, all of this leading to the juvenile court returning the child to the custody of his father. The DSS was again notified of suspected child abuse in March and November 1983, during which time the caseworker of the DSS who visited the home on a monthly basis also recorded suspicions of child abuse, but nothing further was done about the matter.

104 *DeShaney*, 193.

judgment in favour of the DSS. Joshua's mother's appeals to the Court of Appeals of the Seventh Circuit and finally to the United States Supreme Court were also dismissed. In the Supreme Court, Chief Justice Rehnquist held that the State had no constitutional duty to protect a child from his father after receiving reports of possible abuse. The following are key passages from the opinion he wrote for the Court:

> "The Due Process Clause of the Fourteenth Amendment provides that '[n]o State shall ... deprive any person of life, liberty, or property, without due process of law.' Petitioners contend that the State deprived Joshua of his liberty interest in "free[dom] from ... unjustified intrusions on personal security," by failing to provide him with adequate protection against his father's violence. The claim is one invoking the substantive rather than the procedural component of the Due Process Clause; petitioners do not claim that the State denied Joshua protection without according him appropriate procedural safeguards, but that it was categorically obligated to protect him in these circumstances."[105]

> "But nothing in the language of the Due Process Clause itself requires the State to protect the life, liberty, and property of its citizens against invasion by private actors. The Clause is phrased as a limitation on the State's power to act, not as a guarantee of certain minimal levels of safety and security. It forbids the State itself to deprive individuals of life, liberty, or property without "due process of law," but its language cannot fairly be extended to impose an affirmative obligation on the State to ensure that those interests do not come to harm through other means. Nor does history support such an expansive reading of the constitutional text. Like its counterpart in the Fifth Amendment, the Due Process Clause of the Fourteenth Amendment was intended to prevent government "from abusing [its] power, or employing it as an instrument of oppression[.]" Its purpose was to protect the people from the State, not to ensure that the State protected them from each other. The Framers were content to leave the extent of governmental obligation in the latter area to the democratic political processes."[106]

> "Consistent with these principles, our cases have recognized that the Due Process Clauses generally confer no affirmative right to governmental aid, even where such aid may be necessary to secure life, liberty, or property interests of which the government itself may not deprive the individual. As we said in *Harris v. McRae:* "Although the liberty protected by the Due Process Clause affords protection against unwarranted *government* interference... it does not confer an entitlement to such [governmental aid] as may be necessary to realize all the advantages of that freedom." If the Due Process Clause does not require the State to provide its citizens with particular protective services, it follows that the State cannot be held liable under the Clause for injuries that could have been averted had it chosen to provide them. As a general matter, then, we conclude that a State's failure to protect an individual against private violence simply does not constitute a violation of the Due Process Clause."[107]

---

105 *DeShaney,* 194–195.
106 *DeShaney,* 195–196.
107 *DeShaney,* 196–197.

Chief Justice Rehnquist also dealt in detail with the argument that the DSS's knowledge of Joshua DeShaney's situation created a special relationship with him that founded a constitutional duty to protect his rights. At the time of the *DeShaney* hearing, several Courts of Appeal had accepted this argument, but several had also rejected it. Chief Justice Rehnquist opted for the latter approach. He acknowledged the acceptance of such a special relationship and state duty to protect in cases such as *Estelle v Gamble*[108] and *Youngberg v Romeo*[109] where the state had incarcerated individuals or committed them to mental institutions, but this "*Estelle-Youngberg*" duty of care resulted, Chief Justice Rehnquist argued, from the fact that the state had deprived such individuals of the freedom to look after their own interests, not from mere knowledge of their situation.[110] He concluded his opinion as follows:

> "Judges and lawyers, like other humans, are moved by natural sympathy in a case like this to find a way for Joshua and his mother to receive adequate compensation for the grievous harm inflicted upon them. But before yielding to that impulse, it is well to remember once again that the harm was inflicted not by the State of Wisconsin, but by Joshua's father. The most that can be said of the state functionaries in this case is that they stood by and did nothing when suspicious circumstances dictated a more active role for them. In defense of them it must also be said that had they moved too soon to take custody of the son away from the father, they would likely have been met with charges of improperly intruding into the parent-child relationship, charges based on the same Due Process Clause that forms the basis for the present charge of failure to provide adequate protection. The people of Wisconsin may well prefer a system of liability which would place upon the State and its officials the responsibility for failure to act in situations such as the present one. They may create such a system, if they do not have it already, by changing the tort law of the State in accordance with the regular lawmaking process. But they should not have it thrust upon them by this Court's expansion of the Due Process Clause of the Fourteenth Amendment."[111]

We shall return repeatedly to these passages from Chief Justice Rehnquist's opinion in the rest of this chapter but also in later chapters. But as significant for the considerations that this and later chapters explore are a number of key passages from Justices Brennan's and Blackmun's dissenting opinions. The first that demands attention is the following from Justice Brennan's opinion:

> "In a constitutional setting that distinguishes sharply between action and inaction, one's characterization of the misconduct alleged under § 1983 may effectively decide the case.

---

108 429 U.S. 97 (1976).
109 457 U.S. 307 (1982).
110 *DeShaney*, 197–202.
111 *DeShaney*, 202–203.

Thus, by leading off with a discussion (and rejection) of the idea that the Constitution imposes on the States an affirmative duty to take basic care of their citizens, the Court foreshadows – perhaps even preordains – its conclusion that no duty existed even on the specific facts before us."[112]

The second important passage from Justice Brennan's opinion concerns his rejection of Chief Justice Rehnquist's *"Estelle-Youngberg"* analysis. At issue in the *Estelle* and *Youngberg* cases, he argued, were not just instances where the state deprived individuals of the liberty to look after themselves, but more broadly instances where the state acted in a way that may have interfered with that liberty in some way or another. In Joshua DeShaney's case, argued Justice Brennan, the Winnebago DSS took control of the situation in a way that warranted the impression that they would take proper care of his rights, thus making it unnecessary for other individuals, friends or family or neighbours, to pursue the matter further.[113]

"To put the point more directly, [an extensive record of] cases signal[s] that a State's prior actions may be decisive in analysing the constitutional significance of its inaction. I thus would locate the DeShaneys' claims within the framework of cases like *Youngberg* and *Estelle.*"[114]

"It simply belies reality, therefore, to contend that the State "stood by and did nothing" with respect to Joshua. Through its child-protection program, the State actively intervened in Joshua's life and, by virtue of this intervention, acquired ever more certain knowledge that Joshua was in grave danger. These circumstances, in my view, plant this case solidly within the tradition of cases like *Youngberg* and *Estelle.*"[115]

Justice Blackmun agreed fully with this reasoning:

As Justice Brennan demonstrates, the facts here involve not mere passivity, but active state intervention in the life of Joshua DeShaney – intervention that triggered a fundamental duty to aid the boy once the State learned of the severe danger to which he was exposed.

The Court fails to recognize this duty because it attempts to draw a sharp and rigid line between action and inaction. But such formalistic reasoning has no place in the interpretation of the broad and stirring Clauses of the Fourteenth Amendment. Indeed, I submit that these Clauses were designed, at least in part, to undo the formalistic legal reasoning that infected antebellum jurisprudence[.][116]

---

112 *DeShaney*, 204.
113 *DeShaney*, 209–210.
114 *DeShaney*, 208.
115 *DeShaney*, 210.
116 *DeShaney*, 212.

It is a good question whether the formalistic distinction between action and inaction at issue here underpins the formalistic distinction between private and public conduct that informs Chief Justice Rehnquist's opinion or, vice versa, whether the private/public distinction underpins the formalistic distinction between action and inaction. Suffice it to say that the *DeShaney* case illustrates the existence of a conceptual constellation in American constitutional jurisprudence under the auspices of which the public/private divide informs and sustains an action/inaction divide and/or vice versa. This much is abundantly clear from the second passage quoted above from Justice Rehnquist's opinion. One need not tease out this formalistic constellation further to pinpoint whether the chicken or the egg is first. But it is important to understand that it exists as such, and has existed thus right through times that in many ways rendered it conceptually and legal historically implausible, especially when one considers that state *inaction* has been recognised forcefully as state action in a number of Supreme Court Cases, and when one considers further that *The Civil Rights Cases* were amongst them.

That state *inaction* firmly constitutes state *action* has been recognised in United States Supreme Court jurisprudence ever since Justice Stone's decision in *Miller v Schoene*[117] in 1928. The facts of *Miller* made it abundantly clear that both action – destruction of cedar trees to save apple trees – and inaction – leaving the cedars and allowing the apple trees to die from blight – would have constituted a positive governmental choice. Both would therefore inevitably have been subject to the possibility of constitutional review. That the distinction between state action and inaction may never have enjoyed much or any significance as far as a threshold for constitutional review is concerned, may in fact be traced all the way back to the thinking of the very judge who first articulated the state action doctrine in *The Civil Rights Cases*. It would become clear from private correspondence that Justice Bradley never doubted that state inaction could also constitute state action for purposes of the Fourteenth Amendment.[118] Justice Bradley's private correspondence is interesting, but not really important for the point that is at issue here. One need not and should not resort to author's intent or psychological approaches to the interpretation of case law to highlight what is essential here. As Frank Michelman observes, the basic "Hohfeldian point" that state inaction constitutes state action as far as the Fourteenth

117 276 U.S. 272 (1928). Cf. the references to *Miller v Schoene* in Louis Michael Seidman, "The State Action Paradox," *Constitutional Commentary* 10 (1993): 379–401.
118 The letter is quoted in *Bell v Maryland* 378 U.S. 226, 309–310 (1964). Cf. also Ibid, 395.

Amendment is concerned, is written all over Justice Bradley's opinion in the *The Civil Rights Cases.*[119]

Chapter Three returns to Michelman's invocation of the "Hohfeldian point" that state inaction constitutes state action for purposes of the 14th Amendment and it will then become clearer what he means by this. Suffice it to say that the USSC's state action jurisprudence took leave of this Hohfeldian point in no uncertain terms. As *DeShaney* shows clearly, state inaction constitutes an absence of state action in the formalist mind set that *DeShaney* bequeathed to the USSC's jurisprudence. We return to *DeShaney* in later chapters to identify it, along with *Flagg Brothers, Inc. v Brooks*, as a key statement of Justice Rehnquist's judicial abdication of the sovereignty of the people of the United States. Suffice it to observe for now that the refusal to recognise state inaction as state action lies at the heart of the fundamental difference between the USSC's state action jurisprudence and the GFCC's horizontal effect jurisprudence, especially the jurisprudence with which the GFCC moved to supplement or accentuate its earlier jurisprudence in *Lüth* (1957) when it decided the *Erste Abtreibung* (*First Abortion*) case in 1975. In deciding *Erste Abtreibung* as it did, the GFCC introduced a new wave of horizontal effect jurisprudence in Germany in which the *state's duty to protect and promote* the rights embodied in the GG became the principal consideration. This new horizontal effect jurisprudence is generally known as the *Schutzpflicht* or "duty to protect" jurisprudence in Germany.[120] This "duty to protect" jurisprudence avowed in *Erste Abtreibung* made the avowal of state sovereignty already evident in *Lüth* even clearer than it may have been before. Recognition that state inaction could constitute state action for purposes of the Fourteenth Amendment in *DeShaney* would have founded a similar *duty to protect* jurisprudence in the United States. *DeShaney*, however, signalled the USSC's unwillingness to recognise the state's duty to protect constitutional rights against threats by non-state actors in the way the GFCC came to do in *Erste Abtreibung* and the SACC finally came round to do in its *Carmichele* decision in 2002. This then is the major difference between the constitutional jurisprudence of the USSC and the GFCC (and the SACC): The former turns

---

119 Michelman, "The Bill of Rights, the Common Law, and the Freedom-Friendly State," 404.
120 Whether this was really a new turn in the GFCC's jurisprudence is debatable and has been subject to debate. Cf. Martin Oldiges, "Neue Aspekte der Grundrechtsgeltung im Privatrecht," in *Staat Wirtschaft Steuern*, ed. Rudolf Wendt, Wolfram Höfling, and Ulrich Karpen (C.F. Müller, 1996), 300: "Zwar findet sich im Handelsvertreter-Beschluß die Wendung vom Schutzauftrag der Verfassung ... doch ist auch dort wenig von einem dogmatischen Neuansatz zu spüren; in späteren Entscheidungen dominiert dann wieder der Gedanke der Grundrechtsausstrahlung."

largely on a disavowal of state sovereignty, the latter on a clear avowal of state sovereignty.

Erste Abtreibung, however, did more than affirm the avowal of state sovereignty already evident in *Lüth*. It also affirmed this avowal of sovereignty in a way that made the questionable form of this avowal in *Lüth* glaringly obvious. To be sure, the questionable form of the avowal of sovereignty in *Lüth* does not concern the avowal itself, but the questionable notion of the "radiation" or "*Ausstrahlungseffekt*" of constitutional values through which this avowal was articulated. This "radiation of constitutional values" is exactly that which American constitutional scholars and lawyers call substantive due process. It is the substantive due process jurisprudence of the majority judgment in *Erste Abtreibung* that drove the GFCC into the troubled waters from which it only managed to emerge with much difficulty in the *Zweite Abtreibung* case.

The GFCC decided *Erste Abtreibung* two years after the USSC decided *Roe v Wade*. In stark contrast to the USSC, the GFCC insisted that the GG demanded the criminalisation of abortion. It did so on the basis of a substantive due process jurisprudence that it expressly derived from its judgment in *Lüth*. However, substantive due process accusations also came to haunt the majority decision in *Roe*, notwithstanding the fact that it reached the exact opposite of the decision reached in *Erste Abtreibung*. The theory of horizontal effect that will be developed towards the end of this book requires that we take a close look at what happened here.

X The Duty to Protect: *Roe v Wade* and *Erste Abtreibung*

Roe v Wade and *Erste Abtreibung* are not generally regarded as state action and horizontal effect cases. *Roe v Wade* is surely not considered as a state action case in American jurisprudence. This may well be a result of the way the substantive questions in *Roe* dominated the American political and jurisprudential imagination. In contrast to typical state action cases, the substantive demands of the United States Bill of Rights in *Roe* largely eclipsed the procedural question whether the Bill of Rights applies or not. When *Roe* enters the spotlight, attention is usually immediately drawn to the substantive tension between the right to life and freedom of choice. Moreover, *Roe* evidently concerned the question of the constitutionality of legislation, as did *Erste Abtreibung*. How could there be significant questions of horizontal effect in these cases if vertical effect or state action is evidently written all over them? This chapter will nevertheless insist that *Roe* and *Erste Abtreibung* are horizontal effect cases. It will insist, moreover, that the decision of the USSC in *Roe* and the decision of the GFCC in *Erste Abtreibung* and the remarkable differences between them raise crucial questions for any attempt to come to terms with the core questions raised by the horizontal effect of constitutional values and the implications of such horizontal effect for our understanding of constitutional review; hence the need to take a good look at them and to add them to the collection of core horizontal effect/state action cases thus far assembled in this chapter. Given their identical material concerns, we will discuss them together.

A comparative discussion of *Roe v Wade* and *Erste Abtreibung* might begin with the question as to which decision was right and which was wrong. In *Roe* the USSC judged the overly broad criminalisation of abortion in Articles 1191–1194 and 1196 of the Texas Penal Code to fall foul of the Fourteenth Amendment and struck it down. In *Erste Abtreibung* the GFCC judged *the Fünftes Gesetz zur Reform des Strafrechts* (Fifth Criminal Law Reform Act) of 18 June 1974 to fall foul of Articles 2(2)1 and 1(1) of the GG for failing to criminalise abortion broadly enough. Critically at issue in both cases were, in other words, the criminalisation in Texas and the non-criminalisation in Germany of elective (not medically indicated) abortions during the first trimester of pregnancy. *Roe* judged criminalisation of such abortion to be unconstitutional. *Erste Abtreibung* found non-criminalisation to be unconstitutional.

Considering their diametrically opposite outcomes, the question as to which decision was right or better and which wrong or worse is bound to haunt any comparison between them. However, one might also want to steer away from this question by simply insisting that different rules apply for different places and different people and different times. In other words, one can forward a cultural relativist and historicist argument according to which the GFCC got the matter right for Germans and the USSC got it right for Americans. Abortion was acceptable and legal in the United States in 1973 and still is, might one argue. Abortion was correspondingly unacceptable and illegal in Germany in 1975 and only became more acceptable later. And that is the end of the story. This was indeed what the majority opinion suggested in *Erste Abtreibung* in 1975. American jurisprudence regarding abortion, respectable as it may be in the context of America, cannot apply to Germany, given Germany's need to constantly keep in mind the dark years of its National Socialistic past and given the real connection between these dark years and abominable abortion practices. In the words of the GFCC:

> "The express inclusion of the self-evident right to life in the German Foundational Law – quite in contrast with the Weimar constitution – must mainly be understood as a reaction

to the 'annihilation of life that is unworthy of life,' the 'final solution' and the 'liquidation' that the national socialist regime pursued as [fundamental] aims of the state."[121]

"The arrangement concluded in the Fifth Criminal Law Reform Act has up to now been defended with reference to the fact that other democratic states of the West had recently "liberalised" or "modernised" the criminal provisions regarding the termination of pregnancy even further... This consideration cannot influence the decision that has to be made here... The Foundational law is founded on principles of state formation that can only be explained with reference to the historical experience and the spiritual and moral response to the system of National Socialism. This does not imply a judgmental denunciation of other legal orders that have not had similar experiences with their legal systems. Different historical developments, different political circumstances and different political philosophical foundations required and allowed them to make different decisions."[122]

Should one recast these contentions in the language of John Rawls, one could impute to the GFCC an insistence on the significantly different "burdens of judgment" that inform a nation's constitutional law and jurisprudence.[123] Constitu-

---

121 Translated from *Erste Abtreibung* 36: "Die ausdrücklichen Aufnahme des an sich selbstverständlichen Rechts auf Leben in das Grundgesetz – anders als etwa in der Weimar Verfassung – erklärt sich hauptsächlich als Reaktion auf die "Vernichtung lebensunwerten Lebens," auf "Endlösung" und "Liquidierung," die vom nationalsozialistischen Regime als staatliche Massnahmen durchgeführt würden."

122 Translated from *Erste Abtreibung* 66–68: "Die im Fünften Strafrechtsreformgesetz getroffene Regelung wird bisweilen mit dem Hinweis verteidigt, daß in anderen demokratischen Ländern der westlichen Welt in jüngster Zeit die strafrechtlichen Vorschriften über den Schwangerschaftsabbruch in ähnlicher oder noch weitergehender Weise "liberalisiert" oder "modernisiert" worden seien.... Diese Erwägungen können die hier zu treffende Entscheidung nicht beeinflussen.... Dem Grundgesetz liegen Prinzipien der Staatsgestaltung zugrunde, die sich nur aus der geschichtlichen Erfahrung und der geistig-sittlichen Auseinandersetzung mit dem vorangegangenen System des Nationalsozialismus erklären lassen.... Damit wird kein absprechendes Urteil über andere Rechtsordnungen gefällt, "die diese Erfahrungen mit einem Rechtsystem nicht gemacht haben und die aufgrund einer anders verlaufenen geschichtlichen Entwicklung, anderer staatspolitischer Gegebenheiten und staatsphilosophischer Grundauffassungen eine solche Entscheidung für sich nicht getroffen haben."

123 Cf. Frank Michelman, "Human Rights and the Limits of Constitutional Theory," *Ratio Juris* 13, no. 1 (2000): 71 note 9, referring to John Rawls, "The Idea of Public Reason Revisited," in *Collected Papers* (Cambridge, Massachusetts: Harvard University Press, 1999): "John Rawls calls 'burdens of judgment' the causes of unliquidatable disagreement about justice among persons who, as reasonable, all observe and report honestly, argue cogently, and 'share a desire to honor fair terms of cooperation.' Among these causes Rawls lists the likelihood that 'the way we assess evidence and weigh moral and political values is shaped by our total experience, our whole course of life up to now; and our total experiences must always differ. Thus, in a modern society with its numerous offices and positions, its various divisions of labor, its many social groups and their ethnic variety, citizens' total experiences are disparate enough for their judgments to diverge, at least to some degree on many if not most cases of significant complexity.'"

tional rules concerning abortion can accordingly not be included under the uniting commands of an international public reason or "law of peoples" (a set of elementary principles of reason which all citizens of all nations can be expected to endorse despite their different cultural and religious backgrounds). From the perspective of this Rawlsian framework of thinking, the GFCC would seem to have considered abortion law as an element of comprehensive worldviews (the full set of religious and moral convictions that a specific culture or people might endorse). The GFCC also appears to have considered this comprehensive worldview as a crucial criterion for the correct understanding and application of Germany's constitutional law. In this regard they would seem to have moved completely in the opposite direction of the one Rawls had in mind for the articulation, interpretation and application of constitutional law in pluralist societies with competing comprehensive worldviews. In such societies, argued Rawls, constitutional law had best be restricted as far as possible to principles of public reason which every one in those societies could be expected to respect and endorse.[124]

Well, that is Rawls' view, not ours, the GFCC might well have responded to this observation in 1975. Or it may have responded that Germany happens to be one of those countries where no such deep divisions prevail as far as comprehensive worldviews are concerned. Their view was obviously that Germany had one set of values, at least with regard to the criminalisation of abortion, which all Germans apart from a deviant few endorsed. Remarkable in this regard, we shall see below, is the fact that the majority opinion in *Roe* justified its decision in favour of the non-criminalisation of abortion in very similar terms. Despite appearances and protestations to the contrary, Justice Blackmun also handed down a decision that suggested that all Americans, apart from some exceptional deviants, shared the same values regarding abortion in 1973. That these were the positions taken by the majority opinion in both cases will become abundantly clear below. Suffice it to observe for now that these majority opinions in *Roe* and *Erste Abtreibung* basically rule out any significant comparison between United States and German constitutional law regarding abortion. If the difference between the two systems of constitutional law simply relates to their different cultural or historical backgrounds, and if there are no transnational or universal principles with regard to which both systems can be compared, all attempts at comparison must collapse into mere cultural, zoological or ontological description. The international "moot court competition" and normative reflection implicit in all significant comparative studies of law then becomes impossible.

---

124 Cf. Rawls, *Political Liberalism*; Rawls, *The Law of Peoples* (Harvard University Press, 1999).

Normative comparison of *Roe* and *Erste Abtreibung* nevertheless does not seem to be as impossible as the majority opinion in both of them suggested. Both of them were accompanied by minority opinions that in some respects mirrored the normative position reflected in the majority opinion of "the other side." In other words, the minority opinion in *Roe* mirrored features of the majority opinion in *Erste Abtreibung*, and the minority opinion in *Erste Abtreibung* echoed aspects of the majority opinion in *Roe*. The suggestion that deep cultural or historical divisions rendered normative comparison of German and United States abortion law meaningless in the 1970s would therefore seem exaggerated, for the apparent differences *between* the two legal systems were evidently also present *within* the two systems themselves. Both systems were evidently marked internally by the same conflicting burdens of judgement. This not only opened the door for significant comparison of the two sets of judicial responses and the two legal systems. It also would seem to have required from both judiciaries a regard for the internal tensions that marked them, and a method or strategy with recourse to which these tensions could be handled. In other words, both judiciaries may have benefitted considerably from the strategy Rawls recommends under circumstances like these. According to Rawls, all instances of public reason – among which constitutional law is surely one – should withdraw as far as possible from the divergent burdens of judgment that comprehensive worldviews would want to impose on them. Public reason requires that the scope of constitutional deliberation be restricted to the narrow band of values that reflects an overlapping consensus between the competing worldviews that are locked in conflict or contestation. In the end, we shall see presently, only the minority opinion in *Erste Abtreibung* evinced a regard for this wisdom or strategy.

The decisions in *Roe* and *Erste Abtreibung* nevertheless did not only turn on arguments regarding different histories and different "burdens of judgment." The different burdens of judgment were also informed by different convictions regarding the inception of human life. They espoused very different views regarding the point in time in the course of a pregnancy at which human life begins. Justice Blackmun stated expressly in *Roe:*

> "The appellee and certain *amici* argue that the fetus is a "person" within the language and meaning of the Fourteenth Amendment. In support of this, they outline at length and in detail the well-known facts of fetal development. If this suggestion of personhood is established, the appellant's case, of course, collapses, for the fetus' right to life would then be guaranteed specifically by the Amendment. The appellant conceded as much on reargument. On the other hand, the appellee conceded on reargument that no case could be

> cited that holds that a fetus is a person within the meaning of the Fourteenth Amendment."[125]

Now, National Socialism surely had a devastating impact on the termination of both born and unborn life while in power in Germany. And as the arguments of the GFCC in *Erste Abtreibung* make clear, this history would have a lasting influence on how later generations of Germans would come to think about termination of born and unborn life. But National Socialism, for all its deluded imaginations of ever-lasting omnipotence, surely could not affect the moment in time that human life commenced. On this point one would surely think that the inception of human life concerns a biological fact, the recognition of which should command universal consensus. At least as far as the species *homo sapiens* is concerned, the biological or physiological beginning of life cannot vary that much from continent to continent, culture to culture and country to country. At least here then, might one argue, should a certain universalism prevail that disallows the endorsement of different competing conceptions. The exact time at which human life commences can surely not be subject to burdens of judgment and cultural or historical contexts. Yet, the majority opinions of the German and American courts already parted ways on this question. They basically disputed one another's assessment of relevant biological facts. The GFCC insisted that human life basically commences fourteen days after conception. It argued that there is no way of identifying a later moment that significantly divides embryonic development into discernable pre- and post-inception of stages of life. Here is how it articulated the matter:

> "Life in the sense of the historical existence of a human individual commences according to ascertained biological and psychological knowledge in any case on the fourteenth day after conception (nesting, individuation). The process of development that that thus begins is a continuing process that evinces no distinct moments that allow for a precise delimitation of the different phases of human life."[126]

In stark contrast to this reasoning of the GFCC, and not unaware of "new embryological data according to which conception is a 'process' over time and

---

125 *Roe*, 156.

126 Translated from *Erste Abtreibung*, 37: "Leben im Sinne der geschichtlichen Existenz eines menschlichen Individuums besteht nach gesicherter biologisch-psychologischer Erkenntnis jedenfalls vom 14. Tage nach der Empfängnis (Nidation, Individuation) an .... Der damit begonnene Entwicklungsprozeß ist ein kontinuierlicher Vorgang, der keine scharfen Einschnitte aufweist und eine genaue Abgrenzung der verschiedenen Entwicklungsstufen des menschlichen Lebens nicht zuläßt."

not an event,"[127] Justice Blackmun would contend on behalf of the USSC that American common law had always taken the time of the "quickening of life" as its orientation point for purposes of setting a boundary between legal and illegal abortions. And the early anti-abortion statutes that came to replace the common law abortion rules in the course of the 19th century, most of them enacted only towards the middle of the 19th century, continued to be rather lenient with abortions "before quickening."

> "In this country, the law in effect in all but a few States until mid-19th century was the pre-existing English common law. Connecticut, the first State to enact abortion legislation, adopted in 1821 that part of Lord Ellenborough's Act that related to a woman "quick with child." The death penalty was not imposed. Abortion before quickening was made a crime in that State only in 1860. In 1828, New York enacted legislation that, in two respects, was to serve as a model for early anti-abortion statutes. First, while barring destruction of an unquickened fetus as well as a quick fetus, it made the former only a misdemeanor, but the latter second-degree manslaughter. Second, it incorporated a concept of therapeutic abortion by providing that an abortion was excused if it "shall have been necessary to preserve the life of such mother, or shall have been advised by two physicians to be necessary for such purpose." By 1840, when Texas had received the common law, only eight American States had statutes dealing with abortion. It was not until after the War Between the States that legislation began generally to replace the common law. Most of these initial statutes dealt severely with abortion after quickening but were lenient with it before quickening... Gradually, in the middle and late 19th century the quickening distinction disappeared from the statutory law of most States and the degree of the offense and the penalties were increased. By the end of the 1950's, a large majority of the jurisdictions banned abortion, however and whenever performed, unless done to save or preserve the life of the mother."[128]

Justice Blackmun recalled this history to make the point that the broad criminalisation of all abortions (except those for which very clear and specific grounds of justification could be offered) that came to dominate America by the mid-20th century was not really part of the American legal psyche. "All this," he contended, "together with our observation, *supra*, that throughout the major portion of the 19th century prevailing legal abortion practices were far freer than they are today, persuades us that the word 'person,' as used in the Fourteenth Amendment, does not include the unborn."[129]

This basic finding regarding the scope of the word "person" in the Fourteenth Amendment allowed Justice Blackmun to approach the question in *Roe*

---

127 *Roe*, 161.
128 *Roe*, 138–139.
129 *Roe*, 158.

as one that turned on the constitutionality of a legislative curtailment of a right, namely, the claimant's right to privacy and reproductive autonomy. Cast in this way, *Roe* seems to confront our engagement with it in the context of the horizontal effect of fundamental rights with a problem. At issue in *Roe* seems to be a simple vertical application case, a simple case regarding the constitutionality of the vertical relation between state and citizens, not the horizontal relation between citizens. Considering that it is, according to Justice Blackmun, only the pregnant woman's liberty that is at stake, there can be no question here about the state having or not having to protect a Fourteenth Amendment right against threats from non-state third parties. There is simply one person too few around to establish third party relationships here. Going strictly by Justice Blackmun's reasoning, the discussion of *Roe* in a book on the horizontal effect of constitutional rights would seem to be out of place.

The GFCC's approach would seem to at least spare us this problem. The recognition of the existence of an independent life from the moment of conception onwards gathers together enough of a crowd to allow for a meaningful invocation of third persons and third person relationships. Consider the exact way the GFCC phrased the matter:

> "The duty of the state to protect every human life can be inferred directly from Article 2(2)1 of the Foundational Law. It derives, moreover, also from the express stipulation in Article 1 (1)2 of the Foundational law, for it is also implied in the protection of human dignity guaranteed by Article 1(1)2. Developing life is also thus protected. When human life exists, it is entitled to human dignity. This is so irrespective whether the holder of this right is aware of this dignity and able to enforce it. The capacities that are already embedded in human existence when it begins, suffice to found human dignity.
>
> The controversial question whether the nasciturus is a subject of fundamental rights or whether, in view of his lacking legal capacity and constitutional legal capacity, it is just protected by the objective norms of the constitution, is often mooted in case law, scientific writings and also in the matter before this court. This question need not be answered here. This Court has always maintained that the fundamental rights principles of the Foundational Law do not only contain negative individual rights against the state, but also embody an objective normative order. This normative order constitutes a fundamental constitutional decision that governs all areas of law and lays down demands and guidelines for legislation, administration and judicial decisions."[130]

130 Translated from *Erste Abtreibung*, 41: "Die Pflicht des Staates, jedes menschliche Leben zu schützen, lässt sich deshalb bereits unmittelbar aus Art 2 Abs. 2 Satz 1 GG ableiten. Sie ergibt sich darüber hinaus auch aus der ausdrücklichen Vorschrift des Art. 1 Abs. 1 Satz 2 GG; denn das sich entwickelnde Leben nimmt auch an dem Schutz teil, den Art 1 Abs. 1 GG der Menschenwürde gewährt. Wo menschliches Leben existiert, kommt ihm Menschenwürde zu; es ist nicht entscheidend, ob der Träger sich dieser Würde bewusst ist und sie selbst zu wahren weiß. Die von Anfang an im menschlichen Sein angelegten potentiellen Fähigkeiten genügen, um die

The "duty to protect" or "*Schutzpflicht*" jurisprudence that these passages introduced in German constitutional case law would only enter the line of traditional or typical horizontal effect/*Drittwirkung* cases with the *Handelsvertreter* decision of 1990.[131] It is clear, however, that the GFCC moved consciously into the neighbourhood of horizontal effect or *Drittwirkung* here. The reference to its judgment in *Lüth* that accompanies its invocation of an objective order of values leaves little room for doubt in this regard. And should the acceptance that unborn life constitutes a constitutional claimant with fully fledged subjective rights not yet convince one that abortion raises a *Drittwirkung* problematic, the GFCC also wasted no time in driving this point home:

> "The nasciturus is an independent human being that is protected by the constitution. The fact that this is so endows the termination of pregnancy with a social dimension that warrants and requires regulation by the state."[132]

Can one impute a similar social dimension to Justice Blackmun's solitary and solo woman for whom the termination of pregnancy turned exclusively on her right to privacy and reproductive autonomy? For if no sociality or no third party dimension can be restored in the context of *Roe*, one would indeed be facing the puzzling situation that *Erste Abtreibung* constitutes a horizontal effect or *Drittwirkung* case whereas *Roe* does not, notwithstanding the fact that they both dealt with the exact same question. Perhaps this was to be expected. If different jurisdictions and different legal histories can have such remarkably different impacts on moral questions and even on biological facts such as the inception of life, they surely should also be able to effect the taxonomies of their respective

---

Menschenwürde zu begründen. Hingegen braucht die im vorliegenden Verfahren wie auch in der Rechtsprechung und im wissenschafltlichen Schriftum umstrittene Frage nicht entschieden zu werden, ob der nasciturus selbst Grundrechtsträger ist oder aber wegen mangelender Rechts- und Grundrechtsfähigkeit "nur" von den objektiven Normen der Verfassung in seinem Recht auf Leben geschützt wird. Nach der ständigen Rechtsprechung des Bundesverfassungsgerichts enthalten die Grundrechtsnormen nicht nur subjektive Abwehrrechte des Einzelnen gegen den Staat, sondern sie verkörpern zugleich eine objektive Wertordnung, die als verfassungsrechtliche Grundentscheidung für alle Bereiche des Rechts gilt und Richtlinien und Impulse für Gesetzgebung, Verwaltung und Rechtsprechung gibt."

131 BVerfGe 81, 242. Chapter Four returns to this "duty to protect" turn in German horizontal effect jurisprudence and the question whether this was really a turn or basically the commencement of a stronger emphasis on "duty to protect" that was already evident in *Lüth*.

132 Translated from *Erste Abtreibung*, 42: "Da indessen der nasciturus ein selbständiges menschliches Wesen ist, das unter dem Schutz der Verfassung steht, kommt dem Schwangerschaftsabbruch *eine soziale Dimension* zu, die ihn der Regelung durch den Staat zugänglich und bedürftig macht." (emphasis added)

legal systems differently. That which counts as a relation between citizens in one country, should then undoubtedly be able to count as a strictly citizen-state relationship in another. If the court of one country can count three parties in the dispute so as to allow for *Drittwirkung*, another can surely only count two. If courts can bend biology, they should surely also be able to bend maths. Perhaps this is what sovereignty is all about.

The recognition of *the social dimension of abortion* in *Erste Abtreibung* is of profound significance. It is, however, also fundamentally miscued. It is profound for reasons of its emphasis on the social or third party dimension that undoubtedly makes the constitutional review of abortion law an instance of horizontal effect or *Drittwirkung*. It is miscued for reasons of locating this social or third party dimension in the relation between the mother and unborn child. The social and third party dimension that is fundamentally at issue here is a different one. It is the one identified in the dissenting judgment in *Erste Abtreibung*, namely, the relationship between the conflicting convictions that informed the legislative process.

The dissenting opinion in *Erste Abtreibung* recognised that the legislative process and the legislation under review had already gone as far as one can reasonably go to accommodate a deeply divided public (*tief gespaltene Öffentlichkeit*).[133] It was therefore not the role of the court to impose substantive moral postulates on society. This is how the minority opinion phrased the matter:

> "A pluralistic, worldview-neutral and liberal democratic society requires that postulates of fundamental convictions be left to social forces. The state should practice reticence in this regard."[134]

This insight was not far from Justice Blackmun's mind when he articulated the majority opinion in *Roe*. This is clear from his extensive endorsement of Justice Holmes' dissent in *Lochner v New York* merely four paragraphs into his opinion:

> "We bear in mind Mr. Justice Holmes' admonition in his now-vindicated dissent in *Lochner* v. *New York* that [the Constitution] is made for people of fundamentally differing views, and the accident of our finding certain opinions natural and familiar or novel and even shocking ought not to conclude our judgment upon the question whether statutes embodying them conflict with the Constitution of the United States."[135]

133 *Erste Abtreibung*, 85.
134 Translated from *Erste Abtreibung*, 94: "In einem pluralistischen, weltanschaulich neutralen und freiheitlichen demokratischen Gemeinwesen bleibt es den gesellschaftlichen Kräften überlassen, Gesinnungspostulate zu statuieren. Der Staat hat darin Enthaltsamkeit zu üben."
135 *Roe*, 117, referring to *Lochner v New York* 198 U.S. 45 (1905) at 76.

The judicial temptation or inclination to impose substantive readings of the Constitution on patently divided societies became notorious in the United States with the USSC's decision in *Lochner v New York* in 1905. This kind of reasoning subsequently became known as *substantive due process review* and it is against such a substantive reading of the Constitution that Holmes protested with his famous dissent in *Lochner*. The Constitution is not, he insisted, a charter for Herbert Spencer economics.[136] However, Justice Blackmun's reliance on Justice Holmes' vindicated dissent in *Lochner* is patently ironic, if not downright contradictory. For it was indeed Justice Blackmun's majority opinion in *Roe* that was striking down democratic legislation on the basis of its substantive incompatibility with the Constitution. Both Justice Stewart's separate but concurring opinion and Justice Rehnquist's dissenting opinion wasted no time to point this out in *Roe*. Justice Stewart supported the decision, but he realised that he had to square this support with the fact that the USSC had, only ten years before, announced boldly that it had once and for all taken leave of substantive due process review:

> "In 1963, this Court, in *Ferguson* v. *Skrupa*, 372 U.S. 726, purported to sound the death knell for the doctrine of substantive due process, a doctrine under which many state laws had in the past been held to violate the Fourteenth Amendment. As Mr. Justice Black's opinion for the Court in *Skrupa* put it: "We have returned to the original constitutional proposition that courts do not substitute their social and economic beliefs for the judgment of legislative bodies, who are elected to pass laws."[137]

Justice Stewart had no doubt that Justice Blackmun's opinion for the majority evinced a clear case of substantive due process, but he reconciled himself with this because of the fact that the bold resolution in *Skrupa* never to engage in substantive due process again already fell apart two years later, in *Griswold* v. *Connecticut*.[138] Justice Rehnquist was less forgiving. He took the majority opinion to task for invoking Justice Holmes' protest against substantive due process review in *Lochner*, on the one hand, while actually indulging in that same substantive due process, on the other:

> "While the Court's opinion quotes from the dissent of Mr. Justice Holmes in *Lochner* v. *New York*, 198 U.S. 45, 74 (1905), the result it reaches is more closely attuned to the majority opinion of Mr. Justice Peckham in that case. As in *Lochner* and similar cases applying substantive due process standards to economic and social welfare legislation, the adoption of the compelling state interest standard will inevitably require this Court to examine the legisla-

136 Cf. 198 U.S. 45 (1905) at 75.
137 *Roe*, 167.
138 381 U.S. 479 (1965).

> tive policies and pass on the wisdom of these policies in the very process of deciding whether a particular state interest put forward may or may not be 'compelling.'"[139]

The word "compelling" in the last line of this passage points to one of the technicalities that accompany the distinction between substantive and procedural due process in the jurisprudence of the USSC. American constitutional jurisprudence distinguishes three different levels of scrutiny, namely, rational basis review, intermediate review and strict scrutiny. Rational basis review is the standard form of review that simply scrutinises whether the legislation reviewed constitutes a *rational means to a legitimate state end.*[140] Intermediate review scrutinises whether the legislation at issue pursues an *important state end* and does so *effectively.* In other words, if it does not effectively promote or further the important state end, it will not pass scrutiny. Closely associated with and often used interchangeably with intermediate review is the level of scrutiny called "heightened scrutiny" which supposedly adds a third element to the two elements of intermediate scrutiny. Apart from the *effective furtherance* of an *important state end*, it also requires that the legislation is *indispensible* for the furtherance of the important state end.[141] The last and highest form of scrutiny is strict review. Strict review requires that the legislation under review be *narrowly tailored* to pursue a *compelling* state interest. Strict review invariably gives rise to instances of substantive due process review procedures. It allows the court to strike down legislation passed by democratic majorities in the name of some fundamental constitutional value, unless that legislation can be

139 *Roe*, 174.

140 This rational relation test can be traced to the following dictum of Justice Brewer in *Gulf, Colorado And Santa Fe Railway Company v Ellis* 165 U.S. 150 (1897) at 155: "[A classification] must always rest upon some difference which bears a reasonable and just relation to the act in respect to which the classification is proposed, and can never be made arbitrarily, and without any such basis." Tribe (*American Constitutional Law*, 1439–1440) also traces rational purpose scrutiny to *Powel v Pennsylvania* 127 U.S. 678 (1888) where Justice Harlan held state regulation consistent with equal protection provided it "place[d] under the same restrictions, and subject[ed] to like penalties and burdens, all who [were] embraced by its prohibitions; thus recognising and preserving the principle of equality among those engaged in the same [regulated activities]." This test eventually returned to the stricter requirement in *Gulf, Colorado And Santa Fe Railway Company v Ellis* that the classification of those who are singled out by regulation had to be rational and reasonable. Cf. *Rinaldi v Yeager* 384 U.S. 305 (1966) at 308–309 and *McLaughlin v Florida* 379 U.S. 184 (1966) at 191. The argument in the text above suggests that the Texas abortion legislation subject to review in *Roe* should not have passed the weaker form of rational scrutiny articulated by Justice Brewer in *Ellis*.

141 Cf. *Craig v Boren* 429 U.S. 190 (1976): the case in which heightened scrutiny was introduced as a third tier of review alongside rational basis and strict scrutiny.

shown to pursue a compelling state interest while detracting as little as possible from the fundamental constitutional value at stake.

The strict requirement that legislation be narrowly tailored to pursue a compelling state interest usually applies in cases where the legislation under review either negates a fundamental right or effects a "classified" discriminatory measure. "Classified" discriminatory measures are measures that affect classes or groups of individuals that have historically been exposed to debilitating discrimination and/or are known to be vulnerable to such debilitating discrimination. Discrimination on the basis of race would therefore typically elicit strict scrutiny.[142] Legislative or executive action that discriminates on the basis of sex or gender would typically be subjected to intermediate review or heightened scrutiny. Legislation or executive action that merely affects ordinary liberties (that do not constitute fundamental rights) negatively merely requires rational basis scrutiny. In other words, legislation that rationally promotes legitimate state ends can interfere with ordinary liberties without constitutional sanction.

This, then, is the basic jurisprudential framework that informed the disagreement between Justices Blackmun's and Rehnquist's opinions in *Roe*. Justice Blackmun consistently considered the freedom of a woman to terminate pregnancy during the first trimester as a fundamental right, legislative interference with which has to be narrowly tailored to pursue a compelling state interest; hence his finding that the Texas penal code, if taken to pursue a compelling state interest, was not sufficiently narrowly tailored. Its sweep was simply too broad.[143] Justice Rehnquist regarded the freedom to terminate pregnancy during the first semester as nothing more than a liberty that any rational legislation could curtail.[144] The substantive dimension of rational basis review is negligibly thin. It basically reduces constitutional review to procedural due process. The substantive dimension of strict review, on the other hand, is thick. Strict review invariably involves application of substantive norms that underpin fundamental rights. Such rights simply trump ordinary legislative abridgements that do not pursue a compelling state interest in a narrowly tailored fashion.

We saw above how the GFCC made the decision in *Erste Abtreibung* turn on the social or third party relation between the pregnant woman and the unborn life inside her womb. Justice Blackmun steered clear of this option. In fact, he seemed well on the way of locating the third party relationship in the way the dissenting judges did in *Erste Abtreibung*. It looked as if he too was going to

142 Cf. *United States v Carolene Products Co.* 304 U.S. 144 (1938).
143 *Roe*, 164.
144 *Roe*, 172–173.

take deeply divided public opinion regarding abortion as the social or third part dimension in *Roe*. His invocation of Justice Holmes' dissent in *Lochner* surely suggested as much. In the end, however, he stopped short of doing so by considering reproductive autonomy as a right that no other person and therefore no legislator could trump without compelling justification. Reproductive autonomy was not for him, a liberty that others could curtail with recourse to merely rational legislation.

In other words, by viewing reproductive autonomy as a fundamental *right*, Justice Blackmun turned it into a democratically incontestable autonomy. This is essentially what happens when someone invokes a *right*. By calling some instance of autonomy a right – interference with which then requires strict scrutiny – one either dismisses the possibility of any democratic curtailment of that autonomy, or limits such possibility incisively. The invocation of a right basically suggests prevalence of deep consensus with regard to which no reasonable debate or democratic contestation can be contemplated. By taking this step with regard to reproductive autonomy, Justice Blackmun basically destroyed the social and horizontal dimension of the question that he himself had commenced to highlight with reference to Justice Holmes' dissent in *Lochner*.

Was there a way in which Justice Blackmun could have endorsed reproductive autonomy in *Roe* without betraying Justice Holmes' dissent in *Lochner?* There was, as the dissenting opinion in *Erste Abtreibung* shows clearly. The majority opinion in *Erste Abtreibung*, we saw, located the social or third party dimension in abortion cases in the relation between the mother and the unborn child. It did so by insisting on scientific evidence that the development of early embryonic life does not allow for the identification of distinct phases with regard to which the exact inception of individual life can be identified. Separate individual life and the existence of a third party relation between mother and embryo must therefore be assumed from the moment of conception, the majority insisted. Having taken this line of thinking, the majority moved on to affirm the social or third party relationship between pregnant woman and embryo, on the one hand, but also to deny it again, on the other. It firstly affirmed the third party relation by recognising some circumstances under which the two fundamental rights of woman and nasciturus could legitimately compete with one another. However, it ultimately also denied this third party relation again by recognising the "absolute" right to life of the nasciturus when circumstances do not indicate exceptional limits to this right – as would be the case, for instance, if continuation of the pregnancy would seriously threaten the health of the mother.

The absolute right to life of the nasciturus, the majority opinion in *Erste Abtreibung* argued, tolerates no significant competition in cases of merely elective terminations of pregnancy. By casting the competition in these terms, the majority opinion effectively annulled the pregnant woman's reproductive autonomy. Her concerns would only compete with those of the nasciturus if her health and not just her autonomy were at stake. In other words, the pregnant woman's concerns were effectively removed from the scene as far as merely elective (medically unindicated) terminations of pregnancy are concerned. This is how the majority opinion articulated their stance in this regard:

> "The unborn life is destroyed by the termination of pregnancy. The principle of the balancing of competing constitutional right protections in view of article 19(2) of the Foundational Law therefore requires that precedence be given to protecting the life of the nasciturus. This precedence remains valid for the whole pregnancy and may not be questioned during any particular phase of the pregnancy."[145]

The majority in *Erste Abtreibung* could end up with this apparently simple, clear and uncontroversial resolution of the real conflict in the case by turning a reality that is, at best, scientifically and epistemologically ambiguous and subject to continuing and most likely interminable contestation (gradual development of embryonic life does not allow for assessing the exact inception of individual life) into one that is morally, socially and legally unambiguous and incontestable (life and the right to life must therefore be assumed to commence with conception). The concern with the "scientific" or "factual truth" regarding the matter allowed the majority opinion to simply override the moral and social context of interminable disagreement and contestation. This is how it ultimately came to negate the social or third party dimension of abortion that it initially recognised as a crucial element of the question at stake. It invoked "incontestable truths" in response to a question that is ridden with deep uncertainty and strong differences of opinion.

Chapter Six will pay extensive attention to Hans Kelsen's insistence that democratic constitutionalism concerns the sustenance of the third party and horizontal relations between citizens and not the pursuit of truths that would terminate these horizontal third party relations by silencing contestation.[146] Suffice it to observe for now that the sleight of hand with which the majority opinion in *Erste Abtreibung* turned scientific ambiguity into unambiguous moral, political

---

145 Translated from *Erste Abtreibung*, 43: "Das ungeborene Leben .... wird durch den Schwangerschaftsabbruch vernichtet. Nach dem Prinzip des schonendsten Ausgleichs konkurrierender grundgesetzlich geschützter Positionen unter Berücksichtigung des Art. 19 Abs. 2 GG muß deshalb dem Lebensschutz des nasciturus der Vorzug gegeben werden. Dieser Vorrang gilt grundsätzlich für die gesamte Dauer der Schwangerschaft und darf auch nicht für eine bestimmte Frist in Frage gestellt werden."
146 Cf. Chapter Six.

and legal certainty surely falls far short of this Kelsenian understanding of constitutional democratic principles.

The minority opinion in *Erste Abtreibung* is fundamentally different in this regard. As already shown above, it located the third party or horizontal dimension of the review of the Fifth Criminal Law Reform Act of 1974 in a fundamentally divided public (*gespaltene Öffentlichkeit*). It is this third party dimension and this horizontality that the minority opinion endeavoured to respect and sustain with its finding that the Reform Act embodies a proportionality (*Verhältnismässigkeit*) that reflects and sustains the tensions in this divided public in a plausible way. The minority in *Erste Abtreibung* recognised that the Reform Act of 1974 and the legislative process and procedures from which it emerged engaged scrupulously with the political and social tensions in Germany at the time. It is instructive to note one of its key formulations here:

> "In an effort to resolve this very difficult [question] the legislator considered all relevant considerations exhaustively. The legal reform of § 218 of the Criminal Code has already engaged a deeply divided public in this regard. The parliamentary consultations have, because of this background, been conducted with great seriousness and extraordinary diligence."[147]

In view of this express and careful consideration of all concerns that were voiced during the legislative process, the minority opinion in *Erste Abtreibung* rested assured that this was a legislative decision that incorporated compromises on a trial and error basis – *[eine] Entscheidung, die ... Kompromisse voraussetzt und sich im Verfahren des trial und error vollzieht.* As such it complied with the democratic principle of direct accountability to the people (*dem demokratischen Prinzip in die Verantwortung des vom Volk unmittelbar legitimierten Gesetzgebers*).[148] The judiciary may not invoke, argued the justices that signed the minority opinion, the notion of an objective value order to override this democratic process and to assume legislative functions. It may not impose on the democratic process an uncompromising social order – *Der Gedanke der objektiven Wertentscheidung darf nicht zum Vehikel werden, um spezifisch gesetzgeberische Funktionen in der Gestaltung der Sozialordnung auf das Bundesverfassungsgericht zu verlagern.*[149]

147 Translated from *Erste Abtreibung*, 84–85: "Im Bemühen um eine Lösung dieser höchst schwierigen Aufgabe hat der Gesetzgeber alle wesentlichen Gesichtspunkte erschöpfend gewürdigt. Die Reform des § 218 StGB hatte bereits die in dieser Frage tief gespaltene Öffentlichkeit nachaltig beschäftigt. Die parlamentarischen Beratungen sind auf diesem Hintergrund mit großem Ernst und ungewöhnlicher Gründlichkeit durchgeführt worden."

148 *Erste Abtreibung*, 72.

149 *Erste Abtreibung*, 72.

These observations of the minority opinion in *Abtreibung* evidently articulated a significant call for caution regarding substantive due process review procedures. And it evidently identified elements of an undue substantive due process review procedure in the majority opinion's invocation of an objective value decision – "*eine objektiven Wertentscheidung.*" This invocation of an objective value order, the minority opinion noticed clearly, was completely devoid of substance. In other words, it showed up the *lack of substance* that invariably accompanies substantive due process review procedures. Judiciaries invariably resort to substantive due process when they review politically and normatively contentious legislation. And that is the irony. Political and normative contentiousness – lack of sufficient normative substance, in other words – invariably informs judicial resort to substantive due process review procedures.

Invocation of normative substance under circumstances of social contentiousness only serves to undermine the credibility and authority of law. Social contentiousness of substantive due process judicial review does not simply go away once a judiciary has passed its judgment. Political resistance to the judgment will continue and those who can escape from its coercion will systematically seek to do so when they can. In the case of unwanted pregnancies, abortion tourism is the obvious way around coerced full term pregnancies, at least for those who can afford it. The minority opinion in *Erste Abtreibung* was well aware of all of this. It was aware that the legislation would either be ineffective or at best partly effective in fundamentally dubious ways. It would effectively only prevent poor or economically constrained individuals from obtaining abortions elsewhere. And it would predictably move many of these individuals to resort to clandestine abortion practices that invariably involve serious health risks. Such legislation, we shall see presently, cannot comply with basic demands of legislative rationality.

These considerations constituted the crux of the minority opinion in *Erste Abtreibung* and they surely were also acutely relevant in *Roe*. Jane Roe expressly claimed that it was only a lack of means to travel to another state that prevented her from obtaining an abortion.[150] Justice Blackmun could easily have stuck to simple rational basis and procedural due process review to obtain the result he pursued in *Roe*, for there is no rational substance to law that meets with such brazenly selective compliance. It must fail the most basic rational basis procedural due process test.[151] There is just one level of scrutiny in German constitu-

150 *Roe*, 120.

151 Two of the most prominent defenders of *Roe* among American constitutional scholars and legal theorists, Ronald Dworkin and Laurence Tribe, both state their defences of *Roe* in substantive due process terms that invoke the fundamental right of women to determine their

tional review and it is generally expressed in terms of a proportionality (*Verhältnismässigkeit*) test. The test turns on three questions: 1) Does the executive or legislative abridgment of a right pursue a legitimate goal? 2) Does it effectively *promote* this legitimate goal? 3) Does it pursue this goal in the least invasive way possible?[152] It is with regard to the second question that the minority opinion in *Erste Abtreibung* rejected the majority opinion's demand that abortion remain criminalised in Germany. Legislation that would criminalise abortion in the way demanded by the majority would not effectively discourage abortion. It would in fact encourage the avoidance of counselling and consultation – for which the legislation under review provided – that might convince at least some women not to abort. It would thus leave "the right to life" that the majority opinion sought to protect only less protected. It would only encourage abortion tourism and illegal abortions and would effectively expose more women to the grave malpractices that often attach to the latter.[153] It would encourage non-compliance with law that would exactly for reasons of widely known non-compliance be-

---

reproductive lives for themselves. In response to John Hart Ely's argument that there is nothing unacceptable about legislation that subjects the reproductive autonomy of women to constraints of public morality, Tribe argues that such constraints would indeed be unacceptable when at odds with the fundamental rights of someone. Dworkin also regards the rational scrutiny of legislation as much too weak protection of women's fundamental reproductive autonomy, given the way it reduces this autonomy to a mere liberty which any rational legislation may curtail instead of safeguarding it as a right that only narrowly tailored legislation motivated by a compelling state interest may curtail. Cf. John Ely, "The Wages of Crying Wolf: A Comment on Roe v. Wade," *Yale Law Journal* 82 (1973): 926; Laurence H. Tribe, *Abortion: The Clash of Absolutes* (New York: Norton, 1992), 114; Ronald Dworkin, *Life's Dominion: An Argument about Abortion, Euthanasia, and Individual Freedom* (New York: Vintage Books, 1994), 104; Dworkin, *Freedom's Law: The Moral Reading of the American Constitution* (Oxford: Oxford University Press, 1996), 112. The argument forwarded in the reading of *Roe* above is nevertheless that the language of liberties suffices in societies that are both deeply divided by pro-life and pro-choice positions and surrounded by neigbouring states where abortions can be obtained legally. Any legislation that aims to criminalise abortion under these circumstances is bound to be irrational in the way described above. It is only in societies where massive anti-abortion consensus renders exceptional attempts to obtain cross-border abortions policeable (where the whole society basically polices itself willingly) or where basically no person can obtain cross-border abortions (say because of vast or insurmountable distances to facilities where legalised abortion is obtainable) that criminalisation might become rational. In such societies, one would in theory need to rely on something like a fundamental right to abortion and not just on a liberty, but the language of rights would probably be pointless in situations like these in any case.

152 The *Verhältnismäßigkeit* or *Übermaßverbot* is a construct of early decisions of the GFCC, the constitutional status (*Verfassungsrang*) of which was recognised in BVerfGE 23, 127 (1968). Chapter Eight discusses this proportionality principle more extensively.

153 *Erste Abtreibung*, 89.

come ever less capable of demanding respect. The Criminal Law Reform Act of 1974, quite to the contrary, dealt carefully with all these considerations, the minority argued. In this respect it did not only comply with the proportionality demand. It also rehabilitated and strengthened the fundamental respect worthiness of the legal system (*Wiederherstellung der Glaubwürdigkeit der Rechtsordnung*).[154]

Considered against the background of all the observations elaborated above, the essential aim of constitutional review procedures should be to resituate executive and legislative action in the social or third party context from which all legislation emerges. Executive or legislative action that does not respect the third-party or horizontal relations from which it derives, will invariably be selective, ineffective, and counter-productive. It is bound to meet with increasing disrespect and non-compliance. As such it cannot hope to pass the most elementary rational basis scrutiny. This is so because the horizontality and third party background of legislative and executive action cannot be ordered or legislated into oblivion without taking leave of the constitutional principles of liberal democracy that judicial review presupposes. Legislation that seeks to do this – order widespread and increasing disobedience into oblivion – is bound to take leave of the basic principles of liberal democracy. It cannot but become authoritarian and repressive. In other words, legislation that is out of touch with the social reality that it is supposed to govern will either remain ineffective and irrational or attain to rationality by means of oppression.

The same principle also applies to judicial review. Judiciaries cannot perform the task of *constitutional democratic* legislative and executive review when they themselves invoke substantive constitutional norms that ignore the third party or horizontal dimension of constitutional democracy. They themselves then become authoritarian lawmakers. They themselves then invite accusations that impute to them usurpations of sovereignty and juristocratic government. The minority opinion in *Erste Abtreibung* made this point expressly (*[h]ier darf das Bundesverfassungsgericht nicht der Versuchung erliegen, selbst die Funktion des zu kontrollierenden Organs zu übernehmen...*)."[155] The experience with popular sovereignty invariably shows that it is fundamentally "divided" and fundamentally plural, quite to the contrary of all claims from Bodin to Schmitt that sovereignty is undivided oneness. Judiciaries that invoke substantive norms or objective value orders to override duly enacted legislation undermine popular sovereignty. They do not do so because they divide or fragment sovereignty by

154 *Erste Abtreibung*, 84.
155 *Erste Abtreibung*, 70.

constituting a competing power alongside the legislator and executive (the old separation of powers argument against judicial activism). Something much more fundamental is at stake here. Judicial invocations of substantive constitutional norms ruin popular sovereignty because they erase its irreducible divisions by invoking values that tolerate no contestation and no difference of opinion. Substantive due process review does not ruin sovereignty because it splits it. It ruins sovereignty because it ignores its splits. Justice Blackmun need not have gone there. He could have reached a "pro-choice" decision in *Roe* with simple rational scrutiny. Had he done so, he would have shown respect for the ineradicable "divisions" of Texan and American sovereignty instead of ignoring them. In the process, he constructed an illusionary unitary sovereignty, the integrity and credibility of which has remained controversial and suspect ever since *Roe*.

Are we still talking about the horizontal effect of fundamental rights between citizens here? Yes we are, but in a new way that registers the reality that constitutional review is always a matter of horizontal effect. It always concerns relationships between citizens, even when those relations emerge from sovereign legislation. The majority opinion in *Erste Abtreibung* located the third party relationship in the case in the relation between a pregnant woman and the embryonic development of life in her womb. It did so, we saw, in a way that immediately negated that relationship again, given the way it constructed it in a way that rendered the woman's right to reproductive autonomy meaningless. The minority opinion located the third party relationship in a pluralistic legislative context, that is, in the relationship between legislative majorities and minorities. The proportionality test with which it scrutinised the legislation at issue aimed to establish whether it reflected these majority-minority relationships adequately.

What we have just done is to relocate the third party or horizontal relation in constitutional disputes between private individuals from the immediate relation between the litigants to the possible majority and minority legislative relations that inform the litigants' respective claims and defences. This is clearly a whole new concept of horizontal effect that brings with it many new questions. The remaining chapters of this book will dedicate attention to these new questions. One of these questions, however, has bearing on an aspect of the *Lüth* decision to which we need to turn now, before we turn to the discussion of the last case in this chapter. Let us return for this purpose to the sixth main point that we distilled from the *Lüth* decision in the discussion above:

> The nature of this task to review judicial decisions against which constitutional complaints have been filed, also imposes a limit on the GFCC's powers of review in these matters. It is not the task of the constitutional judiciary to test the case against which the complaint is

> directed for all possible mistakes. Its task is only to assess the radiation effect of the constitution on applicable civil law in order to give proper effect to the constitution in the dispute at issue. In other words, the GFCC is not meant to be an instance of higher review, but it cannot shy away from the duty to scrutinise the constitutionality of a trial court decision.[156]

How does one prevent horizontal effect of fundamental rights from turning the practice of *constitutional* review into the higher review of all private law disputes? Or, to use Matthias Kumm's phrase, how does one prevent private law from becoming applied constitutional law?[157] This is the question that the discussion of the *Reiten im Walde* case in the next and last section of this Chapter sets out to answer. However, we need to turn to a preliminary clarification before we move on to *Reiten im Walde.* Does the relocation of the horizontal or social dimension in horizontal effect cases that emerged from the discussion of *Roe v Wade* and *Erste Abtreibung* in this section not render the conception of private law as applied constitutional law inevitable? Does it not necessarily turn the practice of constitutional review into higher review of all private law cases?

The relocation of the horizontal relationship in horizontal effect cases that the discussion above extracted from *Roe* and *Erste Abtreibung* consists in shifting the horizontal dimension from the immediate relation between litigating parties to the relations between legislative majorities and minorities that can ultimately be said to inform the dispute between the parties. It suggests that there is no horizontal effect of fundamental rights at issue in a dispute where no such horizontal legislative relations can be identified. Does this move not turn all or too many private disputes into horizontal effect cases, for has the Hohfeldian argument that we have developed so far in this Chapter not in fact turned all private law into legislation or implied legislation?

The Hohfeldian argument that we have developed has indeed done exactly that. And that means that one can indeed understand all private law rules as reflections of majority-minority legislative relations (in which the minorities are usually negligibly small). However, this does not turn all private law disputes into constitutional disputes, because not all legislation, be it private or public law legislation, raises constitutional issues. Legislation often affects interests of individuals negatively without raising a constitutional issue. And this is what one learns from especially Justice Grimm's dissenting opinion in *Reiten im Walde.*

---

156 *Lüth*, 207.

157 Mattias Kumm, "Who's Afraid of the Total Constitution? Constitutional Rights as Principles and the Constitutionalization of Private Law," *German Law Journal* 7, no. 4 (2006): 341–370.

Justice Grimm's minority opinion in *Reiten im Walde* alerts one to the reality that a constitutional court is not designed to be the highest court of appeal in every administrative proceeding. And this is also the message that his opinion in *Reiten im Walde* holds for the relation between private law and constitutional law. Private law legislation, be this legislation express or implied, does not always constitute "enabling legislation" – legislation aimed at giving effect to constitutional norms. It is not always "applied constitutional law." It is important to remain alert to the distinction between private law that evidently aims at promoting constitutional values and rights and private law that does not. It is of course also crucial to remain alert to the possibility that the latter private law can also sometimes fall foul of constitutional demands. That is what the insistence on the horizontal effect of constitutional rights is surely all about. But the need to maintain a clear regard for the essential difference between private law and constitutional law that the GFCC articulated in the 6th main point of its *Lüth* judgment demands a sober appreciation of the reality that private law limitations of private rights and liberties most often bear no relation at all to constitutional questions.

XI *Reiten im Walde*

Federal legislation regulates access to German forests. Paragraph 14(1) of the Federal Forest Act of 1975 basically allows access (*Betreten*) to forests at own risk. Paragraph 14(2) allows the German states (*Länder*) to regulate the details of access and to limit access for important reasons, among which the protection of woods, economic exploitation of forests and game, as well as the avoidance of damage and the protection of legitimate interests of the owners of forests are specifically listed. Applicable state legislation of Nordrhein-Westfalen of 1975 and 1980 ultimately restricted horse riding to pathways specifically indicated as riding ways and required further that horse riders fasten licence badges (*Kennzeichen*) to their horses which could only be obtained through payment of licence fees. These regulations became the target of the constitutional complaint that became known as the *Reiten im Walde* case that the GFCC decided in 1989. The complaint turned on five assertions:

1) The legislative restrictions on horse riding violated the plaintiff's fundamental right to the free development of his personality that is entrenched in Article 2 (1) of the GG. According to the plaintiff, citizens should be entitled to pursue their enjoyment of horse riding freely in forests. The ends pursued by the regulations, the plaintiff argued, could have been achieved by less intrusive measures.

2) The regulations violated the principle of equality before law entrenched in Article 3 of the GG, considering that similar legislative restrictions were not imposed on skiers and hikers.
3) The regulations violated his fundamental right to freedom of movement guaranteed by Article 11 of the GG.
4) The regulations violated his freedom of professional choice guaranteed by Article 12 of the GG.
5) The regulations violated the rights of horse riders that ensue from the social obligations to which property rights are subject in terms of Article 14 (2) of the GG.

The majority opinion of the court considered the complaint admissible and granted it a proper hearing. However, it ultimately held the claim to be groundless. The relevant legislative regulations, claimed the court, complied fully with the demands of proportionality. They could not be said to burden the claimant's rights more than was necessary.[158] The minority opinion of Justice Grimm also dismissed the complaint. He did not do so, however, on the basis of proportionality considerations. He did so because the complaint did not raise a constitutional concern at all. Horse riding in forests enjoys no constitutional protection (*[d]as Reiten im Walde genießt keinen Grundrechtschutz*).[159] For Justice Grimm that was the end of story. According to him the complaint did not merit the attention of the court. The fundamental right to the free development of one's personality guaranteed by Article 2(1), he averred, does not provide gapless protection for each and every thinkable human activity (*jede beliebige menschliche Tätigkeit*).[160] This trivialisation (*Banalisierung*) of fundamental rights and the proliferation of constitutional complaints to which it would give rise, he added, should be resisted and reversed (*sollte rückgängig gemacht werden*).[161]

Like *Roe* and like *Erste Abtreibung*, *Reiten im Walde* would generally not be considered as constituting a question of horizontal effect. All three cases turned on questions regarding the constitutionality of legislation and therefore would appear to be ordinary cases of vertical constitutional review. Of these three cases, however, *Reiten im Walde* is the only case that indeed does not involve the horizontal effect of fundamental rights. This is not so because it does not involve horizontality or horizontal relations. It surely involves a horizontal and social dimension. But it does not concern the horizontal effect of fundamental

158 *Reiten im Walde*, paragraphs 67–98.
159 *Reiten im Walde*, paragraph 99.
160 *Reiten im Walde*, paragraph 100.
161 *Reiten im Walde*, paragraph 109.

rights because it does not concern fundamental rights. In terms of the argument developed thus far, *Roe* and *Erste Abtreibung* can and should be considered as horizontal effect cases in view of the relations between legislative majorities and minorities that raised constitutional questions in these cases. But *Reiten im Walde* clearly turned on no constitutionally significant majority-minority legislative relationship. Those whose interests were overridden by the legislative measures in question surely count as some sort of minority. But they can hardly be considered a historically significant minority whose interests were significantly affected by majority legislation. The constitutional and constitutive history of Germany did not in any real sense hang in the balance in *Reiten im Walde* as it did in *Erste Abtreibung*, or as the constitutional history of the United States hung in the balance in *Roe*.

De minibus non curat lex constitutionis. This is basically what Justice Grimm communicated to the court in *Reiten im Walde*. At issue here is not a belittling of the interests of horse riders. They are surely not trivial as far as the whole spectrum of human recreational interests and the passions of fellow citizens are concerned. But they become trivial when presented as serious concerns in a forum where they have no proper place. And this, we would like to contend, is the crux of the distinction between constitutional law and private law that the GFCC drew in *Lüth*. The distinction between private law and constitutional law turns on the need not to trivialise constitutional norms and rights with private law issues that have no historical significance. Private law disputes that have no recognisable significance for the histories through which peoples carve out their constitutional identities, cannot raise constitutional concerns. This does of course not mean that private law disputes are trivial. Private law concerns are not trivial in their own proper context, but become trivial when presented as a crucial issue in a constitutional forum. Private law has its own good criteria of triviality, its own good criteria for deciding what counts as a case and what not. The maxim *de minibus non curat lex* also applies in private law for sound reasons. But a non-trivial private law dispute can become trivial when raised in a court that is designed to assess, so to speak, the historical "state of a nation." This is why the South African Constitutional Court can be said to have judged wisely in *Barkhuizen v Napier* that an expiry clause in an insurance contract, however unfair, does not infringe a constitutional right.[162] It should perhaps have gone further by stating, like Justice Grimm in *Reiten im Walde*, that a dispute about such an expiry clause does not even raise a constitutional question.

162 2007 (5) SA 323 (CC).

Let us turn to another example. It is a good question whether the invocation of Article 8 of the Human Rights Act in the context of the unauthorised publication of wedding photographs in *Douglas v Hello*[163] did not constitute a trivialisation of Article 8 that is comparable to the trivialisation of Article 2(1) that Justice Grimm discerned in *Reiten im Walde*. These photographs were, as far as we know, not markedly different from photos that the wedding couple did authorise for publication. Had the unauthorised publication concerned photographs of a more disclosing or sensitive nature, a constitutional rights issue may well have been at stake. But the mere violation of the autonomy to authorise publication cannot constitute a constitutional question. If it could, every minor tort claim would constitute a constitutional question, for every minor tort concerns some violation of private autonomy.

It should have been possible to sort out *Douglas v Hello* with recourse to some ordinary statutory tort (considering the fact that English common law adjudication had after so many years still not managed to forge a simple tort remedy for general privacy infringements). It should not have been necessary to rely on Article 8 of the Human Rights Act to fashion such a tort. Good common law judicial reasoning or good private law legislation could have achieved this goal without much ado.

But why not just rely on the Human Rights Act, one might ask, if it conveniently provides the semantic and normative material for forging ordinary privacy protection in the United Kingdom? This is a good question. Walter Leisner, whose contribution to the German *Drittwirkung* debate will enjoy much attention in later chapters, considers this a possible modus operandi. Constitutional clauses, argues Leisner, can sometimes be direct sources of private law. But when they do function as sources of private law, they do only that. They do not simultaneously function as constitutional principles that inform constitutional review procedures.[164] This seems to be a plausible way of guarding against the trivialisation of constitutional principles in cases where private law needs to borrow language from constitutional texts. The "borrowing" at issue here takes that language out of the constitution and into private law. Private law can be enriched in this way without affecting the constitutional status of constitutional rights. When this Leisnerian understanding regarding the possibility of finding sources of private law within constitutional texts is understood correctly, it clearly does not threaten the distinction between private and constitutional law. The bottom line regarding horizontal effect remains the same. When a constitutional clause

---

163 [2005] EWCA Civ 595.
164 This argument is discussed more extensively in Chapter Four.

is used (borrowed) as a source of private law, it can no longer have the "horizontal effect" of a constitutional right for it no longer reflects a constitutional norm under these circumstances.

XII Summary Reflections

1 Vicissitudes of the State Action Doctrine

The inter-continental state action and horizontal effect tour on which this chapter embarked visited several countries and jurisdictions of the world. There is no doubt that many other countries could have been visited instead. Many other cases could have been discussed. The important aim, however, was to construct a core narrative of horizontal effect jurisprudence that highlights its essential problems and questions.

The crucial development that can be distilled from these cases concerns the vicissitudes of the original state action doctrine laid down in *The Civil Rights Cases*. This original doctrine stipulated that only states could violate the 14th Amendment. This stipulation, we saw from Justice Bradley's judgment, conceptually excluded the possibility that individuals may violate the 14th Amendment. Three subsequent USSC cases basically dismantled this conceptual construction of the state action doctrine. *Labour v Swing* and *New York Times v Sullivan* accepted that common law rules constituted state action for purposes of the protections offered by the Bill of Rights (the 14th and 5th Amendments were respectively at issue in these decisions). *Shelley v Kraemer* accepted that judicial decisions constituted state action for purposes of the 14th Amendment. Between them, these cases created a dispensation under which individuals who abridged 14th or 5th Amendment rights of other individuals, could no longer rely on either common law or judicial interpretations of common law to assert the liberty to abridge such rights. Contrary to Justice Bradley's construction of the state action doctrine, these later cases evidently envisaged a state action doctrine that left private individuals securely bound by the Bill of Rights.

There is, however, one area of fundamental rights abridgments that is not yet properly addressed by this conception of the state action doctrine: What would be the situation when individuals violated the fundamental rights of others "without relying on law at all"? This question, we saw, came expressly to the fore in Justice Kriegler's opinion in *Du Plessis v De Klerk* and we shall return to it below. Let us first take another look at the majority opinion in *Du Plessis* and the rest of the cases discussed in this chapter.

2 The Contradictory Legacies that Informed *Du Plessis*

The majority opinion in *Du Plessis* relied on two other crucial stages in the judicial development of the state action or horizontal effect question that contradicted one another. On the one hand, it relied on the dismantling of the legacy of *Swing*, *Shelley* and *Sullivan* that took place in *Dolphin Delivery*. On the other hand, it relied on the implicit endorsement and consolidation of this same legacy that took place in *Lüth*. *Dolphin* dismantled *Swing*, *Shelley* and *Sullivan* by introducing two rules that re-opened the space for individual abridgments of fundamental rights that *Shelley*, *Swing* and *Sullivan* had effectively closed down. The first rule held that the Canadian Charter of Rights and Freedoms did not apply to the common law unless the state was itself involved in a common law dispute. The second held that the Charter did not bind judicial decisions that did nothing but arbitrate disputes between private individuals. With these two rules, the decision in *Dolphin* secured significant space for individuals to rely on common law rights and defences to abridge the Charter rights of others, and to rely on judicial decisions to enforce those rights or defences. *Lüth*, on the other hand, unambiguously confirmed the rules in *Swing*, *Shelley* and *Sullivan*. It stated clearly that the rights embodied in the GG bind both ordinary private law and judicial decisions. It only added a formal requirement to this confirmation. It insisted that the reach of the constitution into the private sphere be channelled through the language or medium of private law. But nowhere in *Lüth* is there any indication that this formal requirement was introduced to constrain, limit or change the substance of the basic principle that the rights contained in the GG also bind private conduct. In this respect, we observed, there is no tension between the form and substance of the jurisprudence laid down in *Lüth*.

The decisions in *Dolphin* and *Lüth* can evidently not be squared with one another. By relying on both *Dolphin* and *Lüth* for the horizontal effect jurisprudence it developed, the majority opinion in *Du Plessis* created a jurisprudence of which the form and substance no longer held together. In *Du Plessis*, the formal requirement that the effect of fundamental rights in the private sphere be articulated in the language of private law, turned into a rule that constrained the substance of horizontal effect. It somehow created a situation in which private individuals were not quite as bound by fundamental rights as public authorities were.

3 The Dismantling of *Swing*, *Shelley* and *Sullivan* in *Flagg Brothers* and *DeShaney*

Justice Rehnquist, we saw, purposefully and deliberately invoked the absence of common law protection as a ground for not imposing 14th Amendment protection on the people of Wisconsin. The lack of a common law rule in Wisconsin may have allowed him to sidestep *Swing* and *Sullivan*, but the hearing of this violation in both the trial and appeal courts basically prevented him from sidestepping *Shelley*. However, he surely just ignored *Shelley*. Earlier on, in *Flagg Brothers*, he apparently still spared *Shelley* a thought. When he addressed the question of a positive rule of law that is inconsistent with the 14th Amendment in *Flagg* Brothers, he expressly included "decisional law" alongside statutory law. If this "decisional law" was just meant to denote "common law," as it might have, *Shelley* may not have been on his mind in *Flagg Brothers*. But the invocation of "decisional law" may well have been an indication that he specifically wanted to cover the *decisional* aspect of judicial applications of a rule of law as well, and not just the rule as it stands. If so, *Flagg Brothers* can be read to have considered and discarded both *Swing* and *Sullivan*, on the one hand, and *Shelley*, on the other. It is not important to speculate further about this. The substance of Chief Justice Rehnquist's double legacy to state action or horizontal effect jurisprudence is in any case abundantly clear: Ignore *Swing* and *Sullivan* and ignore *Shelley*!

4 Shifting Horizontal Effect Jurisprudence from Private to Legislative Relations

Roe v Wade is not generally discussed in the context of state action or horizontal effect, but the discussion of *Roe* in this chapter highlighted the state action element in *Roe* in view of the GFCC's decision in *Erste Abtreibung. Erste Abtreibung*, we saw, turned the question of the constitutionality of abortion expressly into a *Drittwirkung* or horizontal effect inquiry. The horizontality invoked in the majority opinion in *Erste Abtreibung*, however, is ultimately not the significant horizontality that the *Erste Abtreibung* case brought to the fore. Casting the horizontality question in medically un-indicated abortions in terms of the right to life of the nasciturus and the woman's right to reproductive autonomy, we showed, destroys that horizontality forthwith, given the way the woman's wish to terminate pregnancy can never compete with the child's right to life. The true horizontality at issue in *Erste Abtreibung*, we argued, consists in the one identified in the minority opinion, namely, the relation between the different legislative factions regarding the prior questions *whether* and *when* the un-indicated abortion during the first weeks after conception can at all be said to effect the right to life of a living person. This approach of the minority in *Erste Abtreibung*, we argued further, would have made it possible for Justice Brennan to articulate a pro-choice finding in *Roe* without resorting to substantive due process arguments. The argument of the minority in *Erste Abtreibung* showed that the decision in *Roe* could have been reached on the basis of a procedural due process argument that turned on simple rational purpose scrutiny. It could have turned on a simple finding that an abridgment of basic liberties (not rights) through ineffective legislation that at best achieves partial compliance cannot be deemed rational and therefore falls foul of the Bill of Rights.

5 Substantive and Procedural Due Process and the Question of Sovereignty

The significance of the insights drawn from the analyses of *Roe* and *Erste Abtreibung* for the horizontality question is huge. It shows up a fundamental problem in the jurisprudence developed in *Lüth* that has hitherto never been addressed incisively, namely, the extent to which the notion of an objective order of values or *objektive Wertordnung* asserted in *Lüth* turns on a highly questionable substantive due process jurisprudence. Substantive due process review assumes the existence of an undivided legislative and legal sovereignty. There are cases in which this undivided sovereignty must be assumed, no doubt. Examples of such cases come up with every common criminal trial the normative basis of which reflects no significant social divisions. There are also constitutional cases in which this undivided sovereignty must be assumed, as we shall see below. But the notion of undivided sovereignty and a single substantive system of values cannot be assumed in cases that raise questions with regard to which a society is deeply divided, such as *Roe* and *Erste Abtreibung*. It is with regard to these cases that jurisprudence as such and horizontal effect jurisprudence in particular must develop a consistent notion of "divided" sovereignty and a consistent conception of procedural due process review that matches this notion of "divided" sovereignty. Divided sovereignty is invoked between scarecrows here, for it is an inadequate term that will be replaced with the terms "differential" and "*différantial*" sovereignty towards the end of this book.

The significance of the link between the horizontal effect of fundamental rights and the question of sovereignty should be abundantly clear now. The question of sovereignty is in the first place the question regarding the uninterrupted territorial sovereignty that safeguards the rights of citizens and residents. The lesson that one draws from the horizontal effect or state action theory developed in *Swing*, *Shelley*, *Sullivan* and *Lüth* is indeed that the reach of sovereign power is, in principle, absolute. Empirically speaking, there often are pockets of existence that the sovereign's territorial power fails to reach. There are always some dark woods and desolate corners that sovereign powers fail to police properly. But a proper sovereign would not regard these pockets of existence as evidence of absences of sovereignty. A proper sovereign would own up to these apparent "absences" of sovereignty as mere failures of sovereignty. It would duly compensate those who suffered from such failures of sovereignty so as to acknowledge that it aught to have prevented the harm suffered. The compensation awarded not only concretely restores but also symbolically reconfirms the sovereign's reign. Seen from this perspective, denials of the uninterrupted reach of the sovereign, such as occurred in *DeShaney*, *Flagg Brothers*, *Dolphin Delivery* and *Du Plessis* constitute simple abdications of sovereignty.[165]

To be sure, with the possible exception of *DeShaney* and *Flagg Brothers*, none of the judges that presided in these cases would have admitted to abdications of sovereignty when confronted with the question in the clear terms expounded here. They all would probably have resorted to convoluted conceptions of indirect horizontal effect so as to deny or obfuscate the abdications of sovereignty imputed to them here. Indirect horizontal effect is indeed a convoluted and ambiguous conception that denies direct effect of the constitution in the private sphere, on the one hand, while acknowledging that private law cannot remain inconsistent with the constitution and must be developed so as to make it consistent, on the other. This is a half-hearted affirmation of constitutional sovereignty. And this half-heartedness opens up a vague and opaque space within which two surreptitious destructions of constitutional sovereignty become a real threat. The first concerns the abdication of sovereignty already pointed out above. The second concerns unconstitutional (juristocratic) usurpations of constitutional sovereignty by politically overzealous judges. One should note the irony attached to the latter: jurisprudential half-heartedness may well come to camouflage judicial overzealousness.

None of the judges who presided in *Dolphin Delivery* and *Du Plessis* were prepared to develop a clear and unambiguous horizontal effect jurisprudence that comprises two basic steps that do not compete with one another and thus would not have ended up in the convoluted and ambiguous conceptual mess that goes by the name of indirect horizontal effect. These two steps would have been these:

---

165 Cf. also Van der Walt, "Abdications of Sovereignty in Horizontal Effect Jurisprudence," (forthcoming).

i. *Yes, the constitution of course applies to the private sphere in all cases and under all circumstances where such application makes obvious and simple sense.*
ii. *In such cases where the application of the constitution makes obvious and simple sense, the impact of the constitution on the private sphere must be articulated in the idiom of private law, without allowing that idiom to derogate or diminish the normative demands of the constitution.*

Justice Kriegler came close to this articulation of horizontal effect in his opinion in *Du Plessis*, but suddenly shied away from it in the end. Justice Kentridge's majority opinion for the court, on the other hand, basically fluffed the question of horizontal effect from the beginning to the end. He insisted on the one hand that constitutional rights have no horizontal effect, but nevertheless conceded on the other that they have real impact on the interpretation and application of private law. He inherited this senseless equivocation, we saw above, from the judgment of Justice McIntyre in *Dolphin Delivery.* All of these judges evidently avoided the two clear steps that consistent and practical horizontal effect jurisprudence requires. Why did they shy away from these steps? Why did they end up in such confusion? They did so, it would appear, because of a deep-seated reluctance to affirm the concept of uninterrupted state sovereignty clearly and unambiguously. They were all concerned, as Justice Kriegler was, with exorcising the spectre of the state putting its hands on all private relationships. It is important to also recall these lines of the passage quoted above clearly:

> "Thus, if a man claims to have the right to beat his wife, sell his daughter into bondage or abuse his son, he will not be allowed to raise as a defence to a civil claim or a criminal charge that he is entitled to do so at common law, under customary law or in terms of any statute or contract. That is a far cry from the spectre of the state placing its hand on private relationships."[166]

The acknowledgment that a sovereign state indeed puts its hands on all private relationships from which all the judges who presided in *DeShaney*, *Flagg Brothers*, *Dolphin Delivery* and *Du Plessis* shied away, will of course appear frightening and disturbing to any liberal lawyer, judge or citizen. Justice Kriegler may have got his signals crossed in these lines, as suggested earlier, but he got them crossed in this way because of his profound sense for the liberal concern with liberty deficits that may ensue from full recognitions of constitutional sovereignty. Should one wish to endorse the full recognition of constitutional sovereignty

166 *Du Plessis*, 720 D–I.

evident in cases like *Shelley, Swing, Sullivan* and *Lüth*, on the one hand, and remain mindful of the liberal concern with liberty deficits on the other, one would have to rethink the concept of sovereignty fundamentally. One should in this regard give credit to the profound percipience evident in Justice Kriegler's "crossed signals," for it is from them that the task of rethinking constitutional sovereignty that the horizontal effect of fundamental rights demands receives a most significant prompt.

The recognition and endorsement of full constitutional sovereignty will continue to trouble liberal political and legal theory as long as it understands sovereignty in terms of a monolithic nucleus of undivided political power and authority that *radiates through* the whole geographic space that the sovereign claims as territory. This understanding of sovereignty is evidently no longer adequate in the deeply divided societies that populate most modern states today. Liberal constitutional theory needs to take leave of this radiation conception of sovereignty. It needs to contemplate instead, a popular sovereignty that *reigns between* the state's citizens and/or residents. This sovereignty that reigns between individuals is no longer a vertical sovereignty that towers over the relations between them, but a horizontal sovereignty that emerges from adequately democratic articulations of those relations. Chapter Six will refer to this horizontal sovereignty as "différantial sovereignty."

It is for purposes of articulating this horizontal sovereignty that this chapter analysed *Roe v Wade* and *Erste Abtreibung* as horizontal effect cases. The analysis of *Roe* and *Erste Abtreibung* as horizontal effect cases allows one to direct one's understanding of horizontal effect away from the *Lüth* conception of horizontal effect. The *Lüth* conception of horizontal effect is all too evidently tied to the radiation conception of sovereignty, as is clear from its invocation of the radiation of constitutional values through all strata of law. The concept of sovereignty that informs *Lüth* is tied to the substantive due process review procedure that is reflected in this notion of values that radiate through the legal system. The lesson that one learns from *Roe* and *Erste Abtreibung* concerns the way they reflect the reality that sovereignty, despite its uninterrupted reach, is "divided" in divided societies. The recognition of the uninterrupted reach of sovereignty has hitherto been confused with the notion of the unity of the sovereign and the idea that the sovereign is "one." Uninterrupted sovereignty should nevertheless not be confused with the idea of one undivided monolithic sovereign. Sovereignty can be "divided" without forfeiting its absolutely uninterrupted reach. This is a complex reality to grasp, no doubt. The "division" (again, this is an inadequate term that we shall replace later) of sovereignty at issue here, moreover, must not be confused with the apparent division of sovereignty reflected in the idea of the separation of powers (trias politica). Nor should it be confused with the emergence of supra-statal governments or governance alongside state governments that current legal and political theory has also been describing as "divisions" of sovereignty in recent years.[167]

At issue in the "division" of sovereignty to which *Roe* and *Erste Abtreibung* guide us, is a more complex reality. A coherent grasp of this reality is crucial for a coherent understanding of horizontal effect. That is why the question of horizontal effect and the question of sovereignty, two of the most pressing jurisprudential questions of our time, benefit from being linked in the way they are linked in this book. These two questions should be addressed together and the remaining chapters of this book aim to do exactly this. Suffice it to state for now the two key contentions that will emerge from this combined questioning:

The shift from unitary to "divided" concepts of sovereignty allows one to sever the concept of sovereignty from the demands of substantive due process review procedures. Legal theory has yet to come fully to terms with the irreducible connection between classical conceptions of undivided sovereignty and substantive due process review procedures. Nor has it come to terms with the pressing need to take leave of both the former and the latter.

Replacing the constellation of monolithic sovereignty and substantive due process with a constellation of "divided" sovereignty and predominantly procedural due process review procedures is the essential condition for coming to terms with the challenges that liberal democratic constitutional review faces today.

As we saw in this chapter, the combination of sovereignty and substantive due process conceptions of horizontal effect left its pervasive mark on the world's horizontal effect jurisprudence with the notion of the "radiation effect of constitutional values" on which the GFCC's decision in *Lüth* turned. Contemporary contexts of judicial review – deeply divided and pluralist societies – require a clear break with this constellation of sovereignty and substantive due process.

This chapter nevertheless also stressed the possibility of exceptional cases that demand substantive due process review procedures. In these cases, we said, the resort to assumptions of an "undivided legislative and legal sovereignty" that imposes fundamental liberal democratic values on everyone becomes inevitable. The shift from undivided to "divided" sovereignty and from substantive due process to procedural due process conceptions of constitutional review advocated in this book can therefore never be complete. The shift away from *Lüth*

---

167 Cf. in this regard especially the invocation of divided sovereignty in contemporary Europe discussed in Neil Walker, "Late Sovereignty in the European Union," in *Sovereignty in Transition*, by Neil Walker (Oxford: Hart Publishing, 2003). I return to this invocation of divided sovereignty in Chapters Five and Six.

for which we are arguing here is a shift from the *predominantly substantive* due process horizontal effect jurisprudence embodied in the *Lüth* notion of the radiation of constitutional values, to a *predominantly procedural* due process horizontal effect jurisprudence. The remaining chapters of this book will take on the task of unpacking this problematic carefully. Let us nevertheless begin to explore what is at stake here by taking a provisional look at the essential difference between substantive and procedural due process review procedures from the perspective of the post-*Lüth* understanding of horizontal effect that we need to articulate. We shall do so now in the last section of this chapter with reference to the key concept of "constitutional histories."

6 Constitutional Histories of Peoples

We endorsed Justice Grimm's outright dismissal of the constitutional relevance of the complaints filed in *Reiten im Walde* with the statement that the constitutional history and constitutive history of Germany did not in any real sense hang in the balance in *Reiten im Walde* as it did in *Erste Abtreibung*, or as the constitutional history of the United States hung in the balance in *Roe*. It is the constitutional significance of the latter cases in the history of the two peoples concerned that rendered them *constitutional* cases that demanded *constitutional* review. This was clearly not the case in *Reiten im Walde*. The grievances expressed were simply too personal. They did not concern the history of a people.

What, however, would count as truly historical constitutional questions in alleged violations of personality interests such as bodily integrity and the dignity of the person, the constitutional quality and significance of which no one would question for a moment? Are these concerns not also much too personal, too individual and too private to be construed in terms of the constitutional histories of peoples? Is the constitutional history of a people really at stake every time a violation of a constitutional personality right such as the right to bodily integrity is alleged? It is, but not as obviously so as in the case of historical redefinitions of constitutional majority-minority relations.

At issue in these cases is the absence of majority-minority relations that becomes evident when a legal system considers some or other principle or value inviolable. Constitutional personality rights such as the right to physical integrity are principles that liberal democracies typically consider inviolable. Liberal democracies do not subject these principles to contingent outcomes of majority-minority relations. No *liberal democratic* majority, not even an absolute one, can claim the right to override the constitutional right to physical integrity without offering exceptional justification. No majority legislation, no matter how big the majority, can override this principle. And no minority can claim exemption from it either. That is why the question regarding significant legislative majorities or minorities does not even come into play when this right is at stake. And this is why substantive due process judicial procedures still sometimes play a role in constitutional review. Legitimate substantive due process review procedures are basically the outcomes of instances in which courts justifiably dismiss the possibility of any acceptable historical majority or minority claim to be exempted from the constitutional principle at issue.

Does liberal democracy not betray the fundamental historicity that this chapter attributed to it in such cases? No it does not. In these cases, peoples define their constitutional identities by *historically* confirming their endorsement of rights that have an ahistorical, meta-historical or even unhistorical or natural law-like status or foundation. But the transcendental status or character of the norms thus endorsed does not negate the historicity of their endorsements. Their endorsements remain historical moments, however ahistorical or unhistorical the principle endorsed. They constitute historical moments in the lives of peoples. Hannah Arendt explains well what is at issue here by invoking the enigmatic words of Thomas Jefferson that went into the first lines of the American Declaration of Independence: "We hold these truths [– the laws of nature and nature's God –] to be self-evident."

Why did Jefferson state, "we hold these truths to be self evident"? Why did he not simply say they "are self-evident"? It would appear that Jefferson appreciated and acknowledged the historical commitment that is required to sustain transcendental truths, argues Arendt.[168] Things that are "self-evident" do not remain self-evident by the empirical force of sheer self-evidence. They remain self-evident by the force of the commitment that sustains their self-evidence. And when we forcefully consider something *self-evident*, no one can claim exemption from the demands of this self-evidence, no majority, no minority and no individual. That is the meaning of self-evidence. That is why horizontal effect is also an accurate description of the legal relations that issue from this self-evidence. Self-evidence is the great leveller, the great horizontaliser under the sweep of which we are all fundamentally equal. And when a people commits itself to this *asserted* self-evidence (as the people of Germany did in *Lüth*) or does not commit itself to this self-evidence (as the people of the United States did not in *DeShaney*), that decision to commit or not to commit becomes a conspicuous milestone in the history of their constitutional sovereignty.

---

168 Arendt, *On Revolution*, 193.

Two distinct kinds of horizontal effect can therefore be seen to have emerged from the case law discussed in this chapter, the horizontal effect that results from significant relations between legislative majorities and minorities, and the horizontal effect that results from the historical endorsement of transcendent truths that do not allow any exception for any majority, any minority and any individual. American constitutional jurisprudence refers to procedural due process review in the case of the former horizontality, and to substantive due process in the case of the latter. American judges and jurists have come to realise the problematic nature of substantive due process review in cases where significant social division and significant splits between legislative majorities and minorities prevail. They have largely learned to avoid the temptation to resort to substantive due process under these circumstances, but they still sometimes succumb to it when they should stay far away from it, as Justice Blackmun's judgment in *Roe* shows clearly. *Roe* concerned a divisive issue, the adjudication of which should have turned on nothing more than the rational scrutiny of legislative procedures. As shown above, the conclusion reached in *Roe* could also have been reached through ordinary rational scrutiny review.

But perhaps it is also American apprehensiveness regarding substantive due process that sometimes compels American judges to avoid substantive due process review in cases where they should embrace it, as the case of *DeShaney* makes clear. *DeShaney* was a clear case in which a nation was *historically* required to endorse and sustain transcendent truths regarding the "self-evident" duty of public authorities to protect bodily integrity in cases where they have the means to do so. Justice Rehnquist should have endorsed this truth on behalf of the American people like a true sovereign in a way that made it clear that no one, no legislative majority, no legislative minority and no individual, can claim exemption from this truth. He should not have bowed to the procedural requirement that the people of Wisconsin first vote on the question, for the outcome of this vote should have been deemed immaterial to the decision he was bound to take.

In what proportions do demands for procedural and substantive due process occur in the constitutional history of a nation? Why do we insist that the horizontal effect jurisprudence offered in this book concerns a shift way from the *predominantly* substantive due process conception of horizontal effect in *Lüth* to a *predominantly* procedural due process conception of horizontal effect? These are the key questions that the chapters in *Part Two* of this book will aim to address. The remaining chapters of *Part One* turn now from case law to scholarly jurisprudence. Chapter Three reflects on scholarly engagements with the state action doctrine in the United States. Chapter Four turns to German scholarship on *Drittwirkung* jurisprudence.

Chapter Three: State Action

I Introduction

The state action doctrine may have exploded and gone up in smoke in *Shelley v Kraemer*, but its ashes were collected, put together and restored by the very man who caused the explosion. Five years after his explosive judgment in *Shelley*, Justice Vinson would argue in *Barrows v Jackson*[1] that the principle in *Shelley* only applies when the court's order will be the direct cause of the abridgement of an individual's constitutional rights by enforcing a racially discriminating covenant against the member of the racial minority targeted by that covenant. It does not apply, he argued, when the court only enforces the covenant between the parties to the covenant. An action for damages filed by one party to the covenant against another is therefore not covered by the rule in *Shelley*. This is what he meant, he averred in *Barrows* (now as Chief Justice) when he stated that the racially discriminatory restrictive covenant in *Shelley* was not nil and void for reasons of incompatibility with the rights guarantied by the 14th Amendment.[2]

Charles Black would later refer to the state action doctrine as "the last unexpunged clause of [America's] long settled gentlemen's agreement about racism."[3] Chief Justice Vinson's dissent in *Barrows* openly returns to the fold of this gentlemen's agreement that he appeared to disavow with his majority opinion in *Shelley*. Private racial discrimination, is the clear message here, is constitutionally acceptable as long as it does not seek to curtail the constitutional liberties of another by order of a court of law. The fact that court enforcement of racially discriminatory covenants between parties to the covenant would nevertheless impact *indirectly* on the racial minority targeted by the covenant clearly did not bother Chief Justice Vinson. Had his opinion won the day in *Barrows*, it would have, to invoke a rudimentary law and economics analysis, effectively raised the average purchase price of property for black buyers in white neighbourhoods. The next time Shelley and company would have come round with an offer on a house, they may well have had to contend with expectations that serious offers also reflect penalties attendant upon breaches of restrictive

1 346 U.S. 249 (1953).

2 *Barrows v Jackson*, 260. Cf. also Van der Walt, "Abdications of Sovereignty in Horizontal Effect Jurisprudence."

3 Black, "The Supreme Court, 1966 Term – Foreword: State Action, Equal Protection, and California's Proposition 14," 97.

covenants. To rephrase the matter with reference to a different case: Had Chief Justice Vinson's dissent in *Barrows* had a significant say in *Reitman v Mulkey,*[4] the decision in *Reitman* may have gone the other way, for here too, even though belonging to the targeted racial minority, the plaintiffs were not directly affected by the decision of the court. However, Chief Justice Vinson's dissent in *Barrows* finally triumphed three years later in *Black v Cutter Laboratories,*[5] as we shall soon see.

Chief Justice Vinson's dissent in *Barrows* turned on an assumption that Herbert Wechsler took for granted six years later in his famous article on the neutral principles of constitutional law.[6] Wechsler assumed the constitutional irrelevance of purely private "abridgements" of fundamental rights. To put the matter more precisely: He "assumed" the constitutional irrelevance of private conduct that would appear to abridge fundamental rights, but does not because it only concerns and affects parties and people who voluntarily participate in that conduct. There is a new version of "separate but equal" thinking evident in this assumption, ironically just five years after the USSC's decision in *Brown v Board of Education.*[7] Wechsler's assumption clearly suggests that socially dubious or obnoxious private conduct can be *separated* from the rest of society. It does not affect the *equal* enjoyment of rights by others as long as it remains a private matter. In other words, the private can be separated from the public so as not to affect the equality that public relations exact. As we saw in Chapter Two, *The Civil Rights Cases* turned a blind to the racist (horizontal) effects of the state action doctrine in 1883 by focussing on its function in the distinction between federal and state sovereignties. Seventy years later, from 1953 onwards, the public-private divide would offer a similar distraction from the racist effects of the state action doctrine. Racism would henceforth be sheltered by a gentlemen's agreement regarding people's private practices.

What was really at stake in this refurbished state action doctrine? Was it merely a matter of shielding private racism, or was there more to it? There evidently was more to it. Apart from conveniently serving racism for many years, the state action doctrine also served to appease deep discomfort in the American legal imagination regarding the reach of state and federal sovereignty into private matters. This chapter will elaborate this assertion in four steps. Section II briefly revisits Michelman's "Hohfeldian point." Section III engages with Herbert

4 387 U.S. 369 (1967).
5 351 U.S. 292 (1956).
6 Herbert Wechsler, "Toward Neutral Principles of Constitutional Law," *Harvard Law Review*, 73 (1959): 1–35.
7 Cf. 349 U.S. 294 (1954).

Wechsler's and Laurence Tribe's readings of *Shelley.* Section IV looks closely at Louis Seidman's reading of *DeShaney.* Section V takes issue with the conceptual impasse in American state action scholarship that seems to emerge from especially Seidman's probing essay. Section V also commences to offer a plausible way out of this conceptual impasse by rearranging a number of key concepts on which American state action scholarship turns. It does so in view of arguments that will be offered in more complete form in later chapters of this book.

II Michelman's "Hohfeldian Point"

The engagement with Wechsler's and Tribe's readings of *Shelley* in section III and Seidman's reading of *DeShaney* in section IV will reveal the extent to which the state action doctrine pivots on conceptions of the public/private divide that consider this divide naturally given *before* the question of state action arises. These conceptions of the public/private divide require the state action doctrine to sustain natural private spheres that exist independently of political contentions and conflicts – contentions and conflicts that typically come to a head whenever the state action problematic raises its head. Such conceptions of the public/private divide do not reflect the reality that the state action doctrine – and the political conflicts that it embodies – precedes the public/private divide. They fail to understand that private spheres are not "naturally existing" realities that predate the political conflicts that fuel the state action doctrine, but, realities that emerge *from* these conflicts.

Political and social theory learned from Hobbes that there is no such thing as pre-given private spheres to which the state action doctrine could be subject and which it must respect. The application of the state action doctrine, to the contrary, conditions and determines the public/private divide. The invocation of the state action doctrine is one of the ways in which politics draws the line between the public and the private. Private spheres are accordingly contingent results of applications of the state action doctrine, not vice versa. One can therefore not take recourse to invocations of "private spheres" to determine the correct application of the state action doctrine. This is what one also learns from Wesley Hohfeld's analyses of legal relationships. Seen from this Hobbesian and Hohfeldian perspective, the refurbished state action doctrine that would raise its head in *Black v Cutter Laboratories* is clearly spurious.

Hohfeld's analyses of legal relationships are instructive because of the way they pinpoint the essential dynamics that produce the public/private divide. The *origin* and *inception* of the public/private divide, Hohfeld shows, derive from a decision of the state to act or not to act upon the relationships between parties to a dispute. Phrased in Hohfeldian language: The private sphere emerges from an express or tacit decision of a state, taken by or imputable to its legislatures or judiciaries, to define certain social relations in terms of "liberties" and "no-rights," that is, in terms of the correlative concepts that indicate the liberty of one person to do something under circumstances where another has no right to prevent him/her from doing so.[8] Within the boundaries of such liberties (such absence of ordinary legal duties) is located what one might want to call the most private of private spheres. It is within this space that one cannot rely on regular state law to force anyone to do or not to do something.

The space indicated by the correlatives "liberties" and "no-rights" confronts individuals with high levels of insecurity and they regularly move to bind one another to respect obligations that afford them higher levels of security. They do so by relying on mechanisms that the state makes available for this purpose. And when they do so, they move into spheres of social co-existence that are characterised by the correlation between "rights" and "duties." Legal theory and doctrine for a long time only considered social spheres that are characterised by rights/duties correlatives legally significant. Hohfeld was the first legal theorist to stress consistently that the correlatives liberties/no rights also constitute legally relevant and legally structured private spheres. They do so because of the telling ways in which legal systems not only secure rights but also regularly secure liberties. It is surely not uncommon for a judge to confirm a defendant's liberty to act in some or other way by dismissing a (rights) claim that the defendant has a duty not to act in that way. And it is not uncommon for such liberties to be secured by legislation.

The decision of a state legislature or judiciary to define a relation between individuals in terms of liberties and no-rights can be express or tacit. It can take place in the form of decisive action or simple inaction. The form the decision takes is of little consequence or importance from a Hohfeldian perspective. Of importance is much rather a state's fundamental and foundational *capacity to act or not to act* that gives all state action or state inaction a *decisional* status. Seen from this perspective, social relations that result from state inaction are relations with regard to which, states have decided not to act or have not yet decided to act. They do not constitute realms with regard to which states *cannot act*. This Hohfeldian construction of state action and state inaction may come

---

8 Cf. Wesley Newcomb Hohfeld, "Some Fundamental Legal Conceptions as Applied in Judicial Reasoning," *The Yale Law Journal* 23, no. 1 (November 1, 1913): 16–59. Cf. also Joseph William Singer, "The Legal Rights Debate in Analytical Jurisprudence from Bentham to Hohfeld," *Wisconsin Law Review* (1982): 975–1059. My whole engagement with Hohfeld in this book is deeply indebted to this article and to countless discussions with Joe Singer about Hohfeld.

across as nothing but a ruse or play with words. This is not so, however, when states lay claim to sovereign status. Later chapters of this book will unpack this assertion more carefully. Suffice it for now to observe the simple principle that the claim to sovereignty saddles a state with responsibility for everything that comes to pass within its boundaries. This does of course not automatically imply state liability for all harms to which people may come within state boundaries. But it does translate into the normative requirement that states be able to justify why such liability has not been incurred in some or other specific instance of harm.

Sovereign status accordingly requires the state to explain why failure to prevent violations of constitutional rights does not translate into constitutional liability to compensate for those violations. This line of reasoning has clearly informed the position of many American legal scholars on the state action doctrine over the years, albeit not always with express reference to Hohfeld. Roger Paul Peters already articulated a very forceful assertion in this regard in 1959. Peters wrote:

> "The obvious question at this point is this: May a state deprive a person of due process of law and deny him the equal protection of the laws other than by making or enforcing law? The equally obvious answer is: Yes, by not making or enforcing a law when under duty to do so."[9]

Consistent adherence to this approach would of course render the state action doctrine a non-question that can always be answered positively in advance. Harold Horowitz also made this point forcefully in 1957. Horowitz noted that the USSC has in many situations confirmed the "corollary principle that the constitutional restrictions on state action apply to the manner in which a state regulates legal relations between 'private' persons." The court has done so, he observed, notwithstanding the contrary position it had articulated earlier in *The Civil Rights Cases*. Horowitz had *Shelley v Kraemer* and *Marsh v Alabama* especially in mind and he drew this conclusion from them:

> "[M]uch of the effort in the solution of these problems has been misdirected toward attempting to determine whether in the particular circumstances there has or has not been "state action." It is the thesis of this paper that in all of these problems there *is* state action, and that the sole issue, which tends to become obscured in the search for state action, is whether the particular state action in the particular circumstances, determining legal rela-

9 Roger Paul Peters, "Civil Rights and State Non-Action," *Notre Dame Lawyer* 34 (1959): 320.

tions between private persons, is constitutional when tested against the various federal constitutional restrictions on state action."[10]

---

10 Harold W. Horowitz, "The Misleading Search for 'State Action' Under the Fourteenth Amendment," *Southern California Law Review* 30 (1955): 208–209. The point would be stressed repeatedly in subsequent state action scholarship. Consider especially the following four poignant statements in this regard: 1) Larry Alexander, "The Public/Private Distinction and Constitutional Limits on Private Power," *Constitutional Commentary* 10, no. 2 (1993): 371–372: "[A]ll exercises of private power take place against a background of laws that are paradigmatic state action. Thus, any challenge to the exercise of private power can and should be recharacterized as a constitutional challenge to those background laws." And further, at 377: "Private power is subject to constitutional scrutiny. That is so, not because there is no public/private distinction, but because private power is a product of public laws and has effects on interests of constitutional significance. Some fear recognition of this rather banal point will lead to a nightmare of courts constitutionalising all private decision-making. They would rather, instead, have the courts tell the noble lie that choices of private actors are beyond constitutional scrutiny by omitting to acknowledge that those choices are permitted and enforced by the state itself and thus circumscribed by laws that represent the *state's* choices." 2) C. Edwin Baker, "Private Power, the Press, and the Constitution," *Constitutional Commentary* 10 (1993): 421–441, at 421: "State action is a sea in which everything floats. For this reason, constitutional theorists often conclude that the question is seldom whether there is state action but whether obvious state action (including obvious state inaction) is acceptable." 3) Gardbaum, "The 'Horizontal Effect' of Constitutional Rights," 414–415: "A major thesis of this Article is that ...the threshold search for state action in order to trigger a constitutional claim is entirely unwarranted and unnecessary... [T]he search is entirely misguided... Accordingly, whenever a law is invoked or relied on before a court, there is no threshold issue to be resolved before its constitutionality may be assessed. The only genuine issue in every case is whether that law is consistent with, or violates, the Constitution." Gardbaum argues on this same ground that the whole state action doctrine should be discarded and replaced with a proper regard for the obvious principle that the Supremacy Clause of the U.S Constitution binds all judicial action in the United States, irrespective of state laws that may be at variance with the constitution. The Supremacy Clause (United States Constitution, Article VI, clause 2) reads: "This Constitution, and the Laws of the United States which shall be made in Pursuance thereof; and all Treaties made, or which shall be made, under the Authority of the United States, shall be the supreme Law of the Land; and the Judges in every State shall be bound thereby, any Thing in the Constitution or Laws of any State to the Contrary notwithstanding." 4) Mark Tushnet, "The Issue of State Action/Horizontal Effect in Comparative Constitutional Law," *International Journal of Constitutional Law* 1 (2003): 79: "An important strand of liberalism focuses on creating political structures that simultaneously empower and limit governments. Put crudely, this strand leads constitutionalists to pay primary attention to the threats to human rights that *government* poses. Another strand takes the human rights themselves as a focus. It notes that corporations and nongovernmental actors can threaten human rights, too. Governments and corporations can discriminate on the basis of race; governments and corporations can fire employees for speech with which the employer disagrees. The two strands come together when one observes that the people or corporations exercising "private" power are actually exercising power conferred on them by laws creating and regulating market behavior. Thus government is *always* somehow implicated in private decisions." Cf. also Mark

It is this same recognition that there is always state action that prompted Charles Black to call it an "innocuous truism" that could have gone into "honored retirement" long ago had it not served the racist purposes it served for so many years.[11] The "Hohfeldian" point at issue here would indeed seem elementary enough to consider it a "truism." This is not quite the case. Its truth only becomes "self-evident" when one endorses the basic principle of uninterrupted territorial sovereignty and the presumption of unlimited state responsibility for the well-being and rights of citizens/residents that accompanies such sovereignty.

One scholar who does invoke Hohfeld expressly in his writings about the state action doctrine is Frank Michelman. Chapter Two has already referred to Michelman's invocation of the "simple Hohfeldian point" that state inaction and ordinary common law constitute state action for purposes of the 14th Amendment. The different sections of this chapter are again guided by Michelman's views in this regard. The express focus in the rest of this chapter is nevertheless on a number of other prominent scholars in the American state action debate, at least two of whom – Laurence Tribe and Louis Seidman – evidently concede and even endorse the Hohfeldian point, but nevertheless remain apprehensive of its implications for the American conception of private liberty. It is to these scholars that we turn now by first looking at Wechsler and Tribe's readings of *Shelley* in Section III and Seidman's reading of *DeShaney* in Section IV.

III Wechsler and Tribe: Two Readings of *Shelley*

Chief Justice Vinson's opinion in *Barrows v Jackson* did not convince the majority of the court and for this reason had no immediate effect. But the reasoning that he employed in *Barrows* surely prepared the way for the decision of the majority of the court in *Black v Cutter Laboratories*.[12] In *Cutter Laboratories*, the Supreme Court enforced a collective bargaining agreement that held Communist Party membership as a just cause for dismissal. The Court considered the collective agreement a contract between private parties on which constitutional principles

Tushnet, "State Action, Social Welfare Rights, and the Judicial Role: Some Comparative Observations," *Chicago Journal of International Law* 3 (2002): 435, to which we return right at the end of this book; For a forceful articulation of this line of thinking in the European context, cf. Oliver Gerstenberg, "Private Law and the New European Constitutional Settlement," *European Law Journal* 10, no. 6 (2004): 771–772.

11 Black, "The Supreme Court, 1966 Term – Foreword: State Action, Equal Protection, and California's Proposition 14," 109.

12 *Black v Cutter Laboratories* 351 US 292 (1956).

had no bearing or effect.[13] Chief Justice Warren and Justices Douglas and Black tried in vain to uphold the rule in *Shelley.*[14] *New York Times v Sullivan*[15] had not been decided at the time, but *Labour v Swing*[16] had been. As we saw in Chapter Two, *Swing* had already accepted in 1941 that common law constitutes state action, as *Sullivan* would do again in 1963. The idea that common law rules of contract could constitute state action relevant to the Fourteenth Amendment did nevertheless not convince the judges who decided *Cutter Laboratories* in 1956.

Be it as it may, it is not only against the background of *Shelley*, but also against the background of the deviation from *Shelley* in *Barrows v Jackson* and *Black v Cutter Laboratories* that Herbert Wechsler would ask the following questions in his article on the neutral application of constitutional principles:

> "*Assuming* that the Constitution speaks to state discrimination on the ground of race but not to such discrimination by an individual even in the use or distribution of his property, although his freedom may no doubt be limited by common law or statute, why is the enforcement of the private covenant a state discrimination rather than a legal recognition of the freedom of the individual? That the action of the state court is action of the state, the point that Mr. Chief Justice Vinson emphasizes in the court's opinion is, of course, entirely obvious. What is not obvious, and this is the crucial step, is that the state may properly be charged with the discrimination when it does no more than give effect to an agreement that the individual involved is, by hypothesis, entirely free to make. Again, one is obliged to ask: What is the principle involved?"[17]

This was Wechsler's way of suggesting that the state action doctrine, at least as regards racially discriminatory restrictive covenants, is a "conceptual disaster area," to use Charles Black's phrase.[18] According to Wechsler, *Shelley* provides us with no reasoned argument and therefore with no neutral principle as to when and why one should charge the court's decision with state action instead of taking it as a passive recognition of private liberty and autonomy that do not constitute state action. The remarkable feature of this line of thinking concerns its matter of fact assumption that the neutral application of a legal principle remains pertinent in constitutional review, irrespective of the question whether the principle itself raises substantive neutrality concerns. Wechsler would not seem

13 *Black v Cutter Laboratories*, 294–300.
14 *Black v Cutter Laboratories*, 303. Cf. also Van der Walt, "Abdications of Sovereignty in Horizontal Effect Jurisprudence."
15 376 US 254 (1963).
16 312 US 321 (1941).
17 Wechsler, "Toward Neutral Principles of Constitutional Law," 29.
18 Black, "The Supreme Court, 1966 Term – Foreword: State Action, Equal Protection, and California's Proposition 14," 95.

to be bothered by the possibility that the neutral application of principles that he has in mind may involve principles that are not substantively neutral. If this is indeed the case, he is surely only concerned with the *weak* neutrality reflected by requirements of judicial *consistency*. He surely could then not be concerned, for instance, with the glaring gap that opens up between *neutral* and *consistent* applications of the principle of freedom of contract with regard to contractual clauses that proscribe the selling of property to black people. The evident lack of substantive political and social neutrality that inevitably results from this "neutral application" would evidently be irrelevant according to this reasoning.

The gap between neutral and merely consistent applications of the principle of freedom of contract in the case of contractual agreements not to sell property to black buyers is not only glaringly obvious. It also exposes the way in which the consistent application and enforcement of such agreements *creates* a particular kind of private sphere. It creates a historically contingent private sphere that remains subject to patterns of political contestation and will-formation. These private spheres will not be possible at all times and in all places. They are never just given. The neighbourhood in which only white people can buy property can surely be expected to be offensive to some political actors who could at any time move to defeat it. Should they succeed, the boundaries and definition of the private sphere in this rather racist corner of the world will surely be redrawn. However, should they fail to do so with recourse to ordinary legislative politics and eventually seek recourse to constitutional principles to bring about the desired change, their constitutional challenge can surely not be answered by invoking "a private sphere" as if that "private sphere" is the solution to and not the source of the problem. Put in terms of the terms developed in Chapter One, Wechsler's concern with "neutral principles" evidently regards the substantive neutrality of these principles as baseline questions that fall outside the scope of relevant constitutional considerations. And this is how his arguments reduce principled neutrality to the consistent endorsement of existing status quos.

The human condition, as we know it, surely sustains neither complete nor pervasive agreements regarding proper boundaries of private spheres. The day political liberals and conservatives will see eye to eye with regard to such boundaries – let alone liberals, conservatives and radicals (right and left) – is not looming large on the horizon. Liberals and conservatives differ fundamentally on the question of how private spheres should be styled and they will continue to strive politically to have it styled in ways they respectively prefer. "Styled" is the right word to use here. It points out that private spheres ultimately concern something like life style choices. They are not naturally given. Arguments that Robert Mnookin presented at a 1981 conference on the private/public divide make the point abundantly clear. Mnookin, relying on Daniel Bell, argued that both liberals and conservatives believe in the public/private distinction, they just hold opposite views regarding the question of what is public and what is private. Conservatives believe the economy and financial transactions are private matters that should either not be regulated or regulated as little as possible by public authorities and legislators. According to them, everyone should take care of their own economic interests and politics should play no re-distributive role once market forces have defined society. Sexual and intimate relations, on the other hand, are matters of the highest moral importance to conservatives. They typically believe these matters should be regulated publicly as far as possible. They believe public authorities and legislators should promote heterosexual monogamous marital arrangements as the only proper basis for family and intimate relations. They are against abortion and against homosexual marriages. Many of them may even be against homosexual relationships as such and would prefer to have these relationships criminalised.

Liberals, on the other hand, believe sexual and intimate concerns are private matters that should be left to individual choice. Public authorities and legislation should generally not regulate these concerns. Liberals have no problems with homosexual marriages or relationships, non-marital relationships, etc. They insist that these things should be deregulated as far as possible. What should be regulated publicly, according to liberals, is the economy and financial transactions. Liberals believe public administration and legislation should ensure minimum levels of economic equality and social welfare. The state should constantly be involved in the redistribution of wealth in order to safeguard the human dignity of individuals who fail to fend for themselves. This is a matter of highest moral importance to liberals. To sum up quickly and provocatively: Conservatives believe liberals are "promiscuous" (at least by allowing people to be "promiscuous"). Liberals believe conservatives are "selfish" (at least by allowing people to be "selfish"). But they both believe in the private/public divide insofar as they both believe certain things, especially promiscuity or selfishness, should be publically regulated. As Mnookin puts it well, liberals and conservatives both know the Hudson separates Brooklyn from Manhattan, but they disagree about which side is Brooklyn and which side is Manhattan.[19] Only some radical academics, such as Karl Klare, observes Mnookin, reject the public/private distinction all together. Klare is surely no conservative, but he is also no (ordinary) liberal. He wants both the economy and sexual morality to be regulated.

---

19 Robert H. Mnookin, "The Public/Private Dichotomy: Political Disagreement and Academic Repudiation," *University of Pennsylvania Law Review* 130, no. 6 (June 1, 1982): 1429–1440.

The latter should also be regulated, he believes, not for purposes of conservative pro-marriage and homophobic sexual moralities, but to the contrary, for purposes of ensuring a "public right" to a "sexually pluralistic environment."[20]

One need not go further into this debate here. Its significance for the conception of the state action doctrine that is at issue here should already be clear. From neither a liberal nor a conservative point of view can the private/public be regarded as a natural, spatial or geographical divide that one crosses whenever one leaves public spheres or public offices and enters domestic or business premises. Had this been the case, the debate between liberals and conservatives on this count would not have existed, for few would dispute matters of spatial geography for long. Geographical questions regarding the whereabouts of river X can be settled quickly and enduringly. It is only when the whereabouts of river X becomes economically or politically contentious (is river X the boundary between properties or countries Y and Z?) that they become the subject of enduring debate. The boundaries of the private sphere likewise only remain interesting and contentious because of the way they are drawn by political and social conduct. The private sphere is nothing but a function of legal liberties that temporarily and contingently enjoy legal protection against any imposition of legal duties.

This understanding of the "private sphere" recognises that its temporary enjoyment of legal protection is indeed highly contingent and incidental and always subject to renewed political and social contestation, contestation that may any time render it obsolete or highly contentious. It should be clear from all of this that one cannot invoke "neutral principles" to sustain private spheres that allow for constitutionally acceptable racial discrimination, for the very concern with such private spheres would turn on principles that are already operative in debates or conflicts about how such private spheres should be defined. In other words, the most one can expect from Wechsler's "neutral principles" is the *consistent* application of a set of (obviously non-neutral) principles that sustain some or other preferred conception of private spheres. For these principles to become truly neutral they would have to extract themselves sufficiently from the field of conflicting arguments that sustain the interminably contingent boundaries of the private sphere and they can only achieve this at the cost of becoming largely irrelevant for the boundaries that need to be drawn. They evidently lose their neutrality the moment they become relevant.

---

20 Karl E. Klare, "The Public/Private Distinction in Labor Law," *University of Pennsylvania Law Review* 130, no. 6 (June 1, 1982): 1386–1387.

The quest for neutral principles regarding the application of the state action doctrine is nevertheless not misguided. In fact, the arguments in this book also seek to articulate an understanding of the state action doctrine that would allow for its neutral application. But the concern with neutrality must remain alert to the way neutral application of principles in contexts of (inevitably) non-neutral substantive preferences reduces neutrality to mere consistency. If the concern with neutral principles regarding the application of the state action doctrine were to remain consistent, it would have to relate the neutrality it envisages to recognition of the irreducible and interminable controversiality of all but a very few substantive norms. Neutrality consists in the recognition of conflict, controversy and tension, not on their resolution in some way or another. And it is on the basis of this recognition that the chapters in the second part of this book will set out to articulate a conception of sovereignty that will indeed allow for the "neutral" application of the state action doctrine.

The "neutrality" claimed in this regard is of course not watertight, hence the scarecrows. Those who believe all normative controversy can ultimately be settled with reference to norms that all humans share will be quick to point out that the recognition of irreducible and interminable controversy and contestability takes a typically sceptical side in an old debate about the foundations of normativity. That recognition is therefore hardly as "neutral" as it presents itself. This is indeed an old debate and no one that is familiar with its terms still entertains much hope that it will be settled one day. And since this meta-debate about normative foundations also ends up in unresolved controversy, one seems to have even more reason for resigning oneself to futures of interminable controversy, and to articulate a conception of state action and private/public divides that might allow one to live and deal with deep controversies and differences until such time as better wisdoms befall us all. The solution that Laurence Tribe offers to the state action controversy that resulted from the USSC's decision in *Shelley* would seem to make a tentative move in this direction.

According to Tribe, "the Constitution speaks to state discrimination on the ground of race but not to such discrimination by an individual even in the use or distribution of his property," *provided such discrimination does not have the all over effect of confining minorities to their current disadvantaged positions in society.* This is the "subjugation" thesis that Tribe offers as the real rationale behind the decision in *Shelley.*[21] He offers this subjugation thesis as a response to the "common misconstruction of *Shelley*" that, according to him, is evident in

21 Tribe, *American Constitutional Law*, 1718.

Justice Rehnquist's opinion in *Moose Lodge v Irvis*[22] and in Duncan Kennedy's essay on "The Stages of Decline of the Public/Private Distinction."[23] The "common misconstruction of *Shelley*" consists, for Tribe, in the assumption "that the fourteenth amendment requires states to outlaw all private acts of racism whenever the private party might ultimately seek the security of judicial enforcement."[24] Tribe's claim in this regard is surprising. Common logic surely inclines one to the opposite view that there is no obvious misconstruction of *Shelley* evident here, Chief Justice Vinson's own back-pedalling in *Barrows v Jackson* notwithstanding. The extensive quotes from and engagement with his opinion in *Shelley* in Chapter Two should make this abundantly clear. *Shelley* surely stands for nothing less than a proscription of all unconstitutional private racism that takes recourse to judicial enforcement. And Tribe surely does not exert himself to explain why, according to him, *Shelley* does not stand for this proscription. In fact, he prefers to hedge his bet on this count. "If *Shelley* ever stood for such a bold proposition," he continues, "it certainly does no longer, for in *Washington v Davies* and its progeny the court declared adverse impact on a racial minority is insufficient to make a facially neutral rule or practice unconstitutional or even suspect."[25]

Washington v Davis imposed a restriction on the scope of the rule in *Shelley* by deciding that it only applies in cases where the abridgement of the constitutional right at issue is the result of conduct with discriminatory intent and not only of conduct that happens to have discriminatory effects. Tribe's aim is to offer "a more accurate reading of *Shelley* that survives *Washington v Davis*."[26] One must not get him wrong. His aim is to rehabilitate *Shelley* and the "more accurate reading" of *Shelley* through which he hopes to do so turns on his subjugation thesis. According to this thesis, racial discrimination becomes unconstitutional when it has the effect of entrenching, extending or perpetuating current factual disadvantages of racial minorities, that is, when it attains the effect of state or legally enforced subjugation that makes it impossible for these minorities to escape from their current disadvantaged positions.[27]

---

22 407 US 163 (1972).

23 Duncan Kennedy, "Stages of the Decline of the Public/Private Distinction," *University of Pennsylvania Law Review* 130 (1982): 1349–1357.

24 Tribe, *American Constitutional Law*, 1718.

25 Ibid, 1718 note 24.

26 Ibid. Cf. also Laurence Tribe, *Constitutional Choices* (Cambridge, Mass.: Harvard University Press, 1985), 259.

27 Tribe, *American Constitutional Law*, 1514–1521.

Tribe's subjugation thesis is forceful and resonates in important respects with the understanding of state action and sovereignty pursued in this book. But Chief Justice Vinson surely did not offer this argument nor think of it in *Shelley*, unless one really wants to read this whole argument into his thin statement that racist contracts that do not seek enforcement in a court of law are not nil or nothing. The subjugation theory rather seems to effect a substantive reconstruction of *Shelley* that is not evident in Justice Vinson's opinion.

Be it as it may, the upshot of Tribe's thesis is an acceptance that the Constitution "speaks to state discrimination on the ground of race" but not to any such discrimination by individuals, provided such private discrimination does not have the effect of subjugating a racial minority by confining them by force of law to their current disadvantaged positions in society. In other words, when discrimination passes the legal subjugation threshold, it crosses the public/private divide. Subjugation is necessarily public subjugation, is Tribe's point. Short of subjugation, racial discrimination remains constitutionally irrelevant private racism. It should indeed be clear that Tribe's position on state action still does not expunge what Charles Black called "the last unexpunged clause of [America's] long settled gentlemen's agreement about racism."[28] He too allows for an area of private racism that is constitutionally uncontroversial. This private racism must just not cross the subjugation threshold.

In the final analysis Tribe also comes round to making the "Hohfeldian point" regarding state action. The relevant question is also for him not a threshold inquiry into the presence or absence of state action, but the question whether state *tolerance* of private conduct constitutes a substantive violation of the Fourteenth Amendment. At issue is the question whether a particular instance of "government tolerance of private conduct amounts to state action."[29] Relevant here, for Tribe, "is a decision about the substantive reach of specific constitutional demands rather than a decision about whether the government has *done* anything to which the Constitution speaks."[30] According to him, the "search for state action, properly conducted, ends by identifying the precise substantive constitutional issue to be addressed."[31] In the case of private racial discrimination, that question can be answered, for him, with reference to the subjugation thesis. Private racial discrimination aimed at creating public order that is disadvantageous

28 Black, "The Supreme Court, 1966 Term – Foreword: State Action, Equal Protection, and California's Proposition 14," 97.

29 Tribe, *American Constitutional Law*, 1697.

30 Ibid, 1720.

31 Ibid, 1715.

to racial and other minorities falls foul of the substantive demands of the constitution and can for this reason not be tolerated by the state.

Again, Tribe's position turns on a somewhat creative reconstruction of *Shelley*. This reconstruction nevertheless resonates firmly with one of the central arguments presented in this book. The idea that state action or horizontal effect jurisprudence effects a *horizontalisation* or *levelling* in liberal democracies underpins the key arguments in this book. This is surely also what Tribe's subjugation thesis aims at. It also pivots on the liberal democratic demand that relations between social majorities and minorities sustain minimum conditions of equality and liberty. Cast in terms of the subjugation thesis, the state action doctrine should be understood as a proscription of private endeavours to promote or sustain public inequality.

Tribe's subjugation thesis would seem to work well in the context of discriminatory state action or inaction, but its heuristic value also appears to be limited to this kind of state action/inaction. Can the subjugation thesis be extended to cases of non-discriminatory state inaction such as was at issue in a case like *DeShaney?* This seems unlikely. Those who are happy to endorse the decision that the state inaction in *DeShaney* did not constitute state action may be content to let the matter rest with the conclusion that it did not trigger Tribe's subjugation criterion. The harm suffered as a result of the state inaction in *DeShaney* was too random and too individualised to construe it in terms of general social subjugation. The argument that the state inaction at issue tolerated the entrenchment of the current disadvantages of children just does not seem applicable here. Those who would want to view the state inaction in *DeShaney* as state action, would ultimately have to offer a different argument, for Tribe's subjugation theory surely does not seem to work for *DeShaney* as it does for *Shelley*.

To rephrase the matter in terms that were introduced in the discussion of *Roe v Wade* and *Erste Abtreibung* in Chapter Two: The inapplicability of Tribe's subjugation thesis in a case like *DeShaney* indicates clearly that *DeShaney* did not concern social majority-minority relations. *DeShaney* did not concern some instance of contestability with regard to which citizens/residents can present themselves in terms of legislative majority-minority configurations. *DeShaney* concerned a case of constitutional protection that, I wish to argue, afforded no scope for contestation and disputation, notwithstanding the degree of contestation and disputation – reflected in the majority and dissenting opinions – it in fact happened to elicit. It is important to take another close look at *DeShaney* to understand this well and to determine how the state action in the case can be explained more incisively. This time we will do so through Louis Seidman's reading of the case.

IV Seidman's Reading of *DeShaney*

We saw in Chapter Two how the United States Supreme Court argued little more than twenty years ago that the negligent failure of the Winnebago County Social Services Department to protect Joshua DeShaney from violent assault did not constitute a failure of the state to prevent harm. State employees had for a long time been aware of the violent assaults that eventually led to Joshua DeShaney's severe and permanent brain injuries. They did nothing about it until it was too late. According to the *DeShaney* court, however, these facts reflected a complete absence of the state, and not a failure of the state to act. The decision was based on a formalistic distinction between state action and inaction and an insistence that the Fourteenth Amendment only speaks to the former, not the latter. The distinction between state action and inaction, this line of reasoning suggests, demarcates the public/private divide. The public sphere begins when positive state action commences. The private sphere commences where state action is absent, that is, where the state fails or refuses to act. The *DeShaney* case illustrates the existence of a conceptual constellation in American constitutional jurisprudence under the auspices of which the distinction between state action and state inaction informs and sustains the public/private divide. The violence that befell Joshua DeShaney was private violence perpetrated by his father, not public or state violence. Another look at a key observation in Justice Rehnquist's opinion, already quoted in Chapter Two, makes this abundantly clear:

> "[I]t is well to remember once again that the harm was inflicted not by the State of Wisconsin, but by Joshua's father. The most that can be said of the state functionaries in this case is that they stood by and did nothing when suspicious circumstances dictated a more active role for them."[32]

And as we also saw in Chapter Two, Justices Brennan and Blackmun considered this to be the crucial argument that required refutation:

> "It simply belies reality, therefore, to contend that the State "stood by and did nothing" with respect to Joshua. Through its child-protection program, the State actively intervened in Joshua's life and, by virtue of this intervention, acquired ever more certain knowledge that Joshua was in grave danger."[33]

In Justice Blackmun's words also:

---

32 *DeShaney*, 202–203.
33 *DeShaney*, 210.

> "As Justice Brennan demonstrates, the facts here involve not mere passivity, but active state intervention in the life of Joshua DeShaney – intervention that triggered a fundamental duty to aid the boy once the State learned of the severe danger to which he was exposed."

The sensibility that the public/private divide turns on nothing but a state action/inaction divide would become common course in the wake of the New Deal revolution, argues Louis Seidman.[34] In view of the watershed historical expansion of state regulation of all walks of life in the wake of the New Deal revolution of 1937, the assumption of a "natural" division between state and civil society or public and private life no longer made sense. Against the New Deal background of pervasive state involvement in civil society and the private sphere, specific instances of state inaction could no longer be represented in terms of the simple absence of the state. Against this background, state inaction constituted, not the absence of the state, but the fully present and conscious refusal or failure of the state to act.[35] Under these circumstances, the private/public distinction itself became a function of the state's political *decision* to intervene or not to intervene. No longer was the private sphere the denotation of a natural boundary beyond which the state was not allowed to venture. Henceforth the "private sphere" would signify nothing more than the incidental and historical contours of state or governmental decisions to intervene or not to intervene. No longer the natural boundary that interdicted state intervention, the private sphere became the contingent result or function of non-intervention. And of course, the moment the natural boundary between private and public turned into a historical and incidental contour of state activity, it also became normatively contentious in a way natural boundaries can never be. From this point onwards, the distinction between private and public would be constantly exposed to normative dissent regarding the question whether the state should or should not act or have acted under the circumstances. As we saw above, liberals would generally want the state to concentrate its efforts on the regulation of the economy whereas conservatives would want it to concentrate on sexual morality.

According to Seidman, both Chief Justice Rehnquist and Justice Brennan were well aware of this realist legacy. Both of them were "heirs of the 1937 Revolution," he says.[36] Assuming this to be correct, how then, must one understand Chief Justice Rehnquist's formalist distinction between state action and inaction? His distinction in this regard appears to be guided by a reading of the Fourteenth Amendment that envisages a pre-existing private sphere, a private sphere that

---

34 Seidman, "The State Action Paradox," 397.

35 Ibid, 397–398.

36 Ibid, 399.

exists independently of the question whether the state acted or did not act. This does not seem to be consistent with the thinking one would expect from an "heir of the 1937 Revolution." Consider also this passage again:

> "But nothing in the language of the Due Process Clause itself requires the State to protect the life, liberty, and property of its citizens against invasion by private actors. The Clause is phrased as a limitation on the State's power to act, not as a guarantee of certain minimal levels of safety and security."

It is important to note again that Justice Brennan deemed it necessary to refute this formalist position with an equally formalist retort that there was clear evidence of state action in *DeShaney*. He too did not appropriate the legacy of the realist revolution as fully as one might have expected, argues Seidman. Had he done so, he simply would have dismissed the state action question as a non-issue. He would have accepted state action as a given, or he would have launched "a frontal assault against it," writes Seidman.[37] But it is clear that he did not. His opinion was not based on the view that the state action question is a non-question, one that should evacuate the courtroom so as to allow more space and time for the real question whether the state action or inaction at issue was normatively and constitutionally justifiable. So obvious was the state intervention in *DeShaney* for him, that he based his argument on the conspicuous presence of positive state action. He therefore also did not have to fall back on the argument that he employed thirty-five years before in *New York Times v Sullivan*, as he might have done.[38] The conspicuous presence of positive state action rendered his argument in *Sullivan* regarding deficient common law protection redundant.

So if both these judges were heirs of the realist legacy and the 1937 Revolution, as Seidman contends, why did they both resort to the formalism of a bygone age? According to Seidman, both Justices Brennan and Rehnquist evince deep ambivalence regarding their "realist" inheritance. They are both realists, but they are both deeply bothered by the implications of this realism, he argues. Why is this so? This is how Seidman phrases and responds to this question:

> "[W]hy [do Justices Rehnquist and Brennan] not simply concede that state action analysis ought to be abandoned altogether [and] why [do they] not simply concede that state action

37 Ibid.
38 See again the discussion of *New York Times v Sullivan* in Chapter Two.

> is always present in some form and move directly to an analysis of whether the state action is constitutionally permissible?"[39]
>
> "In light of the confusion produced by the state action inquiry, this approach is certainly attractive. Unfortunately, however, it only shifts the problem without really solving it, because something like the state action doctrine – together with all the uncertainty and incoherence that accompanies it – is built into how we think about constitutional rights."[40]

We want to embrace the New Deal revolution that rendered the distinction between a pre-given private/public divide so implausible, avers Seidman, but

> "we also want to embrace the concept of a private sphere because we know that it preserves a space for individual flourishing that the state may otherwise destroy."[41]
>
> "Political liberals who supported the New Deal therefore could not wholly embrace the skeptical view that individual freedom was a myth. On the contrary, their ultimate aim was to create the material conditions that would free individuals to lead productive and happy private lives."[42]

Judging by the way Seidman phrases the matter, even liberals have or had plausible reason to believe that the New Deal intrinsically threatened to reduce individual liberty to a myth. To be sure, there are individuals who believe, relatively coherently at that, that expansive government programmes (other than the expansive government programme that upholds the principle of freedom of contract, of course) necessarily interfere with individual liberty. One usually calls them libertarians and the likes of Robert Nozick or Friedrich Hayek come to mind when this kind of thinking about the relation between government and liberty is at issue.[43] But Seidman does not seem to be thinking of libertarians in these passages. He is also thinking about Justice Brennan who in most circles would surely not be considered libertarian. One must infer from all of this that Seidman himself has difficulty imagining regulatory politics as the basis of freedom. He himself appears inclined to understand liberty as threatened by politics, and not as conditioned and warranted by politics. And he appears to associate this inclination to view politics as anathema to liberty with many liberal political and legal theorists in the United States.

---

39 Seidman, "The State Action Paradox," 392. This is basically the question asked by all the authors cited in fn. 10 above.
40 Ibid, 392–393.
41 Ibid, 401.
42 Ibid, 400.
43 Cf. Robert Nozick, *Anarchy, State, and Utopia* (Oxford: Basic Books, 1974); Friedrich Hayek, *The Road to Serfdom* (Chicago: University of Chicago Press, 2007).

The appreciation of state action as a condition for civil liberty would understandably create difficulty for libertarians such as Hayek and Nozick, but it is surprising that Seidman would also implicate American liberals – those Americans whom Europeans would tend to call "social democrats" – in this conceptual difficulty. If Seidman is correct in this regard, the state action doctrine would seem to remain fraught with conceptual inconsistences – a conceptual disaster area as Charles Black called it – in the United States, because American liberals, unlike liberal democrats elsewhere in the world, surreptitiously cling to a libertarian concept of liberty, on the one hand, and principles of democratic politics, on the other, without being able to reconcile these two sides of their political commitments. They are "liberals" (libertarians, in fact) on the one hand, and "democrats" on the other, and they lack a conceptual framework for reconciling these two commitments. That is why they are stuck between a realist regard for the contingent political definitions of the private sphere, on the one hand, and a formalist desire for a private sphere that would not entirely be subject to political definition and redefinition, on the other. It is also for this reason that they cannot come to grips with the possibility of "individuals [leading] productive and happy private lives" *because* of robust politics, and not because of the absence of such politics. And this is also why Justices Rehnquist and Brennan, according to Seidman, got stuck between realist and formalist intuitions about action and inaction in *DeShaney*.

It is doubtful whether Seidman's characterisation of Justices Rehnquist and Brennan will resonate with everyone.[44] His argument is nevertheless instructive because of the way it reflects the extent to which the analytical puzzles associated with the state action doctrine may well be the result of a deep-seated ambivalence in American jurisprudence. American jurisprudence is torn, according to Seidman, between the legacy of the realists, on the one hand, and ineradicable convictions regarding a natural private sphere, on the other. In other words, the dream or ideal of a natural private sphere that requires no political delimitation or regulation and warrants constitutional protection against any such delimitation and regulation still drives American legal thinking. The realist movement and the social crises that precipitated the New Deal may have unmasked this dream as a myth, but it has not, it would seem, resolved the deep-seated dependence on this myth in post-realist American legal thought; hence the conundrum of the state action doctrine.

---

44 Cf. for instance Frank Michelman, *Brennan and Democracy* (Princeton University Press, 2005). Michelman gives a very different assessment of Justice Brennan's legacy.

Seidman's intuition regarding this deep tension in the American jurisprudential frame of mind is by no means idiosyncratic. His views in this regard are corroborated by observations of other prominent scholars. Lawrence Tribe's reflections on state action provide a first significant case in point. Tribe is on the one hand duly aware of Michelman's "Hohfeldian point." He is well aware, as he puts it, that the "legal landscape itself [can become] challengeable state action."[45] But Tribe also contends in the same breath that, "to see all social intercourse as behaviour conditioned by and therefore attributable to the state is to deny the existence of a private realm." "Many of us," he continues,

> "therefore, cling to such institutions as freedom of contract and private property, viewing them as a natural, "given" part of the legal landscape which provide a background for our private, consensual transactions."[46]

Here then, is another eminent American constitutional scholar owning up to the deep tension in American legal thinking that informs the state action doctrine. Seidman is evidently not alone in grappling with this tension. However, the lengths to which he goes to also unpack this tension properly make his contribution to the state action debate uniquely instructive. Here are the main lines of this unpacking again: One the one hand, he is fully in favour of a robust post-New Deal state action jurisprudence. He knows the idea of a naturally given private sphere is a myth. On the other hand, he is concerned about the implications of such a robust New-Deal jurisprudence for the space of personal flourishing that he (and many or most Americans) associates with the private sphere. Hence his contemplation of a need to replace the idea of a "natural and pre-existing distinction between public and private" with a concept that would nevertheless "prevent every policy question from becoming an issue for constitutional interpretation."[47] He may have meant, "prevent every *private choice* from becoming an issue for constitutional interpretation," but one can see where he is going.

Seidman knows the position of those – we have been calling them Hohfeldians – who wish to let go of the state action doctrine and accept the simple solution that everything in the legal landscape is state action. This will not help, he argues, because "it shifts the problem without really solving it." It will not help because "something like the state action doctrine – together with all the uncertainty and incoherence that accompanies it – is built into how we think about

45 Tribe, *Constitutional Choices.*

46 Ibid, 264.

47 Seidman, "The State Action Paradox," 399.

constitutional rights."[48] This, however, is as close as one can come to saying that the state action doctrine and the public/private distinction that it sustains are natural after all, without actually saying it. To say that the state action doctrine is built into the way we think about constitutional rights is to forward a very naturalistic contention. Seidman is evidently not ready yet to give up the idea of a "natural and pre-existing distinction between public and private."

What is afoot in this awkward equivocation evident in both Tribe's and Seidman's positions regarding state action? Why this insistence on natural spheres of life against the background of acknowledgments that private spheres are legal landscapes which, like urban gardens, are sculptured and designed by civil authority and state power, remaining wildernesses within which are not original or natural but due to neglect, lack of resources or positive design? Why this apparent concession to decidedly "game ranger" libertarian mentalities that would reserve vast pockets of wilderness in the midst of urban environments? Ira Nerkin offers the following explanation for this apparently ineradicable equivocation:

> "In the post-*Lochner* [and post-New Deal] era, it is widely recognised that non-criminal private action infringing rights of others is sanctioned by law, law that is made or enforced by the state. With this recognition, simple distinctions between what is public and what is private generally have fallen as the complex interrelationship between state power and private economic power has been made apparent. Where once private power could boldly claim a right to be free of state control, now the state is seen to have affirmative obligations to protect individuals from the depredations characteristic of unrestrained action in the private sector. Thus logically, the state action prohibited by the fourteenth amendment is always there. Yet, having come this far, we have avoided re-examining the relationship of private economic power and the state's recognized obligation to protect and extend individual rights and liberties within the context of the fourteenth amendment. It would be more than fair to say that, in the area of state action decision-making, the Court has failed to emerge from the *Lochner* era. Indeed, this would be a highly accurate characterisation of the role of state action doctrine. State action theory has tied the destiny of protection of civil rights and civil liberties to nineteenth century theories of private property and private power and their privileged position vis-à-vis the state."[49]

Chapter One highlighted the very similar observation that Jennifer Nedelsky makes regarding the anachronistic remains of nineteenth century conceptions

---

48 Ibid, 393.

49 Ira Nerken, "A New Deal for the Protection of Fourteenth Amendment Rights: Challenging the Doctrinal Bases of the Civil Rights Cases and State Action Theory," *Harvard Civil Rights-Civil Liberties Law Review* 12 (1977): 298.

of private property that survived post-New Deal understandings of constitutional property rights. "In many crucial respects," she contends,

> "we have accepted the New Deal but rejected its conceptual underpinnings. As a country, we routinely engage in redistribution to ameliorate social ills, but we have not simply accepted property as a mere social construct to be redefined or redistributed without constraint."[50]

What might be the reason for this deep resistance in the American frame of mind to the acceptance of property and private spheres as social constructs that are subject to historical and political disputation and redefinition? Why is this resistance also prominent among liberal or progressive legal theorists who are profoundly schooled and thoroughly seasoned with regard to the socio-historical construction and political disputability of social goods such as property and privacy, and, moreover, deem it just that such social goods be redefined when social need so requires? The problem seems to lie in a confusion of property and private relations, on the one hand, and a very different concern, on the other hand. The "very different concern" at issue here, is the constitutional concern with fundamental rights to life, dignity, liberty (*fundamental* liberty, not private liberty) and integrity of persons that liberal democracies recognise as "inviolable." Liberal democratic Hohfeldians and other liberal democratic social constructionists such as Seidman and Tribe (the social landscape is state action, he concedes) are evidently comfortable with recognising the politically constructed status of property relations, but they quite understandably cannot stomach the idea that the New Deal (or any other programme of social-security legislation for that matter) may have reduced these fundamental rights – the rights that guarantee the fundamental individual liberty to live "productive and happy private lives" – to a "myth." And then, because of some reflex association or equation of these fundamental rights with property and private relations, they suddenly feel themselves compelled to back off from their social-constructionist and state action insights regarding property and private relations.

No doubt, liberal democracies are also social constructions. History teaches us that undemocratic social movements can destroy them. However, as long as they survive, liberal democracies embody the commitment and promise to sustain fundamental rights to liberty, integrity, life and dignity of the person as inviolable. These rights cannot be regarded as contingent social constructions *from within* the definitional boundaries of the social constructions that liberal democ-

50 Nedelsky, *Private Property and the Limits of American Constitutionalism*, 3. Cf. again the discussion of Nedelsky's argument in Chapter One.

racies surely are, without undoing or destroying the whole social construction that goes by the name of liberal democracy. The contingent limitations of these rights to which even liberal democracies sometimes resort, do not constitute reconstructions or destructions that render them contingent or violable "after all." They remain as absolute and inviolable as ever before, notwithstanding the limitations to which they may occasionally become subject. This is so because the over-arching construction of liberal democracy itself depends on sustaining the foundational construction of fundamental rights as inviolable, non-contingent and absolute. The moment that any liberal democracy would begin to give any slack as far as this foundational construction of these rights as "fundamental," "inviolable," "non-contingent" and "absolute" is concerned, would be the moment that that liberal democracy would no longer qualify as a liberal democracy. Social constructions must consider the fundamental (social) constructions on which they pivot non-contingent if they wish to remain the social constructions that they are.

Specific property rights and specific private liberties are very different in this regard. They can be undone, reduced, diminished or reconstructed quite significantly and incisively without threatening the fundamental or essential characteristics of liberal democracy. In fact, their reconstruction may quite to the contrary be required for the sustenance of essential elements of liberal democracy. Stripping private property rights of any potential capacity to entrench racially segregated property relations would surely deprive some individuals of liberties that they may have enjoyed earlier on, but it would not occur to any liberal democrat that one is stripping them of the fundamental liberty to live "productive and happy private lives." One would only be stripping them of a specific (Hohfeldian) liberty that is no longer reconcilable with liberal democracy (assuming rather awkwardly that it was for a time). There may be people who would want to claim that stripping someone of the liberty to create a racially segregated private sphere also strips that person of an element of his or her fundamental liberty. That is their problem and a theory of liberal constitutional democracy cannot solve it for them. They entertain a concept of liberty that is irreconcilable with liberal democracy and irrelevant to liberal democrats. A theory of liberal democracy can only speak meaningfully to people like Seidman and Tribe who evidently are liberal democrats but struggle to make sense of some of liberal democracy's troubling complexities.

The distinction between property relations and the private sphere, on the one hand, and the life, dignity and integrity of the person, on the other, may well be the key that we need to come to terms with the *DeShaney* case. For *DeShaney* had nothing to do with the mere demarcation of private and public spheres. For those who, despite their social constructionist and realist sensibilities, remain profoundly committed to the fundamental liberal democratic undertaking never to reduce the interests of a person in life, liberty and dignity to socially constructed interests, the claim filed in *DeShaney* on behalf of Joshua DeShaney was not subject to any disputation. For them, the fact that the defence and (some of) the presiding judges considered the claim disputable must remain deeply disconcerting. A proper understanding of this point and a proper understanding of that which really came to pass in *DeShaney* may well offer American state action jurisprudence a way out of its seemingly insurmountable impasse.

V One Way out of the American Conceptual Impasse

Thomas Lewis makes the following observation in a thoughtful and meticulous essay on the state action doctrine:

> "Whatever the ultimate results of the cases that will be presented to the Court under the fourteenth amendment, they should flow from consideration of the problems presented, not from a formula that ignores them."[51]

Lewis' argument starts with the observation that there "are few problems whose solution depends more on the starting place of the solver than that presented by the familiar "state action" concept of the fourteenth amendment." This is perhaps another way of saying there are few problems of which the *non-solution* turns so much on formulae that ignore the problem. Be it as it may, the starting point or formula that informs all conceptions of the state action requirement under the 14th Amendment, according to Lewis, is this one:

> "The general statements do, however, provide a starting place by stating the assumption that there is conduct, labelled private, that cannot violate the fourteenth amendment or involve the state in a violation."[52]

"Conduct labelled private that cannot violate the fourteenth amendment" is indeed the formula that has formed and informed the state action doctrine since its first articulation in *The Civil Rights Cases*. But it is clearly not a sufficiently informative formula, for the state action doctrine has been embroiled in deep controversy, we have seen, exactly because "the private" is an empty term that means

51 Thomas P. Lewis, "The Meaning of State Action," *Columbia Law Review* 60, no. 8 (December 1, 1960): 1121.
52 Ibid, 1083.

different things to different people. One well tried but ultimately unsatisfactory way of circumventing this problem is to focus exclusively on the capacity of the person or agent whose conduct is at stake. Is the conduct at stake that of a private individual or a government official? This is the question that some theorists and judges offer as the magic formula that would resolve all confusion regarding state action. For some, however, the fact that a 14th Amendment violation was committed by private individuals makes *almost* as little difference to the violation at hand as the observation that a crime committed by a private individual makes any difference to the nature of the crime at issue. This "*almost*" is nevertheless a crucial qualification, for the fact that some conduct that may count as a 14th Amendment violation in the public sphere should not count as such a violation in a very personal sphere, is not controversial. The personal commitment not to marry outside one's faith is clearly not the same as a governmental selection of employees according to faith. The problem of concern here only begins when the effects of ostensibly "non-governmental" conduct of private individuals begin to exceed the distinctly personal domain and begin to attain a certain "public" or even "governmental" quality. When this happens, however, the simplistic recourse to the private status of the actor evidently no longer resolves the state action question.

This is the problem to which the "public function" line of state action decisions such as the one in *Marsh v Alabama*[53] and *Amalgamated Food Employees Union Local 590 v Logan Valley Plaza*[54] addressed before becoming undone in cases like *Lloyd Corp. v Tanner*[55] and *Flagg Brothers v Brooks.*[56] Notwithstanding their unravelling in later USSC case law, the insights articulated in *Marsh* and *Logan* underline the fact that the invocation of the private capacity of an agent cannot as such decide the question regarding the nature of the conduct in one way or another. And it is really this insight to which Tribe's subjugation theory also returns, as we shall soon see. Private conduct that seeks to perpetuate wide scale racial segregation becomes "governmental." Such private conduct can no longer claim to be private. It follows from all of this that the social effects of allegedly "private conduct" must always be assessed meticulously. The invocation of the formula "private conduct" as an answer to the problematic at stake is not an answer. It is an attempt to avoid answering.

---

53 326 U.S. 501 (1946).

54 391 U.S. 308 (1968).

55 407 U.S. 551 (1972).

56 Cf. again the discussion of *Flagg Brothers* in Chapter Two as well as the short discussion of the development from *Marsh v Alabama* to *Lloyd Corp. v Tanner* in footnote 27 of Chapter Two.

Tribe, we saw towards the end of Section III, invoked the "subjugation" thesis to respond to the problem in *Shelley.* Private conduct becomes "public," according to the subjugation thesis, when it seeks to entrench the substantive disadvantages to which social minorities are exposed. In other words, it attains an evident governmental quality when it seeks to sustain and entrench the social inequality that pertains to current majority-minority relations. Tribe's argument turns on this point: Substantive social inequalities may be a regrettable fact of life that few liberal democracies can claim to have addressed satisfactorily, but liberal democracies can neither actively promote social inequality nor stand by passively when private individuals promote social inequality, without failing an aspiration that liberal democracies dare not fail, namely, the irreducible freedom of individuals and groups to strive for higher levels of equality. When so-called liberal democracies interfere with this freedom or fail to prevent interference with this freedom, they can no longer claim to be consistently committed to liberal democracy. A liberal democracy that fixes or promotes an existing social status quo or allows "private" individuals to fix or promote an existing status quo, betrays what is often called the "open society" with all its attendant implications of unobstructed social mobility. In other words, it betrays the open historicity of liberal democracy that Chapter Two underlined.

However, the "private conduct" formulae can also be offered as an "answer" to state action questions in a very different way. It can be offered as an answer to the question that Justice Rehnquist faced in *DeShaney.* The private conduct at issue in *DeShaney* surely had no governmental or regulatory effect. Tribe's subjugation thesis is clearly not applicable here. At issue is simply private conduct of one individual that violated the fundamental rights of another individual. Let us hear it once more directly from Justice Rehnquist: "the harm was inflicted not by the State of Wisconsin, but by Joshua's father."[57] Here too then, is private conduct offered like a magic formula that simply resolves the question and in this case there is no broad regulatory effect that pulls it back into the category of state action (ignoring for now the arguments of Justices Blackmun and Brennan that government did act in *DeShaney*). So the formula would appear to be watertight in this case. Why might one still want to regard this invocation of "private conduct," in the words of Lewis again, as "a formula that ignores the problem" at stake?

This question takes us right back to Justice Bradley's original articulation of the state action doctrine in *The Civil Rights Cases:* "[C]ivil rights ... such as are guarantied by the Constitution against State aggression, cannot be impaired

57 Cf. again the quote at note 32 above.

by individuals..."[58] For it is already here that a principle regarding private conduct was articulated that could later be invoked like a formula. We saw above that public function cases such as *Marsh v Alabama* and *Amalgamated Food Employees Union Local 590 v Logan Valley Plaza* endeavoured to resist this formula by arguing that some private conduct is sufficiently analogous to governmental or state action. We also saw how Tribe seeks to do the same with his subjugation thesis. Is there a way that one can wrest the private conduct in *DeShaney* from the private conduct formula with a similar analogy? Would it work to argue, for instance, that Randy DeShaney appropriated an exclusively governmental power when he violently assaulted his son, considering that the use of violence is a strictly and exclusively governmental prerogative in liberal democracies? There may be something in this argument, but it does not appear to be very forceful at first glance. It is a shallow analogy that does not reach to the heart of the matter that is at stake here.

The heart of the matter is this: Where does the idea come from that only states or governments can impair or violate a fundamental right? Why did any one ever come to give credence to the idea that the impairment of a fundamental right depends on who violates it? How did a whole history of case law come to accept an idea that appears so fundamentally illogical? Is it not glaringly *self-evident* that someone who suffers the curtailment of a fundamental right suffers a curtailment of a fundamental right? Is it not glaringly *self-evident* that the question regarding the identity of the one who caused the suffering is a secondary question that cannot affect the primary question whether the violation has been suffered or not? Is this not why Justice Harlan's dissent in *The Civil Rights Cases* stated all along that the majority opinion articulated by Justice Bradley played conceptual games that avoided the obvious meaning of the Fourteenth Amendment?[59] Did he not indeed consider it self-evident that the Fourteenth Amendment commanded the Federal Government to prevent impairments of fundamental rights, irrespective of who were responsible for the impairment at issue?

Well, the problem is that all of the above is not self-evident. The problem is that those who insist that a "self-evident" violation of a fundamental right cannot be affected by the question regarding the identity of the violator attribute a metaphysical, transcendental, a-priori, a-historical and socially unconstructed status to the concept of a fundamental rights violation. This attribution cannot be squared with the post-metaphysical, historicist or social-constructionist

58 109 U.S. 3 (1883) at 17. Cf. again Chapter Two for a full quotation of this dictum.
59 Cf. again the discussion of *The Civil Rights Cases* in Chapter Two.

times in which we are today posing these questions. It should be clear that we have returned to Seidman's question and the response to the question that we have started to articulate in Section IV. Seidman, we saw, wants to rely on the socially and politically constructed status of property rights and private spheres to endorse the social democratic reconstruction of America that came about with the New Deal. But he is bothered in the same breath by the possibility that this endorsement of social reconstruction and, by implication, social constructionism as such, would reduce the right to "productive and happy private lives" to a "myth." Seidman's problem is clearly that he wants to embrace a good measure of social constructionism to justify his redistributionist political sentiments, on the one hand, but also wants to hold on to a good measure of a-historical transcendentalism, on the other, to safeguard the right to "productive and happy private lives."

It should also be clear now that any retreat from metaphysical invocations of transcendental, apriori and a-historical rights would seem to deprive one of any incisive retort to the social constructionism evident in the formula of the state action doctrine. It would seem to deprive one from contending that it is simply bizarre to make the existence of a fundamental rights violation dependent on the question of the identity of the violator. When someone else's social constructionism and construction of society happily insist that a fundamental rights violation depends on the identity of the violator, one can no longer invoke the *self-evident* spuriousness of this construction when one has oneself come to concede or endorse social constructionism. One would obviously be contradicting oneself badly. There is however, a deeply significant way in which one can indeed continue to contend that it is simply bizarre, after all, to make the existence of a fundamental rights violation dependent on the identity of the violator. One can consciously, self-consciously and coherently engage in social construction that *renders* this bizarreness self-evident. That is what liberal democrats generally do. That is what one does when one commits to the social construction that goes by the name of liberal democracy. We are back to the argument that we have begun to develop in the previous section. Now is the time to unpack it more carefully.

Liberal democrats, Section IV argued towards the end, engage in a pattern of social construction that holds some elements of liberal democratic societies eternally subject to political reconstruction and redefinition. Among these elements they include private property and private spheres. However, liberal democrats, we saw, also envisage the construction of a society that would deem certain aspects of life as absolutely untouchable by any kind of social reconstruction. Among these elements they include the fundamental liberty, dignity, integrity and equality of all individuals. The latter elements may well be subject to incisive reconstruction, redefinition and even to destruction in other kinds of societies, but they are not in liberal democracies. From the perspective or from within the perspective of this kind of liberal democracy, the idea that a fundamental rights violation can be conditioned by the contingent identity of the violator, is truly and self-evidently bizarre, and coherently so at that.

Let us now rephrase this argument so as to link it also to the other key issues of constitutional review raised towards the end of Chapter Two. Liberal democrats undoubtedly insist on certain forms of transcendental socio-political closure. It is for reasons of this insistence that they typically find the decision in *DeShaney* horrifying. Their "open societies" are evidently not completely open, their liberalism not absolutely liberal. They evidently insist on a minimum of normative closure. They insist in an evidently Kantian fashion on the inviolability of the life, liberty, dignity and integrity of the person. And it is exactly for this reason that they consider the possible outcomes of a Wisconsin vote on the desirability of a public liability tort for failure to prevent serious bodily harm irrelevant. To return to the constitutional review terminology that we invoked towards the end of Chapter Two: There are exceptional circumstances in which liberal democratic constitutional review simply has to resort to substantive due process review procedures.

Does this insistence amount to an ahistorical endorsement of natural law principles that turn these liberal democrats, so profoundly horrified by *DeShaney*, into quaint relics of a bygone age of transcendental metaphysics? The answer to this question is "yes and no" and for this reason "not quite." There is one historical fact that even *DeShaney*-horrified liberal democrats should have come to accept by now with no hesitation. The "natural law" principles regarding the inviolability of life, liberty, integrity and dignity can surely no longer be understood as innate ideas that we all share. It is all too evident that millions and millions of people and many peoples do not entertain this idea at all. It can therefore hardly be regarded as innate. It can hardly be considered to be the moral law "within us," as Kant once put it. But one can endorse the "natural law" principle regarding the inviolability of life, liberty, dignity and integrity of the person *historically*. This is exactly what Thomas Jefferson did, according to Hannah Arendt, when he said, "we hold these truths [that all men are created free and equal] to be self-evident." Jefferson grasped that these truths were not self-evident, argues Arendt.[60] They had to be held as self-evident and they still have to be held thus if one happens to believe, perhaps quite absurdly, in their truth. The American Declaration of Independence, by incorporating Jeffer-

60 Cf. again the discussion of this point towards the end of Chapter Two.

son's words, once held these truths to be self-evident on behalf of all Americans, but it is certainly not evident that all Americans ever held or still hold these truths to be self-evident.

The historical performance or performative act that sustains all constative acts is undeniably present in the liberal democratic ethos that considers the life, liberty, dignity and integrity of the person inviolable. That is why liberal democracy and the state action or horizontal effect jurisprudence that it would come to endorse ultimately remain a question of historical sovereignty. The point will be discussed more incisively towards the end of this book, but suffice it to already mention now: liberals like Kantians, Rawlsians and Kelsenians, on the one hand, and non-liberals like Schmittians, on the other, will probably never see eye to eye with regard to the kind of sovereignty that they choose to exercise or endorse, but they cannot avoid the same boat when it comes to the reality of having to exercise sovereignty with regard to principles that they hold to be self-evident at the expense of others who do not hold those same principles to be self-evident.

This insight into the inevitable role that sovereign closures play in whatever concept of state action one endorses, underlines the significance of Lewis' observations cited above. The formula that private conduct cannot violate the 14th Amendment can indeed not be invoked to resolve the question of state action, for it is deeply embedded in the question itself. It is part and parcel of the question. One cannot refer or defer to "property" and the "private sphere" as if they are independent and external referees that can resolve the issue of state action from the outside. If Kantian concepts like the dignity and integrity of the person must ultimately be conceded to depend on sovereign endorsements, so must concepts of "property" and the "private sphere." All these concepts concern sovereign endeavours to construct a society in some way rather than another. They are not self-evident, they can at best be held to be self-evident by those committed to do so. As Lewis puts it well, "the starting place of the solver" is just as much written all over the solution when one invokes "private conduct" as a response to the state action question as when one would invoke "life," "liberty," "dignity" and "integrity" as a response. At issue are simply two very different exercises of sovereignty, the differences between which cannot be resolved.

The history of a nation's sovereignty is reflected in the historical record of that which that nation held to be self-evident over time. Chapter One has already shown that the history of the United States has from its beginnings been torn between two convictions regarding sovereignty, an Adamsonian and Wilsonian conviction, on the one hand, and a Madisonian and Morrisian conviction, on the other; a conception of sovereignty that subjected property and the private sphere to basic concerns of personal and political liberty and equality, and one that ultimately subjected personal and political liberty and equality to concerns with property and concerns with private spheres that are insulated from political redefinition. The deep tensions between these two kinds of sovereignty in the United States are evidently still reflected in the tensions between decisions such as *Shelley*, on the one hand, and *DeShaney*, on the other.

Tribe's subjugation thesis, we saw, does not work in the case of *DeShaney* as it does in *Shelley*. This explains why state action was recognised in *Shelley* but not in *DeShaney*, one might argue. *Shelley* and *DeShaney* are really two different kinds of cases, one might continue. If one would continue like this, one would of course not be able to allude to tensions between *Shelley* and *DeShaney* as we have just done in the previous paragraph, for there cannot be tensions between things that are fundamentally different. But there is a deeper explanation for *Shelley* that makes clear that *Shelley* and *DeShaney* do deal with the same concern in the final analysis. Louis Henkin articulated this deeper explanation for *Shelley* well in 1962. Evidently sharing the Hohfeldian spirit that we identified in Peters' 1959 observation that a state "may deprive a person of due process of law" and "equal protection of the laws" by "not making or enforcing law when under a duty to do so," Henkin observed:

> "The state is responsible for what it could prevent, and should prevent, and fails to prevent... In *Shelley* for example, the state could have outlawed restrictive covenants. By constitutional provision, by statute, or by development of common law policy, the state could have declared restrictive covenants illegal or unenforceable, whether as restraints on alienation or ... in pursuit of equality as a legitimate public purpose under the state's "police power." Since the state could have forbidden them, it is responsible for their continued existence, surely for their enforcement."[61]

Justice Rehnquist, we saw above, noted with regard to the state functionaries in *DeShaney* that they only "stood by and did nothing when suspicious circumstances dictated a more active role for them."[62] But this failure to act under circumstances that they should have, he stressed, was of no consequence as far as the law is concerned, because the state of Wisconsin had not enacted a public liability tort. And as far as this absence of legislation is concerned, he insisted:

61 Louis Henkin, "Shelley v. Kraemer: Notes for a Revised Opinion," *University of Pennsylvania Law Review* 110, no. 4 (1962): 484–485.
62 *DeShaney*, 202–203.

> "The people of Wisconsin should not have [a system of State liability for failure to act in situations such as the present one] thrust upon them by this Court's expansion of the Due Process Clause of the Fourteenth Amendment."[63]

The common ground and the evident tension between *Shelley* and *DeShaney* are strikingly evident from Henkin's response to *Shelley*, on the one hand, and Justice Rehnquist's response in *DeShaney* to the absence of a public liability tort in Wisconsin, on the other. *Shelley* and *DeShaney* mark the deep ambivalence in American legal consciousness regarding the principle of state responsibility and state sovereignty. There is probably no imminent way out of this tension as far as the historical and political reality of the United States is concerned. But there is a way out of the conceptual impasse that this tension has caused in the minds of liberal democrats. Again, the theory of state action that this book articulates will probably not be convincing to those who subscribe to conceptions of sovereignty that are decidedly not liberal democratic. However, it may well be convincing to theorists like Seidman and Tribe who evidently are liberal democrats but struggle to make sense of some of the deeper complexities of liberal democracy. Private conduct and the private sphere, this chapter has been telling them, have come to be short hand formulas for too many different things or at least two very different things. The first step out of the impasse in the liberal thinking that especially Seidman articulates so well, would consist in distinguishing between "private sphere" and "private property" concerns, on the one hand, and more fundamental personality concerns such as personal freedom, equality, dignity and integrity concerns, on the other. The latter concerns are often tied up with the former concerns, but they also exist absolutely independently of them in liberal democracies. The fact that liberal democrats would want to consider the former to be subject to political definition and the latter not, does therefore not raise a significant problem.

However, there is a second step out of the conceptual impasse of the state action doctrine that may well speak to both liberal democrats and those who would not consider themselves liberal democrats or not liberal democrats of the kind that will be comfortable with the doctrine of state action developed in this book. The second step would consist in simply deciding consistently and coherently whether the state action doctrine is to come to the avail of ordinary private property concerns only or whether it is also to come to the avail of fundamental rights concerns. The question then becomes a very simple one regarding the kind of sovereignty the state action doctrine should come to effect, the kind of sovereignty that asserts the responsibility of the sovereign to warrant

63 *DeShaney*, 202–203.

the fundamental life, liberty, dignity and integrity concerns of citizens, even at the expense of current private or property relations; or the kind of sovereignty that shies away from this responsibility and largely leaves these concerns to their own fates as long as existing private property rights remain well protected. From a liberal democratic perspective, or at least some liberal democratic perspectives, however, the latter sovereignty is an empty or depleted sovereignty that one might describe better as an abdication of sovereignty. It surely begins to look like an abdication of sovereignty when a Supreme Court considers a state's failure to prevent evidently avoidable harm as an absence of state sovereignty (absence of state action) and not as a failure of sovereignty for which proper sovereigns would offer due compensation.

Tribe and Seidman and other liberal and progressive United States scholars may want to reconsider some aspects of their vocabulary against this background, as may many judges. Some of them may come to find themselves less torn between their concerns with the "private sphere," on the one hand, and their endorsement of the New Deal and New Deal-like redefinitions of property and the private sphere, on the other. For their concerns with the "private sphere" may well turn out all along to have been more fundamentally concerned with personal liberty and dignity, concerns with which the New Deal was certainly not at odds but sought to promote and indeed sought to promote by redefining property. If so, they may also find that there need not be "something like the state action doctrine – together with all the uncertainty and incoherence that accompanies it – [built] into how [they] think about constitutional rights."[64]

Not one of the German horizontal effect or *Drittwirkung* theorists to whom we turn now has "something like the state action doctrine ... built into how [they] think about constitutional rights." Even the most reluctant among them – notably Günter Dürig and Claus-Wilhelm Canaris – ultimately acknowledge the ubiquitous presence of the state within the territorial boundaries of a sovereign liberal democracy. In this respect they all basically underline in a very Hohfeldian way an insight that one of their most celebrated sociologists articulated many years ago in an early work:

> Fundamental rights aim to safeguard liberty against the state. This presupposes, however, the prior creation of an oppositional monopoly as far as threats to liberty are concerned. Without such a monopolisation of threats to liberty, the protection of rights would forever be groping in thin air. It would never attain to positive results. It would never manage to effectively secure liberty. The reality that the state is the precondition of all liberty remains constantly forgotten. The state nevertheless does not condition or precondition liberty be-

64 Seidman, "The State Action Paradox," 393.

cause of the way it ensures the realisation of liberty, however incomplete or preliminary this realisation may be. It preconditions liberty because of the way its decision-making programme and organisational framework subjects liberty to rational regulation. In doing so, it gathers up the potential threat to liberty that otherwise would continue to exist diffusely and intangibly in society. Thus does it make the question of liberty decidable, which can result in loss or gains of liberty in specific cases.[65]

65 Translated from Niklas Luhmann, *Grundrechte als Institution: Ein Beitrag zur Politischen Soziologie* (Berlin: Duncker & Humblot, 1965), 57: "Die Grundrechte werden angesetzt, um die Freiheit gegen den Staat zu sichern; aber das setzt voraus, daß zunächst einmal eine Gegeninstanz, ein Monopol auf Freiheitsbedrohung, geschaffen ist, mit deren Bändigung man nicht ins Leere greift, sondern den positiven Erfolg, die Freiheit, wirksam herstellen kann. Der Staat ist, was immer wieder vergessen wird, Vorbedingung aller Freiheit; nicht weil er sie schon partiell oder in elementaren Vorformen gewährleistet, sondern weil sie in der Form des Entscheidungsprogramms für staatliche Organisation rational regulierbar wird. Der Staat faßt das Potential an Freiheitsbedrohung, das in der Gesellschaft diffus und ungreifbar verstreut vorhanden ist, zusammen und macht die Freiheitsfrage entscheidbar – was im Einzelfall Gewinn oder Verlust der Freiheit bedeuten kann." Chapter Five will return to this passage of Luhmann in order to elaborate more extensively the conception of sovereignty that informs it.

Chapter Four: Drittwirkung

I Introduction

The jurisprudence of the GFCC and the debate among German scholars regarding the *Drittwirkung* or horizontal application of the German *GG* have often been discussed in English literature.[1] These discussions focussed predominantly on the essential elements of the GFCC's horizontal effect jurisprudence and on the doctrinal positions taken by three key figures in the early rounds of the scholarly debate, namely Hans Nipperdey, Walter Leisner and Günter Dürig. The basic view that emerged from this literature can be summarised under the following key points:

1) Nipperdey (in 1952 and 1961) and Leisner (in 1960) advocated the direct horizontal application of the GG to private law and private individuals whereas Dürig (in 1956) propounded the indirect horizontal application of the *GG* to private law and private individuals.

2) The GFCC basically followed Dürig's approach in its famous *Lüth* decision[2] in 1957 and confirmed it in its *Blinkfeuer*[3] (1969), *Mephisto*[4] (1971) and a series of other early *Drittwirkung* cases. From the early 1970s onwards the GFCC supplemented this indirect horizontal or radiation effect of fundamental rights (*Ausstrahlungswirkung der Grundrechte*) approach with the "duty to safeguard" (*Schutzpflicht*) principle. The principle derived from the *Schutzgebotsfunktion*

---

1 Cf. especially Kenneth M. Lewan, "The Significance of Constitutional Rights for Private Law: Theory and Practice in West Germany," *The International and Comparative Law Quarterly* 17, no. 3 (July 1, 1968): 571–601.; R Brinktrine, "The Horizontal Effect of Human Rights in German Constitutional Law: The British Debate on Horizontality and the Possible Role Model of the German Doctrine of 'Mittelbare Drittwirkung Der Grundrechte,'" *European Human Rights Law Review* (2001): 421; Basil Markesinis, "Privacy, Freedom of Expression, and the Horizontal Effect of the Human Right Bill: Lessons from Germany," *Law Quarter Review* 115, no. 47 (1999); Basil Markesinis and Stefan Enchelmaier, "The Applicability of Human Rights as between Individuals under German Constitutional Law," in *Protecting Privacy*, ed. Basil Markesinis, The Clifford Chance Lextures Four (Oxford: Oxford University Press, 1999); Hugh Collins, *Utility and Rights in Common Law Reasoning: Rebalancing Private Law Through Constitutionalization*, SSRN Scholarly Paper (Rochester, NY: Social Science Research Network, September 1, 2007), http://papers.ssrn.com/abstract=1011727.

2 BVerfG 7, 198

3 BVerfG 25, 256.

4 BVerfG 30, 173.

der Grundrechte contained in article 1 of the *GG*. It was adopted in horizontal effect cases to stress the duty of the state to protect the fundamental rights of private individuals against other private individuals. The *Schutzpflicht* jurisprudence of the GFCC first came to the fore in the *Erste Abtreibung (First Abortion)* case of 1975.[5] In the wake of *Erste Abtreibung* soon followed other *Schutzpflicht* cases,[6] but the first typical horizontal effect case to follow this approach was the *Handelsvertreter*-decision of 1990.[7]

Chapter Two has already expounded the basic tenets of the radiation effect jurisprudence of the *Lüth* case and the duty to protect jurisprudence of the *First Abortion case*. This chapter will now first take a closer look at the contributions of Nipperdey, Leisner and Dürig in the early years of the scholarly debate on horizontal application in Germany and then turn to two later contributions to the debate by Jürgen Schwabe and Claus-Wilhelm Canaris. The aim of the engagement with these scholars will not be to provide a comprehensive overview of the German *Drittwirkung* debate. There are many other important contributions that will not be discussed here.[8] The focus on Nipperdey, Leisner, Dürig, Schwabe and Canaris is nevertheless justified because of the way these scholars articulated the fundamental terms of the debate with which other scholars continued to engage for a considerable time before Ralph Christensen and Andreas-Fischer Lescano more recently took the debate in a new direction. We return to Christensen and Fischer-Lescano in Chapter Five. This chapter will now only focus on what may be called the first two phases of the debate, the Nipperdey-Dürig-Leisner phase, and the Schwabe-Canaris phase.

The chapter will proceed as follows: Sections II, III and IV will briefly expound the basic positions taken by Leisner, Nipperdey and Dürig in the early exchanges of the *Drittwirkung* debate. Section V and VI will then respectively engage with the writings of Schwabe and Canaris. Section VII will end the

---

5 BVerfG 39, 1.

6 BVerfG 46, 116 (*Schleier*, 1977); BVerfG 49, 89 (*Kalkar*, 1978); BVerfG 77, 381 (*Gorleben*, 1988); BVerfG 88, 203 (*Zweite Abtreibung/Second Abortion*, 1993); BVerfG 96, 56 (*Vaterschaftsauskunft/Illegitimate Children/Right to Know*, 1997).

7 BVerfGe 81, 242.

8 The discussion of the German debate that follows here is also indebted to the contributions of Johannes Hager, "Grundrechte im Privatrecht," *Juristenzeitung* 49, no. 8 (1994): 373–383; Dieter Medicus, "Der Grundsatz der Verhältnismäßigkeit im Privatrecht," *Archiv für Civilistische Praxis* 192 (1992): 35–70; Stefan Oeter, "'Drittwirkung' der Grundrechte und die Autonomie des Privatrechts," in *Archiv des Öffentlichen Rechts*, vol. 119 (J.C.B. Mohr (P. Siebeck), 1994), 529–563; Oldiges, "Neue Aspekte der Grundrechtsgeltung im Privatrecht;" Matthias Ruffert, *Vorrang der Verfassung und Eigenständigkeit des Privatrechts: eine verfassungsrechtliche Untersuchung zur Privatrechtswirkung des Grundgesetzes* (Tübingen: Mohr Siebeck, 2001).

chapter with concluding reflections that highlight the essential issues that informed and still inform the German debate. By the end of the chapter it will be clear that the German debate also reflects the tension between the "Hohfeldian" insistence (see again the discussions in Chapters Two and Three) that horizontal application inevitably involves or turns upon the power of the state to govern every walk of life, on the one hand, and the concern that such an extensive involvement of the state in the lives of citizens will destroy the sphere of private autonomy, on the other. It will also become clear, however, that all five of the key participants in the debate ultimately affirmed the Hohfeldian position regarding the presence of law and the state in every walk of life. This is also true for Dürig, arguably the most "Hohfeld shy" among the German scholars.

II Nipperdey's Position

Nipperdey did not start the *Drittwirkung* debate in Germany,[9] but he deserves specific recognition for the way he made the first bold claims in favour of what many commentators would come to call the "direct horizontal application" of fundamental rights in the private sphere. By making these claims Nipperdey sparked off the crucial or classic phase of the debate in the second half of the 20th century. The essence of his claims are articulated in a couple of concise pages in the 1952 reworked edition of Ludwig Enneccerus' *Allgemeiner Teil des bürgerlichen Rechts*[10] and a short essay, *Grundrechte und Privatrecht*, based on an address held at the University of Cologne and published in 1961. Nipperdey

---

9 The *Drittwirkung* debate in Germany was precipitated by a 1949 essay of Herbert Krüger. Cf. Herbert Krüger, "Die Verfassungen in der Zivilrechtsprechung," *Neue Juristische Wochenschrift* 2, no. 5 (1949): 163–166. Krüger criticised the purely private law jurisprudence of the Weimar civil law judiciary and encouraged the civil judiciary to venture beyond the horizon of pure private law and to enrich their argumentation by also considering constitutional legal principles when appropriate. The essay evoked a stream of publications on the possible impact of constitutional principles on private law jurisprudence, mostly with reference to fictitious cases. The debate came to a head however when H.C. Nipperdey discussed the impact of article 3 of the Constitution on the question of equal pay for men and women for the same work. Cf. Hans Carl Nipperdey, "Gleicher Lohn der Frau für gleiche Leistung," *Recht der Arbeit* (1950): 121. He claimed that article 3 binds all employment contracts directly. Any term of an employment agreement that would affect the position of women adversely would be void. Labour law and constitutional justices initially disputed Nipperdey's stance in this regard, but the Federal Labour Court eventually endorsed his view. For a comprehensive survey of the early stages of the debate, cf. Stern, *Das Staatsrecht der Bundesrepublik Deutschland.* 1509–1595.

10 Ludwig Enneccerus and Hans Carl Nipperdey, *Allgemeiner Teil des bürgerlichen Rechts: ein Lehrbuch* (Tübingen: J.C.B. Mohr, 1952), 51–58.

actually attached little value to the distinction between vertical and horizontal effect of fundamental rights or the distinction between direct and indirect horizontal application. He stressed, instead, the direct and *absolute* normative validity of fundamental rights on private law. His crucial statement in this regard is fully captured in the following passage:

> "The clauses contained in the catalogue of fundamental rights also bind private legal exchanges directly, that is, not only through legislation passed by the legislature for purposes of giving effect to constitutional demands. This function of constitutional clauses, which I have been pointing out for a long time, has in the meantime generally become known as third party effect (*Drittwirkung*). This term is nevertheless inaccurate when one considers that constitutional rights, in the classical and strict sense of subjective public law rights, only apply against the state. More accurate would be to invoke the absolute effect (*absolute Wirkung*) of certain constitutional rights. At issue here is the direct normative effect of specific constitutional clauses in their capacity of objective and binding constitutional law that suspended, amended, supplemented existing private law clauses or created new ones. The constitutional law at issue does not only serve as maxims or interpretive guidelines for other non-constitutional areas of law, but also constitute normative principles for the whole legal system and unitary body of law. Private law subjective rights that apply directly to private individuals also derive from this constitutionally bound unitary body of law and are therefore also subject to the constitution. Any private law transaction that violates a constitutional principle must therefore be void."[11]

It is clear from this passage, that Nipperdey not only deemed the term "indirect horizontal application" or *mittelbare Drittwirkung* to be inaccurate (*ungenau*). He found the very notion of horizontal application or *Drittwirkung* as such to be fundamentally inaccurate. According to him a legal system turns on an inclusive and unitary order, the fundamental norms of which necessarily govern all as-

11 Hans Carl Nipperdey, *Grundrechte und Privatrecht* (Scherpe Verlag, 1961) 14–15: "[Die im Grundrechtskatalog aufgeführten Bestimmungen] binden ... auch den Privatrechtsverkehr unmittelbar, d. h. nicht erst auf Grund von Gesetzen, die vom einfachen Gesetzgeber in Ausführung der Grundsatznormen erlassen worden sind ... Diese Funktion der Grundrechtsbestimmungen, auf die ich seit längerer Zeit hingewiesen habe, ist bisher im allgemeinen als "Drittwirkung" der Grundrechte bezeichnet worden. Das ist allerdings ungenau, weil die Grundrechte im klassischen, engeren Sinne als subjektive öffentliche Rechte sich nur gegen den Staat richten. Richtiger dürfte es sein, von der absoluten Wirkung gewisser Grundrechte zu sprechen. Es handelt sich um die unmittelbar normative Wirkung einzelner Grundrechtsbestimmungen in ihrer Eigenschaft als objektives, verbindliches Verfassungsrecht, das Bestimmungen des Privatrechts aufgehoben, modifiziert, ergänzt oder neu geschaffen hat. Dieses Verfassungsrecht enthält für Rechtsgebiete außerhalb der Verfassung nicht nur "Leitsätze" oder "Auslegungsregeln," sondern eine normative Regelung der gesamten Rechtsordnung als Einheit, aus der auch unmittelbar subjektive private Rechte des einzelnen fließen. Ein Verstoß gegen eine solche auch im Privatrecht wirkende Grundnorm führt in der Regel zur Nichtigkeit des Rechtsgeschäfts."

pects of the law (*eine normative Regelung der gesamten Rechtsordnung als Einheit*), the system of private law self-evidently included. He therefore deemed spurious the view, articulated in *Lüth* and forcefully promoted by Dürig, that fundamental rights needed bridgeheads or *Einbruchstellen* within the system of private law that allowed them to become effective in the private sphere. He accordingly also dismissed the idea that the "general clauses of private law that are capable of and in need of evaluative completion" (*wertausfüllungsfähige und -bedürftige Generalklauseln des Privatrechts*) should serve as such bridgeheads. This view, he maintained, suffers from the historical perspective of the nineteenth century from which it drew its understanding of fundamental rights.[12] He vociferously rejected any suggestion that the system of private law is generally insulated from constitutional law and only provides a limited number of specified ports of entry through which the latter may affect the former. The opening statement of Nipperdey's Cologne address also made this abundantly clear:

> "The Foundational Law, in contrast to Bismarck's constitution and the much further reaching Weimar Constitution, guarantees and protects the foundational principles of the effective private law and economic order. Private law is an integral ingredient of the unitary, liberal and social legal order in its totality (Gesamtrechtsordnung)."[13]

Nipperdey's Cologne address stressed his rejection of the nineteenth century constitutional perspective in terms of which private law concerned an insulated sphere of law that was severed from constitutional law. Germany, he maintained, no longer finds itself in the time of Bismarck and Weimar, times during which a certain dichotomy between state and civil society still informed German thinking about law. The historical background to this rejection is most remarkable. Nipperdey articulated this adamant concern with the total or inclusive legal order with regard to which private law could not insulate itself directly in the wake of a devastating experience with the totalitarian state. He was evidently an early prophet of the "total constitution" that Mattias Kumm would later again

---

12 Ibid, 16.

13 Ibid, 5: "[D]as Grundgesetz, anders als Bismarcks Verfassung und viel weitergehend als die Weimarer Verfassung [gewährleistet und schützt] die Grundprinzipien der geltenden Privatrechtsordnung und Wirtschaftsordnung verfassungsmässig. Das Privatrecht ist ein integrierender Bestandteil der einheitlichen, freiheitlichen und sozialen Gesamtrechtsordnung." Compare also the express statement of the difference between the Weimar Constitution and the GG in Enneccerus and Nipperdey, *Allgemeiner Teil des Bürgerlichen Rechts*, 54: "Es ist deshalb von entscheidender Bedeutung, daß das Bonner Grundgesetz viel weitergehend als die Weimarer Verfassung die Grundprinzipien der geltenden Privatrechtsordnung und Wirtschaftsordnung verfassungsmässig gewährleistet und schützt."

bring to bear on the horizontal application debate.[14] And he obviously saw this total constitution as a remedial response to the totalitarian state. Central to his views in this regard is his strong emphasis on an objective value system that informs this unitary legal totality. He defended this idea vociferously against those who saw democracy as a value-blind and relativistic system (*die das Wesen der Demokratie wertblind im Relativismus sehen*).[15]

This understanding of the constitutional order as an objective normative order found strong resonance in the jurisprudence of the GFCC, as we saw in the discussion of the *Lüth* decision in Chapter Two, notwithstanding the Court's insistence, contra Nipperdey, that this objective value system only enters private law through general principles that are capable and in need of evaluative concretisation. The discussion of the GFCC's *Erste Abtreibung* decision in Chapter Two also showed the prominence of this idea in the *Schutzpflicht* or "duty to protect" jurisprudence that resulted from this decision.

The conception of the constitutional order as an objective value order would become one of the main stays of German *Drittwirkung* jurisprudence among both scholars and judges. A core element of the idea may well be indispensible for any endeavour to articulate a consistent theory of horizontal effect. The arguments regarding an indispensable moment of substantive due process review procedures developed in Chapters Two and Three made this clear. However, the idea also has a vexing side to it that would become increasingly conspicuous in German jurisprudence, especially in the reasoning of the GFCC in its *Erste Abtreibung* decision. The idea of an objective value order can be taken too far or employed too inclusively. Later chapters of this book will therefore articulate a call for adequate caution regarding the unduly *general* or *generalised* substantive due process review procedure to which the idea of an objective value order can lead. As shown in Chapter Two in the discussion of *Roe v Wade* and *Erste Abtreibung*, the idea of an objective value order becomes especially problematic in cases where deep social divisions render the invocation of normative consensus – surely the underlying idea that informs the notion of an objective value order – highly dubious. The problem at issue here was already evident in the *Drittwirkung* jurisprudence that Dürig would come to articulate, as Walter Leisner would point out well. The discussion of Dürig's key arguments that follows now also highlights this.

---

14 Kumm, "Who's Afraid of the Total Constitution? Constitutional Rights as Principles and the Constitutionalization of Private Law," 341–370.

15 Enneccerus and Nipperdey, *Allgemeiner Teil des Bürgerlichen Rechts*, 54.

III Dürig's Position

Günter Dürig's stance on the relation between the constitutional rights entrenched in the GG and the body of private law contained in the *BGB* turn on the following key points:[16]

1) Fundamental rights have no direct bearing on private individuals. The legal relations between individuals are exclusively governed by the body of rules and principles articulated in the *BGB*.
2) The fundamental rights articulated in the GG nevertheless affect the way in which the *BGB* applies to private individuals through the general principles or *Generalklauseln* and abstract concepts of private law that are in need of evaluative concretisations (*wertausfüllungsbedürftige Begriffe*).
3) The impact of the GG on the general principles and abstract concepts of private law generally reflects three degrees of intensity – *drei Intensitätsgrade*. The *first degree* concerns the mere explication (*bloße Verdeutlichung*) of the way a general principle or abstract concept of private law is applied in a particular case. Here the fundamental principles merely have a hermeneutic function that has no significant transformative impact on private law.
4) The second degree of intensity with which the GG can affect private law concerns the rarer cases (*seltenere Fälle*) that require sharpened interpretation (*wertgeschärfte Auslegung*) of private law rules as a result of changed legal sensibilities that have become evident in view of constitutional considerations (*in der Verfassung erkennbar gewordener Auffassungswandel*). At issue here is not a complete lack of private legal protection of constitutional norms (*keine Wertschutzlücken*), but a need to sharpen existing private law rules and remedies to give effect to the protection required by the GG.
5) The third degree of intensity with which the GG can affect private law concerns the rarest cases (*seltenste Fälle*) in which private law protection of constitutional norms evinces gaps (*Lücken*) that require the introduction of supplementary legal protection. Of specific concern in this regard was, for Dürig, the need for new modes of private law protection that safeguarded the fundamental right to a *ureigenster Privat- und Geheimsphäre* (primordial sphere of privacy and secrecy) envisaged by Articles 1 I and 2 I of the GG.
6) For purposes of all of the above, private law recognises the need for the following innovations:[17]

---

16 Cf. Günter Dürig, "Grundrechte und Zivilrechtsprechung," in *Vom Bonner Grundgesetz zur gesamtdeutschen Verfassung: Festschrift zum 75. Geburtstag von Hans Nawiasky*, ed. Theodor Maunz (München: Isar Verlag, 1956), 117–182.
17 Ibid, 180.

a) Interpretation and application of the general principles of private law that explain and accentuate the rootedness of these general principles in the normative values of the GG.
b) The recognition of human dignity (*Menschenwürde*) as a new general principle of private law application alongside "good morals" (*gute Sitten*).
c) The expansion of the bundle of specific private law rights (*einzelne subjektive Privatrechte*) under the notion of "other rights" (*sonstige Rechte*) invoked in § 823 *BGB*.
d) The recognition of a "general right of personality" (*allgemeines Persönlichkeitsrecht*) that crowns the legal protection that private law affords the individual.

These points (1–5 plus 6 a-d) constitute the heart of Dürig's position on the question of how constitutional values affect private law. They constitute the essence of the "solution" (*Lösung*) he offers as far as the relation between constitutional and private law is concerned.[18] This "solution" appears watertight. It surely appears to cover all the ways in which private law can be expected to comply with constitutional norms and should leave no doubt concerning Dürig's real commitment to the substantive effect of constitutional rights on private law. In fact, his "solution" does not appear to detract anything from Nipperdey's emphasis on the unity and totality of the constitutional order with which all law must comply. Dürig's solution acknowledges the possibility that the value order of the constitution may in some cases (albeit the rarest of cases, as he insists) require a full-blown *supplementation* (and not just accentuation or sharpening) of existing private legal protection. Judging by the terms of its basic exposition, no one who is concerned with the progressive realisation of constitutional values in the private sphere should experience any qualms with "Dürig's solution." Any lack of constitutional protection that an existing system of private law may evince, can surely be remedied in terms of this solution. Again, there is surely no deep rift between Nipperdey's position and the position that Dürig put forward in his "solution." However, a rift does seem to open up between them when the fundamental *point of departure* on which Dürig's "solution" is founded, comes into view. It is here, in his *point of departure* – his *Ausgangspunkt*[19] – that Dürig's rejection of Nipperdey's "new doctrine" (*neue Lehre*) comes to the fore.[20] It is here

18 Ibid, 176.
19 Ibid, 157–164.
20 Ibid, 165–176.

that he took the crucial step that cast him as Nipperdey's and Leisner's main antagonist in the *Drittwirkung* debate.

The crux of Dürig's *point of departure* was his insistence that private individuals enjoy a significantly wider liberty to limit the fundamental rights of other individuals than the state does. This greater liberty of individuals to limit the fundamental rights of other individuals, argued Dürig, is stipulated by the constitution itself. The following key statements make his stance in this regard abundantly clear.

> "Our civil law would be damaged irreparably should the following point of departure ever come to be doubted: The primary decision of the Constitution in favour of a general right to liberty against the state ... conceptually includes the liberty vis-à-vis the state, to deviate freely from constitutional principles in its civil law transactions with other individuals in a way the state could never do, provided this deviation takes place in accordance with the current commercial justice (*Verkehrs- und Tauschgerechtigkeit*) of civil law. From this follows the fundamental principle that public authorities – and therefore also the judicial authority – must recognise contracts, unilateral legal transactions, acts and omissions among private individuals as lawful, even when they conflict with the fundamental principles of the constitution, that would bind the state, were it to be the actor in question."[21]

> "Constitutional law always faces situations in which the question of the lawfulness or unlawfulness of an act that abridges the liberty of another person requires two completely different answers, and is constitutionally required to do so, depending on whether the state or a private individual performs that act."[22]

Dürig's insistence in these passages that constitutional principles apply differently to public authorities than they do to private persons should not as such raise alarm among proponents of the horizontal effect of constitutional princi-

---

21 Translated from Ibid, 158–159: "Unser Zivilrecht würde einen *nicht wieder gutzumachenden schweren Schaden* erleiden, wenn folgende *Ausgangserkenntnis* jemals in Frage gestellt würde: Die primäre Entscheidung des Grundgesetzes für ein gegen den Staat gerichtetes generelles Freiheitsrecht ... umschließt begrifflich auch die *Freiheit dem Staat gegenüber, von ihm ungehindert in der unter gleichgeordneten Privaten bestehenden Verkehrs- und Tauschgerechtigkeit des Zivilrechts von Grundrechtssätzen, die für Staatliches Handeln unabdingbar sind, abweichen zu können.* Daraus folgt im Grundsatz die Pflicht der öffentlichen Gewalt – und damit auch der richterlichen Gewalt –, Verträge, einseitige Rechtsgeschäfte, Handlungen und Unterlassungen Privater untereinander als rechtmässig anzuerkennen, auch wenn sie Grundrechtssätzen der Verfassung widerstreiten, die für den Staat, wenn er als Handelnder aufträte, bindend wären."

22 Translated from Ibid, 167: "Das Verfassungsrecht steht permanent Situationen gegenüber, in denen, obwohl an sich der gleiche Lebensvorgang zu subsumieren ist, *Rechtmässigkeit und Rechtswidrigkeit auseinanderklaffen* und verfassungsrechtlich auch auseinanderklaffen *müssen*, je nachdem, ob der Staat oder ein anderer Privater als Beeinträchtiger der Individualsphäre auftritt."

ples. We have already pointed out the typical uncontroversial case in Chapter Three: The decision of a private person not to marry outside the Catholic faith, would not raise a constitutional question in the way a governmental decision to base suitability for employment on considerations of faith would. The issue of course becomes more complicated when a private employer selects employees on the basis of faith, but even here can one see defensible cases for the selection of employees on the basis of faith – for instance by churches – that are unimaginable in the sphere of public employment. If this were all that Dürig meant to say, his qualification of horizontal effect would hardly be questionable. But Dürig seems to have gone further than this. He took another crucial step, one that comes across as an unequivocal rejection of the principle that Chapters Two and Three presented as the rule in *Shelley v Kraemer.*[23] He did this in the very first sentence with which he commenced to expound his basic point of departure:

> "It would be obviously wrong to infer from the fact that civil law adjudication is bound by the constitution in terms of Article 1 III (given that it is state action) that Article 1 III also binds substantive private law [just because] it is entrusted to the judiciary."[24]

Dürig indeed made short shrift of the rule in *Shelley.* He agreed fully that civil law adjudication is bound by the GG in view of Art 1 III, but according to him, this bond only concerns the nature and way (*Art und Weise*) in which such adjudication takes place; it does not concern the extent to which the GG *reaches into the contents* (*inhaltliche Reichweite*) of civil law principles.[25] *The former* – the nature and way in which the adjudication takes place – only concerns procedural mistakes (failures regarding the due process of law) that may occur during civil law adjudication. One such mistake could be a failure to take due consideration of the implications of constitutional norms for the civil dispute at issue. *The latter* – the extent to which the GG *reaches into the contents* (*inhaltliche Reichweite*) of civil law principles – does not depend directly or automatically on Article 1 III. It turns on the contingent extent to which the GG sometimes binds *substantive* civil law. The exact wording of Dürig's point in this regard is important:

---

23 Cf. again the discussions of *Shelley v Kraemer* in Chapters Two and Three.
24 Translated from Dürig, "Grundrechte und Zivilrechtsprechung," 157: "Offensichtlich verfehlt wäre es, wenn man von der Tatsache, daß auch die *Zivilrechtsprechung* (weil staatliche Tätigkeit) *als solche* nach Art. 1 III grundrechtsgebunden ist, irgendwie zurückschließen würde auf das *materielle Zivilrecht*, das der Zivilrechtsprechung zur Entscheidung anvertraut ist."
25 Ibid, 158.

> "The extent to which the contents of civil law are constitutionally bound depends, notwithstanding Article 1 III, on incidental cases in which the constitution naturally binds substantive private law."[26]

In other words, the GG binds substantive civil law only incidentally, that is, in specific cases. At issue is an *incidental* constitutional bond that prevails in some cases (*gegebenenfalls bestehende Grundrechtsbindung*). Whether civil law is bound or not turns on the question whether Dürig's point of departure – his insistence that the GG allows greater freedom to private individuals to affect the constitutional rights of others negatively – actually nullifies the application of the constitution in some cases. Seen in this way, and assuming that the point of departure indeed nullifies the application of the Constitution in some civil law cases, one might want to conclude that the GG *always* binds public authorities and *only* sometimes binds civil law (and private persons) according to Dürig.

Dürig surely knew that his three-pronged method alone (explication, accentuation, supplementation – the last one really being the can opener) extended the scope of potential *Drittwirkung* in a way that would basically erase all the significant or substantive differences between his position and the direct or in fact absolute horizontal application articulated by Nipperdey. This may well be the reason why he articulated the express limitation of the scope of *Drittwirkung* in his point of departure and why he sought to restrict the rule in *Shelley* to formal requirements that do not affect the substantive decisions a judge may take. It is with regard to these two points that he evidently sought to distinguish his position firmly from Nipperdey's position. The crucial difference at issue here surely concerns Dürig's insistence that individuals enjoy greater liberty to abridge the liberties of other individuals than states enjoy. But this insistence, we have seen above, is not remarkable as such. It can only begin to figure as a significant point of disagreement with Nipperdey if Dürig indeed envisaged a significantly wider sphere of "constitutionally untouched" private freedom than Nipperdey envisaged.

All of the above seems to lead one to this conclusion regarding Dürig's position: He may have contemplated a natural private sphere that to a large extent insulates property and contract from constitutional scrutiny, but it is not entirely clear from his text that he did. He seems to have moved in this direction with some of his observations, especially those articulated under his point of departure or *Ausgangspunkt*. And this side of his thinking appears to have been the

---

26 Ibid: "Die *inhaltliche Reichweite* der zivilgerichtlichen Bindung aber ergibt sich trotz Art. 1 III natürgemäß erst aus der gegebenenfalls bestehenden Grundrechtsbindung des anzuwendenden *materiellen* Zivilrechts."

ground of his dispute with Nipperdey. But he also seems to have been well aware, on the other hand, that such completely private spheres do not exist. His recognition of the need for filling gaps where constitutional protection is lacking (*Lückenfüllung*), rare as this need might be, can hardly be reconciled with the notion of a private sphere that is in principle untouched by constitutional scrutiny.

It is important to recall in this regard the insight drawn from the analysis of Justice Kriegler's opinion in *Du Plessis v De Klerk* in Chapter Two: It would only make sense to contend "there is no law that governs a situation and therefore no constitutional protection applicable" should law be considered complete as it is and therefore not amenable to any supplementation or amelioration required by constitutional norms. Such a conception of law would indeed imply existence of spheres of social existence that are devoid of law and therefore beyond the reach of constitutional protections. We also saw in Chapter Two that Justice Rehnquist boldly went far down this avenue in *DeShaney v Winnebago County Social Services Department*. But Dürig's clear recognition that the *GG* demands the closing of any gaps in the protection that constitutional rights demand from private law makes it clear that this is not how he understood the matter.

So one can conclude: If Dürig really intended to articulate a position that was substantively different from Nipperdey's, it is surely in the direction of a "natural private sphere" that is completely untouched by constitutional principles that one would have to look for evidence of such a difference. However, the idea of such a natural private sphere does ultimately not fit into the conception of *Drittwirkung* that he developed. The concept of *Lückenfüllung* is the real can opener in his theory of horizontal effect, we said. It is this clear recognition that horizontal effect can demand a *supplementation* of existing private law so as *to close any gaps* in the protection of fundamental rights that it provides that renders Dürig's position hardly distinguishable from Nipperdey's. It is this recognition that ultimately exposes all spheres of life directly to the sovereign reign of constitutional principles in his so-called indirect horizontal effect approach. *Dürig* also ultimately belongs, however waveringly or unwontedly, to the great tradition of sovereignty-affirming *Drittwirkung* scholarship in Germany that will be invoked towards the end of this chapter.

IV Leisner's Position

Walter Leisner figures, alongside Nipperdey, as the other major proponent of the direct horizontal effect (*unmittelbare Drittwirkung*) of fundamental rights in private legal relations. One could, in view of his endorsement of direct horizontal application, expect to find a systematic and complete subordination of private law to constitutional law in his work. That, however, is not how Leisner saw the matter. According to him, something else is at stake here, and he articulated it as follows:

> "The GFCC is guilty of having created the danger of a two track judicial reasoning by overtaxing the concept of constitutional interpretation as a result of applying it to the general clauses [of private law]. In the process they arrived at some version of indirect horizontal application of constitutional rights. Given that it cannot undo its recognition of direct horizontal application, it should withdraw from this over extension [of the concept of interpretation] and leave private law – now really for once and all! – to private lawyers. For public law should not flow into private law through the elastic concept of "interpretation," but private law should be developed further with reference to constitutional law that stands above both public and private law."[27]

It is important to engage with this multi-layered passage line by line. The first point that requires explication concerns the two-track or *zweispurige* adjudication invoked in the first line. What did Leisner have in mind with this expression? A passage some paragraphs before the one quoted here provides the answer:

> "[The GFCC] thereby exposes itself to the dangerous possibility of double-track adjudication, given that the reliance on fundamental rights as interpretative rules can lead [it] to results that differ from those of the superior civil courts..."[28]

To be sure, at issue for Leisner is not the possibility that constitutional courts and civil courts can come to assess a particular legal position or question differently. Leisner surely has no doubt that this can come to pass. That is after all what the horizontal and indeed the direct horizontal application of constitutional rights is all about. It undoubtedly has the potential to require the overruling of a private law rule in the name of constitutional law. When this happens however,

---

27 Leisner, *Grundrechte und Privatrecht*, 377: "Das Bundesverfassungsgericht trifft die Schuld, [die] Gefahr [einer zweispurigen Rechtsprechung] heraufgeführt zu haben, indem es den "Auslegungsbegriff" überanstrengt und ihn auf die "Generalklauseln" angewendet hat, womit es – im Ergebnis – zu einer Art von mittelbarer Drittwirkung gelangt. Weil es ja die Anerkennung einer unmittelbaren Grundrechtswirkung gar nicht rückgängig machen *kann*, sollte es sich aus dieser Überspannung zurückziehen und – nun wirklich einmal! – das Privatrecht den Privatrechtlern überlassen, denn nicht öffentliches Recht soll über den Kautschukbegriff der "Auslegung" in das Privatrecht einfliessen, sondern dieses soll durch das über dem öffentlichen – wie privatem – Recht stehende Verfassungsrecht fortgebildet werden."

28 Ibid, 366: "Es eröffnet sich so die gefährliche Möglichkeit einer doppelgleisigen Rechtsprechung, indem das Bundesverfassungsgericht durch seine Anwendung der Grundrechte als Auslegungsregeln zu anderen Ergebnissen gelangt, als die oberste Zivilgerichtsbarkeit..."

the simple principle of higher law that supersedes subordinate law kicks in with the result that the constitutional principle simply overrides the private law ruling. No two-track or *doppelgleisigen* adjudication can result from this. However, Leisner stressed in this regard the need to appreciate the difference between private and constitutional law presupposed by the principle of horizontal effect. Private law does one thing and constitutional law something else, he insisted. They are not involved in more or less the same search for the same fundamental norms that according to both govern the legal relation and dispute at issue. It is exactly when private law and constitutional law adjudication are misunderstood as engaged with the same norms that constitutional and civil law courts can end up interpreting these same norms *differently*, he claimed. And this is what runs the risk of a two-track adjudication of the same legal questions according to him. It is then that one ends up with situations in which private law adjudication can come to assess a situation as lawful, only to be overturned on appeal by constitutional adjudication that assesses it as unlawful (or vice versa), with reference to the exact same norms and facts.

The only way to resolve this two-track adjudication so as to restore an unequivocal system of law would be to do away with the notion of *constitutional* review and to simply consider the procedure at issue an instance of higher review that registers no difference between private and constitutional law. And this is effectively what would happen, argued Leisner, were the radiation effect conception of constitutional review in horizontal effect cases to prevail. Constitutional courts would inevitably become final courts of appeal for all private law disputes (*so würde das Verfassungsgericht zur Superrevisionsinstanz*).[29] And private law would thus also lose the degree of institutional independence that Leisner believed it could rightly demand. It may be surprising to hear this from Leisner, the well-recognised exponent of direct horizontal application, but there can be no doubt about his conviction in this regard: The GFCC should now really begin to leave private law to private lawyers – "[*das Verfassungsgericht sollte*] – *nun wirklich einmal! – das Privatrecht den Privatrechtlern überlassen*)."[30]

We shall shortly return to the difference between private and constitutional adjudication that Leisner contemplates. Let us first look at his assessment of the problematic jurisprudence on which the GFCC embarked in *Lüth* according to him. This jurisprudence, he claimed, adopted a substantially coarser (*erheblich vergröberte*) version of Dürig's position on the indirect horizontal application

29 Ibid, 376.
30 Ibid, 377.

of fundamental rights to private legal relations.[31] And Dürig's position, he averred, is already deeply problematic and unconvincing. It leads, according to Leisner, either to complete vagueness or it admits to the very direct horizontality that Dürig sought to avoid (*was ... Dürig vorschlägt führt ... entweder zu völliger Unklarheit oder, doch zu einer mehr oder weniger unmittelbaren Drittwirkung zurück*).[32]

The "complete vagueness" that Leisner imputed to Dürig's position concerns the imprecise and inaccurate way in which Dürig employed the concept of "interpretation" (*Auslegung*). Strictly speaking, the concept of "interpretation" presupposes an *object of interpretation* with *independently interpretable content*. Fundamentally different from such objects of interpretation are concepts that offer no such interpretable content, but simply refer to (*verweisen auf*) other concepts external to them for their meaning. These latter concepts are referential norms (*Verweisungsnormen*) or referential concepts (*Verweisungsbegriffe*). The general clauses of private law such as good morals (*guten Sitten*) and good faith (*Treu und Glauben*) that Dürig proposed as bridgeheads or *Einbruchstellen* for the meaningful and mediated (*mittelbare*) impact of constitutional law on private law are indeed such referential concepts or norms, according to Leisner (*Generalklauselbegriffe sind ja typische Verweisungsbegriffe*).[33] They do not have independent content or meaning and are therefore not interpretable as such. They depend entirely on external points of reference for their meaning. Should constitutional norms be introduced as the relevant points of reference for the open concepts of private law, they would simply displace private law. There would be no way of preventing the eventual replacement of the core principles of private law with constitutional principles; hence Leisner's remarkable insistence: The indirect application of constitutional norms to private law that Dürig espoused threatens rather than protects the institutional independence of private law.

This permeation of private law by constitutional law can only be avoided, contended Leisner, by coming to grips with the true function of the general clauses of private law and the very real difference between this function and the impact of the constitution on private law. What is the difference at issue here? This difference becomes clear, Leisner argued, when one recalls the original function of open clauses of law in legal systems. They were not contemplated as empty vehicles for the introduction of external normative contents ([*sie waren*] *gerade nicht als generelle Analogieinstitute, als Blankett für die Aufnahme anderer*

31 Ibid, 374.
32 Ibid, 361.
33 Ibid, 364.

Norminhalte gedacht...).[34] They were referential concepts that referred to standard views of current practice (*jeweils geltende Verkehrsanschauungen*). These standard views of current practice were simply too in flux to be amenable to foundational conceptualisations of general or abstract norms. They were not amenable to foundational normativisation (*grundsätzlich unnormierbar*). They were for this reason also not intended as open reserves for future legislation and the norms of the constitution were never contemplated as their true content. In the context of private law, "good morals" and "good faith" had to be proved with reference to actual private law practices and not with reference to abstract norms.[35] As Leisner put it:

> "[General principles such as] good morals, good faith and good practice generally differ from fundamental rights and are essentially not articulated with reference to norms, but with recourse to direct articulations of "healthy" perceptions and practices of the legal community."[36]

In other words, the general clauses of private law are vehicles through which good customs and culturally acceptable modes of social exchange in private spheres can be invoked in legal disputes when specific rules of law do not provide satisfactory answers to the questions at issue. They allow judges the limited para-legislative freedom (*paralegislative Tätigkeit*, *nahezu gesetzgeberische Freiheit*[37]) to distil legal rules from general social practices and good customs when positive law fails to provide satisfactory rules. Constitutional norms offer no assistance as far as this para-legislative assessment of these socially acceptable ways of doing is concerned. To the extent that they affect such an assessment, they do so in the same way they affect general parliamentary legislation. In other words, they impose constitutional limits *on* this para-legislative activity of judges in the same way they impose constitutional limits on general legislation. In Leisner's words:

34 Ibid, 365.
35 Ibid.
36 Ibid, 366: "Gute Sitte, Treu und Glauben, Verkehrsitte, sind von den Grundrechten generell verschieden und überhaupt ihrem Wesen nach nicht durch Normen, sondern nur durch unmittelbare Ermittlung der in der Rechtsgemeinschaft bestehenden "gesunden" Anschauungen und Übungen sinnerfüllbar."
37 Ibid, 367 n. 201d.

> "Fundamental rights do not provide the contents of general clauses, they subject general clauses to constitutional limitations."[38]

This then, is Leisner's view of a meaningful division between constitutional and civil law that affirms an acceptable and legitimate degree of institutional independence of the latter without denying its sub-ordinance to the former: Civil law judiciaries are institutionally required and free to interpret and apply civil law in accordance with the intrinsic norms of positive private law and to resort to general or open principles of private law for purposes of considering current practices in private social exchanges when necessary. When this interpretation and application of civil law rules and general clauses conflict with constitutional norms, they must yield to these constitutional norms. This is all that there is to it. Seen from this perspective, constitutional norms have direct *impact* on civil law and civil law disputes when the application of civil law in a dispute conflicts with constitutional norms.

This does not mean that constitutional norms cannot *sometimes* also function as points of reference for the articulation of the general clauses of private law. Many years after Leisner wrote his majestic treatise on the relation between constitutional and private law, the authors of the South African constitution, perhaps quite in contrast to what Leisner considered to be the case in Germany, indeed demanded that common law be developed with reference to constitutional norms. This need not imply a deviation from Leisner's understanding of the relation between constitutional and private law. He does not deny the possibility that constitutional norms can sometimes serve as points of reference for the general clauses of private law. But when they do serve in this capacity, they no longer do so as regulating or validating norms that limit the scope of private law. They then simply become sources of law.[39] There can be no real impact – *Wirkung* – of the constitutional norms on private law in these cases, argued Leisner, unless one simply understands "impact" in a loose sense and not in the specifically legal and constitutional law sense of the word.

The scheme of horizontal application of constitutional norms that Leisner proposed can be outlined with reference to the following key points:

1) Horizontal application of constitutional norms does not concern the interpretation of general principles of private law in view of constitutional norms. This can only give rise to the displacement of rigorous legal reasoning by ab-

---

38 Ibid, 367: "[Die] Grundrechte [sind nicht] Erfüllung der Generalklauseln, sondern Begrenzung ihrer Anwendung."
39 Ibid.

stract philosophical speculation and the pernicious legal uncertainty attendant upon it.[40]

2) Constitutional norms concern a twofold normative order (*zwei Normschichten überlagern sich hier*),[41] one directed at the judiciary as state officials and one directed at private individuals. In their capacity as norms directed at judges, they bind the judiciary to take them duly into account in their interpretation and application of all law. In this capacity they clearly constitute fundamental rules of interpretation (*Interpretationsnormen*) that demand compliance. In their capacity as norms directed at private individuals, they are sources of private law. They then constitute private law rights and duties that supplement the rights and duties that derive from other sources of private law. In this capacity they function as the object of judicial interpretation (*auszulegenden Normen*). Under these circumstances the judge literally takes the constitutional norm as a rule of private law. At issue here *is not* the importation of constitutional law principles into private law,[42] but the due recognition of constitutional norms

---

40 Ibid, 394: "Vermieden werden kann auch der Rückgriff auf die 'Werte' und damit die Gefahr der Anerkennung genereller, willkürlicher 'Höherwertigkeiten' die sich oft nicht auf die Verfassung, sondern auf philosophische Spekulationen gründen." Cf. also 372–373: "Die Werte scheinen eine Auflösung der starren 'Berechtigungen' – die man als solche im Privatrecht nicht glaubt, anwenden zu dürfen – in eine Reihe von 'wertgewichtigen Bausteinen' zu ermöglichen, die man auf die angeblich typisch privatrechtliche Waage der Interessenvergleichung legen kann. Der eindrucksvolle Begriff des Wertes verdunkelt die Möglichkeit der kritischen Analyse eines Vorgangs, in dem tatsächlich nach freiem Belieben 'Wertakzente' verteilt werden können und die subjektiven Berechtigungen auch in ihrem letzten Kern u.U. der angeblichen 'Höherwertigkeit' anderen Interessen zu weichen haben. . . . Es wird nicht nach unklarem richterlichen Belieben bei der Interessenabwägung ein weiteres, grundrechtliches 'Gewicht' auf einer oder beiden Seiten hinzugefügt, sondern es stehen sich ganz konkreten Berechtigungen gegenüber, die unter Umständen eingeschränkt werden können und müssen." Cf. also at 371: "Durch maßstablose derartige 'Wertschärfungen' einer-, unkontrollierbare 'Intensivierung' u.ä. m. anderseits würde jedoch der Rechtsicherheit ein schlechterer Dienst erwiesen, als es durch eine 'unmittelbare' Anwendung droht. Man mag zur Beruhigung des 'zivilistischen Gewissens' BGB-Vorschriften mitzitieren – übernommen werden aus dem Verfassungsrecht keine beziehungslosen Begriffe, sondern Normkomplexe, welche subjektive private Rechte schaffen oder ihnen in gewisser Weise – etwa als schweigender Minimal inhalt – immanent sind." Cf. in this regard also the critique of Ruffert, *Vorrang der Verfassung und Eigenständigkeit des Privatrechts*, 63–71 and especially the following poignant observation at 67: "Wie es zur Rückumwandlung der objektivrechtlichen Ausstrahlungswirkung in ein subjektives, verfassungsbeschwerdefähiges Grundrecht, zur Re-Subjektivierung des objektiven Grundrechtsgehalts kommt, bleibt im Dunkeln." (It remains unclear how the objective order of constitutional values can be translated into a subjective right that can found a constitutional complaint.)

41 Leisner, *Grundrechte und Privatrecht*, 375.

42 *Lüth* incorrectly created this impression – Ibid, 374.

as immediate sources of private law, in the same way constitutional norms can also constitute immediate sources of public law. And when constitutional norms constitute sources of private law in this manner, civil law courts *alone* should have the jurisdiction to adjudicate them. A constitutional court has no jurisdiction here, however much the norms at issue may derive from the text of the constitution.[43]

3) The private law rights to which constitutional norms give rise invariably compete with rights that derive from statutory private law (or judicial private law in countries where private law has not been codified by statute). They can limit such statutory (or judicially determined) private law rights when this happens, or become limited by them, without considerations of a hierarchy of norms affecting these limitations in any way. The task of the civil law judiciary in these cases is to find the correct balance or proportional relationship between those rights that derive from constitutional norms and those that derive from private law legislation or adjudication. The one does not override the other mechanically.

4) No *constitutional* complaint can be filed against civil law adjudication that has *duly considered* the relation between competing private law rights as described under point 3 above. A constitutional complaint can only be filed against a civil court decision when a court has failed to comply with *constitutional* norms in its application of relevant law as described under point 5 below. This cannot happen when a judge has clearly and manifestly considered all private law norms relevant to the dispute – deriving as they may from legislation, judicial decisions or constitutional documents – with due application of mind. Appeals against such judicial findings are *civil law appeals* and must be directed to higher civil courts and the right of appeal runs out when the highest civil court has decided the case.

5) A *constitutional* complaint against a civil law decision can only come into play when the complete disregard for the minimum or essential content of a constitutional right is alleged.[44] Private law rights can limit other private law rights,

---

43 Ibid, 376: "Folgt man nämlich der von Nipperdey und dem BAG vertretenen Auffassung, so verleiht der Grundrechtskatalog den einzelnen öffentliche und private subjektive Rechte in *unmittelbarer* Weise, er ist also privatrechtliches Gesetz! Die Grundrechte sind dann *insoweit* keine Auslegungsregeln, sondern unmittelbare Grundlage von Rechten und Pflichten der Rechtsgenossen untereinander. Dies alles aber gehört zur ausschließlichen Zuständigkeit der höchsten Zivilgerichte, nicht zu der des Verfassungsgericths."

44 Ibid, 389: "Denn dies verlangt die Verfassung unbedingt: daß immer das Wesen, der Kern der einzelnen Bereiche gewahrt werde, was im Privatrecht nicht schwerer abgrenzbar ist, als im öffentlichen Recht, wo das Bestehen der Verfassungsforderung von niemandem in Zweifel ge-

also those that derive from constitutional documents. And when they do so, they may well also come to limit constitutional rights in the process. However, they cannot negate the core content of constitutional rights.[45] When civil law adjudication effectively destroys or completely annuls a constitutional right relevant to the case, the court and the judge as state official effectively fall foul of the *interpretive imperative* contained in the constitutional norm, the imperative that stipulates the way in which all law must be interpreted. Such a judge, it can then be said, fails to appreciate the relevance of a *constitutional* norm to the dispute and thus fails to decide the case with due application of mind. The failure at issue is a procedural failure. Appeals against such civil law decisions to a constitutional court will be in order, for they effectively are appeals against improper judicial procedures.[46] They concern failures of procedural due process.

One can see now why Leisner maintains that Dürig's three-pronged model of "indirect horizontal application" involves either no horizontal application, or direct horizontal application. The invocation of constitutional norms to explain or accentuate the application of private law principles does not constitute an *application* of constitutional norms to private law. Leisner clearly distinguishes between instances where a clause in the constitution functions as a *constitutional* norm and instances where it only serves as a private law rule. In other words, he distinguishes between the application of constitutional clauses *as* private law and *to* private law. The application that is at stake in the horizontal application of *constitutional* rights only concerns the latter. It only concerns those cases where private law is taken on *constitutional review*. When this happens, constitutional norms either validate or invalidate a relevant private law rule. And when they do so, they do so *directly*. There is no way in which this validating or invalidating application of the constitution can be considered indirect (*mittelbar*).

According to Leisner, the GFCC unfortunately opened the door for speculative departures from proper judicial rigour with its notion of the radiation effect (*Ausstrahlungswirkung*) of constitutional norms. According to him, this vague notion should make way for due understanding that constitutional norms either validate or invalidate. Gerard Robbers also makes this point well: Constitutional norms do not radiate, they apply – "Grundrechte strahlen nicht aus, Grundrechte

zogen wird." Cf. also 400: "Ganz allgemein lässt sich also sagen, daß die Grundrechte immer nur einen 'quantitativen Minimalschutz' des betreffenden Freiheitsbereichs bezwecken."

45 Cf. Ibid, 375–380; 397: "wenn ein vernünftiger Rechtsgenosse sich nicht mehr als ein "freier Mann" fühlen kann."

46 Ibid, 375: "Die Verletzung von Auslegungs- und damit i.w.S. von staatlichen "Verfahrensregeln," nicht aber die Anwendung der "Bereichschutzregeln des Zivilrechts" an sich kann hier geprüft werden..."

gelten."[47] They validate when the relevant private law rule can be reconciled with the minimum or essential content of all relevant constitutional rights. They invalidate when the private law rule cannot be squared with this minimum or essential content of constitutional rights.

The significance of Leisner's approach consists in the way it replaces a substantive due process with a procedural due process understanding of horizontal application. This is the heart of his critique of Dürig and of the GFCC's reasoning in *Lüth*. The significance of a shift from a substantive to a procedural due process conception of horizontal effect consists in the way it allows one to move from a socially divisive understanding of constitutional review that undermines the legitimacy of constitution norms, to a socially reconciliatory understanding of constitutional review that sustains their legitimacy. The substance of constitutional rights is irreducibly and irredeemably subject to serious contestation. No system of constitutional law will ever lay such contestation to rest and should therefore not aim to do so. However, the scope for contestation over the core content of constitutional rights is much narrower.

The scope for contestation over the question whether the core of a constitutional right has been recognised at all, is surely not non-existent, but it is significantly narrower than the scope for contestation regarding *the* correct interpretation of fundamental rights. Litigants and lawyers and public opinion can and will dispute the soundness of constitutional decisions indefinitely because of the absence of clearly correct answers to the questions at stake in this kind of dispute. But disputes that strictly concern the procedural question whether judicial deliberation has been proper and sound enough to comply with minimum demands of all relevant constitutional rights can be expected to run out of steam fast. Compared to the substantive question of whether a judge assessed the substance of a constitutional norm correctly, the procedural question whether he or she has applied his/her mind adequately to the matter is a simple one that warrants little disputation. The former question derives from social division and will remain socially divisive. The latter question derives from perceptions that something has gone so obviously wrong in a civil law suit – one has to get something badly wrong to fail minimal constitutional demands – that it warrants inference of failed adjudication. Perceptions of failed adjudication can of course also evoke social dismay, but they are not likely to be socially divisive

---

47 Gerard Robbers, "Für ein neues Verhältnis zwischen Bundesverfassungsgericht und Fachgerichtbarkeit," *Neue Juristische Wochenschrift* 14 (1998): 937: "Grundrechte strahlen nicht aus, Grundrechte gelten. Die Rede von der Ausstrahlungswirkung der Grundrechte gehört einer früheren Rechtssicht an, man sollte sie aufgeben." Cf. again also the critique of Ruffert pointed out in footnote 40 above.

in the long term, especially when due procedures of constitutional review manage to put them right in a timely enough fashion.

The full significance of this understanding of horizontal constitutional review will become clearer towards the end of this book. Suffice it to state for now that it takes one a long way towards a theory of horizontal application that addresses the question of uninterrupted but "divided" sovereignty that emerged from the discussion of *Roe* and *Erste Abtreibung* in Chapter Two. Leisner has much more to tell us in this regard and we return to him in Chapter Six. It is time now to turn to the contributions of Jürgen Schwabe and Claus-Wilhelm Canaris to the *Drittwirkung* debate in Germany, for they also throw considerable light on the question of sovereignty that underpins the question of horizontal effect. We turn to Schwabe first and then to Canaris in section VI.

V Schwabe's Position

Making the Hohfeldian point that all law must be imputed to a sovereign lawmaker may be "child's play," as Frank Michelman avers, but it is exactly by making this point that Jürgen Schwabe created a considerable storm in the German *Drittwirkung* debate in 1971. Substantive private law is part and parcel of the law authored by the state, argued Schwabe. Any private law rule or lack of such rule that allows one private individual to violate the fundamental right of another, he continued, must be considered unconstitutional. This is how he made the point:

> "Purely private force and interventions can only be a source of concern in lawless communities, and at that only for physically weaker individuals. Under the rule of law the burdens that private conduct imposes on others need only be tolerated to the extent that they are supported by the legal order and can, when necessary, be enforced by the state. Private power that imposes inescapable burdens on others is authorised or at least permitted by the state. The coercion that private individuals impose on bearers of fundamental rights is sanctioned by the state. Superior private force that imposes itself on others depends fundamentally on the legal order of the state and not on the personal power of an individual citizen."[48]

48 Jürgen Schwabe, *Die sogenannte Drittwirkung der Grundrechte: zur Einwirkung der Grundrechte auf den Privatrechtsverkehr* (München: W. Goldmann, 1971), 16–17: "[R]ein private Gewalten und Eingriffe können nur in einem rechtlosen Gemeinwesen Besorgnis erwecken und auch da nur für den physisch Schwächeren. Im Rechtstaat erhält der von Privatem ausgelöste und beschwerende, weil zu duldende Eingriff seine Bedeutung daher, daß er von der Rechtsordnung getragen ist – und also notfalls von der staatlichen Vollstreckungsgewalt durchgesetzt wird. Beschwerende, nicht abwehrfähige 'private' Gewalt ist staatlich legitimierte oder doch wenigstens gebilligte Gewalt, der von dort gegen den Grundrechtsträger ausgeübte Zwang ist

Why do so many scholars then find it so difficult to square the constitutional review of private law with ordinary constitutional review? Why do they need this so-called horizontal effect (*sogenannte Drittwirkung*) of constitutional rights to justify the constitutional review of private law? These are the questions that astounded Schwabe and he proceeded to answer them as follows:

> "Almost all the authors that concern themselves with horizontal application distinguish their endeavours carefully from concerns with hitherto well-recognised concepts and practices of constitutional review that restrict constitutional scrutiny to the scrutiny of state action. Whereas the latter is considered to be unproblematic, the former is deemed to require highly complicated and controversial grounds of justification."[49]

The "so-called horizontal effect" cases were, according to Schwabe, nothing but ordinary cases of constitutional review. Considering that private law is no separate sphere of law that somehow does not count as state law, Schwabe could simply not understand why the legal scholars of his time would go to such lengths to explain or justify the constitutional review of private law as a special or separate case of constitutional review. He consequently proceeded to explain to them why private law is not a special but an ordinary product of sovereign law-making. The fact that private law is an instance of state sanctioned power, he argued, is usually sufficiently clear in the case of non-contractual civil law relations.[50] Few legal scholars fail to grasp this point. It is mostly in the context of contractual relationships and contract law, averred Schwabe, that some lawyers entertain conceptions of natural private autonomy as untouched by state action and control. According to him, this line of thinking constituted a misconceived deviation from well-established principles of German legal scholarship that did not make this mistake. Most German scholars, he argued, clearly recognise that the principle of freedom of contract does not create pockets of natural autonomy (*state of nature* autonomy) within the law-governed framework of the state. Among the many that Schwabe cited in this regard, the reference to Franz Laufke was especially poignant. Laufke wrote in 1956:

---

staatlich sanktioniert. Daß gerade der Stärkere einer 'privaten Gewalt' einem 'Eingriff' von Privaten unterliegt, beruht wesentlich auf der staatlichen Rechtsordnung, nicht auf der Macht eines Bürgers."

49 Ibid, 11: "Fast alle Autoren, die sich mit der 'Drittwirkung' befassen, setzen sich sorgfältig von der herkömmlich praktizierten und anerkannten Grundrechtswirkung gegen den Staat ab. Während die letztere unproblematisch ist, bedarf es folglich für die davon ganz verschiedene 'Drittwirkung' mitunter sehr komplizierter und umstrittener Begründungen."

50 Ibid, 17.

> "For purposes of assessing the restrictions that constitutional principles impose on contractual freedom correctly, one must ultimately recognise that legal transactions and contracts derive their status as legal transactions as much from the state as from those that take part in the transaction or contract. The legal status of these transactions does not materialise from the mere communication of the will of an individual, but from the contractual capacity with which the legal order endows an individual and with which it enables the individual to give legal force to expressions of will. The state thus acts as co-author in every legal transaction and as such bears full co-responsibility for the force and consequences of a legal transaction. Seen from this perspective, any contention that constitutional principles have no bearing on private legal transactions would be untenable."[51]

According to Schwabe, this observation by Laufke, as well as many other similar observations by scholars such as Erich Kaufmann, Felix Somló and Hans Heinrich Rupp, makes it abundantly clear that the "scientific misconception of spaces devoid of law" (*wissenschaftliche Fehlleistung von der rechtsleeren Räumen*)[52] should be dismissed once and for all. The law permeates the totality of all space governed by a constitutional state or *Rechtsstaat*. And as far as this uninterrupted reach of the rule of law in constitutional states is concerned, the question whether some or other particular sphere of life is governed by private or public law is of no consequence as far as the application of constitutional norms is concerned. This is so, Schwabe contended, because the constitution applies only to primary rules of law that govern the behaviour of individuals, not to

51 Ibid, 23, referring to Franz Laufke, *Vertragsfreiheit und Grundgesetz, Festschrift für Lehmann*, vol. I (Berlin: Walter de Gruyter, 1956), 180–181: "Schließlich muß man, wenn man die Frage, ob und wie weit sich aus den Grundrechtsbestimmungen Schranken für die Vertragsfreiheit herleiten lassen, richtig würdigen will, beachten, daß die Rechtsgeschäfte und damit auch die Verträge ihre Existenz als Rechtsgeschäft ebensosehr dem Staat wie dem am Rechtsgeschäft Beteiligten verdanken, denn die spezifisch rechtsgeschäftlichen Wirkungen treten nicht schon deshalb ein, weil sie als gewollt bekundet wurden, sondern weil darüber hinaus die Rechtsordnung dem Parteiwillen die Fähigkeit beilegte, als gewollt bekundete Rechtseffekte herbeizuführen. So tritt der Staat schon beim Zustandekommen eines jeden Rechtsgeschäfts als Mittäter auf, der die volle Mitverantwortung für den eingetretenen Rechtseffekt trägt. Unter diesem Gesichtspunkt dürfte es nicht angängig sein zu behaupten, die Grundrechtsbestimmungen seien für die Rechtsgeschäfte schlechtweg bedeutungslos." This imputation (*Zurechnung*) of authorship or at least co-authorship to the state in private legal transactions has been met with vigorous criticism in German *Drittwirkung* scholarship. Apart from Canaris, who will be discussed in more detail in the next session, see also Ernst-Wolfgang Böckenförde "Grundrechte als Grundsatznormen. Zur gegenwärtigen Lage der Grundrechtsdogmatik" 1990 *Der Staat*, 1–31 at 28 fn 108; Robert Alexy, *Theorie der Grundrechte* (Frankfurt am Main: Suhrkamp, 1986), 415–420; Georg Hermes, "Grundrechtsschutz durch Privatrecht auf neuer Grundlage? – Das BVerfG zu Schutzpflicht und mittelbarer Drittwirkung der Berufsfreiheit," *Neue Juristische Wochenschrift* 29 (1990): 1766.

52 Schwabe, *Die sogenannte Drittwirkung der Grundrechte*, 20.

secondary rules that merely organise the application of primary rules. Only primary rules of law that actually govern conduct can abridge or limit constitutional rights and only these rules can have constitutional relevance. The distinction between public and private law is a case in point. It does not constitute a governing rule. It is only a rule that organises government. And this organisational rule, argued Schwabe, cannot clash with the substance of a fundamental right and cannot have any bearing on the application of the constitution.

Schwabe cited as an example in this regard the proscription of defamation and insult with which the GFCC was concerned in the *Schmid* case in 1961.[53] Whether this rule is enforced by public prosecution or in a private suit for damages, he contended, can surely not affect its constitutional status. The normative force of constitutional rights only affects the substance of the proscription, not the manner of its enforcement. He concluded the point with a comical depiction of the absurdity that would result in this case if one were to attribute normative consequences to organisation rules of government:

> "The direct application of constitutional law to (public law) criminal proceedings is uncontroversial. In civil law proceedings parallel to such criminal proceedings the question of horizontal application suddenly raises its head. One can hardly picture this situation realistically enough: When an individual affected by some primary rule of law appears in the criminal court, his reliance on [for example] Section 5 of the GG is immediately recognised as permissible. Should he, however, move on one door further to the civil law hearing, the case is postponed so as to allow the judges to first immerse themselves in the almost limitless literature on horizontal application. Should one consider in addition to this the theoretical possibility that the same judges might be sitting in both courts, the consequences of prevailing conceptions of horizontal application require no further comment." [54]

Schwabe's bottom line is that constitutional norms apply to the substance of all primary legal rules. It is the substance of these primary rules that renders them constitutionally acceptable or not, not the incidental manner of their enforcement. This argument, however, clearly overstates and distorts the very pertinent

---

53 BVerfGe 12, 113.

54 Schwabe, *Die sogenannte Drittwirkung der Grundrechte*, 46–47: "Im (öffentlich-rechtlichen) Strafverfahren ist die unmittelbare Grundrechtsgeltung unbestritten. Im parallelen Zivilverfahren aber ist ein Fall der 'Drittwirkung' gegeben. Dergleichen kann man sich gar nicht realistisch genug ausmalen: Erscheint der durch die Primärnorm Betroffene vor der Strafkammer, ist seiner Berufung auf das Grundrecht des Art. 5 GG sogleich stattzugeben. Geht er aber eine Tür weiter zur Zivilkammer, ist eine Vertagung angezeigt, damit die Richter sich in die fast unübersehbare Literatur zur 'Drittwirkung' vertiefen können. Nimmt man noch hinzu daß beide Kammern theoretisch mit denselben Richtern besetzt sein könnten, dann erübrigt sich zu diesen Konsequenzen der [herrschenden Lehre] jeder weitere Kommentar."

point that he was making. His crucial point regarding the "scientific misconception of spaces devoid of law" (*wissenschaftliche Fehlleistung von der rechtsleeren Räumen*) is exactly the insight that many American legal scholars draw from Hohfeld's analyses of legal relationships or from broader insights that are generally associated with the American realist movement. For these American scholars, we saw in Chapter Three, the basic principle of the rule of law also necessitated an assumption of state tolerance and/or facilitation of all human conduct that is not expressly proscribed by law. And for them too this assumption not only implied the constitutional reviewability of all law, facilitative law (especially contract law) included; it also implied the constitutional reviewability of any absence of express law.

The merit of Schwabe's argument at the time concerned the way it underlined this "realist" insight in a context of "formalist" *Drittwirkung* jurisprudence that appeared to resist it. It is nevertheless a good question whether the *Drittwirkung* jurisprudence at issue was really resisting this insight consistently and whether Schwabe was really confronting it with a point that it had not already conceded, albeit somewhat ambivalently. To return just briefly to Dürig, the scholar whose extensive theory of *Drittwirkung* may appear to single him out as the main antagonist of anyone who would, like Schwabe, dismiss *Drittwirkung* as a non-problem. Dürig clearly recognised that *Drittwirkung* may require *Lückenfüllung*. He acknowledged expressly that constitutional protection deficits might come to require supplementation of private law with additional rules that remedy such deficits. In this respect, the substantive reach of Dürig's theory of *Drittwirkung* is ultimately no less expansive or sweeping than Schwabe's dismissal of the whole *Drittwirkung* question as a pseudo, false or merely so-called (*sogenannte*) question. Dürig's conception of *Lückenfüllung*, we already pointed out above, is really the can opener in his theory of horizontal effect with regard to which Schwabe did not add anything significant. And to the extent that he did seek to add something to Dürig's conception of *Drittwirkung* that was not there already, Schwabe evidently overplayed his hand. What he seemed to add to Dürig's theory is the idea that it makes no significant difference to constitutional review whether the conduct under review is that of a private or public legal subject. If this is really what Schwabe aimed to say, his argument clearly went wrong here. Brief recollection of the conspicuously broader liberty of private persons to discriminate on grounds that public authorities may not – already pointed out above – is enough to make this point clear again. To borrow Schwabe's comical scene of the adjacent court rooms: Racial, gender or faith discrimination by public officials is simply much more likely to end up in constitutional courtrooms than similar discrimination by private individuals in personal spheres of life. The latter discrimination would have to be accompanied by additional elements of tortious or delictual insult to get it into the civil courtroom next door.

The *Drittwirkung* question is not just a "*sogenannte*," so-called or pseudo question. It exists as a real question because instances of private discrimination will, in a constitutional state, sometimes move on from civil to constitutional courtrooms and sometimes not. Schwabe thinks this should happen "often" – *oftmals.* He asks: Should the subjects of fundamental rights not often enjoy more protection against private individuals than against those officials who are subject to proper parliamentary controls – *[m]uß nicht umgekehrt der Grundrechtsinhaber oftmals vor Privaten viel mehr geschützt werden als – in vergleichbaren Fällen – vor parlamentarisch kontrollierten Staatsorganen?*[55] The democratic sentiment expressed with this question surely registers acute regard for the reality that unchecked powers of private actors often surpass the power of states to violate fundamental rights today. But the *Drittwirkung* question is a real and perplexing problem – not just "so-called" or *sogenannt* – because it is not always self-evident when and whether private conduct raises constitutional questions. The answer "often" surely does not answer the question adequately. This is the insight that Schwabe's main interlocutor, Claus-Wilhelm Canaris, offered in response to Schwabe's wholesale dismissal of the *Drittwirkung* question. Canaris, we shall see now, moved to simplify the perplexing aspects of the *Drittwirkung* question by recasting it in terms of the state's constitutional duty to protect the constitutional rights of citizens.

VI Canaris' Response

The crux of Canaris' response to Schwabe consited in the contention that Schwabe never responded to the main question that Dürig's *Ausgangspunkt* or point of departure raised for the theory of horizontal application. Dürig's point of departure asserted a qualitative difference between the power of states to abridge constitutional rights and the liberty of individuals to do so. Schwabe's construction of private autonomy as a mere vehicle for state legislation and state action does not address this difference, argued Canaris. Only when the individual may do nothing to abridge constitutional rights that the state may not do, contended Canaris, is it fair to implicate the state automatically in private abridgment of rights. Only then can one say the state facilitates or tolerates something that it is constitutionally bound not to facilitate or tolerate. Schwabe, wrote

55 Ibid, 49.

Canaris, never responded to Dürig's distinction. He simply ignored it or erased it with recourse to a theory of private legal agency as a reflex of state power that has never enjoyed significant endorsement in Germany. Here is Canaris' crucial statement in this regard:

> "[Schwabe interprets] contractual claims as 'contractually determined legislative commands.' In doing so he reverts to a position that was already current in the 19th century [especially in the work of Thon]. This approach, however, together with the closely related "factual evidence theory" in terms of which the legal transaction is nothing but the factual evidence of legislation, correctly received no following. For this view indeed misses the essential element of the legal transaction that lies in the creative articulation of legal consequences by private legal subjects themselves."[56]

Canaris' response to Schwabe consisted in drawing and maintaining a clear conceptual distinction between the creative construction (*schöpferische Gestaltung*) of private legal relations and the role of the state in facilitating and enforcing those relationships. According to him, the creative construction of private relationships involves a qualitatively different liberty to abridge the rights of other individuals that exceeds the liberty of the state to do so. Canaris went so far as to invoke a wide range of private liberty that is *untouched by law* and accordingly enjoys a-priori exemption from all imputations of unlawful injury to others.[57]

With this rejection of Schwabe's position, Canaris evidently also rejected the recognition of the uninterrupted reach of the rule of law in a constitutional state that we have come to call the Hohfeldian point. This view was already ventured in nineteenth century Germany legal theory, he contended, but it never received significant endorsement. Canaris nevertheless ended up equivocating badly in this regard. He commenced to articulate a conception of the state's duty to safeguard fundamental rights that ultimately contradicts his invocation of a "a wide range of liberty that is untouched by law" (*weiten Bereich allgemeiner Hand-*

---

56 Claus-Wilhelm Canaris, "Grundrechte und Privatrecht," *Archiv für die civilistische Praxis* 184, no. 4 (1984): 217: "[Schwabe deutet] Ansprüche aus Vertrag als 'vertraglich bedingte *Gesetzes*befehle.' Damit wird eine Theorie wieder aufgegriffen, die schon im 19. Jahrhundert [am wichtigsten von Thon] vertreten wurde, sich jedoch ebenso wie die eng verwandte 'Tatbestandstheorie' nach der das Rechtsgeschäft nicht mehr ist als ein tatbestandliches Merkmal des Gesetzes, mit Recht nicht durchgesetzt hat. In der Tat wird durch eine solche Sichtweise das Essentiale des Rechtsgeschäfts verfehlt, das darin liegt, daß die *schöpferische* Gestaltung von Rechtsfolgen durch die Privatrechtssubjekte selbst erfolgt."

57 Ibid, 230: "Richtig ist viel mehr, daß es im Privatrecht einen weiten Bereich allgemeiner Handlungsfreiheit gibt, der rechtlich nicht besetzt ist und in dem rechtswidrige Verletzungen anderer Privatrechtssubjekte daher a priori nicht in Betracht kommen."

lungsfreiheit ... der rechtlich nicht besetzt ist). According to Canaris, the constitutional duty of the state to protect fundamental rights (*Schutzgebotsfunktion der Grundrechte*) necessarily entails a constitutional proscription of insufficient protection (*Untermaßverbot*). This proscription of insufficient protection, he contends, also extends to the zone of constructive legal creativity that individuals enjoy in the private sphere.[58] From this point on, it seems, very little of his critique of Schwabe remains standing.

According to Canaris, constitutional subjective rights can be active or effective within private law in two different ways. They can be operative as defensive rights or *Abwehrrechte*, that is, as the typical negative rights contemplated by classical constitutional law. They function thus whenever coercive private law becomes constitutionally questionable. At issue here in such cases is an *Übermaßverbot*[59] – the constitutional proscription of excessive state interference with private liberty. However, constitutional subjective rights can also function as positive rights that demand minimum state intervention in private liberty. At issue here is the constitutional imperative that the state protect and safeguard constitutional rights adequately, namely the *Schutzgebotsfunktion der Grundrechte* embodied in Article 1 I of the *GG* to which German scholarship also refers as an *Untermaßverbot* – the proscription of inadequate state intervention.

The latter function of constitutional rights in private law, contended Canaris, indeed also affects the creative construction of the contents of private legal relations – *die rechtsgeschäftliche Inhaltsfreiheit*. This can take place through the general clauses of civil law but also through more specific civil law rules that allow for a more differentiated engagement with constitutionally dubious aspects of private relations, such as the rules that render unlawful contracts unenforceable (§ 134 *BGB*). On the basis of these two possibilities of fundamental rights as either defensive rights against excessively coercive private law or positive rights to minimum levels of state protection in private law relations, Canaris ultimately endorsed the *direct horizontal* application of fundamental rights. These two functions of fundamental rights apply directly to the legislator. The notion of indirect horizontal application or *mittelbare Drittwirkung* only make sense, he maintained, when one refers to the impact of fundamental rights on private autonomy as such. This impact is indeed always mediated by the impact of fundamental rights on public authorities. It is never direct.[60]

58 Canaris "Grundrechte und Privatrecht," 245–246.
59 Canaris, "Grundrechte Und Privatrecht," 245.
60 Ibid, 210–212.

VII Schutzpflicht and/or Drittwirkung?

The *Handelsvertreter* case is often considered the beacon of the Federal Constitutional Court's switch from the *Ausstrahlungswirkung* or radiation effect approach to *Drittwirkung* in its earlier decisions, to the *Schutzgebotsfunktion* and *Untermaßverbot* approach in its later decisions.[61] Some scholars doubt whether there really has been such a significant switch in this regard.[62] They may well have a point, given the way the *Schutzgebotsfunktion* is already evident in *Lüth.*[63] It is not necessary to go further into this doctrinal controversy. There is also a line of scholarship that denies the relation between the *Schutzgebotsfunktion* and the *Drittwirkung* problematic altogether.[64] This controversy also need not detain one. Assuming that it does not make much sense to talk about the duty of the state to protect citizens against itself, it is hard to see against whom the duty of the state to protect would find purchase if not indeed against third parties (unless one would want to reduce the state's duty to protect fundamental rights largely to foreign threats).

More pressing than the question whether the *Schutzgebotsfunktion* approach has displaced or just supplemented the *Ausstrahlungswirkung* approach of the GFCC's earlier decisions is the questionability of the *Ausstrahlungswirkung* or ra-

61 BVerfG 81, 242, hereafter *Handelsvertreter.*

62 Oldiges, "Neue Aspekte der Grundrechtsgeltung im Privatrecht," 281–308; Oeter, "'Drittwirkung' der Grundrechte und die Autonomie des Privatrechts," 529–563.

63 Cf. especially *Handelsvertreter* paragraph 49 for the evident link between the *Schutzpflicht* and *Ausstrahlungswirkung* conceptions of horizontal effect: "Vertragsformen zu schaffen, bedeutet keineswegs, daß die Vertragspraxis dem freien Spiel der Kräfte unbegrenzt ausgesetzt wäre. Vielmehr greifen dann ergänzend solche zivilrechtlichen Generalklauseln ein, die als Übermaßverbote wirken, vor allem die §§ 138, 242, 315 BGB. Gerade bei der Konkretisierung und Anwendung dieser Generalklauseln sind die Grundrechte zu beachten (grundlegend BVerfGE 7, 198). Der entsprechende Schutzauftrag der Verfassung richtet sich hier an den Richter, der den objektiven Grundentscheidungen der Grundrechte in Fällen gestörter Vertragsparität mit den Mitteln des Zivilrechts Geltung zu verschaffen hat und diese Aufgabe auch auf vielfältige Weise wahrnimmt..."

64 Cf. Canaris, "Grundrechte und Privatrecht," 226, referring to Josef Isensee, *Das Grundrecht auf Sicherheit – Zu den Schutzpflichten des Freiheitlichen Verfassungsstaates* (1983) 35 and Konrad Hesse, *Grundzüge des Verfassungsrechts der Bundesrepublik Deutschland*, 13 Auflage 1982 Rdnr 351 (I have not consulted these two sources). Dürig, on the other hand affirmed the connection. Cf. Dürig, "Grundrechte und Zivilrechtsprechung," 176. Cf. also the argument that the *Drittwirkung* doctrine and *Schutzpflichtgebot* came together with the *Handelsvertreter* decision of the GFCC forwarded by Georg Hermes "Grundrechtsschutz durch Privatrecht auf neuer Grundlage? – Das BVerfG zu Schutzpflicht und mittelbarer Drittwirkung der Berufsfreiheit," NJW 1990, Heft 29, 1764–1768.

diation effect approach as such. The remaining chapters of this book will take leave of this understanding of horizontal effect. They will put forward an understanding of horizontal effect that pivots on Leisner's insistence that constitutional rights do not radiate. Radiation may be a well-understood and well-defined concept in physics. As far as legal language is concerned, radiation is a vague concept with dangerous consequences. Judges are not trained to deal with it and those who do run the risk of disastrous contaminations. According to Leisner, constitutional rights do two things in the context of private law. On the one hand, they constitute private law rules or rules for private law that private law judges must apply like any other private law. On the other hand they validate or invalidate private law rules. This is a clear and simple conception of the role of constitutional rights in the context of private law that can be entrusted to judges. Canaris' invocation of the *Schutzgebotsfunktion* of constitutional rights and the *Untermaßverbot* that this *Schutzgebotsfunktion* implies provides further clarification of what is at stake in this validating or invalidating role of constitutional rights. The *Untermaßverbot* and *Schutzgebotsfunktion* embodied in constitutional rights invalidate private law that affords too little protection to these rights. This is a transparent doctrinal construction that avoids the vague hermeneutics implied in the term "radiation" or "*Ausstrahlung*." Chapter Six will explain more fully why this vague hermeneutics is not a good basis for constitutional adjudication in liberal democracies. Suffice it to state for now that the proscription of inadequate protection of fundamental rights or *Untermaßverbot* provides liberal constitutional review with a much sounder foundation.

The different positions of Nipperdey, Dürig, Leisner, Schwabe and Canaris discussed in this chapter showed up tensions in German *Drittwirkung* jurisprudence that are similar to those that Chapter Three traced through American state action scholarship. The controversies in German *Drittwirkung* scholarship surely turn on the essential question of the uninterrupted reach of the rule of law in a constitutional state, the question that we have come to explain with reference to Michelman's "Hohfeldian point." The controversies ultimately all seem to derive from the fact that some scholars like Schwabe endorsed the Hohfeldian point unflinchingly, while others, like Dürig and Canaris, resisted it. The latter scholars, we have seen, did nevertheless not dismiss the Hohfeldian point comprehensively or unambiguously. Both Dürig and Canaris appear to have resisted the idea that there are no legal vacuums, no spaces that are simply devoid of law, in a constitutional state. But they both articulated theories of horizontal application that ultimately seem to concede that there are no such spaces after all. Dürig filled these spaces with his concept of *Lückenfüllung*. Canaris filled them with his concept of the *Untermaßverbot*. In the end they both ended up stranded in ambiguities or equivocations that echo the ambiguity that Seidman points out in the context of American state action jurisprudence. Dürig and Canaris also ended up recognising the full territorial sovereignty of the state, on the one hand, while remaining concerned about the implications of this full territorial sovereignty, on the other.

We have reached the end of Part One. Part Two turns now, in Chapter Five, to a significant new development in the horizontal effect debate that has emerged in recent years with the work of especially Matthias Kumm, on the one hand, and Ralf Christensen and Andreas Fischer-Lescano on the other. We can switch to present tense now. Kumm, we shall see, recasts the question of horizontal effect in terms of the totality of the constitution and the unity of the legal system. His emphasis on the totality of the constitution and the unity of the legal system surely evinces the closeness between his position and the Hohfeldian or Schwabian positions discussed in Chapters Three and Four. He ultimately adds little to what we have already gleaned from Hohfeldian or realist state action scholars on the one hand, and Leisner, Schwabe and Canaris on the other. What he does add is an overstatement of their arguments that renders his articulation of these earlier positions questionable.

Christensen and Andreas Fischer-Lescano, however, confront us with a whole new kettle of fish. Not only do these authors present their engagements with the horizontal effect question in a completely new language that requires one to relate it to the broader question of liberal democratic sovereignty in a way that has not been done before. They also, perhaps for the first time in the history of German horizontal effect jurisprudence, endeavour to break incisively with the sovereignty-affirming horizontal effect tradition that is evident among even the most sovereignty-wary scholars – Dürig and Canaris – of the first two waves of *Drittwirkung* scholarship discussed in this chapter.

Part Two: **Sovereignty**

Chapter Five: Uninterrupted Sovereignty

I Introduction

Justice Rehnquist's judicial legacy to the people of the United States, we saw in Chapters Two and Three, consisted in abdicating, on behalf of them, their sovereignty. Through his legacy, one might say, he reduced the sovereignty of the United States to an archipelago of islands of sovereignty. Between these islands of sovereignty the American people find themselves constantly exposed to the absence of sovereign government. As the *DeShaney* case showed, this exposure to the absence of government can take place in the depths of urban environments.

The GFCC's decision in *Lüth*, we argued in Chapters Two and Four, in marked contrast to *DeShaney*, bequeathed to the people of Germany an uninterrupted sovereignty that ensures or at least promises effective sovereign government throughout Germany; through *the whole of Germany*, one might say. When sovereign government fails in Germany, such failure does not, according to the *Lüth* legacy, constitute an affirmation of the absence of government. It constitutes a default on a sovereign guarantee that demands compensation. A sovereign worthy of the name steps in under these circumstances to confirm its sovereignty. It acknowledges the failure and grants the compensation due. It does not deny sovereignty, as Justice Rehnquist did in *DeShaney*.

We also saw in Chapter Three how reluctant some American scholars are to view private spheres as part and parcel of the sovereign's territory. Some basically dismiss the idea (Wechsler most clearly so) and others find themselves caught up in ambivalence on this count (consider again especially the discussion of Seidman's position). Those who dismiss the idea that private spheres form part of the sovereign's territory are evidently concerned about the liberty deficit that would result from accepting the idea. Those who are ambivalent about the idea, are concerned by the liberty deficit that would result from accepting it, and by the sovereignty deficit that would result from dismissing it. One line of scholars, we called them the Hohfeldians, nevertheless accept the idea that private spheres are part and parcel of the sovereign's territory. They accept that private spheres are fundamentally shaped by acts of sovereignty, irrespective whether these acts consist in positive acts or omissions to act and irrespective whether omissions to act are deliberate or incidental. The Hohfeldians accept and stress the principle that the sovereign takes responsibility for everything that happens in its territory. They know that sovereignty, in liberal democracies, guarantees liberty. It does not threaten it. They know liberty deficits result from sovereignty deficits, not from sovereignty.

We saw in Chapter Four that some German *Drittwirkung* scholars also evince ambivalence and discomfort regarding the uninterrupted reign of the German sovereign over its territory. However, none of them endorse the idea that private spheres fall outside the reign of the sovereign. Those concerned about possible liberty deficits that might result from accepting the uninterrupted reign of sovereignty go no further than insisting that the sovereign rules differently in the private sphere than it does in the public sphere. According to them (most notably in the case of Dürig), the sovereign allows private individuals more scope to affect one another's fundamental rights negatively than it allows itself to do. But in the final analysis, the prominent German scholars discussed in Chapter Four basically all come round to accepting the uninterrupted reign of the sovereign over and in private spheres. Those who appear the most hesitant to do so, nevertheless admit to the principle that insufficient intervention of the sovereign in the private sphere would call for *Lückenfüllung* (Dürig), or for the application of a constitutional *Untermaßverbot* (Canaris). Thus do even the most sovereign-wary *Drittwirkung* scholars acknowledge the need for adequate levels of sovereign rule in private spheres. Some German scholars, on the other hand, go so far as to assert bluntly that everything that happens in the private sphere happens in the name of the sovereign and can accordingly be addressed by a regular constitutional *Übermaßverbot* (notably Schwabe).

"The whole is at stake when fundamental rights clash" – "*Wenn Grundrechte kollidieren, geht es ums Ganze.*" This is the dramatic opening sentence of Ralph Christensen and Andreas Fischer-Lescano's work *Das Ganze des Rechts.*[1] This threshold invocation of *the whole of law* surely appears to mark a new decisiveness among German scholars to embrace the willingness of their judiciary to affirm the uninterrupted territorial reign of German sovereignty. With "the whole" or "das Ganze," Christensen and Fischer-Lescano have in mind the overall coherence that the whole system of German law enjoys as a result of the common linguistic horizon that underpins this system of law. They seem to endorse and affirm for Germany the uninterrupted sovereignty that Neil Walker describes as the "continuing source and vehicle of ultimate authority for the juridical order of that polity."[2] This however, is not the case. We shall see below that Christensen

1 Christensen and Fischer-Lescano, *Das Ganze des Rechts – Vom hierarchischen zum reflexiven Verständnis deutscher und europäischer Grundrechte*, 5.

2 Neil Walker, "Late Sovereignty in the European Union," in *Sovereignty in Transition*, ed. Neil Walker (Oxford: Hart Publishing, 2003), 6. Cf. also Ibid, 19. Walker stresses this continuity of sovereignty as an indispensible feature of what he calls late sovereignty.

and Fischer-Lescano's contribution to the *Drittwirkung* debate in Germany dissolves and dispenses with the essential legal sovereignty without which horizontal effect becomes an empty chimera. Christensen and Fischer-Lescano's contribution to the *Drittwirkung* debate, we shall see, amounts to nothing less than an attempt to terminate the great sovereignty-affirming tradition of German *Drittwirkung* scholarship.

In fact, Christensen and Fischer-Lescano's contribution to the horizontal effect debate can be said to represent the far end on a spectrum of ever more incisive or far-reaching subversions of sovereignty apparent in contemporary legal theory and practice. This Chapter engages with three other such subversions of sovereignty in contemporary constitutional theory and practice that progressively ruin the concept of the horizontal effect of fundamental rights and the concept of fundamental rights as such. The three other subversions at stake here are *divisions* of sovereignty, *deistic* conceptions of sovereignty and *dispersals* of sovereignty. Christensen and Fischer-Lescano adds to these subversions of sovereignty a *dissolution* of sovereignty that allows them to *dispense* with it. Their contribution to the horizontal effect debate thus constitutes the fourth and most extreme instance of the progressive subversion of sovereignty that is evident in contemporary legal theory and practice.

The central argument of the chapter is this: The anti-statism on which especially the last three subversions of sovereignty turn underestimates the role that *third party* or *impartial* perspectives play in the effective resolution of social conflict. It underestimates the role that centralised state governments play as impartial third party arbitrators and regulators of social conflict. And it is for purposes of countering this underestimation that the role of state sovereignty, not as the only, but surely as the ultimate guarantor of liberal democratic constitutionalism and constitutional rights in the contemporary world, is stressed towards the end of this chapter. Arguments in favour of dispersals and dissolutions of state sovereignty present themselves regularly today in terms of Luhmannian and Teubnerian concerns with functional differentiation. Consistent constitutional theory requires that we find our way back from Luhmann and Teubner to Hegel, argues Section VI. Section VI articulates a concept of uninterrupted state sovereignty that supplements and qualifies Teubner's invocation of the king's *multiple* bodies with a Hegelian or quasi-Hegelian insistence on the *king's* multiple bodies.[3]

---

3 Gunther Teubner, "Des Königs viele Leiber. Die Selbstdekonstruktion der Hierarchie des Rechts.," *Soziale Systeme* 2, no. 2 (July 1996): 229–255.

Why this atavistic metaphysics of the singular soul and of "monarchy," Teubner, the superb deconstructivist *au-delà* deconstruction may well ask.[4] A brief reference to Schmitt, whom we shall not be following for long, is helpful as far as this question is concerned. This book surely takes leave of Schmitt's *essentialist* insistence on the *existential unity* of sovereignty. As Chapter Six will make abundantly clear, the arguments in this book side unwaveringly with Kelsen's rejection of this unity as metaphysical and simply out-dated in modern societies. And yet, there is one point on which Schmitt cannot be faulted. The exceptional case (and a case would not be a case if it were not exceptional) requires and demands a decision and the one who decides may and must for all practical and logical purposes be called "sovereign." The extent to which some decisions are and must be accepted as indeed decisive or "final," albeit not always for long, renders those decisions sovereign. And the one who is called upon to decide *becomes* the sovereign, the *only* sovereign for the moment.

At issue here is no longer an essentialist but a quasi-functional conception of centralised sovereignty that is not completely at odds with Luhmannian and Teubnerian concerns with functional differentiation. Few would deny the need for high levels of functional differentiation or system formation in contemporary societies. The insistence on the *king's* multiple bodies does not envisage an essentialist or substantive displacement of functional differentiations with monolithic government. At issue in this insistence is, however, a core of legal normativity from which no social system or sub system produced by functional differentiation can claim exemption. Systems of functional differentiation themselves ultimately have to rely on this core legal normativity in non-systemic conflicts with other systems of functional differentiation. To put the matter somewhat bluntly in terms of examples used in earlier chapters: No one can claim that some or other instance of common crime or delict concerns an exigency of functional differentiation with which the demands of state sovereignty should not interfere. One is not at liberty to commit assault within the parameters of functionally differentiated forms of private governance. The same point applies to fundamental or constitutional rights. No one can claim that violations or abridgment of constitutional rights concern exigencies of functional differentiation with which the state has no business. Nothing that happens within the enclaves of systemic differentiation can claim exemption from either common criminal and tort law, on the one hand, or basic precepts of constitutional law, on the other.

4 Ibid, 241–51.

Liberal democracy itself requires that the sovereign commands embodied in common or constitutional law remain largely functional and procedural. That this is so will become especially clear in Chapter Six. But the functional and procedural limitations to which liberal democratic sovereignty inevitably remains subject embody a core of substantive normativity. All conceptions of pure function and pure procedure ultimately remain parasitic on minimal conceptions of substantive normativity.[5] All procedures and all functionalities serve some substantive purpose, however unarticulated or thinly articulated. Liberal democracy, however procedural in practice, likewise presupposes some core normativity and it is this core normativity from which liberal democratic sovereignty exempts no one. That is why liberal democratic sovereignty must be understood as uninterrupted sovereignty. It reigns throughout the territory over which it is sovereign. There are no empty spaces devoid of sovereignty, empty spaces where the liberal democratic sovereign's law does not apply. The assignment or assumption of sovereignty entails, to refer to Walker again, an assignment of "continuing ... and ultimate authority for the juridical order of that polity."[6] Luhmann, we shall see in Section VI, was not always blind to this insight (perhaps he never was). It is indeed through Luhmann that Section VI will find its way back to Hegel, the old philosopher of state sovereignty.

The extensive exploration of Christensen and Fischer-Lescano's impressive redirection of the horizontal effect question in this chapter ultimately takes leave of the irenic concept of linguistic totality on which their redirection of horizontal effect pivots. The aim is to replace the conception of linguistic totality with which they dissolve sovereignty with a coercive concept of linguistic totality that restores sovereignty. At stake is the restoration of the role of sovereigns as ultimate guarantors of linguistic totalities. And this restoration implies a dismissal of Christensen and Fischer-Lescano's understanding of the relation between sovereignty and the linguistic whole. It will become clear in the end that the notion of a linguistic whole within which the interests of individuals can be aligned, be it more or less felicitously or be it more or less coercively by the direct intervention of the sovereign's judiciary, remains part and parcel of an assumption or presupposition of sovereignty. The linguistic whole is itself a command of the sovereign. The sovereign lays down the standardised language within which citizens come to understand or "understand" one another, as Hobbes may al-

5 Frank Michelman, "Constitutionalism as Proceduralism: A Glance at the Terrain," in *Public Law and Politics: The Scope and Limits of Constitutionalism*, ed. Emilios Christodoulidis and Stephen Tierney, The Edinburgh Centre for Law and Society (Aldershot: Ashgate, 2008), 141–161.
6 Walker, "Late Sovereignty in the European Union," 2003, 6.

ready have understood well.[7] This is true for all language at all times, but more evidently so for the official languages within which legal interests must be aligned and reconciled.

The chapter unfolds as follows: It commences in Section II with a discussion of the *division of sovereignty* that threatens horizontal effect of constitutional rights in federal or transnational political units. It then turns in Section III to the *deistic/deontological conception of sovereignty* in ordo-liberal understandings of the relation between politics and economics. Closely related to this *deontological* conception of sovereignty is the *dispersal of sovereignty* to which Section IV turns. Dispersals of sovereignty occur in systems of private governance that claim full or relative insulation from the centralised reign of national constitutions. These self-insulating claims of private governance assert local or localised constitutional controls that serve their functional specificities better than centralised constitutional demands that govern from afar. In the process they effectively contribute to dispersals of sovereignty that fragment, interrupt and disrupt the reign of sovereignty in larger political units. And it is against this background of divided, deistic and dispersed forms of sovereignty that Section V then turns to trace the remarkable way in which Christensen and Fischer-Lescano's linguistic conception of the legal whole ultimately dispenses with the key coercive characteristics of sovereignty without which sovereignty can no longer be recognised

7 Martin Loughlin, *Sword and Scales: An Examination of the Relationship Between Law and Politics* (Oxford: Hart Publishing, 2000), 132, referring to Chapter 4 of the *Leviathan* that deals with language. Cf. Hobbes, *Leviathan*, 18–29. The link between sovereignty and language in the *Leviathan* is not very clear or explicit, but Loughlin's intuition is correct. Hobbes' radical nominalist language and voluntarist understanding of sovereignty would evidently be a productive starting point for an inquiry into the connection between sovereignty and language. With nominalism comes an appreciation of the arbitrariness of words that requires stabilizing social practices if communication is to become possible. As far as sovereignty and the territorial reach of the sovereign's law are concerned, these stabilizing social practices have to attain to the highest possible levels of standardization so that in principle, everyone subject to the sovereign's law, can and must be assumed to understand the law in the same way. Empirically speaking, different persons often do understand the same law differently, which explains the reality of legal conflict and litigation. However, the idea that two people can *rightfully* understand the law differently would of course make a mockery of the sovereignty of law. Sovereignty thus consists in the sacrificial and purifying dismissal of all empirical understandings of law that sovereign law cannot accommodate. Also here on this fundamental level does one recognize the irreducible link between sovereignty and sacrifice that Jean-Luc Nancy describes so well. Cf. Jean-Luc Nancy, *Le Sens du Monde* (Galilée, 1993), 141. Be it as it may, an inquiry into the link between sovereignty and language and the standardisation of language that law demands may well benefit significantly from histories of sovereign involvement in the standardisation of modern languages.

or asserted as sovereignty. Section VI responds to the progressive destruction of sovereignty discussed in Sections II to V with a reconstruction of sovereignty as *uninterrupted* sovereignty.

II Divided Sovereignty

The ECJ famously asserted in *Van Gend en Loos* and *Costa v ENEL* that the law of the member states of the European Union is subject to European law and subject to the interpretation of European law in its own judgements.[8] The GFCC, on the other hand, continues to insist that European law is based on a treaty to which the German state can only remain party as long as (*solange*, the word with which the early decisions in this regard stressed the matter[9]) the treaty provisions and all law that emerges from it can be reconciled with the GG. We return to the GFCC's response to European integration below. Suffice it to note, for now, that a serious problem is evident here as far as jurisdictional sovereignty in Europe is concerned. In terms of the concept of sovereignty bequeathed to modern legal and political theory by Jean Bodin and Thomas Hobbes, sovereignty cannot be divided in this fashion. Bodin and Hobbes tell us that more than one sovereign cannot rule the same territory.[10]

One may observe, however, that the ECJ practices what it preaches whereas the GFCC does not, and that there is therefore no real problem at hand as far as the question of divided sovereignty in Europe is concerned, at least as far as the case of Germany is at issue. Member State sovereignty, a somewhat cynical argument may want to conclude, would appear to have become fake sovereignty, it is nothing more than an ideological construct aimed at pacifying disenfranchised member state citizens.[11] Such cynicism is nevertheless not essential for recognizing that sovereignty has indeed drifted into troubled waters in Europe. Signifi-

---

8 EU: Case 26/26 [1963] (Hereafter *Van Gend en Loos*); EU: Case 6/64 [1964] (Hereafter *Costa v E.N.E.L.*)

9 BVerfG 37, 271 (*Solange I*); BVerfG 73, 339 (*Solange II*).

10 Jean Bodin, *Les Six Livres de la Republique*, vol I (Paris : Librairie Arthème Fayard, 1986), 10 (306): "Et par ainsi nous conclurons que la premiere marque du prince souverain, c'est la puissance de donner loy à tous en general , et à chacun en particulier." Cf. Hobbes *Leviathan*, 167–168 for his famous observation "a kingdom divided in itself cannot stand..." Cf. also Dieter Grimm, *Souveränität: Herkunft und Zukunft eines Schlüsselbegriffs* (Berlin: Berlin University Press, 2009), 24–25.

11 Hans Magnus Enzensberger, "Die politische Enteignung der Europäer," *Der Hauptstadt Brief*, June 9, 2012, http://www.derhauptstadtbrief.de/cms/index.php/84-der-hauptstadtbrief-110/147-die-politische-enteignung-der-europaeer#nav.

cant "divisions of sovereignty" have evidently come to replace erstwhile unitary Member State sovereignties. At issue in this development is not only the forfeiture or transfer of some sovereign powers from one political entity to another that one regularly associates with formations of federal states. The contradicting opinions of the ECJ and the GFCC regarding sovereignty would suggest there is more at stake here. At issue would appear to be an interim phase of federalisation that has become stuck in a lack of sufficient commitment to take things further, on the one hand, and an inability to return to earlier stages of lesser integration and clearer demarcations of competences, on the other. And this impasse, it would seem, has given rise to another division of sovereignty, namely, a division of sovereignty into *de jure* and *de facto* sovereignty.

Dieter Grimm shows well what is at issue here in a recent essay. The institutions of the European Union appear to exercise *de facto* sovereignty without *de jure* sovereignty, the member states appear to exercise *de jure* sovereignty without *de facto* sovereignty. And the question is whether anything worthy of the name sovereignty remains possible in the gap that opens up with this split. There would appear to be several *de jure* sovereigns in the territorial zone that has become known as the European Union, but only one *de facto* sovereign. The Member States are the *de jure* sovereigns and the combined network of European Union institutions constitutes the *de facto* sovereign. Sovereignty however, is fundamentally dependent on its *de facto* existence, that is, on its factual ability to embody and sustain its *de jure* capacities. One learns from both Carl Schmitt and Hans Kelsen that *de facto* sovereignty conditions *de jure* sovereignty. The former founds and maintains the latter. Sovereignty can thus be seen to straddle a *de facto*/*de jure* divide. Some *de facto* assertion, assumption or assignment of sovereignty is indispensable if *de jure* sovereignty is to remain viable. This, we shall see, is also one of the crucial insights to which Grimm's essay on sovereignty in Europe leads one.

Many theorists have come to refer to a "division of sovereignty" in Europe between the governmental institutions of the European Union and those of the member states.[12] Sovereignty can nevertheless not be divided in this way, insists

---

12 Jacques Ziller, "Sovereignty in France: Getting Rid of the Mal de Bodin," in *Sovereignty in Transition. Essays in European Law*, ed. Neil Walker, (Oxford: Hart Publishing, 2003), 261, 276–7; Jacques Ziller (ed.), *L'Européanisation des Droits Constitutionnels à la Lumière de la Constitution pour l'Europe*, Paris, L'Harmattan, 2003, especially the essay of Karine Caunes "La Nature du système juridique européen; retour sur le principe de primauté" 281–298; Monica Claes, "The Europeanization of national constitutions in the constitutionalization of Europe: Some observations against the background of the constitutional expérience of the EU-15," *Croation Yearbook of European Law and Policy*, (2007): 1–38; Cf. also Walker, "Late Sovereignty in the

Grimm along with Bodin and Hobbes. A sovereign can transfer some aspects of its capacity to another agency. Such an agency then exercises these competences on behalf of the sovereign that has transferred them. However, the transferred competences only remain transferred subject to the *de jure* sovereign's continued will to have them exercised by such other agency. The transfer of such competences (*Hohheitsrechte*) does not constitute a transfer of sovereignty as such. Sovereignty remains with the authority that retains the capacity or the first order competence to transfer or not to transfer competences and to revoke any such transfers. Sovereignty, at least *de jure* sovereignty, thus remains with the authority that retains competence regarding competence or *Kompetenz-kompetenz* as Jellinek put the matter.[13] This competence regarding competence, insists Grimm, has never been transferred from the European Member States to the European Union. In this *de jure* respect, he avers, the member states retain undivided sovereignty. They retain the right to revoke the competences transferred but also the right to scrutinise whether the exercise of the competences transferred remains subject to and reconcilable with the terms of transfer. In this respect the GFCC can indeed insist that it retains the jurisdictional power to ensure that the interpretation and application of European law remain reconcilable, not only with the terms on which competences were transferred, but also with terms of transfer that are themselves reconcilable with the constitutional demands embodied in the GG.

The mere retention of *de jure* sovereignty may nevertheless not suffice for purposes of sustaining itself. Grimm argues that a sovereign may come to find itself in a position where it has transferred essential competences that are indispensable for the effective survival of sovereignty. One can expand this argument to also cover the possibility that a sovereign may come to find itself in a position where it still has complete *de jure* capacity to revoke the transfer of all the essential competences that it needs to restore sovereignty effectively, but finds itself for all practical purposes incapable of revoking such transfers. The position of

---

European Union," 2003, 15 n.33, as well as Paul Craig and Gráinne de Burca, *EU Law: Texts, Cases and Materials* (Oxford: Oxford University Press, 2011, 5th ed.), 267 note 36 for further references to literature on shared or divided sovereignty. For two probing recent contributions to this debate, cf. Mattias Kumm, "The Moral Point of Constitutional Pluralism: Defining the Domain of Legitimate Institutional Civil Disobedience and Conscientious Objection" in *Philosophical Foundations of European Union Law*, ed. Julie Dickson & Pavlos Eleftheriadis (Oxford: Oxford University Press, 2012) 216–246; Jörg Gerkrath "The Figure of Constitutional Law of the 'Integrated State': the Case of the Grand Duchy of Luxembourg" *European Constitutional Law Review* 10, no. 1 (April 2014): 109–125.

13 Dieter Grimm, "Wer ist Souverän in der europäischen Union," in *Die Zukunft der Verfassung II* (Frankfurt: Suhrkamp, 2012), 282.

the European member states vis-à-vis the Union may well have reached this point. The member states, or some of them, may well have reached the point where an exit from the Union is *de jure* still in order, but *de facto* inconceivable, especially when the disadvantages of such an exit are properly considered. Many observers probably already regard the Saving Packages and ESM judgements of the GFCC as reflections of *de facto* forfeitures of sovereignty that have reached a point of no return.[14]

What is the problem that such paralysis of sovereignty poses for the question of constitutional review and the horizontal effect of constitutional rights? One might begin to answer this question by noting that the USSC's articulation of the state action doctrine in *The Civil Rights Cases* was significantly informed by the need to stabilise divisions of competences between the individual states and the federal government. The state action doctrine was presented as a rule that prevented federal government from interfering with the sovereign relations between the states and their citizens. This is nevertheless not the problem that prevails in Europe today. It is commonly accepted that European law governs citizens and residents of member states directly.[15] The problem in Europe as far as the question of sovereignty is concerned is this: What is to be done when the European Union ends up governing member states citizens in ways that member state constitutions cannot tolerate? How can minimum requirements of constitutional sovereignty be sustained under such circumstances? How long will it remain possible to talk meaningfully in Europe about the "continuing source and vehicle of ultimate authority for the juridical order" that Walker considers essential for the meaningful survival of legal systems?

The question regarding ultimate authority to create law remained a controversial question in the United States of America for a long time. But in the end, a unitary system of law emerged that combined state law and federal law satisfactorily enough to warrant the assumption of a single system of law in the United States.[16] Americans have by and large come to accept a system of judicial fora that ultimately gives the last say in all matters of law to the Federal Supreme Court. It is this acceptance that warrants the assumption of a single system of law in the United States and it is exactly this acceptance that is still far from evi-

---

14 Cf. in this regard Dieter Grimm, "Prinzipien statt Pragmatismus," *Frankfurter Allgemeine Zeitung: Die Debatte um Europas Zukunft*, June 2, 2013, http://www.faz.net/aktuell/feuilleton/debatten/europas-zukunft/europas-zukunft-prinzipien-statt-pragmatismus-12052280.html.

15 Cf. again *Van Gend en Loos* and *Costa v E.N.E.L.*, fn. 8 above.

16 Jeff Goldsworthy, "The Debate about Sovereignty in the United States: A Historical and Comparative Perspective," in *Sovereignty in Transition*, ed. Neil Walker (Oxford: Hart Publishing, 2003), 423–446, especially at 444.

dent in Europe today. As long as this acceptance remains lacking, precarious or unsettled, the question of sovereignty in Europe will remain controversial.

The concept of sovereignty is nevertheless not that secure in the United States either. The United States may well have been able to lay claim to ubiquitous and uninterrupted sovereignty of law throughout its territory or territories as a result of its unitary system of law, had the USSC's application of the state action doctrine not continued to threaten that sovereignty. The interpretation and application of the state action doctrine in cases like *Flagg Brothers* and *DeShaney* have basically stripped the claim to full territorial sovereignty in the United States of an essential element. Through these cases, we saw in Chapter Two, the American sovereign betrayed the heart of sovereignty by refusing to assume full responsibility for safeguarding fundamental rights throughout its territory (which, again, does of course not translate into unlimited and unconditional public liability). Undivided and uninterrupted sovereignty will only return to the United States when the Supreme Court's jurisprudence returns unequivocally to the jurisprudence in *Labour v Swing, Shelley v Kraemer* and *New York Times v Sullivan.* Only then will the unitary legal system of the United States be able to claim universal and uninterrupted applicability within the United States.

Uninterrupted sovereignty or sovereignties will only return to Europe the day the process of European integration begins to warrant self-evident reliance on a single system of law, or falters to the extent that Member States begin to reclaim ultimate law-making authority. The sovereignty of a single *legal* system would surely be sufficient for establishing the uninterrupted sovereignty on which consistent constitutional review depends. Such sovereignty, however, is not yet evident in Europe. In the meantime, fundamental conceptions and guiding principles of European law, on the one hand, and Member State law, on the other, may well continue to differ significantly. And it may well do so for a considerable time still without providing a settled answer to the question "who has the last say?" Whether Europe will integrate further to higher levels of federalism or ultimately settle for lower and looser levels of inter-governmentalist or confederal integration will surely continue to turn on exactly this question.

Suffice it to state for now that clashing interpretations of the fundamental principles of European law and Member State law may well be on the cards for a considerable time still. According to some observers, the ECJ is driving the process of legal integration with a highly neo-liberal or ordo-liberal jurisprudence at the expense of established social protections in the Member States. This perception came to a head, as we shall see in Chapter Seven, with the ECJ's decisions in the *Laval* and *Viking* cases. Whether this jurisprudence is reconcilable with social state principles of Member States such as Germany is a question that may well invite increasing judicial attention in Member States in the years ahead. The GFCC has thus far preferred not to address this question squarely, as we shall also see in Chapter Seven. Its failure or refusal to do so has been attributed to an ordo-liberal mentality that regards market-integration as an apolitical project that is conceptually incapable of violating fundamental rights and spheres of sovereignty.

Chapter Seven returns to these developments and perceptions. Suffice it to note here that ordo-liberalism, however much originally a product of German soil, appears to have become the driving ideology of European integration. Perceptions that the European treaties and the jurisprudence of the ECJ are informed by ordo-liberal principles are widespread. The next section will address this perception and assess its implications for sovereignty in Europe. The question whether it is the GFCC's own ordo-liberalism or its powerlessness in the face of rampant ordo-liberalism in Europe that explains its acquiescence better, is one that will have to be left unanswered.

III Between Deism and Deontology – Europe and Ordo-Liberalism

Ordo-liberal economic doctrine has its origins in Weimar Germany.[17] Its leading thinkers were Franz Bohm, Walter Eucken, Hans Großmann-Doerth, Alexander Rüstow, Wilhelm Röpke, Constantin von Dietze and Alfred Müller-Armack. Bohm, Eucken and Großmann-Doerth were the editors of the paper series *Ordnung und Wirtschaft* that ordo-liberals still regard as the intellectual cornerstone of their economic thinking. They were also known as the Freiburg School.[18] Friedrich Hayek would later also be associated with them, notwithstanding significant differences between Hayek's thinking and that of the core group of ordo-

17 The brief description of the concept and history of ordo-liberalism in Germany and Europe that follows does not reinvent the wheel. It relies largely on the work that Christian Joerges has done in this regard. Cf. especially Christian Joerges, "Europa nach dem Ordoliberalismus: Eine Philippika," *Postneoliberale Rechtsordnung? Suchprozesse in der Krise* 43, no. 4 (2010): 394–406. A number of the sources that Joerges cites were nevertheless also essential for the understanding of ordo-liberalism that is expounded here. Among them, especially Philip Manow, "Ordoliberalismus als ökonomische Ordnungstheologie," *Leviathan* 29, no. 2 (2001): 179–198 provides an incisive understanding of the historical position the ordo-liberals took in Weimar Germany.
18 Viktor J. Vanberg, "The Freiburg School: Walter Eucken and Ordoliberalism" (Freiburger Diskussionspapiere zur Ordnungsökonomik, n.d.), http://www.eucken.de/fileadmin/bilder/Dokumente/Diskussionspapiere/04_11bw.pdf.

liberals.[19] The school sought a way out of the economic disequilibrium and general economic instability of the time by promoting the idea of an independent market that would be sustained by a strong state, on the one hand, but remain free from political interference, on the other.

The concept of ordo-liberalism undeniably entails a form of market liberalism, considering the way its proponents distinguished it from socialist economic thinking, on the one hand, and the historical school of national economic thinking, on the other.[20] It should nevertheless also be distinguished from laissez-faire liberalism. In contrast to laissez faire liberalism, ordo-liberalism acknowledged the extent to which markets remain dependent on active state support and maintenance. The idea of a night-watchman state that has little or no work to do in the sphere of economics was evidently foreign to it. Walter Röpke invoked the oxymoronic term "liberal interventionism" to stress the need for strong states and forceful state intervention in the maintenance of *free* markets. Hermann Heller perceived this oxymoron clearly and referred deridingly to the "authoritarian liberalism" of the ordo-liberal theorists.[21] Although the ordo-liberals never became National Socialists of note, they did entertain a firm dose of Schmittianism during the National Socialist years in Germany.[22]

The basic ordo-liberalist credo that emerged from these stormy years pivoted on a clear distinction between economic and political activity and stressed the need to keep the latter out of the former. Again, ordo-liberals recognised the need for active state involvement in the construction maintenance of markets, but dismissed any additional need for political interference with market dynamics. The idea that markets should be subject to democratic accountability, supervision and control was anathema to them.[23] In view of its insistence on the with-

---

19 Cf. Manuel Wörsdörfer, "Von Hayek and Ordoliberalism on Justice," *Journal of the History of Economic Thought* 35, no. 03 (2013): 291–317.

20 Political liberalism it surely was not. They were in fact in many respects closely related to the conservative revolution that was afoot in Germany at the time and shared Schmitt's cynicism regarding the parliamentary system unflinchingly. The state should be based on authority not majority – "Der Staat ...muß auf Autorität gegründet sein, nicht auf Majorität," Althaus asserted in 1936. Cf. Manow, "Ordoliberalismus als ökonomische Ordnungstheologie," 181–3, 192.

21 Joerges, "Europa nach dem Ordoliberalismus: Eine Philippika," 395; Manow, "Ordoliberalismus als ökonomische Ordnungstheologie," 182, both referring to Hermann Heller, "Autoritärer Liberalismus," *Die neue Rundschau* (1933): 289–298. To be sure, Heller does not refer to any of the Freiburg ordo-liberals here, but to Carl Schmitt, and specifically to Schmitt's 1932 address "Staat und Wirtschaft" in which Schmitt proposed the complete "Entstaatlichung der Wirtschaft."

22 Joerges, "Europa nach dem Ordoliberalismus: Eine Philippika," 396.

23 Ibid, 397.

drawal of politics from economics after an initial sovereign intervention to create a zone of free competition, ordo-liberalism would appear to promote a deistic conception of sovereignty. Deism was the version of theism to which 18th century scientists subscribed. Stuck between the Biblical narrative of God as the sovereign creator of the universe, on the one hand, and the scientific endorsement of eternal laws of physics with which no "Creator" can interfere, on the other, these scientists resorted to the idea that God created the world but then withdrew from it so that its eternal laws can run their course. The sovereign, believed the ordo-liberals, must likewise create and sustain the market, but refrain from interfering with its natural laws of competition. As Eucken put the matter, the task of the state was simply to give effect to and sustain the "free and natural order willed by God" – "die freie, natürliche, gottgewollte Ordnung zu verwirklichen."[24]

Deism, however, does not quite capture the ordo-liberal understanding of sovereignty. The state *interventionism* required to *sustain* God's order would suggest that they contemplated a more interactive God, or at least a more interactive state that would act constantly to maintain an order that could easily fall apart otherwise, as Weimar Germany would seem to have underlined for them. The ordo-liberals indeed distinguished themselves from laissez-faire liberals and referred to the latter as deists with no regard for the way God's natural order of freedom had to be sustained by authoritarian state intervention.[25] Michel Foucault also emphasised the active governmentalism that informed ordo-liberalism.[26] It therefore seems more accurate to describe ordo-liberalism in

---

24 Walter Eucken, *Grundsätze der Wirtschaftspolitik* (Tübingen: Mohr Siebeck, 1952), as cited by Manow, "Ordoliberalismus als ökonomische Ordnungstheologie," 188.

25 Cf. Manow, "Ordoliberalismus als ökonomische Ordnungstheologie," 187: "Rüstow gilt das laissez-faire Prinzip des klassischen Liberalismus als stoische, deistische 'Harmonietheologie.'"

26 Foucault considered the interventionism of the ordo-liberals to have left little scope for any "free economic" activity in which the state was not involved. According to Foucault, the ordo-liberals did not consider natural economic freedom and competition as a state that could actually be reached, but a goal towards which active government should constantly strive. As such, ordo-liberalism did not at all contemplate the withdrawal of government from the economy, but the constant accompaniment of the economy by government – "Le gouvernement doit accompagner de bout en bout une économie de marché. L'économie de marché ne soustrait pas quelque chose au gouvernement." Similarly to Manow, Foucault argued that the ordo-liberals regarded all notions of a natural sphere of liberty as a naïve naturalism that could not be squared with the significant influence of Husserl's phenomenology on their thinking (Husserlian phenomenology insisted that "natural" essences are never given but always constructed by consciousness). Cf. Michel Foucault, *Naissance de La Biopolitique* (Paris: Gallimard/Seuil, 2004), 105–125, especially 123–125. Cf. also Joerges, "Europa nach dem Ordoliberalismus: Eine Philippika," 397.

terms of a *deontological* sovereignty. Ordo liberalism actively stressed the virtue of free competition and relied on the state to promote this virtue purposefully.[27]

The cultural and moral conservatism of the movement should not be underestimated and Alain Supiot's assessment of it as an ultra-liberalism is questionable. His perception of a deep wish in the ordo-liberal movement to put the affairs of mankind on autopilot is more interesting. He would seem to give a more deistic assessment of the movement that is not in keeping with the way the ordo-liberals understood themselves. This is understandable from the robust social democratic perspective from which Supiot views their beliefs. From such a perspective, the idea that the problems of humanity could be overcome by resolving competition deficits must come across as an unfulfilled deistic dream.[28]

Ordo-liberal thinking survived National-Socialist Germany and continued to enjoy prominence in German economic thinking in the post-war years. Predominantly of Protestant origins, it also joined forces with Catholic socialism in the post-war years. After the war, both Christian churches in Germany were sensitised to the social problems that caused such turmoil in the early phases of capitalism and looked for a third way that would avoid the extremes of laissez-faire capitalism, on the one hand, and centrally planned state socialism, on the other. This alliance between the two churches worked through German society and reached well into the economic order of post-war Germany. The result was a highly successful social market economy (*soziale Marktwirtschaft*) that enjoyed the status of an inclusive and comprehensive social project (*gesamtgesellschaftliches Projekt*) to which even some ordo-liberals warmed up, notwithstanding the social state characteristics of this social market economy. Müller-Armack articulated a concept of *social* market economy in this post-war period and Walter Eucken similarly moved away from classical ordo liberal ideas by developing a framework of thinking in which the strict separation between politics and economics gave way to greater interdependence between them.[29]

---

27 Cf. Manow, "Ordoliberalismus als ökonomische Ordnungstheologie," 190–194; Oles Andriychuk, "Rediscovering the Spirit of Competition – On the Normative Value of the Competitive Porcess," *European Competition Journal,* 6, no. 3, 2010: 575–610; Oles Andriychuk "Thinking Inside the Box: Why Competition as a Process is a Sui Generis Right – A Methodological Observation" 95–118, especially at 110 in Daniel Zimmer ed., *The Goals of Competition* (Cheltenam: Edward Elgar Publishing, 2012).

28 Cf. Supiot, "Le Sommeil Dogmatique Européen," *Revue Française des Affaires Sociales,* 1 (2012) (1) 185–198, at 195: Poursuivant le rêve d'une mise en pilotage automatique des affaires humaines, l'idéologie de la 'gouvernance' s'applique ainsi aux États, après avoir été appliquée aux salariés et aux entreprises."

29 Joerges, "Europa nach dem Ordoliberalismus: Eine Philippika," 397.

This broad social alliance nevertheless did not last long. Old alliances between Catholicism, economic corporatism and Bismarckian conceptions of social welfare returned to prominence. The ordo-liberals, now much more influential than before the war, observed this restoration of the old welfare state with dismay and promoted, instead, the idea of an economic constitution (*Wirtschaftsverfassung*), the gist of which was a demand that politics withdraw from economics so as to allow for a system of undistorted economic competition. The ordo-liberal programme enjoyed broad support in German private law thinking, but received little recognition or support among public lawyers. Public lawyers largely ignored the idea and consequently also made little or no effort to address or articulate the democracy deficit evident in the idea of the economic constitution.[30]

Ordo-liberalism's career would, however, not remain restricted to its predominance in post-war private law thinking in Germany. The emergence of the European Economic Community gave the idea of an economic constitution a second life.[31] To be sure, the development of the European economic order cannot be construed in terms of a conscious promotion or pursuit of ordo-liberal principles, but the key conception of European integration that emerged at the time fitted ordo-liberal thinking like a glove. At issue were especially the following two mainstays of European integration: 1) Europe had to be and could only be integrated through the pursuit of an economic community and European Monetary Union. 2) Economic and monetary union would give rise to a legal order on the basis of which supra-national institutions would ensure economic liberties and free competition.

The integration process commenced slowly, but when it finally gained momentum in the nineteen eighties with Jacques Delors' "White Book" programme for the completion of the internal market, significant endorsement from within ordo-liberal circles ensued. The endorsement came from a second generation of post-war ordo-liberalism in which Friedrich von Hayek played a leading role. Whatever shifts may have marked the thinking of this second generation, the core idea remained the same: The political and economic spheres were to remain separate and the integration of the European market was to remain a strictly economic development. The element of the internal market initiative that res-

30 Ibid, referring to Knut Wolfgang Nörr's puzzlement regarding these two scenes of German law that hardly paid attention to one another. Cf. Knut W. Nörr, *Die Republik der Wirtschaft. Teil I: Von der Besatzungszeit zur grossen Koalition* (Tübingen: Mohr Siebeck, 1999), 84, http://www.mohr.de/nc/rechtswissenschaft/schriftenreihen/detail/buch/die-republik-der-wirtschaft-1.html.

31 Joerges, "Europa nach dem Ordoliberalismus: Eine Philippika," 399.

onated most evidently with this second wave of ordo-liberal thinking was the reciprocal recognition of goods and services and the extension of competition law so as to introduce, alongside measures to prevent private distortions of economic competition (monopoly formations, etc.), proscriptions of Member State regulations that would distort free competition. The ordo-liberal construction of the internal market became the more complete the more the adjudication of the ECJ took over the role of reviewing national legislation to ensure compliance with the principles of the internal market programme, as it began to do at the time.[32]

The phase of deregulation that marked European integration during the consolidation years of the internal market nevertheless turned out to be short-lived. The Maastricht Treaty marked a conspicuous turn towards environmental, labour and consumer regulation that immediately drew criticism from ordo-liberal circles.[33] The adjudication of the ECJ, some would argue, has not really caught up with this new dimension of European integration. A recent series of ECJ preliminary rulings would still seem to reflect a typical ordo-liberal approach to the relation between market freedom and social regulation. At issue are the *Laval*,[34] *Viking*,[35] *Luxembourg*[36] and *Rüffert*[37] preliminary rulings of the ECJ in recent years. In all these cases the ECJ gave precedence to the fundamental economic freedoms entrenched in the TEC (now TFEU) at the expense of the political freedom and competence of European Member States to organise and regulate social security systems and collective trade agreements as they deem fit. Chapter Seven will take a closer look at these cases. Suffice it to observe for now that many observers discern in them the consolidation of an ordo-liberal conception of the relation between economics and politics. This would indeed appear to be the case and Chapter Seven will largely confirm the accuracy of this observation.

---

32 The three processes – mutual recognition of goods and services, prevention of distortions of competition by member states and the ECJ's turn to the review of national legislation – went hand in hand and the 1979 case of *Cassis de Dijon*, EU: C 120/78, is generally regarded as the essential nexus between them.

33 Joerges, "Europa nach dem Ordoliberalismus: Eine Philippika," 402.

34 EU: Case C-341/05, hereafter cited as *Laval*.

35 EU: Case C-438/05, hereafter cited as *Viking*.

36 EU: Case C-346/06, hereafter cited as *Rüffert*.

37 EU: Case C-319/06, hereafter cited as *Luxembourg*. The *Luxembourg* decision is the only one of the four decisions of the ECJ that has become known as the "*Laval* quartet" that will not be discussed in Chapter Seven. The relevant issues in *Luxembourg* are largely covered in the discussion of *Rüffert*.

IV Dispersed Sovereignty – Government and Governance

The twofold narrative that unfolds in recent literature on the self-regulation of systems of "governance" through various modes of private law, on the one hand, and the outsourcing of public powers to private or semi-private agencies, on the other, concern key features of the erosion of national state sovereignties concomitant to globalisation. The decisions of the Israeli and Indian Supreme Courts that respectively struck down privatisations of prisons and police units have become beacons of resistance among constitutional judiciaries to this trend of governance through private law and privatisation.[38] Any attempt to do justice to the wealth of scholarship that already exists in this field of inquiry will take us too far afield for present purposes.[39] The aim in what follows is only to consider the implications of this scholarship for the questions of sovereignty and the horizontal effect revolution.

The discussion that follows is conveniently shaped around two recent volumes of essays, both of which engage with the way the discourse of governance has come to mark the relationship between European private law, on the one hand, and European public and constitutional law, on the other. These volumes, one edited by Fabrizio Cafaggi and one by Cafaggi and Horatio Muir-Watt, [40] pivot on the observation that state-regulation of public relations and public services in Europe is increasingly displaced by non-state institutions of governance. At issue here are not only institutions such as sports and professional associations that "regulate" their commerce firstly by means of internal regulatory procedures and rules and ultimately by private law institutions like contract and de-

---

38 Cf. Judith Resnik, "Globalization(s), Privatization(s), Constitutionalization, and Statization: Icons and Experiences of Sovereignty in the 21st Century," *International Journal of Constitutional Law* 11, no. 1 (January 1, 2013): 162–199, doi:10.1093/icon/mos051. The Israeli decision at issue is *Academic Center of Law and Business v Minister of Finance* (Isr. Aug. 20, 2006). The Indian decision is *Sundar and Others v Chattisgarh* (2011) 7 S.C.C. 547.

39 Resnik, "Globalization(s), Privatization(s), Constitutionalization, and Statization: Icons and Experiences of Sovereignty in the 21st Century" provides an ample record of the wealth of literature that engages with this phenomenon of privatisation, globalisation, and private or semi-private governance.

40 Cf. Fabrizio Cafaggi and Horatia Muir Watt, eds., *Making European Private Law – Governance Design* (Cheltenam/Northampton: Edward Elgar Publishing, 2008); Fabrizio Cafaggi, ed., *The Institutional Framework of European Private Law* (Oxford/New York: Oxford University Press, 2006). For another volume of essays that takes one far into this field of inquiry, especially with regard to the United States context, cf. Jody Freeman and Martha Minow, eds., *Goverment by Contract: Outsourcing and American Democracy* (Cambridge, Mass.: Harvard University Press, 2009).

lict (tort). The same turn towards private law based regulation is also evident in the "commercial" regulation of service provision by companies that emerge from the privatisation of former state run enterprises. A case in point is the network of business relations that resulted from the privatisation and dissolution of British Rail in the 1990s. Out of the single state run enterprise emerged about over 100 separate units, not counting the many more parties involved in the outsourcing of maintenance services.

The aim of this dissolution, in the words of Mark Freedland, was "to replace internal command relationships within the old British Rail by contractual relationships between free-standing autonomous bodies."[41] The spirit of developments such as these is nevertheless not that interested parties involved are intent on or prone to litigate when someone does not stick to the rules, but rather that everyone will naturally comply with the rules in their own interest and would be willing to subject rare cases of intractable disputes to arbitration or disciplinary procedures that are already embodied in the terms of affiliation that condition membership in these associations.[42] As Sir Christopher Foster, the Government's special advisor during the privatisation of British Rail put the matter at the time:

> "Such contracts do not imply resort to litigation... Much reliance must be placed on a common realisation that all parties will gain more from their joint success than from failure, if backed by the appropriate incentivisation the new arrangements will provide..."[43]

One already discerns resonances between the optimism that Sir Foster expresses here, and Christensen and Fischer-Lescano's optimistic faith in linguistic resolutions of conflicts that require no significant sovereign intervention to which we turn below (Section V). Suffice it to note now that the optimism at issue turn in both cases on convictions that sovereign intervention will largely become redundant as a result of constructive private cooperation.

The privatisation drive is informed by the idea that all interested parties will cooperate voluntarily to resolve constitutional and institutional conflicts. And if they ultimately fail to live up to these expectations and refuse to cooperate vol-

---

41 Mark Freedland, "Private Law, Regulation and Governance Design and the Personal Work Contract," in *Making European Private Law: Governmance Design*, ed. Fabrizio Cafaggi and Horatia Muir Watt (Cheltenam/Northampton: Edward Elgar Publishing, 2008), 243.

42 Cf. Colin Scott, "Regulating Private Legislation," in *Making European Private Law: Governance Design*, ed. Fabrizio Cafaggi and Horatia Muir Watt (Cheltenam/Northampton: Edward Elgar Publishing, 2008), 254–268.

43 Christopher Foster, *The Economics of Rail Privatisation* (London: Chartered Institute of Public Finance and Accountancy, 1994), 8. Cf. also the citation of Foster by Freedland, "Private Law, Regulation and Governance Design and the Personal Work Contract," 243.

untarily, private litigation will suffice to address intractable conflicts. This enthusiasm for privatisation is pervasive in European Union institutions, as the convictions of the European Commission in this regard show clearly. The European Commission has expressly stated its confidence in private litigation as an efficient regulatory tool.[44] This is a remarkable development when one considers its implications for the already narrow margin of public interest considerations in economic regulation. The exclusive or dominant concern with economic regulation evident here already signals a substantial and substantive reduction of public interest concerns to the narrow individualistic focus on healthy competition. However, within this narrow focus, traditional competition law still plays a significantly "public" role by subjecting individual concerns with the minimisation of transaction costs to the "public" or "public economic" concerns of general third parties. This public element is no longer evident when private law becomes the principal mode of regulation. Katalin Cseres puts the matter poignantly:

> "The focus of private law is usually the individual private actor and the efficiency of his transactions. Competition law is aimed at the efficiency of the whole economy and at the welfare of society...While private law mainly serves private individual interests, competition law is applied in the interests of the public and is embedded in a public law framework. Private law is first and foremost aimed at the minimization of transaction costs while competition law aims at the general goal of economic efficiency."[45]

As Cseres also observes well, the two sets of "goals and interests" at stake here "might coincide, but they might conflict as well." The confidence that the European Commission expressed in private law litigation as an efficient market regulator communicates the conviction that they mostly coincide and rarely conflict. This is the result of the dominance of the ordo-liberal concept of competition evident in the thinking of the Commission, claims Cseres. The ordo-liberal concept of competition "value[s] individual freedom as an end in itself" and therefore sees less of a gap between sheer individualistic and general competition

---

44 Cf. http://ec.europa.eu/comm/competition/antitrust/others/actions_for_damages/index_en.html (last accessed November 2013): "Facilitating damages claims for breaches of the antitrust rules will not only strengthen the enforcement of competition law, but will also make it easier for consumers, and firms who have suffered damage from an infringement of competition law rules to recover their losses from the infringer." For this reference and further discussion of this point, cf. Katalin Cseres, "Governance Design for the European Private Law: Lessons From the Europeanization of Competition Law in Central and Eastern Europe," in *Making European Private Law: Govermmance Design*, ed. Fabrizio Cafaggi and Horatia Muir Watt (Cheltenam/Northampton: Edward Elgar Publishing, 2008), 143.

45 Ibid, 141.

concerns.[46] Many studies have pointed out that the ordo-liberalism of the Freiburg School of Economics found its way almost directly into Article 81 of the TEC, now Article 101 of the TFEU.[47] Not even ordo-liberals would go so far as to deny the possibility of unhealthy private restrictions of individual liberty and unhealthy private constraints on competition, as is still evident in Articles 81 and 82 of the TEC, but the ordo-liberal understanding of competition "brings [the two] domains [of private interests and public competition concerns] very close," argues Cseres.

Ordo-liberalism, we saw above, has its origins in the neo-liberal Freiburg School of thought that emerged in the 1930s and played a significant role after World War II in German and European economic policy and competition law.[48] This development, still abundantly evident in current thinking of the European Commission, also marks a shift from typically Continental European to more "Anglo Saxon" approaches to regulation. As Tony Prosser contends, the latter approach views regulation as principally concerned with "efficiency maximisation and ... protecting private autonomy." The point of regulation is accordingly to "mimic markets where there is monopoly, and to facilitate market operations where competition is possible." When broader social concerns require intervention into these market principles, such intervention is expected to take place through the political process, "preferably by adjusting initial distributions through taxation and social security provision rather than intervening directly in markets." This approach thus requires "no special body of public service law."[49] The Continental approach, on the other hand, views public service as "an essential legal concept to be applied by administrative courts" and "central symbol of republican legitimacy."[50]

From the perspective of *government* and "classical" public regulation of private relations, the shift to the ordo-liberal and Anglo-Saxon approaches to regulation would seem to promote insulation of commercial concerns from external third party controls and public scrutiny. Regulatory bodies still maintain an overseeing role in the context of the privatisation or liberalisation of former public utilities and services, but their status is quite evidently no longer clearly that of public authorities. They function as "independent regulatory agencies" and

46 Ibid.
47 Ibid, 142–3.
48 Ibid, 141 n.6.
49 Tony Prosser, "Regulatory Agencies, Regulatory Legitimacy, and European Private Law," in *Making European Private Law: Governmance Design*, ed. Fabrizio Cafaggi and Horatia Muir Watt (Cheltenam/Northampton: Edward Elgar Publishing, 2008), 249.
50 Ibid.

have become, as Prosser puts it, a key feature of the "European regulatory scene" on both "EU and national levels."[51] Given that these new regulatory bodies emerged more directly from the common law systems of the UK and USA where the public/private law distinction is often much less emphasized than in the legal systems of Continental Europe, their public law status is already for this reason less clear than was the case in the public regulatory schemes that would emerge in Continental Europe towards the end of the nineteenth century.[52]

Some insistence on public-private classifications is still evident in litigation, especially when the identification of appropriate remedies is at stake. This applies even in the UK.[53] And at first sight the relevant regulatory agencies often appear to be distinctly "public institutions." They are ostensibly "designed to limit the free play of markets" and "to implement public policies." But the reality is much more complex, argues Prosser with reference to recent developments in competition law. Competition law, he observes, is typically administered by independent authorities that are subject to "varying degrees of governmental oversight and intervention." Although this basic pattern or form is still nominally intact, the substance of competition law has changed markedly in the UK in the wake of the 1998 Competition Act and the 2002 Enterprise Act. Under the Fair Trading Act of 1973 and the Restrictive Trade Practices Act of 1976, public interest tests and cabinet ministers who could claim democratic legitimacy of sorts still played a central role in decision-making processes. Private enforcement, moreover, was simply impossible under these acts. The 1998 and 2002 Acts changed these substantive features of pre-1998 competition law in the UK markedly. These acts substituted the public interest based prohibitions of the former legislation with predominantly *competition-based* prohibitions imported directly from EC law and replaced the decision-making role of ministries by that of independent authorities in most cases. "Public interest" tests would henceforth be limited to national security and media mergers.[54] The new acts now also provide for private enforcement of competition law through actions for damages under the auspices of a new Competition Appeal Tribunal that has, in fact, become a "specialist competition law court."[55]

---

51 Ibid, 235.

52 Ibid, 236.

53 Ibid, referring to *R v Panel on Takeovers and Mergers, ex parte Datatfin plc* [1987] QB 815.

54 Ibid, 236–7.

55 Ibid, 237.

This development is particularly striking in the UK, claims Prosser,[56] but is evident elsewhere in the EU. And it is not restricted to competition law. UK regulation of utilities such as gas and electricity increasingly links the interest of consumers to little more than the facilitation of effective competition.[57] The same development is evident on the level of the EU, especially with regard to electronic communications. The EU Commission's regulatory initiatives in the communication sector were crucial for opening up new markets in countries where this sector was formerly regulated by national authorities. The Commission's drive was evidently to simply replace these authorities with regular competition law agencies. In the process, the concern with competitive markets clearly came to enjoy priority over broader public interest.[58]

The greater insulation from democratic scrutiny that characterises these independent regulatory agencies gives rise to modes of "private government" and even of "private legislation," be it through regulatory rules or by means of contractual relationships. This transformation of public into private government is the essence of the transformation of government into governance that is at issue here. The far-reaching independence of these private modes of governance raises serious legitimacy concerns when one views them from the perspective of classical modern or classical "Hegelian" conceptions of government. As Colin Scott puts the matter:

> "[T]he most threatening private legislative regimes are the 'total' ones, where characteristics of interdependence, redundancy, competition and community are all lacking and where the private rule maker has a monopoly not just over the rule making but also over interpretation and enforcement."[59]

The legitimacy concerns that Scott points out here are real and more far-reaching than would appear at first. Not only does this turn to non-state governance and private legislation regimes indeed raise serious and obvious transparency and accountability questions, it also undermines the fundamental distinction between private and public spheres with regard to which modern societies have come to understand basic precepts of sound government. In other words, at issue here is nothing less than the unravelling of key aspects of the normative architecture of modernity. Another passage in Scott's poignant discussion of the matter goes to the heart of the matter at issue here:

---

56 Ibid, 236.

57 Ibid, 238 n.12.

58 Ibid, 238, referring to Art. 8 of Directive 2002/21/EC (The Framework Directive).

59 Scott, "Regulating Private Legislation," 266.

> "The very concept of 'private legislation implies' some normative problem, the appropriation by non-state actors of an essentially public function, the challenge to Weber's idea that the state was characterised by its monopoly of the legitimate use of force against others. Within democratic states the core usage of the term legislation implies rule making through representative legislative institutions, organised variously around principles of majority decision-making or power-sharing, each with mechanisms for the protection of minorities."[60]

No one would seriously suggest that the insulation of these private governance regimes against public modes of scrutiny is completely watertight. These regimes ultimately receive authorisation from elements of statutory or common law, and therefore from some or other instance of state action. They do not escape completely from the reach of the Hohfeldian or Schwabian sensibilities that Chapters Three and Four described and one cannot go so far as to say they are completely beyond the reach of the horizontal effect of constitutional values. To put it in the hyperbolic but clear terms developed in the first chapters of this book: We can still assume with some conviction that private governance regimes cannot authorise common crimes such as murder or assault without forthwith exposing themselves to the criminal prosecution agencies of sovereign states and centralised state governments. In other words, private governance circles do not quite constitute mafia movements; or if they do, they will surely not openly claim to do so. However, two disconcerting aspects of the insularity that characterise governance regimes nevertheless raise serious questions for classical conceptions of public government. The first relates to the systemic pressure towards conformity and acquiescence that any single layer of governmental insulation can be expected to exert. It is not difficult to grasp just how quickly resistance to the systemic pressures at issue here can evaporate in the face of the multiple obstacles it will encounter – requirements to first comply with internal disciplinary procedures, internal channels of review, dispute resolution etc. – before it gets through to anything like a "proper" public hearing.[61]

---

60 Ibid, 261.

61 Cf. Deirdre Curtin and Linda Senden, "Public Accountability of Transnational Private Regulation: Chimera or Reality?" in *The Challenge of Transnational Private Regulation: Conceptual and Constitutional Debates*, ed. Fabrizio Cafaggi, Colin Scott, and Linda Senden (Oxford: Wiley-Blackwell, 2011), 185–188. Curtin and Senden address the problem of public accountability meticulously, but their emphasis is ultimately on the institution of non-judicial processes and fora for mediation. In the process they do not take into account that even these processes and fora can contribute to resistance-paralyzing systemic insulation that can effectively come to eliminate or undermine instead of sustain public accountability. Cf. also Fabrizio Cafaggi, "New Foundations of Transnational Private Regulation," in *The Challenge of Transnational Private Regulation: Conceptual and Constitutional Debates*, ed. Fabrizio Cafaggi, Colin Scott, and Linda

Under these circumstances, public scrutiny of governance structures – what little is left of it – increasingly becomes a notional or nominal consideration with little emancipatory potential worthy of the name. Horizontal effect of fundamental rights does offer some emancipatory potential against this background. Were these inner recesses of self-regulatory regimes of private governance not potentially subject to constitutional scrutiny through the direct horizontal effect of constitutional principles, they would effectively become pockets of society that are largely devoid of law and overarching sovereignty. They would come to constitute, in other words, interruptions of sovereignty, and they will do so by virtue of the sheer conformity inducing weight of systemic pressures.

A second aspect of the insularity that characterises the new forms of governance raises an additional constitutionality concern, namely, the reduction of supposedly "overarching" constitutionality considerations – represented in national constitutional documents, for example – to the systemic logics of governance regimes. Instead of the former remaining a source of critical criteria external to the latter – that for reasons of this *externality* may inform adequate levels of *third* party scrutiny – the latter increasingly assimilates the former so as to render any third party scrutiny worthy of the name impossible. This tendency is abundantly evident in the current phase of constitutional law developments in Europe, both at the level of national constitutional review within Member States and at the level of the "constitutionality" review exercised by the ECJ. Having derived in the first place from international treaties aimed at the creation of a common European market, the principles of "constitutionalisation" that inform European integration predominantly reflect concerns with market liberalisation. They evidently do not seem to include or are not significantly recognised to include counter-weighing principles that subject market liberalisation to other constitutional criteria.

Some tentative concern has been expressed at the level of national constitutional review as far as the promotion of market liberalisation by the jurisprudence of the ECJ is concerned, notably by the GFCC. The GFCC is well aware that developments in European law can come to undermine national constitutional safeguards and national sovereignty. It has expressed its views in this regard in a number of judgments. But it has yet to identify a case where the subversion of national constitutional sovereignty has in fact been jeopardised by an ECJ judgment. Chapter Seven (Sovereignty and the Dual Destiny of *Lüth* in Europe) will return to this concern of the GFCC and the reasons for its reticence

---

Senden (Oxford: Wiley-Blackwell, 2011), 20–49, for poignant assessments in this regard to which we return towards the end of this chapter.

as far as resisting the subversion of German social state principles by market liberalisation in the European Union is concerned. It will become clear then that the close or intrinsic link between sovereignty and horizontal effect review, on the one hand, and the resort of the ECJ to horizontal effect review to pursue market liberalisation, on the other, constitutes one the most significant shifts of sovereignty in Europe today. For now, let us first take a look at a recent contribution to German *Drittwirkung* scholarship that suggests horizontal effect review can and should dispense with its link to sovereignty.

V Dispensed Sovereignty – The Davidsonian Road to Luhmann

In the final analysis, the horizontal effect of fundamental rights always involves a clash between two or more fundamental rights claims. This has correctly been recognised as the specificity of the horizontal application question.[62] As such, horizontal effect indeed appears to threaten the holistic unity of law fundamentally. The law appears to split when rights clash. But there is more to horizontal application than just a conflict of rights. At issue is nothing less than a fundamental break down of social hermeneutics and semantics. Not just legal totality, but social totality as such is at stake when rights clash. It is thus with good reason that Ralph Christensen and Andreas Fischer-Lescano simply refer to an unqualified totality when they invoke the totality that is at stake when rights clash. They simply write: "Totality is at stake when constitutional rights clash – "*Wenn Grundrechte kollidieren, geht es ums Ganze.*" At issue, they suggest clearly, is not only legal totality, but also social totality. That this is a fair interpretation of what is at stake for them, is underlined by the distances they traverse to describe the deep hermeneutic dimension of this totality.

Christensen and Fischer-Lescano trace the hermeneutic totality at issue in the clash between fundamental rights into the deep recesses of analytical theories of science and language. What they achieve in the process is nothing less than a tour de force. Their main concern is the GFCC's jurisprudence in the *Lüth* case, but on their way to *Lüth* they not only engage with Schmitt, Kelsen

62 Stern, *Das Staatsrecht der Bundesrepublik Deutschland*, Band III/1:1513: "Die Besonderheit dieser Konstellation liegt darin, daß hier die Privatrechtssubjekte prinzipiell beide Grundrechtsberechtigte sind; entfalten in diesem Verhältnis die Grundrechte Wirkungen derart, daß hierdurch der eine gegenüber dem anderen Beteiligten geschützt wird, so kann dies zugleich eine Beeinträchtigung der grundrechtlichen Freiheit des anderen beteiligten Privatrechtssubjekts bedeuten. Die Grundrechte würden daher 'in diesen Verhältnissen für alle Beteiligten gleichzeitigt zu Rechten und zu Pflichten führen."

and Smend, but also with Willard van Orman Quine, Donald Davidson and many other significant philosophers and theorists of language and science of our time. Everything is at stake for Christensen and Fischer-Lescano. However much they may protest against the metaphysics of the comprehensive book,[63] they wrote a formidable book to do so. The engagement with this book that follows does not pretend to do full justice to it. It will simply pick out their key argument and then ask some critical questions.

Christensen and Fischer-Lescano's key endeavour is to replace the vertical framework of constitutional jurisprudence that informed the GFCC's reasoning in *Lüth* and subsequent horizontal application cases with a horizontal framework. "*Vom vertikalen zum horizontalen Holismus*" is their heading for the first section of their first chapter. They are evidently embarking here on a veritable horizontal theory of horizontal effect. At issue for them are not so much the decisions and the concrete considerations on which the GFCC's horizontal effect decisions were based, but the theoretical articulation or self-understanding in which the GFCC cast their jurisprudence. Underneath the vertical holism in *Lüth* with which they take issue, they actually discern a hidden sociology – *eine verdeckte Soziologie* – of which they approve.[64] Their concern is with the GFCC's notion of an objective hierarchy of values embodied in the *GG* on the basis of which fundamental rights claims can be balanced so as to resolve clashes between them objectively.

Not only is the invocation of this theoretical framework unhelpful, claim Christensen and Fischer-Lescano, it is also rather disingenuous, for their decisions are not really based on this balancing of claims in view of an objective set of values. Their actual practices surpass the oversimplifications that issue from their erroneous methodology significantly. What the GFCC judiciary really does when it decides horizontal application cases, Christensen and Fischer-Lescano contend, is to engage much more minutely and meticulously with the actual arguments and counter arguments before it. The process of communication that actually takes place in the court is much more refined than the notion of "*balancing rights in view of the objective hierarchy of values embodied in the* GG" would suggest; hence their invocation of the hidden sociology of the courts – *die verdeckte Soziologie der Gerichte* – the sophistication of which surpasses the sophistication of their jurisprudential self understanding by far.[65]

63 Christensen and Fischer-Lescano, *Das Ganze des Rechts*, 80.
64 Ibid, 175.
65 Ibid.

We shall presently turn to Christensen and Fischer-Lescano's positive portrayal of the actual communication process and real sociology of the courts and will then proceed to question the excessive optimism apparent in this portrayal. Suffice it for now to observe that their approval of the actual practices of the GFCC is so confident that they do not find it necessary to point out one seriously wrong or truly problematic decision. This makes one wonder. Why make such an extensive fuss of the GFCC's erroneous vertical holism if it has not really lead the Court astray in at least some cases? The arguments forwarded in this book may well assist them on this count. What Christensen and Fischer-Lescano calls *Lüth's* questionable vertical holism is exactly that to which Chapter Two referred as the dubious substantive due process jurisprudence in *Lüth* that led to the highly questionable majority opinion of the GFCC in *Erste Abtreibung*.

What Christensen and Fischer-Lescano correctly find questionable about this vertical holism or substantive due process is the idea that one can generally extract precise enough guidelines from the broad principles or values embodied in constitutional documents for purposes of addressing the highly specific exigencies of concrete legal conflicts. This procedure is all the more questionable, one should note, under circumstances where both parties to the conflict can rely on one or more of these broad constitutional principles, often the very same ones. Indeed, until such time as constitutional judiciaries attain better theoretical insight into the procedural due process review that should mostly (not always, as we have seen in Chapter Two and will see again in Chapter Six and Eight) inform their jurisprudence, their better practices will continue to just muddle through largely unexplained. And they will of course continue to be lured into their worse and worst performances. They will continue to be tempted by problematic substantive due process decisions that are not called for and they will do so more often than Christensen and Fischer-Lescano seem to realise.

The message that Christensen and Fischer-Lescano extract from 20th century analytical philosophy of language and science concerns the way this philosophy developed an increasing regard for the irreducible margin of indeterminacy, undecidability, double contingency and open-eventfulness that accompanies and conditions all instances of significant human communication. This irreducible margin of indeterminacy is a constant source of misunderstanding and failed communication. Understanding and communication in fact only become possible to the extent that they manage to stabilise and contain the indeterminacies that constantly haunt them. And they manage to do so through practices of temporalisation that relate present acts of communication to *recollections of past* and *imaginations of future* acts of understanding. Christensen and Fischer-Lescano take one on a well-organised tour through 20th century philosophy of language to make this point.

The tour begins with Bertrand Russell's rejection of the holism of Hegelian theories of meaning that reduce the meaning of individual instances of communication to the semantic wholes or totalities within which the communication takes place. Russell sought to oppose and dismiss these holistic theories of meaning with an atomistic building-block concept of meaningful communication. Communication would accordingly consist for Russell in the building of sound compositions and combinations of elementary units or atoms of meaning, each and all of which derive their meaning exclusively from within themselves. The whole building-block endeavour rested on the assumption that elementary facts or data could be perceived, identified and understood in isolation. It soon came tumbling down, however, when especially three theorists started shaking this assumption incisively. The beginning of the holistic turn can be linked to Gottlob Frege's 1892 contention that meaning cannot be attached to words, only to sentences.[66] But the crack in the building-block theory really opened up as a result of especially two posthumous works of Ludwig Wittgenstein.

Wittgenstein, who himself also articulated a building-block theory of language in his early work *Tractatus Logico-Philosophicus* (1922), articulated a fundamental critique of the building-block theory in writings on which he was working at the time of his death, the essay *Über Gewissheit* and the larger work *Philosophische Untersuchungen*, both of which were only published after his death in 1952. The former dismissed the possibility of reliable knowledge of basic facts and units of meaning and the latter developed a game or practice theory of language. The game theory of language articulated in the latter work explained the possibility of common linguistic meaning with reference to linguistic practices current in language communities.

Another nail in the coffin of the building-block theory of language was Willard Van Orman Quine's 1951 essay on the dogmas of empiricism with which he exposed the prior conceptual and theoretical comprehension that precedes and therefore interferes with any attempt at direct empirical observations of reality. A whole web of conceptual material conditions every instance of empirical observation, argued Quine. Holism was suddenly back with a bang in linguistic theory and Donald Davidson would soon become one of the most prominent spokesmen of this holistic turn in English analytical philosophy. In 1967 Davidson expanded Frege's sentence-based conception of meaning into one that made any

---

66 Ibid, 94, referring rather implausibly to Gottlob Frege, *Grundlagen der Aritmethik*, 1884, Breslau, § 106. Should the reference rather have been to *Über Sinn und Bedeutung* 1892, *Zeitschrift für Philosophie und philosophische Kritik*, NF 100, 1892, 25–50?

instance of communication dependent on the totality of possible meaningful utterances within a language.[67] This totality of meaningful utterances could of course never be known and overseen, it could only be assumed as the horizon of possible meaning. Davidson's turn to this assumption of a horizon of possible meaning marks a crucial moment in Christensen and Fischer-Lescano's narrative. It is this horizon that they wish to invoke as the totality or *Ganze* that is at stake in the conflict of rights.

The assumption of linguistic horizons is not a once off act but a constant *practice* of understanding that turns on active ascriptions of meaning to words and actions. These ascriptions can be sustained as long as and to the extent to which these words and actions fit into an imaginable and anticipatable "totality" of meaningful utterances that everyone involved in the relevant acts of communication appears to *hold* in common. In other words, the totality of meaningful utterances is *assumed*, *imagined* and *anticipated* in common. At issue in acts of communication are reciprocal acts of "radical translation" through which individuals re-situate the words and acts of others within the totality of their own assumptions of possible meaning.[68]

However, holistic language theory soon began to collect its own bag of worries. The most disconcerting among them was the constant subversion of reliable communication that must result from the constant variation of linguistic horizons. Since communicants can at no point in time oversee the totality of their own linguistic expectations, let alone those of others, they always only contemplate current horizons of meaning that are discernibly incomplete, highly variable and indeed constantly varying. If the part can only be understood with reference to the whole and the whole is constantly changing, the part itself will also be subject to constant change. And given that any individual act of significant communication and understanding must itself contribute to the constant transformation of the comprehensive horizons of meaning within which they take place – given that the transformation of the part must also contribute to the transformation of the whole – communication basically becomes impossible. A problem of *double variation* thus began to preoccupy holistic language theory. Meaning must constantly be slipping if communication alters horizons of communication and vice versa.

---

67 Cf. Donald Davidson "Truth and Meaning" in *The Essential Davidson* (Oxford: Oxford University Press, 2006) 159; Christensen and Fischer-Lescano, *Das Ganze des Rechts*, 94.

68 Donald Davidson, "Radical Interpretation," in *Inquiries into Truth and Interpretation* (Oxford: Oxford University Press, 2001), 125–139; Christensen and Fischer-Lescano, *Das Ganze des Rechts*, 95, 129.

Davidson's ultimate response to the slippery qualms of this radical strand of holistic linguistic theory invoked the metaphor of figures that can be observed by virtue of the backgrounds against which they appear. Backgrounds indeed always exceed capacities of observation and different acts of observation by different observers (and also by the same observer) indeed constantly vary and transform backgrounds. Backgrounds therefore never appear as comprehensively observable figures themselves, but enough of them can be observed in common for long enough to allow for sufficiently stable and common observations of foreground figures.[69] Holistic language theory thus came to locate the condition for reliable communication in communicative practices that sustain and maintain common linguistic horizons for sufficient lengths of time. And this is also the language theoretical insight from the basis of which Christensen and Fischer-Lescano proceed to interrogate the theory of constitutional meaning that informed the jurisprudence in *Lüth*: Instead of determining its parts from above, the linguistic whole is maintained from within by particular linguistic practices and by specific acts of communication that maintain and sustain the whole as an open horizon of meaning. Language constitutes a horizontal, not a vertical whole. Its operation is two directional, not one directional. The linguistic horizon is sustained by communicative practices and vice versa.

The GFCC's reasoning in *Lüth*, Christensen and Fischer-Lescano argue, mainly with reference to Thomas Henne,[70] was informed by the vertical holistic theory of the state that Rudolf Smend developed in response to the positivist approach to fundamental rights during the Weimar era. The meaning and scope of the various rights should be determined strictly with reference to the text of the consti-

---

69 Christensen and Fischer-Lescano, *Das Ganze des Rechts*, 97. They ascribe this idea to Davidson while referring up to this point only to the essays "Radical Interpretation" and "A Coherence Theory of Truth and Knowledge" For the latter essay, cf. Donald Davidson, *The Essential Davidson* (Oxford: Oxford University Press, 2006), 225–241. None of these essays forward this argument regarding backgrounds that sustain stable observations of foreground figures expressly or clearly. Christensen and Fischer-Lescano may be reconstructing it from the many other authors that they also cite, or from the notion of "passing theories" that Davidson discusses in "A Nice Derangement of Epitaphs" – cf. Ibid, 251–265. They also cite this essay, but only later. Cf. Christensen and Fischer-Lescano, *Das Ganze des Rechts*, 127–8. Be it as it may, the point here is not to put their reading of Davidson in doubt. I am surely not enough of a Davidson reader to offer firm judgment here, but on the whole, the reading of Davidson that they offer surely appears plausible and reliable.

70 Cf. Thomas Henne, "'Von 0 auf Lüth in 6 1/2 Jahren.' Zu den Prägenden Faktoren der Grundsatzentscheidung," in *Das Lüth-Urteil aus (rechts-)historischer Sicht – Die Konflikte um Veit Harlan und die Grundrechtsjudikatur des Bundesverfassungsgerichts*, ed. Thomas Henne and Arne Riedlinger (Berlin: Berliner Wissenschafts-Verlag, 2005), 197–222.

tution, maintained the positivists. They should not be inferred from "Hegelian" or organic totalities that endow them with meaning from above. For the positivists, such holistic approaches to constitutional interpretation would only serve to legitimate authoritarian abridgements of constitutional rights. This positivist approach, argued Smend, reduced constitutional rights to the simple principle of government by law. They are much more than that, argued Smend. They are vehicles for the continual renewal and further development of the collective will of the state (*dauernde Erneuerung und Weiterbildung des staatlichen Willensverbandes*) and the continuing life of the state (*Lebensvorgang des Staates*).[71]

Fundamental rights thus came to perform a double task in Smend's thinking. On the one hand they effected necessary exclusions that defined the limits and thus the unity of the state. On the other hand, they served as legitimation for new courses of conduct that renewed public life and resisted the stagnation of collective convictions.[72] Smend's thinking thus articulated a dynamic holism that, in clear contrast with the classical bourgeois constitutional thinking that separated state and society, turned on a dynamic interaction between them. It recognised the multiplicity of agents that contributed to the collective and constitutional life of the state and the different meanings that normative texts could attain in different contexts. It explained the collective life of the state in terms of dialectic mediations between private and public life. It emphasised the quality of dynamic integrity in terms of which the whole constantly integrated its individual parts. Indeed the state appeared in Smend's thinking as a constant process of integration:

> "The constitution is the legal order of the state, more specifically, of the life in which the state has its living reality, that is, its process of integration. The meaning of this process is the perennial renewal of the living totality of the state and the constitution is the statutory articulation of norms with which some aspects of this integration must comply."[73]

---

71 Christensen and Fischer-Lescano, *Das Ganze des Rechts*, 38.

72 Ibid.

73 Cf. Rudolf Smend, "Verfassung und Verfassungsrecht," in *Staatsrechtliche Abhandlungen und andere Aufsätze* (Berlin: Duncker & Humblot, 1994), 189, also quoted by Christensen and Fischer-Lescano, *Das Ganze des Rechts*, 40. Smend would appear to be much more interesting for the theory of sovereignty and constitutional review contemplated in this book than could be reflected here properly. His integration theory views the existence of a people in terms of a daily plebiscite (ein sich täglich erneuernden Plebiszit) and a continuing dialectic interrogation with one another (eine dauerende dialektische Auseinandersetzung miteinander) – cf. also his 1964 essay "Integration" in *Staatsrechtliche Abhandlungen* 482–486 at 483. Suffice it to say that these descriptions of the life of a people resonate strongly with the Hohfeldian and Kelsenian (and Hegelian) theory of sovereignty, state action and horizontal effect that will come together towards the end of this book. Whether Christensen and Fischer-Lescano's assessment of Smend's

One can be forgiven for thinking that Smend herewith, already in 1928, basically already coined for constitutional theory the dynamic holism that Christensen and Fischer-Lescano distil from linguistic theories that, as we saw above, would emerge only much later in the 20th century. But this would not be correct according to Christensen and Fischer-Lescano. For them there is still much too much Hegel in Smend. The integrated totality of the state that Smend invokes is, according to them, not an open and indefinite horizon, but a defined whole – "diese Einheit is kein indefiniter Horizont [sondern] eine definierte Grösse als Totalität des staatlichen Lebens."[74] The concession it makes to the life and living experience of the whole (*Erlebnis der Totalität*) is typical of the Neo-Hegelianism of the time to which Karl Larenz also belonged, they argue. Larenz's hermeneutic re-articulation of these Neo-Hegelian theories of the state, observe Christensen and Fischer-Lescano, basically precipitated the value-oriented jurisprudence (*Wertungsjurisprudenz*) that would find its way into the *Lüth* decision. Smend's theory, they contend, is still part and parcel of the metaphysics of the book that Hegel articulated paradigmatically – "*die von Hegel paradigmatisch formulierte Metaphysik des Buches.*" Smend's holistic conception of integration is not at all a matter of text and textuality, the margins of which *expose* rather than *enclose*; it is by far not yet an intimation of hyper-textuality, the margins of which dissolve completely into infinite referentiality.[75] Whatever intimations of open horizontality it may contain or appear to contain, are ultimately swept up by a vertical thrust (*Zug ins Vertikale*).[76]

Christensen and Fischer-Lescano's critique of Smend is truly impressive, but they ultimately pay much too dear for it. They purchase the hypertextuality of their post-metaphysical theory of horizontal constitutional adjudication by removing from it the very element of critical adjudication and the irreducible "moment of verticality" that adjudication always entails. They pay for their hypertextuality with the typical hype of yet another new fangled fashion of alternative dispute resolution. As will soon become clear, the removal of the state from their hypertextual scene culminates in removing judges from the scene of constitutional litigation. One may well ask here whether the term "litigation" is still ap-

conception of integration in terms of a defined whole (definierte Grösse) really does justice to the "openness" of the process that Smend evidently envisaged, is doubtful. I nevertheless offer this reflection tentatively, for here too (as in the case of Davidson above) I surely am not sufficiently familiar with Smend's work to offer firmer judgment of Christensen and Fischer-Lescano's reading of his texts.

74 Christensen and Fischer-Lescano, *Das Ganze des Rechts*, 40.

75 Ibid, 78–83.

76 Ibid, 40.

posite for the optimistic discourse ethics that they propose for the resolution of legal conflict. Niklas Luhmann, one of their principal mentors, does much better on this count, as we shall soon see.

As already indicated, Smend's Hegelianism found its way into the *Lüth* jurisprudence of the GFCC through Larenz's hermeneutics. Larenz turned Smend's dialectics into an evaluative jurisprudence (*Wertungsjurisprudenz*) that ultimately generated the notion of an objective hierarchy of values. According to Larenz, the coherence of this objective hierarchy of values could be invoked to find the right balance between the colliding constitutional rights that set the scene for the horizontal application of these rights. The reasoning launched in *Lüth* thus came to turn on nothing less than an optimistic idea with mythic proportions: however general and broad banded the objective framework or normative values embodied in constitutional rights may be, they also possess within their broad ranges the fine calibration that allows for the correct and just resolution of specific conflicts between them. However much they may be lumbered onto the battlefield like heavy clubs, the judiciary will miraculously turn them into high-tech surgical tools that hardly draw blood. Whatever one may say of Hegel's original mythological optimism, he did not take things this far.[77]

Christensen and Fischer-Lescano's alternative to the *Lüth* approach is indeed to have the judiciary exchange their course instruments for the precision tools of a finer sociology. The latter equipment will enable them to line up the specificities of competing arguments so as to facilitate and demand precise communicative exchanges. And in the wake of these communicative exchanges the quarrelsome parties will reflect upon their sins or ignorance and the conflict between them will simply evaporate. In the end, it seems, even the needlepoint entries of fine surgery get replaced by mere psychological or counselling interventions that move the quarrelsome parties to grasp whatever misconceptions fuelled the conflict between them so that they may come to kiss and make up again.

Or so it appears when one retraces Christensen and Fischer-Lescano's steps carefully. They surely commence with a clear grasp of the aporias of serious legal

---

77 Hegel may have been somewhat optimistic about the healing of historical wounds – cf. G. W. F. Hegel, *Phänomenologie des Geistes*, in *Werke in 20 Bänden*, vol. III (Frankfurt: Suhrkamp, 1970), 492: "Die Wunden des Geistes heilen, ohne daß Narben bleiben" – but he had no illusions about the historical infliction of death and destruction that marked history. Cf. also Ibid, III: 36: "Aber nicht das Leben, das sich vor dem Tode scheut und von der Verwüstung rein bewahrt, sondern das ihn erträgt und in ihm sich erhält, ist das Leben des Geistes. Er gewinnt seine Wahrheit nur, indem er in der absoluten Zerissenheit sich selbst findet." One might also want to heed in this regard that philosophy, according to Hegel, should not be edifying – "Die Philosophie aber muß sich hüten, erbaulich sein zu wollen."

conflict. They accordingly set the scene with an apposite invocation of the incommensurability and abyssal heterogeneity between language games that Lyotard describes in *The differend.*[78] Wittgenstein may have recognised the fundamental heterogeneity of language games, argue Christensen and Fischer-Lescano, but compared to Lyotard's relentless regard for the hermetic closure of language games, he still assumed a degree of semantic overlapping that disqualifies him from grasping the catastrophic closures of mutually exclusive hermeneutic practices. And it is these practices that inform hardened legal conflict. Their superb description of this cataclysmic scene is worth quoting in full:

> "The language games that thus cross one another are not connected by anything with which some mediation can commence. They face one another across a gorge of brutal difference. Mediation or compromise is no longer conceivable between them. Not even an aside that might register some mutual recognition is apparent here. And a decision regarding propriety and justification is also no longer feasible here, for they have no common ground between them. A groundless decision must in the most real sense of the word be imposed on them. In short, discord necessarily returns here as an instance of conflict between (at least) two parties that cannot be resolved appositely, for there is no rule of judgment that applies to both arguments. The legitimacy of the one argument does not provide for the legitimacy of the other. Should one nevertheless apply a rule of judgment under these circumstances so as to [at least] resolve the legal conflict at hand, one subjects at least one of the parties to injustice (or both, considering that neither may recognise the rule)."[79]

This is fine legal theory, as fine as it gets. One hardly has anything meaningful left to say about *Lüth's* invocation of the "best balancing" or *schonendste Ausgleich* between competing values after reading this exacting passage. Against this background the notion of "best balancing" sounds so hollow that it warrants no further comment. However, the climb to these high altitudes and thin air of contemporary social theory must have taken its toll, for Christensen and Fischer-Lescano reach these heights only to scramble down fast into a valley where coarser thoughts can breath again. They turn around with a contention from nowhere that the injustice that this passage describes, the injustice (Unrecht) of decisions that simply terminate incongruity that cannot be resolved, would be fatal for juridical processes. It would turn them into acts of violence that would destroy the distinctions between legitimate and illegitimate authority

78 Christensen and Fischer-Lescano, *Das Ganze des Rechts*, 202.
79 Ibid.

and good and bad judgements without which the constitutional state becomes inconceivable.[80]

One wonders what Christensen and Fischer-Lescano might make of the suggestion that at least some judiciaries, among them also the GFCC, have been doing exactly the kind of thing they describe for centuries and/or decades now without visibly forfeiting either their claims to constitutional legitimacy or their ability to command respectful distinctions between their better and worse judgments. However, they do not wish to contemplate the possibility that legitimacy can survive deficits of normative justification. Obviously thinking that all concerns with legitimacy would have to be dropped if one were to admit to the reality of (ultimately arbitrary) judicial terminations of incommensurability, they deem it wiser to rather drop the idea of incommensurability:

> "The question is surely whether one can assess incommensurability really this strictly. For if one would do that, the modest question as to how such "completely heterogeneous" language games can at all end up in conflict becomes unanswerable."[81]

The suggestion that language games can only end up in conflict if there is enough commensurability between them to allow for conflict is transparently spurious. This kind of moderate semantic or hermeneutic conflict does occur, true enough, but conflict also and often manifests as nothing but mute clashes between irreconcilable wills and desires to occupy the same space at the time; they often concern nothing more than inexplicable miasmic doublings for which no sufficient rhyme or reason is evident. When this happens, as it often does, conflict requires hermeneutics only for fuel, not for ignition. It comes to demand articulation of sufficiently semantic juridical claims for the sake of libidinal fires that are already burning. Hermeneutics only tend to spread such fires; they do not cause them. Parties rarely end up in conflict because of prior semantic constructions that go by the name of rights claims. They resort to these constructions when conflict has already materialised. It is a good question whether inceptions of "hermeneutic" conflict that reflect the minimum of commensurability that Christensen and Fischer-Lescano attribute to them, do not also turn invariably on extraneous moments of non-hermeneutic inflamma-

---

80 Ibid, 202–3: "Für das juristische Verfahren als der institutionalisierten Regulierung von Streit wäre dies fatal. Jede Entscheidung im Konflikt der Rechtsmeinungen und Lesarten der Normtexte ließe sich nur noch einen Akt der Gewalt, durch das Machtwort fällen. Und das juristische Verfahren selbst verlöre jede Legitimität. Die für den Rechtsstaat zentrale Unterscheidung von legitimer und illegitimer Gewalt, von guten und schlechten Entscheidungen würde damit keinen Boden mehr finden."

81 Ibid, 203.

tion that require no common ground and no commensurability. Anyone who suggests conflict requires commensurability underestimates the levels of sheer a-rationality evident in most conflict (*a-rational* because it can only be deemed *irrational* from the perspective of some or other commensurable criterion of rationality that is imposed from somewhere else). And it is this underestimation that evidently causes the rapid deterioration and disintegration of the fine line of argument that Christensen and Fischer-Lescano have developed so painstakingly before taking their fateful discourse ethical turn. What follows thereafter would have merited little comment had the "sociological" jurisprudence that they propose as an alternative to the reasoning in *Lüth* not turned on exactly this assumption of minimal hermeneutic commensurability.

The horizontal holistic approach that they advocate culminates in the proposal that the collision of fundamental rights at stake in horizontal application cases cannot be resolved with recourse to vertical holism. Colliding rights cannot be balanced with recourse to an objective scale of values that endows every right with its due measure of respect and recognition. Judges should take leave of this lofty idea and lofty language, as they invariably do in fact. Their jurisprudence should descend to the horizontal plane of their actual practices, the horizontal plane where the conflicting arguments of litigants clash face to face. They should demand from all arguments involved that they meet one another's terms satisfactorily enough. The judicial process should thus come to effect something akin to the process of *radical translation* that Davidson identified as the condition for all communication. The judicial process should come to understand itself for what it really is when it functions properly. It does not involve judgment. It simply stabilises the communications between the litigants and removes the potential for slippery misunderstandings between them. And when this happens, the conflicting parties basically begin to resolve their differences themselves. The conflicts between them miraculously simply commence to evaporate into thin air and no one ends up subjected to coercive criteria of judgment that are foreign to their self-understanding. Should anyone begin to think this is a perniciously hyperbolic rendition of what Christensen and Fischer-Lescano are suggesting, listen to this:

> "The law fends off imperialistic impositions on the claims of the parties. The legal battle nevertheless compels their incongruous semantic expectations to enter the space of language. In doing so, however, the law does not coerce them directly. It much rather forces them to engage in self-reflection and to engage in a learning process. It does not lay

down a framework of reference for them. It compels the social systems party to the conflict to become aware of their own frameworks of reference and to try out others."[82]

"Conflict is sociologically speaking a highly integrated system of communication. The reality of controversy does not mean that the parties must talk past one another hopelessly. To the contrary, competitive action such as is the action at stake in semantic disputes constitutes instances of interaction in which the respective moves of the speakers take recourse to one another at the highest level of reciprocity. Every misinterpretation of the other is punished with the disappointment of one's own endeavours. In other words, success in legal conflict requires that the parties listen carefully to one another."[83]

"Davidson employs the idea of triangulation in this regard. The speaker and listener understand one another in the common world of communication. This world [rather: between-world/Zwischenwelt] between them is decisive. Both participants articulate from within their own languages a sense of the other's language and develop this sense further when it fails or runs into difficulty. From successful communication processes then derives, as a third level phenomenon, the social bond of communication. At issue here is a horizontal linguistic understanding that constantly develops further in the practices of the participants. And it is in this way that the linguistic totality constitutes a practical and horizontal whole."[84]

At this point Christensen and Fischer-Lescano finally call upon Niklas Luhmann to team up with Davidson:

"Language thus becomes precisely a medium of difference and dissent, as Niklas Luhmann avers. Luhmann, just like Davidson, does not view communication as an act of information in the course of which the agents merely exchange messages that they then decipher together with reference to a common scheme. Language is also for him a process of understanding."[85]

We have followed Christensen and Fischer-Lescano far enough for present purposes. The exposition above cannot claim to have done justice to the four hundred pages of *Das Ganze des Rechts* in the couple of pages dedicated to it above.

82 Ibid, 206.

83 Ibid, 208.

84 Christensen and Fischer-Lescano, *Das Ganze des Rechts*, 208–209: "Davidson verwendet hier den Gedanken der Triangulation. Sprecher und Hörer verständigen sich in der gemeinsamen Welt der Kommunikation. Diese Zwischenwelt ist entscheidend. Jeder der beiden Beteiligten stellt aus seiner Sprache heraus vermutungen über die Sprache des anderen an, die er bei Scheitern und Schwierigkeit und weiterentwickelt. Aus dem gelungenen Verständigungserfahren entsteht dann als Phänomen der dritten Art das soziale Band der Kommunikation. Es ist ein offener Horizont sprachlicher Verständigung, der im praktischen Verhalten der Beteiligten ständig weiter-entwickelt wird. Darin liegt das Ganze der Sprache als praktischer und horizontaler Holismus."

85 Christensen and Fischer-Lescano, *Das Ganze des Rechts*, 209.

There is much more to this formidable book than just this. But the engagement with their book above surely highlights their central concern and most of their key points. Among them are some of their best and some of their worst arguments. Their best arguments not only take the theoretical reflection on horizontal effect to levels of sophistication that it has rarely if ever reached since the work of Walter Leisner. They also direct future reflection on horizontal effect jurisprudence into a new direction that is bound to be highly productive still. By taking leave of the lofty language of the vertical holism and overarching value jurisprudence articulated in *Lüth* and by re-focusing the question of horizontal effect more closely on the actual dynamics of judicial processes, they contribute towards a new kind of jurisprudence in which the operative economics of constitutional review can become more visible. Chapter Eight returns to the productive insights they offer in this regard. However, their optimistic vision of this operative economics unfortunately lures them into their worst arguments. And it lures them into wasting one of the crucial insights that they have to offer.

The crucial thought that they offer the theory of horizontal effect concerns the way they relate the question of horizontal effect and the collision of rights on which it turns to a totality that is not closed and defined, but undefined and open. They stress the conception of a transcendent horizon that remains transcendent throughout the process of judicial review and never gets reduced to immanence on the way to the resolution of conflicts. This is indeed a crucial thought from which the theory of horizontal effect and the theory of constitutional review as such stand to gain significantly.

However, Christensen and Fischer-Lescano's optimistic vision of this open horizon turns on a rather naïve underestimation of the sovereign role of the state in successful or at least relatively stable social communication processes. Their rosy view of courts as planes on which judges simply activate the irreducible rests of linguistic commensurability between the clashing arguments of litigants, without having to impose on the self-understanding of one or both of them criteria of judgment that are foreign to that self-understanding, is out of touch with the anthropological reality of significant conflict.[86] And their failure to take conflict seriously prevents them from taking a closer look at the dynamics of constitutional review that would explain why sovereign judicial impositions sometimes function in the felicitous way they envisage and sometimes not. One need not counter their optimistic vision with a pessimistic or negative

---

86 The anti-statism that informs *Das Ganze des Rechts* is evident from the opening pages onwards in which Christensen and Fischer-Lescano expound the problematic of the book. Cf. Ibid, 17–22. It would not be an exaggeration to say that a Luhmannian or rather Teubnerian anti-statism (Luhmann's anti-statism is not that evident) is the driving energy throughout the book.

one. One need not assume that litigants never learn from litigation and never find judicial explanations of their misguided recourse to litigation helpful. One need not assume that litigants never come to new self-understandings. There may well be cases in which failed litigation prompts self-reflexion that leads to "better" understanding. But one also needs to take a closer look at these felicitous cases than Christensen and Fischer-Lescano do in order to understand better why these happy outcomes occur, when they do, and why it is *realistic and wise* to assume that they do not occur nearly as often as they fail to occur. A much finer sociology than the one they are offering is required here.

In fact, one needs to explain why it is *realistic and wise* to assume that losing litigants regularly leave courtrooms in states of confusion, anger and deep anxiety. One needs to understand that they bear in their breasts the seed of civil war and insurrection, however minimal and insignificant for the moment. Only then will one begin to understand that the erasure of the state from the open horizon of law is naive and unhelpful. A clear regard for the iron hand needed to back up judicial decisions that send losing litigants stumbling back into worlds that fail to meet their self-understandings ought to dispel the naive anti-statism that systems theory propounds so persistently. And it ought to give these theorists enough reason to ponder the possibility of the state itself becoming the open horizon that they stress with such flamboyance and with such good reasons.

Constitutional review is understandably less concerned with forces that stabilise felicitous communication than it is haunted by the coercive force that stabilises the utter speechlessness of those who live under law they do not understand. Quite to the contrary of what Justice Kriegler averred in *Du Plessis v De Klerk*, horizontal effect does invite the state to put its hands on all private relations when these relations turn sufficiently bad or problematic. It pervasively commands the state to do so to stabilise failures of communication coercively. Linguistic and constitutional theory cannot and should not deny this reality. It should seek to understand it better. Christensen and Fischer-Lescano's triumphant optimism prevents one from doing so. We shall turn away from them now in order to engage with Luhmann on somewhat less optimistic terms that may well do more justice to his thought. After all, considering the caution Habermas expressed many years ago regarding Luhmann,[87] one would assume that there is a sharper sting to Luhmann's thinking than the irenic discourse ethics attributed to him in *Das Ganze des Rechts* would suggest.

---

87 Cf. Jürgen Habermas, *Der philosophische Diskurs der Moderne* (Frankfurt a.M: Suhrkamp, 1989), 426–445; Jürgen Habermas, *Theorie des kommunikativen Handelns I* (Frankfurt a.M: Suhrkamp, 1988), 173–295; Habermas, *Faktizität und Geltung – Beiträge zur Diskurstheorie des Rechts und des demokratischen Rechtsstaats*, 573–81.

VI Uninterrupted Sovereignty – A "Luhmannian" Return to Hegel

Luhmann would indeed seem much more cautious about the communication outcomes of systemic differentiation than Christensen and Fischer-Lescano would seem to suggest. The last pages of *Grundrechte als Institution* clearly convey a much more realistic regard for the possible failures of communication that may result from processes of functional differentiation. He expressly dissociates himself here from the "much criticised harmonic picture of society of early functional analysis" – "*das viel kritisierte harmonische Gesellschaftsbild des frühen Funktionalismus.*"[88] Especially the closing lines of *Grundrechte als Institution* reflect a real sense of the precariousness of functional differentiation and an acute awareness of the critical disturbances (*kritische Störungen*) with which systemic integration always contends.[89]

Luhmann, one should add, evidently also does not seem to be the ideal authority for a theory of the horizontal effect of fundamental rights. *Grundrechte als Institution*, in any case, dismisses the notion expressly and completely. The text could not be clearer in this regard:

> "The constitution protects the individual against the state, and only against the state. The idea that every individual must respect the integrity of every other individual is unimaginable..."[90]

Grundrechte als Institution also takes care to ensure that horizontal effect does not slip in through the backdoor of the state's positive duty to protect fundamental rights. Consider for instance the assessment of the right to equality that it proposes. The right to equality is not really a right *to equality*, argues Luhmann, for the state cannot guarantee or provide equality. It is at most a rightful demand that the state justifies any conduct that amounts to unequal treatment.[91] Cast in this way, the right to equality clearly closes the door on the horizontal effect of equality rights conclusively. Positive state action becomes the only possible target of equality review. The *failure* of states to ensure equality or minimum levels of equality is surely not part of Luhmann's vision in *Grundrechte als Institu-*

---

88 Niklas Luhmann, *Grundrechte als Institution* (Berlin: Duncker & Humblot, 1965), 197.
89 Ibid, 216.
90 Ibid, 75–76 (starting on the page and following on into fn. 60): "Darin gewährt die Verfassung [dem Mensch] vor dem Staat. Und zwar: nur vor dem Staat. Daß die Würde jedes Menschen jeden Menschen verpflichtet, ist unvorstellbar..."
91 Ibid, 167–9.

tion. Whence this classic "negative rights against the state" vision of constitutional rights in *Grundrechte als Institution?* The answer to this question can be traced to the dismissal of Hegel's political and legal philosophy in the early pages of the book. There we find a remarkable paragraph that warrants close attention:

> "The necessity to provide foundations – of which the profound rootedness in the division between thought and existence cannot be discussed here – splits social reality with cleaving force into a sphere of the state and a sphere of society. The state has to justify itself to and in society. (Hegel's conception, which takes over this principle of division but inverses the foundational relation, never received a real following)."[92]

One of the key features of Luhmann's theory of social systems comes firmly to the fore in this paragraph. Luhmann writes that it is not the split between state and society that brings about the necessity of foundation (*Notwendigkeit der Begründung*), as one might easily think would be the case. It is the necessity of foundation that brings about the split between state and society with cleaving force (*die mit bohrender Kraft die soziale Wirklichkeit aufspaltet*). In other words, social realities split because they require foundation; they do not require foundation because they are split. It is the very split that founds, or the very foundation that splits. The self-evident "foundations" of pre-modern societies required no such splitting, contends Luhmann. They did not turn on significant divisions. The three different orders of medieval societies, for instance, sustained rather than severed their unifying embeddedness in the overarching metaphysical idea of the *Corpus Christi.*[93] It is the absence of such self-evident metaphysical embeddedness that requires modern societies to reflect on and articulate its foundations actively and consciously. For purposes of this reflection they need to create a double register, for no reflection or re-flection is possible without two registers. Modern societies create this double register by splitting itself into two separate spheres, the sphere of the state and the sphere of civil society. They then found themselves by requiring the state to justify itself to civil society. And right here does one find the almost casual dismissal of Hegel that runs through the whole negative rights conception of fundamental rights in *Grundrechte als Institution*. The splitting self-foundation of modern societies turns on the demand that the state justify itself to civil society, stresses Luhmann, and not vice versa as Hegel suggested – "die Auffassung Hegels, die das Trenn-

---

92 Ibid, 27.

93 Duby, *The Three Orders: Feudal Society Imagined* (Chicago: University of Chicago Press, 1982); *Ullman, The Individual and Society in the Middle Ages* (London: Methuen and Company, 1967).

schema übernimmt, aber das Begründungsverhältnis umkehrt, blieb ohne reale Folgen." Luhmann is referring here to Hegel's insistence that the state guarantees a minimum of Kantian morality vis-à-vis the egocentric individualistic pursuits of civil society.

It is important to take a closer look at Hegel's conception of the relation between state and civil society, for it should be clear that it is the Hegel that Luhmann dismisses so casually here – "[er] blieb ohne reale Folgen"/ "he received no real following" – who would have been and might still become the champion of the horizontal effect of fundamental rights that Luhmann surely does not want to be. Hegel's idea that the state must subject the pursuits of civil society to the demands of Kant's morality obviously lays a solid foundation for the horizontal effect of constitutional rights. Why the casual dismissal of this idea just because it did not receive any following, might one ask. Why not rather, like Franz Wieacker, lament this failure to learn from Hegel as one of the very unfortunate features of nineteenth century legal science?[94]

And why, might one ask further, does this rejection persist in *Das Ganze des Rechts*, a book that expressly aims to promote the horizontal effect of fundamental rights. Why do Christensen and Fischer-Lescano persist with this dismissal of Hegel, whose reversed conception of the relation between state and civil society – in terms of which the latter must justify itself to the former – makes him a very likely champion of horizontal effect? The answer may well lie in an anti-Prussianism that has marked the resistance to Hegel's political philosophy ever since the publication of Rudolf Haym's *Vorlesungen über Hegel und seine Zeit* in 1857.

The perception that Hegel was nothing but an apologist for the authoritarian Prussian state of his time became pervasive during the second half of the 19th century and survived well into the 20th. As we saw from the engagement with Christensen and Fischer-Lescano's work above, it informed the positivist rejection of holistic understandings of the Weimar constitution and spawned an atomistic philosophy of language that tried for decades to suppress the insight

94 Franz Wieacker, *Privatrechtsgeschichte der Neuzeit* (Göttingen: Vandenhoeck & Ruprecht, 1967), 415: "Dass die Philosophie Hegels, die als erste die Möglichkeit eines geschlossenen Systems der Rechtstheorie mit der geschichtlichen Dimension vereinbart hat und die also der Entdeckung der Geschichtlickkeit für die Rechtswissenschaft eine ähnliche normative Bedeutung hätte geben können, wie einst die naturrechtliche Anthropologie den ungeschichtlichen Rechtsentwürfen der Aufklärung, – dass diese Philosophie ohne Einfluss blieb auf eine Zivilrechtswissenschaft, die die Ungeschichtlichkeit des Vernunftrechts durchschaute, sich auf die Geschichtlichkeit der Kultur und des Volksgeistes berief und endlich gerade der Restauration diente: dies alles ist eines der vielen Paradoxe der Geschichte des Geistes."

that conceptual frameworks and practices condition empirical observation. Apprehension regarding Prussian authoritarianism thus goes a long way towards explaining why Quine and Davidson would be hailed in the second half of the 20th century for advancing analytical philosophy of science and language to a frontier of insights that Hegel had already taken for granted more than a century before.[95] Some of this anti-Prussian apprehension still appears to inform Christensen and Fischer-Lescano's dismissal of Smend's neo-Hegelian vertical holism. Anti-Prussianism may well explain their radically horizontal holism in terms of which language itself absolves the state from duty and steers it into retirement.

Anti-Prussianism is surely not an unpalatable thought among liberal democrats, but not all liberal democrats are ad idem as far as making Hegel one of their principal Prussian adversaries. The perception that Hegel's philosophy was nothing but an apology for Prussian authoritarianism cannot be squared with plausible contentions, to the contrary, that it was nothing of the kind. It cannot be squared with contentions that it was not the battle of Austerlitz (some years after his death), but the battle of Jena and before that the storming of the Bastille that inspired Hegel. It cannot be squared, in short, with Joachim Ritter's masterful 1956 portrayal of the revolutionary Hegel, the Hegel that saw the French Revolution as the historical realisation of the Kantian idea of moral autonomy and thus as the culmination of the history of the world as the history of liberty. It cannot be squared with the Hegel that entrusted the institutional protection of this Kantian autonomy to the state, or at least to an idea (or Idea) of the State as the ultimate embodiment of the world-historical advance of human liberty.[96]

Hegel's subjection of the particularity of the (material) pursuits of civil society to the universalism embodied in the institutions of the (ideal) state is the core of his political and legal philosophy. Ritter makes it abundantly clear that Hegel's endorsement of the universalism of the French Revolution did not concern a subjection of the particular pursuits of the state to the universalist concerns of citizens, as one might think. Quite to the contrary, it concerned the subjection of the particular pursuits of citizens in civil society to the universalist ideals of the revolution.[97] For Hegel, the private sphere, or civil society, ultimately posed the gravest danger to the Kantian ethics of moral autonomy that, according to him, was the very telos or aim of world history. The French Revolution and the rise of the constitutional state were, for him, the historical embodiment of this world

95 Cf. Wolfgang Welsch, Hegel und die analytische Philosphie, http://www2.uni-jena.de/welsch/Hegel%20Analytik.pdf.

96 Ritter, "Hegel und die französische Revolution," 183–255.

97 Ibid, 219–233.

historical idea of freedom in his own time. But he was percipient enough to realise that this idea was as much threatened as it was realised in the times he lived. And the principal threat to moral autonomy, he believed at the time he was writing, did not come from the state, but from civil society. He saw civil society as the gruesome power that would ultimately destroy all freedom. As he put it:

> "Civil society is the monstrous power that ties the human being to itself. It demands of the human being that it works for it and that it does everything for and through it."
>
> "When civil society functions without constraints, it becomes completely self-enclosed and locked into a process of increasing population and industrialisation. The reduction of all human relations to needs and to the means to provide for these needs, increases the hoarding of wealth, on the one hand, and the atomisation and insulation of specific labour as well as the dependence and need of the labouring classes, on the other. From this ultimately results the inability to enjoy the liberties and especially the spiritual benefits of civil society."[98]

It is not necessary that one reconcile Haym's and Ritter's interpretations of Hegel. It is also not necessary for present purposes to decide which vision is the more accurate one. Much more instructive would be to contemplate the profundity of Hegel's elegiac suggestion that felicitous human communication (reason) is a function of fatigue and a product of old age. When one begins to grasp the depth of this insight, one not only begins to grasp the function of state coercion, but also why modernity wrested constructions of coercion from feudal rulers so as to entrust them to the centralised and bureaucratised corridors of state authority. The owls of Minerva begin their flight when the exuberant cruelty of youth, to which Nietzsche still clung so melancholically,[99] has grown old and

---

98 G.W.F. Hegel, *Grundlinien der Philosophie des Rechts* in *Werke in 20 Bänden*, Vol. VII, (Frankfurt a. M: Suhrkamp Verlag 1970), 386, 389: "Die bürgerliche Gesellschaft ist vielmehr die ungeheure Macht, die den Menschen an sich reißt, von ihm fordert, daß er für sie arbeite und daß er alles durch sie und vermittels ihrer tue." "Wenn die bürgerliche Gesellschaft sich in ungehinderter Wirksamkeit befindet, ist sie innerhalb ihrer selbst in *fortschreitender Bevölkerung* und *Industrie* begriffen. Durch die *Verallgemeinerung* des Zusammenhangs der Menschen durch ihre Bedürfnisse und der Weisen, die Mittel für diese zu bereiten und herbeizubringen, vermehrt sich die *Anhäufung der Reichtümer* ... auf der einen Seite, wie auf der andern Seite die *Vereinzelung* und *Beschränktheit* der besonderen Arbeit und damit die *Abhängigkeit* und *Not* der an diese Arbeit gebundenen Klasse, womit die Unfähigkeit der Empfindung und des Genusses der weiteren Freiheiten und besonders der geistigen Vorteile der bürgerlichen Gesellschaft zusammenhängt." Cf. hereto also Ritter "Hegel und die französische Revolution," 232.

99 Friedrich Nietzsche, *Zur Genealogie der Moral* in *Sämtliche Werke, Kritische Studienausgabe*, vol. V (Berlin: Walter de Gruyter, 1999).

grey.[100] The ascent and consolidation of centralised structures of government reflect the extent to which the disorderly exuberance of feudal and ancient oppression and cruelty has yielded to a sedentary desire for routine security. Much talk is going around today regarding the end of the modern era of centralised state authority, much of it also in the name of Luhmann.[101] Suffice it to respond to this talk about the end of the state by observing that centralised state authorities will probably survive as long as the perception persists that individuals have more to fear from one another than they have from routine and centralised structures of government. Already in pre-modern times were the centralised jurisdictions of Royal courts perceived as a safeguard against the avarice and caprice of so many princes.[102] Hegel's early *Ständeschrift* also pivoted on this insight.[103]

100 G. W. F. Hegel, *Grundlinien der Philosophie des Rechts*, 28: "Wenn die Philosophie ihr Grau in Grau malt, dann ist eine Gestalt des Lebens alt geworden, und mit Grau und Grau lässt sie sich nicht verjüngen, sondern nur erkennen; die Eule der Minerva beginnt erst mit der einbrechenden Dämmerung ihren Flug."

101 Cf. Teubner, "Des Königs viele Leiber. Die Selbstdekonstruktion der Hierarchie des Rechts," 252; Teubner, Globale Zivilverfassungen: Alternative zur staatszentrierten Verfassungstheorie, *Zeitschrift für ausländisches öffentliches Recht und Völkerrecht*, 63 (2003): 1–28; Teubner, Globale Privatregimes: Neo-spontanes Recht und duale Sozialverfassungen in der Weltgesellschaft, in *Zur Autonomie des Individuums*, ed. Dieter Simon/Manfred Weiss (Baden-Baden: Nomos Verlagsgesellschaft, 2000), 437–453; Gunther Teubner, "Societal Constitutionalism: Alternatives to State-Centred Constitutional Theory?" in *Transnational Governance and Constitutionalism*, ed. Christian Joerges, Inger-Johanne Sand, and Gunther Teubner, International Studies in the Theory of Private Law (Oxford: Hart Publishing, 2004), 3–28; Gunther Teubner, "Fragmented Foundations: Societal Constitutionalism beyond the Nation State," in *The Twilight of Constitutionalism?*, ed. Martin Loughlin and Petra Dobner (Oxford: Oxford University Press, 2010), 327–341; Christensen and Fischer-Lescano, *Das Ganze des Rechts*, 21. For a firm statement that it is not the erosion of the national state but only of the Keynesian welfare national state that is at issue in the process of globalisation and transnationalisation, cf. Bob Jessop, *The Future of the Capitalist State* (Cambridge: Polity Press, 2002), 210–213. For a forceful critique of Teubner's conception of societal constitutionalisation from one who is surely not unsympathetic to Teubner's work, cf. Emilios Christodoulidis, "On the Politics of Societal Constitutionalism" *Indiana Journal of Global Legal Studies* 20 (2013): 629–663; "A Default Constitutionalism? Some Cautionary Remarks on the Many Constitutions of Europe," in *The Many Constitutions of Europe*, ed. Kaarlo Tuori and Suvi Sankari (Farnham: Ashgate, 2013), 31–48.

102 Cf. Chris Thornhill, *A Sociology of Constitutions: Constitutions and State Legitimacy in Historical-Sociological Perspective*, Cambridge Studies in Law and Society (Cambridge: Cambridge University Press, 2011). Thornhill is also a close reader of Luhmann, but the course of thinking that he develops in this book, differs remarkably from the anti-statism of the "societal constitutionalisation" line of thinking that Teubner develops. As I have shown more extensively elsewhere – cf. Van der Walt, "Abdications of Sovereignty in Horizontal Effect Jurisprudence," (forthcoming), Thornhill relies on a Luhmannian analysis to trace the remarkable consolidation and expansion of centralised state powers and public law that resulted from the coupling of

And *Grundrechte als Institution*, one must add, in the final analysis comes round to making a point that is hardly distinguishable from Hegel's concern with the sovereign responsibility of the centralised state. Its anti-Hegelian thrust, we shall see presently, ultimately unravels dramatically.

Luhmann's rejection of the horizontal effect of constitutional rights, his rejection of the state's positive duties regarding constitutional rights, one can see now, is fully consistent with his dismissal of Hegel's conviction that civil society should justify itself to the state, instead of the state justifying itself to civil society. It is fully consistent with his inversion of Hegel's position on this point. However, Luhmann's own refined position on the function of fundamental rights ultimately commits him to invert his own position as well. He ultimately comes round to endorsing a position that can hardly be distinguished from the Hegelian position he rejected (or inverted).

Constitutional rights are not expressions of values, argues Luhmann. They function. They organise autonomous social spheres in which the systemic articulation of individual personality (shielded by personal dignity and liberty rights) and wealth (shielded by property rights) become possible. In the process, however, they also rid the political system of excessive burdens and excessive complexity. And in doing so, they actually contribute to the functional integration of the political system. To the same extent that they constrain the state, they also empower it.[104] Constitutional rights have the double effect of empowering, not only the claimants of rights, but also the political system that has to observe their claims. There can be little doubt that Luhmann is indeed convinced of the deep rationality apparent in the mutual and reciprocal benefits of this logic of functional differentiation. But this two-directional thrust is ultimately exactly what ruins his anti-Hegelian position. For if constitutional rights, according to the double logic of systemic differentiation, simultaneously constrain and empower the state, they not only subject the state to limits but also and simultaneously burden it with duties. And Luhmann recognises this in the clearest terms:

---

governmental power with fundamental rights discourses. This line of thought is also central to Thornhill's argument in "The Future of the State" in *The Financial Crisis in Constitutional Perspective: The Dark Side of Functional Differentiation*, ed. Poul Kjaer et al, Oxford, Hart Publishing, 2011, 357–394. Thornhill here again forcefully makes the point that the state will survive as long as the concern with fundamental rights survives.

103 Cf. Ritter, "Hegel und die französische Revolution," 206.

104 Luhmann, *Grundrechte als Institution*, 140 and especially 146: "[D]urch die Institutionalisierung der Entscheidungsverbindlichkeit als gängiges Symbol, das im sozialen Verkehr fraglos und routenemässig akzeptiert wird, wächst die Legitimität der staatlichen Entscheidungstätigkeit." Cf. also Thornhill, *A Sociology of Constitutions: Constitutions and State Legitimacy in Historical-Sociological Perspective*, 162–168.

> "Fundamental rights aim to safeguard liberty against the state. This presupposes, however, the prior creation of an oppositional monopoly as far as threats to liberty are concerned. Without such a monopolisation of threats to liberty, the protection of rights would forever be groping in thin air. It would never attain to positive results. It would never manage to effectively secure liberty. The reality that the state is the precondition of all liberty remains constantly forgotten. The state nevertheless does not condition or precondition liberty because of the way it ensures the realisation of liberty, however incomplete or preliminary this realisation may be. It preconditions liberty because the way its decision-making programme and organisational framework subjects liberty to rational regulation. In doing so, the state gathers up the potential threat to liberty that otherwise would continue to exist diffusely and intangibly in society. Thus does it make the question of liberty decidable, which can result in loss or gains of liberty in specific cases."[105]

"I rest my case," the grey old philosopher with the wary and weary eyes would have observed. It is indeed Ritter's Hegel who speaks through these lines, the Hegel whom Luhmann – at least in *Grundrechte als Institution* – understood clearly but refused to follow. It is surely also the Hohfelds and Schwabes of this world who speak here. Both Hohfeld and Schwabe, we saw in the first chapters of this book, basically heaped the myriad of diffuse and unpredictable ways in which private individuals can come to threaten one another's *fundamental* rights (*private* law rights suffice to deal with the distinct and predictable threats) on the shoulders of the state where they can be identified, assessed and processed properly.

That Luhmann would ultimately basically come to embrace the Hegel that he dismissed was ironically on the cards from the moment he commenced to wield the double-sided logic of his concept of integration and differentiation. This double-sided logic basically also committed him to the Hohfeldian and Schwabian positions regarding state action and horizontal effect with which Chapters Three and Four engaged, notwithstanding his own dismissal of horizontal effect. If constitutional rights are grasped as institutions of functional differentiation that empower the state as much as they constrain it, that is, if constitutional rights are understood to empower the state through constraining it, the idea is clearly that the state is not just at liberty to act in accordance with this constrain-

---

105 Luhmann, *Grundrechte als Institution*, 57," (fully quoted in German in Chapter Three above, fn. 65). Cf. also at 16: "Die Spezialisierung des politischen Systems auf Problementscheidungsaufgaben bedeutet einerseits eine funktionale Spezifikation, also einen Funktionsverlust gegenüber älteren weniger differenzierten Sozialordnungen; anderseits – und das ist kein Widerspruch, sondern gerade das Kenzeichen dieser Umstrukturierung – eine gewaltige Steigerung der Staatsaufgaben und des Staatseinflusses. Denn in einer differenzierten Sozialordnung entwickeln sich zahlreiche Spannungen und ein solcher Alternativenreichtum, daß in allen Sphären der Gesellschaft mehr Probleme durch Entscheidung gelöst werden müssen."

ing empowerment or empowering constraint, it is constitutionally required, or better, *constitutionally constrained* to do so. The fine logic that Luhmann develops basically erases the distinction between empowerment and constraint. If constitutional rights have the double-sided quality of negatively constraining and positively empowering the state, the empowering at issue is evidently also defined by the constraining.

The state thus constrained/empowered is not just constrained by the demand not to violate or abridge constitutional rights, it is also constrained by the demand not to allow these rights to be violated and abridged. This may not be the necessary implication of ordinary logic and language, but it surely seems to be the implication of the sophisticated double-edged conception of system formation that Luhmann has in mind. And it is exactly here that Luhmann appears to meet Hohfeld. One is not at liberty to act in compliance with a duty, Hohfeld teaches us. One is obliged to do so. If the state's empowerment is defined and indeed constrained by such double-sided constitutional constraints, it is not at liberty to act or not to act according to its empowerment. Constitutional constraints thus necessarily constrain both the acts and omissions of the state. They thus necessarily entail constitutional duties. And this double constraint/duty, we have seen from the first chapters of this book, is the fulcrum on which the horizontal effect of fundamental rights turns.

Luhmann's implicit endorsement of the Hohfeldian/Schwabian point elaborated in Chapters Three and Four turns on his clear insight into the immediate connection between the constraints on and empowerment of the state. The moment of constitutional constraints is the moment of constitutional empowerments. The exceptional clarity that Luhmann brings to the table on this point contributes much to a consistent understanding of the horizontal effect of fundamental rights that he dismisses so vociferously. The contribution that he makes in this regard concerns the incisive sociological explanation of the uninterrupted sovereignty without which, we saw in the first chapters of this book, horizontal effect cannot be understood properly.

In short, Luhmann himself ultimately comes round to affirming a conception of the state that is not just constrained to respect fundamental rights, but also constrained to enforce fundamental rights because of this obligatory respect. And it is exactly with regard to this point that certain Luhmannian conceptions of societal constitutionalisation miss something essential. The constitutions that emerge from these processes of social constitutionalisation are considered to be independent of national state constitutions. A case in point is the theory of social constitutionalisation that Gunther Teubner proposes. Dieter Grimm's recent response to Teubner's proposition in this regard explains well what is at stake here and we shall turn to it presently. Let us first retrace our steps for a moment.

The different sections of this chapter have thus far elaborated reflections on the *de jure* retention but *de facto* loss of Member State sovereignty (section II), ordo-liberalism and the deistic/deontological conception of sovereignty that drives the process of market integration (section III) and the dispersal of sovereignty concomitant to the rise of systems of private governance that are likewise informed by the ordo-liberal insistence to keep politics out of economic competition (section IV). Considered together, these reflections tell the story of significant interruptions of sovereignty in Europe. One could assess this interruption as an interim phenomenon that marks a phase of "sovereignty in transition" in the wake of which uninterrupted sovereignty will eventually settle again. Sovereignty can accordingly either settle again as simple Member State sovereignty after an eventual demise and dissolution of federal conceptions of European integration. Or sovereignty can eventually settle again as the sovereignty of a federal European state.

One may also, on the other hand, come to assess the current interruptions of sovereignty as preludes to a more conclusive termination of sovereignty in the wake of which modern political systems may well give way again to forms of government akin to the exercise of political power in feudal Europe.[106] Should this

---

106 I have argued before that the state sovereignty presupposed by proper horizontal effect constitutes a resistance to returns of feudalism and all sorts of neo-feudalism in contemporary forms of government. Cf. Van der Walt "Rethinking the Fundamental Structures of the State with Reference to the Horizontal Application of Fundamental Rights" in *Der grundrechtsgeprägte Verfassungsstaat. Festschrift für Klaus Stern zum 80. Geburtstag*, ed. Michael Sachs et al, (Berlin: Duncker & Humblot, 2012), 627–648; Van der Walt, "Blixen's Difference: Horizontal Application of Fundamental Rights and the Resistance to Neo-Colonialism," *Journal for South African Law* no. 2 (2003): 311–331. For a forceful recent articulation of this argument, cf. Alain Supiot, "The Public–private Relation in the Context of Today's Refeudalization," *International Journal of Constitutional Law* 11, no. 1 (January 1, 2013): 129–145. The argument is not new though. Several of the authors associated with the American realists and sociological movements in jurisprudence in the early 20th century already employed the notion of a "return to feudalism" to describe the increasing delegation of governmental powers to private corporations. Cf. in this regard, Roscoe Pound, "The New Feudalism," *American Bar Association Journal* 10 (1930): 553; Roscoe Pound, "Liberty of Contract," *The Yale Law Journal* 18, no. 7 (May 1, 1909): 454–487; Morris R. Cohen, "Property and Sovereignty," *Cornell Law Quarterly* 13 (1928 1927): 8–30; Robert L. Hale, "Coercion and Distribution in a Supposedly Non-Coercive State," *Political Science Quarterly* 38, no. 3 (September 1, 1923): 470–494; Robert L. Hale, *Freedom through Law: Public Control of Private Governing Power* (New York: Columbia University Press, 1952). For an illuminating discussion of these works, cf. William J. Novak, "Public-Private Governance: A Historical Introduction," in *Government by Contract: Outsourcing and American Democracy*, ed. Jody Freeman and Martha Minow (Cambridge, Massachusetts: Harvard University Press, 2009), 23–40, especially at 34–35. Cf. also in this regard Daphne Barak-Erez, "Civil Rights in the Privatized State: A Comparative View," *Anglo-American Law Review* 28 (1999): 503–524.

possibility materialise, territorial sovereignty may well enter an epoch of far-reaching fragmentation and competences of government will again become personal or corporate as they were during much of pre-modern Europe. The major achievement of modernity, the achievement of modern states to wrest power from multiple powerful subjects (or multiple subjects of power as Foucault might have put it) would have become undone again. These multiple powerful subjects, either personal or corporate, would again come to vie with one another for territorial control or influence at the expense of any attempt to construct formalised systems of law that pivot on principles of general legislation and universalization. The Hegelian aspiration to subject the endless competition and concurrency of particular interests to the universalising demands of centralised states would then only be remembered as the dream that marked the Kantian imagination of an ancient modernity.

This apocalyptic vision of the demise of uninterrupted territorial sovereignty is unfounded or ill founded, some would say. One can imagine Gunther Teubner among them. This apocalyptic vision, one can imagine him saying, stems from a logo-centric melancholy that resists the radical democratic and micro-historical (as opposed to grand-historical) proliferation of societal constitutionalisation processes.[107] Constitution-making no longer requires modernity's conception of centralised state constitutions to establish functional legal systems, his argument might continue. The systems of law that will result or are already resulting from "deconstructive" processes of societal constitutionalisation are well capable of salvaging modernity's normative heritage. They are as capable of maintaining operative differentiations between primary and secondary law in terms of which the latter orders (codifies) the former so as to provide for adequate review and transformation processes. Nothing need therefore be feared from these poli-centric systems of law that will and are coming to displace state centred visions of law.

Teubner assesses the processes of societal constitutionalisation at issue here as historical processes of radical deconstruction that take leave of the transcendentalisms (hospitality, the gift, justice, forgiveness) that still burden Derridean deconstruction. There is an adventurous Nietzschean spirit afoot in the radical deconstruction of modern constitutionalism that Teubner contemplates. And yes, one should concede to this youthful Nietzschean deconstructivist that Derrida – the thinker who first taught us deconstruction – retained considerable el-

107 Cf. again Teubner, "Des Königs viele Leiber," 251–2. For a more incisive engagement with the problems that attach to this constitutional fragmentation and poli-centric constitutionalisation to which we shall also return below, cf. again Teubner, "Fragmented Foundations: Societal Constitutionalism beyond the Nation State," 327–41.

ements of old Hegel in his thinking – enough to be well aware of the remaining emancipatory potential of state structures and the universality of formal law; *and* well aware of the terror that lurks in the resistance to these universalist claims of the state and modern rule of law.[108]

"This concession figures," one can imagine Teubner responding. It reflects the very remnants of logo-centrism in Derridean deconstruction that Luhmannian "deconstruction" seeks to overcome.[109] One would hope, however, that the Hegelian Luhmann constructed above might complicate Teubner's vision somewhat. There are other system theorists around who do seem to grasp the "Hegel" in Luhmann well.[110] However, let us return to Grimm for a crystal clear statement of the concerns that may well have informed Derrida's Hegelian caveat regarding the emancipatory potential of states in the time of globalisation.

Societal constitutions (*Zivilverfassungen*), argues Grimm, ultimately pivot on a set of private norms and rationality criteria that reflect exclusively their own particular or sectorial interests. They heed or consider concerns of others – concerns of other particular sectors or general concerns of the social whole – only to the extent that these concerns affect their own interests.[111] Against this background, democratic perspectives on the resolution of conflicts that exceed concerns with sectorial interests become highly unlikely. Teubner is not unaware of this problem, concedes Grimm. He envisages an evolutionary system of co-operation between intra-systemic control mechanisms and arbitrators, on the one hand, and the legal and judicial systems of international organisations and national states. At issue for Teubner, is a transnational legal order that maintains a

---

108 Jacques Derrida, *L'autre Cap* (Paris: Les Éditions de Minut, 1991), 39: "[C]ar il peut même arrive, on peut l'espérer prudemment, que dans certains cas de vieilles structures étatiques nous aident à lutter contre des empires privés et transnationaux[.]" And at 76: "Le *même devoir* dicte de respecter la difference, l'idiome, la minorité, la singularité, mais aussi l'universalité du droit formel, le désir de traduction, l'accord et l'univocité, la loi de la majorité, l'opposition au racisme, au nationalisme, à la xenophobie."

109 Teubner, "Des Königs viele Leiber," 244: "Der dekonstruktiven Tanz, wenn es ihn den gibt, mag seine Lahmung überwinden ... wenn Dekonstruktion selbst dekonstruiert werden kann." For an instructive and truly exquisite comparison (*Auseinandersetzung*, rather) of systems theory and deconstruction, cf. also Teubner, "Ökonomie und Gabe – Positivität der Gerechtigkeit: Gegenseitige Heimsuchungen von System und Différance," in *Widerstände der Systemtheorie – Kulturtheoretische Analysen zum Werk von Niklas Luhmann*, ed. Albrecht Koschorke and Cornelia Vismann (Berlin: Akademie Verlag, 1999), 199–212.

110 Thornhill's narrative in *A sociology of Constitutions* parches from the theory of functional differentiation precisely the genesis of a universal or universalizing public law and constitutionalism that extracted itself from the particularities of medieval hierarchies. And this line of thinking is also evident in Luhmann. Cf. again fn. 104 above.

111 Dieter Grimm, *Die Zukunft der Verfassung II* (Frankfurt a.M: Suhrkamp, 2012), 310.

loose coherence of fragmented and partial legal orders (*fragmentierten Teilrechtsordnungen*). And it is on this loose coherence of partial legal orders in a transnational order, comments Grimm, that Teubner relies to subject the system-egoistic pursuit of particular interests to appropriate limits.[112]

In the final analysis, argues Grimm, Teubner correctly recognises the participation of national states in this loose coherence of transnational legal orders, but underestimates the pivotal role that they play in holding the whole order together. None of the private legal orders that take part in this transnational legal order command the coercive powers required for making this order functional (*in der fragmentierten globalen Zivilgesellschaft gibt es per se keine Zwangvollstreckung*). This also applies to the European Union, which constitutes one of the most integrated transnational legal systems of the kind Teubner envisages;[113] hence Grimm's Hegelian assessment of Teubner's vision of transnational law: It is ultimately not so devoid of state law as Teubner suggests.[114] It can ultimately only work in the shadow of public authority – "*[n]ur im Schatten der öffentlichen Gewalt hat er eine begrenzte Wirkungschance.*"[115] "Under these circumstances," argues Grimm, system theoretical enthusiasm for transnational functional differentiation "should not be too inclined to sacrifice the state ... Despite evidence of erosion, national states still offer the best chance for the modern achievement of constitutional government."[116]

Grimm's analysis of Teubner's system theoretical conception of social constitutionalisation shows clearly why social constitutionalisation cannot be offered as a panacea for current interruptions of sovereignty in Europe. Social constitutionalisation is evidently itself dependent on the sovereignty that it seeks to replace. The fundamental problem that the system theoretical analysis of the social whole in terms of spontaneous functional differentiation fails to take seriously is the need for legitimate coercion – the need to enforce the law against the will of interested parties for the sake and in the name of the sovereign's conception of a general public good. As Grimm points out well, the factional or sectorial interests of social systems are, in the final analysis, vehicles of private interest. As such, they must in principle always remain subject to scrutiny as far as their compliance with fundamental principles of law is concerned. Not on one count and not for one minute can they legitimately claim exemption from the possibility of such scrutiny.

112 Ibid, 311.
113 Ibid.
114 Ibid.
115 Ibid, 312.
116 Ibid.

Teubner recognises some role for national sates in the interplay between transnational orders, observes Grimm. His point is that Teubner does nevertheless not appreciate the crucial role that actual or potential law enforcement by states play in making this interplay possible. This assessment is cogent. Much of the polemical strength of Teubner's theory of social constitutionalisation would simply evaporate if he would too obviously concede that the whole discourse ultimately depends on statal enforcement of law and constitutional rights. But this concession does slip into his discourse despite his best attempts to keep it out. This is abundantly clear in a 2010 essay that once again explains the proliferation of social constitutions and the marginalisation of state law in the time of globalisation.

The essay addresses the question of harm and injury that may result from the competing maximisations of systemic rationalities concomitant to these processes of social constitutionalisation. Teubner starts off by arguing, as Frank Michelman also does, that ordinary constitutional review will be of little significance in this context because of the insignificant role national states play in these processes of social constitutionalisation.[117] He then turns to the question whether one can take recourse to the horizontal effect of constitutional rights to address the harm and injury that may ensue from the maximisation of systemic rationalities. At first his answer appears to be a rather confident "no," because horizontal effect review of fundamental rights would either have to turn the conflict into a question of state responsibility again, or address it as a conflict between two private legal subjects. Neither of the two options would work, argues Teubner. The former cannot work because the state is not involved in the conflict, and the latter cannot work because the parties to the conflict can no longer be identified as legal subjects.

The anonymous processes of system formation at issue here, asserts Teubner with regard to the latter problem, do not have the profiles of personal identities or legal subjects. The problem comes to a head for him with the following question: "[C]an fundamental rights ever be asserted against the structural violence of anonymous social processes?" And it is here, in the response that he offers that he not only admits to the crucial role of the state in addressing the question, but also seems to acknowledge the problem is not much of a problem after all. As predicted above, any recognition of state responsibility in the redress of systemic harm would divest his argument of whatever polemic force it may have ap-

117 Cf. Teubner, "Fragmented Foundations: Societal Constitutionalism beyond the Nation State," 327. Frank Michelman forwarded a similar argument some years earlier. Cf. Michelman, "W(h)ither the Constitution?" 1063–1083.

peared to have. And this is exactly what happens when Teubner moves to answer the question he has posed.

What must one do to redress the problem of systemic harm according to Teubner? *One must resort to civil litigation in courts of law.* And there can be no doubt that the courts he has in mind are state courts, for he proceeds to ask how this litigation can be processed in a way that would address the problem of anonymous systemic harm, on the one hand, and satisfy the doctrinal demands of the black letter lawyers who work in these state courts, on the other. The answer, contends Teubner, lies in *suing an institution.* In the end, this is all there is to it. Let us nevertheless here it from Teubner himself:

> "[C]an fundamental rights ever be asserted against the structural violence of anonymous social processes? The only way this can happen is to use individual suits against private actors to thematise conflicts in which human rights of individuals are asserted against structural violence of the matrix. In more traditional terms, the institutional conflict that is really meant has to take place within individual forms of action... Translated into the language of law, this becomes a problem of attribution: Who dunnit? Under what conditions can the concrete violation of integrity be attributed not to persons but to collective actors, or to anonymous communication processes? If this attribution could be achieved, the genuine problematic of human rights would have been formulated even in the impoverished rights talk of the law. In an extreme simplification, the 'horizontal' human rights problematic can perhaps be described in more familiar legal categories as follows: the problem of human rights in private law arises only where the endangerment of body-mind integrity comes from social 'institutions' (and not just from individual actors). In principle, institutions include private formal organisations and private regulatory systems. The most important examples here would be business firms, private associations, hospitals, schools, and universities, as formal organisations on the one hand; and general terms of trade, private standardisation, and similar rule-setting mechanisms as private regulatory systems on the other ... The concept of the institution could accordingly re-specify fundamental rights in social sectors. The outcome would be a formula of 'third party effect' which could seem plausible also to a black letter-lawyer. It would regard horizontal effect no longer as balancing between the fundamental rights of individual bearers, but instead as the protection of human rights and rights of discourses vis-à-vis expansive social institutions."[118]

The black letter lawyers that Teubner invokes here may well wonder what it is that he finds so complicated here. Litigation against institutions would not strike any relatively capable lawyer as a particularly novel enterprise. What is it then that the systems theorist finds so particularly challenging as far as this litigation against social institutions is concerned? Is it the difficulty of identifying the perpetrator, the "who dunnit?" difficulty, as he puts it? Teubner has already stepped

---

118 Teubner, "Fragmented Foundations: Societal Constitutionalism beyond the Nation State," 339.

down considerably in this passage from the extra-terrestrial discourse that often characterises system theory, but he needs to step down a bit more if the "who dunnit?" question is bothering him this much. What, after all, is one talking about when one talks about horizontal effect of fundamental rights? One is talking about the violation of fundamental rights. A fundamental right is not the kind of thing that can easily be violated anonymously, not for long in any case. One can imagine a once-off assaulter of psychological or bodily integrity fleeing the scene without having been identified, but a serial assaulter is very unlikely to remain unidentified for long in a state where the sovereign runs a half-decent police force. And the institutional assault on physical or psychological integrity that Teubner has in mind is much like a serial assault.

The systemic assault that is at issue for him is likely to endure in time (unless brought to book). And even if this institutional harm is of a once-off kind, the institutional perpetrator itself is surely not something that is that capable of simply "fleeing the scene." We are talking, after all, about entities with well-developed "social constitutions." So all that is required to get on with the task of suing Teubner's corporate violator of human rights is the constitutional will of a sovereign state to bring fundamental rights violations to book, wherever these violations may occur. System theorists, we know now, have the penchant to dismiss the applicability of the crude fundamental rights normativity of national state constitutions (the impoverished language of rights, Teubner calls it in the passage above) in the folds of finely calibrated functional differentiations. But on this occasion, they themselves have come knocking at the door of the state – the door of the state's courts – for purposes of redressing violations of human dignity and integrity. They would seem to have come to acknowledge after all, that the Jurassic old state still offers the only door to knock on when fundamental rights violations are at stake.

"At long last," might one want to add, but this would not be right, for Luhmann, at least, already acknowledged this long ago in a passage that we have already quoted twice. It is apposite to quote a part of this passage again in response to Teubner's "who-dunnit?" question. The "who-dunnit?" problem, the problem of giving a recognisable profile to potential human rights violations, is exactly the one that prompted Luhmann to identify the state as the precondition for any protection of human rights:

> "[T]he state gathers up the potential threat to liberty that otherwise would continue to exist diffusely and intangibly in society. Thus does it make the question of liberty decidable, which can result in loss or gains of liberty in specific cases."[119]

---

119 Luhmann, *Grundrechte als Institution*, 57. Cf. also again the passage quoted in fn. 105 above.

This does not mean to say the capacity of state sovereignty to perform this task of safeguarding the liberty of citizens is not in question in the times of ever increasing globalisation and privatisation in which we find ourselves. Systems theorists should nevertheless not feel vindicated by this reality. They should not relish it. They should be as concerned and alarmed about it as anyone else who is concerned about the liberty, integrity and dignity of human existence.[120] The crisis and the task that we are facing can hardly be articulated better than Fabrizio Cafaggi articulates it in the following poignant passage:

> "[Transnational private regulation] regimes are sector specific and often represent conflicting interests at the global level. These include conflicts between industry and NGOs and trade unions, between large multinational corporations and small suppliers that require co-ordination and rules. Often domestic courts have provided techniques to define the boundaries and the jurisdiction over regulated entities and to secure compliance with democratic principles. Still these regimes – whose regulatory effects go well beyond the sphere of the regulator, encompassing regulated entities and beneficiaries that did not voluntarily opt in at the time of drafting – pose serious accountability challenges. They challenge states' sovereignty when regulating matters traditionally subject to domestic legislation. Their private nature limits the scope for judicial review by domestic courts and often allows escape from accountability mechanisms deployed in the domestic arena. Those challenges require normative responses that call for changes in the governance of private regulators and in the regulatory process to enhance voice and exit options for regulatory beneficiaries."[121]

---

120 Some signs of such concern seem to be emerging from the essays in Poul Kjaer et al, ed., *The Financial Crisis in Constitutional Perspective: The Dark Side of Functional Differentiation*, (Oxford; Portland, Oregon: Hart Publishing, 2011). In his contribution to this volume, Teubner proposes a mixture of external social pressures and internal experimentation as a way out of the malaise of functional differentiation that became manifest with the global financial crisis. The needed reforms will have to come from within the capillary processes of social and economic constitutionalisation themselves, for external interventions will simply not be able to address the complexities of the malfunctioning that has become evident. But the reforms will probably only commence as a response to external pressures, argues Teubner, and among these he expressly recognises the significance of protecting constitutional rights through the recognition of the horizontal effect of these rights. Cf. Gunther Teubner, "A Constitutional Moment? The Logics of 'Hitting the Bottom,'" in *The Financial Crisis in Constitutional Perspective: The Dark Side of Functional Differentiation*, ed. Poul F Kjaer, Gunther Teubner, and Alberto Febbrajo (Oxford; Portland, Oregon: Hart Publishing, 2011), 18. A reality check surely seems to have left its mark here on the discourse of societal constitutionalisation and functional differentiation, but one's jaw still tends to drop when noticing how much trust this discourse has (at least up to now) been bestowing on the internal ethical self-regulation of insulated social sub-systems. Teubner writes (at 17): "Historically, it was collective bargaining, co-determination, and the right to strike, which enabled new forms of societal dissensus. In today's transnational organisations, ethical committees of conduct fulfil a similar role."

121 Cafaggi, "New Foundations of Transnational Private Regulation," 49.

This is the context within which the thinking about the horizontal effect of fundamental rights and the relation of this horizontal effect to state sovereignty must commence today. It is this context that renders hollow-back doctrinal concerns with distinctions between direct and indirect horizontal application so passé and so critically out of touch with the work that lawyers and legal theorists have to do today. The times in which we live call for incisive thinking about the possibility of coercive enforcement of basic legal norms in all walks of life for the sake of safeguarding basic human liberty, dignity and integrity. A normative jurisprudence that is also a realistic jurisprudence must contemplate law as a coercive linguistic whole. As we have seen in this chapter, and will again see in the next, one can also rely meaningfully on Luhmann for this insight. With some exceptions, however, Luhmannian scholars have nevertheless not contributed much thus far to the work that has to be done in this regard, notwithstanding the remarkable and promising conceptual innovations with which they have enriched the horizontal effect question.

To the contrary, we have seen in this chapter how two very able followers of Luhmann and Teubner, Christensen and Fischer-Lescano, have gone to extraordinary lengths to ignore or deny the coerciveness of law. This is to be lamented, for they surely command highly refined and penetrating conceptual strategies that can contribute much to the critical analyses and thinking that horizontal effect jurisprudence needs today. However, anyone who would want to contribute meaningfully to the jurisprudence of horizontal effect would have to have no illusions about the sacrificial coerciveness of this jurisprudence. Horizontal effect would not have become the problematic field of legal theoretical inquiry had it not been driven by burdensome questions regarding the legitimacy of sovereign coercion.

Chapter Six: Différantial Sovereignty

I Introduction

The conception of the sovereign rule of law in terms of a coercive linguistic whole to which Chapter Five guided us can but need not be invoked to underpin authoritarian exercises of sovereignty. Coercive linguistic systems need not be authoritarian. Not only can they comply fully with the liberty ideals of the Enlightenment. Their coerciveness can serve these ideals and, moreover, have the exclusive end of serving them. The liberty demands of the Enlightenment, articulated in Chapter Five expressly with reference to Kant and Hegel (Ritter's Hegel), and the need to enforce them with coercive sovereignty, is exactly what was at stake in Chapter Five and is at stake again in this chapter.

Section II of this chapter will briefly elaborate this coerciveness of the political ideals of the Enlightenment further, for an understanding of this coerciveness is crucial for a proper grasp of the concept of sovereignty that will be articulated in the rest of the chapter. The key insight that emerges from this elaboration concerns the requirement that the coerciveness of Enlightenment political ideals always remain justified with reference to criteria of minimum and inevitable coercion. Coercion in the name of Enlightenment political ideals must in principle be accompanied by *plausible* and *persuasive* claims that the coercion at stake is absolutely inevitable and limited to an absolute minimum.

Two absolutes are at issue here then, absolute necessity and an absolute minimum. Connecting them both to *plausibility* and *persuasiveness* of course raises enigmatic hermeneutic questions. These questions will receive some attention, but cannot be addressed extensively in what follows. Suffice it to state for now that compliance with the two absolute demands contemplated here – necessity and minimum intrusion – can never be proved. The best that can be achieved in this regard – for instance in procedures of judicial review – is to establish *plausible* compliance with reference to *persuasive* grounds. At issue then are lesser or more modest criteria – not proof but *persuasiveness* and *plausibility*. However, it is exactly with regard to these lesser criteria that current conceptions of indirect horizontal application, currently the predominant understanding of how horizontal effect should take place in many jurisdictions of the worlds, cannot be justified. Turning as they do on vague notions regarding the radiation of constitutional values through all spheres of law, they fall foul of the transparency demanded by the plausibility and persuasiveness at issue here. That this is so is argued in Section III with reference to elements of the jurisprudential thinking that Carl Schmitt would articulate in 1933.

The jurisprudential thought that Schmitt articulated in 1933 is typical of a confidence that a people stands existentially united by constitutional values that inform and infuse every walk of life. In terms quite comparable to that developed by the GFCC in *Lüth* and by Dürig, Schmitt argued that the open principles of law should be utilised to transmit the foundational values of the National Socialist movement throughout the legal system and into every judicial decision. It surely need not be argued extensively here that the kind of jurisprudence and review procedures that Schmitt envisaged for Germany in 1933 stood little chance of offering plausible and persuasive grounds for claiming that its coerciveness complied with the demands of minimum and necessary intrusion. They – the review procedures that Schmitt contemplated and those that actually materialised after 1933 – most likely never even embodied any conscious aspiration to offer such grounds, and if they did, were most likely bound to fail this aspiration dismally and fatally. This is beside the point. Of interest in what follows is this question: Is one necessarily better off with the *form* of the jurisprudence that Schmitt contemplated in this regard when the constitutional values at stake – the *content* of this jurisprudence – are not the *völkische* (ethnic-populist) values that Schmitt endorsed in 1933, but values that are generally associated with cosmopolitan liberalism?

This is the key question posed in Section III to which the answer may well be affirmative, but not without evidently forfeiting all plausible and persuasive claims that one's enforcement of law complies with requirements of minimum and necessary coercion. An overzealous cosmopolitan liberalism may well turn out to be more coercive and intrusive than is necessary for the *sustenance* of the normative ideals of the Enlightenment. The word *sustenance* is emphasised for good reason here. An overzealous cosmopolitanism would be *overzealous* for reasons of striving to fulfil (some or other particular conception) of Enlightenment ideals. Enlightenment ideals can, however, not be fulfilled. They embody a paradoxical structural incapacity as far as complete fulfilment is concerned. They can at best be *sustained*, section III will argue, and the way of sustaining them is to sustain well functioning liberal democracies. There is thus a slippage from Enlightenment ideals to liberal democracy evident in the arguments presented in this chapter. That is inevitable.

The only way to restore the plausibility and persuasiveness of the claim to minimal and inevitable coerciveness, argues Section IV, is to acknowledge that modern societies are divided to such an extent that the enforcement of a set of substantive values in all walks of life, be they *völkisch* or cosmopolitan, is bound to require higher levels of coercion and intrusion than is absolutely necessary to maintain well-functioning liberal democracies. Even predominantly liberal societies need to contend with individuals or groups that are not liberal. Liberal cosmopolitan majorities invariably need to share space with, say, parochial and conservative minorities. These minorities cannot be coerced to live by cosmopolitan values in every aspect of their existence without evidently raising levels of coercion to higher levels than are absolutely necessary to sustain liberal democracy. In order to uphold plausible and persuasive claims to the principle of minimal coercion and intrusion, liberal democracies evidently have to refrain, as far as absolutely possible, from any authoritarian attempt to enforce a truly liberal society on anyone who does not share that particular view of the true society. That is why liberal democratic constitutional jurisprudence in general and liberal democratic horizontal effect jurisprudence in particular need to rethink the key concepts on which they pivot fundamentally. And this rethinking, argues Section IV, can hardly do better than commencing with Kelsen's response to Schmitt and Kelsen's understanding of constitutional democracy in terms of the sustenance of majority-minority relations.

Section V reconnects the Kelsenian insights developed in Section IV directly to the horizontal effect question. It shows that Kelsen's understanding of liberal democracy finds deep echoes in the concept of horizontal effect review that Walter Leisner articulated in his contribution to the German *Drittwirkung* debate. Leisner's understanding of horizontal effect turns on the very principle that Kelsen would highlight as the essence of liberal democratic constitutionalism, namely, the sustenance of majority-minority relations in terms of which democratic majorities obtain their majority status via minorities and vice versa. The consequence of this principle is that majorities may not coerce minorities more than is absolutely necessary and minorities may not constrain majorities more than is absolutely necessary to sustain liberal democracy.

It is for purposes of articulating this Kelsenian and Leisnerian understanding of liberal democratic sovereignty that Section VI proposes the concept of *différantial* sovereignty. At issue in this invocation of *différantial* sovereignty is the Derridean insight into the irreducibly split origination of all "unitary" essences. Essences have no stable core that endows them with nodal or punctual presence. They derive from relations of deference and difference between multiple "unitary" essences (written between scare crows because no unitary essences ultimately escape from the play of differentiation and deference, they all derive *from* this play). "Unitary" essences irreducibly remain functions of deference and difference. There is no essence outside the deferential and differential relationship. To denote this combination of deference and difference Derrida famously invoked the then still neologistic term "*différance*" and it is on the basis of this notion of *différance* that this chapter elaborates the concept of *dif-*

férantial liberal democratic sovereignty.[1] And it does so for purposes of explaining what is at stake in the open coercive totality of liberal democratic sovereignty.

II Coercive Enlightenment Ideals

The Enlightenment language of sovereignty commenced with a clear regard for and acceptance of the coercive potential of sovereignty. The Enlightenment thinkers entertained no illusions regarding the coerciveness of law. It was from Rousseau that we received the clearest possible statement in this regard:

> "In order that the social contract do not become an empty formula, it contains tacitly the obligation that gives power to others to enforce it; so that anyone who would refuse to obey the general will, would be constrained by the whole body [politic]. This can only mean one thing: Those who do not want to be free will be forced to be free."[2]

Those who would want to read an authoritarianism into this passage from the *Contrat Social* should think twice, for the legitimation for the coercive force of the body politic that Rousseau invokes here is thoroughly based on the principles of universalization and reciprocity that Kant and Rawls would articulate later. The categorical moral imperative, proposed Kant, demands conduct of which the maxim could be made a universal law.[3] And the law that would serve this moral imperative, he maintained, would consist in the general [coercive] system of rules with reference to which the arbitrary liberty of *everyone* – die Freiheit der Willkür *eines jeden* – can be reconciled with everyone else's liberty – *jedermanns Freiheit*.[4] According to Rawls' reciprocity principle, the exercise of political power is proper only when we sincerely believe that the reasons

1 Derrida, *Marges de La Philosophie*, 3–29. Derrida derived the concept of différance from the structural linguistic insight (of principally Ferdinand de Saussure) into the way meaning is produced by the difference between linguistic signs (A is A because A is not B or C, etc.) and by the temporal relations of anticipation and postponement between them (A is A because of the ways in which A simultaneously anticipates and postpones B or C, etc.).

2 Freely translated from Jean Jacques Rousseau, *Du Contrat Social* (Paris: Gallimard, 1964), 186: "Afin donc que le pacte social ne soit pas un vain formulaire, il renferme tacitement cet engagement qui seul peut donner de la force aux autres, que quiconque refusera d'obéir à la volonté générale y sera constraint par tout le corps: ce qui ne signifie autre chose sinon qu' on le forcera d'être libre."

3 Kant, "Metaphysik der Sitten," 140; *Grundlegung zur Metaphysik der Sitten*, in *Werke in 10 Bänden*, ed. Wilhelm Weischedel, vol. VI (Darmstadt: Wissenschaftliche Buchgesellschaft, 1983) 51

4 Ibid, 337.

we offer for our political actions may reasonably be accepted by other citizens as a justification of those actions.[5] Rousseau made it abundantly clear in the first books of the *Contrat Social* that the coercive general will is not just the will of the majority of particular wills, but the will of *everyone* – *chacun*.[6] Hegel recognised clearly that Kant's principle of universalization derived from these passages in the *Contrat Social*.[7]

Why would coercion be necessary at all, might one ask, if the general will is the will of everyone? Before we move to answer this question, let us first recall that Rawls too, had no illusions about the coercive force of government, even when based on public reason and the principle of reciprocity:

> "[G]overnment's authority cannot be evaded except by leaving the territory over which it governs, and not always then. That its authority is guided by public reason does not change this."[8]

Rawls clearly does not seem to have entertained the idea that the sovereign coerciveness of law necessarily ruins the ideal of the rule of law. Yet this is exactly the notion that seems to inform Christensen and Fischer-Lescano when they argue that that the imposition of a judicial decision on someone without that person actually agreeing with it as opposed to merely accepting it, ruins the distinction between legitimate and illegitimate force on which the rule of law (*Rechtsstaat*) is based.[9] Luhmann – on whose authority they rely for the communicative or discourse ethics on the basis of which such judicial force would no longer be necessary – nevertheless also appears to have had different views in this regard. "Threats of coercion and naked force is an insufficient basis for government ... and the shrinking of the state to a mere agency of coercion must be avoided," writes Luhmann. "The coercive potential [of the state] must be re-

5 Rawls, *Political Liberalism*, xlvi.

6 Rousseau, *Du Contrat Social*, 195.

7 Hegel, "Vorlesungen über die Geschichte der Philosophie III," in *Werke in 20 Bänden*, vol. XX (Frankfurt a.M: Suhrkamp, 1970), 365, 413.

8 Rawls, *Political Liberalism*, 222.

9 Christensen and Fischer-Lescano, *Das Ganze des Rechts*, 202–203: "[Wenn jede] Entscheidung im Konflikt der Rechtsmeinungen und Lesarten der Normtexte [sich nur noch durch einen Akt der Gewalt, durch das Machtwort fallen ließe, verlöre das juristische Verfahren jede Legitmität]. Die für den Rechsstaat zentrale Unterscheidung von legitimer und illegitimer Gewalt, von guten und schlechten Entscheidungen, würde damit keinen Boden mehr finden." The background to these assertions is their rejection of Lyotard's principle of radical heterogeneity in terms of which common understanding on the basis of which conflicts can actually be resolved (instead of just terminated) are impossible/often not possible. Cf. again the discussion of *Das Ganze des Rechts* in Chapter Five and the unaltered quotation of this passage in fn. 80.

served for emergencies," he continues, but not without adding: "This coercive potential is nevertheless indispensible because there are always people who do not accept the authority of government dutifully and voluntarily" – "*[Das Zwangspotential des Staates bleibt freilich unentbehrlich] ... [denn] es [gibt Menschen], welche die Herrschaft nicht freiwillig-pflichtmässig akzeptieren.*"[10]

Whence then this paradox? Why this need for force when the will of everyone is contemplated in this Enlightened or liberal democratic exercise of force? If no one really dissents, who is there to coerce? This is the old question that never ceases to haunt Rousseau's paradox and the Kantian and Hegelian conceptions of law. The criminal is not executed, he commits suicide, *es ist die Tat des Seinigen*, Hegel insisted.[11] The sense of paradox that prevails here, stems from the failure to distinguish between the transcendental *idea* of law articulated in the constructions of Rousseau, Kant and Hegel, on the one hand, and the empirical reality of the law, on the other. It is a fact of earthly existence that Rousseau's "will of everyone" is hardly ever and very likely never the actual empirical will of everyone. The will of everyone is an idea or idealistic construction, the actual substance of which probably does not exist and, even if it did, could not be known; hence the inevitability of interminable disagreement and contestation, and deep conflict regarding these contents; hence also the frequent need for sovereign and coercive terminations of this contestation and conflict. The liberal democratic signifier – the freedom of everyone – indeed remains empty (devoid of any signified) as Claude Lefort puts it well,[12] but this emptiness does not absolve liberal democratic sovereignty from the responsibility to exercise power coercively. It is exactly the emptiness of the liberal democratic signifier that founds that responsibility and demands it. Only if lasting empirical agreement (signifiers replete with stable content) regarding all matters of governmental importance were to become an earthly reality, would the use of force become superfluous and, of course, illegitimate. The idea that the emptiness of the liberal democratic signifier would proscribe the exercise of coercive power – more or

---

10 Luhmann, *Grundrechte als Institution*, 141–143.

11 Hegel, *Grundlinien der Philosophie des Rechts, Werke in 20 Bänden*, VII: 374: "[Strafe is nicht mehr nur zufällige Vergeltung durch die Rache, aber die] Versöhnung des Rechts mit sich selbst und durch Aufheben des Verbrechens sich selbst wiederherstellende und damit als *gültig verwirklichende Gesetze*, und in subjektiver Rücksicht des Verbrechers als *seines von ihm gewussten* und für ihn und *zu seinem Schutze gültigen Gesetzes*, in dessen Vollstreckung an ihm er somit selbst die Befriedigung der Gerechtigkeit, nur die Tat *des Seinigen* findet." (text somewhat adjusted for the sake of brevity).

12 Claude Lefort, *L'Invention Démocratique: Les Limites de la Domination Totalitaire* (Paris: Fayard, Artheme, Librairie, 1994), 92: "[L]'image de la souveraineté populaire se joint celle d'un lieu vide, impossible à occuper..."

less what Christensen and Fischer-Lescano are getting at – is evidently deeply misguided.

However, the absence of substantive truths (signifiers replete with signifieds) with reference to which the substantive legitimacy of any coercive sovereign decision can actually be proved and approved (instead of just imposed and accepted) does burden liberal democracy with an inevitable imperative. It burdens it with the demand to subject sovereign coercion to criteria of minimum and inevitable intrusion. Liberal democratic coercion must indeed present itself plausibly as an emergency control (*Notfallskontrolle*) as Luhmann puts it. Its coercive decisions cannot impose more normative substance on its citizens than the minimum substance required for purposes of sustaining their civil coexistence. The invocation of a minimum normative substance required for sustaining civil coexistence of course again simply begs the question. This "minimum" can also not be proved or emphatically approved. The "minimum" signifier also remains empty. That is why the history of liberal democracy remains a history of sovereignty. It remains a history of sovereign decisions, the "minimal intrusion" of which remains *imposed* on citizens in sovereign decisional and sacrificial fashion.

Liberal democracy surely does not escape from the sacrificial history of sovereignty that Jean-Luc Nancy describes so forcefully,[13] but it subjects itself to the demand that liberal democratic sacrifices remain justifiable in terms of inevitability and minimality. And it recognises that justification in terms of minimum and inevitable coercion does not constitute proof of minimum and inevitable intrusion. That is why the ultimate test for liberal democracy ultimately consists in the capacity of governments to sustain liberal tolerance of governmental intrusion as *plausibly* and *persuasively* complying with the demands of minimum and inevitable intrusion.[14]

It should be clear that liberal democracy ultimately turns on criteria of *plausibility* and *sufficient persuasiveness* that might sustain durable acceptance. That is why lasting sovereignty, at least in liberal democracies, is always a function of

---

13 Nancy, *Le Sens du Monde*, 141.

14 Another thought enters here that takes us beyond questions of sacrifice. In the liberal tolerance of intrusion invoked here inheres something that is deeper than mere tolerance. At issue in this tolerance is an element of forgiveness that accepts putting up with margins of intrusion that may well have been avoidable but cannot be proved to have been avoidable. Chapter Eight returns to this thought. Suffice it to say this for now: Liberal democratic citizenship turns on coping and putting up with a significant margin of ignorance regarding the difference between evitable and inevitability intrusion and this margin of ignorance commits it to a daily forgiveness of intrusion that is quite possibly not inevitable.

plausibility and *sufficient persuasiveness.* It is a function of elementary reasonableness and a sufficiently effective rhetoric regarding this reasonableness. And it is this plausibility and sufficient persuasiveness that is ultimately at stake in the horizontal effect of constitutional rights and the judicial assessment of this horizontal effect. However, it is exactly this plausibility and persuasiveness that the currently dominant understanding of horizontal effect jurisprudence cannot sustain. For this jurisprudence regularly invokes vague key terms like "radiation," "*Ausstrahlung*," "development" and "amelioration" of ordinary law to "promote" constitutional values, "schonendste Ausgleich," etc. None of these terms adequately reflect or embody the empirical precision required to sustain plausible and persuasive claims that no more than absolutely necessary and minimum coercion and intrusion will be imposed by any decision reached.

The kind of empirical precision required here can be attained much more convincingly by ordinary proportionality tests that are usually employed in the review of legislation. That this is so will be explained further in Chapter Eight. Suffice it to state for now that current horizontal effect jurisprudence with its predominant emphasis on the "indirect method" not only fails to match the empirical precision required to sustain minimum levels of coercion. It all too often aspires to do the opposite. It all too often aspires to maximise the impact of constitutional values in ways that show no regard for the demands of minimal coercion and intrusion. The dangerous war games that become possible in this bushy terrain of "radiation," "*Ausstrahlung*," "development," "amelioration" of ordinary law to "promote" constitutional values, "schonendste Ausgleich," and so forth, can hardly be illustrated better than by recalling Carl Schmitt's reliance on similar terms in 1933.

III Carl Schmitt's Unitary Substantive Due Process and Indirect Horizontal Effect Jurisprudence

It is no simple matter to plot a course through the puzzling conceptual frameworks of Carl Schmitt. He attached, for instance, much significance, on the one hand, to constitutional amendment clauses that shield constitutions against change by ordinary parliamentary majorities,[15] but he insisted, on the other, on the irreducible freedom of the pouvoir constituant to change constitutional arrangements at whim.[16] He made a great deal out of the structural division be-

15 Schmitt, *Verfassungslehre*, 101–102.
16 Ibid, 79–80.

tween state and civil society that characterised 19th century European polities. He lamented the erasure of this structural division and the resulting totalisation of the state to which popular democracy gave rise. He viewed these developments as the root of the turmoil that plagued the Weimar republic and of the "decadent" party political parliamentarianism of the time.[17] But his response to this crisis would ultimately not consist, as one would expect, in stressing the importance of structural divisions in the state. On the contrary, he responded to the crises of Weimar with a concept of the political and the constitutional that turns on total unity and unitary totality.[18]

This chapter will leave the task of squaring these circles in Schmitt's thought to more seasoned readers of his work. It will only pay close attention to two concerns or concepts that come up repeatedly in Schmitt's texts, namely, *totality* and *neutrality.* It is especially Schmitt's concern with the latter, with neutral power or *pouvoir neutre*, as he called it with reference to Benjamin Constant, which makes his work more interesting than his biography would suggest. It is this aspect of his thought that will concern us most in what follows. What we will trace in his work is a shift that takes place from *plurality*- to *unity*-based concepts of totality and neutrality. When exactly this shift occurred is probably impossible to pinpoint and doing so is also not important for present purposes. Suffice it to say that one can distinguish between earlier writings of Schmitt that pivot on an implicit concern with plurality, and later writings that expressly opt for a unity-based understanding of neutrality and totality.

Schmitt's engagement with the total state started with a critique of the weakness of the Weimar republic (the weak total state) but soon moved on to an endorsement of the totalitarian National Socialist *movement* (the *mobilised* state) the totality of which was also it strength. Schmitt explained this shift in his assessment of the total state by distinguishing between totality that results from weakness and totality that results from strength.[19] The weakness of Weimar, the weakness and decay of its party political parliamentarianism, argued

---

17 Cf. especially Carl Schmitt, *Der Hüter der Verfassung* (Berlin: Duncker & Humblot, 1996), 73–91; but also Carl Schmitt, *Die geistesgeschichtliche Lage des heutigen Parlamentarismus* (Berlin: Duncker & Humblot, 1996), 10–11.

18 Schmitt, *Verfassungslehre*, 3; Schmitt, *Der Begriff des Politischen* (Berlin: Duncker & Humblot, 1996), 39; Schmitt, "Die Wendung zum totalen Staat," in *Positionen und Begriffe: im Kampf mit Weimar – Genf – Versailles : 1923–1939* (Berlin: Duncker & Humblot GmbH, 1994), 166–178; Schmitt, "Weiterentwicklung des totalen Staat in Deutschland," in *Positionen und Begriffe: im Kampf mit Weimar – Genf – Versailles : 1923–1939* (Berlin: Duncker & Humblot GmbH, 1994), 211–216.

19 Schmitt, "Neutralität und Neutralisierungen," in *Positionen und Begriffe: im Kampf mit Weimar – Genf – Versailles : 1923–1939* (Berlin: Duncker & Humblot GmbH, 1994), 213.

Schmitt, was due to the erasure of the distinction and division between state and civil society. The 19th century state, he contended, maintained a separate existence and *raison d'être* that could not be reduced to the concerns of civil society. From this position the state could maintain internal political neutrality. The concern of the state was simply to ensure its continued existence and strength vis-à-vis other states, not to impose substantive normativity on its subjects. As regards its internal affairs, the state basically upheld an institutional framework within which religious and other differences and conflicts could be resolved or at least contained. A quasi-Hegelian argument can be read into this construction. Although by far not the Kantian *Allgemeinheit* or universality that Hegel entrusted to the state or at least to the idea of the state,[20] the 19th century state maintained a certain internal universalism to the extent that it did not demand nor promoted any particular or factional loyalty. It only demanded and commanded the general (internally universal) allegiance that would ensure its future. In this respect the state could be said to exercise neutral power.[21]

In other words, by maintaining the whole, the totality of its institutions and institutional concerns, the 19th century state remained neutral. This internal neutrality of the state contributed to another crucial neutrality, the neutrality of parliament. Parliament, functioning during this time as the political representation of the concerns and interests of civil society vis-à-vis the state, sought to establish true consensus regarding these concerns and interests. Basically united in the enterprise to safeguard their concerns against a potentially overbearing state, the parliamentary representatives of civil society were not prone to factionalism. Parliamentary debate was fundamentally informed by the ethos of establishing and promoting the true concerns of everyone.[22] According to Schmitt, this ethos disintegrated in the parliamentarian struggles of the 20th century and gave way to intransigent factionalism. It disintegrated because popular sovereignty (as opposed to imperial sovereignty) turned parliament into a struggle for the control of the state itself. No longer united against the external figure of the imperial state or the emperor, the parliaments of popular democracy became factional. The stakes of parliamentary democracy suddenly became too high to be left to the vicissitudes of open and impartial debate; hence the drawing of fixed and intractable party lines, increasing party mobilisation and the maintenance of strict party discipline that eventually destroyed the open politics of free

---

20 Cf. again Chapter Five.

21 Schmitt, "Neutralität und Neutralisierungen," 309–334; Schmitt, *Der Hüter der Verfassung*, 132–140.

22 Schmitt, *Der Hüter der Verfassung*, 73–91; Schmitt, *Die geistesgeschichtliche Lage des heutigen Parlamentarismus*, 61–61.

conviction that could plausibly claim to serve everyone's interests. This, in a nutshell, is Schmitt's devastating critique of Weimar politics. The Weimar state, he warned, was bound to be torn apart by the factional interests that clamoured to control it. All that had to happen was the materialisation of any narrow majority intent on the forthwith dissolution of the majority principle itself; hence also Schmitt's later concern with entrenched constitutional amendment clauses mentioned above.[23]

For a time Schmitt indeed continued to look at ways in which the Weimar constitution could be protected. Remarkable in this respect is his exploration of constitutionally commissioned dictatorial institutions aimed at safeguarding the state against factional abduction. These institutions included the office of the imperial president, the maintenance of a professional civil service and state bureaucracy (*Beamtentum*), an independent central bank and public transport services.[24] Of special interest in this regard is the trust he invested in the office of the imperial president and the special powers this office commanded under the emergency provisions of Section 48 of the Weimar constitution. The president could rely on these powers, claimed Schmitt, to fend off factional threats to the constitution and the state.[25] Most remarkable in this regard is the institutional concepts on which Schmitt relied in this regard. He described the role and function of the imperial president, relying on Benjamin Constant, as a *pouvoir neutre*. And the picture of the president that comes to the fore in the process reminds one vividly of Kantorowicz's narrative of *the king's two bodies*.[26]

The office of the imperial president, averred Schmitt, represents no particular interests, not even and especially not his personal interests. It represents only the universal or general interests of the state, that is, of the whole state or the state as a whole. And it is for this reason that the president can act as a neutral power that can arbitrate and act impartially in the face of factional conflicts.[27] At issue here for Schmitt was an institution that embodies or rather *disembodies* the integrity and totality of the law.

It is interesting to note that the very early Schmitt also articulated a concept of law that warranted the notion of the totality of the law and the totality of the state that is at issue here. His very first publication describes the law as a *com-*

---

23 Schmitt, *Verfassungslehre*, 101–112.
24 Schmitt, *Der Hüter der Verfassung*, 149–159.
25 Ibid, 132–159.
26 Ernst Hartwig Kantorowicz, *The King's Two Bodies: A Study in Mediaeval Political Theology* (Princeton: Princeton University Press, 1981), 383–450.
27 Schmitt, *Der Hüter der Verfassung*, 135–137.

plexio oppositorum, a complex (set or system) of oppositions. The law, Schmitt maintained here, could not be reduced to one of the terms in the set of opposites that it holds together. It always transcends the one term so as to keep in contention both terms.[28] Understood in this way, the law is never fully embodied in any particular or single legal term or concept. It thus maintains a disembodied existence. Any single legal term is surely an embodiment of the law, but the law is always more than this embodiment. It always also withdraws from this singular and exclusive embodiment so as to always also remain something more than this embodiment.

The particular embodiments of law can never be separated and insulated from the irreducible surplus of law that holds sway in its margins. This inexhaustible and irreducible surplus of law disembodies the law. It deprives it of complete substance. Schmitt's conception of the law as a *complexio oppositorum* invites one to contemplate, again with reference to Kantorowicz, *the law's two bodies*. The notion of a *complexio oppositorum*, the embodied body of law or *corpus iuris* that results from positing the law remains irreducibly accompanied by law that cannot be posited. And this law that cannot be posited disembodies all posited embodiments of law. The disembodiment at work here results from the surplus of law that transcends positive law, withdraws from it, and deprives it of complete substance.

These concerns in Schmitt's early work reflect an understanding of totality and neutrality in terms of a whole that is sustained by a split or divided reality. They reflect an understanding of totality that contemplates an internal plurality, a plurality *within* the state and *under* law. This would change in Schmitt's later work. *Der Begriff des politischen* (*The concept of the political*) is renowned for emphasising the *unity of the political* and its denunciation of divisions within the political unit. Well-known lines from this work put this move in a nutshell, foremost among which are these:

> "The political group is always the group that finds its orientation in the serious case."[29]
>
> "[The political group] is therefore always the decisive human grouping, the political unity from which derives always, when it is present at all, the decisive unity and sovereignty in the sense that the decision of the decisive case, even when it is the exception, belongs to it

---

28 Schmitt, *Römischer Katholizismus und politische Form* (Stuttgart: Klett-Cotta, 1923), 11, 14, 31, 49–50.

29 Translated from Schmitt, *Der Begriff des Politischen*, 39: "Politisch ist jedenfalls immer die Gruppierung, die sich an dem Ernstfall orientiert."

as a logically necessity... The word "sovereignty" makes good sense here, as does the word "unity."[30]

Schmitt published these lines in 1932. The unitary political sovereignty that is at issue in them, nevertheless already appeared prominently in the *Verfassungslehre* of 1928. And the *Verfassungslehre* gives one good reason to believe that it is nothing less than the constitution of a people that is at stake for Schmitt when he writes about the "decisive human grouping," "die *maßgebende* menschliche Gruppierung," in 1932. The opening page of the *Verfassungslehre* makes this clear:

"The word "constitution" must be understood strictly with reference to the constitution of the *state*, that is, to the political unity of a people... it then signifies the *totality* of political unity and *order*."[31]

Schmitt presented this understanding of the word "constitution" as the concrete totality of political unity and order as "the absolute concept of the constitution" (*absoluter Verfassungsbegriff*). This absolute concept of the constitution concerned a "unitary totality" (*einheitliches Ganzes*). He distinguished the absolute from the relative concept of the constitution. The latter denoted for him the collection of multiple singular laws or statutes (*die Verfassung als eine Vielheit einzelner Gesetze*) and he expressly exempted the former from the reach of the latter. The political totality of unity and order inheres in the political existence of the state (*politischen Existenz des Staates*), not in statutes, rules or some or other normativity (*Gesetze, Regeln und irgendwelchen Normativitäten*). In fact, it is the latter, the relative constitution, that is completely subject to the whiles and whims of the former, the absolute constitution. This becomes abundantly clear in Schmitt's description of the pouvoir constituant:

"All constitutional competences and arrangements depend on constituent power. Constituent power, however, cannot constitute itself constitutionally. The people, the nation, remain the primal foundation of all political developments. The people are the source of all strength. The nation expresses itself constantly in new forms and perennially brings

30 Translated from Ibid: "Sie ist deshalb immer die *maßgebende* menschliche Gruppierung, die politische Einheit infolge dessen immer, wenn sie überhaupt vorhanden ist, die maßgebende Einheit und "souverän" in dem Sinne, daß die Entscheidung über den maßgebenden Fall, auch wenn das der Ausnahmefall ist, begriffsnotwendig immer bei ihr stehen muß. Das Wort "Souveränität" hat hier einen guten Sinn, ebenso wie das Wort "Einheit."

31 Schmitt, *Verfassungslehre*, 3: "Das Wort "Verfassung" muß auf die Verfassung des *Staates*, d.h. der politischen Einheit eines Volkes beschränkt werden... dann bedeutet es den *Gesamtzustand* politischer Einheit und *Ordnung*."

> forth new forms and organisations, but never subjects its political existence to an ultimate formation.
>
> In its relation to all constituted powers, constituent power appears in many statements of Sieyès in terms of the metaphysical relation between 'natura naturans' and 'natura naturata' in the philosophy of *Spinoza:* It is the inexhaustible primal source of all forms that can itself not be contained in any form; it brings forth ever new forms from within itself; formless does it construct all forms."[32]

It is against the background of his concern with this formlessness of the absolute constitution – the concrete existential freedom of a people to decide who and what it wants to be – that Schmitt's concern with the raised majority requirements in constitutional amendment clauses must strike one as puzzling. There is probably only one explanation for his concern with constitutional clauses that subject constitutional changes to the requirement of exceptional majorities. These clauses were essential for his distinction between revolutionary acts that found new constitutions (*Verfassungsgebung*), on the one hand, and constitutional amendments (*Verfassungsänderungen*) that bring about circumscribed changes within a constitutional order that remains largely intact, on the other.[33]

Constitutional amendment clauses, reasoned Schmitt, only apply to constitutional reforms or amendments. They bear no relation to the revolutionary founding of new constitutions. They have no effect on the absolute constitution – the pouvoir constituant and existential will of the people to decide freely who and what it wants to be – and can for this reason not impose any conditions on any positive constitution through which the existential freedom of the people choose to give expression to itself. The positive constitutions that result from founding acts are entirely and exclusively conditioned by the existential freedom of the people. They too already presuppose the existential existence and will of a people. They are creations or expressions of that will and can therefore not limit it.

---

32 Ibid, 79–80: "Auf der verfassunggebenden Gewalt beruhen alle verfassungsmässig konstitutiertien Befugnisse und Zuständigkeiten. Sie selbst aber kann sich niemals verfassungsgesetzlich konstituieren. Das Volk, die Nation, bleibt der Urgrund alles politischen Geschehens, die Quelle aller Kraft, die sich in immer neuen Formen äussert, immer neue Formen und Organisationen aus sich herausstellt, selber jedoch niemals ihre politische Existenz einer endgültigen Formierung unterordnet ... In manche Äusserungen von Sieyès erscheint der 'pouvoir constituant' in seinem Verhältnis zu allen 'pouvoirs constitués' in einer metaphysischen Analogie zu der 'natura naturans' und ihrem Verhältnis zur 'natura naturata' nach der Lehre *Spinozas:* ein unerschöpflicher Urgrund aller Formen, selber in keiner Form zu Fassen, ewig neue Formen aus sich herausstellend, formlos alle Formen bildend."

33 Ibid, 26.

What then, is the place (or non-place) of the absolute constitution in Schmitt's conceptual framework? The answer to this question becomes clear when one takes a schematic look at the whole framework. The framework pivots, we saw, on three clear moments or terms: *a) The absolute constitution, b) the positive constitution* and *c) the relative constitution.* The absolute constitution *(a)* concerns the existential will of the people. It basically exists as sheer potential and thus remains a state of relative *negativity* (greater or lesser negativity, depending on the degree of restless dissatisfaction with its existing form and the forms of government that result from it). It gives *positive form* or expression to itself through collective decisions about basic *forms of government* (for example popular democracy) and these decisions become or produce the *positive constitution (b)* of a people. The positive constitution, in turn, provides the basis for *(c), the relative constitution,* that is, the particular arrangements and institutions of government that it decides to maintain. It is among these arrangements that one also finds any constitutional amendment clauses that may be contained in the constitutional framework. These constitutional amendment clauses, as part and parcel of *(c),* provide the means for changing *(c)* but not for changing *(b).* Only *(a)* can change *(b)* and does so through revolutionary decisions.[34]

It should be clear that *(a)* and *(c),* the *absolute* and *relative constitutions,* have no direct bearing on one another. This is so, in the first place, because *(a)* does not need *(c)* to change *(b)* and would be abusing *(c)* rather meaninglessly and cynically should it proceed to do so. This is so, in the second place, because the derailment of *(c)* is at best the derailment of the last carriage in the train smash that occurs when *(a)* decides to derail *(b)*; *(a)* surely does not need *(c)* to derail *(b)* and can, moreover, simply do away with *(c)* by doing away with *(b).* No one is concerned with constitutional amendments in times of real revolution and it would be ludicrous to rely on them to suppress, justify or obfuscate real revolutions; hence Schmitt's quite consistent insistence that the *Reichsgesetz* of 24 March 1933, fully compliant as it was with the two third majority stipulated by Article 76 of the Weimar Constitution, was not the constitutional ground of the National Socialist State. The real ground for this new state was the will of the people that became evident with the *Reichstagswahl* of 5 March 1933 which acknowledged Hitler as the *Führer,* an election that Schmitt assessed juridically as a direct plebiscite or *Volksabstimmung.*[35]

---

34 Ibid, 20–23. Cf. also 99–121.

35 Schmitt, *Staat, Bewegung, Volk* (Hamburg: Hanseatische Verlaganstalt, 1933), 7: "[diese Wahl war in Wirklichkeit, rechtswissenschaftlich betrachtet, eine Volksabstimmung, ein Plebiszit, durch welches das deutsche Volk Adolf Hitler ... also politischen Führer des deutschen Volkes anerkannt hat."

The most important aspect of Schmitt's constitutional scheme for our concern with the threat of totalising constitutionalisations consists in the way *(a)* effectively permeates and conditions *(b)* and *(c)* unconditionally and unilaterally. No internal political differentiation that may ensue from either *(b)* or *(c)* has, in turn, any real differential effect on *(a)*. In other words, *(a)* remains the totalising principle on which neither *(b)* nor *(c)* has any constraining effect. As a consequence of this, *(a)* always threatens to simply flood *(b)* and *(c)* in whichever way it wants. The fundamental political and existential unity of the people *(a)* that constitutes the state as absolute constitution remains untouched by any historical differentiations that fundamental forms of government *(b)* or particular institutions *(c)* may bring about within a polity. And it is to be expected that *(a)* will not tolerate any significant forms or differentiations that *(b)* or *(c)* may threaten to impose on it. It will, to the contrary, always ensure that *(a)* permeates *(b)* and *(c)* thoroughly and conclusively without *(b)* and *(c)* ever attaining any hold on *(a)*. And it is exactly this scheme that lurks in understandings of horizontal effect that turn on the idea that all strata of law should be infused by constitutional principles. Schmitt, we shall see presently, was himself an advocate of such an understanding of horizontal effect.

It should be clear now that Schmitt's constitutional scheme would never tolerate a significant or deep distinction between constitutional law and private law. It would underwrite and pursue actively the radiation of constitutional principles through all aspects of law, private law included. Schmitt's scheme is thus well in line with the concept of horizontal application that the GFCC would later articulate in *Lüth*. Anyone who would want to consider this claim to be farfetched should consider the following passage from the heady days of his National Socialist fervour:

> "Law in the substantive sense of the word entails, in the first place, the securing of political unity. Only on the basis of uncontroversial and in this regard positive political decisions can the law develop freely and autonomously in all areas of public life."[36]

In 1933, Justus Wilhelm Hedemann published a remarkable critique of the "flight into the general clauses of the law" (*die Flucht in die Generalklauseln*) that he

36 Schmitt, *Staat, Bewegung, Volk*, 15: "Zum Recht im substantiellen Sinne gehört als Erstes Sicherstellung der politischen Einheit; nur auf der Grundlage der unbestrittenen, und in diesem Sinne positiven, politischen Entscheidungen kann sich dann in allen Gebieten des öffentlichen Lebens Recht in freiem und autonomen Wachstum entfalten."

considered current at the time.[37] Considering the demand in Schmitt's constitutional scheme that all law reflect the fundamental constitutional decisions of the German people, it can hardly be surprising that Schmitt would, in 1933, come to the defence of the "flight into the general clauses of the law" that Hedemann criticised. Schmitt's apology for the general clauses of law would not only stress their inevitability in modern legal systems. It would also plead for the expansion of their generality and openness into every legal concept so as to facilitate better the permeation or radiation of National Socialist constitutional principles into all areas of law. He concluded in this regard that the law should be understood as nothing but a collection of undetermined concepts – "*so betrachtet gibt es heute überhaupt nur noch 'unbestimmte' Rechtsbegriffe.*"[38]

It should be clear from the above that one can hardly imagine a stronger rejection of the 19th century division between state and civil society than the one Schmitt articulated in his 1933 text *Staat, Bewegung, Volk.* Schmitt explained this rejection in terms of changed political-economical circumstances that no longer warranted or justified invocation of private liberty against the powers of the state. This invocation may have made sense in a time when state and isolated individual stood directly opposed to one another, a situation that warranted the protection of the poor isolated individual (*arme, isolierte Einzelperson*) against the all powerful Leviathan state (*vor dem mächtigen Leviathan "Staat"*). It stopped making sense, however, when gigantic private corporations began to wield power that was in many respects equal to that of the state, without having to assume political responsibility and accountability. They could avoid political accountability and responsibility, just because they could claim to be part of the private sphere.[39] These were the main lines of his argument.

One may understandably feel apprehensive about endorsing or taking instruction from anything that comes out of *Staat, Bewegung, Volk,* but Schmitt's observation regarding the obsolete foundations of classical liberal democracy and the need for political control of private power that often constitutes nothing less than vast political power is poignant. It echoes a sentiment that is visibly current among legal theorists and judges who endorse the horizontal effect of fundamental rights. It is doubtful whether these theorists and judges will ever

---

37 The political sentiments behind Hedemann's little book would appear not to have differed much from Schmitt's (considering the note on which the book ends), but he evidently still articulated a concern with juridical rigor that Schmitt no longer found compelling in 1933. Cf. Justus Wilhelm Hedemann, *Die Flucht in die Generalklauseln. Eine Gefahr für Recht und Staat* (Tübingen: J.C.B. Mohr (Paul Siebeck), 1933), 76.

38 Schmitt, *Staat, Bewegung,Volk*, 43–44.

39 Schmitt, *Staat, Bewegung,Volk*, 24–25.

or should ever part company with him on this point.[40] The real question remains, however, whether they should also choose to keep company with that part of his thinking that endorsed the transmission of basic National Socialist political foundations through the whole legal system. Do they really want to embrace that part of his thinking that facilitated this transmission theoretically by embracing a flight into the general principles of law that effectively reduced all legal concepts to open legal concepts?

The problem that is evident here does not simply go away when one replaces whatever dark and obnoxious *volkische* values may be lurking in the foundations of a legal system with transparent Enlightenment and liberal ideals. A careful concern with horizontal effect cannot afford to merely rest its case with the replacement of *volkische* with liberal values (however relieved about such replacements it may well be). At issue here is the problematic nature of a mode of constitutional hermeneutics which Christensen and Fischer-Lescano aptly call "vertical holism." Vertical holism entails the hermeneutic demand that detailed deliberation of specific legal judgments reflect or embody the fundamental legal values at the base or foundation of the legal system directly. Vertical holism does not allow for any degree of normative or semantic independence within sub-spheres of law. It sees to it that overarching principles of law remain directly operative within all areas and sub-areas of law.

This vertical operation invariably undermines whatever legal certainty and secure expectation of rights one might hope for from judicial decisions in specific cases. The exigencies of the specific case are just too narrow and specific to accommodate the broad values at the base in a relatively determined fashion. Broad values can pan out in a myriad of ways and are bound to destroy, frustrate or dismay whatever specific expectations might be entertained at the level of the specific case. Once one accepts this vertical semantic transmission as one's principal mode of legal reasoning, it is only consistent to argue that all legal concepts should become *open concepts*. The problematic nature of this vertical holism is one of the key points that Christensen and Fischer-Lescano bring to bear on the horizontal effect debate. Especially poignant in this regard is their observation that it was not a mindless or mechanical judicial positivism that destroyed individual rights and secure legal expectations under National Social-

40 Cf. Justice Madala in *Du Plessis v De Klerk* 1996 (5) BCLR 658 727 H-J: "Those who would widen the scope of the operation of the Bill of Rights hold the view that the verticality approach is unmindful of the modern day reality – that in many instances the abuse in the exercise of power is perpetrated less by the State and more by private individuals against other private individuals."

ism, but conscious and conscientious interpretivism that transmitted fundamental values through the whole legal system.[41]

The concurrence on this point between latter day conceptions of horizontal effect (extreme versions of which would simply reduce private law to "applied constitutional law") and Schmitt's thinking in *Staat, Bewegung, Volk* should therefore give pause for careful reflection. One may well, indeed in agreement with Schmitt, wish to promote the political control of powerful private entities. But should one do so with recourse to an expanded or exploded concept of general legal clauses that basically turn all legal concepts into *open* legal concepts? An engagement with Schmitt on this point alerts one to the precarious and thorny territory that one enters when one endorses this conception of the horizontal effect of fundamental rights. Again, at issue here is not the facile dismissal of thoughts just because a prominent and fervent National Socialist jurist also happened to think them.[42] At issue is a critical call for caution regarding the totalisation of constitutional principles. Should one embrace such a totalisation just because one is confident that one's fundamental constitutional values are acceptable in a way that Schmitt's were not?

Some years ago I argued that Justice Kriegler's concern in *Du Plessis v De Klerk* about the spectre of the totalitarian state that rises with the horizontal application question is simply miscued.[43] How can one be concerned with a totalising destruction of private spheres when the totalisation at issue concerns, in fact, the systematic enforcement of liberal constitutional values in all spheres of life? Liberal jurists and judges should welcome and not fear such systematic enforcement of principles of fundamental human dignity and individual freedom, I contended. This argument, however, did not and does not respond adequately to the complexity of the problem that is at issue here. The failure to address the complexity of the problem of horizontal effect is also evident in Matthias Kumm's endorsement of private law as applied constitutional law. This kind of argument should be worrisome to anyone who endorses the horizontal application of fundamental rights. This is not so because liberal constitutional values can as easily degenerate into hysteric totalitarian regimes of the National Socialist kind. One is probably on much safer ground with liberal than one is with *volkische* values in this respect, but one should not underestimate the

41 Christensen and Fischer-Lescano, *Das Ganze des Rechts*, 48.

42 Had scholarship been such a simplistic exercise, one would also have had to avoid relying on Joachim Ritter for the main argument in Chapter Five.

43 Johan van der Walt, "Perspectives on Horizontal Application: Du Plessis v De Klerk Revisted," *South African Public Law* 12 (1997): 1–31, Van der Walt, "Horizontal Application of Fundamental Rights and the Threshold of the Law in View of the Carmichele Saga," 517–540.

wide shoulders of abstract concepts such as human dignity and personal liberty. One should not underestimate the many things they can carry. Schmitt himself found significant common ground in Rousseau's "democratic" and Enlightenment conception of the identity of ruler and ruled – *Identität von Regierenden und Regierten.*[44]

Justice Kriegler's concern in *Du Plessis v De Klerk* accurately expressed the intuition that a certain conception of horizontal effect may lead to the erasure of essential differences between citizens and government without which liberal democracy cannot be understood. Liberal constitutional values are indeed less likely to lead to totalitarian conceptions of society than *volkische* values. But a certain totalitarian imagination already lurks in strong or expansive conceptions of liberal values as *substantive values.* Frank Michelman's claim that substance cannot be removed completely from form is of course correct.[45] However, it is crucial to understand the liberal values of liberal democracy *as far as possible* as procedural principles on the basis of which differences can be managed and *as little as possible* as substantive principles that can be imposed on everyone in a "homogenous" society.

It is ironic that one of Schmitt's most illustrious scholars, Ernst-Wolfgang Böckenförde, would come to argue exactly this point most poignantly with reference to the jurisprudence that the GFCC developed in *Lüth.* According to Böckenförde, the jurisprudence of the GFCC in *Lüth* turned the GG into a founding order for the whole of society, instead of construing it narrowly as a framework that organises essential features of the relation between state and citizens. As this book of has argued throughout, these essential features of the relation between citizens and state surely have real and absolute implications for some horizontal relations between citizens. This is not how Böckenförde sees the matter and we shall take issue with him on this count in Chapter Eight. But his critical assessment of *Lüth's* transformation of the constitutional framework of the state (*Rahmenordnung des Staates*) into a substantive ordering of society (*rechtliche Grundordnung des Gemeinwesens*) is acute and of crucial significance for the concept of horizontal effect forwarded in this book.[46]

The wide shoulders of liberal political principles can indeed carry many things, but the concern here is not that they will easily invite illiberal values and sentiments in contemporary constitutional democracies. The real cause of concern in contemporary constitutional democracies is the very real possibility

44 Schmitt, *Die geistesgeschichtliche Lage des heutigen Parlamentarismus*, 19–20.
45 Michelman, "Constitutionalism as Procedrualism: A Glance at the Terrain," 141–161.
46 Cf. Ernst-Wolfgang Böckenförde "Grundrechte als Grundsatznormen" 1990 *Der Staat* 1–30.

that totalising or de-differentiating promotions of liberal constitutional values can lead, to the contrary, to the ordo-liberal totalisation of private spheres at the expense of proper public political and constitutional scrutiny. Kumm's conception of private law as *applied constitutional law* can easily turn constitutional law into an extension of private law. Once totalisation of this kind sets in, there is no way to control the course it will take, for there will be no resistance from "elsewhere" within the legal system.

We have seen in Chapter Two how constitutional principles were reduced to private law principles in the course of the nineteenth century. This can easily happen again. Chapter Five showed that such a totalisation of private spheres – described by Cafaggi and others as the rise of "the new private law" – might well be afoot again in Europe and the globalised world. The trends at issue here, we have seen, are also presented and promoted under banners of *functional differentiation*. Really at stake in them, however, may well be pervasive modes of *functional de-differentiation* in terms of which human coexistence is increasingly reduced to an agglomeration of private spheres from which public power, wielded by independent and impartial public authorities, can no longer be distinguished. At issue here is the deep de-differentiation that threatens to render the Hegelian distinction and differentiation between state and civil society obsolete. Theorists of functional differentiation have come to recognise disastrous deregulation as "the dark side" of functional differentiation.[47] There is, however, real cause for suspecting that this "dark side of functional differentiation" is not incidental to functional differentiation, but a reflection of the general darkness that sets in when deregulation removes government from private spheres.

Suffice it to stress that there is much to which Schmitt's seamless constitutional scheme, even rid of its *völkische* baggage, can alert us. This seamless constitutional scheme rides on the back of the externalisation of social differences and differentiations that Schmitt's antagonistic concept of the political effects. At issue is his conception of the political in terms of a friend enemy decision (*Freund/Feind Entscheidung*) that has made a considerable comeback in recent radical democratic theory.[48] This undertaking has not been devoid of interesting insights and may well have contributed to the articulation of a theoretical basis for a refreshing pluralisation of politics. The friend-enemy decision can indeed in one respect be understood as the emergence of plurality, that is, the emergence

---

47 Poul F Kjaer, Gunther Teubner, and Alberto Febbrajo, eds, *The Financial Crisis in Constitutional Perspective: The Dark Side of Functional Differentiation* (Oxford; Portland, Oregon: Hart Publishing, 2011).

48 Chantal Mouffe, *The Return of the Political* (New York: Verso Books, 1993), 117–134.

of a plurality of political contenders. The friend and the enemy count for more than one, to be sure. And yes, there is something friendly and forgiving, even touching, in Schmitt's portrayal of the public enemy.[49] But the friend-enemy decision is in another evident respect also exactly that which sustains unitary political totalities. The friend-enemy decision effects an externalisation of plurality that sustains internal unity. As we saw above, it is exactly in the context of the friend-enemy decision that Schmitt described the emergence of the political in terms of sovereign unity. It is the enemy that unites a people. An element of this logic may even be present in Schmitt's analysis of 19th century parliamentary solidarity vis-à-vis imperial threats to their common interests.[50]

One might describe this externalisation of plurality and internalisation of unity as characteristic of the military spirit or soldier-ethics that Schmitt happily saw returning to Germany in 1937.[51] There are probably very few among us who are completely impervious to the romantic fascination with warriors and the ethics and aesthetics of soldiers. That is probably why good war films invariably remain box-office hits. It is a good question, however, whether this fascination offers any helpful insights when it comes to regular constitutional review of internal social conflict within civil states. Horizontal constitutional review is not civil war. It turns on the ethics of citizens, not soldiers. For better insight into this ethics, we must turn to Schmitt's legendary antagonist, Hans Kelsen.

---

49 Schmitt, *Der Begriff des Politischen*, 29–30. Cf. hereto Ulrich K. Preuss, "Vater der Verfassungsväter – Carl Schmitts Verfassungslehre und die verfassungspolitische Diskussion der Gegenwart" in *Politisches Denken Jahrbuch 1993*, ed. Volker Gerhardt, Henning Ottmann, and Martyn P Thompson (Stuttgart: Metzler, 1993), 117–133, especially at 120.

50 Cf. hereto also Marcus Llanque, "Die Theorie politischer Einheitsbildung in Weimar und die Logik von Einheit und Vielheit (Rudolf Smend, Carl Schmitt, Hermann Heller)," in *Metamorphosen des Politischen: Grundfragen politischer Einheitsbildung seit den 20er Jahren*, ed. Andreas Göbel, Dirk van Laak, and Ingeborg Villinger (Berlin: Akademie Verlag, 1995), 157–176, especially 165–171.

51 Cf. Carl Schmitt, "Totaler Feind, totaler Krieg, totaler Staat," in *Positionen und Begriffe: im Kampf mit Weimar – Genf – Versailles : 1923–1939* (Berlin: Duncker & Humblot GmbH, 1994), 273: "Deutschland hat diesen Zwiespalt [zwischen bürgerlicher Gesellschaft und preußischem Soldatendstaat] heute überwunden und entfaltet in geschlossener Einheitlichkeit seine soldatische Kraft."

IV Hans Kelsen and the Open Duality of the Constitutional Democratic Whole

It is instructive to begin an analysis of the Kelsen-Schmitt debate along the lines that Schmitt himself drew between him and Kelsen. Kelsen's theory of the state, contended Schmitt, turns on empty positivist normativism. Kelsen is clearly the main antagonist of Schmitt's political and constitutional theory and therefore the consistent negative point of reference in the *Verfassungslehre, Der Begriff des Politischen* and *Politische Theologie.* Schmitt wrote in his *Verfassungslehre:*

> The theory of the state that H. Kelsen repeats in many books presents the state as a system and unity of legal norms, without offering the slightest effort to explain the material and logical principle of this unity. It also fails to explain how it came about and why it was necessary that the many positive legal determinations of a state and the various constitutional norms on which they turn constitute such a system or unity. The political *existence* and *development* of this statal unity and order thus gets transformed into a mere matter of *functioning.*[52]

Having said this, Schmitt went on to explain Kelsen's political theory as one of the last outgrowths of the theory of the bourgeois constitutional state (*letzte Ausläufer der ...Theorie des bürgerlichen Rechtsstaates*) of the 17th and 18th centuries. The normativity of the authentic version of these theories turned on individualistic conceptions of natural law. These conceptions of natural law endowed these bourgeois constitutional conceptions with real meaning and a real sense of compelling normativity (*echtes Sollen*), argued Schmitt. But in Kelsen's system of law, contended Schmitt further, this real and compelling normativity is replaced by an empty normativity. Kelsen's legal system turns on a bottomless positivism in terms of which a norm applies simply because and when it applies – "[e]twas gilt wenn es gilt und weil es gilt[, d]as ist Positivismus."[53]

Not only does Kelsen's system fail to explain why norms are compelling, insisted Schmitt, it also insulates itself juridically against all facticity and all fac-

52 Schmitt, *Verfassungslehre*, 9.: Die in vielen Büchern ... wiederholte Staatslehre von H. Kelsen stellt ebenfalls den Staat als ein System und Einheit von Rechtsnormen dar, freilich ohne den geringsten Versuch, das sachliche und logische Prinzip dieser "Einheit" und dieses "Systems" zu erklären, und ohne auseinanderzusetzen, wie es kommt und nach welcher Notwendigkeit es sich fügt, daß die vielen positiven gesetzlichen Bestimmungen eines Staates und die verschiedenen verfassungsgesetzlichen Normen ein solches "System" oder eine "Einheit" bilden. Das politische *Sein* und *Werden* der staatlichen Einheit und Ordnung wird in ein *Funktionieren* verwandelt."

53 Ibid.

tual foundations of law. It insulates itself against any act of a constituent power and the actual will of a people to give itself law. And it prevents such concrete lawgiving from becoming the foundation of law.[54] As Schmitt put it in *Der Begriff des Politischen,* Kelsen belonged to the Gerber-Laband school of pure legal theory. This pure legal theory, he claimed, separated law from its political roots, that is, from its foundations in political and sovereign lawgiving and law-making.[55]

Kelsen, however, was surely not unaware of the counter-intuitive character of his "positivist" project. He was surely not oblivious to the fact that his abstraction of the legal system from its political roots left the law hanging in thin air. It is again ironic that no one other than Böckenförde would come to note this well.[56] Kelsen knew, Böckenförde observed, that questions regarding the origin and end of legal systems ultimately takes one out of the realm of the "*ought*" and into the realm of the "*is*;" out of the sphere of normativity and into the sphere of facticity or existence. He referred in this regard to this passage from Kelsen's *Hauptprobleme der Staatsrechtslehre:*

> "It is extraordinarily significant that the question regarding the beginning and end of norms can only be answered by moving from the world of normativity [*Soll*] to the world of existence [*Sein*]. The inverse also applies. The question regarding the beginning and end of existence invariably takes one out of the world of existence and into the world of normativity. That makes clear that the question regarding the beginning and end of normativity exceeds normative observation and the methods of normative knowledge."[57]

Kelsen's awareness regarding the factual or ontic origins of legal norms was indeed acute, perhaps much more acute than it appears from this remarkable passage. His "pure theory of law" in fact never claimed to have left the realm of fac-

---

54 Ibid.

55 Schmitt, *Der Begriff des Politischen*, 21.

56 Ernst Wolfgang Böckenförde, *Staat, Verfassung, Demokratie: Studien zur Verfassungstheorie und zum Verfassungsrecht* (Frankfurt am Main: Suhrkamp, 1991), 91.

57 Hans Kelsen, *Hauptprobleme der Staatsrechtslehre: Entwickelt aus der Lehre vom Rechtssatze* (Aalen: Scientia Verlag, 1984), 9–10: "Es ist außerordentlich bezeichnend, daß man die Frage nach dem Anfange und dem Ende, der Entstehung und Zerstörung des Soll nur insofern beantworten kann, als man aus der Welt des Soll in die des Seins übergeht; und daß man bei derselben Frage in bezug auf das Sein in die Welt des Soll gerät. Daran zeigt sich deutlich, daß die Frage nach Entstehung und Zerstörung des Soll nicht mehr in der nur auf das Soll gerichteten Beobachtungsebene und innerhalb der normativen Erkenntnismethode liegt." On Kelsen's consistent methodological anti-sociological refusal to engage with questions of existence and to restrict jurisprudence to a pure concern with the legal sphere of normativity or "ought," cf. Hans Kelsen, *Über Grenzen zwischen juristischer und soziologischer Methode: Vortrag, gehalten in der Soziologischen Gesellschaft zu Wien* (Aalen: Scientia-Verlag, 1970).

ticity behind it. Such was his awareness of law's entanglement in historical life that he based the idea of pure law on the force of a fiction or pretension. To talk meaningfully about *law* (law that is significantly valid and binding), he maintained, one had to assume or presuppose the existence of pure law, that is, of law that is not rooted in factual or existential origins. The logic of his system of course already compelled him to rely on this fiction or presupposition. However, we shall see presently that there was more to this presupposition than the logical or epistemological demands of his system of law. Let us nevertheless first take a look at these demands.

Kelsen's predicament is well known. The logic of his system turns on the demand that every norm be validated by a higher norm. This logic must run into trouble every time the ultimate foundational norm – the *Grundnorm* – comes into sight, for the *Grundnorm* itself lacks validation by a higher norm. Hence Kelsen's instruction that the *Grundnorm* must never be equated with any real historical constitution for no historical constitution contains its validation within itself. Considered in terms of Schmitt's scheme of absolute *(a)*, positive *(b)* and relative constitution *(c)* that we analysed above, the following becomes abundantly clear as far as Kelsen's construction of pure law is concerned: the normative validity or legitimacy of *(b)* and *(c)* cannot be derived from *(a)* because *(a)* itself lacks the normative foundation (the prior norm) on the basis of which it can endow *(b)* and *(c)* with validity. The normativity of *(b)* would have to be assumed or presupposed for the system to get started so that the question of the normativity of *(a)* can be suspended or ignored while we talk about law as law. Kelsen was abundantly clear on this count. The *Grundnorm* can never be equated with any real instance of historical constitution-making that emanates from the real will and existence of a people. It can thus never be equated with *(a)*. The *Grundnorm* is not an instance of positive or posited law. It is neither *Gesetz*, nor *gesetzt*. It is presupposed (*vorausgesetzt*).[58] Quite to the contrary of Schmitt's observations above, and of pervasive perceptions of Kelsen as a positivist, there is in fact little or no positivism at work in his system of pure law. In the final analysis it is quite evidently a highly idealist construction.

In comparison with Kelsen's pure theory of law, Schmitt's constant obsession with the ultimate factuality or factual foundations of law would seem to slip into a mundane or common sense obsession with sufficient causes. The positing of *(a)* in the scheme pointed out above surely requires no rocket science and no theoretical sophistication; it is a simple reflection of a commonly shared causal imagination that informs lay understandings of law as the law *of* a peo-

58 Kelsen, *Reine Rechtslehre*, 66–67.

ple, that is, law that comes *from* a people as if *caused by* a people. This causal concern is abundantly evident in Schmitt's comment on Kelsen quoted above. It is this common sense causal imagination that ultimately exposes and abandons law to its normative deficit, not Kelsen's counter-intuitive avoidance of this common sense imagination.

Kelsen understood the need for an imaginative effort through which law could be insulated from constant factual demands upon it. He knew that such an effort or move was necessary if law were not to be reduced to a set of factual demands, that is, if law were to be given (or contemplated as having) some autonomous institutional existence beyond these factual demands. If this were not doable, one would simply never be able to entertain a concept of law that distinguishes law significantly from other social concerns. Law is sociologically speaking undoubtedly part and parcel of a dense and complex social fabric, but in order to understand what is uniquely at issue in that part of this complex social fabric that one calls "law," one also needs to be able to extract law from this social reality so as to create an abstraction that can properly be called "law." When one does not do that, law indeed becomes nothing more than a set of open organisational principles or nominal husks through which anything and everything can pass. One then has exactly what Schmitt proposed in *Staat, Bewegung, Volk*. The law would begin and end, so to speak, with every judicial decision. "Legal" conflicts would constantly embroil one in questions about first and last things. The essential identity of a people would be at stake in every legal decision.

In Kelsen's words, judges would constantly have to reconsider *sollen* in view of *sein*. They would constantly have to adjust general norms in view of the specificity of particular political or moral considerations. Instead of Kelsen's apparently complete or absolute separation of law and politics, one would have a complete replacement of law by politics. Questions of the beginning and end of law would turn the quotidian business of law into a constant cataclysmic ritualism that stages or restages the factual existence of a people on a daily basis. The exception would become the rule. This is bound to happen when the legal rule is conceived exclusively or predominantly from the perspective of the exception, when every legal decision involves the ultimate foundations of a people, as Schmitt conceived of it in *Staat, Bewegung, Volk*.[59] It is when this happens that

59 Cf. in this regard the poignant observation of Preuss, "Vater der Verfassungsväter? Carl Schmitts Verfassungslehre und die verfassungspolitische Diskussion der Gegenwart," 133: "[Schmitt] ist einer der Intellektuellen, die sich theoretisch und praktisch von den Abgründigkeiten der Politik haben fesseln lassen und das in ihr enthaltene humane Rationalisierungspotential ausgeschlagen haben."

positive facts become everything and norms become nothing but the empty husks or forms through which these facts are transmitted. It is Schmitt's concept of law that turns on naked positivism, not Kelsen's.

Does Kelsen's theory of law, on the other hand, deprive one completely of a link between law and politics? Does it tell us that factual questions about the beginnings and ends of law should never enter the theory, practice and administration of law? A careful reading of Kelsen's texts does not suggest this. Kelsen's demand that the theory of law imagines the existence of pure law does not necessarily incorporate a demand that the empirical reality of law and daily legal practice never consider extra-legal concerns. And there is also no evidence in Kelsen's work of such a naive demand. His pure theory of law *does* convey the message that a constant or frequent failure to talk about the law *as law* and the constant or frequent failure to distinguish law from morals or politics or literature or whatever else, *will* deprive the word law of any particular meaning. But the "pure theory of law" does not portray the picture of a theorist who has lost all sight and sense of reality. His regard for the factual political context of constitutional adjudication was so acute that he proposed the parliamentary election of constitutional judges for purposes of making the court more representative of actual democratic relations.[60] This proposal may well have been half-baked,[61] but it reflects the extent of his realism.

Any suggestion that Kelsen was oblivious to issues that spring from the historical origins and contingency of legal systems would surely be false. He was patently aware of law's dependence on the historical vicissitudes power relations. He expressly articulated his pure theory of law against the background of an awareness of the historical beginnings and ends of legal systems, new foundational norms, etc. He was patently aware that such new foundations would reverberate throughout every aspect of old law that survives the transition from old to new systems of law.[62] His pure or purifying theory of law would of course suggest that new legal systems had better move soon enough from questions of specific facts (margins of superior military force, incidental power relationships, contingent political bargaining) to questions of generally valid norms if claims that a new *legal* system has been founded are ever to be taken seriously.

---

60 Kelsen, "Wesen und Entwicklung der Staatsgerichtsbarkeit" in Hans Kelsen and Robert Christian van Ooyen, *Wer soll der Hüter der Verfassung sein? Abhandlungen zur Theorie der Verfassungsgerichtsbarkeit in der pluralistischen, parlamentarischen Demokratie* (Tübingen: Mohr Siebeck, 2008), 27.

61 Frank Michelman, "Dilemmas of Belonging: Moral Truth, Human Rights, and Why We Might Not Want a Representative Judiciary," *UCLA Law Review* 47 (2000): 1221–1252.

62 Kelsen, *Reine Rechtslehre*, 67–70.

The possibility of ever again *presupposing* or *imagining* the "immaculate" emergence of a *Grundnorm* that is not soiled by the facticity of its origin will most likely always depend on successful and sufficiently rapid transitions from specific historical facts to general normative considerations. Only thus will the citizens of the new legal system gain the courage and confidence to imagine their new constitution as a *Grundnorm* and their legal system as "pure law" or something close enough to it to get on with things. Only retrospectively will such new law receive solid (enough) foundations and only retrospectively will these foundations be recognised, maintained and sustained.[63] This is the lesson that we can take from Kelsen's pure theory of law: He did not offer us metaphysical assurance of ever present and pre-existing foundations of law that inhere in the mere existence of a people, as Schmitt did or attempted to do. In fact, Kelsen went so far as to insist that the existence of people as *a people* depends on their ability to retrospectively maintain law that turns them into a people.[64] His legal constructivism was deconstruction par excellence.[65] It left no scope for romanticist and metaphysical conceptions of peoples as living presences and living causes of law.

The significance of this rather lengthy engagement with Kelsen's famous stand-off with Schmitt for the question of horizontal effect at issue in this book concerns the way this stand-off raises serious doubts regarding the horizontal effect jurisprudence articulated in *Lüth*. The notion of the radiation of constitutional values through the open principles of private law surely suggests the existence of a broad semantic continuum between the first principles and the specific concretisations of a legal system. This suggestion is evidently at odds with Kelsen's pure theory of law. The latter evidently demands more specific validatory links between higher and lower legal norms. The *Stufenbau* or hierarchical structure of this pure theory of law casts the legal system into relatively independent strata of law that need not answer constantly to the implications of first principles. The more specific a legal question, the more specific the norms that apply to it.[66] This does not mean that specific legal norms exist com-

63 For an engagement with this process in the context of the South African constitutional transition, cf. Johan van der Walt, "Vertical Sovereignty, Horizontal Constitutionalism, Subterranean Capitalism: A Case of Competing Retroactivities," *South African Journal on Human Rights* 26 (2010): 102.

64 Kelsen, *Vom Wesen und Wert der Demokratie*, 31–32. Cf. also Kelsen, *Das Problem der Souveränität und die Theorie des Völkerrechts* (Aalen: Scientia Verlag, 1960), 9–53.

65 For similar line of thought, cf. Jacques Derrida, "Declarations of Independence 1," *New Political Science, 1986, Vol.7(1), pp.7–15* 7, no. 1 (1986): 7–15.

66 Kelsen, *Reine Rechtslehre*, 73–89.

pletely independently of more general norms. They can surely be checked for minimal levels of conformity with more general norms without which no legal system can sustain adequate levels of coherence. But they do not act as mere transmitters or conveyers of the content of general norms. They answer firstly to the exigencies of the specific social practices from which legal disputes arise. In this regard they place a huge question mark behind the broad band horizontal effect jurisprudence articulated in *Lüth*. This question mark goes to the heart of the critique that Leisner directed at Dürig and *Lüth*, as Section V will make clear.

But there is another respect in which Kelsen's thought offers a much more incisive understanding of horizontal effect than the one articulated in *Lüth*. Kelsen's concept of liberal democratic constitutionalism affords legal theory profound regard for the liberal democratic demand that *all* constitutional review remain a matter of *horizontal* constitutional review. Considered from within the liberal democratic paradigm of Kelsen's thoughts on constitutional democracy, there can evidently be no such thing as vertical constitutional review or vertical effect. When a legal system's *Grundnorm* happens to be the *Grundnorm* of constitutional democracy, it inscribes into that system of law an understanding of law as an expression of the will of the majority of citizens. This majority principle, however, especially as phrased here, signifies only half of the constitutional democratic principle that is at stake here. Constitutionalism and the constitutional scrutiny of majority legislation, argued Kelsen in classical liberal fashion, concerns the protection of minorities. Constitutional democratic law therefore does not only concern the constitutional validation of majority legislation; it also and more fundamentally concerns the sustenance of majority-minority political relationships. The majority principle, argued Kelsen, is in fact a majority-minority principle.[67] The constitutionality of constitutional democratic law consists, in other words, in the maintenance of compromises between majorities and minorities.[68] As such, it cannot and must never take part in the pursuit of truth in politics. Invocations of truth in political debate, Kelsen saw clearly, must fall foul of liberal democratic constitutions. Invocations of truth claim access to knowledge or insights with regard to which there can be no minority opinion. They entertain the idea of a politics that justifiably demands unanimous consent.[69]

One of the important elements or implications of Kelsen's thought in this regard consists in the astoundingly simple way in which he resolves the paradox of

---

67 Kelsen, *Vom Wesen und Wert der Demokratie*, 53, 57, 58.

68 Ibid.

69 Kelsen, *Vom Wesen und Wert der Demokratie*, 100–104. Cf. also Kelsen, *Was ist Gerechtigkeit?* (Stuttgart: Reclam Philipp Jun, 2000).

constitutional democracy and the enigma of the co-originality of democracy and rights to which Habermas has paid extensive attention.[70] Given that the meaning of the *concept of the majority* (as opposed to or in contrast with the sheer fact of mute overpowering force) depends on the *concept of the minority*, the constitutional identification and protection of minorities also constitutes the constitutional recognition and safeguarding of majorities. This recognition clearly underpins the democratic right of majorities to enact legislation and make law. Kelsen saw clearly that there is no democracy-rights conflict at issue here, but the necessary co-existence of both.[71] This recognition is crucial for the conception of horizontal effect review that will be developed in the rest of this chapter and in Chapter Eight.

The importance of this recognition of the majority principle as a majority-minority relation for the understanding of horizontal effect review proposed in this book also concerns its *levelling* or *horizontalising* effect. The majority-minority principle deprives everyone involved in political debate and law-making of any (vertical) appeal to truths that would, by definition, silence dissent. Constitutional democracy reduces all political contention and all outcomes of political contention, all enactments of law included, to configurations of competing value claims. It reduces all law to configurations of competing value claims that survive in political compromises. In the final analysis, these configurations remain reflections of personal assessments or particular concerns and evaluations, none of which can claim any intrinsic, ontological or natural superiority in the struggle for law and legislation.

Kelsen's sound reasons for the deliberate non-foundationalism that so irked Schmitt should be clear from the above. To rephrase Schmitt somewhat: Not only does Kelsen not make the slightest attempt to explain the necessity of legislation and constitutional principles; *he also refuses to do so.*[72] He refuses to do so, one can argue, because any such grounding would be irreconcilable with the foundational norm of constitutional democracy, that is, with the principle that law ultimately turns on compromises and not on truth. Kelsen knows that the existential, concrete, natural or whatever substantive grounding of the law that Schmitt

---

70 Habermas, *Faktizität und Geltung – Beiträge zur Diskurstheorie des Rechts und des demokratischen Rechtsstaats*, 112–135; 167–187.

71 I rely here on an articulation that I also used in Johan Van der Walt, "Rethinking the Fundamental Structures of the State with Reference to the Horizontal Application of Fundamental Rights," in *Der grundrechtsgeprägte Verfassungsstaat: Festschrift für Klaus Stern zum 80. Geburtstag*, ed. Michael Sachs and Helmut Siekmann (Berlin: Duncker & Humblot GmbH, 2012), 627–648.

72 Schmitt, *Verfassungslehre*, 9.

demands is the beginning of the externalisation of plurality and the internalisation of unity that runs through Schmitt's thinking (no plurality is possible in the face of truth/no truth is possible in the face of plurality); Schmitt's foundationalism necessarily implies termination of civility and citizenship for the sake of military and missionary unity. Enter the ethics of soldiers.

The ethics of citizenship – the non-foundational foundation of constitutional democratic law – is the heart of Kelsen's contribution to an incisive conception of constitutionalism and constitutional review. It is the heart of his contribution to the insight that all instances of constitutional review concern the horizontal effect of constitutional rights and principles, that is, the effect of these rights *between* citizens and not *on* citizens. Kelsen and Leisner speak the same language on this count. It is exactly with regard to this point – this horizontalisation of constitutional relations – that Leisner made his most profound contribution to the theory of horizontal effect, as we shall see now.

V Leisner's "Kelsenian" Horizontal Effect Jurisprudence

What remains to be highlighted in this chapter are two key points with regard to which Leisner's understanding of horizontal effect underlines key elements of Kelsen's theory of constitutional review. The first point concerns Leisner's critique of the imprecise notions of "indirect horizontal effect" and "radiation of constitutional principles through all levels of law." The second point concerns his insistence that *all constitutional review* turns on the horizontal effect of constitutional principles.

The discussion of Kelsen's thought in section IV already unmasked the extent to which the *jurisprudential concept* of unspecified levels of value-radiation through whole systems of law falls short of the idea of law or the idea of pure law. It is this concept of value-radiation – especially as conceived by Dürig in terms of an "amelioration" of private law through the consideration of constitutional norms in private law adjudication – that loosens the screws of normative transmission and exposes the law just too much to Schmitt's expanded vision of general clauses of law that turns all legal concepts into open legal concepts. This ameliorative understanding of value-radiation may well also be lurking in constitutional clauses that stipulate the "development" of common and customary law so as to "promote" constitutional values throughout the legal system.[73] It is exactly this critique that Leisner levelled against Dürig's theory and against the

73 Cf. Articles 8(3) and 39(2) of the Constitution of South Africa of 1996.

elastic or rubbery concept of interpretation (*der Kautschukbegriff der Auslegung*) in *Lüth.*[74]

Leisner proposed in this regard, as we saw in Chapter Four, a more precise understanding of the relation between constitutional rights and private law. Constitutional norms, he argued, either apply directly to private conduct as positive norms of private law, or as minimal or essential constitutional criteria with which the adjudication of private law must comply. In both cases, however, the constitutional norms at issue either apply or do not apply. There is no third way in terms of which they serve as general ameliorating or developmental guidelines. What Dürig proposed in this regard, argued Leisner, either descends into complete vagueness or admits to the direct effect of the constitution on private law.[75] Direct effect, argued Leisner, concerns the principle that private law rules and principles, the general principles of private law included, must comply with constitutional demands. When they do not conform thus, one can now say clearly with reference also to Kelsen, they do not comply with the system of normative validation and are, therefore, simply invalidated and invalid. Their validity cannot be improved by interpretive reflection on constitutional principles. They cannot be made *more valid.* They cannot be *more* or *less valid.* And the general principles of private law can accordingly not be invoked to transmit more or less constitutional validity into private law. The open principles of private law are part and parcel of substantive private law. They too (their application) are either valid or invalid; they are either applicable law, or inapplicable law, or not law at all. This then is the first point with regard to which Kelsen and Leisner can be heard to speak the same language. Leisner, we can say, forwarded a veritable *Stufenbau* conception of horizontal effect jurisprudence.[76]

There is however, a second point of resonance between Kelsen and Leisner that also underlines the significance of Leisner's contribution to a consistent understanding of horizontal effect and liberal democratic constitutional review. According to Leisner, we saw in Chapter One, the early manifestation of "constitutional review" during the time of the French Revolution firstly concerned the "horizontal effect" of the principles of the revolution. In the mind-set of the revolutionary generation, he argued, "constitutional review" was in the first place aimed at bringing to book old private liberties and privileges that derived from feudal law and could no longer be squared with a constitution – the *Déclaration*

---

74 Leisner, *Grundrechte und Privatrecht*, 377.

75 Cf Ibid, 361.: "[W] as ... Dürig vorschlägt führt entweder zu völliger Unklarheit oder, doch zu einer mehr oder weniger unmittelbaren Drittwirkung."

76 For the way Kelsen understood the invalidation of all law that would contradict constitutional norms, cf. Kelsen, *Reine Rechtslehre*, 84–89.

– the very goal of which was to destroy feudal liberties and privileges so as to establish a framework of equality before the law. Only in the second place did it occur to the revolutionaries that exercises of state power could also be subjected to constitutional review. And whenever they in fact proceeded to subject state action to constitutional review, they also approached such instances of review as the review of private exercises of power, as if it were *conceptually* beyond the state *as state* to abuse its own power. The revolutionary generation considered instances of abuse of state powers as abuses of state powers by private individuals. The inverse of the state action doctrine in *The Civil Rights* cases was at stake (see again the discussion in Chapter Two). Only private individuals were considered capable of abusing fundamental rights, not the state.

This mind-set of the French revolutionary generation can be argued to have created an *idea* of the state in terms of which the state is always the guarantor and never the violator of fundamental rights. The use or abuse of state machinery to violate rights is of course pervasively possible, but according to the late eighteenth/early nineteenth century revolutionary mind-set at issue here, such abuses were also considered private abuses. They were considered private corruptions or abductions of the state. We return to this argument below. Important to note for now is the fact that Leisner supplemented this historical argument with a conceptual one. According to him, it is not only historically but also conceptually compelling to consider all constitutional review procedures as horizontal effect review procedures. This is how he made the point:

> "From a natural law conception of the human person, all values must be considered to derive from [evaluations by] human beings. From this perspective, liberty does not lose its value because of collisions with the state, but because of collisions with the [collective] values of other individuals. All abridgments of liberty that result from such collisions must accordingly be considered horizontal abridgments of liberty. The principle that all evaluations are human evaluations disrobes the state from independent aims or ends that are not the ends of individuals. Clashes with the state are therefore in the first place clashes with the values of other individuals."[77]

77 Leisner, *Grundrechte und Privatrecht*, 144: "Weil 'Werte' aber nach der naturrecthlich-personalen Auffassung nur vom Menschen ausgehen können, verliert eine Freiheitsbetätigung ihre 'Werthaftigkeit' stets bei Kollision, nicht primär mit der staatlichen, sondern mit der 'Wertsphäre' anderer Individuen. Der Bedeutungswandel zur Werthaftigkeit führt also ... zu einer grundsätzlich-primären 'Drittwirkung' aller Freiheit, weil ein Zusammenstoß mit dem 'Staat,' der seines 'Selbstzwecks' entkleidet ist, nur mehr eine Verletzung (vieler, mediatisierter) anderer persona-Werte ist." The translation above took some liberties for the sake of readability in English.

When values are strictly understood to derive from evaluations, that is, from the evaluating practices of human individuals, the state itself, *the state as state*, cannot have values. The state as state can then also not entertain and pursue ends of its own which are not the ends of citizens. The state is then disrobed, so to speak, of all ends of its own – *"der 'Staat,' der seines 'Selbstzwecks' entkleidet ist,"* writes Leisner. He invokes in this passage "a natural law conception of the human person." He has something in mind, however, that does not quite accord with the transcendental quality of natural law conceptions. At stake for him is evidently an insight that philosophers would much rather articulate in terms of a post-Nietzschean regard for the role of subjective evaluation in the articulation of all values. In the context of the post-metaphysical conviction that all values are but human evaluations, constitutional review can by definition not scrutinise the goals and pursuits *of the state* as if they were objective or subject-independent. The state has no independent goals or purposes that can be scrutinised. Constitutional review can at best scrutinise the goals and pursuits of those citizens who are in control of state resources and state machinery. In other words, it can at best scrutinise the pursuits of democratic majorities so as to prevent them from disregarding the fundamental rights of minorities.

The point that Leisner makes is this one: The state cannot abuse its powers, only individuals or groups can abuse the powers of the state. And the resonance of this idea with Kelsen's conception of constitutional democracy should be clear. Leisner's post-metaphysical reduction of values to personal evaluations echoes Kelsen's expulsion of truth from democratic politics with perfect pitch. Under the Kelsenian concern with the constitutional democratic sustenance of majority-minority compromises, majority democratic pursuits, deprived as they are of claims to superior or conclusive knowledge, effectively remain pursuits of fellow citizens. The constitutional review of such majority pursuits therefore effectively concerns horizontal effect review. It concerns the horizontal effect of constitutional rights and principles *between* citizens. The counter-argument that majority pursuits represent the state and thus turn into something that transcends the mere pursuits of *some* citizens does not impress the Kelsenian and Leisnerian mind-set elaborated here. Majority pursuits may represent the state momentarily, but they do not embody the state, not unilaterally, in any case. They are not the state nor do they constitute the conduct of the state. The constitutional democratic state can only be embodied by bilateral majority-minority relationships and compromises, and this embodiment constitutes in fact, in fundamental respects, a disembodiment of the state and a disembodiment of sovereignty.

VI Différantial Sovereignty

The dis-embodied or disrobed concept of sovereignty that emerges from the Kelsenian and Leisnerian conceptions of constitutional review discussed above evinces interesting similarities with the invocation of neutral power in Schmitt's early work. As we saw above, the early Schmitt invoked a distinction of Benjamin Constant in this regard that elucidates very well what is at stake in the *idea of the state* that cannot violate its own constitution. Schmitt, we saw, elaborated the notion of neutral power with reference to Constant's idea of the *pouvoir neutre*. Constant explained this concept of the *pouvoir neutre* with reference to the distinction between reigning and governing, a distinction that Schmitt then also related to the Roman distinction between auctoritas and potestas. The imperial presidency, wrote Schmitt in *Der Hüter der Verfassung*, reigns, it does not govern. It does not pursue governmental goals. Its reigning is restricted to securing the continued existence of the state and the capacity of this reigning is circumscribed by the exceptional powers with which the constitution empowers it in times of emergency. If any *one* office or person can be said to embody the state, it would be someone or something like Schmitt's president or presidency that reigns without governing. Schmitt would later again refer to the state as the neutral power that neutralises the factional or unilateral threats that civil society might pose to the continued existence of the state.[78] Kelsen articulated a devastating critique of Schmitt's ideas in this regard, the crux of which turned on the question why the imperial president, advised by a presidential committee, should be a more neutral protector of the constitution than a constitutional court.[79]

The political neutrality of the office of the president is undoubtedly a highly contentious idea. And Schmitt surely also did not waste the opportunity to use this idea in 1933 in order to *neutralise* the president and give the *Führer* exclusive powers of government.[80] It is nevertheless unfortunate that Kelsen was not a little more sympathetic to the historical background of this idea, however much Schmitt's appropriations and misappropriations of the idea in times for which it was surely no longer fit were bound to be highly dubious. Schmitt simply came too late – after Kant, after Nietzsche – to entertain the idea that the political neutrality of any single person could still enjoy the metaphysical credibility with which pre-modern monarchs could claim to have received their earthly

78 Schmitt, "Neutralität und Neutralisierungen," 309–334.
79 Kelsen and Ooyen, *Wer soll Hüter der Verfassung sein?* 61–79.
80 Schmitt, *Staat, Bewegung, Volk*, 9–10.

powers directly from God.[81] The idea was undoubtedly spent by the time Schmitt tried to revive it for better (1922) and for worse (1933) purposes. However, the idea of neutrality that is still evident in the concept of a power that reigns without governing, and reigns so as to keep in check the biases and lack of neutrality of all positive political programmes, should not be dismissed too quickly. It may still be one of the best denotations available for the constitutional sustenance of horizontal majority-minority relations and compromises that Kelsen and Leisner identified as the essence of constitutional democracy. In this last section of this chapter, this idea of *reigning that does not govern* will be developed further with reference to the Derridean concept of *différance*. At issue will be the articulation of a concept of sovereignty that reigns as an instantiation of *différance*, hence the invocation of a *différantial* sovereignty. Derrida might have simply invoked in this regard, the reign of *différance*.

The problem that one discerns in Schmitt's concept of the reign of sovereignty concerns the way he invariably linked this reign to an underlying subjectivity that founds and informs the atomic unity of the political group. Schmitt always fell back on this conception of underlying subjectivity, even at times when he came close to articulating thoughts that might have led him away from it. His atomistic and unitary conception of the political evidently resurfaced in his invocation of Constant's distinction between reigning and governing. Here too did he end up identifying this reigning with subjective powers, namely, the powers granted to the imperial president under Section 48 of the Weimar Constitution. The moment that such identification of reigning with subjective powers takes place it becomes almost impossible to sustain the distinction between reigning and governing. One then inevitably ends up cladding reigning with governmental powers or simply reducing reigning to governing. That is why Hindenburg, in respective phases of Schmitt's thinking comes across as either a potential autocrat (with or without an advising committee, this is immaterial) with exclusive emergency powers,[82] or a powerless figure that leaves all governing to Hitler. And that is also why Schmitt could so easily describe Hitler in 1933

---

81 In 1849, the Prussian King Friedrich Wilhelm IV would still or again resist the horizontalisation of constitutional sovereignty by rejecting the invitation of the Paulskirche Assembly to become the King of a United Germany. He insisted that he obtains his sovereignty from the higher authority of the heavens. This is a remarkably late invocation of a vocabulary that was surely running out of steam, also in Germany, in the course of the nineteenth century. Cf. Lothar Gall, ed., *Fragen an die deutsche Geschichte: Ideen, Kräfte, Entscheidungen von 1800 bis zur Gegenwart* (Bonn: Deutscher Bundestag, 1987), 147–148.
82 Cf. Schmitt, *Der Hüter der Verfassung*, 132–140.

as having assumed the capacities of both reigning and governing.[83] Be it as it may, Derrida had no doubt that Schmitt's conception of the political never departed from the metaphysics of underlying subjectivity.[84] It is also this metaphysics that ultimately sustained Schmitt's understanding of the sameness and unity of the ruler and the ruled.

Kelsen's thought very clearly offers us the possibility of a very different understanding of the political and of the concept of reigning, one that moves markedly away from conceiving the political in terms of atomic origins and subjective powers. As we saw above, Kelsen refrained from positing the presence of a *Grundnorm* or foundational value for his hierarchy of legal norms. He insisted, we saw, on the *presupposed* or *vorausgesetzte* status of the *Grundnorm*. The *Grundnorm* is a fiction that sustained the coherent hierarchy of law, he argued. It is therefore not a metaphysical ground that anchored the system of norms in a foundational truth. And this non-foundationalism is clearly also repeated within the assumed *Grundnorm* itself when we assume the *Grundnorm* to be that of liberal democracy.

The liberal democratic *Grundnorm* safeguards the system of legal norms from infusion by truth or truths. It consists in the functional imperative to sustain democratic relationships between majorities and minorities. It sees to it that the political process remains undistorted by claims to higher wisdom or more authoritative convictions that only some share. It prevents exclusion and marginalisation by disqualifying from politics all convictions that cannot plausibly and persuasively be argued to be convictions that everyone shares.

Liberal democracy is a system of government that requires persons with different convictions to simply live together as equals. It begins and ends with the demand that the coexistence of more than one opinion or conviction be preserved as its foundational principle. As such, liberal democracy evidently concerns a legal and political system that is founded on the *assumption* of split origins, and not on the assertion of atomic foundations and exclusive truths. The emphasis on *assumption* is crucial here, for it is through this *assumption* that the sovereignty of liberal democracy or liberal democratic sovereignty shows its sovereign hand. The notion of split origins also has no preferential ontological status. It is fundamentally or foundationally dependent on a sovereign decision to uphold or presuppose the principle of split origins as the keystone of a political and legal system.

This description of Kelsen's conception of liberal democratic constitutionalism has already moved far into a field or mode of inquiry and analysis that Jac-

---

83 Schmitt, *Staat, Bewegung, Volk*, 9–10.

84 Jacques Derrida, *Politiques de l'amitié* (Paris: Galilée, 1994), 86–87.

ques Derrida opened up with the concept of *différance*. The crux of this mode of inquiry and analysis consists in the decision (no doubt!) to resist readings of texts that aim to establish one coherent meaning. It engages in this resistance for purposes of showing that textual meaning is invariably the outcome of multiple tensions that are never laid to rest completely. In the later phases of his work, Derrida expanded this mode of inquiry for purposes of showing how political sovereignty too, despite its attempt to construct itself in terms of nuclear selfness or ipseity, always remains suspended in tensions with alterity. It always remains significantly exterior and foreign to itself. Seen from this perspective, classical sovereignty consisted in the denial and exclusion of difference and alterity. Derridean deconstructions of sovereignty, on the other hand, consists in reminding sovereignty of its irreducible entwinement with outsides that are crucial for the construction of its most inner insides. It is not necessary to engage more incisively with these thoughts of Derrida's here.[85] Suffice it to say that these thoughts evidently provide one with productive conceptual strategies with which the following Kelsenian and Leisnerian understanding of liberal democracy can be ventured:

Liberal democracy inclines, as far as it *plausibly* can, towards the *inclusion* of its outsides. As such, liberal democratic sovereignty is a peculiar kind of sovereignty that inverses – again, as far as *plausibly* possible – the typical or classical thrust of sovereignty towards externalisation of alterity and difference (typically through friend/enemy distinctions). It reverses the inclination towards homogenisation and the establishment of a nuclear self. It does not resist the insight that its origin has always been split. Liberal democratic sovereignty does not resist the insight that it derives from a split that it cannot mend. It is in this respect that one can call liberal democracy *horizontal* instead of *vertical* sovereignty. It is sovereignty that is spread between multiple points of reference that figure on horizontal planes. It is sovereignty that reigns between citizens. The idea of perpendicular sovereignty that towers over and overshadows everything around it is foreign to it.

It is this peculiar sovereignty of liberal democracy that we have come to call différantial sovereignty in this chapter. It turns, not on one pivot, but on more than one, at least two. And these pivots themselves, be they two or more than two, constantly mutate. Liberal democratic sovereignty becomes manifest over time as a dynamic of differentiations, differences, deferrals and mutations that never come to rest. By grace or by force of these differentiations, differences, deferrals and mutations unfolds the sheer *historicity* of liberal democracy (see

85 Cf. Derrida, *Voyous: deux essais sur la raison* (Paris: Galile´e, 2003), 19–66.

Chapter Two again). It is this *historicity* or *temporality* that reveals the constitutive liberty of liberal democracy, namely, the liberty to reveal and show itself differently.

Liberal democracy inevitably depends on governments and governing officials. These governing officials come and go as the history of liberal democracy unfolds. But none of them ever come to *reign*. Nobody – no person, no subject – reigns in liberal democracies. Only liberal democracy reigns in liberal democracies. Only liberal democracy is sovereign in liberal democracies. But there are officials who are crucial for the reign and sovereignty of liberal democracy and they are the judges. Liberal democratic judges are state officials, no doubt, but they are not government officials. Their task is to monitor and sustain the reign of liberal democracy by monitoring and sustaining the differential and deferential relations between governing majorities and governed minorities. They would of course not be able to do this if they were to be elected by these majorities and minorities so as to "represent" them proportionally, as Kelsen once suggested they should be. This is the surest way of having judiciaries of whom the members favour either majorities or minorities. It is the surest way of electing judges who become either government or anti-government officials. Judges are neither of these. Their task is to sustain plausibly proper relations between governing majorities and governed minorities without governing (or anti-govering) themselves. That is how judiciaries represent the reign of liberal democracy.

How do judges sustain plausibly proper relations between majorities and minorities? They do so by maintaining and applying the principle of minimal coercion, which is, in the same breath, surprisingly perhaps, not a principle of maximal constraint, but of minimal constraint. Liberal democracy that is both intrinsically liberal and intrinsically democratic – and not just an unstable compound of monolithic liberalism and monolithic democracy – requires that governing majorities do not coerce minorities more than necessary, and governed minorities do not constrain majorities more than necessary. It is the task of judiciaries to ensure this minimal constraint and minimal coercion. This may appear thoroughly implausible, but it is not.

One might think minimal coercion of minorities must turn on maximal constraint of majorities, but only libertarians really think this, and they are not liberal democrats and do not understand liberal democracy. If democratic majorities receive *democratic* status from the way they respect the freedom of minorities, as Kelsen suggested, democratic minorities also receive their *democratic* status from the way they respect the freedom of majority governments to govern freely. Kelsen taught us that proper minority protections require proper majority powers, and vice versa. A moment's reflection makes the neat simplicity of this insight abundantly clear. Majorities do not need *democratic* majority powers to protect themselves and their own interests. Being majorities, they can surely do so by other means, even outright undemocratic means, should they wish to do so. They need *democratic* powers for one thing only, namely, for governing in ways that will sustain the democratic respect of minorities. And if the confounding conundrums of the New Deal with which Seidman, Nedelsky and Nerkin engage so thoughtfully (see Chapter Three again) clarify at least one thing, they surely clarify the other side of the coin that is at issue here: Minority protections remain largely meaningless when majorities cannot launch forceful governmental programmes that give meaning to them.

That is why judiciaries do not pose any counter-majoritarian obstacles when consistent liberal democratic sovereignty prevails. Public power cannot be an impediment to liberty if it is to remain *public* power. Public power is the condition for liberty, as the New Deal in the United States made abundantly clear. The task of judiciaries is to sustain minority protections exactly through the sustenance of the freedom of majorities to govern properly. When judiciaries engage in review of legislation they do not engage in anti-majoritarian practices. They engage in pro-majoritarian practices as much as they engage in pro-minority practices. When judicial review is properly practiced – something that requires abstinence from substantive due process review in all but a few exceptional cases – it endorses the right of majorities to govern. This is the classic lesson that we learn from Justice Holmes' dissent in Lochner.

This is surely the underlying wisdom that informs the classic proportionality tests that judiciaries regularly employ or employed in the "vertical" review of legislation. But this wisdom has perhaps become too faded and obscure in current review practices and in constitutional theory. And the reason for this obscuration may well be the increasing displacement of this classical form of judicial review with practices of "balancing rights" that judiciaries inherited from the kind of jurisprudence that the GFCC developed in *Lüth*. It is this concept of balancing that turns judges into governing officials. It is high time that constitutional theory rearticulates the wisdom of classical review procedures in a way that refreshes them fundamentally. This is what the last chapter of this book – Chapter Eight – sets out to do. It will endeavour to do so by showing, true to the insights of Leisner articulated in this chapter, that the proper application of proportionality tests always concerns the horizontal effect of constitutional rights. Going this route requires, however, that one rehabilitate the proper or classic proportionality test for horizontal effect review, or something akin to it. Again, we return to this task in Chapter Eight.

Chapter Seven, however, will first turn now to other business. It will first turn now to a current example of how classical judicial review procedures have become displaced by the kind of review procedures articulated in *Lüth*. At issue will also be a current example of a judiciary that governs instead of reigns, with devastating results for liberal democracy. The jurisprudence of *Lüth* has again been imported from Germany in the way South Africa imported it in 1996. This time the importing agent was the ECJ and the significant date of importation (it actually started earlier) was 2007. And this importation of *Lüth* (or the kind of jurisprudence developed in *Lüth*) by the ECJ, we shall now see in Chapter Seven, would, ironically be disastrous for *Lüth's* future in Germany.

Chapter Seven: Sovereignty and the Dual Destiny of *Lüth* in Europe

I Introduction

Chapter Five already engaged with some of the key issues of the "transfer" of sovereignty that is taking place in Europe today.[1] Two elements of this transfer are again of concern in this chapter. The first is the shifting of sovereignty from the Member States to the European Union that section II of Chapter Five discussed extensively with reference to Dieter Grimm's question "Who is sovereign in Europe?" The second concerns the dispersal of sovereignty that section IV of Chapter Five discussed with reference to the shift from government to governance that is taking place in contemporary societies. The first element – the rise of European Union sovereignty at the expense of Member State sovereignty – will be the main concern of most of this chapter. The second element – the dispersal of European sovereignty – will only come into the picture towards the end of the chapter.

The central argument of this chapter concerns the shift or transfer of sovereignty from the Member States to the European Union that is taking place in the judicial practices of the ECJ. The essence of these sovereignty-transferring or sovereignty-appropriating judicial practices, it will be contended, consists in the ECJ's resort to a jurisprudence that is essentially the same jurisprudence that the GFCC developed in *Lüth*. The argument has two sides that relate to the two sides of the jurisprudence in *Lüth*. On the one hand, earlier chapters of this book argued, the jurisprudence in *Lüth* constituted a statement of full territorial sovereignty because of the way it acknowledged the reach of the fundamental rights protections embodied in the GG into all spheres of law and life in Germany. Already on this count was the ECJ's appropriation of the jurisprudence in *Lüth* bound to have significant implications for sovereignty in Europe, for it surely signalled a bold confirmation of its insistence – evident ever since *Van Gend en Loos* and *Costa v E.N.E.L.* – that its interpretations of European law have direct and by implication direct horizontal effect throughout the European Union. Relations between individuals in the European Union are evidently directly governed by the "constitutional" principles embodied in the European Treaties. The express articulation of this horizontal effect of the treaties in later cases

1 Cf. Neil Walker, ed., *Sovereignty in Transition*, (Oxford: Hart Publishing, 2003).

such as *Bosman*, *Defrenne* and again in *Viking* and *Laval* was the logical extension of the position already taken in *Van Gend en Loos* en *Costa v E.N.E.L.*

The other side of the argument concerns the nature of the sovereignty that has thus been or is thus being transferred from Member States to the Union. This is the disconcerting side of the story that relates to the disconcerting side of the jurisprudence developed in *Lüth*. The basic affirmation of constitutional sovereignty in *Lüth* is essential for the proper recognition of horizontal effect and it has been commended as such throughout this book. There is therefore no reason why one should question the ECJ's jurisprudence on this count. If the court's jurisdiction and authority is to have any sovereign significance, its judgments must obviously apply directly to individuals and to the horizontal relations between them. The disconcerting side of this assertion of sovereignty, however, relates to the ECJ's "*Lüthian*" understanding of this sovereignty (the court does of course not base its judgments expressly on *Lüth*, hence the scarecrows).

Chapter Two described the jurisprudence in *Lüth* in terms of the substantive due process review procedure that American legal theorists associate with the judgment of the USSC in *Lochner v New York*. It also showed how the problematic side of these substantive due process review procedures became manifest in the GFCC's judgment in *Erste Abtreibung*. The ECJ's endorsement of direct effect and direct horizontal effect has all along been accompanied by similar substantive due process review procedures. The trouble that came to the GFCC in *Erste Abtreibung* could therefore be expected to also hit the ECJ sooner or later. All that was needed for this to happen was a case or a series of cases that turned on deeply divisive political and social concerns in Europe. And this happened in the *Laval, Viking, Rüffert and Luxembourg* cases. By resorting to the practice of balancing competing values that is so central to the jurisprudence in *Lüth*, the ECJ proceeded to make substantive due process rulings in these cases that simply ignored the deep social and political divisions that informed the disputes in them.

This resort of the ECJ to substantive due process review procedures in *Laval*, *Viking*, *Luxembourg* and *Rüffert* is an essential characteristic of the sovereignty that the European Union is asserting in Europe today. The transfer of sovereignty that is at issue here is neither a liberal democratic transfer of sovereignty nor a transfer of liberal democratic sovereignty. It is a transfer of sovereignty that is driven and managed by a judiciary that has brazenly taken over functions of government. And the sovereignty transferred in the process reflects no regard for divisive social concerns and the majority-minority relations concomitant to them. Considered in terms of the concepts elaborated in Chapter Six, the ECJ is not a court that *reigns*. It is not a court that monitors constitutional majority-minority relations. It is a court that *governs*. And as courts often do when they govern (when they resort to substantive due process review), the ECJ governs in a brazenly counter-majoritarian fashion. Widespread perceptions of the deep democratic deficit that marks European integration today will surely be emboldened by the ECJ's decisions in *Laval*, *Viking*, *Luxembourg* and *Rüffert*. The question whether this development will promote or frustrate the process of European integration is not difficult to answer.

The significance of *Lüth* cannot but fall into decline if the sovereignty of which it is the expression is falling into decline. If the jurisprudence in *Lüth* is indeed a statement of full jurisdictional sovereignty in Germany, as is argued in this book, any appropriation of that jurisprudence by another court for a jurisdiction to which all the jurisdictions of German judiciaries are subject, must self-evidently lead to the complete subordination of the latter jurisdictions to the former jurisdiction. This was bound to happen ever since the ECJ's assertion of the direct effect and direct horizontal effect of European law pointed out above. All that still had to happen for the confirmation of this displacement of *Lüthian* sovereignty in Germany itself was the application of this jurisprudence to a case that would come from German soil and this happened when the ECJ passed its judgment in *Rüffert*. The fact that *Rüffert* was not strictly or formally a horizontal effect case (it is that in terms of the views developed in this book) does not matter, for it is the substance of the "balancing" jurisprudence in *Lüth* that in the end came around to inform the ruling in *Rüffert*. Something similar also happened when the ECHR heard and decided the *Görgülü* and *Hannover* cases,[2] but the arguments in this chapter will focus on *Laval*, *Viking* and *Rüffert* because of the significantly more divisive potential of these cases.

The arguments outlined above will be developed as follows in this chapter. Section II traces the rise and increasing consolidation of European Union sovereignty that has resulted/is resulting from the ECJ's appropriation of the substantive due process horizontal effect jurisprudence that the GFCC developed in *Lüth*. This rise and consolidation of European Union sovereignty may for a while still remain *de facto* sovereignty that lacks *de jure* foundations. However, it is well-established knowledge in the domain of legal theory that *de facto* sovereignty always precedes *de jure* sovereignty. It is in fact the precipitating condition for *de jure* sovereignty. And when it is not met with resistance soon enough, it is bound to establish itself as *de jure* sovereignty before long. The significance of such *de facto* transfers of sovereignty should not be underestimated.

2 *Görgülü v Germany* [2004] ECHR 88; *Von Hannover v Germany* (2005) 40 E.H.R.R. 1.

Section III describes what one can plausibly call the demise of German sovereignty that has been taking place in Germany in recent years. This demise, section III contends, is bound to lead to the marginalisation of *Lüth* in Germany. *Lüth* can plausibly be said to have been very instrumental in its own demise. Its "triumph" in Europe is in many respects the cause of its downfall in Germany, and it is this combination of triumph and decline that will be described as *Lüth's* dual destiny in Europe.

Section IV assesses the nature of the European Union sovereignty that is emerging from the adjudication of the ECJ and finds it fundamentally wanting as far as the différantial concept of sovereignty developed in Chapter Six is concerned. The substantive due process review procedure taken over in *Laval*, *Viking* and *Rüffert* is typical of a monolithic and vertical sovereignty. It is definitely not horizontal and différantial. At work in these cases was a court that governs, not a court that reigns. A court that believes it has the authority and wisdom from the basis of which conflicts that spring from deep socio-political divisions can be resolved correctly – by "balancing" fundamental economic freedoms with social rights – assumes nothing less than superhuman powers for itself. A court with any sense of mortal modesty, not to mention a sense of democratic accountability, should not do this. It should not enter the fray of disputes like these. It should only monitor them and see to it that they do not get completely out of hand. And the way to do this is to stay away from any substantive due process review procedures until such time as it becomes absolutely impossible to avoid them. In other words, the way to do it is to defer to democratic legislation as far as possible, be this legislation express or implicit.

Judiciaries often have to decide questions of empirical incommensurability in coercive ways. They do so, we saw, whenever they act on behalf of the general will of a people that Rousseau, Hegel and Kant contemplated. They then ignore empirical incommensurability for the sake of an ideal commensurability that they believe they can ascribe to the will of each and everyone involved. They do so whenever they find grounds for criminal conviction or delictual damages. But they cannot do so, however, when empirical incommensurability reflects deep social divisions that render the notion of "the will of everyone" implausible. Under these circumstances, the task of reconciling incommensurabilities should be entrusted to the heavens. And the heavens themselves, it would appear, simply leave this task to the dissipating force of time. Mortals invariably respond to this temporal processing of the incommensurable with agony, but when they also do so with wisdom, they organise themselves by ballot into democratic majorities and minorities. That is the only way in which the incommensurable can be "reconciled" or "balanced" without widening the gaps from which it springs.

II The Rise of European Union Sovereignty

Earlier Chapters of this book contended that the GFCC's judgment in *Lüth* constituted the consummation of the principle of full territorial constitutional sovereignty in post-war Germany. The indirect but effective acceptance of the horizontal effect of fundamental rights in *Lüth*, went the argument, signalled the GFCC's firm assertion that there is no part of German territory that is not governed by the sovereign demands of the GG. The idea that a private sphere could somehow be exempted from these sovereign constitutional demands basically perished when the GFCC passed its judgment in *Lüth* in 1957. It is surely ironic, but it could not have come as a surprise that the claim to full territorial constitutional sovereignty in Germany would become seriously jeopardised the moment that another judicial power would appropriate the principles of the GFCC's judgment in *Lüth* for purposes of claiming a similarly full territorial sovereignty in large parts of Europe that would also include the Federal Republic of Germany. This is what happened when the ECJ asserted the horizontal effect of Articles 39, 43 and 49 of the TEC (now Articles 45, 49 and 56 of the TFEU) in its judgments in *Viking* and *Laval* in December 2007. One can say *Lüth* had a 50-year run in Germany before it walked over to the European Union.

It of course did not all happen in that one (constitutionally) eventful December when *Laval* and *Viking* were decided. As these judgments make clear, the principle of the horizontal effect of the fundamental freedoms was already accepted in earlier ECJ case law. The *Bosman* and *Defrenne* cases were clear precedents by that time.[3] And the claim to sovereignty embodied in the recognition of the horizontal effect of the fundamental freedoms was also evidently prepared by the ECJ's decisions regarding the direct effect of European Union law in *Van Gend en Loos* and *Costa v E.N.E.L.* in 1963 and 1964.[4] When one considers these two groundbreaking cases, one may want to conclude that *Lüth's* run in Germany may well have been much shorter than the half-century suggested here. However, we know from the United States' experience with the state action doctrine that the resistance to the direct effect (and therefore direct horizontal effect) of the Federal Bill of Rights and especially the Fourteenth Amendment played a significant symbolic role in the way the individual states guarded their sovereignty vis-à-vis the Federal Government (see again the discussion of *The Civil Rights Cases* in Chapter Two). In view of the historical significance of the resistance to horizontal effect as an instance of anti-federal resistance, the

3 EU: Case 415/93 [1995] (*Bosman*); EU: Case 43/75 [1976] (*Defrenne*)
4 EU: Case 26/26 [1963]; EU: Case 6/64 [1964].

firm recognition and acceptance of the horizontal effect of the Union Treaties under the controversial circumstances of the *Viking* and *Laval* cases may well one day be recognized as crucial moments in the federalization of Europe.

Again, there were earlier horizontal effect judgments in the case law of the ECJ. But the divisive circumstances under which the court adopted horizontal effect so unflinchingly in *Laval* and *Viking* tell the story of a court that was prepared to stage a revolutionary act of federalization. European constitutional scholars may well come to refer one day with much rhetorical force to that watershed December of 2007. *Laval* and *Viking* may well become as significant milestones in the ECJ's "quietly revolutionary" case law as the milestones that *Van Gend en Loos* and *Costa v E.N.E.L.* have become.[5]

Both *Laval* and *Rüffert* concerned cases in which the union action or the invocation of an existing collective agreement at issue sought to secure host state working conditions for workers of other Member States. At issue, in other words, was an attempt to include workers under existing working conditions, not an attempt to exclude them from those conditions. Articles 3(1) and (8) of the Posted Workers Directive of the European Council and Parliament, Directive 96/71, essentially proscribe the exclusion of workers from existing working conditions and agreements in the host state. If anyone was aiming to exclude workers from such working conditions, it was the claimants in these cases, Laval and Rüffert, not the Swedish trade unions and not the state of Niedersachsen. At stake in the articles of the Directive are anti-discrimination measures, not measures that are evidently or expressly aimed at promoting freedom of movement at the cost of Member State legislation or collective bargaining agreements that are evidently not discriminatory.[6]

Laval concerned the question whether industrial action in the building sector aimed at securing collective bargaining agreements for Latvian workers in Sweden was reconcilable with Directive 96/71/EC and article 49 of the TEC (freedom to provide services – now article 56 of the TFEU). *Viking* turned on the conflict between Finnish seamen and Viking, the owner of a Finnish-registered ferry, in the wake of the latter's decision to reflag the ferry in Estonia so as to benefit from less burdensome Estonian labour agreements and regulations. At stake on the one hand were the rights that the Finnish seamen claimed under collective bargaining agreements secured in terms of Finnish Labour Law, as well as the fundamental rights to collective bargaining warranted by Article 13 of the Fin-

5 Joseph Weiler, "A Quiet Revolution. The European Court of Justice and its Interlocutors," *Comparative Political Studies*, 26 (1994): 510–534.

6 Cf. Catherine Barnard, "A Proportionate Response to Proportionality in the Field of Collective Action," *European Law Review*, 37 (2012): 118.

nish Constitution and Article 28 of the European Charter of Fundamental Rights. At stake on the other hand was the liberty Viking claimed to re-register the ferry in Estonia in terms of article 43 of the TEC (freedom of establishment – now article 49 of the TFEU). *Rüffert* concerned the compatibility of Niedersachsen legislation on compliance of posted workers with local collective bargaining agreements with the freedom of movement of workers guaranteed under article 49 of the TEC (now 56 of the TFEU) as regulated in Directive 96/71/EC.

In *Laval*, a Latvian building company won a government contract to renovate school premises in Vaxholm, Sweden. The company posted a number of Latvian workers to Sweden to build the school. The Swedish builders' union (Svenska Byggnadsarbetareförbundet) opened negotiations with Laval's Swedish subsidiary with the aim of extending the relevant collective bargaining agreements to the posted workers in order to negotiate wages for them. The negotiations failed and the union began to blockade Laval's building sites. All work on Laval's sites basically came to a halt and Laval's Swedish subsidiary went into liquidation. Laval consequently sought a declaration in the Swedish Courts that the industrial action was unlawful. It also sought an injunction to stop the action as well as compensation from the unions for damages suffered. The Arbetsdomstolen referred questions to the ECJ on the interpretation of Directive 96/71 and Article 49 TEC, on freedom to provide services.

Directive 96/71 seeks to ensure that workers from one member state posted to another receive minimum protection as regards terms and conditions of employment. It also aims to ensure that member states do not treat foreign firms with posted workers less favourably than local firms. The ECJ accepted that industrial action can be used to procure the minimum protections stipulated in the Directive, but it deemed the industrial action at issue in the case unlawful for two reasons:

1) Foreign firms can be demanded to comply with local collective bargaining agreements with general application in the relevant sector of work, but they could not be required to engage in "case by case" negotiations within the sector.
2) The Directive can be used to negotiate minimum wages and protections, but it does not allow for the negotiation of more generous terms. This finding is most remarkable in view of Article 3(7) of the Directive that states clearly that the Directive should not be used to preclude the negotiation of more favourable conditions. We return to this point presently.

The ECJ's ruling in *Viking* endorsed the freedom of Viking to reflag its Finnish-registered ferry in Estonia. It considered the industrial action in question an unlawful restriction of freedom of establishment under article 43 because it "has the effect of making less attractive, or even pointless ... Viking's exercise of its right to freedom of establishment." The Court held that Viking would evidently enjoy less favourable treatment than other firms established in the host state. It nevertheless stressed that this subordination was not a matter of simply disregarding social considerations and objectives but of recognising that economic and social objectives are "co-original" in European law. In other words, at stake in the case was the proper "balancing" and "harmonising" of social and economic concerns in the dispute, as Advocate General Kokott stressed with regard to the *Laval* ruling.[7] Some commentators accept this rhetoric of "balancing" and "harmonising" with enthusiasm,[8] some do so more cautiously.[9] Many others, however, have decidedly pointed out the privileging of economic liberties (and the economic constitution of Europe) over fundamental social rights that is evident in these rulings of the ECJ.[10]

---

7 Juliane Kokott, "The ECJ's Interpretation of the Posting Directive in the Laval and Rüffert Judgements" http://www.bmas.de/portal/27236/property=pdf/2008__07__16__symposium__eugh__kokott__englisch.pdf.

8 Charles F. Sabel and Oliver H. Gerstenberg, "Constitutionalising an Overlapping Consensus: The ECJ and the Emergence of a Coordinate Constitutional Order," *European Law Journal* 16, no. 5 (2010): 511–550. These authors provide a careful account of the balancing the ECJ undertook in these cases, but remarkably without any concern with the question whether this balancing should have taken place in the first place. It is this question that will be our main concern in this chapter.

9 Probing inquiries into the deeply contradictory issues involved in the balancing process in which the ECJ engaged in *Laval* and *Viking* which nevertheless also ends up commending the courts endeavours in this regard can be found in Loïc Azoulai, " "The Court of Justice and the Social Market Economy: The Emergence of an Ideal and the Conditions for its Realisation," *Common Market Law Review*, 45 (2008): 1335–1356 and Dragana Damjanovic, "The EU Market Rules as Social Market Rules: Why the EU Can be a Social Market Economy?" *Common Market Law Review*, 50 (2013): 1685–1718. In the final analysis Azoulai and Damjanovich retreat remarkably easily from their more critical insights, but their analyses of the key issues are instructive.

10 Barnard, "Employment Rights, Free Movement Under the EC Treaty and the Services Directive," in *EU Industrial Relations v. National Industrial Relations* (Alphen aan den Rijn: Kluwer Law International, 2008), 137–168, especially at 151: "It could be argued that this is, in fact, balance in name, not substance... Community law automatically puts the 'social' on the backfoot... Despite the recognition of the right to strike as a fundamental right ... this recognition has little more than rhetorical value." Cf. also Barnard, "Social Dumping or Dumping Socialism?," *The Cambridge Law Journal* 67, no. 02 (2008): 262–264; A. C. L. Davies, "One Step Forward, Two Steps Back? The Viking and Laval Cases in the ECJ," *Industrial Law Journal* 37, no. 2 (June 1, 2008): 126–148, doi:10.1093/indlaw/dwn001; Christian Joerges and Florian Rödl, "Informal Politics, Formalised Law and the 'Social Deficit' of European Integration: Reflections after the Judgments of the ECJ in Viking and Laval," *European Law Journal* 15, no. 1 (2009): 1–19, doi:10.1111/j.1468-0386.2008.00448.x; Robert Rebhahn "Grundrechte und Grundfreiheiten im

In *Rüffert* the ECJ appeared to have no qualms with dismantling elements of procedurally sound social democratic legislation that German social democrats may well have hoped to retain as democratically accountable and settled law. Dirk Rüffert, liquidator of the assets of the company *Objekt und Bauregie*, pursued a claim of *Objekt und Bauregie* against Niedersachsen for services rendered in the building of the Göttingen-Rosdorf prison. The Hannover Landgericht (Regional Court) offset the claim with a penalty incurred by Objekt und Bauregie for contravening Niedersachsen legislation. The legislation at issue, the *Landesvergabegesetz*, required contractors and subcontractors to comply with Niedersachsen social security regulation and collective bargaining agreements whenever they tender for building and public transport service contracts with Niedersachsen authorities. The preamble of the legislation stated expressly that the aim of the legislation was to avoid "distortions of competition which arise in the field of construction and local public transport services resulting from the use of cheap labour" and to alleviate "burdens on social security schemes."[11] On appeal to the Celle Oberlandesgericht (Higher Regional Court), the latter Court referred the case to the ECJ for a preliminary ruling regarding the compatibility of the legislation at issue with European law, notably Article 49 TEC and Council Directive 96/71, Article 3(1).

According to the ECJ, the restriction of the legislative requirements to building and transport service agreements with Niedersachsen public authorities made it clear that the regulations did not apply "universally" to "all similar undertakings in the geographical area and in the profession or industry concerned" as Article 3 (8) of Directive 96/71 stipulated. The legislation therefore fell foul of Article 3 (4) of the Directive which requires Member States to guarantee workers from other Member States posted to their territories the terms and conditions of employment that are "universally applicable within the meaning of Art. 3 par 8." Thus did the Niedersachsen legislator lose its right to determine the working and social security conditions of employees involved in contracts (or subcontracts) with Niedersachsen public authorities. And thus did Dirk Rüffert vindicate Ob-

kollektiven Arbeitsrecht vor dem Hintergrund der neuen EuGH Rechtsprechung," referenced on this page, http://www.etui.org/fr/Themes/Dialogue-social-et-negociation-collective/Legislation-sociale/Interpretation-de-la-Cour-europeenne-de-Justice/Reaction-aux-jugements/Articles-Presse-etc, but no longer accessible (Prof. Rebhahn kindly provided me with a copy on request); Rebhahn, "Grundfreiheit vor Arbeitskampf," *Zesar* (2008): 57–65; Fritz Scharpf, "'The Only Solution is to Refuse to Comply with ECJ Rulings,'" *Social Europe Journal*, April 6, 2009, http://www.social-europe.eu/2009/04/interview-the-only-solution-is-to-refuse-to-comply-with-ecj-rulings/. Cf. also Supiot, "Le Sommeil Dogmatique Européen," 185–198.

11 *Rüffert* paragraph 5.

jekt und Bauregie's right to sub-contract 53 Polish workers to build the Göttingen-Rosdorf prison in Niedersachsen at 46.7 % of the minimum wage laid down by the "Building and Public Works Collective Agreement" in Niedersachsen.

The different academic and political responses that the *Laval*, *Viking* and *Rüffert* rulings elicited were to be expected. There is little point in joining the fray here as far as the substantive outcomes of these cases are concerned. The responses would have been as controversial had the court made similar substantive rulings in favour of the other parties in these cases. The more pressing questions that should be asked here concern the decision of the ECJ to engage with the questions in these cases in a way that was bound to be deeply controversial and contentious.[12] Why did it appropriate for itself the capacity or jurisdiction to suggest judicial resolutions for conflicts that are deeply political and should therefore have been deferred, as far as possible, to political authorities? What alternatives were available to the court and what is the effect of the options it exercised? These are the key questions that are of concern in what follows.

The rulings in *Laval* and *Rüffert* could not have been reached on the strength of Directive 96/71 alone. In fact, a proper or at least very plausible reading of Directive 96/71 would suggest that its articles should never have been invoked as grounds for the unlawfulness of the union action in *Laval* and the implementation of the legislation and collective agreements in *Rüffert*. The Directive is very clearly aimed at securing for posted workers the minimum benefits (minimum salaries, minimum holidays, resting hours, etc.) and the limitation of maximum burdens (maximum working hours) to which host state nationals are entitled in terms of legislation and collective bargaining agreements. In other words, the aim of the Directive is clearly that host states should ensure that posted workers

12 Cf. in this regard Harm Schepel, "Constitutionalising the Market, Marketising the Constitution, and to Tell the Difference: On the Horizontal Application of the Free Movement Provsions in EU Law," *European Law Journal*, 18 (2012): 177–200; and again Barnard, "A Proportionate Response to Proportionality," 124–129. Both Schepel and Barnard question the ECJ's method of balancing fundamentally. Schepel concludes with the following observation: "Absent a clear hierarchy of norms and values, without a coherent conception of the 'fundamental freedoms,' and with no clear conflict rules, [the ECJ's approach of 'striking a fair balance between competing interests'] is bound to end up in highly indeterminate and unpredictable 'weighing and balancing' of everything involved." Schepel's and Barnard's critiques of this insufficiently normatively constrained balancing evidently also join the earlier critigues of this kind of judicial freedom associated with horizontal effect judicial review articulated earlier by Böckenförde, Leisner and Ruffert in response to *Lüth*. Cf. again in this regard the discussions of the German Drittwirkung debate in Chapter Four and also the discussion of proportionality in Chapter Eight.

do not have worse working conditions than host state nationals. As already pointed out above, article 3(7) of the Directive makes it clear that this guarantee of the same working conditions for posted workers also does not imply prescriptions of better working conditions for them.[13] What the Swedish unions sought to achieve in *Laval* and the Niedersachsen government sought to achieve in *Rüffert* were surely not at odds with this reading of the Directive. Read in this way, the Directive itself postulates the social considerations that the ECJ retrieved from Article 28 of the Charter of Fundamental Rights and the social principles recognised in the treaties. It seeks to guarantee acceptable social conditions for posted workers in host states. The ECJ was evidently reading the Directive against its grain.

Why and how did it come to do so? It did so it seems, because it believed the circumstances of these cases warranted priority of freedom of movement and services stipulated by Article 49 of the TEC over the social goals pursued by the Swedish Unions and the Niedersachsen government. And it managed to do so by taking recourse to a balancing of values that gave them leeway to articulate a ruling for which neither Directive 96/71 nor any other clear legislative text provided concrete legal grounds. Article 49, as such, also provided no concrete legal grounds for the ruling. Article 49 does not articulate the specific conditions for its application. The ECJ simply extracted from it the fundamental principle of market freedom for which it stands.

The balancing took place explicitly in *Laval* and *Viking* and implicitly in *Rüffert*.[14] We shall return presently to the specifics of the balancing process in *Rüffert*. It is important to first reflect well on the outcome of the balancing procedures in these cases. What emerged from these balancing procedures was a "case specific" prioritising of the market freedom for which articles 43 and 49 TEC stood under circumstances where a *social* democratic legislator may well have given precedence to the social security and collective bargaining rights claimed by the unions, without tolerating anything that a *liberal* democrat could have considered constitutionally intolerable.

In other words, the court ultimately made a political decision that may well have been made otherwise had it started with different premises. There is nothing in the European Treaties that commanded it to give precedence to the market

---

13 Article 3(7): Paragraphs 1 to 6 shall not prevent application of terms and conditions of employment which are more favourable to workers.

14 *Laval*, paragraph 94 (proportionality), *Viking*, paragraph 79 (balancing). "Balancing" or "proportionality" is not invoked expressly in *Rüffert*, but an implicit balancing or proportionality test is evident in paragraphs 40 to 42 where the court dismisses the justification for the *Landesvergabegesetz* offered by the German authorities.

freedoms under the circumstances of *Laval* and *Rüffert.* The jurisdictional restriction that limits its competence to the scrutiny of alleged violations of one of the market freedoms does also not compel it to find a violation whenever it recognises a curtailment of a market freedom. The ECJ's own (misplaced) rhetoric of "balancing" indicates that is it not merely scrutinising curtailments of market freedoms as if it can do so without taking into account other considerations that compete with these freedoms. Under circumstances like these, a strictly or predominantly legal judgment was simply impossible. Courts that are mindful of the limits of *judicial* competence may well want to refrain from judgment when the circumstances would seem to demand a political decision that it in principle is not competent to take.[15] The ECJ evidently had no qualms with making bold judgments under just such circumstances in these cases.

The *legal* basis of the ECJ's ruling in *Viking* is equally contentious. The European legislation that the ECJ invoked was Article 1(1) of Regulation No. 4055/86 that provided for the basic freedom to provide maritime services in Member States by nationals established in another Member State. The court nevertheless found that this regulation did not apply as such in *Viking,* because actual reflagging of Viking's ferry had not yet taken place. The decision therefore simply turned on the general right to freedom of establishment guaranteed by the article 43 of the TEC, and on the requirement that any limitation of this freedom must be justified. The court recognised that such justified limitations could issue from principles of social protection embodied in Community law.[16] The question therefore finally came to turn on the need to balance the "free movement of goods, persons, services and capital ... against the objectives pursued by social policy..."[17] The question here cannot be whether the court got this balancing right. The question is again why and whether the court should have embarked on this process of balancing at all.

The actions taken by the Finnish Seaman's Union surely affected Viking's article 43 rights to reflag its ferry in another Member State negatively, but it did not render that right meaningless. It did not create a situation that any liberal democratic legislator should have considered intolerable. It was therefore not for the court to intervene as if the legislative status quo in *Viking* reflected an intolerable legislative failure. It was simply not the court's task to find the "right balance"

15 Both Damjanovic, "The EU Market Rules as Social Market Rules: Why the EU Can be a Social Market Economy?" 1708–1712 and Azoulai, "The Court of Justice and the Social Market Economy: The Emergence of an Ideal and the Conditions for its Realisation," 1339–1347 argue this point well but do not seem to take its implications seriously in their conclusions.

16 *Viking*, paragraph 104.

17 *Viking*, paragraph 105.

between rights to collective bargaining and union activities, on the one hand, and the right to reflag or establish elsewhere, on the other. As Dragana Damjanovic puts it well with reference to the "quasi-legislative approach" of the ECJ in these cases, the court could have refrained from "mak[ing] use of the discretionary powers given to it under the proportionality principle when the use of it could have considerable – in particular market-opening – effects on the Member States' welfare regimes."[18]

Let us return now to the specifics of the implicit balancing procedure that the ECJ conducted in *Rüffert*. An objection is imaginable that *Rüffert* did not involve the balancing of interests evident in *Laval* and *Viking*. It might be argued that the legislation and collective agreement for public workers in the case simply failed to comply with the requirements stipulated by Directive 96/71. The collective agreement for public workers, the argument might hold, did not apply throughout the region of Niedersachsen and thus did not comply with Articles 3(4) and 3(8) of the Directive, end of story. This apparently "strictly legal" argument, however, is surely not warranted in view of the very plausible reading of Directive 96/71 as an anti-discriminatory measure pointed out above. Assuming that this is indeed the overall purpose of the Directive, Articles 3(4) and 3(8) must surely be read as ensuring that some sub-regional collective agreement – that happens to allow for worse working conditions than those that are generally applicable in the region as a whole – does not create a loophole that would justify those worse working conditions for posted workers in the region. The fact that some sub-regional collective agreement (such as the public workers agreement at issue in *Rüffert*) *improves* the working conditions for some workers can surely not be the malaise that these articles seek to prevent.

---

18 Damjanovic, "The EU Market Rules as Social Market Rules: Why the EU Can be a Social Market Economy?" 1710, 1712. Significant in this regard is also Azoulai's question how the ECJ might retreat from this judicial activism. Cf. Azoulai, "The European Court of Justice and the Duty to Respect Sensitive National Interests" 167–187, at 176–179 in *Judicial Activism at the European Court of Justice*, ed. Mark Dawson, Bruno de Witte and Elise Muir (Cheltenham /Northampton: Edward Elgar Publishing, 2013). Astounding on the other hand is the suggestion of Clemens Kaupa in the same volume that the ECJ is not activist enough and should engage more incisively with the economics of integration. Cf. Kaupa, "Maybe not activist enough? On the Court's alleged Neoliberal Bias in its Recent Labor Cases" 56–75, at 58 in *Judicial Activism at the European Court of Justice*, ed. Mark Dawson, Bruno de Witte and Elise Muir (Cheltenham /Northampton: Edward Elgar Publishing, 2013). Kaupa writes (at 58): "Judicial Diligence in internal market law would require an active engagement of the Court with competing economic regulatory concepts." He is evidently under the impression that a substantive engagement with the economics of integration would enable the ECJ to get its balancing right.

In other words, what really seems to have occurred in *Rüffert* was not non-compliance with the Directive. At stake here was much rather the Court's concern with the negative or limiting impact of legislation and collective agreements on the freedom to provide services guaranteed by article 49 of the TEC that was evidently not foreseen in the Directive.[19] But again, article 49 surely does not stipulate or envisage completely unlimited freedom to provide services and it does not provide concrete criteria for how this freedom is to be limited and applied. The only way that such limits can be determined judicially is by either deferring to concrete limits laid down by legislators or by embarking on substantive "balancing" procedures in the course of which it draws those limits itself. The ECJ resorted to the latter procedure with far reaching consequences for the sovereign right of Niedersachsen and German authorities to regulate working conditions within their territorial boundaries.

"Schonendste Ausgleich" is the concept that the judges in *Lüth* used to describe this "balancing" procedure. It is on the basis of such a balancing procedure that it allowed the "objective value order" or "objektive Wertordnung" of the GG to radiate through all strata of German law. "Substantive due process" is the concept that American legal theory invokes for such balancing procedures. It should not be forgotten that the substantive due process review in *Lochner v New York* duly engaged in such a balancing procedure (and established that no serious health concerns of employees weighed up to the freedom of contract of employers).[20]

This "substantive due process" review procedure passed unproblematically in *Lüth*, argued Chapter Two, because it turned on a fundamental value – freedom of expression – which all Germans shared or could be considered to share at the time *Lüth* was decided. But it was bound to run into trouble, Chapter Two contended further, the moment it would be employed in a conflict that reflected deep divisions in German society. Such a conflict came to the fore in *Erste Abtreibung* and the rest is history. But this history explains best what came to pass in

19 That the Directive did not stand for everything that the Court wanted to base on it would appear to be corroborated by the proposals for new legislation that followed in the wake of the public controversies that ensued from the *Laval, Viking, Rüffert* and *Luxembourg* cases. Cf. the *Proposal for a Directive of the European Parliament and of the Council on the Enforcement of Directive 96/71/EC Concerning the Posting of Workers in the Framework of the Provision of Services*, Brussels, 21 March 2012; *Proposal for a Council Regulation on the Exercise of the Right to Take Collective Action within the Context of the Freedom of Establishment the Freedom to Provide Services*, Brussels, 21 March 2012. The contents of these proposals need not be analysed here. The fact that the Council and European Parliament saw the need for them speaks volumes. I am indebted to Eleftheria Neframi for bringing these proposals to my attention.

20 198 US 45 (1905) at 55–60.

Laval, Viking and *Rüffert.* These cases turned on the same substantive due process horizontal effect review procedure that the GFCC developed in *Lüth.* It did so under circumstances of social division that was as deep as the social division that informed the conflict in *Erste Abtreibung.* And this combination of substantive due process and deep social division, we shall see presently, is precisely what has come to threaten the *Lüthian* duty of federal Germany and the individual German states to protect the fundamental rights of their citizens today, for it effectively suppresses any claim to significant political difference or differentiation as far as this duty to protect (*Schutzpflicht*) is concerned.

Germany is just the example here. There is no reason why the citizens of any other Member State should feel less threatened by this development. Ask the members of the Finnish Seamen Union in *Viking.* Ask the members of the Svenska Unions in *Laval.* Viking and the Finnish Seamen's Union surely entertained different and contradictory views regarding the "balancing" and "harmonising" of their conflicting concerns, surely as different and contradicting as the views expressed by legal scholars in the wake of the case. What is new, one might well ask. Winners and losers of court cases do not feel the same about the outcome of the court battles between them and there is no reason for being overly precious about this fact, might one continue. This is just the way things are in the best of liberal democracies, as Chapter Six may seem to have underlined. This cavalier response, however, becomes somewhat problematic under circumstances where the losers in these battles may justifiably feel that they have been subjected to rules that are "foreign" to them, rules that they cannot identify as "their own." It has become a pervasive observation that this is exactly what is afoot in Europe today. The best way of coming to grips with this sense of alienation among so many people and peoples of Europe is to look more closely at the kind of sovereignty that is currently emerging from the judicial integration of Europe driven by the ECJ. We shall return to do so in Section IV below. Let us first take a look at the loss of sovereignty in the Member States that has resulted/is resulting from this process of judicial integration.

III The Demise of German Sovereignty and the Marginalisation of *Lüth* in Germany

The successful insolation of an instituted ordo-liberal economic order from the political and constitutional contexts in which it operates (see again the discussion in Chapter Five) is, according to Joerges, the reason why the GFCC, despite its many warnings to do so, has not moved to protect the constitutional sovereignty of the German people against any emaciation of their constitutional rights by developments in European Union law. The GFCC, argues Joerges with reference to the court's Maastricht decision, evidently regards the basic economic order reflected in the legal institutions and practices of the European Union as apolitical. And it is also for this reason, suggests Joerges, that the GFCC does not consider it necessary to subject these institutions and practices to constitutional scrutiny.[21] In other words, according to Joerges, the GFCC has basically bought into the ordo-liberal understanding of the relation between economics, law and politics.

Joerges' explanation does not pretend to tell the whole story of the demise of German constitutional sovereignty in the jurisprudence of the GFCC. There are other complex issues such as the GFCC's constitutional commitment to European integration articulated in article 23 of the GG and the historical and factual momentum of the integration process that also play crucial roles here. One must also add to this the calamitous way in which the GFCC has slowly but surely been painting itself into a corner as Dieter Grimm points out well.[22] But Joerges' explanation is instructive as regards the GFCC's obiter response to *Laval* and *Viking* in *Lisbon*, and especially with regard to the GFCC's omission to even mention the ECJ's decision in *Rüffert* at the time.

It is already remarkable that the GFCC could rest so easily content in *Lisbon* to defer to the ECJ's decisions in *Viking* and *Laval*. The court did so, we saw, on strength of the ECJ's mere assertion that they had weighed up and balanced the fundamental liberties and social protection principles embodied in the Treaties and Charter of Rights. It did not scrutinise incisively whether the balancing performed by the ECJ could indeed be squared with the social protection demanded by the GG. One would have thought that this assessment called for more careful argument and inquiry, even though German constitutional concerns were not directly at issue in *Laval* and *Viking*. That *Rüffert* did not warrant citation and incisive scrutiny, according to the GFCC, is exponentially more remarkable, for German constitutional concerns were evidently at stake in *Rüffert*. The failure to address *Rüffert* in *Lisbon* may well be a reflection of the state of constitutional sovereignty in Germany. The ECJ delivered its ruling in *Rüffert* on 3 April 2008. It is unlikely that it came too late to be taken into consideration by the GFCC in *Lisbon*, for *Lisbon* was delivered on 30 June 2009. It would appear that the GFCC artfully turned a blind eye to *Rüffert* when it cited *Viking* and *Laval* in *Lisbon*. It is inconceivable that it would not have considered itself under incircum-

---

21 Joerges, "Europa nach dem Ordoliberalismus: Eine Philippika," 406.

22 Grimm, "Prinzipien statt Pragmatismus." *Frankfurter Allgemeine Zeitung: Die Debatte um Europas Zukunft*, June 2, 2013. http://www.faz.net/aktuell/feuilleton/debatten/europas-zukunft/europas-zukunft-prinzipien-statt-pragmatismus-12052280.html

ventible pressure to explain meticulously and expressly why the decision in *Rüffert* did not violate the social state or *Sozialstaat* principle contained in Art. 20(1) of the GG. An engagement with *Rüffert* may well have compelled it to incline towards more than mere obiter observations, and this may well have been the real reason why it decided not to mention or engage with *Rüffert* when it commented on *Laval* and *Viking.*

One of the key passages in which the GFCC communicated its intention to protect German constitutional sovereignty in *Lisbon* is surely this one:

> "The unification of Europe on the basis of a contractual federation of sovereign states may surely not be realised in a way that deprives the member states of sufficient space for the political formation of economic, cultural and social relations. This applies especially to areas that determine the living conditions of citizens, especially their constitutionally protected private sphere of individual responsibility and social security, but also to political decisions that are especially dependent on cultural, historical and linguistic pre-understandings and which take form discursively in the party political and parliamentary based space of the political public sphere."[23]

The GFCC stated clearly in *Lisbon* that it would generally defer to European Community law on the basis of trust that the ECJ would generally safeguard the fundamental rights embodied in the German Constitution sufficiently. The court nevertheless reserved for itself the right not to comply with European law in exceptional cases when this is the only way of averting violations of German Constitutional rights. At issue in this statement would appear to be nothing less than a judicial endorsement of German sovereignty.

The GFCC has articulated this protective stance vis-à-vis developments in European law in similar passages in a veritable series of judgments now. Not once, however, has it regarded it necessary to actually intervene and identify a treaty provision or development in European law as irreconcilable with the German GG. This has led to Joseph Weiler's 2009 assessment of the GFCC as the dog that

23 BVerfG, 2 BvE 2/08 vom 30.6.2009, Absatz-Nr. (1–421), http://www.bverfg.de/entscheidungen/es20090630_2bve000208.html (hereafter *Lisbon*) paragraph 249 (also highlighted as *Leitsatz* 3): "Die europäische Vereinigung auf der Grundlage einer Vertragsunion souveräner Staaten darf nicht so verwirklicht werden, dass in den Mitgliedstaaten kein ausreichender Raum zur politischen Gestaltung der wirtschaftlichen, kulturellen und sozialen Lebensverhältnisse mehr bleibt. Dies gilt insbesondere für Sachbereiche, die die Lebensumstände der Bürger, vor allem ihren von den Grundrechten geschützten privaten Raum der Eigenverantwortung und der persönlichen und sozialen Sicherheit prägen, sowie für solche politischen Entscheidungen, die in besonderer Weise auf kulturelle, historische und sprachliche Vorverständnisse angewiesen sind, und die sich im parteipolitisch und parlamentarisch organisierten Raum einer politischen Öffentlichkeit diskursiv entfalten."

barks but never bites.[24] The meek acceptance of the ECJ's jurisprudence in *Viking* and *Laval* and its omission to engage with the judgment in *Rüffert* would appear to be little more than another bout of the court's toothless barking.

The GFCC's promise in *Lisbon* that it would see to it that the GG remains the final criterion for the constitutionality of power relations in Germany surely reflects key elements of *Lüth* and of the Hegelian conception of the state articulated in Chapter Five. It surely echoes the principle that the state remains the final authority regarding constitutional acceptability of social relations within its territory, be these relations private or public. As a whole, however, the *Lisbon* decision left much doubt as to whether the GFCC is ever going to live up to its promise. Its acceptance of the jurisprudence in *Laval* and *Viking* as reconcilable with the social state principle of the GG,[25] notwithstanding having taken due notice of the forceful academic criticism of these cases,[26] would seem to tell the story of a court that is seriously losing ground as far as its pronounced claims to sovereignty is concerned. And its failure to even engage with *Rüffert* would appear to tell the even more ominous story of a court that is no longer willing to stand what ground it still has left to stand. It is against this background that one can plausibly begin to talk of an evident demise of German constitutional sovereignty.

But this is not all. The decisions of the ECJ in *Laval*, *Viking* and *Rüffert* also reflect the other side of the coin. One discerns in these cases the confident rise of European Union territorial sovereignty. And these two sides of the coin reflect the dual destiny of *Lüth* in Europe and Germany today. *Laval*, *Viking* and *Rüffert* signal the end of *Lüth's* force in Germany. Private economic resistance to the sovereignty of German constitutional rights that once demanded and fuelled the assertion of constitutional sovereignty in *Lüth* will from now on not need to resort to German private law to stake its claim. It will be able to do so in terms of law that offers it a better chance, namely the protection of economic liberties offered by the European Treaties and the ECJ. Why would one resort to law that is subject to the GG if one could resort to law to which the GG is subject? In other words, *Laval*, *Viking* and *Rüffert* signal the commencement of *Lüth's* second life in European Union law, and in this second life it may well come to defend some of the private interests that it would have resisted in its former life. One may well wonder how the *Laval*-court would have balanced the interests in *Lüth*.

24 Joseph Weiler, "The 'Lisbon Urteil' and the Fast Food Culture," *European Journal of International Law* 20, no. 3 (2009): 505.
25 *Lisbon*, paragraph 398.
26 Cf. again fn. 10 above.

IV European Union Sovereignty – Vertical and Monistic or Horizontal and Différantial?

A general perception has been spreading that European Union law is depriving Member States citizens of democratic participation in the making of the law by which they are governed, given the way law-making in intransparent corridors of European bureaucracies has come to subvert and displace the participation of citizens in domestic law-making.[27] The rulings of the ECJ in *Laval*, *Viking* and *Rüffert* will surely strengthen this perception, not weaken it. They will add to the perception of pervasive bureaucratic law-making in Europe the perception of conspicuous judicial law-making that has come to complement this bureaucratic law-making.

When one loses in the game of democratic law-making, one can at least to some debatable extent argue that one has participated in that law-making. When one loses in a game constructed by unknown players, the context turns rather Kafkaesque. When social security concerns become marginalised by neo-liberal policies in a process of adequate political participation by everyone involved (as happens whenever the Tories are voted in for a term of government in the United Kingdom and the Republicans in the United States), the triumph of neo-liberalism is a political outcome that all liberal democrats, also the defeated social liberal democrats among them, must accept as legitimately binding until such time as a more social democratic politics regains political ascendancy. The decisions of a court that are informed by ordo-liberal, neo-liberal or any other substantive vision, differ fundamentally from any such substantive convictions that emerge

27 Cf. Larry Siedentop, *The Wall Street Journal*, 17 June 2005: "Democratic political cultures are being weakened in the Member States, without being replaced." This source could not be accessed. For this quotation, cf. Jean-Claude Piris, *The Constitution for Europe: A Legal Analysis*, Cambridge Studies in European Law and Policy (Cambridge: Cambridge University Press, 2006), 18. For a more specific discussion of the way domestic bureaucracies increasingly passes contentious policy decisions that they would struggle to get passed in domestic legislatures onto the European level where democratic controls will not interfere, cf. Stefan Oeter, "Federalism and Democracy," in *Principles of European Constitutional Law*, ed. Armin von Bogdandy and Jürgen Bast (Oxford: Hart Publishing, 2007), 78. For a further analysis of how the intergovernmental composition of the Council, for all its claims to democratic representation, only strengthens the hand of the Commission, cf. 68. At issue here is of course also the point regarding "executive federalism" and "democratic deficit" in the European integration process that Habermas has been making forcefully and repeatedly in recent writings. Cf. for instance Jürgen Habermas, *Zur Verfassung Europas. Ein Essay* (Frankfurt a.M: Suhrkamp, 2011), 39–129. For one of the significant early contributions to this question, cf. Giandomenico Majone, "'Europe's Democratic Deficit': The Question of Standards," *European Law Journal*, 4 (1998): 5–28.

triumphantly from democratic political conflicts. Substantive judicial visions do not present themselves as political *positions.* They present themselves as reflections of transcendent legal orders on which politics and political *positions* have and should have no significant bearing. Under these circumstances, political *opposition* cannot even present itself as *a position.* It no longer has any standing in the debate.

To rephrase the point in terms that Chapter Six elaborated with reference to Hans Kelsen's majority-minority principle: In circumstances under which a judicial majority espouses substantive social visions, any dissenting judicial minority is basically reduced to an edifying adornment of case reports. Unlike a parliamentary minority that loses out to a parliamentary majority, it can no longer assert itself conspicuously and forcefully as a legitimate minority position that continues to command significant constitutional (not to mention political) support.

This is one of the key reasons why a jurisprudence with a sound regard for the difference between law and politics (without having to be naïve about the instability of this difference) would insist that judiciaries stay as far away as possible from decisions that are evidently political. The rulings that the ECJ made in *Laval, Viking* and *Rüffert* surely were political in this sense. They concerned the deep and well-known political battle lines between labour and capital that have been drawn more than a century ago and have been dividing democratic societies ever since. The ECJ nevertheless addressed the questions raised in these cases as if they were legal questions that could be resolved with reference to black letter legal documents. In doing so, it evidently engaged in the kind of substantive due process review procedure that Chapter Two identified in the judgements of the GFCC in *Lüth* and *Erste Abtreibung* and in the opinion of Justice Blackmun in *Roe v Wade*, not to mention *Lochner* again. In the process the ECJ came to stand for a monistic and monolithic embodiment of sovereignty that simply ignores and suppresses the deep differences that come to the surface in European politics and in European socio-economic conflicts. This is surely the profile it earned for itself with its decisions in *Laval, Viking* and *Rüffert.*

This monistic or monolithic sovereignty would appear to have established itself as the *de facto* sovereign in Europe today. It will perhaps only be a matter of time before it establishes itself as the *de jure* sovereign as well, as we learn from both Kelsen and Schmitt. Seen from this perspective, Bodin and Hobbes would still seem to be correct as far as contemporary Europe is concerned. Sovereignty cannot be divided, in any case not in the way it is being "divided" in Europe today. Two powers cannot indefinitely claim sovereignty over the same territory without a clear delimitation and separation of their respective competences. When dual sovereignties are claimed without such delimitation and separation of competences, both sovereignties claimed must be considered to find themselves locked in a process of transition that had better come to an end before one or both claims at issue become utterly meaningless. In other words, when two powers both claim either unlimited or insufficiently delimited sovereign competences over the same territory, they are either preparing for a showdown of sorts for purposes of finally settling the matter, or the one is basically being laughed off in silence by the other for reasons of making meaningless noise. Joseph Weiler, we saw above, has come very close to saying just this with regard to the GFCC's position in Europe.

Functional "divisions" of sovereignty are possible, as functional federal political systems show well. But such divisions of sovereignty require adequate processing of political sentiments and differences if they are to become and remain functional. And when they manage to do so, they are no longer divided in the simple sense of the word. They attain the "unitary effect" of significant political differentiation. Chapter Six referred to this "unitary effect" of political differentiation as the *reign of sovereignty* that results from difference and not from the suppression of difference. It developed in this regard a concept of différantial sovereignty that takes leave of the monistic or monolithic conception of sovereignty on which the jurisprudence of the ECJ in *Laval*, *Viking* and *Rüffert* evidently turned. The concept of différantial sovereignty turns instead, on relations of difference and deference between democratic majorities and minorities that always keep both in play but ultimately insist on the general duty of democratic minorities to respect the legislation of democratic majorities.

There are of course exceptions where the duty to respect majority legislation no longer applies and it is for reasons of such exceptions that the institution of constitutional review will always remain an integral feature of liberal democracies. Chapter Eight will articulate a way in which these exceptions can be understood. For now, let us consider for a moment the question whether the ECJ could plausibly have decided *Laval*, *Viking* and *Rüffert* in a way that would have reflected the différantial sovereignty of majority-minority relations and the deferential duty of minorities to respect majority legislation. At stake here is the simple question whether it could have complied with the elementary principle of general judicial deference to duly enacted legislation.

The problem that the ECJ faces in this regard is of course the absence of a true or fully-fledged European legislator to which it can defer with the same conviction that a national court can refer to a national legislator.[28] But however im-

28 Cf. in this regard the poignant reflections on the lack of legislation with which the ECJ must contend in Mark Dawson, "The Political Face of Judicial Activism," 11–31 at 27 in *Judicial*

perfect this constellation of a European "state" judiciary and "state" legislator may still be in Europe today, some of the structures required for such a constellation can be said to have been established sufficiently for purposes of requiring the ECJ to defer as far as possible to existing legislation. Deferring as far as possible to existing legislation also implies interpreting and applying that legislation as strictly as possible. Any expansive reading of applicable legislation would always run the risk of judicial legislation in matters with regards to which the legislator has decided not to act or has not yet decided to act.

To be sure, Chapter Two argued and Chapter Eight will argue again that judiciaries sometimes have to intervene in cases where a legislator has failed to legislate. *DeShaney v Winnebago Social Services Department* was our example of such a case. The criterion for the necessity of judicial intervention in the absence of legislation that we forwarded then and will forward again pivots on this two-step argument: An existing status quo that is not addressed by clear legislation should firstly be understood as a reflection of legislative tolerance. And any existing status quo that accordingly reflects legislative tolerance of something that *no* liberal democratic legislator worthy of the word would tolerate, should secondly be considered as an indication of legislative failure in response to which a judiciary not only may, but also must intervene. Again, *DeShaney* is the prime example of such a case. The absence of a public liability tort on the basis of which claims for damages can be processed in cases like *DeShaney*, surely points to a legislative failure that no liberal democracy worthy of the word can tolerate. But exactly here lies the problem. None of the claims at issue in *Laval*, *Viking* or *Rüffert* can in any way be compared to the claim for damages in *DeShaney*.

Laval, *Viking* and *Rüffert* ended with rulings that were not strictly or comprehensively underpinned by any articles of legislation that the ECJ invoked. The ECJ may well have come to the ordo-liberal conclusion that the questions that these cases raised were not adequately addressed by applicable legislation. Should it have done so, it could have brought this perceived inadequacy to the attention of the relevant legislature as judiciaries have done for ages. It may for instance have indicated to the European Parliament and Council, the legislator that drafted Directive 96/71, that the Directive does not in its opinion reckon well with the various ways in which union action and collective agreements can come to frustrate the fundamental liberties guaranteed by the Treaties. But

---

Activism at the European Court of Justice, ed. Mark Dawson, Bruno de Witte and Elise Muir (Cheltenham /Northampton: Edward Elgar Publishing, 2013). New Legislation is fortunately now in the offing with regard to the issues that came to the fore in *Laval*, *Viking* and *Rüffert*. Cf. footnote 19 above.

whatever legislative "inadequacy" may be at stake here according to whatever judiciary with whichever political sentiments, that "inadequacy" is not such that it cannot possibly be regarded as the reflection of the legitimate legislative will of a liberal democratic legislator worthy of that label. For this reason, they would have had to live and deal with the "inadequacy" as if it were in fact the express will of a liberal democratic legislator.

To rephrase the matter in terms of the discussion of the *DeShaney* case in Chapter Two: None of the claims raised in *Laval*, *Viking* or *Rüffert* can be compared with the claim raised on behalf of Joshua DeShaney in the *DeShaney* case. Chapter Two took Justice Rehnquist to task for tolerating (absence of) legislation that no liberal democratic legislator worthy of this constitutional label could possibly pass. This was not the case in *Laval*, *Viking* and *Rüffert*. The judiciary that heard these cases simply had to contend with the possibility that a liberal democratic legislator – say one that happened to be led for the moment by a robust social democratic majority – may well have been endorsing the legislative regimes that allowed for the union activities or collective agreements at issue in these cases. This legislator may well have regarded the plights of the claimants in each of these cases as the lesser of two evils without falling foul of liberal democratic constitutional demands (in a way that no such legislator could do – so went the argument in Chapter Two – with regard to the harm that came to Joshua DeShaney as a result of public negligence).

As we saw above, the rulings in *Laval* and *Rüffert* could not have been reached on the strength of Directive 96/71 alone. In fact, if reached to some extent on the back of Directive 96/71, they were reached on the back of a very implausible reading of the Directive. The substance of these rulings must have come from a perception of the negative impact of any strict reading of the Directive on the freedom to provide services guaranteed by article 49 of the TEC. And it is here that the substantive due process judicial activism of the ECJ commenced in these cases – the political process of balancing that guided all three rulings towards a prioritisation of economic liberty over social security concerns for which there was no clear legal ground. Considering the very real perception of a democracy deficit in Europe, a perception that surely and understandably undermines rather than promotes felicitous European integration, the ECJ should not have moved to fill "the gaps" in existing legislation by resorting to the balancing of values in these cases. Again, had it been so concerned with the impact of the developments in *Laval*, *Viking* and *Rüffert* on the economic liberties provided in the Treaties, it could have alerted the European Parliament and Council to this concern with ample obiter dicta. The latter institutions may by far not yet provide an adequate basis for the différantial and horizontal sovereignty that this book contemplates, but they do reflect a degree of political representativeness that the ECJ surely cannot claim and should also not wish to claim.

It is important to stress once again that the arguments elaborated above do not take sides in any of the conflicts discussed. There may well be some kind of wisdom in the arguments that the ECJ forwarded in these three cases as far as the integration of Europe is concerned. The phenomenon of "social dumping" that dismay many commentators who responded to these cases, may, in ways that are evidently not readily assessable, be conducive to some kind of social redistribution in Europe. The ECJ may well have believed with some justification that it ultimately promoted a classical "invisible hand" social solidarity in Europe – even if at the expense of some of the better-off workers in the industrial powerhouses of Europe who may well have a thin concept of solidarity when it comes to considering the plights of workers of Member States with struggling or weak economies.[29] Those who believe that the destruction of achieved levels of social security in some countries will not contribute to the rise of social security in others will surely doubt this wisdom. For them the destruction of achieved social security will just contribute to spreading vulnerability. But all of this is beside the point here. The point is that the kind of decision-making that was required in these cases (if any were required) should have been left to democratically elected legislators. It is not for courts to decide (or make authoritative preliminary rulings with regard to) questions like these.

Of primary concern in this chapter were not the social consequences of the *Laval, Viking* and *Rüffert* cases. It is the political consequences of these cases that are deeply disconcerting. Talk about the democracy deficit in Europe is not as rife as it is for no reason. It reflects a pervasive sentiment that bureaucratic and judicial processes are taking government away from democratic deliberation by citizens. Again, if the rulings in *Laval, Viking* and *Rüffert* achieved anything, they surely strengthened these perceptions. They surely did not weaken them. And the source of this perceived juristocratic usurpation of political powers can be traced all the way to *Lüth.*

The decisions in *Laval* and *Viking* exemplified the kind of horizontal effect jurisprudence that *Lüth* bequeathed to Europe. These decisions surely pivoted on the Hohfeldian insistence that the sovereign's law apply everywhere and to everyone. They cannot be faulted on this count. But they also wrested sovereignty away from the horizontal relations between democratic majorities and minorities and put it in the hands of a judiciary that decides matters from above as if it

29 Even Barnard concedes this point. Cf. Barnard, "A Proportionate Response to Proportionality,"122–123.

had access to celestial wisdom from which everyone involved would self-evidently benefit. It is indeed a very vertical or celestial sovereignty that the ECJ assumed in *Laval Viking* and *Rüffert.* If it is so that the jurisprudence of the ECJ is fundamentally informed by ordo-liberal thinking, as so many academic observers contend, these celestial claims of the court should come as no surprise. As Walter Eucken put it, the aim of ordo-liberalism was to realise the free and natural order willed by God – "die freie, natürliche, gottgewollte Ordnung [zu] verwirklichen."[30]

It is important to note again that the judicial exercise of sovereignty that is evident in these cases constitutes a *de facto* assumption of sovereignty. It is not contemplated by the European Treaties. How this kind of judicial activism can be squared with Articles 4(2) and 5(1–4) of the TEU must remain confounding in view of basic principles of national and international law that surely apply here. The rulings of the ECJ in *Laval, Viking* and *Rüffert* surely do not seem to reflect due respect for either national political and constitutional identity stipulated in Article 4(2). The Court can of course claim that Article 4(2) was not applicable at the time when they decided *Laval, Viking* and *Rüffert.* It is a good question whether it would be prepared to raise this argument. Would this judiciary really be prepared to argue and admit openly that it was not bound and did not considered itself bound to respect political and constitutional identities of Member States in 2007 and 2008 when *Laval, Viking* and *Rüffert* were decided? One can only hope it is still rational to assume the answer to this question is negative.

Article 5 of the TEU deals with the principles of conferral, subsidiarity and proportionality. The pin that holds the whole article and all these principles together is the principle of conferral of competences contained in Articles 5(1) and (2). The moment one undoes the screws that hold the principle of conferral together, the principles of subsidiarity and proportionality will also fall apart so as to end up drifting in an ocean of governmental caprice. Sub-Articles 5(3) and 5(4) cannot be invoked to restore order once this has started to happen; nor can the Protocol on the application of the principles of subsidiarity and proportionality of the Lisbon Treaty offer any help under these circumstances. And this is precisely what happens when the judicial institution that is supposed to keep the screws of conferral tight begins to loosen them in the way the ECJ has done in *Laval, Viking* and *Rüffert.* Judicial activism of the kind that came to pass

30 Walter Eucken, *Grundsätze der Wirtschaftspolitik*, as cited by Manow, "Ordoliberalismus als ökonomische Ordnungstheologie," 188.

in these decisions makes a mockery of the distinction between conferred and non-conferred competences. As Catherine Barnard puts the matter bluntly:

> "The essence of the criticism [levelled against] Viking is that the Court used the single market provisions to reach deep into an area of national law, an area over which the European Union has ... no competence to (re)regulate."[31]

It is for reason of this subversion of the contractual conferral of competences for which the European Treaties provide that the judicial activism of the ECJ in *Laval*, *Viking* and *Rüffert* can be considered to constitute a *de facto* assumption of sovereignty that has no *de jure* backing. This is why one can refer in this regard to a quiet revolution of massive proportions that appears to be taking place in Europe today.

The revolution that might be at issue here would appear to be another horizontal effect revolution – it is taking place through a consistent endorsement of the horizontal effect of the fundamental freedoms. It is nothing of the kind. The substantive due process horizontal effect review that the ECJ inherited from *Lüth* seems to be transferring sovereignty in Europe to the hands of a vertical, monistic and unitary sovereign. At issue here is not a sovereignty that reflects the constitutive differences from which it derives. It is a sovereignty that suppresses these differences. Suppression is another form of externalising differences. It may not be as (overtly) bellicose, but it is ultimately a deeply Schmittian sovereignty that the ECJ is appropriating for the European Union.

To the extent that this new sovereign appears simultaneously content to delegate much of its decision-making power to structures of private governance and to private law, as a group of scholars associated with Fabrizio Cafaggi argue convincingly, it would appear to bear many resemblances with the peculiar mix of governmental structures that adorned pre-modern Europe, namely, the monistic and vertical sovereignty of monarchs or emperors, on the one hand, and the fragmentation of this sovereignty in the hands of so many private princes, on the other. It is no wonder then that the ever-acute Alain Supiot would perceive in this regard a re-feudalisation taking place in Europe today.[32]

The fragmentation of sovereignty evident in this "re-feudalisation of Europe" may also come to evince a horizontality of sorts. We know that the vertical rule of kings and emperors did not wield significant power vis-à-vis their nobles before consolidating their powers toward the end of the middle ages. They were

---

31 Barnard, "A Proportionate Response to Proportionality," 135.

32 For these references to Cafaggi and Supiot, see again the discussion of governance and dispersed sovereignty in Chapter Five.

rarely towers of strength that significantly overshadowed the powers of lesser feudal rulers. The latter rulers in many respects ruled their estates independently. Perhaps it is a fascination with this kind of horizontality – this absence of normative hierarchy – that prompts Gunther Teubner to invoke the notion of the king's multiple bodies as the symbol of societal constitutionalism.[33]

Be it as it may, it is not this kind of sovereignty – however weak and horizontalised it may well end up despite its very vertical aspirations – for which this book is arguing. This sovereignty will ultimately only be horizontalised because of its weakness. Its "horizontality" will be the blind function of incidental vicissitudes of competition and conflict with other major and minor sovereigns. The normative communication that will reign in the context of this sovereignty will not be a horizontal and différantial communication from which may emerge discursive relations between democratic majorities and minorities. It will in all significant respects remain the reign of sovereigns (major and minor) over subjects, not the reign of sovereignty between citizens.

The kind of horizontal effect and the kind of sovereignty – a truly horizontal and truly différantial sovereignty – for which we are arguing has been described extensively in Chapter Six. It is now time to take a close look at the judicial review procedures on which this horizontal and différantial sovereign would want to rely.

33 For this reference to Teubner, see again Chapter Five. Three more recent horizontal effect decisions of the ECJ, EU: Case C-555/07 (*Kücükdevici*), EU: Case C-282/10 (*Domingez*) and EU: Case C-176/12 (*Association de médiation sociale*) decided respectively in 2010, 2012 and 2014 raise new issues the implications of which for the horizontal effect jurisprudence in *Laval* and *Viking* (to which they do not refer at all) were not yet sufficiently clear to me at the time this manuscript went into print. These implications will be addressed in future work. Suffice it to say for now that the ECJ appears to have taken to indirect horizontal effect jurisprudence in these decisions without taking leave of the (effectively direct) ordo-liberal economic philosophy that informed *Laval* and *Viking*, as especially the *Association de médiation sociale* decision would suggest.

Chapter Eight: Liberal Democratic Constitutional Review

I Introduction

Ernst-Wolfgang Böckenförde's assessment of the jurisprudence that the GFCC developed in *Lüth* highlighted the way this jurisprudence introduced a "balancing" or "*Abwägung*" conception of proportionality into constitutional review. Since *Lüth*, claimed Böckenförde, this "balancing" conception of proportionality came to take up a place alongside the classic model of the proportionality test in German constitutional review. This "balancing" test, he argued, envisages a *propriety*-proportionality – *eine Angemessenheits-Verhältnismäßigkeit*. It contemplates the reconciliation of competing normative principles that contradict each other. This reconciliation requires a creative construction of a rule and as such moves far away from the interpretive application of the existing legal rules that constitute a legal order – *[sie] ist eher Aufgabe der Gestaltung als der (interpretativen) Andwendung einer Rechtsordnung.* This process of reconciliation – also called *schonendste Ausgleich* in *Lüth* – is much less a matter of clarifying meaning than it is one of giving meaning – *[sie] ist mehr Sinngebung als Sinndeutung.*[1]

Böckenförde may well have overestimated the stability of the distinction between construction and interpretation and between clarifying and giving meaning. Those sensitive to the lessons of modern/postmodern hermeneutics and linguistics would be less inclined to draw such firm distinctions in this regard. Böckenförde nevertheless responded poignantly with these observations to a concern that other German scholars had also been raising for some time in response to the GFCC's horizontal effect jurisprudence. The task of jurisprudence is surely to constrain the instabilities of interpretation, not to indulge in them or to aggravate them. Leisner already invoked the elastic concept of interpretation – *Kautschukbegriff der Auslegung* – that accompanies the radiation jurisprudence articulated in *Lüth.*[2] Matthias Ruffert pointed out the dark cloud under which the transformation of broad objective values into narrow subjective rights

1 Ernst Wolfgang Böckenförde, "Grundrechte als Grundsatznormen," *Der Staat* (1990): 20–23.
2 Leisner, *Grundrechte und Privatrecht*, 377. Cf. also Leisner, *Die Abwägungsstaat* (Berlin: Duncker & Humblot), 223–242 for an extensive critique of this "balancing" conception of proportionality as a weakening of the state and a return of the personalisation of power. This critique evidently builds on the concerns that Leisner developed earlier in Walter Leisner, *Demokratie – Selbstzerstörung einer Staatsform* (Berlin: Duncker & Humblot, 1979).

take place whenever the radiation conception of horizontal effect jurisprudence comes into play – *[w]ie es zur Rückumwandlung der objektivrechtlichen Ausstrahlungswirkung in ein subjektives, verfassungsbeschwerdefähiges Grundrecht kommt ... bleibt im Dunkeln.*[3]

Again, some of this darkness and elasticity also attaches to the classical interpretation and application of negative rights against the state. These classical rights are also broad semantic concepts the narrowing down of which in specific cases requires interpretive processes that are not fully transparent. No act of interpretation is fully transparent. But classical proportionality tests have established clear points of reference that serve and manage to constrain the margins of creativity and construction in legal reasoning more incisively than the balancing conception of proportionality that predominantly informs horizontal effect jurisprudence.

Why this hermeneutic conservatism, may some well want to ask? The answer is an old one, the significance of which the engagement with proportionality in this chapter seeks to revitalise. Less circumscribed methods of legal interpretation widen judicial powers. And, as Böckenförde observed cogently, the widening of judicial powers in any society necessarily narrows the scope of democratic politics in that society.[4] In other words, the widening of judicial powers concomitant to loose conceptions of legal interpretation takes the articulation of legal normativity away from the formation of majority-minority relations that Chapter Six forwarded as the crux of the horizontal effect problematic. This is one of the surest ways of reintroducing towering and vertical "reasons of state" that remain untouched by the horizontal evaluation and articulation of norms that take place in actual democratic political exchanges. It is the surest way of taking law away from the actual play of différance and différantial politics. And it is also the surest way in which, for instance, the neo- or ordo-liberal visions of society discussed in Chapter Five can entrench themselves in law while insulating themselves from democratic processes that might come to question and challenge them (see Chapter Five again). Judicial practices of the ECJ discussed in Chapter Seven may well be some of the most pronounced examples the world has seen in this regard in recent years. Those who confuse hermeneutic rigor with political conservatism are indeed confused.

---

3 Ruffert, *Vorrang der Verfassung und Eigenständigkeit des Privatrechts*, 67. Compare in this regard also Harm Schepel's critique of the Laval, Viking and Rüffert cases cited in Chapter Seven, fn. 12.

4 Böckenförde, "Grundrechte als Grundsatznormen," 25: "Es vollzieht sich ein gleitender Übergang vom parlamentarischen Gesetzgebungsstaat zum verfassungsrechtlichen Jurisdiktionstaat."

Böckenförde's obvious endeavour to restrict constitutional review to the application of classical negative rights against the state ultimately moves in a direction that will surely not be followed here. His apparent identification of horizontal effect as such as the inevitable cause of all problems attendant upon the jurisprudence articulated in *Lüth* was miscued. In this regard he would appear to have been oblivious to the problem of private power for which his mentor Schmitt had an acute regard (see again the discussion of Schmitt in Chapter Six). The problems that Böckenförde analysed so masterfully do not lie with the horizontal effect of fundamental rights as such. They lie with the particular understanding of horizontal effect articulated in *Lüth* and with the particular understanding of proportionality that would emerge from *Lüth*. But moving away from *Lüth* on this count does not require moving away from horizontal effect as such. As we shall see in this chapter, the proper or classical proportionality test that Böckenförde sought to rehabilitate pivots fundamentally on the horizontal and not the vertical effect of constitutional rights. To grasp this, however, one has to make the switch from the traditional or standard to the Leisnerian and Kelsenian understanding of horizontal effect elaborated in Chapter Six.

The proportionality test that this chapter will put forward as the cornerstone of liberal democratic constitutional review pivots on Leisner's conception of horizontal effect in terms of horizontal relations between citizens that are no longer subject to vertical reasons of state. The conception of the liberal democratic state that will come to the fore is indeed one of a state that is disrobed of all separate reasons of state that are not articulated in the horizontal relations between democratic majorities and minorities. At issue here is indeed the democratic state that Leisner had in mind, "*der 'Staat,' der seines 'Selbstzwecks' entkleidet ist.*" Böckenförde was correct to identify the surreptitious return of vertical reasons of state – "*[so] kehren die verlorengegangenen Staatszwecke wieder*" – in the wide margins of constructive judicial interpretation for which the concretisation of an objective value order – the key conception developed in *Lüth* – allowed.[5] This move in *Lüth* surely suggested the existence of a broad band of values that are not subject to democratic discussion and the decision of the GFCC in the *Erste Abtreibung* case surely confirmed this.

This chapter will again relate this problematic of the interpretive return of democratically unarticulated reasons of state to that which American constitutional scholars call *substantive due process review*. Substantive due process, we

5 Böckenförde "Grundrechte als Grundsatznormen," 23: "Wird den Grundrechten ein objektivrechtlicher Gehalt in der Form von Prinzipien-Normen, d.h. Optimierungsgeboten ... zugesprochen, kehren die – verlorengegangenen – Staatszwecke wieder als zielgerichtete ... Handlungsaufträge."

shall see, indeed concerns the same assumption that Böckenförde identifies in *Lüth*, namely, the assumption of transcendent constitutional values that exist independently of democratic deliberation. But again, the problem of substantive due process or vertical reasons of state should not be attributed or linked to the recognition of the horizontal effect of fundamental rights. To the contrary, it is exactly the classical notion of the vertical effect of constitutional rights that presupposes or assumes the existence of vertical reasons of state. The "vertical effect" of fundamental rights surely registers the standard or traditional "rule of law" demand that such reasons of state generally remain subject to the limits that constitutional rights of citizens impose on them, but it does not deny the existence of such reasons of state as such. The recognition of the horizontal effect of constitutional rights, as articulated by Leisner, turns on a more radical democratic principle. It turns on an *almost* complete denial of the existence of any such vertical reasons of state. And the proportionality test that should accompany the Leisnerian horizontal effect review envisaged in this book must reflect this *almost* complete denial of vertical reasons of state by steering away as far as possible from substantive due process conceptions of constitutional review. It should, to begin with, do so in all cases where empirical evidence of deep social divisions indicates the existence of significant majority-minority relations.

Almost complete denial of vertical reasons of state? What marginal remainder of vertical reasons of state and substantive due process review procedures does this "almost" salvage? Envisaged here are exceptional cases of fundamental rights curtailments or violations in which majority-minority democratic relations are *self-evidently* not at stake or relevant. This chapter has again quite a bit to say about this "*self-evidently*." Suffice it for now to simply say that there are exceptional cases in which a court can justifiably invoke *self-evident* values that everyone shares or must share, values that thus transcend and render irrelevant any real or imagined majority-minority relationship that might negate them. These cases should be extremely rare in well functioning liberal democracies. The *self-evidence* of the values or principles on which they turn should largely suffice to keep them out of court. No one should and few would want to litigate about things that should move everyone and will move many or most to invoke the notion of *self-evidence*. However, adamant denials of *self-evidence* do occur and sometimes they litigate themselves into the highest of judicial fora and finally get away with it. This is what happened in the *DeShaney* case, as this chapter will again contend.

It is in cases like *DeShaney* that the idea of absolutely inviolable human or fundamental rights must become an overriding reason of state or non-negotiable substantive constitutional principle that overrides any argument against it. In these principles is embedded the core and irreducible substance of sovereignty without which liberal democracies cannot claim to found sovereign systems of law. The substantive nature of the principles at stake here cannot be denied, but the substance of concern here does allow for the kind of proceduralisation that Rousseau and Kant had in mind, when they respectively contemplated the general will and the categorical imperative. And this proceduralisation, we shall see, can be embodied or is in fact embodied in the first leg of classic or standard proportionality tests. Seen in this way, the normative substance of fundamental rights can be argued to embody a proceduralised normativity that does not require a significant departure from procedural due process review procedures. In fact, by limiting the essential substantive normativity (or reasons of state) that founds liberal democratic sovereignty to concerns that are amenable to Rousseauian or Kantian proceduralisations of normativity, this essential normativity turns into a narrow normative zone within the parameters of which procedural and substantive due process review procedures cannot and need not be distinguished. Within the limits of this zone, due process review can be characterised as adequately substantive and adequately proceduralised. Constitutional theory lacks good coinage for this adequately proceduralised substantive due process and adequately substantivized procedural due process review procedures. Perceptive readers of Rawls would grasp that "public reason review" may be a good term to use in this regard. Suffice it to say that it is this adequately proceduralised substantive/adequately substantivized procedural due process review procedure that is at stake in the liberal democratic constitutional review that this chapter elaborates with reference to the classical three-step proportionality test.

This is the concluding chapter of this book and the time has come to bring together the key themes that have been developed in preceding chapters. This will be done in three steps or sections. Section II will revisit the question of horizontal effect and the recognition of full territorial sovereignty that the chapters in Part One addressed. Section III returns to the question of the kind of sovereignty that requires recognition in contemporary liberal democracies with which Part Two engaged. Section IV distinguishes between substantive and procedural due process review procedures, stresses the importance of largely reverting to procedural due process review and highlights the possibility of rare cases in which substantive due process becomes inevitable. Section V commences to relate the horizontal conception of liberal democratic sovereignty described and highlighted in Section III to the kind of judicial review-procedures that might support and underpin it. It does so by linking the concept of liberal democratic sovereignty to the first step of a three-step proportionality test that is loosely based on the proportionality test that is applied in Germany and South

Africa. Sections VI and VII bring the second and third steps of this proportionality test into focus. In the course of elaborating these second and third steps, comparative references will also be made to the different "levels of scrutiny" on which constitutional review turns in the United States. Section VIII returns briefly to the distinction and difference between constitutional and ordinary law and the importance of sustaining this distinction consistently. Section IX brings the reflections in this Chapter and also in this book to a close by looking at how the horizontal liberal democratic judicial review procedures proposed in Sections IV to VII might address one of the most vexing problems liberal democracies face today, namely, the problem of socio-economic rights and adequate social equality.

II The Recognition of Sovereignty

The problem with the state action and indirect horizontal effect jurisprudence that has become current in the world today, argued this book, concerns the way it invariably seeks to frustrate the recognition of full territorial sovereignty without which a functional and coherent legal system cannot be contemplated. Some judges and some legal scholars have recognised this problem well. Three judicial decisions of the USSC stand out for their unflinching recognition of the sovereign as the source and author of all law and all absences of law, and for their unflinching recognition that the sovereign's law and lack of law (the latter being nothing less than a different format of the former) should be reconcilable with the demands of the Constitution of the United States. These decisions are those of Justices Vinson, Frankfurter and Brennan in *Shelley v Kraemer*, *Labour v Swing* and *New York Times v Sullivan*. There is also a strong line of thought among some American scholars, we called them the Hohfeldians, that recognises what Frank Michelman calls the simple "Hohfeldian point." At issue in the recognition of the "Hohfeldian point" is the simple contention that all law, undoubtedly also private law, can be traced to the law-giving authority of the sovereign, and must therefore be subject to constitutional demands.

There is, however, also a strong line of thought in American jurisprudence that shies away from this Hohfeldian point. This line of thought is also well represented in a matching line of judicial decisions that simply reject the Hohfeldian point as unflinchingly as the decisions in *Shelley*, *Swing* and *Sullivan* accepted it. The two twentieth century decisions that we highlighted in this regard are those of Justice Rehnquist in *Flagg Brothers v Brooks* and *DeShaney v Winnebago County Social Service Department*. However, a rejection of the Hohfeldian point long before Hohfeld came around to articulate it is already evident in *The Civil*

Rights Cases, the USSC decision with which Justice Bradley founded the state action doctrine in 1883.

The judgment with which the GFCC founded the principle of the horizontal effect or *Drittwirkung* of fundamental rights in the *Lüth* case, we argued in Chapter Two, also recognised without qualification or hesitation the basic principle that all law, private law included, can be traced to the law-giving source that we call the sovereign. However, Chapter Two also showed that the *Lüth* decision has been a source of inspiration for judicial opinions elsewhere in the world that either failed or refused to recognise the law-giving role of the sovereign in all spheres of law, or only recognised it reluctantly and equivocatingly. Notable in this regard is the opinion of Justice Kentridge in the South African case *Du Plessis v De Klerk*. The appropriation of *Lüth* in *Du Plessis*, we argued in Chapter Two, did not do justice to it. It paid little more than lip service to it while actually endorsing the very evident refusal to recognise the principle of sovereignty in the Canadian case *RWDSU v Dolphin Delivery Ltd.*

Chapter Four discussed the various positions taken by the first and second generations of German *Drittwirkung* scholars. Not one among them, we saw, could be singled out for completely rejecting the recognition of sovereignty evident in *Lüth*. There were some, most notably Dürig and Canaris, who evinced considerable reluctance to recognise the sovereign as the source of all law and thus also of private law. But all of them, Dürig (with his concept of *Lückenfüllung*) and Canaris (with his *Untermaßverbot*) included, ultimately came round to recognising the lawgiving role of the sovereign in all areas of law. All of them ultimately recognised, in other words, that all law, private law included, is subject to (some kind of) constitutional scrutiny; hence their endorsement of the horizontal effect of constitutional rights, albeit it not always without equivocation.

The most express and least equivocating "Hohfeldian" contribution to the German *Drittwirkung* debate was surely that of Jürgen Schwabe, but Nipperdey and Leisner (earlier in time of course) surely followed short on his heels. For an unambiguous rejection of sovereignty in German *Drittwirkung* scholarship one has to turn to what might be called a third generation of *Drittwirkung* scholars. Notable among them are Christensen and Fischer-Lescano (discussed in Chapter Five). These scholars dismiss the concept of sovereignty, remarkably, not for purposes of resisting the doctrine of *Drittwirkung*, but for purposes of providing it, they believe, with the sound sociological and linguistic foundation that they find lacking in *Lüth*.

III Liberal Democratic Sovereignty

Chapters Five (Uninterrupted Sovereignty) and Six (Différantial Sovereignty) proceeded to articulate a concept of liberal democratic sovereignty on the basis of which the essential concerns of horizontal effect or state action jurisprudence can be addressed more adequately and less ambiguously and equivocatingly than they were dealt with hitherto. For this purpose Chapter Five articulated a conception of *uninterrupted* sovereignty that dismissed the notion of areas of sovereign territory – signposted as "private spheres" – that are not subject to the sovereign's law. And if the sovereign at issue is a constitutional sovereign, as one assumes is the case when one contemplates a liberal democratic sovereign, one must also assume that areas signposted as private spheres are not just subject to the sovereign's law, but also to the sovereign's constitution and constitutional law.

The problem that results from this unequivocal recognition of the uninterrupted reign of the sovereign's law and constitutional law over its whole territory concerns the perceived liberty deficits that would result from this recognition. The whole horizontal effect debate, we argued from the beginning of this book, is in fact a debate between those scholars and judges who are concerned by the sovereignty deficits that would result from dismissing horizontal effect, and those who are concerned by the liberty deficits that would result from recognising horizontal effect. It is to both these concerns that Chapter Six responded with the notion of a *différantial* sovereignty (taken over from the Derridean concept *différance*) in terms of which horizontal effect is no longer conceived in terms of the application of the sovereign's law *to* private relations, as if from above, vertically. With the concept of *différantial* sovereignty Chapter Six sought to articulate a veritably *horizontal* concept of horizontal effect, in terms of which horizontal effect is understood as the sovereign reign of law, constitutional law included, *between* citizens.

The concept of *différantial* sovereignty contemplates the horizontal reign of sovereign law between equal citizens, not the application or imposition of the sovereign's law *to* the "non-sovereign" horizontal relations between citizens. Chapter Six developed this concept of *différantial* sovereignty with recourse to the difference between Schmittian and Kelsenian conceptions of sovereignty (ultimately dismissing the former and endorsing the latter) and with recourse to the concept of the state that is disrobed of separate reasons of state – "*der 'Staat,' der seines 'Selbstzwecks' entkleidet ist*" – that Leisner developed in his majestic contribution to the *Drittwirkung* debate to which this book is deeply indebted. In fact, the concept of *différantial* sovereignty developed in Chapter Six is evidently little more than an articulation of the implications of Kelsen's and Leisner's thought for our understanding of horizontal effect review and constitutional review in general.

The upshot of the engagement in Chapter Six with Kelsen and Leisner is the insight that all constitutional review should categorically be understood as horizontal effect review, given the way it concerns the constitutional law that reigns horizontally between equal citizens and not some elevated sovereign's constitutional law that occasionally also applies to the relations between his non-sovereign citizens. And it is from this perspective of the horizontal reign of sovereign law (we can now begin to take leave of the concept of *the* sovereign's law with much equanimity) that one now, to conclude this book, needs to take a closer look at the constitutional review procedures that might corroborate it.

IV Substantive and Procedural Due Process Constitutional Review

The GFCC's judgment in the *Lüth* case has been hailed widely as one of the world's key statements of horizontal effect adjudication. This assessment of *Lüth* is spurious. The *Lüth* judgment can and should be hailed as one of the key judgments in the constitutional case law of the world for the way it recognised the uninterrupted reign of constitutional principles over the whole territory of a liberal democratic sovereign. Compared to the express denial or abdication of sovereignty that Justice Rehnquist's state action judgments in *Flagg Brothers* and *DeShaney* bequeathed to the people of the United States, *Lüth* clearly constitutes a formidable recognition of the principle of sovereignty on which the horizontal effect of fundamental rights turns. It reflects no recognition, however, of the horizontal reign of sovereign law that the concept of liberal democracy and the concept of the horizontal effect of constitutional principles demand from constitutional adjudication.

Alongside its recognition of sovereignty, the *Lüth* judgment also articulated and endorsed the notion of an objective value order that radiates through all strata of ordinary law. In doing so it articulated a substantive due process conception of "horizontal effect" (note the scarecrows) that cannot be reconciled with the demands of true horizontality on which any horizontal effect jurisprudence worthy of the name must insist. Unless one assumes the prevalence of a normatively undivided society, something that probably no contemporary society can still do today, the notion of an objective value order – one single objective value order – simply allows too much scope for the imposition of "foundational values" on some individuals or groups who do not share them. In other words, as it stands articulated, the jurisprudence in *Lüth* is bound to end up in authoritarian and vertical impositions of values that cannot be reconciled with the non-authoritarian horizontality envisaged under the concept of liberal democracy and the strictly *horizontal* effect of constitutional values.

The link between substantive due process review procedures and vertical or authoritarian conceptions of sovereignty is inseverable. This was not that evident yet in the *Lüth* decision, because the substantive decision in *Lüth* could not be faulted for obviously riding roughshod over deep social divisions. It is for reasons of having turned on a relatively unproblematic substantive decision that the judgment could hitherto survive as a plausible and persuasive instance of liberal democratic constitutional review. But the problematic nature of its substantive due process concept of horizontal effect would become glaringly evident in a judgment from which the GFCC soon had to retreat, namely, its judgment in the *Erste Abtreibung* case. The highly contentious nature of the notion of an "objective value order" became clear for the world to see in *Erste Abtreibung* because Germans could in 1975 no longer be said to share one objective value order as far as the question of the constitutionality of the decriminalisation of abortion was concerned. They could at best be subjected to such a value order, in vertical sovereign fashion.

Two years earlier, in 1973, the USSC more or less ended up doing the same thing in *Roe v Wade* that the GFCC did in *Lüth*. As in the case of *Lüth*, the substance of the decision in *Roe* could plausibly pass as a statement of liberal democracy and the horizontal sovereignty implied by the concept of liberal democracy. Unfortunately, it also did so by articulating a substantive due process and vertical sovereignty judgment that betrayed the lessons that the USSC had already learned from earlier substantive due process judgments, most notably from its judgment in *Lochner v New York* in 1905. It was to be expected that Justice Rehnquist would take Justice Blackmun's judgment to task for its recourse to substantive due process review procedures. As we know now from our discussion of *Flagg Brothers* and *DeShaney* in Chapter Two, Justice Rehnquist was not one for endorsing statements of sovereignty, let alone the vertical sovereignty evident in Justice Blackmun's judgment.[6]

For purposes of passing as a true statement of the horizontal sovereignty of liberal democracy, *Roe* should have been decided like the minority opinion in *Erste Abtreibung* wanted to decide *Erste Abtreibung*. *Roe* should have been decided by a finding that state legislation that criminalises abortion does not pass a

6 This is not completely true though. When it came to reading substantive property rights into the constitution, Justice Rehnquist was much less reticent. Cf. *Kaiser Aetna v United States*, 444 US 164 (1979). I am indebted to Joe Singer for bringing this case to my attention.

basic proportionality or rational purpose scrutiny test. State legislation that criminalises abortion under circumstances where individuals with adequate financial means can easily cross state borders to obtain abortions, while others without those means cannot, is neither effective nor rational. Such legislation, observed the minority opinion in *Erste Abtreibung*, undermines the credibility of the sovereign's legislation and legal system.[7]

There are cases, however, the liberal democratic adjudication of which cannot, it seems, avoid substantive due process considerations. *DeShaney* would appear to have been such a case. We argued in Chapter Two and Three that Justice Rehnquist basically turned *DeShaney* into a procedural due process case of sorts. He expressly invoked the absence of legislation in the State of Wisconsin that created a public liability tort for negligent failure of public officials to prevent harm. Such legislation should not be imposed on the people of Wisconsin, he said, through an interpretation of the 14th Amendment. What he said can be re-construed fairly as follows: The absence of legislation in Wisconsin that creates some or other public liability tort is an expression of the legislative will of the people of Wisconsin. There may be many things that one might say about the wisdom or lack of wisdom of a legislative will that expresses itself through the refusal or failure to legislate, but such failure or refusal, it seems, cannot easily be faulted procedurally. Justice Rehnquist may well have had an argument like this in mind. Or he may have thought that there is a sufficiently rational purpose evident in the absence of a Wisconsin public liability tort that might have provided Joshua DeShaney with a remedy. He may well have had in mind typical public immunity considerations that often govern this area of law. Public liability torts, goes the well-known reasoning, would burden the delivery of public services and the execution of public duties to the extent of actually hampering them. It is a good question whether blanket public immunity rules comply with basic rationality criteria. Other judiciaries in the world have come to doubt this.[8] But this is beside the point. The question is whether one

---

7 Ronald Dworkin regards simple rational scrutiny as too weak protection when it comes to something as fundamental as the concerns of women to exercise their own responsibility in matters of reproduction. But the dissenting opinion in *Erste Abtreibung* shows clearly that rational scrutiny provides adequate protection in cases such as *Erste Abtreibung* and *Roe*. Note again the discussion of *Roe* and *Erste Abtreibung* in Chapter Two.

8 The judgment of the South African Constitutional Court in *Carmichele v. Minister of Safety and Security and Another* 2001 (1) SA 489 (SCA) led to a fundamental revision of the public immunity rule in South African public liability case law, the upshot of which was a clear rejection of blanket public immunities. Cf. especially *Minister of Safety and Secuirity v Dirk van Duivenboden* 2002 (6) SA 431 SCA. There was a time that English courts also moved in this direction. Cf. *Dorset Yacht Co.Ltd. v Home Office* [1970] A.C. 1004 and *Anns and Others v London Borough of Merton*

might fault Justice Rehnquist for implicitly relying on rational purpose scrutiny in *DeShaney.*

One might begin by saying that it is not a curtailment of a liberty that is at issue here, but the abridgment of a fundamental right to bodily integrity. For purposes of constitutional clearance in the United States, this kind of abridgment requires the identification of a "compelling state interest" and "sufficiently narrow tailoring" of any legislation that is said to serve this compelling interest. *DeShaney*, might one therefore say, demanded substantive due process review. But Chapter Two and Three of this book criticised Justice Blackmun for taking recourse to this reasoning in *Roe*. We criticised him for identifying the wrong horizontal effect or *Drittwirkung* relationship in *Roe*. Following the minority opinion in *Erste Abtreibung*, we faulted him for basically locating the horizontal effect relationship in the relation between the pregnant woman and the embryonic nasciturus (the latter being the other or "third" person – hence *Drittwirkung* – as the majority judgment in *Erste Abtreibung* reasoned[9]), instead of locating it in the relation between the legislative majority and minority that differed fundamentally and vehemently with regard to the question whether the embryonic nasciturus can be regarded as a third person in the first place (as the minority opinion in *Erste Abtreibung* reasoned).

Should one follow the same reasoning in *DeShaney*, it would no longer be Joshua DeShaney's constitutional right to physical integrity that would be at issue, but indeed the constitutional liberty of a legislative majority to curtail the constitutional liberty of a legislative minority by enacting legislation that one might deem rational, or by failing to enact such legislation, or by preventing the minority from enacting such legislation.[10] And if it should then turn out that such legislation or absence of legislation could indeed be deemed rational, Joshua DeShaney would surely no longer be in this picture. Those who would want to bring "poor Joshua's" constitutional right to bodily integrity back into the picture, would have to turn to "compelling state interest" and narrowly "tailored

[1978] A.C. 728. However, a turn away from this development became evident again in *Caparo Industries plc v Dickman and Others* [1990] 1 All ER 568. *Caparo* was not a public liability case, but it showed the first signs of a turn away from the open application of the neighbourhood test (devised in *Donoghue v Stevenson* in 1932) in *Dorset* and *Anns* which finally led to the overruling of *Anns* in *Murphy v Brentwood District Council* [1991] 1 AC 398.

9 Of course ignoring for a moment that the review of legislation was at stake in the case.

10 All of these options fit into the category of legislation for purposes of the horizontal constitutional scrutiny that we are contemplating here: enacting legislation, failing to enact legislation and/or preventing legislation by opposing it.

legislation" jurisprudence. They would have to turn to substantive due process review, in other words.

Why might one want to return to substantive due process in the case of *DeShaney* but not in *Roe?* The reason why we criticised Justice Blackmun's substantive due process reasoning in *Roe*, following the minority opinion in *Erste Abtreibung*, related to the deep social divisions that are also evident in the United States as far as the criminalisation of abortion is concerned. These deep social divisions are also reflected in real majority-minority legislative relationships. Recourse to substantive due process review in such cases of deep social division simply imposes the substantive morality of parliamentary minorities on parliamentary majorities. And this imposition ruins the horizontal relations between those majorities and minorities. Might this then be a reason for not resorting to substantive due process in *DeShaney?* Should one indeed contemplate or imagine in this case a majority-minority standoff between those in favour of public immunity rules and those against? And should one then insist that a judge should not interfere from above by imposing some substantive constitutional norm on this majority-minority configuration regarding public immunities? This may well have been, we suggested above, the kind of reasoning that may have moved Justice Rehnquist in *DeShaney* when he said legislation should not be imposed on the people of Wisconsin. Should this indeed have been the reasoning that moved him, one would have to assume that he also contemplated a legislative majority in the state of Wisconsin, and perhaps elsewhere in the United States of America, that reckoned Joshua DeShaney's rights are not at issue here.

Should this reconstruction of Justice Rehnquist's reasoning in *DeShaney* be correct, it would surely be a grave cause of concern for those who would like to associate the United States with liberal democratic sovereignty. For if there is one thing that makes a huge difference between *Roe* and *DeShaney*, it must surely be the fact that Joshua DeShaney was surely no longer an unborn foetus. At issue in the *DeShaney* case was not a medically unindicated abortion in the first trimester of pregnancy. Joshua DeShaney was a fully born child, four years old. Let us change the question in *Roe* just slightly to see what is at stake here. Suppose the question had been whether the criminalisation of medically un-indicated abortions any time up to birth was constitutional or not. Would any relatively sound-minded American judge have contemplated and respected a legislative majority in favour of non-criminalisation? But perhaps we are not exactly fair to Justice Rehnquist yet. Perhaps we need to refine our analogy a little more: Would any sound-minded American judge have contemplated and respected a legislative majority that would have wanted public immunity rules to apply to police officers and other public officials who had reason to suspect occasional occurrence, in some clinic, of duly criminalised medically un-indicated abortions during the second and third trimesters of pregnancy, but did nothing about it?

There are dark times, Hannah Arendt tells us, when even legislative majorities, and not just some lunatic fringes of society, lose their minds.[11] During such dark times, things that rational and reasonable people generally consider to be self-evident principles of civil coexistence evidently lose their self-evidence. The judgment of the USSC in *DeShaney* would appear to have been such a dark moment in the history of the United States, a dark moment in which a Supreme Court judiciary apparently assumed the existence of some bizarre and dark legislative spirit and, in the process, for the sake of respecting this dark legislative spirit, abdicated, on behalf of the people of the United States, their liberal democratic sovereignty.

V The Proceduralisation of Minimum Substance and the First Proportionality Question

DeShaney would appear to ruin our critique of *Lüth*, *Erste Abtreibung* and *Roe* if that critique would require a complete rejection of substantive due process review procedures. It should be clear from our reading of *DeShaney* that a complete restriction of judicial review to procedural due process review procedures would end up with bizarre consequences that liberal democratic constitutional review cannot tolerate. *DeShaney* impresses on a liberal democratic understanding of horizontal effect jurisprudence the necessity of substantive due process review procedures in some cases. These cases, however exceptional they may be, would seem to ruin the concept of an exclusively *procedural* conception of liberal democratic constitutional review that would refrain completely from imposing substantive values with a vertical downwards thrust on horizontal relations between individuals. In other words, the strict proceduralisation of all horizontal effect review would seem to demand supplementary arguments if the whole project of this book were not to founder. Can such arguments be offered in this regard? The history of moral and political thinking does seem to offer some help.

The history of moral thinking distinguishes between typically substantive and typically procedural conceptions of moral deliberation. Substantive conceptions of moral deliberation – one may want to call them communitarian or Aristotelian, as they are often called – commence with a number of recognised sub-

11 Hannah Arendt, *Men in Dark Times* (Middlesex: Penguin Books, 1973), 12–38; Arendt, *Eichman in Jerusalem* (New York: Penguin Books, 1994), 56–111.

stantive values, arrange them according to their relative importance in a hierarchy of norms, and work out how tensions between them can be reconciled or mediated. Procedural conceptions of moral deliberation on the other hand – typically called Kantian – proceed by invoking the principle of universalization. The principle of universalization demands the ability to imagine the maxim of one's conduct as a universal law with which the conduct of everyone must comply. We saw in Chapter Six that Kant derived this principle of universalization from Rousseau's description of the *volonté général* as the will of each and every one – *chacun*. The general will is accordingly not just the will of a majority of citizens for this would only reduce the general will to the numerical preponderance of some *particular* wills. The general will is *definitively* the will of *everyone – chacun*. We also showed in Chapter Six how this principle of universalization and the notion of the will of *chacun* return as key concepts in Hegel's philosophy of law and Rawls' principle of reciprocity. Coercive actions must be supported by reasons that one believes can be respected by everyone coerced by these actions, argues Rawls. Even convicted criminals must be able to conceive of punishment as self-inflicted, argued Hegel before him.

However, Chapter Six also noted that Rousseau's conception of the general will as the will of each and everyone, Kant's principle of maxim-universalization and Rawls' principle of reciprocity are all idealist constructions. There are no conclusive empirical or logical grounds available on the basis of which one can prove that some action complies or does not comply with the principle of the general will, universalization or reciprocity (all Kant's attempts to do so failed and no one is well known for having done better since). In the final analysis, the "universality" of any concern depends on an act of sovereignty, that is, on the sovereign decision to present some or other course of conduct as a universal concern. The most that a sovereign with Rousseauian, Kantian or Rawlsian (Kantian will do from now on) aspirations can do, Chapter Six averred, is to claim *plausibly* and *persuasively* that some or other course of conduct pursues a universal concern that every human individual shares with all others.

That any Kantian aspirations that a sovereign might have are ultimately dependent on concerns of *plausibility* and *persuasiveness* – as opposed to "pure self-evidence" – is clear even in the case of concerns that one might consider "self-evidently" universal. One may want to consider in this regard concerns with bodily integrity, dignity and liberty that liberal democratic constitutions invariably posit as absolute principles of liberal democracy. The best arguments one may invoke to prove that these concerns are the concerns of *everyone* can ultimately only raise the plausibility and persuasiveness of the claim that these concerns are universal. They do not leave the plane of mere plausibility and persuasiveness behind them so as to arrive at *proven* universality. Kant tried to do this by taking recourse to the notion of performative contradictions that ruin all normative claims that cannot be universalised. But, again, all his efforts in this regard failed.

Now, if moral philosophy gets one no further than this under pure conditions of abstract thought, constitutional review procedures would surely be hard pressed to get one any further under the complex conditions of constitutional review. Constitutional review procedures, however *procedural* one may wish to make them, would then ultimately also seem to turn on sovereign decisions to hold some things as rational, justifiable, self-evident, etc. The only thing that a sovereign can do to keep the spectrum of its sovereign decisions within range of what one may call "plausible universality" or "plausible reciprocity" is to restrict the range of such sovereign decisions to a very narrow spectrum of concerns that can be expected to meet with general acceptance. The concerns of "public reason," one might call these concerns, following Rawls. These principles of public reason, being few and quite "self-evidently" indispensible for civil co-existence, may well answer to most demands for "universal" or at least general justification. However, they ultimately also remain dependent on sovereign endorsements and restatements, especially after dark times during which their apparent self-evidence was quite evidently eclipsed by black humours.

Consider again the significance of Jefferson's words in the first lines of the American Declaration of Independence to which Arendt points us: "We hold these laws of nature and nature's god to be self-evident truths." Jefferson would not have used this strange performative expression, writes Arendt, had the self-evidence of these truths really been self-evident; had this self-evidence been able to stand on its own legs, so to speak (see again the discussion in Chapter Six). But having said this, and having acknowledged the performative act of sovereignty that ultimately sustains the self-evidence of principles of public reason, one can confidently assume with Rawls that the principles of public reason indeed provide one with *adequate* levels of "universalization" or generalisation.

Why "adequate"? They appear adequate because they do not seem to be socially and politically divisive. One may reasonably assume that they sustain the minimal "overlapping consensus" that guarantees the cohesion on which liberal democratic sovereignty depends. This minimal overlapping consensus need therefore not be imposed on anyone as an alien and alienating substantive norm. And it is from the perspective of this minimal overlapping consensus that one may also proceed to invoke the notion of *adequate* proceduralisation. To put the matter in the Kelsenian terms developed in Chapter Six: One can honestly imagine, or a judge conducting a process of constitutional review can plausibly and persuasively claim, that there is no minority or majority in the territory of the liberal democratic sovereign that does not share in this minimal overlapping consensus.

One knows, of course, as Rawls also knows well,[12] that this argument does not take one very far. The application of these principles of overlapping consensus – all of them being so abstract, general and minimal as they are – soon leads one straight into interpretive difficulties, differences and disagreements. That is why constitutional review procedures require supplementary rules that are usually reflected in proportionality tests. We shall presently turn to the profound historical significance of these supplementary rules. Suffice it to say for now that liberal democratic horizontal effect review must be able to assume a number of minimal substantive principles that can be proceduralised adequately by inviting and receiving a negative answer to the question whether there is any significant majority or minority that does not endorse them. Constitutional review procedures could conduct this adequate proceduralisation with recourse to the first step of a three-step proportionality test that may read as follows:

Is the legislative or common law rule or administrative act (or as we have seen, absence of legislation, absence of common law or absence of administrative action) in question reconcilable with the norms of an open and free democratic society?[13]

With this almost ritual or formulaic first step of standard proportionality tests, constitutional judiciaries would implicitly pose and receive a negative answer to the question whether any of the interested parties before them reject the minimal substantive principles that sustain an open and free democratic society. No counsel of sound mind leads a serious client into court with the intention of questioning the applicability of this question. For this to happen, truly dark

12 Rawls, *Political Liberalism*, 240 – 241.

13 This "first leg" of the proportionality test is drawn from Art 36 of the Constitution of South Africa of 1996. It is not reflected in all proportionality tests elsewhere in the world. The German *Übermaßverbot* (alternatively *Verhältnismässigkeitsgebot*) is a product of early GFCC case law, the constitutional status (*Verfassungsrang*) of which was expressly recognised by the GFCC in BVerfGE 23, 127 (1968). The exact contents of the *Übermaßverbot* were much debated since then, but a consensus developed during the 1970s that it comprised three elements: 1) Geeignetheit/ Tauglichkeit (efficacy/appropriateness), 2) Erforderlichkeit/Notwendigkeit (compelling reason/ necessity), 3) Verhältnismäßigkeit/Zumutbarkeit/Angemessenheit (proportionality). Cf. Stern, *Das Staatsrecht der Bundesrepublik Deutschland*, Band III/1: 762, 775. It should be clear that the reconstruction of the proportionality test proposed here is based on a reconstruction that loosely relates to Stern's description. Some references will also be made to the different levels of scrutiny in American constitutional review along the way, but for a more precise description of these different levels of scrutiny (rational purpose, heightened, intermediary and strict), cf. again the discussion of *Roe v Wade* in Chapter Two).

times will have had to descend on that court. But the troubles start soon after this initial question and it is to these troubles that we must turn next. However, one can conclude for now, that this little ritual[14] saves the concept of *procedural* due process horizontal effect review from the substantive trouble with which *DeShaney* confronts it. *DeShaney* may have ended up with a bizarre assessment of the particular legislation or absence of legislation in question in the case, but *DeShaney* surely could not have gone so far as to openly question the validity of the minimal substantive normativity contained in the first leg of our proportionality test without precipitating a constitutional crisis.[15]

One can assume that Justice Rehnquist knew this. One can assume that he understood as well as anyone else that any attempt to reconcile the negligent failure of due administrative care in the *DeShaney* case with this minimum sub-

---

14 The idea is not to suggest that it is procedurally perfunctory and therefore otherwise actually insignificant. Constitutional Courts can of course easily find some or other legislation to fall foul of the principles of an open and democratic society, so much so that the rest of the proportionality test becomes redundant. Two good USSC examples are *Roy Romer v. Richard Evans et al* 517 US 620 (1996) and *City of Cleburne v Cleburne Living Centre* 474 US 432 (1985). In both these cases the possibility of resorting to stricter review procedures was expressly considered and avoided. *Cleburne* concerned the requirement that a special permit be obtained to use premises as a home for the mentally handicapped. Justice White judged the requirement to rest on an irrational prejudice against mentally handicapped persons, thus making it possible to strike down the requirement as unconstitutional by resorting to a basic rationality test, and thus avoiding the difficulty that mentally handicapped persons could not be regarded as a quasi-suspect classification as far as constitutional review is concerned (which would have blocked stricter review). *Romer* concerned an amendment to the Colorado constitution – Amendment 2 – that that would have made any specific Colorado state action aimed at the special protection of homosexual persons unconstitutional. Having considered a similar case of discrimination that deprived Mormons of the vote which passed scrutiny (*Davis v. Beason* (133 U.S. 333 (1890) cited by dissenting Judges Scalia and Thomas and Chief Justice Rehnquist) as no longer good law for reasons of having had to pass stricter scrutiny, Justice Kennedy nevertheless simply concluded (at 635) that the discrimination in *Romer* did not even pass rational scrutiny – "in addition to the far-reaching deficiencies of Amendment 2 that we have noted, the principles it offends, in another sense, are conventional and venerable; a law must bear a rational relationship to a legitimate governmental purpose ... and Amendment 2 does not." I am indebted to Joe Singer for pointing out these two cases for me. Cf. also the discussion of *Gulf, Colorado And Santa Fe Railway Company v Ellis* 165 US 150 (1897), *Powel v Pennsylvania* 127 US 678 (1888), *Rinaldi v Yeager* 384 US 305 (1966) and *McLaughlin v Florida* 379 US 184 (1966) in Chapter Two, fn. 140.
15 This format of the proportionality test is not applied in the United Sates, but the various levels of scrutiny applied in the Unites States do correspond with the different elements of the proportionality test devised above. Rational purpose scrutiny appears to echo the second leg of the proportionality test (effectiveness) and strict scrutiny (narrow tailoring) would appear to correspond with the third leg of proportionality test (minimum intrusion). Cf. again sections IV and V of this chapter.

stantive normativity of liberal democracy would be futile. And then one can also begin to assume the real reason for articulating his judgment with reference to bold formalistic distinctions between action and inaction (presence or absence of due administrative care/presence or absence of legislation that created public liability torts). One can assume that his formalistic reasoning was effectively a ploy to simply avoid these questions of basic substantive normativity. Why would he have wanted to avoid these questions? Only one assumption seems warranted here: to avoid overt approval of a bizarre legislative will that no judiciary can approve without forfeiting defining credentials of liberal democratic judiciaries.

Liberal democracy and liberal democratic constitutional review embody a minimal substantive normativity. We saw above that this minimal substantive morality can be proceduralised adequately, but not fully. Justice Rehnquist nevertheless refused to be tied to this minimal substantive normativity. He basically refused to be a liberal democratic judge. But he could not admit to this refusal openly; hence his resort to formalism; hence his resort to the surreptitious betrayal of liberal democracy and the surreptitious abdication of liberal democratic sovereignty for which *DeShaney* came to stand.

VI The Second Proportionality Question: Rationality and Effectiveness

The regular rational purpose scrutiny test in American constitutional review meets the typical European or German proportionality test when one moves to the second leg of the latter test. Here the relevant question in both the American and German tests is simply whether any curtailment of constitutional rights or liberties that result from legislation or administrative acts (or any absence of both when considered in view of the horizontal effect jurisprudence proposed here), is rational and effective. It is worthwhile observing again that many questions that at first glance appear to involve substantive constitutional concerns can be turned into questions of simple rationality and effectiveness (rational purpose), provided the rationality and efficacy questions were asked rigorously enough. At issue here is again the way the minority opinion in *Erste Abtreibung* provides one with a way around or out of the substantive due process review into which Justice Blackmun slipped too quickly in *Roe*. At stake in this regard is not only the avoidance of divisive substantive due process judgments that the option of rational review offers. At stake is also the higher level of clarity and precision that this translation of substantive normative questions into questions of rationality and efficacy promises.

One of the major weaknesses of the *Lüth* concept of substantive radiation or *Ausstrahlung* of fundamental rights, we pointed out in Chapters Two, Four and Six, is the wide scope that it leaves for "speculative" judicial interpretations of the meaning and implication of abstract fundamental rights principles for concrete questions of constitutional review. At issue here was especially Leisner's observation regarding the *vagueness – Unklarheit* – of this method, but also his and Robbers' contention that fundamental rights do not radiate, but validate or invalidate – *Grundrechte strahlen nicht aus, Grundrechte gelten.*

If one's aim is to move away from the huge potential for vertical judicial impositions of constitutional values on horizontal relations between citizens – recollection of the *"Ausstrahlung"* jurisprudence that Schmitt articulated in 1933 should be one's call for extreme caution here – the substantive considerations of concern in the notion of "radiation" should be restricted to the minimal substantive assumptions of a narrow range of (adequately proceduralised) values that everyone can plausibly and persuasively be expected to share. Once it is clear that a review question at hand concerns the narrow range of constitutional values that everyone can be expected to share and respect, they have to take leave of the abstractness of these values so as to ask the most concrete and specific questions that can be asked under the circumstances of the case. As Rawls also points out with regard to the principle of public reason, they are too abstract to allow for concrete answers. The concrete answers must be derived from very specific questions regarding the effect of any course of action or decision on the horizontal relations between equal citizens.

These concrete questions would invariably concern the real impact of any decision on the fundamental horizontality and equality between citizens that liberal democratic sovereignty demands and guarantees. Any decision or course of action or lack of these that obviously and for no good reason treats them differently – that fails to establish "general legislation," so to speak – and any such decision or course of action that curtails their equal liberty without good reason should accordingly be deemed either ineffective or irrational or both. Chapter Five expressed much incredulity and scepticism with regard to Christensen and Fischer-Lescano's rather irenic or rosy view of the application of these concrete review procedures, but one must concede in all fairness that they too ultimately share exactly this concern, namely, the need to move away from vague notions – with high potential for vertical impositions (*Züge ins Vertikale*, they call it aptly) – such as "schonendste Ausgleich" and "balancing of rights." It is for the same reason that we emphasise here the need to move as quickly as possible from abstract substantive considerations (considered adequately under the first leg of the proportionality question) to concrete questions regarding the rationality and efficacy of the impact of any decision on the relations between equal citizens. One can surely endorse in this regard Christensen and Fischer-Lescano's plea for the substitution of an abstract hermeneutics of fundamental rights with a more accurate and precise sociology of fundamental rights concerns.

VII The Third Proportionality Question: Minimal Intrusion

One should not fail to discern the ancient historical drama that finds its final resolution – we are speaking deliberately like Hegel here – in the third leg of the proportionality test.[16] For here, more conspicuously than anywhere else, does one see the history of sovereign law – a history that begins with the maxims *princeps legibus solutus est*[17] and *quod princeps placuit legis habet vigorem*[18] – finally resolving into the aspiration that guided this history from its very beginnings. For jurists and political thinkers have through the ages invariably, as soon as they had articulated or acknowledged these maxims of sovereignty, always retreated from them so as to tie them to another source of authority. One might say the history of sovereignty is the history of splits that ends with the splitting evident in the third leg of the standard constitutional proportionality test. We find this history of split sovereignties already evident in the institutions of the Roman Republic, notably in the Roman distinction between the *auctoritas* of the senate and the *potestas* of the magistrates.[19] This early splitting of Roman republican sovereignty falls into considerable obscurity with the advent of imperial rule, but it does not disappear, for the emperor, the history of political thought tells us, was also always considered to be somehow bound by principles of the common good of the people that he ruled, as if the *auctoritas* for his *potestas* still lay outside him. Here again, still very vaguely but evidently enough, does one see early traces of the original splitting or *split origin* of sovereignty that would culminate in the concept of a differentiated or différantial sovereignty that Chapter Six borrowed from the thinking of Jacques Derrida.

---

16 The telegraphic summary of the early history of sovereignty invoked here, although mostly inspired by the texts of Agamben, Figgis and Kantorowicz cited below, is also much indebted to Joseph Canning, *A History of Medieval Thought 300–1450* (London: Routledge, 1996).

17 Digest 1.3.31 (Ulpian) in Justinian, *Corpus Iuris Civilis* I, ed. Paulus Krueger and Theodor Mommsen (Clark, New Jersey: Lawbook Exchange, 2010).

18 Digest 1.4.1 (Ulpian); Institutes 1.2.6 in *Corpus Iuris Civilis* I.

19 Cf. Giorgio Agamben, *State of Exception* (Chicago: University of Chicago Press, 2005), 41–51, 74–88.

The original splitting of sovereignty soon takes on quite clear contours in the Middle Ages. During the middle and high Middle Ages, the Pope increasingly managed to claim, for the good of the Christian church and community, the *auctoritas* that ultimately governs the *potestas* of the Emperor. This claim prevailed until such time as the Pope began to lose this authority again towards the end of the Middle Ages and especially after the Reformation.

When the Eusebean claims of Kings to be the ultimate representative of God on Earth finally began to triumph over similar claims of Popes and Emperors towards the end of the Middle Ages so as to establish the doctrine of the divine right of kings,[20] they did so, however, already fundamentally informed by the condition of another original splitting, the splitting of the King's body into two. One need not contemplate seriously the notion of the two bodies of the emperor as far as medieval Europe is concerned (as far as we know no historian has ever done this), for emperors had practically disappeared from the scene by this time, notwithstanding the nominal persistence of the Holy Roman Empire till the battle of Jena in 1806 – speaking here again deliberately like Hegel. The narrative of the King's two bodies pivoted on medieval and Renaissance symbolism regarding the split between the earthly government of the King and the reign of the celestial office of kingship.[21] Benjamin Constant would tap into this symbolism to articulate the distinction between *governing* and *reigning* invoked in Chapter Six. Carl Schmitt would revive this distinction in his early writings, but only to ultimately instrumentalise it in ways that betrayed its essence. Schmitt would appropriate this differentiation and splitting of sovereignty into modes of governing and reigning, Chapter Six showed, only to undo this splitting again with atomic or unitary conceptions of sovereignty. The distinction is a significant one, Chapter Six nevertheless insisted, lamenting the fact that Kelsen, the ultimate theorist of originally-split sovereignties, did not perceive its significance for the split sovereignty that his conception of liberal democracy contemplated.

Kelsen would conceive constitutional liberal democracy in terms of the political exigency to maintain majority-minority relations in divided societies. These majority-minority relations, argued Kelsen, endow both majorities and minorities with *democratic* status. *Democratic* majorities derive their *democratic* status from the extent to which they use their majority powers to safeguard mi-

20 The crucial turns in this direction were the publication of John Wycliffe's *De Officio Regis* (1378) and the reign of Richard III of England (1452–1485) and the reign of Henry III of France (1551–1589). Cf. Figgis, *The Divine Right of Kings*, 66–80, 118.

21 The symbolisation of the Kings two bodies through the construction of a funeral effigy dates back to the death of Edward II in 1327 and the practice was transplanted to France with the death of Charles VI in 1422. Cf. Kantorowicz, *The King's Two Bodies*, 420–421.

norities, and *democratic* minorities derive their *democratic* status from the extent to which they respected the right of democratic majorities to govern. In a socially divided liberal democracy, Chapter Six, argued, majorities *govern*, but liberal democracy *reigns*. Liberal democracy *reigns* by subjecting majority government to the exigencies of sustaining majority-minority relations.[22] Chapter six elaborated this Kelsenian conception further with reference to Leisner's concept of "*der 'Staat,' der seines 'Selbstzwecks' entkleidet ist*" – the state that is deprived or disrobed of any separate or independent reasons of state that are not the concerns of equal citizens in horizontal relations. This is how Chapter Six arrived at the concept of a différantial and horizontal concept of liberal democratic sovereignty in terms of which the sovereign reign of liberal democracy results from the differences between democratic majorities and minorities. Within the reign of these differences, the identities or essences of both majorities and minorities are always deferred and displaced by one another. The Kelsenian recognition of the différantial displacements with which minorities and majorities constantly defer but also co-constitute one another's identities reflects what might be called the end phase of the epochal historical deconstruction of the nodal or atomic conception of sovereignty reflected in the maxim *princeps legibus solutus est.* And it is this historical deconstruction, we wish to conclude now, that liberal democratic constitutional review finally came to articulate in the third leg of the proportionality test, namely, the demand that no majority legislation or administrative act, or the absence of any of these, may come to interfere more with the equal and horizontal liberties of citizens than can be justified to them in *plausible* and *convincing* terms that they can *plausibly be persuaded* to respect.

---

22 The concepts elaborated here, the différantial splitting of popular sovereignty into irreducible majority-minority relationships and the distinction between governing and reigning sovereignty are key elements of questions with which one would need, from the perspective of liberal democratic sovereignty and liberal democratic judicial review developed here, to engage with the forceful critiques of judicial review articulated by authors such as Ran Hirschl and Jeremy Waldron. Cf. Waldron, *Law and Disagreement*; Waldron, *The Dignity of Legislation*; Hirschl, *Towards Juristocracy*; *Tushnet, Taking the Constitution Away from the Courts*. One would have to inquire whether these arguments in favour of judicially unfettered majoritarian democracy accommodate or could accommodate the differential understanding of sovereignty and democracy developed here. If not, these critiques may prove to be less pertinent or instructive for the socially deeply divided contexts of many if not most contemporary democracies. However, it should be clear from the endorsement above of much of Böckenförde's critique of the jurisprudence articulated in *Lüth* (a forceful critique of juristocracy in its own right) that the conception of horizontal effect review that is forwarded in this book shares many of the sensibilities of these authors.

It should be obvious from these demands of plausibility and persuasiveness that the liberal democratic reasons for curtailing any liberty or right should be clear and exact. The abstract rights and principles that can and must be invoked for purposes of the first leg of the proportionality test, can no longer play a role here in the third leg of the test, especially not with reference to vague notions of balancing and *schonendste Ausgleich* of these abstract rights. These notions allow much too much scope for obfuscating undemocratic impositions of substantive decisions on individuals or groups that may well have very different convictions and sensibilities. They may come to baffle and instil acquiescence, but they will not constitute serious attempts to convince and persuade. At issue here is again the point that Christensen and Fischer-Lescano make with regard to the need for a more accurate sociology of fundamental rights than invocations of vague notions such as balancing and *schonendste Ausgleich* might facilitate. Much more specific questions need to be asked under the third leg of proportionality tests, many or most of which should be open to strict demands for rigorous empirical observation and control. This is, perhaps, exactly what American constitutional law language seeks to denote with the "narrow tailoring" of any legislation or regulation that abridges fundamental rights in pursuit of "compelling interests." When one engages rigorously with the specific questions or narrow tailoring envisaged here, and when one does this, moreover, *after already* having restricted the substance of substantive due process review to the confirmation of a small handful of abstract normative principles that everyone involved can be expected to endorse *before* moving on to more controversial and divisive issues, one may well begin to rid the notion of substantive due process of the stigma that currently attaches to it.

At issue here is not the suggestion that the method articulated in *Lüth* always leads to unacceptable results. One can acknowledge, as Christensen and Fischer-Lescano do, that the *Lüth* method resulted more often than not in convincing enough judgments, notwithstanding the unrefined language of *schonendste Ausgleich*, *Ausstrahlung*, etc., that it employed. This is most likely so because a more accurate sociology of the issues at stake in any case accompanies the *Lüth* method surreptitiously. Christensen and Fischer-Lescano invoke in this regard the hidden sociology – *eine verdeckte Soziologie* – that is at work in the more precise reasoning of the GFCC.[23] But when the notions of *schonendste Ausgleich*, *Ausstrahlung*, etc., end up in trouble, as it did in *Erste Abtreibung*, one can be sure that the finer sociology of fundamental rights that Christensen and Fisch-

23 Christensen and Fischer-Lescano, *Das Ganze des Rechts*, 175.

er-Lescano have in mind, was surely neglected with the result of and perhaps for the sake of leaving things vague.

It is crucial to clarify exactly what is at stake in the assessment of *minimal intrusion* that the finely calibrated sociology of fundamental rights should aim to assess. At issue in this assessment of minimum intrusion is definitely not a libertarian or neo-liberal concern with minimal or minimum government. At issue is, fundamentally to the contrary, a concern with maximum or maximal government. Here lies, perhaps, the resolution of the New Deal conundrums that Seidman and Nirken raise in the context of the state action doctrine, and which Nedelsky raises in the context of property rights. As we saw in Chapters One and Three, these scholars invoke the difficulty that progressive Americans experience with reconciling their endorsement of redefinitions of property and the private sphere demanded by vicissitudes of social need, on the one hand, with their liberal recognition of the need to safeguard a personal sphere of life from undue governmental interference, on the other. The conundrums at issue here would seem to result from the assumption that maximum protection of the person implies a maximal reduction of government. However, the Kelsenian concept of horizontal minority-majority relations elaborated in this book suggests the exact opposite logic is at stake in liberal democracies, namely, maximal protection of minorities coupled with maximal tolerance for majority government. There is no libertarian or neo-liberal plea for the minimal or night watchman state in either Kelsen's conception of liberal democratic minority-majority relations or in Leisner's concept of the state that is disrobed of separate reasons of state.

This may come across as counter intuitive. However, this is exactly what is at stake in a finely calibrated sociology of constitutional rights that one should hope to see embodied in the second and third legs of proportionality tests. At stake is exactly the need to establish accurately just *how far* liberal democratic government can go to safeguard and maximise fundamental personality concerns with life, liberty and equality without imposing unnecessary demands on anyone. At issue in liberal democracy is, as its name indicates, both maximal government and maximal protection of fundamental personality concerns, both maximum sovereignty and maximum liberty. From this perspective, the idea that maximum sovereignty implies a liberty deficit, or maximum liberty implies a sovereignty deficit, would seem completely miscued.

The understanding of liberal democracy as a concern with maximal sovereignty for the sake of maximal liberty requires one more crucial conceptual move. It requires that one no longer refer to the fundamental concerns of liberty – the concerns with life, liberty, equality, physical integrity and dignity – in terms of privacy and the private sphere. These concerns are, in a very fundamental way, *public concerns that concern everyone*. The terms privacy and private sphere should be reserved for incidental aspects of life that do not concern anyone but the individual to whom they happen to matter for reasons of personal taste and inclination. These things are not private because the state and public authorities are categorically proscribed from interfering with them, but because they are, for the time being at least, simply irrelevant to public life. Hobbes knew, as well as Rawls did, that comprehensive government is not a good idea and not necessary to uphold civil order.[24] *De minibus non curat rex*. A very similar consideration – or perhaps it is the same one – informs the distinction between private and constitutional law to which we turn now.

VIII The Difference between Ordinary and Constitutional Law

The recasting of horizontal effect review jurisprudence in terms of the three components of the proportionality test proposed above (Sections V to VII), evidently proposes for horizontal effect review the very method that judiciaries have hitherto been applying in "vertical review procedures." This recasting surely confirms and concludes the erasure of the distinction between the horizontal and vertical effect of fundamental rights for which the chapters in this book have argued. Over the years, the question regarding the apposite proportionality test in *Drittwirkung* cases evoked different opinions among German scholars. Some scholars favoured the regular proportionality or *Verhältnismäßigkeit* test.[25] Others believed a balancing of rights or *schonendste Ausgleich* to be more apposite.[26]

---

24 Loughlin, *Sword and Scales*, 135 referring to Hobbes, *Leviathan*, 239–40.

25 As we saw above, Böckenförde was evidently skeptical about the balancing approach, but he also seemed to be skeptical of *Drittwirkung* as such and for this reason can be said to have stood somewhat outside the debate. Cf. again "Grundrechte als Grundsatznormen," 20–23. Canaris' "duty to protect" or "state action" approach to the question basically committed him to adopt the regular proportionality test in the form of the *Übermaßverbot* in cases where a civil law rule positively limits a fundamental right and in the form of the *Untermaßverbot* in cases where civil law rules fail to provide sufficient protection of a fundamental right. Cf. Canaris, "Grundrechte und Privatrecht," 201–246. Martin Oldiges, "Neue Aspekte der Grundrechtsgeltung im Privatrecht," 308 basically followed Canaris and noted that this approach spares the judiciary the "rechtsgestaltende Charakter" of the balancing approach, evidently responding to the reservations that Böckenförde voiced in this regard.

26 Klaus Stern, "Ehrenschutz und 'allgemeine Gesetze,'" in *Festschrift für Heinz Hübner zum 70. Geburtstag am 7. November 1984*, ed. Gottfried Baumgärtel et al. (Berlin: De Gruyter, 1984), 827–828; Wolfgang Rüfner, *Handbuch Des Staatsrechts*, ed. Josef Isensee and Paul Kirchof, Bnd V (Heidelberg: C.F. Müller, 2007), 38. In other words, these scholars basically endorsed the approach in *Lüth*.

According to the latter scholars, the regular *Verhältnismässigkeit* or proportionality test had to be reserved for regular vertical review procedures. For them balancing or *Ausgleich* was the correct approach to horizontal effect review, given the way this horizontality review always concerns a conflict between rights, whereas under the former, the state has no rights that can or need to be balanced with the rights of citizens. Some scholars also believed the constitutional proportionality test only applied in highly exceptional cases to private legal disputes. According to them the proportionality tests that have been developed within private law doctrine over centuries (already in Roman law) and private law legislation should generally be applied in disputes between private parties.[27]

It should be clear by now that this book aims to steer constitutional review away from the balancing or *Ausgleich* approach and towards the regular proportionality approach. This conclusive erasure of the difference between regular "vertical" constitutional review, on the one hand, and "horizontal effect" review, on the other, may well seem to also erase the difference between private law and constitutional law. The erasure of the difference between the method of constitutional review of private law and the method of constitutional review of public law would seem to confront one once more with a potential translation of all private law questions into constitutional law questions. And this translation again raises the question whether there remains any other significant difference between private law and constitutional law that might prevent constitutional courts from becoming final appeal courts in all private law questions.

This question, however, is misplaced. The proportionality test proposed here need not and does not translate all private law concerns into constitutional concerns, not even potentially so. The proportionality test surely does not turn all public law cases into constitutional law cases, so why should it do so in the case of private law? The method of review has obviously nothing to do with the selection of cases one takes on review, be these cases private or public law cases. Yet, the suggestion that the same method be used in the review of both private and public law provides an opportune moment for revisiting the question of the difference between private and constitutional law, for the comparison of the methods of review respectively applicable in private and public law cases shows clearly why the suggestion that horizontal effect erases the difference between constitutional law and private law is evidently wrong.

---

27 Cf. Medicus, "Der Grundsatz der Verhältnismäßigkeit im Privatrecht," 35–70. Medicus notably relied on Böckenförde for his key points regarding the inapplicability of the constitutional proportionality test in private disputes.

Not all public law disputes constitute constitutional cases and it would be obviously wrong to suggest public law is just "applied constitutional law." Yet, this is exactly what has come to be suggested by one of the more recent contributions to the horizontal effect debate, notably by Matthias Kumm. Kumm expressly describes private law as "applied constitutional law," we saw in Chapter Six. He does so, we saw, in what is perhaps nothing more than a somewhat overzealous endeavour to promote the idea of the sovereign reign of constitutional law over and in all other spheres of law. Recognising the sovereign reign of the constitution in all spheres of law is undoubtedly an important endeavour that also goes to the heart of the arguments elaborated in the chapters of Part One of this book. But this recognition should not mutate into the very different idea that private law is nothing but an extension of constitutional law. Again, the discussion in Chapter Five of Schmitt's endorsement of this idea in 1933 should serve as a clear call for caution in this regard. Someone like Kumm might of course object to this point by responding that the catastrophic misuse of an idea for obnoxious purposes does not necessarily ruin it forever. The whole of Chapter Six was aimed, however, at showing that it is not just the particular use that Schmitt made of this idea, but the idea as such that calls for serious caution, irrespective of the kind of constitution that one hopes to see "applied" in all particular fields of law. For this idea is the root of the dubious inclination towards substantive due process methods of review that Section III and IV of this chapter, and Chapters Five and Six before that, seek to eradicate.

Be it as it may, it is exactly for purposes of showing why the recognition of the sovereign reign of the constitution over all areas of law does not amount to a blanket translation of all private disputes into potential constitutional disputes that Chapter Two ended with a discussion of Justice Grimm's dissenting opinion in the GFCC's *Reiten im Walde* judgment. The discussion of *Reiten im Walde* in Chapter Two showed how the translation of all ordinary law disputes into constitutional disputes cannot but end up trivialising constitutional law and constitutional jurisprudence. The claim in *Reiten im Walde* concerned an administrative law claim that had no standing in a constitutional court, contended Justice Grimm. Similar findings can surely become pertinent and necessary in private law disputes and Chapter Two cited the British case *Douglas v Hello* (claims of privacy infringements with regard to unauthorised publication of photographs that were not significantly different from other photographs of which publication was duly authorised at a price) and the South African case *Barkhuizen v Napier* (late registration of an insurance claim) as possible examples.

This argument does not suggest disputes in ordinary courts are trivial. Ordinary law, be it administrative, private or criminal law, has it own criteria of triviality that are usually announced with the maxim *de minibus non curat lex*. The fact that an ordinary court has given a dispute a hearing and possibly even several appeal hearings is already enough indication that that claim is not trivial as such. But even non-trivial claims can become trivial when raised in the wrong context. Private law claims can become trivial in a context where the aim is to consider only fundamental constitutional concerns that literally mark the decisive beacons of a people's constitutional history. There is a second order triviality that constitutional law needs to weed out from claims that duly merit constitutional review. The maxim *de minibus non curat lex constitutionis* would announce well what is needed in this regard and the essential difference between private and constitutional law, argued Chapter Two, should be seen to turn on exactly this maxim. When a private law dispute suddenly turns into a significant historical beacon of a people's constitutional history, argued chapter Two, it surely demands a hearing in that people's highest constitutional forum. If not, it should neither be taken nor allowed there.[28]

---

28 The question of "jurisdictional design" and the extent to which the distinction between ordinary law and constitutional law requires a complete separation or partial overlap of judicial competences has not been addressed in this book. For a meticulous engagement with this question, cf. Frank Michelman, "The Interplay of Constitutional and Ordinary Jurisdiction," in *Comparative Constitutional Law*, ed. Tom Ginsburg and Rosalind Dixon (Edward Elgar Publishing, 2012), 278–297. The position proposed here would be reconcilable with the idea that all courts should in principle always be alert to the potential constitutional implications of an ordinary law dispute, and competent to make judgments in this regard. Some such judgments – those that strike down legislation as unconstitutional – should best be reserved for constititutional courts, as Article 167 of the Constitution of South Africa of 1996 stipulates for South African judiciaries. This position is thus also in line with Articles 168 and 169 that allow the Supreme Court of Appeal and High Courts to judge constitutional questions, subject to the stipulation in Article 167 (that only the Constitional Court may strike down National and Provincial Legislation). The position taken here nevertheless deviates significantly from the South African position as far as Article 39(2) of the Constitution of 1996 is concerned, considering its clear apprehension regarding adjudication that would "promote the spirit, purport and objects of the Bill of Rights." There is a big difference between being alert to common or customary law that is irreconcilable with the Bill of Rights and being ready to change or reject such law, on the one and, and the duty to constantly "promote the spirit" of the Bill of Rights, on the other. The notion of "promoting the spirit" of the Bill of Rights evidently risks or effects an expansion of substantive due process judicial review that the position taken here seeks to avoid for the sake of restricting judicial review to minimal considerations of substance that condition a *liberal* democratic judicial review. At issue here is exactly the proto-liberal inspiration that guides all dualist conceptions of constitutionalism that Michelman invokes in a related essay. Cf. Frank Michelman, "Constitutions and the Public/Private Divide," in *The Oxford Handbook of Comparative Constitutional Law*, ed. Michel Rosenfeld and András Sajó (Oxford: Oxford University Press, 2012), 298–317. All dualist conceptions of constitutionalism contemplate some distinction between exercises of rulership to which the constitution applies and a space of society to which

IX Social Liberal Democracy?

A procedural conception of liberal constitutionalism, writes Frank Michelman, understands this constitutionalism as a way of living with our most fundamental and divisive differences. It does not understand constitutionalism as a way of resolving those differences with reference to some substantive norm with regard to which all our differences can be deemed settled. The constitution does not resolve our deep differences, says Michelman, "it helps us to get over them, vault us past them."[29] The committed engagement in this book with the conception of constitutionalism in terms of the sustenance of majority-minority relations that Kelsen articulated in *Vom Wesen und Wert der Demokratie* was from the beginning as much inspired by what Kelsen wrote there, than by that which Michelman writes here about a constitutionalism that requires and helps liberal democrats to live with their deepest differences. Majorities and minorities simply have to learn to live with their differences and get over them, one might say with combined reference to both Kelsen and Michelman. But there is a third inspiration that also guided the articulation of the procedural liberal democratic horizontal effect jurisprudence articulated in this book. That inspiration comes from Hannah Arendt's articulation of the crucial role that forgiveness plays in politics. The world cannot begin anew, writes Arendt in *The Human Condition*, if we are doomed to return again and again to ancient wrongs. Politics is fundamentally conditioned by the ability to forgive and get over wrongs done in the past.[30] Following this thought, one might venture yet another version of the

---

the constitution does not apply, claims Michelman (cf. the articulation at 306). How is this proto-liberal inspiration to be reconciled with the "challenge from the left" the ultimate contention of which is the "ubiquity of the state" and the "inference ... that every case at law falls within the purview of a constitutional bill of rights no matter how strictly "vertically" directed? Michelman's answer is that even very left oriented or "post-liberal" constitutional dispensations such as that of South Africa find themselves on a scale of possible positions from left to right, together with more right oriented constitutional dispensations such as that of the United States, all of which positions still maintain the proto-liberal government-society distinction evident in dualist conceptions of constitutionalism (cf. 311–312). It is ultimately the sustenance of this proto-liberal spirit (or "ghost," as Michelman also calls it) that is at issue with the invocation of the maxims *de minibus non curat rex* and *de minibus non curat lex constitutionis* above. It is exactly this proto-liberal spirit that is threatened by the notion of "promoting the spirit of the Bill of Rights." The position taken here would have been much more at ease with a wording of article 39(2) that stipulated the simple duty of courts to ensure the basic conformity of all law with the demands of the Bill of Rights.

29 Frank Michelman, "Constitutional Legitimation for Political Acts," *The Modern Law Review* 66, no. 1 (2003): 1–15.

30 Hannah Arendt, *The Human Condition* (Chicago: University of Chicago Press, 1989), 236–243.

Kelsen-Michelman conception of liberal constitutionalism offered above, now with Arendt's voice added: Constitutionalism demands from majorities and minorities that they forgive one another for the injurious ways in which they differ and apparently cannot stop differing. "Help us to forgive one another our daily differences," might one hear these Kelsenian-Michelmanian-Arendtian liberal democrats pray in due constitutional worship.[31]

Might this daily democratic forgiveness also include forgiveness for not granting one another our daily bread? If we follow Arendt on this point, the answer would be "of course not." Arendt, we know, was wilfully blind with regard to deprivations of daily bread. She defined politics, political forgiveness included, in terms of the ability to ignore and forget questions of material need and poverty.[32] But not so Michelman, or at least not the Michelman writing in the 1960s and 70s. We find him arguing boldly in 1969 that the United States constitution guarantees American citizens a right to a certain social minimum that exists independently of the right to the equal protection of the laws and does not raise the (absence of positive) state action and semantic questions (does the right also include access to golf courses and theatres?) that the equal protection route raises. And he did all of this, one notices, without serious concerns about the substantive due process review procedures on which such a right will turn inevitably.[33]

---

31 Arendt, *On Revolution*, 196, referring to Woodrow Wilson's invocation of Americans' worship of their constitution.

32 Arendt, *On Revolution*, 59–114; Van der Walt, "Law and the Space of Appearance in Arendt's Thought," 72–76; Christodoulidis, "Depoliticising Poverty: Arendt in South Africa," *Stellenbosch Law Review* 22, no. 3 (2011): 515.

33 Frank Michelman, "The Supreme Court, 1968 Term-Foreword: On Protecting the Poor through the Fourteenth Amendment," *Harvard Law Review* 83, no. 7 (1969): 7–59. The article notes the substantive due process worries that moved the USSC during this time to rather address minimum socio-economic guarantees via the Fourteenth Amendment (equal protection of the laws) at 17–18. It also basically concedes the substantive due process status of the social minimum right that it contemplates as the more consistent and coherent option at 33 (considering that the poor cannot be considered to constitute a constitutionally invidious classification that should otherwise prompt stricter review), and does not deem it necessary to justify further what conspicuously stands out as an instance of the substantive constitutional legitimations against which Michelman would later argue forcefully. The closest that the article comes to returning to the problem of substantive due process review consists in the concession right at the end (at 57) that the absence of a judiciable standard for specifying the social minimum does shunt the social minimum approach somewhat onto equal protection rails again. As for the state action questions that might burden the review of equal protection but not to the review of a right to a social minimum, cf. 39, 55–57.

A second article from this period would appear to already have been somewhat more cautious. Still undoubtedly remarkably adventurous, we see Michelman basing the right to a social minimum in 1979 largely on John Ely's conception of the "representation-reinforcing" demands of the constitution. At issue here, in brief, was Ely's view that the constitution contains a substantive demand that participation in democratic decision-making procedures should be fully representative – everyone should be able to participate, not just in principle but also as a matter of social reality or substance. Dire poverty, argued Michelman then, following Ely, is evidently one of the social realities that distort political representation by preventing some persons from exercising their political rights properly. The "representation-reinforcing" thrust of the constitution therefore stipulates a right to a social minimum that would rectify or minimalize this distortion of political representation. Close to the end of the article the argument confidently reached the high note for which it had been preparing:

> "Through a lawyerlike parsing of constitutional text, history, and structure, Ely makes a plausible case for the Constitution's own express recognition of a class of general constitutional rights and ... an overwhelming ... case for inclusion in that class of minimum welfare rights – rights to the indispensible means of effective participation in the institutional system itself."[34]

But it also immediately returned to considerable caution:

> "[T]he duty [to ensure a social minimum nevertheless] seems to be one that courts acting alone cannot or ought not undertake to define, impose and enforce. Indeed, the texts themselves would hardly tolerate judicial enforcement in the face of legislative passivity."[35]

Ironically enough, Michelman sounded this more cautionary note with reference to Hohfeld, but evidently not in order to make the Hohfeldian point that we have been attributing to him throughout this book. At issue for him here, was rather the opposite of the Hohfeldian point. Activation of the Fourteenth Amendment requires more than "the purely quiescent state," he says, it requires positive "making or enforcement of laws." Was Michelman, of all people, really invoking a standard state action requirement for the possible adjudication of the right to a social minimum, here in 1979? If so, it would surely have been quite out of character. Already in 1969 did he recognise the "moribund" status of that "letter"

---

34 Frank Michelman, "Welfare Rights in a Constitutional Democracy," *Washington University Law Quarterly* 3 (1979): 684.
35 Ibid, 684–685.

with reference to Charles Black,[36] and that recognition would evidently stay with him in work that would follow later (see again Chapter Three). More in line with the overall development of his thought would be the inference that it was not Hohfeld, but John Rawls that was already beginning to temper and even restrain his confidence regarding a judiciable right to a social minimum in 1979.

Notwithstanding the strong recognition of social equality concerns as a principle of justice in *A Theory of Justice*, Rawls would already in this book, in 1971, express clear reticence regarding the possibility of turning this principle of justice into a justiciable constitutional right. Rawls would become a major influence in Michelman's thought and one can already see, here in 1973, Rawls turning Michelman away from his earlier confidence regarding the justiciability of social rights. The critical issue for Michelman, responding to Rawls in 1973, was surely not Hohfeld, as the reference to both state action and inaction in this passage makes clear:

> "Given Rawlsian premises, acceptance of judicial review thus reflects a belief that it is possible and useful to cultivate a special capacity for evaluating the compliance of legislative action (inaction) with principles of justice or their derived constitutional embodiments, *and for persuading the generality of citizens to recognise discrepancies when they occur.*"[37]

That legislative action includes legislative inaction is acknowledged casually here within a set of parentheses. This is evidently not the fish that Michelman wanted to fry in this passage. That fish swims in the line that he italicised. Judiciaries lack the means for "persuading the generality of citizens to recognise discrepancies when they occur" when social rights are at issue. Of concern here for Michelman was "another interpretation of the [remedial] incompetence notion." At issue in the standard conception of "remedial incompetence" is the notion that enforcement of rights "involves a complex of subsidiary but vitally important choices which the judiciary lacks all basis for making." However, this conception of remedial incompetence envisages a standard lack of judicial competence that pertains to the enforcement of all rights and not only the enforcement of social rights. The "other" interpretation of remedial incompetence that Michelman, following Rawls, specifically had in mind in 1973, was this one:

---

36 Michelman, "On Protecting the Poor through the Fourteenth Amendment," 57.

37 Frank Michelman, "In Pursuit of Constitutional Welfare Rights: One View of Rawls' Theory of Justice," *University of Pennsylvania Law Review* 121, no. 5 (May 1, 1973): 1008.

> "[T]he court lacks modes of articulation and explanation under which it can decide the case and maintain its appearance of answering to external principle, the moral source of its influence on other parts of government."[38]

The social rights that would ensue from Rawls' principles of justice, in other words, are just too stuck in intractable normative controversy. There is no way that judges can generally convince citizens that they have access to external criteria of judgment that raise them above general normative controversy regarding social rights and this lack of sufficiently obvious external criteria deprives them of the normative authority to tell other branches of government – democratically elected as they are or acting in accordance with democratically enacted legislation – what they are to do. This Rawlsian line of argument would become increasingly important in Michelman's later work, so much so that Michelman would later appear reluctant to follow suit when Rawls himself commenced to soften his stance in this regard. In 1993 and 2001 Rawls would commence to regard the right to a social minimum as a constitutional essential. Ironically he now found himself endorsing Michelman's earlier position.[39] A remarkable crossing would appear to have taken place here. Rawls would seem to have departed from his earlier position to follow Michelman's earlier argument in the same time that Michelman would exchange his earlier position for the one Rawls articulated earlier on. They both would appear to have thought the other had the better idea. Be it as it may, perhaps as a result of this exchange, Michelman later also began to experiment with the possibility of *non-justiciable* constitutional essentials. However, the conviction regarding the ultimate non-justiciability of a social minimum right, on the one hand, and apprehension regarding the questionable wisdom of including non-justiciable rights in the constitution of a people (such as the people of the United States) with excessively legalistic expectations regarding their constitution, on the other, ultimately also cautioned him not to venture too far down the avenue of non-justiciable rights.[40]

The reasons for not accepting the right to a social minimum as either a justiciable or a non-justiciable constitutional essential, writes Michelman, do not concern a tension between liberalism and socioeconomic constitutional guarantees. Rawls argues convincingly, writes Michelman, that the basic individual

---

38 Ibid, 1007.

39 Cf. Rawls, *Political Liberalism*, 228–229; Rawls, *Justice as Fairness: A Restatement*, ed. Erin Kelly (Cambridge, Mass.: Harvard University Press, 2001), 47–48, 162. Cf. also the reference to Michelman on footnote on 162, fn. 40 and the similar reference in *Political Liberalism* 237, fn. 23.

40 Cf. Frank Michelman, "Socioeconomic Rights in Constitutional Law: Explaining America Away," *International Journal of Constitutional Law* 6, no. 3–4 (July 7, 2008): 663–686.

rights on which liberalism turns are conditioned by and therefore presuppose minimal socioeconomic guarantees. There is therefore no tension between liberalism and social guarantees as such, as many critics of liberalism argue. The problem pertains much rather to the non-ideal conditions under which any adjudication of social guarantees would have to be contemplated, namely, conditions of irreducible social division and moral controversy regarding the very existence of such constitutional guarantees (irreducible disagreement between those who believe they exist and those who believe they do not), on the one hand, and irreducible disagreement or lack of certainty regarding the extent of such guarantees, even among those who believe they exist, on the other. [41] Under these conditions, especially in the United States where constitutional rights raise expectations of strict constitutional legality that are irreconcilable with merely aspirational or utopian moral considerations, argues Michelman, there is a strong case for restricting judicial review to questions regarding the constitutional framework with reference to which implacable differences and deep disagreements can be resolved procedurally. And among these differences and disagreements, differences and disagreements with regard to constitutional guarantees of social minimums just happen to be among the most divisive cases in point.

On another occasion one may well want to return to Rawls' principles of justice and specifically his difference principle, to investigate certain resonances that these principles appear to have with Kelsen's majority-minority principle. Especially the difference principle appears to potentially reflect the same double maximisation configuration (maximum sovereignty–maximum liberty/maximum majority government–maximum minority protection) that is apparent in Kelsen's majority-minority principle. It would be worthwhile, it seems, to ponder the question whether the latter, the majority-minority principle, does not show us the way towards an adequate proceduralisation of the former, the difference principle. Should this turn out to be the case, it may well also facilitate a productive break with the maxim-minimum configuration (maximum sovereignty–minimum liberty or maximum liberty–minimum sovereignty) that has confounded state action and horizontal effect jurisprudence so enduringly. But all of this would put enormous weight on Kelsen's shoulders, weight that he surely never offered to carry. For him, the majority-minority principle was a principle of liberal democracy, not of justice.[42]

---

41 Cf. Frank Michelman, "Poverty in Liberalism: A Comment on the Constitutional Essentials," *Drake Law Review* 60 (2012 2011): 1001–1021.

42 Cf. Kelsen, *Was ist Gerechtigkeit?*, 49–50: "Wenn die Geschichte der menschlichen Erkenntnis uns irgend etwas lehren kann, ist es die Vergeblichkeit des Versuches, auf rationalem

So for now, we may conclude that Michelman, Rawls and Kelsen would seem to have put the substantive social requirements for liberal principles of justice beyond the reach of constitutional review.[43] One may well want to agree with all of them that it is more important and "more urgent" to sustain the framework of procedural principles with reference to which deep disagreement can be overcome, than to insist on substantive constitutional guarantees in a way that may come round to threaten the very framework of procedural principles. The thirteenth chapter of St. Paul's letter to the Romans are written all over the solution that Rawls and Michelman contemplate here. And it would also seem to be written between the lines of Kelsen's conception of constitutional review in terms of the need to sustain viable majority-minority relations. So *for now*, in this *meantime*, or *in the time that remains*, one might say with Giorgio Agamben,[44] social liberal democrats, if there are or will be some, would have to accept that there is not much material horizontality coming from the horizontal effect revolution as yet. To the contrary, in Europe we have seen, another European "constitutional" court, the ECJ, is bringing about what many consider an anti-social revolution, exactly in the name of the horizontal effect of fundamental liberties. The ECJ earned this reputation for its horizontal effect jurisprudence through its decisions in the *Laval* and *Viking* decisions discussed in Chapter Seven. Horizontal effect has been presented in this book as an endeavour to undo hierarchy and inequality. If these perceptions of the ECJ's jurisprudence in *Laval* and *Viking* were correct, they would surely suggest that horizontal effect jurisprudence could easily also have a hierarchy-entrenching effect. Sobering arguments of Mark Tushnet would appear to underline this reality.

In two articles that link the question of horizontal effect directly to social democratic concerns, Tushnet argues, on the one hand, that states with strong social democratic commitments tend to have less difficulty with recognising

---

Wege eine absolut gültige Norm gerechten Verhaltens zu finden, d.h. aber eine solche, die die Möglichkeit ausschließt, auch das gegenteilige Verhalten für gerecht zu halten."

43 It is noteworthy, however, that Michelman has again taken up the idea of non-justiciable socio-economic rights in his recent work in what appears to be an endeavour to reconsider its plausibility and possible cogency. Cf. Frank Michelman, "Constitutionally Binding Social and Economic Rights as a Compelling Idea: Reciprocating Perturbations in Liberal and Democratic Constitutional Visions," forthcoming in *Social & Economic Rights in Theory and Practice: A Critical Assessment*, ed. Helena Alviar Garcia, Karl Klare, and Lucy Williams (London: Routledge, 2014).

44 Giorgio Agamben, *The Time That Remains: A Commentary on the Letter to the Romans* (Stanford: Stanford University Press, 2005). Assuming that we are no longer bound by "author's intention hermeneutics," this exquisite book may well be understood as a forceful defence of liberal democracy.

the horizontal effect of constitutional rights in its constitutional jurisprudence.[45] This part of Tushnet's argument evidently recognises an egalitarian and social democratic thrust in horizontal effect review procedures that warrants the assumption that horizontal effect is fundamentally reconcilable and indeed concerned with social democracy. But this assumption only remains plausible, argues Tushnet further, as long as legislative commitments within these social democratic states remain moderate or less than moderate. More progressive legislative commitments to social democracy may well bring about a configuration that renders any kind of constitutional review at odds with levels of social democracy that have in fact been achieved. Seen from this perspective, horizontal effect review may well become a counterweighing force in social democracies. Tushnet cites in this regard the examples of the Netherlands and Sweden, countries with "thick" social democratic commitments in which constitutional review of parliamentary legislation is constitutionally either proscribed or highly restricted.[46] However, the judgments of the ECJ in *Laval*, *Viking* and *Rüffert* seem to provide an even more striking example of the point Tushnet is making. "Constitutional" review of legislative regimes with strong social democratic commitments had disastrous consequences for these commitments in all three cases.

Or so some perceive the matter. There are also others, we have seen in Chapter Seven, who discern "an invisible hand" social redistribution programme in the market liberalising jurisprudence of the ECJ. The subversion of established social security standards in wealthier Member States of the European Union is just a sad consequence of opening richer employment markets to workers of poorer Member States, they contend. Perhaps. Perhaps they really believe this. And perhaps they are even right. But how shall one ever know? And how can judiciaries know? What puts judiciaries in a better position to know? This brings one back to Michelman's invocation of "remedial incompetence" of judiciaries in 1973. Just like other mortals, judiciaries also lack modes of decision-making on the basis of which they can "maintain [their] appearance of answering to external principle" when they deal with the unfathomable questions that socio-economic rights raise. For this reason, they lack "the moral source of [their] influence on other parts of government."

One may want to conclude from this that judiciaries should simply refrain from exerting such influence on other parts of government, but this would be going too far. Chapter Seven suggested ways in which courts – the ECJ in that

45 Cf. Tushnet, "State Action, Social Welfare Rights, and the Judicial Role," 435–453, Tushnet, "The Issue of State Action/Horizontal Effect in Comparative Constitutional Law," 79–98.
46 Tushnett, "State Action, Social Welfare Rights, and the Judicial Role" 445.

case – can communicate their perceptions to other parts of government without taking over the functions of other parts of government. This would seem to be quite feasible and that is perhaps also why Michelman's most recent work is again looking into the significance that the right to a social minimum may have when conceived as a "non-justiciable constitutional essential." Perhaps courts do have sufficient moral standing for exercising influence on other parts of government after all, but they surely cannot claim to "answer to external principle" in matters of socio-economic equality and for this reason have neither the right nor the moral standing to take over the functions of other parts of government.

To be sure, other parts of government also cannot claim to answer to "external principle" and also do not have the unique moral standing that endows them with the right to govern. No one has. Other parts of government surely do not obtain the right to govern from unique moral standing. They obtain that right from procedures devised for selecting those who are to govern under circumstances where no one has the unique moral standing that warrants the moral right to govern. Or so, in any case, is how things work in liberal democracies.

The ambiguity of the practice of horizontal effect judicial review is nevertheless not restricted, argues Tushnet, to the way it allows for the judicial subversion of social democracy. Its very existence, as a kind of last-ditch remedy, can be ascribed to the weak commitment to social democracy that ultimately characterises liberal democracies, he contends. This is how he makes the point:

> "I offer no normative recommendations, but observe only that we are likely to live with thin social democratic systems for quite a long time and that, as a result, the state action/horizontal effect issue will be with us for a long time as well."[47]

The gloomy ambiguity of a legal construction on which many social democratic lawyers and legal theorists have been fixing much hope for many years now, the horizontal effect of constitutional rights, can hardly be portrayed more realistically than Tushnet portrays it here. Those who are still awaiting a more distinct parting of the wicked and the worthy, but not anxiously enough to cast caution in the wind and take leave of liberal democracy for the sake of a more radical politics, may well have to wait, like St. Paul and St. Augustine instructed, for a day of final reckoning at the end of time. Only then might mortals come to know whom the heavens favoured, those who were more concerned about prenatal and less concerned about postnatal abortions, or those who were more concerned about postnatal and less about prenatal (at least first trimester) abor-

47 Ibid, 453.

tions. For this is strangely how the morals of mortals often pan out on this planet. Those who are uniquely concerned about medically unindicated abortion of life during first trimesters of pregnancy would seem to be much less concerned about the post-natal abortion of life that results from inadequate social security measures (see again the discussion of conservative and liberal conceptions of the public private divide in Chapter Three).

The United States and Europe and many other "developed" and relatively rich regions or countries of the world abort fully born children and adults of all ages on a daily basis by systemically depriving them of adequate nourishment, medicine, housing, education and employment; not only "elsewhere" in the world but also in these countries themselves. Until such time as all of this comes to an end, and considering that the prospects of real change in this regard do not come across as encouraging, social liberal democrats may well want to consider another kind of forgiving as the truest reflection of the human condition and of liberal democracy as we know it now, namely, the condition of having to forgive one another, on a daily basis, the unforgivable.

The forgiving of the unforgivable is the only forgiving worthy of the name, we learned, now already so many years ago, from French philosophers.[48] From the doubled coil of this paradox leap forth, simultaneously, intertwined and mutually obscuring, both the remarkable achievement and nagging embarrassment of liberal democracy: by embracing compromise as a key constitutional virtue and a key constitutive practice, liberal democracy can surely claim to constitute a plausible way of avoiding the kind of humanitarian disasters for which the uncompromising politics of the twentieth century became notorious. But it purchases this achievement by also renouncing deep commitments to social justice that might lose patience with the perennial practice of compromising that sustain existing social hierarchies. Horizontal effect constitutional review can also be traced into this double coil of an unforgivable forgiving.

Liberal democracy is then, an endeavour to live on and muddle through under conditions of strict epistemological horizontality, conditions under which no one can, as yet, convincingly claim conclusive celestial insights. Again, it is an endeavour to live on in the time that remains. Under these seemingly incircumventible conditions of irreducible mortal ignorance, the grace to forgive one another the unforgivable may well remain the essence of liberal democratic ethics. There is however, one mischievous question with which *social*

---

48 Cf. Paul Ricoeur, *La Mémoire, l'Histoire, l'Oubli* (Paris: Seuil, 2000), 630–637. Whether this spectral forgiving of the unforgivable that Ricoeur discusses here was envisaged as the daily and perfunctory business that it has become, is another question social liberal democrats should ask themselves honestly.

democrats may well want to continue their *liberal* democratic conversation with other liberal democrats. It is a question that concerns basic logic and does therefore not, it seems, need to involve the wisdom of the heavens: What is the big deal about first trimester abortions if postnatal abortions are not a big deal?

Bibliography

Ackerman, Bruce A. *We the People: Foundations.* Cambridge: Harvard University Press, 2000.

Agamben, Giorgio. *State of Exception.* Chicago: University of Chicago Press, 2005.

—, *The Time That Remains: A Commentary on the Letter to the Romans.* Stanford: Stanford University Press, 2005.

Alexander, Larry. "The Public/Private Distinction and Constitutional Limits on Private Power." *Constitutional Commentary* 10, no. 2 (1993): 361–378.

Alexy, Robert. *Theorie der Grundrechte.* Frankfurt am Main: Suhrkamp, 1986.

Amar, Akhil Reed. "Remember the Thirteenth." *Constitutional Commentary* 10 (1993): 403–408.

Andriychuk, Oles. "Rediscovering the Spirit of Competition – On the Normative Value of the Competitive Process," *European Competition Journal,* 6, no. 3, 2010: 575–610.

—, "Thinking Inside the Box: Why Competition as a Process is a Sui Generis Right – A Methodological Observation" in *The Goals of Competition* edited by Daniel Zimmer. 95–118. Cheltenam: Edward Elgar Publishing, 2012.

Arendt, Hannah. *Eichman in Jerusalem.* New York: Penguin Books, 1994.

—, *Men in Dark Times.* Middlesex: Penguin Books, 1973.

—, *On Revolution.* New York: Penguin Books, 1963.

—, *The Human Condition.* Chicago: University of Chicago Press, 1989.

—, *The Origins of Totalitarianism: Imperialism.* New York: Harcourt Brace Jovanovich, 1968.

Atiyah, Paul. *The Rise and Fall of Freedom of Contract.* Oxford: Clarendon Press, 1979.

Azoulai, Loïc. " "The Court of Justice and the Social Market Economy: The Emergence of an Ideal and the Conditions for its Realisation," 45 (2008) *Common Market Law Review,* 1335–1356 and Dragana Damjanovic, "The EU Market Rules as Social Market Rules: Why the EU Can be a Social Market Economy?" *Common Market Law Review,* 50 (2013): 1685–1718.

—, "The European Court of Justice and the Duty to Respect Sensitive National Interests" in *Judicial Activism at the European Court of Justice* edited by Mark Dawson, Bruno de Witte and Elise Muir. 167–187. Cheltenham /Northampton: Edward Elgar Publishing, 2013.

Baker, C. Edwin. "Private Power, the Press, and the Constitution." *Constitutional Commentary* 10 (1993): 421–441.

Barak-Erez, Daphne. "Civil Rights in the Privatized State: A Comparative View." *Anglo-American Law Review* 28 (1999): 503–524.

Barnard, Catherine. "Employment Rights, Free Movement Under the EC Treaty and the Services Directive." In *EU Industrial Relations v. National Industrial Relations,* 137–168. Alphen aan den Rijn: Kluwer Law International, 2008.

—, "Social Dumping or Dumping Socialism?" *The Cambridge Law Journal* 67, no. 02 (2008): 262–264.

—, "A Proportionate Response to Proportionality in the Field of Collective Action," *European Law Review,* 37 (2012): 118–135.

Berlin, Isaiah. *Four Essays on Liberty.* London: Oxford University Press, 1969.

Black, Charles. "The Supreme Court, 1966 Term – Foreword: State Action, Equal Protection, and California's Proposition 14." *Harvard Law Review* 81 (1967): 69–109.

Böckenförde, Ernst Wolfgang. "Grundrechte als Grundsatznormen." *Der Staat* (1990): 1–30.

—, *Staat, Verfassung, Demokratie: Studien zur Verfassungstheorie und zum Verfassungsrecht.* Frankfurt am Main: Suhrkamp, 1991.

Bodin, Jean: *Les Six Livres de la Republique*, vol I. Paris: Librairie Arthème Fayard, 1986.

Brinktrine, R. "The Horizontal Effect of Human Rights in German Constitutional Law: The British Debate on Horizontality and the Possible Role Model of the German Doctrine of 'Mittelbare Drittwirkung der Grundrechte.'" *European Human Rights Law Review* (2001): 421–432.

Brüggemeier, Gert, Aurelia Ciacchi, and Giovanni Comandé, eds. *Fundamental Rights and Private Law in the European Union – Vol. I: A Comparative Overview.* Cambridge: Cambridge University Press, 2010.

Bürge, Alfons. *Das französische Privatrecht im 19. Jahrhundert: zwischen Tradition und Pandektenwissenschaft, Liberalismus und Etatismus.* Frankfurt a.M.: Vittorio Klostermann, 1991.

Buxton, Richard. "The Human Rights Act and Private Law." *Law Quarterly Review* 116 (2000): 48–65.

Cafaggi, Fabrizio. "New Foundations of Transnational Private Regulation." In *The Challenge of Transnational Private Regulation: Conceptual and Constitutional Debates*, edited by Fabrizio Cafaggi, Colin Scott, and Linda Senden, 20–49. Oxford: Wiley-Blackwell, 2011.

—, ed. *The Institutional Framework of European Private Law.* Oxford/New York: Oxford University Press, 2006.

Cafaggi, Fabrizio, and Horatia Muir Watt, eds. *Making European Private Law – Governance Design.* Cheltenam/Northampton: Edward Elgar Publishing, 2008.

Canaris, Claus-Wilhelm. "Grundrechte und Privatrecht." *Archiv für die civilistische Praxis* 184, no. 4 (1984): 201–246.

Canning, Joseph. *A History of Medieval Thought 300–1450.* London: Routledge, 1996.

Carré de Malberg, Raymond. *La Loi Expression de la Volonté Générale.* Paris: Economica, [1931] 1984.

Carter, Ian. "Positive and Negative Liberty." In *The Stanford Encyclopedia of Philosophy*, edited by Edward N. Zalta, 2012. http://plato.stanford.edu/archives/spr2012/entries/liberty-positive-negative/.

Cherednychenko, Olha O. "Fundamental Rights and Private Law: A Relationship of Subordination or Complementarity?" *Utrecht Law Review* 3, no. 2 (December 20, 2007): 1–25.

Christensen, Ralph, and Andreas Fischer-Lescano. *Das Ganze des Rechts – Vom hierarchischen zum reflexiven Verständnis deutscher und europäischer Grundrechte.* Berlin: Duncker & Humbolt, 2007.

Christodoulidis, Emilios. "A Default Constitutionalism? Some Cautionary Remarks on the Many Constitutions of Europe." In *The Many Constitutions of Europe*, edited by Kaarlo Tuori and Suvi Sankari, 31–48. Farnham: Ashgate, 2013.

—, "Depoliticising Poverty: Arendt in South Africa." *Stellenbosch Law Review* 22, no. 3 (2011): 501–520.

—, "On the Politics of Societal Constitutionalism." *Indiana Journal of Global Legal Studies* 20 (2013): 629–663.

Claes, Monica. "The Europeanization of national constitutions in the constitutionalization of Europe: Some observations against the background of the constitutional expérience of the EU-15." *Croation Yearbook of European Law and Policy* 2007: 1–38.

Clapham, Andrew. *Human Rights in the Private Sphere.* Oxford: Clarendon Press, 1993.

—, *Human Rights Obligations of Non-State Actors.* Oxford: Oxford University Press, 2006.
Caunes, Karine. "La Nature du système juridique européen; retour sur le principle de primauté" in *L'européanisation des droits constitutionnels à la lumière de la Constitution pour l'Europe*, edited by Jacques Ziller. 281–298. Paris: L'Harmattan, 2003.
Clements, Richard. "Bringing It All Back Home: 'Rights' in English Law Before the Human Rights Act 1998." *Human Rights Law Journal* 21 (2000): 134–142.
Cohen, Morris R. "Property and Sovereignty." *Cornell Law Quarterly* 13 (1928 1927): 8–30.
Collins, Hugh. *Utility and Rights in Common Law Reasoning: Rebalancing Private Law Through Constitutionalization.* SSRN Scholarly Paper. Rochester, NY: Social Science Research Network, September 1, 2007. http://papers.ssrn.com/abstract=1011727.
Cooper, Jonathan. "Horizontality: The Application of Human Rights Standards in Private Disputes." In *An Introduction to Human Rights and the Common Law*, edited by Rosalind English and Philip Havers, 53–69. Oxford: Hart, 2000.
Coussirat-Coustère, Vincent. "Convention européenne des droits de l'homme et droit interne: Primauté et effet direct." In *La Convention europeénne des droits de l'homme. Actes de la Journée d'étude du 16 novembre 1991.* Brussels: Nemesis, 1992.
Craig, Paul and Gráinne de Burca *EU Law: Texts, Cases and Materials.* Oxford: Oxford University Press, 2011, 5th ed.
Cseres, Katalin. "Governance Design for the European Private Law: Lessons From the Europeanization of Competition Law in Central and Eastern Europe." In *Making European Private Law: Governmance Design*, edited by Fabrizio Cafaggi and Horatia Muir Watt, 138–193. Cheltenam/Northampton: Edward Elgar Publishing, 2008.
Curtin, Deirdre, and Linda Senden. "Public Accountability of Transnational Private Regulation: Chimera or Reality?" In *The Challenge of Transnational Private Regulation: Conceptual and Constitutional Debates*, edited by Fabrizio Cafaggi, Colin Scott, and Linda Senden, 185–188. Oxford: Wiley-Blackwell, 2011.
Daly, James. "Cosmic Harmony and Political Thinking in Early Stuart England." *Transactions of the American Philosophical Society* 69, no. 7 (1979): 1–41.
Damjanovic, Dragana. "The EU Market Rules as Social Market Rules: Why the EU Can be a Social Market Economy?" *Common Market Law Review* 50 (2013): 1685–1718.
Davidson, Donald. "Radical Interpretation." In *Inquiries into Truth and Interpretation.* Oxford: Oxford University Press, 2001.
—, *The Essential Davidson.* Oxford: Oxford University Press, 2006.
Davies, A. C. L. "One Step Forward, Two Steps Back? The Viking and Laval Cases in the ECJ." *Industrial Law Journal* 37, no. 2 (June 1, 2008): 126–148.
Dawson, Mark. "The Political Face of Judicial Activism." in *Judicial Activism at the European Court of Justice*, edited by Mark Dawson, Bruno de Witte and Elise Muir, 11–31. Cheltenham /Northampton: Edward Elgar Publishing, 2013.
De Vos, Bart J. "The Netherlands." In *Fundamental Rights and Private Law in the European Union: Vol I, A Comparative Overview*, edited by Gert Brüggemeier, Aurelia Ciacchi, and Giovanni Comandé, 405–484. Cambridge: Cambridge University Press, 2010.
Debet, Anne. *L'influence de la Convention européenne des droits de l'homme sur le droit civil.* Paris: Dalloz, 2002.
Derrida, Jacques. *De la Grammatologie.* Paris: Les Éditions de Minuit, 1967.
—, "Declarations of Independence 1." *New Political Science* 7, no. 1 (1986): 7–15.
—, *L'autre cap.* Paris: Les Éditions de Minuit, 1991.
—, *Marges de la Philosophie.* Paris: Les Éditions de Minuit, 1972.

—, *Politiques de l'amitié*. Paris: Galilée, 1994.
—, *Voyous: deux essais sur la raison*. Paris: Galilée, 2003.
Dreyer, Frederick A. *Burke's Politics: A Study in Whig Orthodoxy*. Waterloo: Wilfrid Laurier Univ. Press, 1979.
Duby, George. *The Three Orders: Feudal Society Imagined*. Chicago: University of Chicago Press, 1982.
Dürig, Günter. "Grundrechte und Zivilrechtsprechung." In *Vom Bonner Grundgesetz zur gesamtdeutschen Verfassung: Festschrift zum 75. Geburtstag von Hans Nawiasky*, edited by Theodor Maunz, 117–182. München: Isar Verlag, 1956.
Dworkin, Ronald. *Freedom's Law: The Moral Reading of the American Constitution*. Oxford: Oxford University Press, 1996.
—, *Life's Dominion: An Argument about Abortion, Euthanasia, and Individual Freedom*. New York: Vintage Books, 1994.
Ely, John. "The Wages of Crying Wolf: A Comment on Roe v. Wade." *Yale Law Journal* 82 (1973): 920–949.
Enneccerus, Ludwig, and Hans Carl Nipperdey. *Allgemeiner Teil des Bürgerlichen Rechts: ein Lehrbuch*. Tübingen: J.C.B. Mohr, 1952.
Enzensberger, Hans Magnus. "Die Politische Enteignung der Europäer." *Der Hauptstadt Brief*, June 9, 2012. http://www.derhauptstadtbrief.de/cms/index.php/84-der-hauptstadtbrief-110/147-die-politische-enteignung-der-europaeer#nav.
Eucken, Walter. *Grundsätze der Wirtschaftspolitik*. Tübingen: Mohr Siebeck, 1952.
Fedtke, Jörg, and Dawn Oliver, eds. *Human Rights and the Private Sphere: A Comparative Study*. Abingdon: Routledge-Cavendish, 2007.
Figgis, John Neville. *The Divine Right of Kings*. London: Cambridge University Press, 1934.
Ford, John. *The Man Who Shot Liberty Valance*. Western. Paramount Pictures, 1962.
Foster, Christopher. *The Economics of Rail Privatisation*. London: Chartered Institute of Public Finance and Accountancy, 1994.
Foucault, Michel. *Naissance de la Biopolitique*. Paris: Gallimard/Seuil, 2004.
Freedland, Mark. "Private Law, Regulation and Governance Design and the Personal Work Contract." In *Making European Private Law: Governmance Design*, edited by Fabrizio Cafaggi and Horatia Muir Watt. Cheltenam/Northampton: Edward Elgar Publishing, 2008.
Freeman, Jody, and Martha Minow, eds. *Goverment by Contract: Outsourcing and American Democracy*. Cambridge, Mass.: Harvard University Press, 2009.
Friedmann, Daniel, and Daphne Barak-Erez, eds. *Human Rights in Private Law*. Oxford: Hart Publishing, 2001.
Friendly, Henry J. "The Public-Private Penumbra: Fourteen Years Later." *University of Pennsylvania Law Review* 130, no. 6 (June 1, 1982): 1289–1295.
Gall, Lothar. *Fragen an die deutsche Geschichte: Ideen, Kräfte, Entscheidungen von 1800 bis zur Gegenwart*. Bonn: Deutscher Bundestag, 1987.
Gardbaum, Stephen. "The 'Horizontal Effect' of Constitutional Rights." *Michigan Law Review* 102, no. 3 (December 1, 2003): 387–459.
Gerhardt, Volker, Henning Ottmann, and Martyn P Thompson, eds. *Politisches Denken Jahrbuch 1993*. Stuttgart: Metzler, 1993.
Gerkrath, Jörg. "The Figure of Constitutional Law of the 'Integrated State': the Case of the Grand Duchy of Luxembourg." *European Constitutional Law Review* 10, no. 1 (April 2014): 109–125.

Gerstenberg, Oliver. "Private Law and the New European Constitutional Settlement." *European Law Journal* 10, no. 6 (2004): 766–786.

Goldsworthy, Jeff. "The Debate about Sovereignty in the United States: A Historical and Comparative Perspective." In *Sovereignty in Transition*, edited by Neil Walker, 423–446. Oxford: Hart Publishing, 2003.

Grimm, Dieter. *Die Zukunft der Verfassung II.* Frankfurt a.M: Suhrkamp, 2012.

—, "Does Europe Need a Constitution?" *European Law Journal* 1, no. 3 (November 1995): 282–302.

—, "Prinzipien statt Pragmatismus." *Frankfurter Allgemeine Zeitung: Die Debatte um Europas Zukunft*, February 6, 2013. http://www.faz.net/aktuell/feuilleton/debatten/europas-zukunft/europas-zukunft-prinzipien-statt-pragmatismus-12052280.html.

—, *Souveränität: Herkunft und Zukunft eines Schlüsselbegriffs.* Berlin: Berlin University Press, 2009.

—, "Wer ist Souverän in der Europäischen Union." In *Die Zukunft der Verfassung II.* Frankfurt: Suhrkamp, 2012.

Habermas, Jürgen. *Der philosophische Diskurs der Moderne.* Frankfurt a.M: Suhrkamp, 1989.

—, *Faktizität und Geltung – Beiträge zur Diskurstheorie des Rechts und des demokratischen Rechtsstaats.* Frankfurt am Main: Suhrkamp, 1992.

—, "Remarks on Dieter Grimm's 'Does Europe Need a Constitution?'" *European Law Journal* 1, no. 3 (November 1995): 303–7.

—, "Schluss mit der Feigheit der Politiker." *Vorwärts*, February 2, 2012. http://www.vorwaerts.de/Politik/Europa/23482/schluss_mit_feigheit.html.

—, *Strukturwandel der Öffentlichkeit.* Frankfurt a.M: Suhrkamp, 1990.

—, *Theorie des kommunikativen Handelns I.* Frankfurt a.M: Suhrkamp, 1988.

—, *Zur Verfassung Europas. Ein Essay.* Frankfurt a.M: Suhrkamp, 2011.

Hager, Johannes. "Grundrechte im Privatrecht." *Juristenzeitung* 49, no. 8 (1994): 373–383.

Hale, Robert L. "Coercion and Distribution in a Supposedly Non-Coercive State." *Political Science Quarterly* 38, no. 3 (September 1, 1923): 470–494.

—, *Freedom through Law: Public Control of Private Governing Power.* New York: Columbia University Press, 1952.

Hayek, Friedrich. *The Road to Serfdom.* Chicago: University of Chicago Press, 2007.

Hedemann, Justus Wilhelm. *Die Flucht in die Generalklauseln. Eine Gefahr für Recht und Staat.* Tübingen: J.C.B. Mohr (Paul Siebeck), 1933.

Hegel, G. W. F. *Grundlinien der Philosophie des Rechts, Werke in 20 Bänden.* Vol. VII. Frankfurt: Suhrkamp, 1970.

—, *Phänomenologie des Geistes Werke in 20 Bänden.* Vol. III. Frankfurt a.M.: Suhrkamp, 1970.

—, "Vorlesungen über die Geschichte der Philosophie III." In *Werke in 20 Bänden.* Vol. XX. Frankfurt a.M.: Suhrkamp, 1970.

Heller, Hermann. "Autoritärer Liberalismus." *Die Neue Rundschau* (1933): 289–298.

Henkin, Louis. "Shelley v. Kraemer: Notes for a Revised Opinion." *University of Pennsylvania Law Review* 110, no. 4 (1962): 473–505.

Henne, Thomas. "'Von 0 auf Lüth in 6 ½ Jahren.' Zu den prägenden Faktoren der Grundsatzentscheidung." In *Das Lüth-Urteil aus (rechts-)historischer Sicht – Die Konflikte um Veit Harlan und die Grundrechtsjudikatur des Bundesverfassungsgerichts,* edited by Thomas Henne and Arne Riedlinger. Berlin: Berliner Wissenschafts-Verlag, 2005.

Henne, Thomas, and Arne Riedlinger, eds. *Das Lüth-Urteil aus (rechts-)historischer Sicht: die Konflikte um Veit Harlan und die Grundrechtsjudikatur des Bundesverfassungsgerichts.* Berlin: Berliner Wissenschafts-Verlag, 2005.

Hermes, Georg. "Grundrechtsschutz durch Privatrecht auf neuer Grundlage? – Das BVerfG zu Schutzpflicht und mittelbarer Drittwirkung der Berufsfreiheit." *Neue Juristische Wochenschrift* 29 (1990): 1764–1768.

Hirschl, Ran. *Towards Juristocracy: The Origins and Consequences of the New Constitutionalism.* Cambridge: Harvard University Press, 2004.

Hobbes, Thomas. "Leviathan." In *The English Works of Thomas Hobbes of Malmesbury*, Vol. III, edited by Molesworth. London: John Bohn, 1839.

Hogg, Peter. *Constitutional Law of Canada: Vol. II.* 5th ed. Ontario: Thomson Carswell, 2008.

Hohfeld, Wesley Newcomb. "Some Fundamental Legal Conceptions as Applied in Judicial Reasoning." *The Yale Law Journal* 23, no. 1 (November 1, 1913): 16–59.

Holmes, Oliver Wendell. *The Common Law.* Cambridge, Massachussetts; London, England: The Belknap Press of Harvard University Press, 2009.

Horowitz, Harold W. "The Misleading Search for 'State Action' under the Fourteenth Amendment." *Southern California Law Review* 30 (1955): 208–221.

Horwitz, Morton J. *The Transformation of American Law, 1780–1860.* Cambridge: Harvard University Press, 1977.

Hunt, Murray. "The Horizontal Effect of the Human Rights Act." *Public Law* (1998): 423–433.

Jellinek, Georg. *Allgemeine Staatslehre.* Berlin: Julius Springer, 1922.

Jessop, Bob. *The Future of the Capitalist State.* Cambridge: Polity Press, 2002.

Joerges, Christian. "Europa nach dem Ordoliberalismus: Eine Philippika." *Kritische Justiz* 43, no. 4 (2010): 394–406.

Joerges, Christian, and Florian Rödl. "Informal Politics, Formalised Law and the 'Social Deficit' of European Integration: Reflections after the Judgments of the ECJ in Viking and Laval." *European Law Journal* 15, no. 1 (2009): 1–19.

Justinian. *Corpus Iuris Civilis I.* Edited by Paulus Krueger and Theodor Mommsen. Clark, New Jersey: Lawbook Exchange, 2010.

Kant, Immanuel. "Metaphysik der Sitten." In *Werk in 10 Bänden*, edited by Wilhelm Weischedel, 7:85–102. Darmstadt: Wissenschaftliche Buchgesellschaft, 1983.

—, "Mutmasslicher Anfang der Menschengeschichte in 10 Bänden." In *Werk in 10 Bänden*, edited by Wilhelm Weischedel, 9:85–102. Darmstadt: Wissenschaftliche Buchgesellschaft, 1983.

Kantorowicz, Ernst Hartwig. *The King's Two Bodies: A Study in Mediaeval Political Theology.* Princeton: Princeton University Press, 1981.

Kaupa, Clemens. "Maybe not activist enough? On the Court's alleged Neoliberal Bias in its Recent Labour Cases" in *Judicial Activism at the European Court of Justice*, edited by Mark Dawson, Bruno de Witte and Elise Muir, 56–75. Cheltenham/Northampton: Edward Elgar Publishing, 2013.

Kelsen, Hans. *Das Problem der Souveränität und die Theorie des Völkerrechts.* Aalen: Scientia Verlag, 1960.

—, *Hauptprobleme der Staatsrechtslehre: Entwickelt aus der Lehre vom Rechtssatze.* Aalen: Scientia Verlag, 1984.

—, *Reine Rechtslehre.* Aalen: Scientia Verlag, 1994.

—, *Über Grenzen zwischen juristischer und soziologischer Methode: Vortrag, gehalten in der Soziologischen Gesellschaft zu Wien.* Aalen: Scientia-Verlag, 1970.
—, *Vom Wesen und Wert der Demokratie.* Aalen: Scientia Verlag, 1981.
—, *Was ist Gerechtigkeit?* Stuttgart: Reclam Philipp Jun, 2000.
Kelsen, Hans, and Robert Christian van Ooyen. *Wer soll der Hüter der Verfassung sein? Abhandlungen zur Theorie der Verfassungsgerichtsbarkeit in der pluralistischen, parlamentarischen Demokratie.* Tübingen: Mohr Siebeck, 2008.
Kennedy, Duncan. "Form and Substance in Private Law Adjudication." *Harvard Law Review* 89, no. 8 (June 1, 1976): 1685–1778.
—, "Stages of the Decline of the Public/Private Distinction." *University of Pennsylvania Law Review* 130 (1982): 1349–1357.
—, *The Rise & Fall of Classical Legal Thought.* Cambridge: AFAR, 1998.
Kiefner, Hans. "Der Einfluss Kants auf die Theorie und Praxis des Zivilrechts im 19. Jahrhundert." In *Philosophie und Rechtswissenschaft: Zum Problem ihrer Beziehung Im 19. Jahrhundert.* Frankfurt a.M.: Jahrhundert, Vittorio Klostermann, 1969.
Kinsch, Patrick. "Dean Spielmann *L'Effet Potential de la Convention Européenne des Droits de l'Homme entre Personnes Privées.*" *Annales du Droit Luxembourgeoise* (1995): 493–496.
Kirchof, Paul. "Verfassungsnot." *Frankfurter Allgemeine Zeitung*, July 12, 2012. http://www.faz.net/aktuell/feuilleton/debatten/europas-zukunft/paul-kirchhof-zur-krise--der-eu-verfassungsnot-11817188.html.
Kjaer, Poul F, Gunther Teubner, and Alberto Febbrajo, eds. *The Financial Crisis in Constitutional Perspective: The Dark Side of Functional Differentiation.* Oxford; Portland: Hart Publishing, 2011.
Klare, Karl E. "Legal Subsidiarity & Constitutional Rights: A Reply to AJ van der Walt" (2008) 1 *Constitutional Review* 129–154.
—, "The Public/Private Distinction in Labor Law." *University of Pennsylvania Law Review* 130, no. 6 (June 1, 1982): 1358–1422.
Kokott, Juliane. "The ECJ's Interpretation of the Posting Directive in the Laval and Rüffert Judgements" http://www.bmas.de/portal/27236/property=pdf/2008__07__16__symposium__eugh__-kojott__englisch-pdf.
Krüger, Herbert. "Die Verfassungen in der Zivilrechtsprechung." *Neue Juristische Wochenschrift* 2, no. 5 (1949): 163–166.
Kumm, Mattias. "Who's Afraid of the Total Constitution? Constitutional Rights as Principles and the Constitutionalization of Private Law." *German Law Journal* 7, no. 4 (2006): 341–370.
—, "The Moral Point of Constitutional Pluralism: Defining the Domain of Legitimate Institutional Civil Disobedience and Conscientious Objection" in *Philosophical Foundations of European Union Law*, edited by Julie Dickson & Pavlos Eleftheriadis. Oxford: Oxford University Press, 2012.
Laband, Paul *Das Staatsrechts des Deutschen Reiches Vol I.* Tübingen: J.C.B. Mohr (Paul Siebeck), 1911.
La Torre, Massimo. "'Rechtsstaat' and Legal Science. The Rise and Fall of the Concept of Subjective Right." *Archiv für Rechts-und Sozialphilosophie* (1990): 50–68.
Laufke, Franz. *Vertragsfreiheit und Grundgesetz, Festschrift für Lehmann.* Band I. Berlin: Walter de Gruyter, 1956.

Lefort, Claude. *L'Invention Démocratique: Les Limites de la Domination Totalitaire.* Paris: Fayard, Artheme, Librairie, 1994.
—, "Permanence du Théologico-politique?" In *Essais sur le Politique XIXe-XXe siécles*, 275–329. Paris: Seuil, 1986.
—, "The Permanence of the Theologico-Political?" In *Democracy and Political Theory*, 213–255. Minneapolis: University of Minnesota Press, 1988.
Leigh, Ian. "Horizontal Rights, the Human Rights Act and Privacy: Lessons from the Commonwealth?" *International & Comparative Law Quarterly* 48, no. 01 (1999): 57–87.
Leisner, Walter. *Demokratie – Selbstzerstörung einer Staatsform.* Berlin: Duncker & Humblot, 1979.
—, *Die Abwägungsstaat.* Berlin: Duncker & Humblot, 1997.
—, *Grundrechte und Privatrecht.* München: Beck, 1960.
Lewan, Kenneth M. "The Significance of Constitutional Rights for Private Law: Theory and Practice in West Germany." *The International and Comparative Law Quarterly* 17, no. 3 (July 1, 1968): 571–601.
Lewis, Thomas P. "The Meaning of State Action." *Columbia Law Review* 60, no. 8 (December 1, 1960): 1083–1123.
Liboreiro, Andrea Rodriguez. "Spain – A Jurisdiction Recognising the Direct Horizontal Application of Human Rights." In *Human Rights and the Private Sphere: A Comparative Study*, edited by Jörg Fedtke and Dawn Oliver, 379–398. Abingdon: Routledge-Cavendish, 2007.
Llanque, Marcus "Die Theorie politischer Einheitsbildung in Weimar und die Logik von Einheit und Vielheit (Rudolf Smend, Carl Schmitt, Hermann Heller)," in *Metamorphosen des Politischen: Grundfragen politischer Einheitsbildung seit den 20er Jahren*, edited by Andreas Göbel, Dirk van Laak, and Ingeborg Villinger, 157–176. Berlin: Akademie Verlag, 1995.
Locke, John. "Two Treatises of Government." In *The Works of John Locke.* Vol. 5. Aalen: Scientia Verlag, 1963.
Lokin, J.H., and W.J. Zwalve. *Hoofdstukken uit de Europese Codificatie-geschiedenis.* Groningen: Tjeenk Willink, 1992.
Loughlin, Martin. *Sword and Scales: An Examination of the Relationship Between Law and Politics.* Oxford: Hart Publishing, 2000.
Loughlin, Martin, and Neil Walker, eds. *The Paradox of Constitutionalism: Constituent Power and Constitutional Form.* Oxford: Oxford University Press, 2008.
Luhmann, Niklas. *Grundrechte als Institution: Ein Beitrag zur politischen Soziologie.* Berlin: Duncker & Humblot, 1965.
Macpherson, Crawford B. *The Political Theory of Possessive Individualism: Hobbes to Locke.* Oxford: Oxford University Press, 2010.
Maine, H.S. *Ancient Law: Its Connection with the Early History of Society and Its Relation to Modern Ideas.* London: John Murray, 1920.
—, *Dissertations on Early Law and Custom.* London: John Murray, 1891.
Majone, Giandomenico. "'Europe's Democratic Deficit': The Question of Standards," 4 (1998) *European Law Journal*, 5–28.
Mak, Chantal. *Fundamental Rights in European Contract Law: A Comparison of the Impact of Fundamental Rights on Contractual Relationships in Germany, the Netherlands, Italy and England.* New York, Alphen aan den Rijn: Kluwer Law International, 2008.

Manow, Philip. “Ordoliberalismus als ökonomische Ordnungstheologie.” *Leviathan* 29, no. 2 (2001): 179 – 198.

Markesinis, Basil. “Privacy, Freedom of Expression, and the Horizontal Effect of the Human Right Bill: Lessons from Germany.” *Law Quarter Review* 115, no. 47 (1999): 47 – 88.

Markesinis, Basil, and Stefan Enchelmaier. “The Applicability of Human Rights as between Individuals under German Constitutional Law.” In *Protecting Privacy*, edited by Basil Markesinis. The Clifford Chance Lextures Four. Oxford: Oxford University Press, 1999.

Marx, Karl. “Critique of the Gotha Programme.” In *Karl Marx Friedrich Engels: Collected Works Vol.24*, by Karl Marx and Friedrich Engels, 75 – 99. London: Lawrence & Wishari, 1989.

—, “Kritik des Gothaer Programms.” In *Karl Marx und Friedrich Engels: Werke-Artikel Entwürfe*, edited by Friedrich Engels, 5 – 25. Berlin: Dietz Verlag, 1985.

Massaro, John. *No Guarantee of a Gun: How and Why the Second Amendment Means Exactly What It Says*. Bloomington: AuthorHouse, 2009.

McCarthy, Cormac. *Blood Meridian*. Picador Books, 1990.

—, *No Country for Old Men*. London: Picador Books, 2007.

Medicus, Dieter. “Der Grundsatz der Verhältnismäßigkeit im Privatrecht.” *Archiv für civilistische Praxis* 192 (1992): 35 – 70.

Mensch, Elizabeth. “The Colonial Origins of Liberal Property Rights.” *Buffalo Law Review* 31 (1982): 635 – 736.

—, “The History of Mainstream Legal Thought.” In *The Politics of Law: A Progressive Critique*, edited by David Kairys, 23 – 53. New York: Pantheon Books, 1998.

Michelman, Frank. *Brennan and Democracy*. Princeton University Press, 2005.

—, “Constitutional Legitimation for Political Acts.” *The Modern Law Review* 66, no. 1 (2003): 1 – 15.

—, “Constitutionalism as Proceduralism: A Glance at the Terrain.” In *Public Law and Politics: The Scope and Limits of Constitutionalism*, edited by Emilios Christodoulidis and Stephen Tierney, 141 – 161. The Edinburgh Centre for Law and Society. Aldershot: Ashgate, 2008.

—, “Constitutionally Binding Social and Economic Rights as a Compelling Idea: Reciprocating Perturbations in Liberal and Democratic Constitutional Visions.” In *Social & Economic Rights in Theory and Practice: A Critical Assessment*, edited by Helena Alviar Garcia, Karl Klare, and Lucy Williams. London: Routledge, 2014.

—, “Constitutions and the Public/Private Divide.” In *The Oxford Handbook of Comparative Constitutional Law*, edited by Michel Rosenfeld and András Sajó, 298 – 317. Oxford: Oxford University Press, 2012.

—, “Dilemmas of Belonging: Moral Truth, Human Rights, and Why We Might Not Want a Representative Judiciary.” *UCLA Law Review* 47 (2000): 1221 – 1252.

—, “Human Rights and the Limits of Constitutional Theory.” *Ratio Juris* 13, no. 1 (2000): 63 – 76.

—, “In Pursuit of Constitutional Welfare Rights: One View of Rawls’ Theory of Justice.” *University of Pennsylvania Law Review* 121, no. 5 (May 1, 1973): 962 – 1019.

—, “Poverty in Liberalism: A Comment on the Constitutional Essentials.” *Drake Law Review* 60 (2012): 101 – 121.

—, “Socioeconomic Rights in Constitutional Law: Explaining America Away.” *International Journal of Constitutional Law* 6, no. 3 – 4 (July 7, 2008): 663 – 686.

—, "The Bill of Rights, the Common Law, and the Freedom-Friendly State." *University of Miami Law Review* 58 (2003): 401–447.
—, "The Interplay of Constitutional and Ordinary Jurisdiction." In *Comparative Constitutional Law*, edited by Tom Ginsburg and Rosalind Dixon, 278–297. Edward Elgar Publishing, 2012.
—, "The Supreme Court, 1968 Term-Foreword: On Protecting the Poor through the Fourteenth Amendment." *Harvard Law Review* 83, no. 7 (1969): 7–59.
—, "W(h)ither the Constitution?" *Cardozo Law Review* 21 (2000): 1063–1083.
—, "Welfare Rights in a Constitutional Democracy." *Washington University Law Quarterly* 3 (1979): 659–693.
Mnookin, Robert H. "The Public/Private Dichotomy: Political Disagreement and Academic Repudiation." *University of Pennsylvania Law Review* 130, no. 6 (June 1, 1982): 1429–1440.
Mouffe, Chantal. *The Return of the Political.* New York: Verso Books, 1993.
Nancy, Jean-Luc. *L'Expérience de la Liberté.* Paris: Galilée, 1988.
—, *La Communauté Désoeuvrée.* Paris: Christian Bourgois, 1999.
—, *Le Sens du Monde.* Galilée, 1993.
Nedelsky, Jennifer. *Private Property and the Limits of American Constitutionalism: The Madisonian Framework and Its Legacy.* Chicago: University of Chicago Press, 1990.
Nerken, Ira. "A New Deal for the Protection of Fourteenth Amendment Rights: Challenging the Doctrinal Bases of the Civil Rights Cases and State Action Theory." *Harvard Civil Rights-Civil Liberties Law Review* 12 (1977): 297–366.
Neuner, Jörg, ed. *Grundrechte und Privatrecht aus rechtsvergleichender Sicht.* Tübingen: Mohr Siebeck, 2007.
Nietzsche, Friedrich. *Zur Genealogie der Moral.* In *Sämtliche Werke, Kritische Studienausgabe.* Vol. V. Berlin: Walter de Gruyter, 1999.
Nipperdey, Hans Carl. "Gleicher Lohn der Frau für gleiche Leistung." *Recht der Arbeit* (1950): 121–128.
—, *Grundrechte und Privatrecht.* Krefeld: Scherpe Verlag, 1961.
Nörr, Knut W. *Die Republik der Wirtschaft. Teil I: Von der Besatzungszeit zur Grossen Koalition.* Tübingen: Mohr Siebeck, 1999. http://www.mohr.de/nc/rechtswissenschaft/schriftenreihen/detail/buch/die-republik--der-wirtschaft-1.html.
Novak, William J. "Public-Private Governance: A Historical Introduction." In *Government by Contract: Outsourcing and American Democracy*, edited by Jody Freeman and Martha Minow, 23–40. Cambridge, Massachusetts: Harvard University Press, 2009.
Nozick, Robert. *Anarchy, State, and Utopia.* Oxford: Basic Books, 1974.
Oeter, Stefan. "'Drittwirkung' der Grundrechte und die Autonomie des Privatrechts." In *Archiv des öffentlichen Rechts*, 119: 529–563. J.C.B. Mohr (P. Siebeck), 1994.
—, "Federalism and Democracy." In *Principles of European Constitutional Law*, edited by Armin von Bogdandy and Jürgen Bast, 78. Oxford: Hart Publishing, 2007.
Oldiges, Martin. "Neue Aspekte der Grundrechtsgeltung im Privatrecht." In *Staat Wirtschaft Steuern*, edited by Rudolf Wendt, Wolfram Höfling, and Ulrich Karpen, 281–308. Heidelberg: C.F. Müller, 1996.
Peters, Roger Paul. "Civil Rights and State Non-Action." *Notre Dame Lawyer* 34 (1959): 303–334.

Piris, Jean-Claude. *The Constitution for Europe: A Legal Analysis.* Cambridge Studies in European Law and Policy. Cambridge: Cambridge University Press, 2006.

Plato. *Republic.* Cambridge, Mass.: Harvard University Press, 1935.

Polanyi, Karl. *The Great Transformation: The Political and Economic Origins of Our Time.* Boston, MA: Beacon Press, 2001.

Pound, Roscoe. "Liberty of Contract." *The Yale Law Journal* 18, no. 7 (May 1, 1909): 454–487.

—, "The New Feudalism." *American Bar Association Journal* 10 (1930): 553.

Preuss, Ulrich K. "Vater der Verfassungsväter – Carl Schmitts Verfassungslehre und die verfassungspolitische Diskussion der Gegenwart" in *Politisches Denken Jahrbuch 1993,* edited by Volker Gerhardt, Henning Ottmann, and Martyn P Thompson. Stuttgart: Metzler, 1993.

Prosser, Tony. "Regulatory Agencies, Regulatory Legitimacy, and European Private Law." In *Making European Private Law: Governmance Design,* edited by Fabrizio Cafaggi and Horatia Muir Watt, 235–253. Cheltenam/Northampton: Edward Elgar Publishing, 2008.

Puchta, G.F. Vorlesungen über das heutige römische Recht. Leipzig: Verlag von Bernhard Tauchnitz, 1862

Rawls, John. *Justice as Fairness: A Restatement.* edited by Erin Kelly. Cambridge, Mass.: Harvard University Press, 2001.

—, *Political Liberalism.* New York: Columbia University Press, 1996.

—, "The Idea of Public Reason Revisited." In *Collected Papers.* Cambridge, Mass.: Harvard University Press, 1999.

—, *The Law of Peoples.* Cambridge, Mass.: Harvard University Press, 1999.

Rebhahn, Robert. "Grundfreiheit vor Arbeitskampf – der Fall Viking." *Zesar* (2008): 57–65.

Reid, John Phillip. *Constitutional History of the American Revolution: The Authority to Legislate.* Madison: University of Wisconsin Press, 1986.

Resnik, Judith. "Globalization(s), Privatization(s), Constitutionalization, and Statization: Icons and Experiences of Sovereignty in the 21st Century." *International Journal of Constitutional Law* 11, no. 1 (January 1, 2013): 162–199.

Ricoeur, Paul. *La Mémoire, l'Histoire, l'Oubli.* Paris: Seuil, 2000.

Rimanque, K., and P. Peeters. "De toepasselijkheid van grondrechten in de betrekkingen tussen private personen – algemene probleemstelling." edited by K. Rimanque. Antwerpen: Kluwer, 1982.

Ritter, Joachim. "Hegel und die französische Revolution." In *Metaphysik und Politik,* 183–255. Frankfurt a.M.: Suhrkamp, 2003.

Rittstieg, Helmut. *Eigentum als Verfassungsproblem: zu Geschichte u. Gegenwart d. bürgerl. Verfassungsstaates.* Darmstadt: Wissenschaftliche Buchgesellschaft, 1975.

Robbers, Gerard. "Für ein neues Verhältnis zwischen Bundesverfassungsgericht und Fachgerichtbarkeit." *Neue Juristische Wochenschrift* 14 (1998): 935–941.

Rose, Carol. "The Ancient Constitution vs. the Federalist Empire: Antifederalism from the Attack on 'Monarchism' to Modern Localism." *Faculty Scholarship Series* no. Paper 1823 (January 1, 1989). http://digitalcommons.law.yale.edu/fss_papers/1823.

Rousseau, Jean Jacques. *Du Contrat Social.* Paris: Gallimard, 1964.

Ruffert, Matthias. *Vorrang der Verfassung und Eigenständigkeit des Privatrechts: eine verfassungsrechtliche Untersuchung zur Privatrechtswirkung des Grundgesetzes.* Tübingen: Mohr Siebeck, 2001.

Rüfner, Wolfgang. *Handbuch des Staatsrechts.* edited by Josef Isensee and Paul Kirchof. Vol. Bnd V. Heidelberg: C.F. Müller, 2007.

Sabel, Charles F., and Oliver H. Gerstenberg. "Constitutionalising an Overlapping Consensus: The ECJ and the Emergence of a Coordinate Constitutional Order." *European Law Journal* 16, no. 5 (2010): 511–550.
Salmond, Sir John William, and R. F. V. Heuston. *Salmond on the Law of Torts.* London: Sweet & Maxwell, 1973.
Scalfari, Eugenio. "Das wäre die vierte Schuld." *Die Zeit,* March 15, 2012.
Scharpf, Fritz. "'The Only Solution Is to Refuse to Comply with ECJ Rulings.'" *Social Europe Journal,* April 6, 2009. http://www.social-europe.eu/2009/04/interview-the-only-solution-is-to-refuse-to-comply--with-ecj-rulings/.
Schepel, Harm. "Constitutionalising the Market, Marketising the Constitution, and to Tell the Difference: On the Horizontal Application of the Free Movement Provsions in EU Law," 18 (2012) *European Law Journal* 177–200.
Schmitt, Carl. *Der Begriff des Politischen.* Berlin: Duncker & Humblot, 1996.
—, *Der Hüter der Verfassung.* Berlin: Duncker & Humblot, 1996.
—, *Die geistesgeschichtliche Lage des heutigen Parlamentarismus.* Berlin: Duncker & Humblot, 1996.
—, "Die Wendung zum totalen Staat." In *Positionen und Begriffe: im Kampf mit Weimar – Genf – Versailles : 1923–1939.* Berlin: Duncker & Humblot, 1994.
—, "Neutralität und Neutralisierungen." In *Positionen und Begriffe: im Kampf mit Weimar – Genf – Versailles : 1923–1939.* Berlin: Duncker & Humblot, 1994.
—, *Römischer Katholizismus und politische Form.* Stuttgart: Klett-Cotta, 1923.
—, *Staat, Bewegung, Volk: die Dreigliederung der politischen Einheit.* Hanseatische Verlagsanstalt, 1933.
—, "Totaler Feind, totaler Krieg, totaler Staat." In *Positionen und Begriffe: im Kampf mit Weimar – Genf – Versailles : 1923–1939.* Berlin: Duncker & Humblot, 1994.
—, *Verfassungslehre.* Berlin: Duncker & Humblot, 2003.
—, "Weiterentwicklung des totalen Staat in Deutschland." In *Positionen und Begriffe: im Kampf mit Weimar – Genf – Versailles : 1923–1939.* Berlin: Duncker & Humblot, 1994.
Schwabe, Jürgen. *Die sogenannte Drittwirkung der Grundrechte: zur Einwirkung der Grundrechte auf den Privatrechtsverkehr.* München: W. Goldmann, 1971.
Scott, Colin. "Regulating Private Legislation." In *Making European Private Law: Governmance Design,* edited by Fabrizio Cafaggi and Horatia Muir Watt, 254–268. Cheltenam/Northampton: Edward Elgar Publishing, 2008.
Seidman, Louis Michael. "The State Action Paradox." *Constitutional Commentary* 10 (1993): 379–401.
Seifert, Achim. "L"effet horizontal des droits fondamentaux : quelques réflexions de droit européen et de droit comparé." *Revue Trimestrielle de Droit Européen* 48 (2012): 801–826.
Singer, Joseph William. "The Legal Rights Debate in Analytical Jurisprudence from Bentham to Hohfeld." *Wisconsin Law Review* (1982): 975–1059.
Smend, Rudolf. "Verfassung und Verfassungsrecht." In *Staatsrechtliche Abhandlungen und andere Aufsätze.* Berlin: Duncker & Humblot, 1994.
Spielmann, Dean. *L'Effet Potentiel de La Convention Européenne des Droits de l'Homme entre Personnes Privées.* Brussels: Nemesis/Bruylant, 1995.

—, "Obligations Positives et Effet Horizontal ses Dispositions de la Convention." In *L'Interprétation de la Convention Européenne des Droits de l'Homme*, edited by Frédéric Sudre, 133–174. Brussels: Nemesis/Bruylant, 1998.

Stern, Klaus. *Das Staatsrecht der Bundesrepublik Deutschland*. Band III/1. München: C.H. Beck, 1988.

—, "Ehrenschutz und 'allgemeine Gesetze.'" In *Festschrift für Heinz Hübner zum 70. Geburtstag am 7. November 1984*, edited by Gottfried Baumgärtel, Hans-Jürgen Becker, Ernst Klingmüller, and Andreas Wacke, 815–829. Berlin: De Gruyter, 1984.

Sudre, Frédéric. "Les 'Obligations Positives' dans la Jurisprudence Européenne des Droits de l'Homme." In *Protection des Droits de l'Homme: la Perspective Européenne: Mélanges à la Mémoire de Rolv Ryssdal*, edited by Paul Mahoney, 1359–1376. Köln: Carl Heymanns, 2000.

Sunstein, Cass R. *The Partial Constitution*. Cambridge, Mass: Harvard University Press, 1993.

Supiot, Alain. "Le Sommeil Dogmatique Européen" 1 (2012) *Revue Française des Affaires Sociales* 185–198.

—, "The Public–private Relation in the Context of Today's Refeudalization." *International Journal of Constitutional Law* 11, no. 1 (January 1, 2013): 129–145.

Teubner, Gunther. "A Constitutional Moment? The Logics of 'Hitting the Bottom.'" In *The Financial Crisis in Constitutional Perspective: The Dark Side of Functional Differentiation*, edited by Poul F Kjaer, Gunther Teubner, and Alberto Febbrajo, 3–42. Oxford: Hart Publishing, 2011.

—, "Des Königs viele Leiber. Die Selbstdekonstruktion der Hierarchie des Rechts." *Soziale Systeme* 2, no. 2 (July 1996): 229–255.

—, "Fragmented Foundations: Societal Constitutionalism beyond the Nation State." In *The Twilight of Constitutionalism?* edited by Martin Loughlin and Petra Dobner, 327–341. Oxford: Oxford University Press, 2010.

—, Globale Privatregimes: Neo-spontanes Recht und duale Sozialverfassungen in der Weltgesellschaft, *Zur Autonomie des Individuums*, edited by Dieter Simon/Manfred Weiss. Baden-Baden: Nomos Verlagsgesellschaft, 2000.

—, "Globale Zivilverfassungen: Alternative zur staatszentrierten Verfassungstheorie," *Zeitschrift für ausländisches öffentliches Recht und Völkerrecht* 63 (2003): 1–28.

—, "Ökonomie und Gabe – Positivität der Gerechtigkeit: Gegenseitige Heimsuchungen von System und Difference." In *Widerstände der Systemtheorie – Kulturtheoretische Analysen zum Werk von Niklas Luhmann*, edited by Albrecht Koschorke and Cornelia Vismann, 199–212. Berlin: Akademie Verlag, 1999.

—, "Societal Constitutionalism: Alternatives to State-Centred Constitutional Theory?" In *Transnational Governance and Constitutionalism*, edited by Christian Joerges, Inger-Johanne Sand, and Gunther Teubner, 3–28. Oxford: Hart Publishing, 2004.

Thornhill, Chris. *A Sociology of Constitutions: Constitutions and State Legitimacy in Historical-Sociological Perspective*. Cambridge: Cambridge University Press, 2011.

—, "The Future of the State" in *The Financial Crisis in Constitutional Perspective: The Dark Side of Functional Differentiation*, edited by Paul Kjaer et al. 357–394. Oxford: Hart Publishing, 2011.

Tribe, Laurence. *American Constitutional Law*. 2nd ed. New York: Foundation Press, 1988.

—, *Constitutional Choices*. Cambridge, Mass.: Harvard University Press, 1985.

Tribe, Laurence H. *Abortion: The Clash of Absolutes*. New York: Norton, 1992.

Tuck, Richard. *Natural Rights Theories: Their Origin and Development.* Cambridge: Cambridge University Press, 1979.
Tully, James. *A Discourse on Property: John Locke and his Adversaries.* Cambridge: Cambridge University Press, 1980.
Tushnet, Mark. "State Action, Social Welfare Rights, and the Judicial Role: Some Comparative Observations." *Chicago Journal of International Law* 3 (2002): 435–453.
—, *Taking the Constitution Away from the Courts.* Princeton: Princenton University Press, 1999.
—, "The Issue of State Action/Horizontal Effect in Comparative Constitutional Law." *International Journal of Constitutional Law* 1 (2003): 79–98.
Ubillos, Juan María Bilbao. "Die Einwirkung der Grundrechte auf das spanische Privatrecht." In *Grundrechte und Privatrecht aus rechtsvergleichender Sicht*, edited by Jörg Neuner. Tübingen: Mohr Siebeck, 2007.
Ullman, Walter. *The Individual and Society in the Middle Ages.* London: Methuen and Company, 1967.
—, *Medieval Political Thought.* Baltimore: Penguin, 1975.
Unger, Roberto Mangabeira. *Democracy Realized: The Progressive Alternative.* New York: Verso, 1998.
—, *What Should Legal Analysis Become?* New York: Verso, 1996.
Vanberg, Viktor J. "The Freiburg School: Walter Eucken and Ordoliberalism." Freiburger Diskussionspapiere zur Ordnungsökonomik, http://www.eucken.de/fileadmin/bilder/Dokumente/Diskussionspapiere/04_11bw.pdf.
Van den Bergh, G. C. J. J. *Eigendom: Grepen uit de Geschiedenis van een Omstreden Begrip.* Deventer: Kluwer, 1988.
Van der Walt, Johan. "Abdications of Sovereignty in Horizontal Effect Jurisprudence." forthcoming in *Boundaries of State, Boundaries of Rights: Human Rights, Private Actors, and Positive Obligations*, edited by Tsvi Kahana and Anat Scolnicov. Cambridge: Cambridge University Press.
—, "Blixen's Difference: Horizontal Application of Fundamental Rights and the Resistance to Neo-Colonialism." *Journal for South African Law* no. 2 (2003): 311–331.
—, "Constitution-Making as a Learning Process: Andrew Arato's Model of Post-Sovereign Constitution-Making" 26 (2010) *South African Journal on Human Rights:* 1–18.
—, "Horizontal Application of Fundamental Rights and the Threshold of the Law in View of the Carmichele Saga." *South African Journal on Human Rights* 19 (2003): 517–540.
—, "Johannesburg: A Tale of Two Cases." In *Law and the City*, edited by Andreas Philippopoulos-Mihalopoulos, 221–236. Routledge-Cavendish, 2007.
—, *Law and Sacrifice: Towards a Post-Apartheid Theory of Law.* London: Birbeck Law Press, 2005.
—, "Law and the Space of Appearance in Arendt's Thought." In *Hannah Arendt and the Law*, edited by Marco Goldoni and Christopher McCorkindale. Oxford: Hart Publishing, 2012.
—, "Law, Utopia, Event." In *Law and the Utopian Imagination*, edited by Austin Sarat, Lawrence Douglas, and Martha Merrill Umphrey. Stanford: Stanford University Press, 2014.
—, "Perspectives on Horizontal Application: Du Plessis v De Klerk Revisted." *South African Public Law* 12 (1997): 1–31.

—, "Progressive Indirect Horizontal Application of the Bill of Rights: Towards a Co-operative Relation between Common-law and Constitutional Jurisprudence" *South African Journal on Human* Rights: 17, no. 3 (2001): 341–363.
—, "Rethinking the Fundamental Structures of the State with Reference to the Horizontal Application of Fundamental Rights." In *Der grundrechtsgeprägte Verfassungsstaat: Festschrift für Klaus Stern zum 80. Geburtstag*, edited by Michael Sachs and Helmut Siekmann, 627–648. Berlin: Duncker & Humblot, 2012.
—, "Vertical Sovereignty, Horizontal Constitutionalism, Subterranean Capitalism: A Case of Competing Retroactivities." *South African Journal on Human Rights* 26 (2010): 102–129.
Van der Walt, André. "Normative Pluralism and Anarchy: Reflections on the 2007 Term" 1 (2008) *Constitutional Review:* 77–128.
—, *Property and Constitution.* Pretoria: Pretoria University Law Press, 2012.
Vandevelde, Kenneth J. "A History of Prima Facie Tort: The Origins of a General Theory of Intentional Tort." *Hofstra Law Review* 19 (1991 1990): 447–497.
—, "The Modern Prima Facie Tort Doctrine." *Kentucky Law Journal* 79 (1991 1990): 519–555.
Verhey, Luc. *Horizontale Werking van Grondrechten, in het Bijzonder van het Recht op Privacy.* Zwolle: W.E.J. Tjeenk Willink, 1992.
—, "Horizontale Werking van Grondrechten: de Stille Straatsburgse Revolutie." In *Geschakeld Recht: Verdere Studies over Europese Grondrechten ter Gelegenheid van de 70ste Verjaardag van Prof. mr. E.A. Alkema*, edited by Tom Barkhuysen, M.L. van Emmerik, and J.P. Loof, 517–536. Alphen aan den Rijn: Kluwer, 2009.
Villey, Michel. *La Formation de la Pensée Juridique Moderne.* Paris: Quadridge/PUF, 2009.
Von Jhering, Rudolf. *Gesammelte Aufsätze aus den Jahrbüchern für die Dogmatik des heutigen römischen und deutschen Privatrechts Bnd I.* Jena: Gustaf Fischer, 1881.
—, *Geist des römischen Rechts auf den verschiedenen Stufen seiner Entwicklung* Leipzig: Breitkopf und Härtel, 1894.
—, *Im Begriffshimmel der Jurisprudenz* in *Scherz und Ernst in der Jurisprudenz: eine Weihnachtsgabe für das juristische Publikum.* Leipzig: Breitkopf und Härtel, 1909.
Von Savigny, F.C. System des heutigen Römischen Rechts, Vol I. Berlin: Deit und Comp, 1840.
—, *Vermischte Schriften.* Aalen: Scientia Verlag, 1968.
Wade, H.W.R. "Horizons of Horizontality." *Law Quarterly Review* 116 (2000): 217–224.
Waldron, Jeremy. *Law and Disagreement.* Oxford: Oxford University Press, 1999.
—, *The Dignity of Legislation.* Cambridge: Cambridge University Press, 1999.
Walker, Neil. "Late Sovereignty in the European Union." In *Sovereignty in Transition*, edited by Neil Walker. Oxford: Hart Publishing, 2003.
Weber, Max. "Die protestantische Ethik und der Geist des Kapitalismus." In *Gesamtausgabe*, edited by Horst Baier, Wolfgang J. Mommsen, and Rita Aldenhoff. Vol. 18. Tübingen: Mohr Siebeck, 1993.
Wechsler, Herbert. "Toward Neutral Principles of Constitutional Law." *Harvard Law Review* 73 (1959): 1–35.
Weiler, Joseph. "The 'Lisbon Urteil' and the Fast Food Culture." *European Journal of International Law* 20, no. 3 (2009): 505–509.
—, "A Quiet Revolution. The European Court of Justice and its Interlocutors." *Comparative Political Studies* 26 (1994): 510–534.
Welsch, Wolfgang. Hegel und die analytische Philosophie, http://www2.uni-jena.de/welsch/Hegel%20Analytik.pdf.

Wieacker, Franz. *Privatrechtsgeschichte der Neuzeit: unter besonderer Berücksichtigung der deutschen Entwicklung.* Gottingen: Vandenhoeck & Ruprecht, 1967.
Windscheid, B. *Lehrbuch des Pandektenrechts.* Aalen: Scientia Verlag, 1963.
Wörsdörfer, Manuel. "Von Hayek and Ordoliberalism on Justice." *Journal of the History of Economic Thought* 35, no. 03 (2013): 291–317.
Ziller, Jacques. "Sovereignty in France: Getting Rid of the Mal de Bodin." In *Sovereignty in Transition*, edited by Neil Walker, 261–278. Oxford: Hart Publishing, 2003.
—, ed. *L'Européanisation des Droits Constitutionnels à la Lumière de la Constitution pour l'Europe.* Paris: L'Harmattan, 2003.

Case Law

Canada

RWDSU v. Dolphin Delivery	573 2 (S.C.R. 1986)

European Court of Human Rights

Appleby and Others v. The United Kingdom	(2003) 37 E.H.R.R. 38
Costello-Roberts v. The United Kingdom	(1995) 19 E.H.R.R. 112
Görgülü v Germany	[2004] ECHR 88
Gustafsson v. Sweden	(1996) 22 E.H.R.R. 409
Hatton and Others v. The United Kingdom	(2002) 34 E.H.R.R. 1
Marckx v. Belgium	(1997) 24 E.H.R.R. 143
VgT Verein gegen Tierfabriken v. Switzerland	(2002) 34 E.H.R.R. 4
Von Hannover v Germany	(2005) 40 E.H.R.R. 1

European Court of Justice

Association de médiation sociale	EU: Case C-176/12 [2014]
Bosman	EU: Case 415/93 [1995]
Costa v E.N.E.L.	EU: Case 6/64 [1964]
Defrenne	EU: Case 43/75 [1976]
Domingez	EU: Case C-282/10 [2012]
Kücükdevici	EU: Case C-555/07 [2010]
Laval	EU: Case C-341/05 [2007]
Luxembourg	EU: Case C-319/06. [2008]
Rüffert	EU: Case C-346/06 [2008]
Van Gend en Loos	EU: Case 26/26 [1963]
Viking	EU: Case C-438/05 [2007]

Germany

Zeugen Jehovas	BVerfG 23, 127 (1968)
Blinkfeuer	BVerfG 25, 256 (1969)

Bürgschaftsverträge	BVerfG 89, 214 (1993)
Erste Abtreibung	BVerfG 1, 39 (1975)
Gorleben	BVerfG 77, 381 (1988)
Handelsvertreter	BVerfG 81 242 (1990)
Kalkar	BVerfG 49 89 (1978)
Lissabon	BVerfG 123, 267 (2009)
Lüth	BVerfG 7, 198 (1958)
Mephisto	BVerfG 30, 173 (1971)
Reiten im Walde	BVerfG 80, 137 (1989)
Schleier	BVerfG 46, 116 (1977)
Solange I	BVerfG 37, 271 (1974)
Solange II	BVerfG 73, 339 (1986)
Zweite Abtreibung	BVerfG 88, 203 (1993)
Vaterschaftsauskunft	BVerfG 96, 56 (1997)

Luxembourg

Engel v Engel — *Cour de Cassation*, Judgment no 2/85 of 17 January 1985

South Africa

Barkhuizen v Napier	2007 (5) SA 323 (CC)
Carmichele v. Minister of Safety and Security and Another	2001 (1) SA 489 (SCA)
Du Plessis v De Klerk	1996 (5) BCLR 658 (CC)
Minister of Safety and Security v Dirk van Duivenboden	2002 (6) SA 431 SCA
Minister van Polisie v Ewels	1975 (3) SA 590 (A)
Van Eden v Minister of Safety and Security	2003 (1) SA 389 (SCA)

United Kingdom

Anns and Others v London Borough of Merton	[1978] A.C. 728.
Aston Cantlow Parochial Church Council v Wallbank	[2003] UKHL 37
Caparo Industries plc v Dickman and Others	[1990] 1 All ER 568.
Donoghue v Stevenson	[1932] UKHL 100
Dorset Yacht Co.Ltd. v Home Office	[1970] A.C. 1004
Douglas v Hello	[2005] EWCA Civ 595
Murphy v Brentwood District Council	[1991] 1 AC 398
R v Panel on Takeovers and Mergers, ex parte Datatfin plc	[1987] QB 815

United States

Amalgamated Food Employees Un. v Logan Valley Plaza	391 U.S. 308 (1968)
Barrows v Jackson	346 U.S. 249 (1953)
Bell v Maryland	378 U.S. 226 (1964)

Black v Cutter Laboratories	351 U.S. 292 (1956)
Blum v Yaretsky	457 U.S. 991 (1982)
Brinkerhoff-Faris Trust & Savings Co. v Hill	281 U.S. 673 (1930)
Brown v Board of Education	349 U.S. 294 (1954)
Buchanan v Warley	245 U.S. 60 (1917)
Burton v Wilmington Parking Authority	365 U.S. 715 (1961)
City of Cleburne v Cleburne Living Centre	474 U.S. 432 (1985)
Craig v Boren	429 U.S. 190 (1976)
Davis v. Beason	133 U.S. 333 (1890)
DeShaney v. Winnebago County Dept of Social Services	489 U.S. 189 (1989)
Flagg Brothers Inc. v. Brooks	436 149 (U.S. 1978)
Fuentes v. Shevin	407 U.S. 67 (1972)
Gulf, Colorado And Santa Fe Railway Company v Ellis	165 U.S. 150 (1897)
Harmon v Tyler	273 U.S. 668 (1927)
Hudgens v NLRB	424 U.S. 507 (1976)
Jackson v Metropolitan Edison Co	419 U.S. 345 (1974)
Kaiser Aetna v United States,	444 US 164 (1979)
Labour v. Swing	312 U.S. 321 (1941)
Lloyd Corp. v Tanner	407 US 551 (1972)
Lochner v New York	198 U.S. 45 (1905)
Marbury v Madison	5 U.S. 137 (1803)
Marsh v Alabama	326 U.S. 501 (1946)
McLaughlin v Florida	379 US 184 (1966)
McCulloch v Maryland	17 U.S. 316 (1819)
Miller v Schoene	276 U.S. 272 (1928)
Moose Lodge No. 107 v Irvis	407 US 163 (1972)
New York Times v. Sullivan	376 U.S. 254 (1963)
Nixon v Condon	286 U.S. 73 (1932)
North Georgia Finishing, Inc. v Di-Chem, Inc.	419 U.S. 601 (1975)
Powel v Pennsylvania	127 US 678 (1888)
Reitman v Mulkey	387 U.S. 369 (1967)
Rendell-Baker v Kohn	457 U.S. 830 (1982)
Rinaldi v Yeager	384 U.S. 305 (1966)
Roe v Wade	410 U.S. 113 (1973)
Roy Romer v. Richard Evans et al	517 U.S. 620 (1996)
Smith v Allwright	321 U.S. 649 (1944)
Sniadach v Family Finance Corporation	395 U.S. 337 (1969)
Shelley v. Kraemer	334 U.S. 1 (1948)
Terry v Adams	345 U.S. 461 (1953)
The Civil Rights Cases	109 U.S. 3 (1883)
Twining v New Jersey	211 U.S. 78 (1908)
The Civil Rights Cases	109 U.S. 3 (1883)
United States v Carolene Products Co.	304 U.S. 144 (1938)
Washington v Davis	426 U.S. 229 (1976)

Abbreviations

BGB	Bürgerliches Gesetzbuch
ECJ	European Court of Justice
ECHR	European Court of Human Rights
GFCC	German Federal Constitutional Court
GG	Grundgesetz für die Bundesrepublik Deutschland
SACC	South African Constitutional Court
USSC	United States Supreme Court

Index of Persons

Arendt, Hannah 29, 37, 65, 68, 77, 164, 195, 374, 376, 390 f.
Austin, John 52 f., 55 f., 76 f.

Bismarck, Otto von 205
Blackmun, Justice 126 f., 133 f., 136 – 140, 142 f., 146, 149, 165, 181, 192, 353, 370, 372 f., 379
Blackstone, William 50 – 52, 55
Böckenförde, Ernst-Wolfgang 224, 312, 316, 343, 361 – 364, 383, 386 f.
Bohm, Franz 246
Bradley, Justice 38, 86, 88 – 92, 94, 128 f., 155, 192 f., 367
Brennan, Justice 100 f., 126 f., 158, 181 – 185, 192, 366

Cafaggi, Fabrizio 252 – 255, 258, 291, 313, 359
Canaris, Claus-Wilhelm 199, 202, 222, 224, 227 – 232, 236, 367, 386
Christensen, Ralph 31 f., 73, 202, 232, 236 f., 239 f., 253, 260 – 262, 264 – 275, 277 f., 280, 292, 297, 299, 310 f., 367, 380 f., 384
Christodoulidis, Emilios 239, 280, 391
Claes, Monica 242
Constant, Benjamin 301, 303, 327 f., 382
Cseres, Katalin 254 f.

Davidson, Donald 261, 263 – 265, 267, 271 f., 278
Delors, Jacques 250
Dietze, Constantin von 246
Dürig, Günter 199, 201 – 203, 205 – 212, 214 f., 220 f., 226 – 228, 230 – 232, 236, 294, 321, 323 f., 367

Eucken, Walter 246, 248 f., 358

Fischer-Lescano, Andreas 31 f., 73, 202, 232, 236 f., 239 f., 253, 260 – 262, 264 – 275, 277 f., 280, 292, 297, 299, 310 f., 367, 380 f., 384 f.
Foster, Christopher 253
Frankfurter, Justice 8, 98 f., 244, 349, 366
Freedland, Mark 253
Frege, Gottlob 263

Gerkrath, Jörg 243
Grimm, Dieter 8, 150 – 154, 163, 241 – 244, 283, 286 – 288, 334, 349, 388
Großmann-Doerth, Hans 246

Harlan, Justice 89, 91, 141, 193
Harlan, Veit 76, 107, 265
Hayek, Friedrich 184 f., 246 f., 250
Haym, Rudolf 277, 279
Hedemann, Justus Wilhelm 308 f.
Hegel, Georg Wilhelm Friedrich 31, 64, 68 – 70, 73, 237, 239, 267 f., 275 – 282, 286, 293, 297 f., 302, 337, 375, 381 f.
Henne, Thomas 76, 265
Hirschl, Ran 30, 383
Hobbes, Thomas 12, 18, 28, 41, 168, 239 – 241, 243, 353, 386
Hogg, Peter 105 f.
Hohfeld, Wesley Newcomb 168 – 170, 172, 203, 226, 282 f., 366, 392 f.
Holmes, Oliver Wendell 52 – 54, 139 f., 143, 332
Horowitz, Harold 170 f.
Horwitz, Morton 38 f., 48 f., 51, 57

Jefferson, Thomas 164, 195 f., 376
Jellinek, Georg 60, 71 f., 78 f., 243
Jhering, Rudolf von 66 f., 70 f.
Joerges, Christian 246 – 251, 280, 341, 348 f.

Kant, Immanuel 37, 65, 67 – 69, 73, 195, 277, 293, 296 – 298, 327, 337, 365, 375
Kantorowicz, Ernst Hartwig 303 f., 381 f.
Kelsen, Hans 14, 20, 29, 32, 72, 144, 238, 242, 260, 295, 314 – 324, 326 – 329, 331, 353, 368 f., 382, 385, 390 f., 395 f.

Kennedy, Duncan 38 f., 48–53, 55–57, 65, 75, 83, 178, 378
Kent, James 50, 53, 55
Klare, Karl 30, 175 f., 396
Klein, Ernst Ferdinand 62
Kriegler, Justice 11, 16, 90 f., 117–119, 155, 160 f., 212, 274, 311 f.
Kumm, Matthias 150, 205 f., 232, 243, 311, 313, 388

Laband, Paul 71 f., 316
Larenz, Karl 267 f.
Laufke, Franz 223 f.
Lefort, Claude 81, 298
Leisner, Walter 24, 32, 38 f., 42, 59–62, 64 f., 68, 71, 80 f., 154, 201 f., 206, 209, 212–218, 220–222, 231 f., 273, 295, 321, 323–326, 328, 332, 343, 361, 363 f., 367–369, 380, 383, 385
Lewis, Thomas 190, 192, 196
Locke, John 12, 41–44, 65
Luhmann, Niklas 31, 200, 237, 239, 260, 268, 272–277, 280–283, 286, 290, 292, 297–299
Lyotard, Jean-François 269, 297

Macpherson, C.B 41 f.
Maine, Henry Sumner 52–56, 76
Malberg, Carré de 61
Mansfield, Lord 51
Marshall, Chief Justice 89, 96
Martini, Karl Anton Freiherr von 62 f., 68
Marx, Karl 77
McIntyre, Justice 102–106, 160
Mensch, Elizabeth 38 f., 45 f., 66, 81, 275, 279, 298, 325
Michelet, Jules 81
Michelman, Frank 99, 101, 123, 128 f., 132, 167 f., 172, 185 f., 222, 231, 239, 288, 312, 319, 366, 389–398
Mnookin, Robert 174 f.
Morris, Governor 46, 284
Muir-Watt, Horatio 252
Müller-Armack, Alfred 246, 249

Nancy, Jean-Luc 25, 77, 240, 299
Nedelsky, Jennifer 38 f., 46 f., 187 f., 332, 385
Neframi, Eleftheria 347
Nerkin, Ira 187, 332
Nietzsche, Friedrich 279, 327
Nipperdey, Hans 201–206, 208 f., 211 f., 219, 231, 367
Nozick, Robert 184 f.

Orlando, Vittorio Emanuele 71

Parsons, Talcott 51–53, 55
Peters, Roger Paul 170, 197
Polanyi, Carl 71
Preuss, Ulrich 314, 318
Prosser, Tony 255–257
Puchta, G.F 66

Quine, Willard van Orman 261, 263, 278

Rawls, John 18, 132–134, 296 f., 365, 375–377, 380, 386, 393–396
Rehnquist, Justice 27 f., 86, 119–129, 140, 142, 157, 165, 178, 181–183, 185, 192, 197 f., 212, 235, 356, 366, 369–373, 378 f.
Ritter, Joachim 69, 73, 278 f., 281 f., 293, 311
Rittstieg, Joachim 42 f.
Robbers, Gerard 220 f., 380
Roosevelt, Franklin Delano 57
Röpke, Wilhelm 246 f.
Rousseau, Jean-Jacques 296–298, 312, 337, 365, 375
Ruffert, Matthias 202, 218, 221, 343, 361 f.
Russell, Bertrand 263
Rüstow, Alexander 246, 248

Savigny, Friedrich Carl von 66–69
Scharpf, Fritz 342
Schmitt, Carl 13 f., 32, 72, 148, 238, 242, 247, 260, 294 f., 300–309, 311–320, 322 f., 327–329, 353, 363, 380, 382, 388
Schwabe, Jürgen 202, 222–229, 231 f., 236, 282, 367

Scott, Colin 253, 257f.
Seidman, Louis 47f., 128, 168, 172, 180–189, 194, 198f., 231, 235, 332, 385
Singer, Joseph 169, 370, 378
Smend, Rudolf 73, 261, 265–268, 278, 314
Sonnenfels, Joseph von 62f., 68
Sunstein, Cas 74f.
Supiot, Alain 249, 284, 342, 359
Svarez, Carl Gottlieb 62

Teubner, Gunther 237f., 280, 283, 285–292, 313, 360
Thornhill, Chris 280f., 286
Tuck, Richard 41–43
Tully, James 41f.
Tushnet, Mark 30, 171f., 383, 396–398

Unger, Roberto 83

Van der Walt, André 30
Van der Walt, Johan 96, 117, 123, 159, 166, 173, 280, 284, 311, 391
Verhey, Luc 1, 4, 8f.
Villey, Michel 70
Vinson, Justice 94–97, 166f., 172f., 178f., 366

Waldron, Jeremy 30, 383
Walker, Neil 13, 162, 236, 239, 242, 244, 334
Wechsler, Herbert 167f., 172–174, 176, 235
Wieacker, Franz 68f., 277
Wilson, James 46, 391
Windscheid, Bernhard 66
Wittgenstein, Ludwig 263, 269

Zeiller, Franz von 62f., 68

Subject Index

Abwägung 361
adequate proceduralisation 30, 376 f., 395
Allgemeines Bürgerliches Gesetzbuch 25, 32
allgemeines Persönlichkeitsrecht 208
Amalgamated Food Employees Union Local 590 v Logan Valley Plaza 92, 191, 193
Angemessenheits-Verhältnismäßigkeit 361
anti-Prussianism 277 f.
applied constitutional law 150 f., 311, 313, 388
auctoritas 327, 381 f.
Ausgangspunkt 45, 208, 211, 227
Auslegung 213, 215, 220
Ausstrahlungseffekt 32, 130
Ausstrahlungswirkung 26, 114, 201, 218, 220 f., 230, 362

balancing 144, 261, 269, 289, 332, 335–337, 341, 343–349, 356, 361 f., 380, 384, 386 f.
Banalisierung 152
Barkhuizen v Napier 23 f., 388, 417
Barrows v Jackson 166, 172 f., 178, 417
baselines 1, 4, 38 f.
Begriffsjurisprudenz 3
Black v Cutter Laboratories 167 f., 172 f., 418
Blinkfeuer 201, 416
Brown v Board of Education 167, 418
Bürgerliches Gesetzbuch 33, 108, 419

Canadian Charter of Rights and Freedoms 102, 156
Carmichele v Minister of Safety and Security 18, 118–120, 129, 311, 371, 417
chacun 241, 297, 375
chain of being 44
Civil Code 25 f., 107 f.
Civil Rights Act 87 f.
classical legal consciousness 2 f., 14, 17 f., 20, 22, 39
Commonwealth of Virginia v Rives 95
competition law 251, 254–257
complexio oppositorum 304
conceptual disaster area 15, 173, 185
constitution 2–4, 8, 10–14, 16, 22–24, 27–30, 33, 38 f., 86 f., 89–91, 93, 96, 101, 104, 106, 109–111, 113, 115, 117–119, 123, 127, 131, 137–140, 147, 150, 154, 156, 159 f., 171, 173, 177, 179 f., 192, 203–206, 208–211, 215–217, 219–221, 224 f., 232, 240, 242, 244, 266, 275, 277, 280 f., 283, 285 f., 288, 290, 300, 303, 305–307, 317, 320 f., 324, 327 f., 340, 343, 350, 352, 366, 368, 370, 375, 378, 383, 388–392, 394
– absolute constitution 305–308
– positive constitution 306 f.
– relative constitution 305, 307, 317
constitutional 1, 3–18, 20–27, 29 f., 32, 34–39, 44, 47, 85 f., 89–92, 95, 97–101, 105–120, 125–134, 137 f., 140–142, 144–155, 158–167, 170–174, 177–181, 184–189, 197, 199, 201, 203–221, 223–231, 236–240, 242–244, 252 f., 258–262, 265–268, 270, 274, 276–278, 280–285, 287 f., 290 f., 293–295, 300 f., 303, 305–313, 315, 319–324, 326–328, 332, 334 f., 338 f., 341, 348–353, 356, 358, 363–370, 372 f., 377–382, 384–399
– constitutional essentials 394 f.
– constitutional histories 163
– constitutional review 4 f., 7, 9 f., 12, 15, 18, 21–23, 25–27, 30, 32 f., 37, 44 f., 107, 116, 128, 131, 139, 142, 147–150, 152, 154, 162–164, 173, 195, 214, 220–223, 226, 231, 244 f., 259, 266, 273 f., 288, 314, 321, 323–327, 354, 361, 363–366, 369 f., 374, 376–380, 383, 387, 389, 396 f., 399
constitutionalism 2 f., 10 f., 13–15, 19 f., 24, 30, 44 f., 144, 188, 239, 280, 285 f., 288 f., 312, 320 f., 323, 360, 389–391
– liberal democratic constitutionalism 5, 13–15, 19, 21, 29, 32, 237, 295, 321, 329
Constitution of South Africa 323, 377, 389
– 1993 Constitution 115–117
– 1996 Constitution 115, 117

contract 2, 9, 12–18, 20–22, 42, 46, 90, 93, 99, 105, 153, 160, 172f., 179, 203, 209, 211, 223f., 226, 229, 252f., 284, 296, 340, 342f.
Contrat Social 296f.
coordinates 1, 4, 6, 38, 42

dark times 29, 33, 374, 376, 378
Déclaration des Droits de l'Homme et du Citoyen 8, 23–25, 45, 324
deeply divided public 139, 143, 145
de facto 33, 242, 244, 284, 336, 353, 358f.
deism 237, 240, 246, 248f., 284
de jure 242–244, 284, 336, 353, 359
delict 17f., 21, 27, 120, 238, 253
de minibus non curat lex 153, 388
de minibus non curat lex constitutionis 23f., 153, 389f.
de minibus non curat rex 386, 390
deontological 240, 249, 284
DeShaney v Winnebago County Social Services Department 9, 212
DeShaney v Winnebago Couunty Social Services Department 9, 27–29, 85f., 119f., 123–129, 157, 159f., 164f., 168, 172, 180–183, 185, 189f., 192f., 195, 197f., 235, 245, 355f., 364, 366, 369–374, 378f., 418
différance 286, 295f., 328, 330, 362, 368
différantial 21, 32f., 158, 161, 293, 295f., 327f., 330, 337, 352, 354, 356, 360, 362, 368, 381, 383
dispersal of sovereignty 237, 240, 284, 334
Donoghue v Stevenson 21f., 372, 417
double variation 264
Douglas v Hello 5, 23f., 154, 388, 417
Dred Scott v Sandford 90
Drittwirkung 4, 12, 25f., 31f., 40, 91, 110, 138f., 154, 157, 165, 199, 201–204, 206, 209, 211f., 222–227, 230–232, 236f., 260, 295, 325, 343, 367f., 372, 386
– *mittelbare Drittwirkung* 4, 114, 201, 204, 213, 224, 229f.
– *sogenannte Drittwirkung* 222–225
– *unmittelbare Drittwirkung* 212, 215, 324
due process 28, 87, 119, 125f., 170, 183, 197f., 210, 365
– procedural due process 26, 29f., 32f., 141f., 146, 158, 162f., 165, 220f., 262, 365, 369, 371, 374, 378
– substantive due process 26, 29f., 32f., 130, 140f., 146, 149, 158, 161–165, 195, 206, 221, 262, 300, 332, 335–337, 347f., 353, 356, 359, 363–365, 369–374, 379, 384, 388f., 391
Du Plessis v De Klerk 3, 17, 85, 90, 102, 114f., 120, 155, 212, 274, 310–312, 367, 417

economic constitution 250, 341
Eigentum 6f., 28
Einbruchstellen 108, 205, 215
Enlightenment 4, 26, 293f., 296, 310, 312
Erste Abtreibung 26f., 85, 129–135, 137–139, 142–150, 152f., 157f., 161–163, 180, 202, 206, 222, 262, 335, 347f., 353, 363, 370–374, 379, 384, 417
Estelle v Gamble 126
European Court of Human Rights 1–5, 7, 336, 416, 419
European Court of Justice 7–9, 12, 33, 241f., 245f., 251, 259f., 333–360, 362, 396f., 416, 419
evaluative jurisprudence 268
Ex Parte Common Wealth of Virginia 95

federalisation 242
Ferguson v. Skrupa 140
feudalism 284
feudal privileges 4
Flagg Brothers, Inc. v Brooks 28, 85f., 120–123, 129, 157, 159f., 191, 245, 366, 369f., 418
Fourteenth Amendment 8, 28, 39, 88, 95–101, 119, 121–129, 131, 134–137, 140, 171, 173, 178f., 181f., 187, 190, 193, 198, 338, 391–393
freedom of contract 2f., 12f., 15, 17f., 20–22, 28, 174, 184, 186, 223, 284, 347
freedom of testation 28
friend enemy decision 313

functional differentiation 237f., 275, 281f., 286f., 290f., 313
Fünftes Gesetz zur Reform des Strafrechts 131

Generalklausel 114, 207, 213, 217, 230, 308f.
German Federal Constitutional Court 8, 12, 24, 26, 32, 37, 40, 85, 107–110, 112f., 115, 129–133, 135, 137f., 142, 147, 149–151, 153, 157, 162, 201f., 206, 213f., 220f., 225, 230, 235, 241–244, 246, 259–262, 265, 268, 270, 294, 308, 312, 332, 334–336, 338, 348–351, 353f., 361, 363, 367, 369f., 377, 384, 388, 419
Glaubwürdigkeit der Rechtsordnung 148
gottgewollte Ordnung 248, 358
governance 162, 238, 240, 252–254, 257–259, 280, 284, 291, 334, 359
Griswold v. Connecticut 140
Grundgesetz 97, 108–110, 112f., 129–132, 137, 144, 151f., 156, 201f., 205, 207–212, 224f., 229, 241, 243, 261, 312, 334, 338, 347, 349–351, 419
Grundordnung 312
Grundrechte 4, 8, 23, 26, 28, 32, 37, 45, 200–204, 207, 210, 213, 216–222, 224f., 228–230, 236, 260, 275f., 281f., 290, 298, 312, 324f., 341, 350, 361–363, 380, 386
– *Grundrechte gelten* 221, 380
– *gute Sitten* 208, 215

Handelsvertreter 129, 138, 202, 230, 417
Harris v. McRae 125
Herzog v Herzog 16
hidden sociology 261, 384
historicity 19, 21, 24f., 164, 192, 330f.
Hohfeldian point 128f., 167f., 172, 179, 186, 222, 228, 231, 366, 392
holism 263, 266f., 278
horizontal effect 4f., 7–13, 15f., 18–26, 29–33, 37f., 41, 44, 47, 85, 92–94, 96f., 102, 107, 110–118, 123, 129–131, 137–139, 149–166, 171, 173, 180, 196, 199, 201f., 204, 206, 209f., 212, 214, 221f., 226, 230–232, 237, 239f., 244, 258–261, 266, 273–275, 277, 280–284, 288–293, 295, 300, 308–312, 320–326, 332, 334–336, 338f., 343, 348, 357, 359–365, 367–370, 372, 374, 377–379, 383, 386–388, 390, 395–399
– direct horizontal effect 4, 10, 111f., 115f., 212, 259, 334–336, 338
– horizontal effect revolution 7–10, 252, 359, 396
– indirect horizontal effect 3–5, 10, 15, 23, 29f., 47, 111–114, 117, 159, 212, 300, 323, 360, 366
– so-called horizontal effect 223
horizontalising effect 7, 322
Human Rights Act 5, 24, 154

idea of the state 25, 37, 302, 325, 327
implied contracts 15–17, 19
impoverished language of rights 290
individual 1f., 5f., 14, 16, 18f., 21–23, 25, 27f., 30–35, 37, 41–44, 47, 85–87, 90, 93f., 104, 107–113, 118, 125–127, 135, 137, 142–144, 146, 149f., 155f., 161, 163–166, 169, 173, 175, 177, 179, 184f., 187–189, 191–194, 201f., 204, 207–209, 211, 218, 222, 224–229, 236, 239, 244, 254f., 263f., 266, 275f., 280–282, 289, 295, 309f., 325f., 334f., 338, 348, 350, 369, 371, 374f., 384, 386, 394
– individual flourishing 184
– individual freedom 147, 184, 254, 311

Jackson v Metropolitan Edison Co 121, 418
judicial review 9, 15, 29f., 146, 148, 162, 273, 291, 293, 332, 343, 360, 365f., 374, 383, 389, 393, 395, 398

Kautschukbegriff der Auslegung 324, 361
king's two bodies 303, 382

Labour v Swing 11, 16, 18, 23, 85, 98f., 101f., 110–113, 120, 156–158, 161, 173, 366, 418
Labour v Swing 11, 17, 85, 93, 98, 110, 155, 173, 245, 366

Laval 7–9, 12, 33, 245, 251, 335–341, 343–360, 362, 396 f., 416
legal consciousness 3, 13 f., 31, 39, 198
Legalität 31, 37
legality 37, 395
legal subjectivity 3, 39, 46
liberal democracy 14–16, 19–21, 24–27, 148, 164, 189, 192, 194–196, 198 f., 239, 294 f., 299, 309, 312, 329–331, 333, 355, 369 f., 375, 379, 382 f., 385, 390, 395 f., 398 f.
liberality 14
libertarian 184 f., 187, 331, 385
liberty deficit 15–17, 20 f., 160 f., 235 f., 368, 385
life, liberty and property 1, 5 f., 8 f., 15, 18, 24, 30, 33 f., 41, 47, 87, 89, 101, 108, 112, 115, 119, 124 f., 127, 130–132, 134–138, 142–144, 147, 149, 157 f., 174, 181–183, 187–190, 192, 194–196, 199, 203, 212, 224, 226, 250, 266 f., 292, 294, 308, 311, 317, 334, 351, 385 f., 399
Lloyd Corp. v Tanner 92, 191, 418
Lochner v New York 139 f., 335, 347, 370, 418
Lockean legacy 6
Lückenfüllung 212, 226, 231, 236, 367
Lüth 3, 12, 17 f., 26, 29, 32 f., 37 f., 40, 85, 107–115, 129 f., 138, 149–151, 153, 156, 158, 161–165, 201 f., 205 f., 214, 218, 221, 230, 235, 259–262, 265, 267–269, 271, 273, 294, 308, 312, 320 f., 324, 332–338, 343, 347 f., 351, 353, 357, 359, 361, 363 f., 367, 369 f., 374, 380, 383 f., 386, 417
Luxembourg 5, 7, 9, 243, 251, 335 f., 347, 416 f.

Madison 7, 10
Madisonian legacy 11
majority-minority relations 21 f., 27–29, 32, 163, 180, 192, 295, 328, 335 f., 354, 362, 364, 382 f., 390, 396
Marbury v Madison 44, 96, 418
Marsh v Alabama 92, 122, 170, 191, 193, 418
Menschenwürde 137 f., 208
Mephisto 201, 417
Miller v Schoene 128, 418
monolithic 15, 19 f., 26, 32, 161 f., 238, 337, 353 f.
– monolithic democracy 331
– monolithic liberalism 20, 331
Moose Lodge v Irvis 178
Moralität 31, 37
morality 31–33, 37, 147, 175, 182, 277, 373, 379

nasciturus 47, 137 f., 143 f., 157, 372
neutral principle 167, 173 f., 176 f.
New Deal 11, 21 f., 86, 182, 184–188, 194, 199, 332, 385
New York Times v Sullivan 11, 16–18, 23, 85, 93, 98–101, 110–113, 120, 155–158, 161, 173, 183, 245, 366, 418
New York Uniform Commercial Code 121 f.

ordo-liberalism 246–248, 250, 255, 284, 358
originally-split sovereignties 382
owls of Minerva 279

Pandectists 3, 25, 30–36, 39
paralegislative Tätigkeit 216
Paulskirche 29, 33, 328
– Paulskirche Constitution 3
– Paulskirche debates 29
philosophy of language 262, 277
Plessy v Ferguson 90
potestas 327, 381 f.
pouvoir neutre 301–303, 327
Preussisches Allgemeines Landrecht 62
princeps legibus solutus est 381, 383
private conduct 18, 23, 93, 95, 120, 156, 167, 179, 191–193, 196, 198, 222, 227, 324
private government 257
private legislation 253, 257 f.
private racism 39, 167, 178 f.
privatisation 3, 5, 23, 252–255, 291
proceduralisation 365, 374
property 2, 5–15, 22, 28–30, 39, 47, 86 f., 89 f., 92–94, 103, 119, 123, 125, 152,

166, 173 f., 177, 183, 186–189, 194, 196–199, 211, 281, 284, 370, 385
proportionality 33, 145, 147–149, 152, 300, 332, 339, 343 f., 346, 357–359, 361–366, 371, 374, 377–381, 383–387
public function 92, 122, 191, 193, 258
public liability tort 124, 195, 197 f., 355, 371, 379
public/private divide 128, 168, 179, 181 f.

quasi-contracts 12, 16 f., 21

radiation 113, 130, 161, 163, 231, 293, 300, 308 f., 320, 323, 362, 380
– radiation effect 26, 32, 109, 114, 117, 150, 162, 201 f., 214, 220, 230 f.
– radiation jurisprudence 32, 361
radical translation 264, 271
Rahmenordnung 312
reasons of state 362–365, 368, 383, 385
rechtsleere Räumen 224, 226
Rechtsstaat 19, 35 f., 224, 270, 274, 315, 322
reign 26, 29 f., 32, 159, 161, 212, 236, 239 f., 327 f., 330 f., 333, 335, 337, 354, 360, 368 f., 382 f., 388
Reiten im Walde 85, 150–154, 163, 388, 417
Reitman v Mulkey 93, 167, 418
Relativismus 206
revolution 1–10, 21–23, 32 f., 37, 40 f., 44 f., 164, 182–184, 247, 278 f., 281, 307, 324, 339, 359, 391, 396
– American Revolution 1, 6 f., 21
– French Revolution 1, 3, 10, 28 f., 44 f., 278, 324
– 1848 Revolution 28
Roe v Wade 85, 130 f., 133–143, 146 f., 149 f., 152 f., 157 f., 161–163, 165, 222, 370–374, 379
Roe v Wade 26 f., 85, 130 f., 150, 157, 161, 180, 206, 353, 370, 377, 418
Rüffert 7, 9, 12, 33, 251, 335–337, 339–359, 362, 397, 416
RWDSU v Dolphin Delivery Ltd 3, 17, 85, 101–107, 110–114, 156, 159 f., 367, 416

schonendste Ausgleich 144, 269, 300, 347, 361, 380, 384, 386
Schutzpflicht 129, 138, 201 f., 206, 224, 230, 348
Schutzgebotsfunktion der Grundrechte 201, 229–231
self-evidence 3 f., 25, 43, 89, 131, 164 f., 172, 193–196, 227, 245, 276, 364, 374–376
Shelley v Kraemer 10, 16–18, 23, 85, 92–99, 101–103, 105 f., 110–114, 116, 120, 155–158, 161, 166, 168, 170, 172 f., 177–180, 192, 197 f., 210 f., 245, 366, 418
significant encouragement 93
significant entanglement 93
social market economy 249, 341, 345 f.
sonstige Rechte 208
South African Constitutional Court 90, 102, 107, 114 f., 117 f., 120, 129, 153, 371, 419
sovereignty 6 f., 9 f., 12–15, 17 f., 20–23, 25–29, 31–33, 88, 94, 96, 115, 119–123, 129 f., 139, 148 f., 158–162, 164, 166 f., 170, 172 f., 177, 179, 196–200, 212, 222, 232, 235–246, 248 f., 252, 259 f., 266, 280, 284, 287, 291–293, 295 f., 299, 302, 304 f., 320, 326–331, 334–338, 348–354, 356–360, 365–370, 375 f., 381–383, 385, 395
– liberal democratic sovereignty 13, 15, 19–21, 25 f., 33, 232, 239, 295 f., 298, 329 f., 332, 335, 365, 368, 373 f., 376, 379 f., 383
– sovereignty deficit 15–17, 19–21, 26, 235 f., 368, 385
– uninterrupted sovereignty 31 f., 161, 235 f., 239, 241, 245, 275, 283 f., 368
soziale Marktwirtschaft 249
Staat 28, 32, 45, 108, 129, 137–139, 200, 204, 209, 223 f., 247, 266, 275, 298, 301, 305, 307–309, 311 f., 314–316, 318, 325–327, 329, 350, 361, 363, 368, 383
Staatszwecke 363
– der 'Staat,' der seines 'Selbstzwecks' entkleidet ist 326, 363
state action doctrine 2, 11 f., 15, 22–24, 28, 38–40, 85 f., 91, 97, 101, 105, 120, 123, 128, 155, 165–168, 170–173, 176 f., 180,

184–187, 190, 192, 194, 198 f., 244 f., 325, 338, 367, 385
Stufenbau 32, 320, 324

technicality 14
territorial sovereignty 32, 158, 172, 232, 245, 285, 334, 338, 351, 365 f.
Testierfreiheit 28
The Civil Rights Cases 2, 12, 40, 85–92, 94–97, 105, 111, 128 f., 155, 167, 170, 187, 190, 192 f., 244, 325, 338, 367, 418
tief gespaltene Öffentlichkeit 139, 145
torts 12, 14, 17 f., 20–22, 27
Treu und Glauben 215 f.
Tribe's subjugation thesis 177–180, 192 f., 197
trivialisation 24, 152, 154

Übermaßverbot 147, 229 f., 236, 377, 386
United States Supreme Court 9 f., 12, 26, 40, 44, 85, 92 f., 98, 100, 105, 110, 113, 121, 125, 128–131, 136, 140 f., 155, 167, 170, 177, 181, 191, 244 f., 335, 366 f., 370, 374, 378, 391, 419
Untermaßverbot 229–231, 236, 367, 386
ureigenster Privat- und Geheimsphäre 207

Verdeutlichung 207
Verfassung 129, 132, 138, 202–205, 207, 209, 218 f., 230, 243, 266, 275, 286, 301–303, 305, 316, 319, 327 f., 352, 362
– *Verfassungsänderungen* 306
– *Verfassungsbegriff* 305
– *Verfassungsgebung* 306
Verhältnismässigkeit 145, 147, 387
vertical holism 261 f., 271, 273, 278, 310
Vertragsfreiheit 28, 224
Verweisungsbegriffe 215
Verweisungsnormen 215
Vgt Verein gegen Tierfabrieken 1
Viking 7, 9, 12, 33, 245, 251, 335–341, 343–360, 362, 396 f., 416
Volk, Bewegung, Staat 32, 107, 145, 305–309, 311, 314, 318, 327, 329
vorausgesetzt 317, 329

Washington v Davis 97, 178, 418
Weimar 37, 131 f., 203, 205, 246, 248, 265, 277, 301, 303, 307, 314, 328
wertausfüllungsbedürftige Begriffe 207
wertausfüllungsfähige und -bedürftige Generalklauseln 205
wertblind 206
wertgeschärfte Auslegung 207
Wertschutzlücken 207
Wertungsjurisprudenz 267 f.
Whig association of political liberty with property 10
Whig political philosophy 7
„White Book" programme 250
Wirtschaftsverfassung 250

Youngberg v Romeo 126

Bei Fragen zur Produktsicherheit wenden Sie sich bitte an:
If you have any questions regarding product safety,
please contact:

Walter de Gruyter GmbH
Genthiner Straße 13
10785 Berlin
productsafety@degruyterbrill.com